Unwanted Visionaries

OXFORD STUDIES IN INTERNATIONAL HISTORY

JAMES J. SHEEHAN, SERIES ADVISOR

The Wilsonian Moment: Self-Determination and the International Origins of Anticolonial Nationalism
Erez Manela

In War's Wake: Europe's Displaced Persons in the Postwar Order
Gerard Daniel Cohen

Grounds of Judgment: Extraterritoriality and Imperial Power in Nineteenth-Century China and Japan
Pär Kristoffer Cassel

The Acadian Diaspora: An Eighteenth-Century History
Christopher Hodson

Gordian Knot: Apartheid and the Unmaking of the Liberal World Order
Ryan Irwin

The Global Offensive: The United States, the Palestine Liberation Organization, and the Making of the Post–Cold War Order
Paul Thomas Chamberlin

Unwanted Visionaries: The Soviet Failure in Asia at the End of the Cold War
Sergey Radchenko

Lamaze: An International History
Paula A. Michaels

Unwanted Visionaries

The Soviet Failure in Asia at the End of the Cold War

Sergey Radchenko

OXFORD
UNIVERSITY PRESS

OXFORD
UNIVERSITY PRESS

Oxford University Press is a department of the University of Oxford.
It furthers the University's objective of excellence in research, scholarship,
and education by publishing worldwide.

Oxford   New York
Auckland   Cape Town   Dar es Salaam   Hong Kong   Karachi
Kuala Lumpur   Madrid   Melbourne   Mexico City   Nairobi
New Delhi   Shanghai   Taipei   Toronto

With offices in
Argentina   Austria   Brazil   Chile   Czech Republic   France   Greece
Guatemala   Hungary   Italy   Japan   Poland   Portugal   Singapore
South Korea   Switzerland   Thailand   Turkey   Ukraine   Vietnam

Oxford is a registered trademark of Oxford University Press
in the UK and certain other countries.

Published in the United States of America by
Oxford University Press
198 Madison Avenue, New York, NY 10016

Library of Congress Cataloging-in-Publication Data
Radchenko, Sergey, author.
Unwanted visionaries : the Soviet failure in Asia at the end of the Cold
War / Sergey Radchenko.
pages ; cm.—(Oxford studies in international history)
Includes bibliographical references and index.
ISBN 978–0–19–993877–3 (alk. paper)
1. Soviet Union—Foreign relations—Asia.   2. Asia—Foreign
relations—Soviet Union.   I. Title.   II. Series: Oxford studies in
international history.
DK68.R28 2014
327.4705—dc23
2013040054

9 8 7 6 5 4 3 2 1
Printed in the United States of America
on acid-free paper

For Onon, the Asia of my innermost thoughts.

CONTENTS

ACKNOWLEDGMENTS

This book was great fun to write. It brought me face to face with an Asia I never knew. I met dozens of former policy makers, historians, and people from different walks of life, some who appear on the pages of this book, some who have left an intellectual imprint on my still malleable conscience, and some who have simply become great friends. With apologies to those I have accidentally omitted, I would like to thank the following scholars for helping me understand how the Cold War ended in Asia, for commenting on the book manuscript, and for sharing important sources: Jordan Baev, Csaba Bekes, Laszlo Borhi, Gregg Brazinsky, Choi Lyong, Malgorzata Gnoinska, Iwashita Akihiro, Jeremy Friedman, Izumikawa Yasuhiro, Yurii Kruchkin, Li Danhui, Alexander Lukin, Lorenz M. Lüthi, Vojtech Mastny, Elizabeth McGuire, Mircea Munteanu, Niu Jun, Svetlana Savranskaya, Bernd Schaefer, Shen Zhihua, Doug Selvage, Shimotomai Nobuo, Onon Perenlei, Mikhail Prozumenshchikov, Shin Jong-Dae, Pavel Stroilov, Balazs Szalontai, Lisbeth Tarlow, William Taubman, Péter Vámos, Robert Wampler, Katherine Weathersby, and Vladislav Zubok.

Additional thanks are due to Chen Jian and Tsuyoshi Hasegawa, who, through their writing and personal advice, have shaped my thinking about Chinese and Japanese politics and foreign policy. James Hershberg, Mark Kramer, Gilbert Rozman, Odd Arne Westad, and David Wolff have helped me conceptualize the key arguments of the book. Artemy Kalinovsky, then working on his own book on Soviet foreign policy, was a great partner in research adventures across the former Soviet Union.

In the course of writing this book I was fortunate to have interviewed former politicians, diplomats, and key witnesses of the era. I would like to express my gratitude to the following individuals for their time: Arai Nobuo, Georgii Arbatov, Amb. Romulus Budura, Stephen Bryen, Anatolii Chernyaev, Amb. Gong Ro-myung, Joseph M. Ha, Hwang Byongtae, H. E. Kim Young-sam, Vadim Medvedev, H. E. Nakasone Yasuhiro,

Vladimir Ovsyannikov, Pavel Palazhchenko, Park Chul-un, Amb. Vladimir Rakhmanin, Keith B. Richburg, Vasilii Saplin, Konstantin Sarkisov, H. E. Eduard Shevardnadze, Daniel Sneider, Joun-yung Sun, Vadim Tkachenko, Amb. Togo Kazuhiko, Alisher Vakhidov, Yurii Vanin, Nikolai Vasil'ev, and Wu'er Kaixi.

This book is based on multi-archival research. I would like to thank the following archives for their understanding and cooperation: (in China) Shanghai Municipal Archive; (in France) Archives Nationales; (in Germany) Foundation Archive of Parties and Mass Organizations, and the Stasi Archive; (in Hungary) Hungarian National Archive; (in India) Nehru Memorial Library and Museum; (in Italy) Italian Communist Party Archive; (in Mongolia) Mongolian Foreign Ministry Archive, especially T. Nergui, and the Government Archive; (in Russia) Archive of Foreign Policy of the Russian Federation, especially Elizaveta Guseva, State Archive of the Russian Federation, the Gorbachev Foundation Archive, especially Olga Zdravomyslova, Russian State Archive of Recent History, especially Mikhail Prozumenshchikov, Russian State Archive of Social and Political History, IMEMO Archive, and the Sakhalin State Archive; (in South Korea) Olympic Research Center; (in Switzerland) International Olympic Committee Archive; (in the United Kingdom) Foreign and Commonwealth Office; (in the United States) George Bush Presidential Library, Ronald Reagan Presidential Library, Archive of the United Nations, National Security Archive, especially Tom Blanton and Svetlana Savranskaya, Harvard University's Lamont Library, and the Archive of the Hoover Institution. In addition, I am most grateful to the History and Public Policy Program at the Woodrow Wilson Center, in particular to Christian Ostermann and James Person, for allowing me to draw on their institutional resources and collections.

I wrote most of this book while at the University of Nottingham Ningbo China (UNNC). I wish to thank my friends at UNNC for their patience with their restless colleague. In addition, I am grateful to the Slavic Research Center at the University of Hokkaido in Japan, to the Kyungnam University in South Korea, and to the Woodrow Wilson Center for hosting me at different stages of writing.

This book would not have been possible without the generous support of the British Academy, the Korea Foundation, and the Scowcroft Institute of International Affairs, which I acknowledge with gratitude.

Owing to its international scope and multilanguage research base, this book was difficult to write. It was, however, even more difficult to edit and I am truly fortunate to have had Susan Ferber of Oxford University Press guide me in revising the manuscript so that I am not the only one who can understand what it says. Thank you for that lesson, Susan. I would also like to thank Maureen Cirnitski and Elina Carmona for their hard work in preparing this book for publication.

Last but not least, all these years I have enjoyed the unfailing support of my family. My wife, Onon, stoically tolerated my regular disappearance into various archives all over the world, and my son, Nikita, often found his father buried in papers and books, too absorbed in uncovering hidden historical plots to check that math homework. I am also grateful to my parents, Sergey Radchenko Sr. and Tamara Radchenko, as well as my mother-in-law, Tsetsegnyam Lombodorj, who have long reconciled themselves to the fact that their son lives more in the past than in the present.

NOTE ON TRANSLITERATION

This book relied extensively on non-English sources. When transliterating Russian names, I used the Library of Congress system, modified to allow the common sense spelling of ya andyu. I shunned the use of umlauts in the English transliteration of Mongolian sources, which resulted in partial obscurity in the spelling of some Mongolian terms in the endnotes. Chinese names are spelled in pinyin in the book, except in the endnotes, where I provided the original characters for those interested in pursuing the sources further. Korean and Japanese sources in the endnotes are also spelled out in Korean and Japanese only. In view of the complexities of the competing spelling systems, Korean names in the text are rendered in their most recognizable form. Vietnamese names are written without accents.

Unwanted Visionaries

Introduction

On a wintry day of March 13, 1985, thousands of mourners gathered under the Kremlin walls to bid farewell to General Secretary Konstantin Chernenko, who had succumbed, at age seventy-three, to a combination of heart, lung, and liver disease. As his casket rolled into Red Square, soldiers stood guard in front of Lenin's mausoleum, keeping away the crowds with black-edged portraits of the deceased leader. New General Secretary Mikhail Gorbachev towered atop the mausoleum with other Politburo members. Delegations from foreign countries were seated on the long benches at the flanks. Gorbachev read his eulogy to the "faithful servant of our party and people," while foreign guests stared at the spectacle. Perhaps the only person who truly cared about Chernenko's death was his widow, Anna, who kissed him on the forehead before the casket was lowered into a grave near the Kremlin wall. Afterward, an observer reported, "the Politburo members discarded their red-and-black mourning armbands and returned to the mausoleum to watch soldiers march to shouted commands and military music."[1]

Chernenko's death surprised no one. For the brief months that he steered the Soviet Union, the ailing, asthmatic General Secretary struggled to live yet another day, but everyone knew that he was running out of time. Chernenko's death bore with it a promise of change, not only for the Soviet Union but also for the world. That promise was personified by Mikhail Gorbachev, the big unknown with as yet little to boast of but his youth and charm. Foreign dignitaries at the funeral eagerly awaited their chance to meet the new Soviet leader and get a sense of his intentions. There was a brief opportunity to do so at a reception held after Chernenko's burial in the Kremlin's grand St. George's Hall. Hundreds of visitors—from world statesmen to guerrilla leaders—assembled under the golden chandeliers to shake Gorbachev's hand and exchange a few words. Foreign correspondents watched carefully as Gorbachev greeted the delegations, counting the seconds he spent with each and making judgments, on this basis, about the new leader's foreign policy priorities.

The correspondents were in for a surprise. The British Prime Minister, Margaret Thatcher, who commanded everyone's attention at the previous Soviet funeral and had the longest and the warmest conversation with the ailing Chernenko, had to wait in line for half an hour. The Iron Lady "watched coldly" as first the young and charismatic Rajiv Gandhi of India and then the Chinese technocrat Li Peng were each whisked off to the front of the long queue of world leaders in a gesture of unmistakable symbolism: for Gorbachev, Asia came first.[2] The new Soviet leader looked East with anticipation unseen since the great Asian love affair of Nikita Khrushchev, who thirty years earlier steered his enthusiastic efforts toward an ever closer friendship with the world's first and second most populous countries. The ménage à trois did not last, but the idea survived and was rehabilitated as Gorbachev made his first unsure steps at the helm of an empire.

Gorbachev had been to neither China nor India. His first-hand experience of Asia amounted to two brief trips to Mongolia and Vietnam. But he was fascinated by Asia: by its population, its resources, and its potential. Time and again in his early months and years in power, Gorbachev addressed the subject of Asia's rise, and the importance of Soviet engagement with the region: "The development of civilization is moving in the direction of the Pacific," Gorbachev argued at a Politburo meeting in April 1986. And again: "A huge number of various countries and peoples coexist in Asia and in the Pacific Ocean. And we are building a bridge.... Let us raise our assessments of China, India, Japan. This is serious. This is politics. This will stimulate our relations with them." And on another occasion: "Civilization in the 21st century will move to the East. There are huge forces, huge potential of a future civilization in Asia."[3]

In time, all of this was cast aside, and it was the European and the American dimensions of Gorbachev's foreign policy that captured the imaginations of contemporary observers and, later, historians. The dramatic events of the late 1980s—Reykjavik and Malta, the collapse of socialism in Eastern Europe, and the fall of the Berlin Wall—have overtaken earlier events, so that in retrospect Gorbachev's Asian first love appears as nothing but a flirtation, a temporary distraction from the grand European finale of the Cold War. A recent mammoth book by the Gorbachev Foundation entitled "Responding to the Challenges of the Times" explores in some 926 pages the former General Secretary's foreign policy between 1985 and 1991, but only the last 137 pages touch on Asia. The region has been all but relegated to a side note even by the leader himself. The end of the Cold War was celebrated in style in Europe, but who can tell what happened to the Asian Cold War, and what happened to that spirit of 1985, when Gorbachev set his sights on closer engagement with the ancient civilizations of the East?

The Cold War ended differently in Asia than it did in Europe. There was no easy closure, no date to celebrate, no great fanfare, no great liberation, and little credit to be had for changing the world. In Asia, 1989 has a different sound to it, a sound of roaring tanks and thumping bullets. Apart from the Tiananmen massacre, all else has been forgotten as somehow irrelevant to the course of world history. The Soviet Union's Asia policy in the 1980s has received scant attention. Maybe it is because Gorbachev failed to make an impact on Asia in the same way he made an impact on Europe. Certainly, his vision of a Soviet pivot to the East went up in smoke, briefly replaced by promising relationships with Western Europe and America. Even the great achievement of the Sino-Soviet normalization, symbolized by Gorbachev's memorable trip to Beijing in May 1989, has faded in historical memory, despite being one symptom of a tectonic change in Asia, a change still taking place.

I watched Chernenko's funeral at home on a black-and-white TV in my family's small one-room flat on the fourth floor of a dilapidated Khrushchev-era building in the town of Korsakov, a bleak outpost on Sakhalin Island. I was only a child and did not appreciate the significance of what was about to happen. But even among the adults, few Sakhaliners realized that the Cold War was ending. It simply faded. On Army and Navy Day I was no longer allowed to run amok with other kids aboard the formidable cruisers docked in the heavily guarded port; the cruisers disappeared one day, never to return. The old Japanese carton factory across the street from our Khrushchevka had its fence rebuilt with fancy metal plates intended for a military helicopter base on the outskirt of town; who knows what happened to the choppers? Then, one day in 1990, I received a present from my father who had for the first time boarded a fishing boat to Japan, just across the Soya Strait: a Nintendo console. The Cold War was over.

Soon, every fishing boat would come from Japan loaded beyond capacity with second-hand cars. They were a wonder at first—these rusting symbols of technological progress—but before long almost every family bought one. Markets were flooded with cheap Chinese goods and angry customers wanting their money back for defective products. Bearded oilmen from Alaska and Texas congregated in the Pacific Café in Yuzhno-Sakhalinsk, biting into exotic hamburgers. There was a sense of great changes happening, but little did we know that the truly great changes were actually taking place elsewhere, in China, Japan, South Korea, further out in Southeast Asia. The region was booming and prospering, but Russia was left on the sidelines. It was never able to tap into the Asian miracle. "Civilization"—to use Gorbachev's vague term—moved to the East. Russia stayed behind.

* * *

This book recounts Soviet policy in Asia between 1982, when Leonid Brezhnev died, and 1991, the year of Soviet collapse. Chapter 1 challenges the conventional wisdom that Sino-Soviet rapprochement, which began in 1982, was a natural or inevitable outcome of Deng Xiaoping's foreign policy pragmatism and a consequence of China's reform and opening. Instead, the beginning of the dialogue between the two countries was a reaction to prevailing international circumstances. The early 1980s were a time of dramatic worsening of Soviet-American tensions. The détente was dead. In its wake came the Second Cold War, laden with promises of Ronald Reagan's crusade against the Evil Empire, crisis in Poland, war in Afghanistan, US economic sanctions, and the chilling nuclear missile controversy in Europe. Fearful of growing Soviet international isolation, the aging Soviet leadership arrived at the necessity of breaking new ground with China, although not without an internal struggle and backtracking.

Deng Xiaoping reciprocated Soviet feelers. He had invested himself heavily into a better relationship with the United States, but, with Ronald Reagan in the White House, the sort of strategic partnership Deng had envisioned proved well beyond his reach. The sale of American weapons to Taiwan and Reagan's reluctance to offer sensitive technology to China exposed Deng to internal criticism that he had done too much for the United States without American reciprocity. Distancing from the United States under the banner of the so-called independent foreign policy, and the beginning of the Sino-Soviet dialogue, helped Deng Xiaoping in redressing criticism from other party leaders while exerting pressure on the Americans to live up to his expectations, a tactic that worked extremely well.

But if there was a lot of tactical thinking in both Moscow and Beijing at the beginning of the Sino-Soviet dialogue, in both countries there were proponents of rapprochement whose sights were set higher than the immediate requirements of the geopolitical poker. For them, the Sino-Soviet normalization was first and foremost an ideological imperative, the natural consequence of the two countries' adherence to the socialist path. Tactics and strategy therefore combined in unforeseen ways to bring about silent, step-by-step improvement of Sino-Soviet relations from the second half of 1982. Gorbachev tapped into this dynamic, but the process began years before he had become the General Secretary.

Chapter 2 explores Soviet-Japanese relations from 1982 through 1987. Realizing Japan's growing importance to the region, the Soviet leadership, from Brezhnev to Gorbachev, worked hard to improve relations with Tokyo and tap into Japan's capital and technology, so sorely needed by the Soviet economy. Moreover, the Soviet leadership recognized that frigid political relations with Japan only strengthened the Americans and their system of alliance aimed at containing the Soviet threat. The key problem in the Soviet-Japanese relationship was the disagreement over the fate of the Southern Kurile Islands, called "northern territories" by the Japanese, which had been occupied by the Soviets in the closing days of the Second World War.

In the early 1980s the Soviet leadership briefly considered making concessions in the territorial dispute, hoping to split Japan from the United States and neutralizing it in the context of heightening tensions in East Asia. That did not happen. Japan was too firmly and comfortably lodged within its American alliance to attempt a rapprochement independent of Washington. Gorbachev's arrival on the scene failed to break the territorial deadlock in Soviet-Japanese relations. The Soviets and the Japanese had inflated perceptions of their countries' importance vis-à-vis the other, believing that the other would eventually give in rather than lose out in economic and security terms. Gorbachev failed to find a place for Japan in his global vision. The Japanese leaders, too, often sacrificed better relations with the USSR to appease the United States in the context of divergences over trade and Washington's claims that the Japanese did not do enough to share the burden of defending their country from communist threat.

Chapter 3 explores the rise and fall of Gorbachev's vision for Asia. One of the main pillars of this vision was Moscow's relationship with India. Although India was unaligned during the Cold War, between 1985 and 1987 Gorbachev made impressive inroads with the Indians, thanks to his close relationship with Rajiv Gandhi. A dynamic Soviet-Indian relationship was for Gorbachev the vital core of a new foreign policy, one that he thought should replace the hapless hole-patching of the Soviet octogenarians, the self-entrapping web of increasingly costly commitments that had led the Soviet Union down a blind alley by the early 1980s. Gorbachev labored to bring about a triangle—USSR, India, and China—to offset US influence in the region. This was the new General Secretary's strategy for rescuing the Soviet Union from its increasingly obvious international isolation. Yet Gorbachev overrated his ability to snatch victory from the jaws of defeat, for neither China nor India was as keen on triangular politics as Gorbachev was. The two powers had their own plans for bolstering regional hegemony, ones in which the Soviet Union had no role to play.

Soviet relations with India withered in the late 1980s. This was partly related to the imperative of quitting Afghanistan, and the rapprochement with Pakistan that this entailed for the USSR. The chapter recounts Gorbachev's decision to end the war in Afghanistan, explaining how he hesitated in making a choice between leaving that quagmire and maintaining Soviet credibility in the Third World. The signing of the peace accords on Afghanistan in April 1988 left Rajiv Gandhi out in the cold. India was being bypassed in the train of events that would lead, in a matter of months, to the end of the Cold War and to the death of non-alignment as a strategic concept. Gorbachev realized that his engagement with the West ruled out the sort of geopolitical arrangements he was once so desperate to sell to the Indians. From 1987 his attention was increasingly diverted away from India and China toward Europe and the United States, and, indeed, toward mounting difficulties at home. Gorbachev needed the West and the moral and financial support that a broad-ended engagement with the West could bring to bear on his weakening domestic standing. The divergence between former geopolitical imperatives and the realities of Soviet policy of the late 1980s was most evident in Gorbachev's refusal to sanction the deepening of Soviet-Indian military cooperation and closer ties in the nuclear field. The slow demise of the promising Soviet-Indian relationship was a symptom of Gorbachev's reorientation from the geopolitical thinking that marked his policy from the very beginning toward hope for a superpower détente born of brave but naïve idealism.

Chapter 4 explores the origins of the political settlement in Indochina. Since Vietnam invaded Cambodia to overthrow the Pol Pot regime, the Chinese insisted that Hanoi's withdrawal from Cambodia was a prerequisite for Sino-Soviet normalization. Deng Xiaoping saw the Vietnamese occupation as a part of the Soviet plot to encircle China. This assessment began to change in the mid-1980s thanks to budding rapprochement with Moscow, but Deng kept up the pressure, hoping to use the promise of better relations as an incentive for the Soviets to help China in containing Vietnam's regional ambitions. Gorbachev was not responsive to Deng's probes because he was mindful of the geopolitical importance of the Soviet-Vietnamese alliance and did not want to squander his influence by pressing Hanoi to concede to China's demands. Nevertheless, as economic costs of supporting Vietnam's occupation of Cambodia mounted, the Soviets worked behind the scenes to effect a peace settlement.

Chapter 5 looks at the making of the Sino-Soviet summit of 1989. China and the USSR were both on the road with destinations yet unknown.

They were locked in an implicit competition as pioneers of reform social-ism. Gorbachev felt upstaged by Deng and criticized the Chinese for their failure to understand that political reforms had to precede reforms in the economic sphere. The Gorbachev phenomenon was initially welcomed in China, although by 1988–89 this assessment was questioned by Chinese conservatives. Events in Eastern Europe influenced the mindset of the Chinese leaders, none more powerfully than the fall of the Berlin Wall and the death of Nicolae Ceaușescu in Romania. Deng chose to avoid differ-ences over ideology in his landmark meeting with Gorbachev days before the Tiananmen crackdown. For the author of China's rise, the handshake with Gorbachev represented a new departure for China as a player on the international stage.

Gorbachev's visit to Beijing coincided with the student demonstrations in the Tiananmen Square, but the crushing of the protesters on June 4 did not elicit Gorbachev's condemnation. In spite of his personal aver-sion to the use of force, Gorbachev was all too ready to excuse the violent suppression of dissent in China, and even utilized Tiananmen to expand relations with Beijing at US expense. The Bush Administration was seri-ously concerned about the turn of the events, as the prospect of a rein-vigorated Sino-Soviet alliance loomed large in 1989. Bush misread Chinese foreign policy: 1989 was not 1949. China was not in the game of leaning to one side or the other. Deng steered a neutral course. Not even Yeltsin's rise derailed Beijing's careful policy, for although Yeltsin was detested in Beijing, and the Chinese government secretly sympathized with the plan-ners of the coup d'état, Yeltsin's victory in 1991 was quickly accepted; in a few years China and Russia moved toward a "strategic partnership."

Chapter 6 retells the story of the Soviet Union's engagement with the two Koreas. Under Gorbachev the Soviets' traditional partnership with Pyongyang reached its apogee; the Soviets valued this relationship, because North Korea, like Vietnam, was an important geopolitical asset in the Asian Cold War. But Pyongyang's resistance to political reform irked Gorbachev, while North Korea's persistent requests for military aid took a toll on his patience. By 1988 Gorbachev began to reciprocate South Korea's probes for establishing better relations. For South Korean President Roh Tae-woo, a rapprochement with the USSR was a sine qua non of his country's emer-gence as a prominent regional player; not only would it boost Seoul's inter-national standing, but it would also strengthen South Korea in dealing with the North. On the other hand, rapprochement with USSR would bring huge political dividends to any South Korean politician who could make it hap-pen, and a real competition ensued between 1988 and 1990 amid leading political factions in Seoul for the chance to be the first. Gorbachev, after resisting South Korea's approaches for longer than necessary, gave in, persuaded by the promise of credits from Seoul desperately needed for the empty Soviet coffers. Soviet–South Korean normalization was not taken kindly in Pyongyang; in the face of its own growing isolation, North Korea sought assurance of survival in the pursuit of a nuclear deterrent.

Chapters 7 and 8 trace the ups and downs of Soviet-Japanese relations until 1991. In 1988 through 1989 Gorbachev appeared willing, for the first time, to discuss the merits of Japan's claims to the "northern territories." This encouraged the Japanese to think that Soviet concessions were within reach. However, evidence suggests that Gorbachev deliberately sought to appear flexible to entice Japan to develop relations despite the territorial deadlock. He had no intention to return the islands. Tokyo's emphasis on economic incentives was misplaced. The Soviets wanted to develop Siberia and the Far East but thought they could do it even without Japan's involvement or by playing the Japanese against their competitors. By the turn of the decade such hopes had proven illusory, highlighting the importance of mending fences with Japan. But a breakthrough was more difficult than ever, as Gorbachev's policy of glasnost gave rise to public opinion that, especially in regions bordering Japan, proved vocally hostile to territorial concessions.

In 1990, inspired by the changes that had just taken place in Europe, a powerful Japanese politician, Ozawa Ichiro, attempted to arrange a secret deal that would involve the transfer of the islands to Japan in return for massive Japanese investments in the Soviet economy. The desperate Soviet economic situation made Ozawa think that Gorbachev would be open to a compromise. He miscalculated the extent to which Gorbachev's opponents—especially Boris Yeltsin—would use the threat of territorial concessions to question Gorbachev's patriotism and undermine his political base. Gorbachev was unwilling to sell the islands, and his visit to Tokyo in April 1991—a long-awaited chance to open a new page in Soviet-Japanese relations—produced little for Tokyo in the way of tangible results. In the closing months of 1991 the Russian leadership maneuvered carefully in an attempt to gain Japanese economic aid in exchange for an unclear promise to return the islands. Yeltsin was not willing to put his nationalist credentials on the line, and the issue went unresolved. Absorbed in back-and-forth haggling over the ownership of the islands, Japan missed out on the chance to improve relations with the USSR. The Cold War's end caught Tokyo by surprise, and it failed to formulate a new foreign policy for the changing era while comfortably relying on the familiar bedrock of US-Japanese alliance.

The main protagonist of this book is Mikhail Gorbachev, remembered for having brought about the end of the Cold War and the Soviet rapprochement with the West. *Unwanted Visionaries* shows that this was not what he had started out to do. At the outset he looked to China and India as allies in the global struggle against the United States. Gorbachev worked hard to maintain relations with longtime clients like Vietnam and North Korea in order to strengthen Soviet geopolitical standing in Asia. Gorbachev, like his predecessors, saw Asia as a Cold War theater where the Soviet Union could lead by winning the sympathies and loyalties of the regional players. His vision collapsed for lack of followers, however, and Gorbachev turned his attention to Soviet-American dialogue, which in due course led to the dismantling of the Soviet Union's imperial enterprise and the decline of its global influence. Unwelcome in the West, unwanted in Asia, Russia retreated inward, nurturing visions of a comeback recycled from Gorbachev's portfolio of unrealized dreams.

CHAPTER 1

Card Players: The Origins of Sino-Soviet Rapprochement, 1982–85

In March 1982 Soviet General Secretary Leonid Il'ich Brezhnev visited Tashkent, in Uzbekistan, to spend a few days in the company of his friend Sharaf Rashidov, a corrupt local tyrant who had made millions from a massive cotton scam. The official purpose of Brezhnev's trip to the Central Asian republic was to present Uzbekistan with the Order of Lenin on account of Rashidov's successes in cotton-growing, but, in view of Tashkent's proximity to the border with Chinese Xinjiang, Brezhnev planned to make a statement about improving relations with China. It almost never happened. On March 23, Brezhnev was touring an aviation plant with Rashidov when scaffolding bearing numerous onlookers suddenly collapsed, burying the Soviet leader and his entourage. Brezhnev survived but broke his collarbone.[1] It was under these dramatic circumstances that on March 24 the enfeebled and anesthetized General Secretary delivered his policy statement on China, one of the most important policy statements he had ever made.[2]

Brezhnev said that the Soviet Union was not threatening China and that it would be willing to resume border talks. The Soviet Union, he said, still considered China to be a socialist country and wanted to develop relations with it in all fields without preconditions, if there was reciprocity on China's part. He added that the Soviet Union recognized China's sovereignty over Taiwan.[3] While nothing in what the General Secretary said was a spectacular departure from existing policy, Brezhnev's statement was by far the friendliest since relations with China reached a new low in 1980. Few thought so at the time, but Brezhnev's Tashkent initiative became a new point of departure for Moscow's relationship with Beijing and a turning point for international politics that would change the dynamic of the relationship among China, the USSR, and the United States.

This chapter explores the origins of Sino-Soviet rapprochement between 1982 and 1985, when the two sides took tentative steps to improve relations after more than two decades of hostility. This process cannot be understood except in the broader international context. Indeed, the unseen presence in Sino-Soviet dialogue was that of the United States. Each country approached the other in light of fears and hopes they had for their relations with Washington. The Reagan Administration's hawkish policies vis-à-vis the Chinese and the Soviets in effect strengthened the hand of supporters of Sino-Soviet rapprochement in both countries, paving way to a difficult but ultimately constructive engagement. While the talks that followed Brezhnev's Tashkent probe pursued tactical goals at first, they inadvertently led to something greater, reshaping both countries' foreign policies in the direction of cooperation unseen since the Sino-Soviet alliance fell apart in the 1960s.

THE TASHKENT LINE

Brezhnev was well past the point when he should have made policy statements or even appeared in public. He had experienced physical and mental decline since the mid-1970s, and for the three years before the Tashkent trip was as good as a walking corpse, the subject of endless hypocritical praise in Soviet propaganda and the biting ridicule of the man in the street. Suffering from asthenia and cerebral vascular sclerosis, slurring his speech and unsure in gait, Leonid Il'ich refused to die, starring in the sorry spectacle of Soviet decay, bathing in the sea in the Crimea, reading from his prepared notes on well-timed occasions (as in Tashkent), perhaps not entirely oblivious of what was happening in his country and in the world, but certainly resigned and helpless in altering the course of events.[4] In the meantime, the Soviet Union slid deeper and deeper into international isolation.

It may or may not have registered in the depths of Brezhnev's dim conscience that, as he was driven around in a black limousine with Rashidov through the streets of Tashkent, Soviet soldiers were losing a war across the border in Afghanistan. The Soviet Union invaded this country in December 1979. The decision bore Brezhnev's signature but he was hardly in a position to appreciate the consequences of Moscow's fatal misadventure;

others in the Politburo had decided for him.[5] The invasion caused an international uproar, especially in the United States. President Jimmy Carter, who had planted kisses on Brezhnev's bloated cheeks the previous June at the Vienna summit, now refused to submit the hard-bargained nuclear treaty SALT II for ratification to the US Senate. The détente this treaty symbolized was pronounced dead, buried somewhere in the mountains of Afghanistan.

Or, some say, it was already dead before Afghanistan, and "lies buried in the sands of Ogaden," in Ethiopia—in the words of Zbigniew Brzezinski, Carter's National Security Adviser. Brzezinski claimed that the Soviets killed détente by their lack of moderation in Third World conflicts and by building up overseas commitments at US expense from the Caribbean to the South China Sea.[6] If anyone shed tears over the unrealized promise of détente, it was not the anti-Soviet champion Brzezinski, who worked hard to derail a more accommodating policy toward the USSR. Brzezinski schemed tirelessly to undermine his rival in the policy establishment, Secretary of State Cyrus Vance, who had been careful not to do something that the Soviets would interpret as obviously hostile.[7]

Brzezinski held no inhibitions in this respect. Between 1978 and 1980 he did more than just about anyone else to kill détente and, inadvertently, to precipitate Tashkent, by playing the China card in the face of Moscow's dire warnings. He did so against resistance from the State Department, not least the US Ambassador to the USSR, Thomas J. Watson, who argued for a more "evenhanded" approach to the two communist giants. Watson wondered why the Chinese, "who had a tendency to jump around from bed to bed," received much better treatment than the Soviets.[8] "You have to remember," Brzezinski told Watson, "that we are very sexy people."[9] Brzezinski's successful flirtation with China—resulting in the normalization of Sino-US relations on January 1, 1979—had far-reaching consequences, deeply unsettling to keen observers in Soviet policy-making circles.

By 1980 the United States and its allies in Western Europe were providing military technology to China. It was a time when Beijing singled out the Soviet Union as China's number one enemy, fought a war with Soviet ally Vietnam, and helped the anti-Soviet mujahedeen in Afghanistan with weapons and covert training. The Soviets mailed countless letters of protest to the West and resorted to desperate measures to avert China's military modernization, such as forcing their allies in Eastern Europe to curb the flow of technology to the Chinese through a series of export control meetings. After one such meeting in Lovech, Bulgaria, in October 1980, the Hungarian participants noted, "they [the Soviets] are scared of strengthening the Chinese military potential. . . . The Soviet representative generally urged great caution in all forms of new cooperation proposed by the Chinese . . . in the interest of avoiding harmful leaks of technical-scientific findings."[10]

On October 2, 1980, the Soviet Politburo discussed military cooperation between China and the United States and passed a resolution to counteract this cooperation by explaining (through Soviet ambassadors posted overseas) what China's long-term designs really were and how the naïve Americans had been taken in by China's anti-Soviet stand. "[B]eing realistic, one should recognize that a 'strong' China will probably choose a different direction for its expansionist plans: it will swallow neighboring countries, take over regions vital for the entire world, and will not serve as an instrument in the hands of the USA or some other country."[11] By helping China's modernization, the Soviets prophesied, Washington hastened the arrival of America's own doom. Foreign Minister Andrei Gromyko, who, unlike Brezhnev, had not lost capacity for analytical thinking, memorably said of the West's cooperation with Beijing, "you may be in a euphoric mood now about China but the time will come when you will all be shedding tears."[12]

By 1980, when Gromyko "bleated" about isolation in unproductive meetings with the Americans, and Brezhnev passed his time in harmful indulgence in sleeping pills, Sino-Soviet relations were as warm as permafrost and had been so for a generation.[13] In the early 1960s, Mao Zedong accused Moscow of betraying revolution and abandoning Marxism-Leninism, and the Soviets responded with ideologically charged tirades of their own. It was not long before polemical debates over communist theology gave way to a frigid standoff, punctuated by sudden flares of tensions. In 1969 China and the Soviet Union nearly went to war over a disputed islet on the Ussuri River, and in 1979 the Sino-Vietnamese war necessitated a show of Soviet military force on the border with China for the sake of deterrence. In the intervening years, both sides built up huge military forces at their mutual border, and the Soviets stationed troops in Mongolia and concluded an anti-Chinese defensive pact with Vietnam.

Brezhnev, before his irreversible slide into senility, had become so apprehensive of the Chinese threat that he sought a quasi alliance with the archenemy—the American imperialists—to offset the sinister designs of that "perfidious" neighbor that, he conceded, as a "European" he never understood.[14] He had no doubts about his own fate—or that of the other Soviet leaders—at the Chinese hands, should it come to the worst: "For me they have ordained an honorable death. They plan to shoot me. Mr. Kosygin [Prime Minister] they plan to hang, and Mr. Mikoyan [Politburo member] they will boil alive. At least I have an honorable fate, not like Mikoyan, like those who will be boiled alive."[15] That was said in 1972, when the Chinese and the Soviets were at least talking to each other and were bound by a treaty of alliance. By 1980, this was no longer the case. China had pulled out from the defunct treaty, moving, in the words of American policy maker Mike Oksenberg, "into a new era of leaning to one side, this time toward the US."[16]

Oksenberg, Brzezinski's China hand at the National Security Council, had experience in academia, something few Soviet foreign policy experts could boast of, and took a long view of China-US relations that was anything but euphoric. "The Chinese believe the quest for a world order is quixotic," he wrote to Brzezinski. "They wish to position themselves, as in a horse race, so that [as] our strength ebbs—which they see as inevitable—and as the Soviet power peaks, they will be in a position to surge forward."[17] This logic would have impressed the more pragmatically inclined minds in the Soviet corridors of power, especially the old China hand Mikhail Stepanovich Kapitsa, who, as Deputy Foreign Minister, played a key role in defining Moscow's policy toward China at this low ebb in Sino-Soviet relations.

The tall, bald, broad-shouldered, and humorous Kapitsa, nicknamed Mikhstep, was the living legend of the Soviet foreign policy establishment, and not only because of his reputation as a hopeless womanizer, a heavy drinker, and a connoisseur of quality cigars. His occasional lectures for young diplomats at the Foreign Ministry were packed; he was known to say things that bordered on heresy—and get away with it.[18] Above all, he was a pragmatist in the best realpolitik tradition of Russia's foreign policy. He and Oksenberg would have agreed about the general thrust of China's intentions on the world stage. "The Chinese never befriend anyone for a long time," Kapitsa pronounced some weeks after Brezhnev's performance in Tashkent.[19] Whereas for Oksenberg this was a bad thing—"we must harbor no private illusion that the Chinese see this convergence [with the US] as enduring," he warned Brzezinski[20]—for Kapitsa, China's propensity to "jump from bed to bed" was the one great hope for breaking out of the Soviet impasse of the early 1980s.

At a time when few could foresee the consequences of China's reform and opening, Kapitsa knew the Chinese would abandon socialism. "They have advanced the motto 'let's get rich' and everyone has escaped into trading." "In ten years," he ominously predicted in June 1982, "the capitalists and kulaks will multiply, and there will be no other way but to crush them with tanks."[21] For a pragmatist like Kapitsa, this did not really matter. Whatever the Chinese did at home was their business. In foreign policy, China's alignment with the United States was only temporary, because the Chinese "wish to modernize [their] economy using Western technological help and credits, and have no other capital to pay for this help but anti-Sovietism."[22]

At some point, they would realize that one-sided reliance on the United States hurt China's international standing. "Maybe in 10–15 years the Chinese will open their eyes and take up an equal distance from both the US and the USSR," noted Kapitsa.[23] This prediction was borne out by events and occurred much earlier than Mikhstep would have predicted.

In the meantime, after the Chinese announced that they would indefinitely postpone bilateral consultations with the Soviet Union (as a penalty for the Soviet invasion of Afghanistan) and even refused to send their athletes to the Moscow Olympics, Kapitsa was one of the very few people who would still occasionally go back and forth between Beijing and Moscow. Supposedly he was visiting with the Soviet Ambassador, but in reality he was testing the waters to see if the Chinese were interested in developing a dialogue. Kapitsa turned up in Beijing in March 1980 and met privately with his counterpart in the Chinese Foreign Ministry, Yu Hongliang.[24] He repeated the experiment in 1981 and then again in May 1982, when he met with the deputy Foreign Minister Qian Qichen.[25] During these meetings, the Chinese insisted that, before Sino-Soviet relations could improve, the Soviets had to remove the "three obstacles" to normalization—first, cut troops at the border and pull forces out of Mongolia; second, make Vietnam withdraw from Cambodia (Vietnam had invaded neighboring Cambodia in December 1978, prompting Chinese accusations of Soviet complicity); and finally, leave Afghanistan. These were ambitious demands, and Kapitsa's one-man missions could not even begin to address them.

This was the context in which Brezhnev made his policy pronouncement, his speaking notes set in big letters for ease of reading. It would be an exaggeration to say that he was fully cognizant of the new policy direction. A good illustration of Brezhnev's mental state was an episode not long after Tashkent when, in a public speech in Azerbaijan, he confused Azerbaijan with Afghanistan and launched into reading a classified memo, not noticing the mistake until his foreign policy aide pulled him by his elbow.[26] There was no telling what the General Secretary would sign into policy. Much depended on his aides, who would read this or that memo out to him and then get his signature. But, as Aleksandr Bovin, one of his speech writers and the editor of the national daily *Izvestiya* explained in September 1982, "if you tell him about this memo in the morning, or even about the subject that it is devoted to, he will stare at you, as if this is the first time he is hearing about it, and then will brush you aside like an annoying fly: don't spoil my vacation. He just doesn't remember what he is doing and what he is signing."[27]

But if Brezhnev's lips uttered those words, who was behind the idea? Bovin, as one of the speech writers, most certainly played a role in the formulation of what became known as the "Tashkent line."[28] The paragraph about China was "consciously inserted" into that speech, perhaps by Bovin, who had for several years tried unsuccessfully to persuade the Soviet leadership that changes were happening in China after Mao's death.[29] Another candidate for the authorship of the new policy line was Brezhnev's aide Viktor Golikov, who had gone on record earlier for inserting similar passages into Brezhnev's speeches, most recently in August 1980.[30] Despite some uncertainty as to who pioneered rapprochement with China, there is no doubt as to who opposed it: Oleg Borisovich Rakhmanin.

Rakhmanin was the First Deputy Head of the Department for Relations with Socialist Countries, known simply as The Department, in the Central Committee of the Soviet Communist Party. Born in 1924, he was not even sixty at the time of Tashkent, a relatively young man by the standards of the Soviet ruling elite. Rakhmanin's professional career began in 1946, when he was posted as a Soviet diplomat to China, then still in the throes of a civil war. In the 1950s he studied and worked in Beijing, reaching the senior position of a counselor at the Soviet Embassy by the turn of that decade, just as the Sino-Soviet friendship went up in smoke. Many Soviet diplomats who had invested themselves heavily into learning China's language, history, and culture found China, swept up by the tide of the Cultural Revolution, hostile, xenophobic, and anti-Soviet. Many would-be diplomats drowned their sorrows in academia. Rakhmanin, though, made the best of the situation. In 1968 he took up a job at the Central Committee and soon made a name for himself as the top Soviet authority on anything China-related.[31]

During a period when his boss in the Central Committee, Konstantin Rusakov, spent weeks at a time on vacations and in the hospital, Rakhmanin assumed formidable power, since his Department was in charge of relations not just with China but all socialist countries.[32] There was also another International Department in the Central Committee, one that liaised with communist parties in the West and in the Third World. Together the two departments played a role similar to that of the National Security Council in the United States; but of the two, The Department was by far the more important. With the ailing Soviet leadership unwilling and unable to shoulder the daily burdens of policy making, Rakhmanin's influence in the corridors of power soared. Rakhmanin's pronouncements on China assumed the character of immutable truths, which were delivered through party decisions and publications in flagship journals to the broader audience of academics, journalists, and the Soviet public. Through annual consultations known as "the Interkit," Rakhmanin's decrees were passed on to obliging policy communities in the socialist commonwealth.[33]

In his many publications Rakhmanin was ferociously critical of the Chinese, even after Mao Zedong, long demonized in Soviet propaganda, passed from the stage.[34] Romanian diplomat Romulus Budura, who had known Rakhmanin in Beijing in the 1950s, noted that "he loved China."[35] "He loved China and the Chinese people, and always believed in their huge potential," remarked Rakhmanin's son, who followed in his father's footsteps to become a China expert at the Soviet Foreign Ministry.[36] But his coworkers and acquaintances in the Central Committee remembered a temperamental, heavy-handed man, deaf to opinions different from his own. Georgii Arbatov, one of the Soviet Union's most prominent public intellectuals, labeled him "a Buddhist bonze."[37] It was an apt characterization of a man the Chinese memorably called "the fourth obstacle to normalization."

In the run-up to Tashkent, Rakhmanin "was trying to prove that nothing has changed in China after Mao's death," Bovin recalled.

> Mao had turned away from the socialist road, and there is no sign that the Chinese are amending Mao's anti-socialist principles. Present-day China has no smell of socialism. Golikov, however, thought that even under Mao China remained socialist even though it cannot be ruled out that the "Great Helmsman" had gone overboard in terms of his revolutionary-ness and anti-Sovietism. We have to support the Chinese who are trying to correct Mao. And it's time to be friends. . . . I am not sure that Brezhnev understood these details. His logic was simpler: Mao is gone, the "Gang of Four" [who helped orchestrate the Cultural Revolution] is in jail, so something must be changing, and not for the worse. A probe will not hurt.[38]

The Tashkent probe thrust Rakhmanin into a dilemma. It came at a time when the Soviet Union was running into increasing resistance among its allies to Rakhmanin's hardline anti-Chinese policy. Economic difficulties in Eastern Europe in the early 1980s prompted interest in increasing trade with China, while the Chinese, despite open hostility toward the Soviet Union, seemed willing to improve relations with the East Europeans.[39] Soviet allies hoped that Tashkent would signal change in the rigid Soviet position, which would make it easier for the East Germans, among others, to mend fences with China. Rakhmanin hurried to put an end to such speculations, announcing at a meeting of socialist bloc party functionaries in Moscow in early April that Tashkent did not mean a change of policy for Moscow, that there was full continuity with the past, and that there was a unanimity of views about China's "rightist, pro-imperialist course" within the Central Committee, the Foreign Ministry, and the Soviet academic institutes.[40] He was lying.

In May 1982, Rakhmanin left for the annual meeting of the Interkit in Sofia in a bid to reassert his authority over the wavering anti-Chinese ranks in the Soviet bloc. Interkit had been running into trouble for some time. This time the disagreements could no longer be papered over. The SED (East German Communist Party) delegation had explicit instructions from the East German leader Erich Honecker to pursue an "active policy towards China, corresponding to the long term interests of socialism and peace."[41] The head of the delegation, Bruno Mahlow, challenged Rakhmanin's pessimistic take on China and refused to sign the Interkit report.[42] One of the key disagreements was over the correct interpretation of the Tashkent line—whether (as the East Germans claimed) it was a major departure or whether (as Rakhmanin insisted) it was just a tactical move.[43]

Rakhmanin returned from Sofia determined to have his line approved by the highest leadership and submitted a report to this end to the Politburo's Chinese Commission, of which he was the Secretary.[44] He insisted that efforts to "expose Chinese hegemonism" would have to be continued and interpreted recent developments in China as a "move towards the right." The Chinese Commission reportedly disagreed on the course of action to take. Yurii Andropov (soon to be the General Secretary) and Boris Ponomarev (the head of International Department) called for a rapprochement with the Chinese—while "giving them a rebuff when needed." Gromyko, though, "demanded to push the Chinese, not to let them off lightly." In the end, the Commission adopted a twelve-page document in Rakhmanin's style, singling out Honecker for criticism and proposing several measures to silence the domestic champions of better Sino-Soviet relations. The Politburo endorsed these measures on May 20, despite Brezhnev's lip service in defense of the Tashkent line.[45]

Rakhmanin's Interkit report was clearly directed against Sino-Soviet rapprochement, although the publication on the same day of a relatively softcore *Pravda* editorial by a certain "Igor Aleksandrov" (who quite possibly stood for the KGB)[46] predicting that "sooner or later unsolved problems [in Sino-Soviet relations] will have to be removed" assured readers that the Tashkent line had not been abandoned.[47] Rakhmanin, who sought the Politburo's permission to "toughen" the Aleksandrov article, fell short of his ambitions this time. Nevertheless, the endorsement of his report suggested that the proponents of a rapprochement faced a formidable battle, as Anatolii Chernyaev found out first hand when he refused to sign his name to Rakhmanin's report. Chernyaev, who was then the Deputy Head of the International Department,[48] remembered an angry Rakhmanin "storming" into his office, demanding a signature, and even threatening (over the phone) to take up the matter with the higher authorities.[49]

Undaunted, Chernyaev complained to his immediate boss Boris Ponomarev:

I don't know if you are aware of this, but in the last 15 years when Rakhmanin was responsible for China in the CC Department, and especially after he became the First Deputy, he wrote dozens of articles, brochures and even books. And all of this is about one thing: how to smash China. He perfectly understands that if relations changed, all of his "literature" will go into the trash bin. But he has already nominated himself for the elections to the Academy of Sciences and has no intention to abandon this plan. So he will do anything to make sure that our line in relation to China remains such as depicted in his articles and brochures written under his four pen-names. But I think it is not appropriate to surrender this vital area of our state interests to Rakhmanin's personal ambitions.[50]

Ponomarev signaled agreement. He had endorsed Rakhmanin's report at the Chinese Commission and supported it at the Politburo, as did Yurii Andropov, who should have known better than most that Rakhmanin was advising a harmful course of action. Inertia was a strong force, however, and Rakhmanin enjoyed a great clout. Having imposed his opinions on the Politburo, he continued to press for conformity among allies, as he did in a conversation with the Hungarian Ambassador in Moscow, Mátyás Szűrös, on July 7: "Colleagues working in the field...hold excessively positive opinions which may incite the leadership of fraternal Parties toward exaggerated development of relations. The socialist countries could objectively become part of the Chinese 'broad anti-Soviet united front.'" Szűrös asked, anxiously, whether Hungary had fallen out of step and learned, to probable relief, that the Hungarians were doing all right; it was the East Germans who were giving Rakhmanin a headache.[51]

Empowered by the May 20 Politburo decision, Rakhmanin ventured to bring Honecker to heel. He had a letter prepared and sent to the East German leader on July 14, 1982. It began "Dear Comrade Erich Honecker," implying a direct personal appeal, as if from Brezhnev to Honecker, but was signed as "the Central Committee of the CPSU."[52] Odds are Brezhnev never saw this letter. Rakhmanin effectively appropriated the Central Committee for his ends, hijacking China policy, as Brezhnev, reduced to senility, went on a semi-permanent vacation, and other key players in the Soviet leadership jockeyed for the power.

In the letter, Rakhmanin repeated his conventional take on China's duplicity and hostility. "One gets the impression," the letter went, "that the current leaders of the PRC have no desire to conduct a serious political dialogue with us, they are not prepared for it." He noted, however, that Beijing was attempting by means of "small steps" to improve relations with some Eastern European countries at the Soviet Union's expense. Under these circumstances, the Chinese approaches had to be rebuffed resolutely. Should any relations be maintained with China, these should be limited strictly to trade, science, culture, and sport—party-to-party ties should definitely not be developed. In economic relations, Rakhmanin called on the East Germans to consult with the USSR before taking any steps and certainly not allow anything that could "strengthen the potential of the Chinese hegemonism." The same conclusion applied to the development of exchange in science, culture, and sport, because, in Rakhmanin's assessment, Beijing used "people's diplomacy" to "undermine our friendship and cooperation. Ties, which manifest such intentions, are unacceptable."[53]

In conclusion, Rakhmanin wrote:

> The CC CPSU believes that the German friends will correctly understand our deep concern about the dangerous consequences of China's differentiated approach in relations with the fraternal countries, and this policy will be rebuffed. It is clear that if Beijing obtained a basis to speculate on the fact that someone from the closest allies and friends of the USSR shows neutralism or submissiveness with regard to the anti-Soviet "widest united front," being hammered together by the Chinese leaders, this would have extremely negative consequences for socialism, peace and our bilateral cooperation.[54]

The letter was written in a rather heavy-handed, intimidating manner, interlaced with implicit and explicit threats. It is not difficult to imagine how Honecker felt about receiving it from none other than the "Central Committee of the CPSU," though he may not have realized the extent to which it reflected Rakhmanin's personal preferences.[55] Upon considering Rakhmanin's letter at the Politburo on July 27, 1982, the East Germans resolved to tell the Soviets off, while moving ahead with the gradual normalization of relations with China.[56] With the power vacuum increasingly evident in Moscow, Honecker refused to be cowed by Rakhmanin's threats; his quiet rebellion showed the limits of Soviet influence in Eastern Europe years before this influence formally collapsed. Rakhmanin did not necessarily get the message.

The May 20 Politburo decision also gave Rakhmanin remit to publish an article in the leading Communist Party journal *Kommunist*. The following month the Department submitted a piece that rubbed the Chinese into dust on all counts. Other than repeating the well-known Rakhmaninite claims about the sins of Maoism and the evil plotting of the "Chinese hegemonists" in coup with various dark forces, the article specifically addressed heretics among unnamed communist parties that had responded to Beijing's calls for rapprochement. "A certain ideological closing of ranks between anticommunists like Reagan, social-chauvinists in Beijing and the opportunists has taken place," said the article.[57] Rakhmanin's team made it unclear who the opportunists were, but Erich Honecker would have known.

The piece went to the *Kommunist*'s editorial committee, which discussed it on June 27, with several members expressing grave concern about the jaw-dropping formulations. "About the word 'hegemonism'—'Chinese hegemonism,' 'Soviet hegemonism'—this makes a terrible impression," complained Stepan Salychev, who, as a former KGB agent in Paris, had known better style than Rakhmanin's—"Maybe we could do without these things." Another member of the board agreed that the article made a "strange impression" and contained many "contradictions" and "unclear thoughts." Several people spoke in favor of "postponing" publication despite the "difficult position of the editor": "One should take into account that this material will be read by very different readers through a huge magnifying glass. This is serious political material; therefore one should approach it very seriously."[58]

No one knew this better than the editor of *Kommunist*, Richard Kosolapov. Since the article had come from Rakhmanin, it could not be "postponed." "Accepted for publication with due regard to the comments voiced," was all that Kosolapov could bring himself to say.[59] The matter appeared closed, and the Chinese were on track to be served a nasty installment of propaganda at a very fragile time in Sino-Soviet relations. Just then Chernyaev intervened. A member of the editorial board of the *Kommunist*, Chernyaev hardly showed up at the meetings, presumably keeping himself busy at the Central Committee. However, he, too, received Rakhmanin's article and found that it amounted to "a complete denunciation of Tashkent." "Shocked," he phoned Kosolapov, but the editor could only say that "Rakhmanin is sitting on my head."[60]

Chernyaev took up this matter with Ponomarev, but the tired apparatchik was wary of stirring up trouble:

[PONOMAREV]: Do you know what the Chinese write about us every day? And what a bad speech the Chinese made in the UN?

[CHERNYAEV]: I know. But I also know that they stopped writing much of what they used to write half a year ago. The whole world sees this. It's enough to flip through TASS [bulletins]. But Rakhmanin is hiding this from the C[entral] C[ommittee]. The main thing, though, is: will Tashkent be continued or not? If yes, then one must not allow for propaganda to diverge from policy.

[PONOMAREV]: A lot of water has flowed under the bridge since Tashkent...

[CHERNYAEV]: Is that so? That means...

[PONOMAREV]: No, no. You misunderstood me (becoming afraid). What am I proposing? Let Kosolapov, if he sympathizes with you, call Andropov. But in general, be careful, one should not make it look as if we (the International Department) are pro-Chinese, and Rakhmanin is the only one who struggles.[61]

As a result, Kosolapov took up the matter with his immediate boss in the Central Committee, Mikhail Zimyanin, who discussed it with Rakhmanin's boss, Konstantin Rusakov (the ailing head of The Department) and agreed that the article should be pulled from *Kommunist* and circulated to the Chinese Commission of the Politburo. That was not the end of the story. Andropov was unhappy with Chernyaev's meddling and reproached Ponomarev for allowing his staff to stir up conflicts between CC departments. He also instructed Rakhmanin to amend the article in particular, cutting the criticism of China's domestic affairs. Rakhmanin supplied only marginal amendments but was able to monopolize the editing process so that not only the editorial board (including Chernyaev) but also the editor of *Kommunist* (who in the meantime went on vacation, probably to dodge the trouble) were effectively removed from the process. Chernyaev, after attempting to appeal to Brezhnev and Andropov through their aides and through his good friend Georgii Arbatov (the director of the Institute of USA and Canada Studies), all but gave up, resigning himself to the imminent publication of the "anti-Chinese nonsense."[62]

On August 6 Ponomarev called up Chernyaev. As the latter recounted, Ponomarev

thr[ew] some text at me with the words "read this. You have won!": It is a note from Brezhnev [who was then vacationing in the Crimea], addressed to Andropov, a very short one, just one paragraph: I am attaching a memorandum by my aide c[omrade] Golikov on Chinese affairs. I think it has reasonable ideas. I request that it is discussed at the Chinese Commission of the Politburo. And Golikov's memo—about 15 pages—says the following: one gets the impression that we are underestimating the importance of normalization with China. Our propaganda does not strongly support the Tashkent line, and sometimes comes out with materials which undermine it. No one wants to notice the changes in China but they are happening. Our main enemy is US imperialism, so the main strike should be made in that direction. Because otherwise what we have is that in terms of negotiations, contacts and exchanges we allow ourselves with the US (even at such a tense moment) what we do not allow ourselves with China. We have to have a strategic, Tashkent-like approach to the problem of China. Every day everything must be done to relieve the tensions, develop cooperation, achieve mutual understanding, not to push China in the US direction, etc.[63]

The memorandum was of "completely anti-Rakhmanin essence," even though it lacked a single mention of the *Kommunist* article. "But who suggested this to Golikov," mused Chernyaev—"or perhaps he is the source of the Tashkent line? And 'arrived' at this memorandum 'independently,' maybe without any knowledge of the *Kommunist* article? But he had to know about the Interkit." Whatever the case, the result of this timely intervention was that Rakhmanin was taken down a peg or two, and Andropov even reportedly threatened that, unless he changed his behavior, "we will have to look for another place for him."[64] Rakhmanin, wrote Chernyaev nearly two months after his "victory"—"as well as many others, cannot wait for the Chinese to pull something off that will cause Leonid Il'ich [Brezhnev]'s 'wrath' so that the whole Tashkent line—especially the Politburo course adopted in August after Golikov's memo—would go to hell. Absolute incapacity to think in historical categories, lack of understanding what a state policy is. Yet, the fact that we and Chinese clawed each other for an extra 7–8 years is Rakhmanin's doing."[65]

Brezhnev addressed himself to the subject of China in a conversation with Erich Honecker on August 11. Rakhmanin would have been pleased to know that Brezhnev castigated Honecker for sticking his neck out in relations with Beijing. He would have been much less pleased to hear the General Secretary admit that he, too, saw changes happening in China. Brezhnev told his East German visitor: "Don't get me wrong: we are for normalization of relations with China. But we seek a real normalization, which means not at the cost to third countries, and not at the price of concessions on the questions of war and peace or our revolutionary theory. We have worked and continue to work with an eye to the future."[66] Normalization with China was a part of that future, hence Tashkent, hence Brezhnev's support for Golikov's intervention to save the fragile sprouts of better Sino-Soviet relations from the winter of Rakhmanin's sinophobia.

The emergence and the resilience of the Tashkent line cannot be explained by any single circumstance. At least two factors were in play. Probably the most important consideration on the Soviet side was the climate of Soviet-American relations. Things had been on the decline since the late 1970s: the Soviet meddling in Africa and deployment of mid-range nuclear missiles in the European theatre, invasion of Afghanistan, and crackdown against Poland's Solidarity in 1981 were poorly received in Washington, so that by the time Reagan emerged as President in January 1981, only faint memories remained of Brezhnev's most treasured foreign policy accomplishment—the fabled détente. In the wake of the demise of détente came the Second Cold War, marked by US-led economic sanctions, effective breakdown of nuclear disarmament talks fraught with a missile stand-off in Europe, and the body count of the Afghanistan quagmire. The Soviets had not yet seen the American President's most memorable anti-Soviet rhetoric, but already after his first year in office many in the Soviet leadership must have thought that the Chinese had not been so bad, after all.

There was thus a strong temptation to play the China card against Washington, just as ten years earlier Washington had played the China card against the USSR. At that time the United States was the apparent power in decline, or so it seemed after the defeat of Vietnam and the economic travails of the 1970s. The Soviets, by contrast, were confident and up-and-coming. In the early 1980s the roles were reversed but the game was the same. This was a simple matter of tactical insight, something obvious to pragmatists like Kapitsa, who, as late as February 1983, still characterized Soviets' effort at normalization with China as a "tactical question," a goal the Soviets pursued with an eye to the "troublesome, complicated international situation."[67]

For some, however, this tactical consideration combined with an ideological imperative: China and the USSR, as two socialist countries, should not be on the opposite sides of the barricades, not after Mao's death had depersonalized this long-running feud. After all, the threat of "Maoism without Mao," as Rakhmanin would have it, was less evident to an informed observer than the challenge—military, economic, and ideological—posed by the United States. Brezhnev put the point across to Honecker in the starkest terms: "There has never been such an unbridled and aggressive administration in the USA as that of Reagan."[68]

CHINA'S RESPONSE TO TASHKENT

Deng Xiaoping's response to Tashkent proposals was swift. On March 25 he held a meeting of the Politburo to decide what China should do. The East German intelligence, which got wind of this meeting, noted that there was "an intense discussion" of the available options. Deng himself appeared rather skeptical, saying that Brezhnev "apparently assumed that the announcement of readiness for a new policy towards China can already produce an improvement of relations. China, by contrast, should still be prepared for war with the Soviet Union. Even a small border conflict can escalate into a war." On the other hand, Deng did not rule out that the Soviets were "genuinely interested" in improving relations with China. The circumstances called for the creation of a special "working group" to study what the Soviets were up to.[69]

For the moment, Deng called up Foreign Minister Huang Hua and asked for immediate reaction to the Soviet proposals.[70] On March 26 Hua's deputy Qian Qichen summoned a crowd of reporters and read out three sentences from his notepad: "We have noted the remarks on Sino-Soviet relations made by President Brezhnev in Tashkent on 24th March. We firmly reject the attacks on China contained in the remarks. What we attach importance to are actual deeds of the Soviet Union in Sino-Soviet relations and international affairs."[71]

The statement sounded very tough, and it was seen as such by the foreign media, which for several days published headlines such as "Brezhnev overture rebuffed by China" and "Peking denounces Brezhnev."[72] In fact, the purpose of the brief statement was to tell Moscow that China was willing to improve relations, but the message was coded. By saying that China attached importance to "actual deeds" of the Soviet Union, Qian Qichen implied that what Brezhnev *said* was actually quite reasonable, but it would have to be backed by actions. More important still was what the statement *did not* say: it was uncharacteristically constrained and stripped of the usual rhetoric of "struggle against Soviet social-imperialism." In the statement, Brezhnev was for the first time recognized as President (as opposed to being the head of a reactionary clique)—something the East German intelligence, for example, immediately noticed. The Stasi was also impressed that in referring to Brezhnev's comments about China, the Chinese used a relatively mild word: "attacks," rather than the usual "slander."[73] Unsurprisingly, these nuances were lost on most foreign journalists, though not on the Soviet one who, Qian recalls, "put his thumbs up and told me: 'ochen khorosho'" (very good, in Russian).[74]

The Soviets perfectly realized what the Chinese meant by "actual deeds." Normalization continued to depend on the Soviet removal of the "three obstacles." A few weeks after Tashkent, Deng Xiaoping took an opportunity to remind the Soviet leadership about these "obstacles" by sending a message via Romania's old-time ruler Nicolae Ceaușescu. Since the mid-1960s Ceaușescu had raised his international profile by carrying messages between Beijing and Moscow. He managed to keep Romania out of the Sino-Soviet split and, indeed, used the quarrel in the communist world to pretend, credibly, that his country was not a Soviet satellite. On April 16 Deng told Ceaușescu that the Chinese paid attention to the speech at Tashkent. But, he said, "we attach importance to actual deeds; the actual deeds include the Afghanistan and Cambodia problems, and include the troops on our border." He hammered the point: "A million troops! If we do not talk about these concrete deeds, what would be the basis [of the talks]?" Dodging Ceauşescu's call to respond to the Tashkent proposals, Deng said, with a hint of irritation: "In general, he [Brezhnev] needs to change his hegemonism. Brezhnev's talk is not bad but we look at deeds. When you see Brezhnev, you can tell him, ask him to do one or two things first: he can start with Cambodia and Afghanistan, or from the Sino-Soviet border or Mongolia. If there are no deeds, we cannot approve, and the people of the world cannot approve."[75]

Deng reiterated the same points, though with some sense of optimism, when he secretly met North Korean "Great Leader" Kim Il-sung in Pyongyang on April 27. "Sino-Soviet relations," he said, "should eventually improve. But it seems that there are no conditions now to resume normalization. The so-called conditions are that there should be actual deeds on the problem of the Soviet Union in Afghanistan, the Cambodian problem, and the problem of Soviet troops at the Sino-Soviet border and in Mongolia."[76] Just making a little progress on any of these obstacles would indicate Soviet good intent, and "only then," Deng argued, "can we have the foundation of trust."[77]

Deng's cautious willingness to seek improvement of Sino-Soviet relations after two years of escalating confrontation must be understood within a broader context of Chinese foreign policy. Two things had happened in the months before Tashkent to prepare the ground for the seed Brezhnev would plant on March 24; without them, the Soviet initiative would have led nowhere.

China's positive response was on the one hand a product of worsening Sino-American relations and Deng's reasonable estimate that he could play the Soviet card against the Americans, much as the Americans had played the China card against the Soviet Union for years. On the other hand, the Soviet threat appeared less ominous once the Soviets were obviously bogged down in a quagmire in Afghanistan and suffered from international isolation and the breakdown of détente. Under these circumstances, improving relations with Moscow was not a bad idea, seeing, in particular, that China needed a peaceful environment for the economic reforms Deng had unleashed. There was also a third factor: some people in the ranks of China's top leadership wanted better relations with the Soviet Union for "ideological" reasons. Deng, though not always in agreement with them, could not ignore what they had to say.

Between November and December 1978, Deng Xiaoping, the frail, chain-smoking survivor of years of political turmoil, the "ass-kicker" (in Oksenberg's matter-of-fact phrase), consolidated power in China. He did so at the expense of his rival, Hua Guofeng, Mao's anointed successor, who was known for the "two whatevers": following whatever policies Mao had followed and obeying whatever instructions Mao had made.[78] Deng rejected such a rigid approach. Although in important respects he adopted Mao's policies (in particular, building a closer relationship with the United States), for Deng the United States meant something greater than what it had meant for Mao, whose decision to seek rapprochement with Washington was very much a function of the Soviet threat to China in the late 1960s. For Deng, alignment with the United States was part and parcel of China's plans to modernize. As Deng reportedly told his assistant after visiting the United States in January 1979, "If we look back, we find that all of those [Third World countries] that were on the side of the United States have been successful [in their modernization drive], whereas all of those that were against the United States have not been successful. We shall be on the side of the United States."[79]

From 1979 to 1980 Deng Xiaoping put all his efforts into building a de facto alliance with the United States. With the beginning of military exchanges—Carter's Defense Secretary, Harold Brown, turned up in Beijing, and his Chinese counterpart Geng Biao toured the United States—the Americans encountered a very strong Chinese push for military technology, even weapons.[80] Not all were in favor of arming the communist power. Cyrus Vance and Thomas Watson in Moscow were bitterly opposed.[81] The US military brass eyed Chinese requests with suspicion. "We foresee a number of problems," wrote Assistant Secretary of Defense David McGiffert. "The gap between Chinese expectations and US inclinations on technology and equipment is still wide. The Chinese have already requested some of the most sophisticated equipment we have. We are trying to limit this effort to probe the limits of our policy by telling them beforehand that we will not at this time consider such requests."[82]

All of that was immensely annoying to Deng, who had gone out on a limb for the sake of a closer relationship with China's former imperialist foe. He even agreed to allow the Americans to set up an intelligence gathering station in Xinjiang to monitor Soviet nuclear tests; he had first asked for American weapons in return, but, after being rebuffed, agreed nonetheless, becoming the first leader of the Chinese Communist Party to cooperate with the CIA.[83] He ordered China into a war with neighboring Vietnam. There were many reasons, to be sure, not least defending China's credibility in Asia in the face of Vietnam's clumsy pretensions to regional hegemony, and frustrating perceived Soviet efforts to "encircle" China in a web of hostile alliances—but, at a deeper level, to show that China was America's reliable ally in the Cold War. How could the Americans drag their heels in embracing Deng after all that he had done for America? By 1981 grievances began to build up in the relationship, and Brzezinski's flirtation did not suffice to redress them.

Deng's unhappiness with the scope of US technology transfers and, more generally, with the scope of technology transfers from the West, mounted in spite of significant progress in the US export policy. With Brzezinski's commitment to a strategic relationship and to most-favored-nation status for China—something the Soviets had long sought but could not get—trade restrictions were progressively lifted. The process had begun back in the Nixon Administration, when China could not even get what the Soviets were getting. This was called the "China differential."[84] In the face of mounting Chinese pressure, the differential was abandoned, and, during the Carter Administration, the differential was increasingly in favor of China, to Moscow's undoubted anger.

Reagan continued to gradually lift restrictions on technology transfers. Yet as late as 1983, China's treatment, for the purposes of US export controls, was only marginally better than the Soviet Union's but a lot worse than India's.[85] Deng's frustration with these restrictions is understandable. In the better days of the Sino-Soviet alliance, the Soviets supplied cutting-edge technology to the People's Republic, including in such sensitive fields as nuclear physics and military industry. Even then the Chinese complained incessantly that they were not getting all they could be getting. The Soviet Union had transferred blueprints for entire factories to China—completely free of charge. The Americans were not willing to go nearly as far.

Deng's impatience became manifest very early in the Reagan Administration. If in the late Carter years the Chinese patriarch had limited himself to occasional complaints that "the scope of technology transfer is too narrow," as he had told Harold Brown in January 1980,[86] by late 1981 the tone of his remarks had become much sharper. "It may be surprising to you," Deng told Donald Regan, the Secretary of the Treasury, who visited China in November 1981, "but America had not given China a single item of advanced technology." Deng exaggerated but went on to make a point: "Perhaps this problem is one of how the US treats China. I wonder whether the US is still not treating China as a hostile country. It's a question of the way US-China relations are perceived. We have been waiting. Frankly, we have been very patient."[87]

By early 1982, just as the Soviets made first moves toward accommodation with China, Deng Xiaoping and other Chinese leaders were cynical about Reagan's technology transfer policy, indicative as it was to Deng of US unwillingness to see China as a "partner." Foreign Minister Huang Hua called this policy "loud thunder with little raindrops"—that is, ample promises but little action.[88] At the dawn of his career in the late 1940s, Huang Hua was party to a back channel between the Chinese communists and the White House, which at the time hit a dead end, prompting subsequent scholarly speculations as to whether Harry S. Truman "lost China." Now he witnessed a similar turning point in Sino-American relations. If between 1948 and 1949 Mao Zedong was interested in "leaning to one side"—that is, the Soviet side in the Cold War—now China was clearly leaning to the US side, but it was not getting the support it needed.

Failure to deliver technology was confounded, in Deng's eyes, by an even greater transgression on Washington's part. The problem was Taiwan. Deng recognized that Taiwan's continued independent existence hinged to a large extent on the US willingness to support Jiang Jingguo's regime. This support—political or military—strengthened Jiang's hand vis-à-vis the mainland or, as Deng liked to say, made him "thrust his tail to the skies and think that he has nothing to fear."[89] That was perhaps not that bad compared to what Deng could have expected once the seventy-year-old Taiwanese patriarch passed from the scene and new players emerged in Taipei. Indeed, Deng may have counted on US assistance in the reunification talks, much as George Marshall had mediated talks between the CCP and the Guomindang in 1946.[90]

This prospect was a non-starter for the Carter Administration. But Deng did not know that. He hoped to make the Americans understand that they did not need Taiwan. He was hopeful on this score in January 1979 when he went to the United States and, in a *Time* interview, even spoke of reunification within a year.[91] He remained hopeful even after the US Congress passed the Taiwan Relations Act in March 1979, although perceptive observers like Oksenberg could already sense that Deng's policy orientation was "coming under some attack for having produced too little and having cost too much."[92] By the end of 1980 Deng was running out of patience.

Reagan rode into office laden with campaign promises on Taiwan that did not bode well for China. As he canvassed in the summer of 1980, he made some seriously provocative remarks about his intentions to restore official relations with Taiwan. The Chinese were outraged and issued public warnings of ominous consequences. Privately, for the first time since normalization, US Ambassador Leonard Woodcock was informed that the United States "must 'rescind' the Act if our relations are to develop meaningfully." "PRC should understand this will not be done," Carter wrote in the margins of Woodcock's briefing, but Deng continued to press for the cancellation of the Act.[93] Did Carter, or Reagan after him, understand the problem the Taiwan issue was causing for Deng—how he could not simply swallow rhetoric like Reagan's for fear of undercutting his own legitimacy and that of the Chinese Communist Party? In the heat of US electoral politics, parochial sentiments sometimes mattered more than strategic insight. Even among the insiders, however, opinions diverged over whether Deng's rage over Taiwan was genuine or simply a tactical ploy aimed to extract concessions in other areas of bilateral relations.[94]

By early 1982 Sino-American relations had reached the crisis point. As policy makers in Washington debated the scope of weapons sales to Taiwan, including, controversially, whether or not to provide the island with a new generation FX fighter aircraft, Beijing's tone became more intolerant and accusatory. Deng drew a line and showed no signs of willingness to back away from it, even if this meant backtracking for Sino-US relations. "No matter what changes take place in the world," he told former Vice President Walter Mondale, who visited with Deng in November 1981, "China will survive. China has lived in isolation and poverty in the past for long periods. Historically, we went through difficult times in Yan'an and we managed to survive and did very well."[95] In a conversation with Mondale's successor, George Bush, on May 8, 1982, Deng referred to the "erroneous US view" that "China is insignificant and that the US has no need for any help from China while China needs US help. Those holding this view feel that as long as the US is tough with the Soviet Union you can do what you feel about China and China will swallow it."[96]

Just as Brezhnev in Tashkent reassured China of Soviet respect for the Chinese sovereignty over Taiwan, Reagan's unclear position on the Taiwan arms sales prompted Deng to reconsider the whole framework of Sino-American relations. The days of enthusiastic leaning to one side were over. Already, at an enlarged Politburo meeting on June 13, 1981, Deng urged his party comrades to "plan for the worst" in Sino-US relations and not to be afraid of their degradation: if the United States supplies weapons to Taiwan, he said, "we cannot talk vaguely."[97] What the United States did in Taiwan was symptomatic of the broader problem of the Sino-American relationship. Deng had bargained for an alliance of equals against the common threat of "Soviet hegemonism." In this alliance China would respect US interests, but the United States would have to take into account China's interests because of potential confusion with "recognizing" Taiwan. Instead, the Chinese patriarch found himself a party to a game, in which China was only a card in the global US strategy. Who was the hegemon then?

Deng presented the unpleasant realities at an enlarged Politburo meeting in October 1981: "what the US does in Taiwan is actually hegemonism." Playing "cards," Deng said, drawing on his experience as an accomplished bridge player, was not profitable to China, because "when you play cards, a card can be changed at any time, and one can also lose at any time."[98] China needed a more stable policy. Deng unwittingly rediscovered Lord

Palmerston's dictum, with Chinese specifics: China had no permanent friends or enemies, just permanent interests. Henceforth, China would not just struggle with Soviet "hegemonism" but would, in Deng's words to a foreign visitor, "oppose superpowers and hegemonism, no matter what circumstances, and no matter where hegemonism comes from."[99] In September 1982 this new imperative was publicly proclaimed from the platform of the 12th CCP Congress as China's "independent foreign policy."[100]

Offering a positive response to the Tashkent probe was easier than it had been just a few years earlier. Indeed, the Soviet Union no longer appeared as menacing as it was in 1979 when Deng could feel the Kremlin's tentacles all along the Chinese perimeter. One of the reasons for Deng's eagerness to normalize relations with the United States was that in the late 1970s he was clearly unsettled by what he, in the spirit of 19th-century geopolitics, christened Moscow's "southern policy." Like Brzezinski, Deng believed that the Soviet Union thirsted for warm water ports of the Indian Ocean and the oil of the Middle East. By controlling "choke-points" in the Middle East, the Soviets could starve Europe of oil and force it to "capitulate." Likewise, Soviet expansionism in Southeast Asia was a consequence of their ambition to control another "choke-point," the Malacca Straits.[101]

But Deng was overoptimistic about the Soviet chances. The Soviet Union never did get to the Middle East, much less to the Malacca Straits. Its perceived push in Southeast Asia (primarily through a proxy—Vietnam) stalled, as most of Southeast Asia sided with China against the Soviets and their allies. In the meantime, Afghanistan had turned into a quagmire, with the Arab nations opposed to the Soviet invasion. Reflecting on these developments, Deng told Kim Il-sung in September 1982 that the Soviet Union "is having a hard time."[102]

In a conversation with the Pakistani President Mohammad Zia ul-Haq the following month, Deng said that although, in his opinion, Moscow's southern policy would not change even after Brezhnev left the scene, the Soviets were facing "great difficulties" internally and externally, including poor economic prospects and international isolation.[103] But did this mean that the Soviet Union no longer posed the greatest threat to China's security, as it had, in the Chinese estimates, since 1969? Opinions diverged. Deng himself and his protégés Zhao Ziyang and Hu Yaobang continued to emphasize that the greatest "hegemonic" danger still emanated from the USSR, though by late 1982 they did so with much less rigor and conviction than even a year earlier.[104] On the other hand, even such anti-Soviet stalwarts as Peng Zhen, who in the heat of Sino-Soviet polemics in the 1960s called the Soviets "tsars" and "gods" and who still regarded the northern neighbor as a "tiger" that "sees China as a piece of meat, and really wants to eat it," now argued that it was, after all, only a "paper tiger," and that it would not invade China "unless it went crazy." The Soviet Union sank a hundred thousand troops into the Afghan quagmire, but, Peng Zhen added, "ten Afghanistans don't have as much population as China."[105]

In short, gradually the Chinese leaders were rethinking the Soviet menace. Huang Hua, discussing this reappraisal, later recalled: "We believed that such an attitude on Brezhnev's part [i.e., his Tashkent proposals] was a requirement of the difficult internal and external environment the Soviet Union faced." Internally, the high rate of investment in the military-industrial complex and poor agricultural output resulted in shortages and kindled popular discontent. In Huang Hua's assessment, the Soviet Union was losing the intense competition with the United States at the time of sour relations with China: "the triangular strategic position was obviously unfavorable to the Soviet Union."[106]

When Brezhnev made his speech in Tashkent, he was hardly aware of the thinking of Chinese ruling elites, but his initiative came just in time to allow Deng to turn the tables on the United States. "China," Deng told the Pakistani Foreign Minister in April 1982, "will neither play the US card against the USSR, nor allow others to play the China card."[107] This left one possibility. Indeed, Beijing's actions after Tashkent clearly show that Deng was not in fact averse to playing a card—the Soviet card—against the United States.

The opening of a dialogue with the Soviets did not mean Deng Xiaoping despaired about the Sino-American relationship. On the contrary, developing this relationship was still his key strategic priority, because it remained crucial to the project of modernization, which Deng could not endanger. But there was also a discernible difference between Deng's attempt to build a "united front" against the USSR in 1979 and the more balanced approach of 1982. The post-normalization honeymoon was over; China did not become America's ally. Whether there was a missed opportunity is an open question. Some would say no, echoing Oksenberg's and Kapitsa's contemporary assessments that China could not become anyone's ally. Yet the beginning of the Chinese shift toward equidistance, although it may have been conditioned by powerful historical currents, was nevertheless a product of specific circumstances at a particular time.

Richard Nixon, the card player par excellence who pioneered the opening to China, had the foresight to recognize that playing China as a "card" in the Cold War was not a good strategy for the United States. After meeting in September 1982 with Deng and other senior Chinese leaders, Nixon sent a long report to Reagan, arguing: "Juvenile talk about 'playing the China card' should be knocked off. We should make it clear to the Chinese and to the world that *even if there were no Soviet threat*, we consider it in our interest to help China to become economically strong so that it will better be able to resist any threat posed by the Soviet Union or any other potentially aggressive power."[108] Views like Nixon's were not common in Washington, especially not on Capitol Hill among the fire-breathing anti-communists who pressed Reagan to strengthen American support for Taiwan.

The President had enough sense to resist this pressure by refusing to sell FX aircraft to Taiwan. The decision was made on January 10, 1982, a little too late to undo the damage that the speculations of the forthcoming sale had caused since the summer of 1980. In any case, not selling FX did not mean that Reagan refused to sell other weapons to Taiwan, and the tug-of-war with the Chinese continued until August 17, 1982, when Washington promised to eventually cease weapons' sales. However, the communiqué did not say when this would happen, and Reagan's National Security Adviser William P. Clark characterized the uncertainty as a "major gain" for the United States.[109] Whether it really was a "major gain" or a lost opportunity for the United States is another open question.

Even so, by August 1982 it seemed as if the worst had passed in Sino-US relations. Four days after the communiqué with the Americans, Deng, in a meeting with a foreign visitor, hardly uttered a word of criticism against the United States. Instead, he chose to bash the Soviets for their aggressive designs and their efforts to "outflank" China's "European allies" by pushing toward warm water ports on the Indian Ocean and controlling the Middle East.[110] Anyone listening to Deng's explanations would have found it hard to believe that the Chinese and the Soviets were just then secretly talking to each other. Deng kept his hand well concealed.

In mid summer 1982, just as Deng turned up the heat on the Americans in the unhappy negotiations over the Taiwan arms sales (even refusing for a time to meet with the US Ambassador),[111] he called a meeting at his home with China's senior leaders Chen Yun and Li Xiannian. The three decided to send a secret emissary to Moscow with a proposal to reopen political talks. The task fell to Yu Hongliang, the head of the Soviet Union and Eastern Europe section at the Chinese Foreign Ministry. To avoid arousing the suspicion of foreign observers, Yu Hongliang went under the pretext of "inspecting the work of the embassy" in Moscow and in Warsaw.[112]

On August 10 Yu Hongliang told Deputy Foreign Minister Leonid Il'ichev and Mikhail Kapitsa that China was in favor of political consultations with the Soviet Union, but only if the "three obstacles" were on the table for discussion. Il'ichev beat around the bush, and only Kapitsa remarked that Deng's message had new aspects and speculated that something positive might come out of it. Yu Hongliang was told that his information would be passed up the command chain to the Soviet leadership for decision.[113]

Yu Hongliang continued on to Poland to inspect the work of the Chinese Embassy there and give the Soviets a week to think about Deng Xiaoping's proposals. On August 18 he was back in Moscow, and once again met with Il'ichev. The Soviet official came across much warmer than on the previous occasion, which was probably a reflection of the triumph of Golikov's and Chernyaev's line over Rakhmanin's. He told Yu that the Foreign Ministry would deliver an official response to the Chinese proposal in a few days. Indeed, on August 20, 1982, Deputy Foreign Minister Viktor Mal'tsev gave the Soviet reply to the Chinese Charge d'affaires, Ma Xusheng: the Soviet side was prepared to hold consultations at whatever time, in whatever place, and at whatever level to discuss the problems of Sino-Soviet relations and overcome obstacles to the normalization. After further exchange, it was agreed to hold the first round of political consultations in Beijing in October 1982.[114]

Reviewing the latest developments in Sino-Soviet relations at a Politburo meeting on September 9, 1982, Brezhnev talked about the "new aspects" in the Chinese policy. "It looks like my speech in Tashkent keeps working....Let's see how the Chinese behave themselves at the forthcoming consultations. We also should treat them seriously, on the big scale, in a balanced manner, not forgetting, of course, about our state interests. We could provide comrades, who will conduct the consultations, with an aim: to feel out the possibilities, for a start, for freeing Sino-Soviet relations from unnecessary sharpness and prejudice. One cannot allow for some hawkish statement in the press or some other awkward step to complicate the already difficult dialogue with China."[115] The last statement was no doubt a criticism of Rakhmanin, who, despite his earlier setback with the *Kommunist* article, and despite ominous predictions by those in the know that he would "lose his head," continued to sabotage the Tashkent line. But, as Chernyaev noted with satisfaction, Rakhmanin's resistance was now only an episode.[116] Sino-Soviet relations had reached a new point of departure.

TALKS BEGIN

On October 3, 1982, Leonid Il'ichev arrived in Beijing for the first round of political consultations at the Deputy Foreign Ministers' level. Il'ichev, well-known in China, had been the head of the Soviet delegation at the border talks since August 1970, which had dragged on for a decade without progress. He also represented the Soviet Union at the only round of political consultations in the fall of 1979, when Afghanistan buried early hopes of normalization. In his earlier days, Il'ichev headed the ideology department in the Central Committee, where he helped reverse the tide of Khrushchev's thaw. Perhaps for these reasons, Kapitsa recalled, the Chinese became downhearted when he told them that Il'ichev would be the Soviet negotiator once again: "they knew very well his love for long speeches and his grimacing, and were not inclined to talk to him."[117]

The talks, from October 5 to 21, did not bring the two sides closer together on the main questions. Qian Qichen, who headed the Chinese delegation, outlined the "three obstacles" to normalization (with emphasis on Vietnam), and Il'ichev in turn insisted on talks without preconditions and not to the detriment of "third countries"—Afghanistan, Mongolia, Vietnam, and Cambodia. Il'ichev declared that the Soviet Union did not threaten China and called for expanding economic, cultural, and scientific ties. Qian Qichen refuted Il'ichev's "precondition" of having "talks without preconditions" and returned to the "three obstacles," proposing that the Soviets, for a start, use their influence to make Vietnam pull out of Cambodia. In this spirit, Il'ichev and Qian Qichen held six meetings before the talks adjourned.[118]

Before his departure from Beijing, on October 24, Il'ichev had a meeting with Foreign Minister Huang Hua, demanding to know whether China expected that the Soviet Union would pay for improvement of relations through the worsening of its relations with other countries. Huang Hua responded that "whoever tied the bell [to a tiger's neck] must also untie it." By this he meant that it was the Soviet Union that had created the "three obstacles" in the first place, so it must take the initiative to remove them.[119] The fact of holding a meeting itself represented a noticeable upgrade in the level of Sino-Soviet contacts. "We consider the actual fact of having consultations to be a positive development, and we intend to continue such meetings," the Soviets concluded, suspecting, however, that the Chinese had only agreed to these talks in order to "blackmail their imperialist partners, first and foremost the USA."[120] These sentiments were echoed by Deng Xiaoping, who thought the Soviets had wanted the talks to escape international isolation.[121] Both sides were right to a certain extent, though as it subsequently turned out, both underestimated the other side's interest in genuine rapprochement.

Even though nothing of substance was achieved at the first round of talks, the two sides maintained a generally optimistic outlook. Andrei Gromyko, in a meeting with his counterparts from Eastern Europe on October 21, announced that "the Soviet side will work patiently. We'll try to find out whether the Chinese side has positive intentions, or whether this is just a Chinese maneuver, which also cannot be ruled out. As they say, we'll see."[122] Deng Xiaoping made a similar comment a few days later: "the Sino-Soviet dialogue should be continued, one cannot imagine Sino-Soviet relations in a perpetual deadlock."[123] The real value of these negotiations for Moscow and Beijing was that the two sides were now talking to each other after years of estrangement.

In the meantime, Brezhnev died peacefully in his sleep on November 10, 1982. The dead General Secretary would have been pleased and intrigued to know that the Chinese propaganda did not make a celebration of his passing and even offered a very kind obituary. Released in the form of Huang Hua's statement to the Xinhua News Agency, the obituary praised Brezhnev as an "outstanding statesman of the Soviet Union," extended "deep condolences on the death of President Brezhnev and our sincere sympathy to the Soviet government, the Soviet people and the members of President Brezhnev's family," and ended with the uplifting message that "the Chinese people sincerely wish that the national construction of the Soviet Union will develop with each passing day, the material and cultural life of the Soviet people will continue to improve and the unity of the multi-national Soviet Union will be more consolidated."[124]

It was the warmest statement the Soviets had heard from China in twenty years. Huang Hua himself had little to do with it: Deng sent him as a special emissary to Moscow, and he simply did not have the time to meet with the Xinhua reporters. The statement was written by General Secretary Hu Yaobang and approved personally by Deng Xiaoping.[125] It was seen in the foreign media as "an unmistakable olive branch" to the new Soviet leaders.[126] The Soviets repaid this kindness with special attention to Huang Hua's delegation: a motorcade, a personal guide (the grimacing Deputy Foreign Minister Il'ichev), and even a special standing arrangement at the funeral.[127] It was the highest Chinese delegation to visit Moscow since Prime Minister Zhou Enlai's trip in 1964 shortly after Nikita Khrushchev's ouster. At the reception after the funeral, Yurii Andropov spent the most time—three minutes—with Huang Hua, whose hand was shaken earlier than that of US Vice President George Bush, the head of the American delegation.[128]

Foreign correspondents watched intensely as Huang Hua spoke to Andropov, "gesturing emphatically during the conversation."[129] They could not hear what was being said, however. Huang Hua, lamenting Brezhnev's death—"a great loss for the Soviet country and its people"—congratulated Andropov on his new leadership role and voiced a hope that Sino-Soviet relations would be gradually normalized. Andropov said that he was happy to see Huang Hua in Moscow and that he also hoped that Sino-Soviet relations would improve. It was a short, formal exchange, but after Huang Hua and his entourage left for his hotel, the Soviet interpreter chased them down and asked for a verbatim record of what Huang Hua said. Apparently, the Soviets wanted to scrutinize the Foreign Minister's every word to see if, somewhere between the lines, there was a hint of a change of the Chinese position.[130]

Huang Hua's meeting with his counterpart Andrei Gromyko on November 16 was more substantial, lasting an hour and fifty minutes. Gromyko called for closer ties in economic, cultural, and scientific relations as a first step to normalization, while Huang Hua insisted on the big problems being solved first: "the current tensions in the relationship between the two countries, with the armies confronting each other at the border, with tensions at other borders, threatening our country's security—if these circumstances do not change, even if there is some increase in trade, economic cooperation, cultural exchange and other aspects, it cannot help the overall situation." Gromyko repeated that "China should not be afraid of the Soviet Union. The Soviet Union in no way threatens China." Huang Hua and Gromyko at least agreed to disagree, and the meeting was cordial enough that Gromyko, well known for his tough looks, managed a faint smile and saw Huang Hua off to the elevator.[131]

Two days later Gromyko reported on his meeting with Huang Hua at the Soviet Politburo, with Andropov now in charge: "The conversation with Huang Hua was, on the whole, friendly. But he once again raised the question of Cambodia, our forces in Mongolia, Afghanistan and cutting the troops located near the borders. For now, one cannot cling to anything, judging by the conversation. But I think we should discuss this question separately in some way and think seriously from what we could begin our subsequent talks with China."[132]

The big question facing the Soviet leadership was whether or not they could make any concessions to China on the "three obstacles" without undermining what Andropov deemed to be essential Soviet interests. Speaking in Prague on January 4, 1983, at the Political Consultative Meeting of the Warsaw Pact, Andropov said that "we do not intend to pay for normalization by concessions to the detriment of our friends, nor do we intend to ask China to pay."[133] This meant that Andropov was dead set against any movement on Afghanistan, Vietnam, or Mongolia. That left open the question of the Soviet troops in the border area, half an obstacle by the Chinese measure.

On the last point, Andropov suddenly indicated some flexibility: "We think that during the next round of consultations, which will take place in

Moscow, [we will] let it be understood that steps are possible in this direction. If it comes to genuine normalization, to the establishment of at least minimal trust, the prospect of mutual force cuts in the border region will become more real." Andropov made a reservation, however: some of these forces were actually stationed in the Far East to counter the "increasing military preparations of the USA and Japan."[134] Nevertheless, he did not rule out a force cut in principle. It was a cautious step in the Chinese direction, perhaps too cautious for the Chinese to discern.

Andropov's caution reflected a lingering uncertainty about China—in his own mind and in the Politburo as a whole. More and more officials recognized that it was a good idea to mend fences. But where was the thin line that divided reasonable concessions from careless policy fraught with undesirable strategic consequences for the USSR? This problem was discussed at length in the Politburo meeting on May 31, 1983. Only Gromyko was in favor of making further concessions to China in the political dialogue. The Foreign Minister had the reputation of a die-hard orthodox, for which reason his eventual replacement by Eduard Shevardnadze, after Gorbachev's rise to power, has been seen as an important breakthrough on the path to a more liberal Soviet foreign policy. Granted, Gromyko was no liberal. But in 1983 he showed some awareness of the long-term benefits of a better relationship with China, and he was willing to go an extra mile where other Politburo members, whether because of political conservatism or simply lack of understanding, erred on the side of caution.

> GROMYKO: ...One of the terms for normalization of our relations is the with drawal of our troops from Chinese borders. It seems to me that we could think about that....Regarding Mongolia. Maybe we should withdraw part of the army away from the border....
>
> USTINOV [MINISTER OF DEFENSE]: Regarding Mongolia I should say that if we move the Soviet army, that's now located there back to our territory then we will lose a very good post. Everything is already equipped there. That's why we have nowhere to move on the Soviet border....
>
> TIKHONOV [PRIME MINISTER]: ...Regarding removal of the troops from the Chinese border, to me it seems like an unrealistic act.[135]

Andropov did not make his position clear, and this ambiguity indicates that, though he thought Gromyko's proposals were worth consideration, he was not yet prepared to overcome serious objections by people like Dmitrii Ustinov, who had a long-standing obsession with the "Chinese peril." On the other hand, the Soviet security dilemma that had precipitated the

Tashkent line in the first place did not disappear; if anything, it worsened in the months after Tashkent so that by mid-1983 the Soviets were more nervous about the international situation than at any time since perhaps the Cuban Missile Crisis. The breakdown of arms control talks with the West and the pending deployment of Pershings in Western Europe, the fall-out after the Polish crackdown, unrest in the Middle East, persistent failings in Afghanistan—all these issues piled up as the Soviet leadership came to a conclusion that the Reagan Administration, packed with anti-Soviet madmen (first and foremost, the President himself) was leading matters toward a war.

Under these circumstances, playing the China card was a viable policy option. The question was how to do it in the face of the Chinese obsession with the "three obstacles." Andropov could not quite square that circle, although he tried a few things in the first half of 1983, before his deteriorating health knocked the General Secretary out of action. One was an appeal to China by member states of the Warsaw Pact, whose top leaders gathered in Moscow on June 28, 1983, for an unscheduled meeting called by the Soviets to work out a response to the deployment of US nuclear missiles in Western Europe. The appeal emphasized that the forces of imperialism threatened the interests of all socialist countries, including China, and proposed that the Chinese leaders "join efforts" with the socialist camp in opposition to the United States. Signed by all but the Romanians, the appeal was then forwarded to the Chinese Embassy in Moscow. It was rejected in Beijing.[136]

The same fate befell another Soviet appeal, sent to the Chinese and the North Koreans in May 1983, which proposed "cooperation" between the three in the work against the imperialists. The Chinese did not respond, nor, for that matter, did the North Koreans, although, unlike the Chinese, Kim Il-sung at least liked the idea of working against the imperialists, just not, he said, "in cooperation" with anyone.[137] These sorts of appeals had been a staple of Soviet propaganda in the 1960s, and they were aimed to show the Soviet allies that the Soviet Union was principled and reasonable, unlike China. Clearly, this time the Soviets meant what they said. The situation was grave and this was no time to fool around.

Another important signal was issued by Andropov in an interview with the Soviet daily *Pravda* on August 27, 1983. Voicing himself in favor of normalization, Andropov said that such normalization should not "harm" the interests of third countries.[138] This was very similar to what the Soviets had said before, but there was an important difference. Previously, Moscow's position was that normalization should not "affect" the interests of third countries, which was a more sweeping formulation than Andropov's chosen "harm." The latter allowed the Soviets much more room for bargaining with the Chinese. An uninformed observer would have easily overlooked these differences, but not the Chinese. Deng Xiaoping was quick to point out the discrepancy to Kim Il-sung: "recently Andropov's way of talking changed; previously he said that improvement of relations between the two countries should not affect third countries, and now he says it should not harm the interests of third countries."[139]

The Sino-Soviet dialogue picked up pace in September 1983, when Mikhail Kapitsa visited Beijing for foreign policy consultations. These were different from the familiar semiannual political consultations. Foreign policy consultations resurrected an old Soviet practice of sharing important foreign policy information with friends in the socialist camp. This time, the Chinese were happy to listen and the Chinese Foreign Minister Wu Xueqian even offered some useful information in return.[140] Gromyko reported to Soviet allies that during these consultations the Chinese and the Soviet views "coincided" on a number of international problems, including the Middle East, Korea, and Central America.[141]

Little did he know that, after Defense Secretary Caspar Weinberger's consultations in Beijing that same September, the Americans had likewise concluded that Beijing "shares with us an 'identical' view as regards Soviet designs in Africa, the Middle East, and Central America."[142] Perhaps the Chinese were telling both the Soviets and the Americans what they wanted to hear. In relative terms, however, this was a gain for the Soviets, since until then, the Chinese had consistently conveyed the impression that they were with the United States on most key international issues. The change wasn't lost on the policy makers in Washington. As Secretary of State George Shultz noted at a meeting of the National Security Council on September 20, 1983: "The Chinese, despite their statements, *do* have a card mentality. It is clear that that is what they are doing at present with the US in respect to their talks with the USSR." The one positive element, according to Shultz, was that "the Chinese do not appear to be getting too far in their talks with the Soviets."[143] Appearances, however, can be deceptive. Shultz was right that the Chinese were playing cards. But he was not fully aware of the complexity of the game in Beijing, and what the United States and the Soviet Union meant to different players on China's political stage.

CARD PLAYERS AND IDEOLOGUES

Even as Sino-American relations improved in the late 1970s, the more cautious observers in Washington worried whether the Chinese were in fact as anti-Soviet as they claimed or whether their propensity to "jump beds" would one day lead to China's defection to the Soviet camp. Washington had an arsenal of carrots to avert this unfavorable scenario, most importantly technology transfers and export credits, which, Mike Oksenberg and David Aaron argued in August 1979, could be used effectively in order to "dissuade the Chinese from thinking they can play a 'Soviet' card against us." "This [the dissuasion] has to be done indirectly and very subtly, but they should know that if their flirtation with Moscow assumes serious proportions[,] technology transfers and credits are less likely to be forthcoming."[144]

Deng knew this already, which was why he went out of his way in 1979 through 1980 to prove to the Americans that he had no such intentions as Oksenberg and others suspected. In fact, he did not. Deng was a very intelligent man, and he had been saying for years that the Soviet Union was itself a "backward" country and therefore could not help China with its modernization.[145] What he also seems to have realized was that Washington was apprehensive of the prospects of China mending fences with the USSR and so through doing exactly what the Americans hinted he should not do—talking to the Soviets—he could gain greater leverage in Washington at a time when Sino-American relations had deteriorated. By responding to Brezhnev's Tashkent initiative, Deng played the proverbial Soviet card that the Americans had so hoped to dissuade him from playing.

Deng did not want to overdo it, though, so even after the resumption of the Sino-Soviet dialogue in the fall of 1982, he continued to assure the Americans that nothing would change in relations with Moscow and that rapprochement was not in the cards. Even if Brezhnev died, Deng told Nixon in September, the "expansionist nature of the 'Soviet social system' and the Czarist imperialist heritage" would remain unchanged no matter who ruled in the Kremlin.[146] Yet even as he denied any intention to mend fences with Moscow, Deng continued to play the Soviet card, because his denials only served to remind the Americans of the possibility that there was in fact such intention in Deng's mind. If so, one way to avert the possibility was to continue giving Deng what he wanted: technology, access to financing and markets, and compromise on Taiwan. This was the course the Reagan Administration eventually adopted, and after August 1982 Sino-American relations resumed forward movement.

Despite Deng Xiaoping's claims to the contrary, Sino-Soviet relations continued to improve after 1982 with almost imperceptible momentum. It was not exactly what Deng had in mind. Ever since Tashkent he had lingering doubts about Brezhnev's long-term intentions and erred on the side of caution. Skeptical as he was that the Soviet Union would unleash a war, he still continued to believe, despite Tashkent, that the Soviet Union posed the greatest threat to China. Recounting his meeting with Deng in September 1982, Nixon reported that "while he [Deng] gave the US some shots, he hit the Soviet Union much harder. He nodded vigorously in agreement when I said that there was a major difference between the two superpowers: the Soviet Union has designs on China, and the US does not."[147] A few days after this meeting, Deng complained to his associates that Brezhnev "should not think that he can mislead China with his 'fraudulent maneuver'"—that is, Tashkent.[148]

The "three obstacles" proved a useful weapon in Deng's hands to forestall movement toward normalization and, at the same time, to appease his critics in the Chinese leadership who favored a speedy rapprochement with the Soviet Union. At the time of Tashkent there were two different groups of ruling elites, which could be called, for simplicity, right-leaning and left-leaning. The right-leaning—Deng and his protégés and associates, such as Premier Zhao Ziyang and General Secretary Hu Yaobang—looked to the West. The left-leaning were *not* the same leftists who between 1975 and 1976 obstructed Sino-American relations. Those leftists—the so-called Gang of Four—were defeated in the party struggles years before Tashkent. Now the critics of Deng's West-looking policy were a much more formidable force: they had worked for China's socialist future hand in hand with Soviet planners at the height of Sino-Soviet cooperation in the 1950s, and included people like Chen Yun and Li Xiannian.[149]

Chen and Li were only the most visible functionaries suspected of nostalgia for Soviet-style economic planning. Many more in the party and the state apparatus were favorably disposed toward economic rapprochement with the Soviets, realizing the urgency of modernization of Soviet-built factories and perhaps doubting the entire framework of Deng's policy of "opening to the outside" as basically incompatible with Maoist principles, or socialism itself.[150] According to contemporary East German intelligence reports, Deng Xiaoping was even criticized at a Politburo meeting in March 1983 for putting too much faith into cooperation with the United States, which had failed to deliver what had been promised.[151]

It is hard to imagine anyone openly challenging Deng at the Politburo; if anyone could do it, however, it was the seventy-eight-year-old political heavyweight Chen Yun, who was gravely concerned about China's economic performance and criticized the State's economic policies in fairly acrimonious terms at a Politburo meeting on March 17. Chen warned against "idealism" in economic policies, criticized careless spending on projects that China could not afford, and urged careful planning for the next ten years to establish the foundation for economic growth.[152] Significantly, in his statement, Chen Yun praised China's experience with the Soviet-supported 156 industrial projects of the First Five-Year Plan, claiming it was incorrect to say that they "went astray."[153] This criticism was probably directed at Hu Yaobang, as well as Premier Zhao Ziyang, although Zhao, partly to protect himself, also lashed out at Hu and sided with the cautious planners.[154] In the subsequent months, Chen Yun would still pound on Zhao and Hu for doing things too quickly.[155] In a sense, criticism of Zhao and Hu *was* criticism of Deng, as no one could be under any illusion as to the source of their support in the ruling circles.[156]

Reagan's relaxation of export controls in June 1983, raising China to a "friendly, non-aligned country"—despite angry denunciations on Capitol Hill by the likes of Jesse Helms, who urged him to keep "Red China" at bay—went a long way toward relieving some of the pressure from Chinese reformers like Zhao and Hu, and, indirectly, Deng.[157] Chen Yun still complained, putting an ideological spin on the question of learning from the West in his speech at a party plenum on October 12, 1983: "Some people see foreign [Western] skyscrapers, highways, etc., and think that China is not as good as the foreign, and socialism is not as good as capitalism, that Marxism is ineffective." These people, Chen proposed, should be reeducated, lest they forget that "the continued existence in the world of socialist countries headed by communist parties is an irrefutable proof that communism will replace capitalism."[158]

While Deng's love for the West had its limits—he was, for example, dead set against Western-style democracy as ineffective and unsuitable for China—he never manifested anything comparable to Chen Yun's affinity for the socialist camp. For Deng, normalization with the USSR was only a matter of tactics; for Chen Yun, it was more a matter of long-term strategy. Zhao Ziyang recalled that "Chen Yun retained a deep-rooted admiration for the Soviet Union and a distrust of the United States. His outlook was very different from that of Deng Xiaoping, and there was friction between the two."[159] Chen Yun could not understand why China could live with US support for Taiwan, but not with Soviet support for Vietnam; the reason, in Chen Yun's view, was his comrades' (i.e., Deng's) love for American technology, though it could well be replaced by technology purchases from the socialist camp.[160] As a result of these disagreements, progress toward Sino-Soviet normalization became both a tactical ploy and a strategic choice, resulting in a stalled process over the "three obstacles" and yet a move forward in practical exchanges of all kinds, especially trade.

Deng gradually yielded to the mounting pressure for economic cooperation with the Soviets. For example, on July 20, 1982, when reviewing a joint report by the Ministry of Foreign Trade and the Foreign Ministry about using the Soviet help to upgrade China's industrial and mining enterprises, Deng wrote: "Contacts with the Soviet Union should begin with political questions."[161] For the same reason, Deng urged the two ministries on another occasion, in December 1982, "not to rush headlong" into scientific and technical cooperation with the USSR. One should not have the attitude of "a hungry man who will eat anything," he warned, but granted that "one or two things could be done."[162]

The trickle of "one or two things" continued, widening until it had to be acknowledged that Sino-Soviet contacts in all spheres were expanding at an impressive pace. Thus, from 1982 to 1983, Sino-Soviet trade turnover (excluding increasingly substantial cross-border trade) increased from 275 million dollars to 673 million dollars, followed by another increase to 1.321 billion dollars in 1984 and nearly two billion dollars in 1985. Overall, from 1981 to 1985, Sino-Soviet trade expanded nearly nine times. The initiative for this broadened economic exchange actually came from the Chinese, to the great surprise of the Soviet Politburo.[163] Unlike Deng, Chen Yun was very supportive of developing trade with the USSR, as well as with Eastern Europe, recalling that such trade was very profitable to China in the 1950s. At a time when the United States shunned China's textiles, Soviet willingness to buy Chinese-made goods was good news: "in the past," Chen Yun said, "they wanted [to buy] everything, even paste [jianghu]!"[164]

The Soviet Union and China exchanged delegations of coal and steel specialists in 1983; in 1984 the Chinese negotiators asked for Soviet involvement in the development of a major coal field in the Chinese northeast. The Soviets were asked to supply equipment for coal enrichment plants and thermal and nuclear power plants, and were invited to upgrade a textile and a wood processing factory in China. There were dozens of smaller projects, too, from arrangements for cross-border trade to retail distribution of periodic literature in Beijing and Moscow.[165] Although Sino-Soviet trade remained unimportant in comparison with the overall trade turnover for both countries, there is no denying that Sino-Soviet economic relations were expanding with astonishing speed. This was a far cry from the "one or two things" envisioned by Deng Xiaoping in 1982.

ARKHIPOV COMES TO CHINA

When Andropov was on his deathbed, he called up "Mikhstep" Kapitsa and told him that he wanted to take yet another step toward bringing the Soviet Union and China closer together. His idea—penciled on a piece of paper Kapitsa later delivered to the Politburo—was to send First Deputy Premier Ivan Arkhipov to China as a messenger for improved relations.[166] Arkhipov, who would later speak of China as his "Second Motherland," explaining poetically that half of his heart was in China and the other half in Russia, was a living legend of Sino-Soviet solidarity.[167] In 1950 Stalin sent him as the chief economic adviser to the Chinese government. For a good part of the 1950s Arkhipov was in China, coordinating massive Soviet economic and technical aid. The aged administrator symbolized the golden years of Sino-Soviet fraternity and solidarity.

The idea was pitched to the Chinese and met with a positive response. On February 8, 1984, one day before Andropov's death, Arkhipov's visit was discussed at a meeting of China's Central Committee Leading Group on Foreign Affairs Work. Li Xiannian, who presided, proposed to use the visit to cover a "certain distance" in relations with the USSR. Signing economic and technological agreements with Arkhipov, Li explained, would not only advance the four modernizations but also put "a kind of pressure" on the United States.[168] Li's comments registered continued ambiguity of Chinese policy. The talk of "pressure" reflected Deng Xiaoping's tactic: the prospect of Arkhipov's visit could raise the stakes for Reagan, also shortly due in China. On the other hand, the Chinese leaders understood that Arkhipov was more than a card in the Sino-US exchange, and that improved Sino-Soviet relations were important on their merit.

Arkhipov was supposed to go to China in May 1984 but at the last moment the trip was called off by the Soviets. The foreign media speculated that the Vietnamese, apprehensive of Sino-Soviet rapprochement, were able to block this Soviet initiative. Vietnam's relations with China reached another low point in April when the PLA fired tens of thousands of shells into the Vietnamese territory and dispatched battalions to occupy three hills in Vietnam. Probably Hanoi turned up the heat on the Soviets on this account. There is also evidence that Arkhipov's trip was vetoed by either Gromyko (who was unhappy that Soviet economic proposals went too far and, moreover, did not want Arkhipov to steal his thunder by precipitating rapprochement outside the framework of foreign ministry consultations) or, even more likely, by Rakhmanin (who did not want Arkhipov in Beijing at all).[169]

Whatever the cause of this postponement, its news was badly received in Beijing. It was a big loss of face for the Chinese, especially for the proponents of prompt normalization who would have found it difficult to argue that the Soviet Union had mended its ways and no longer resorted to "bullying." Unsurprisingly, at another Foreign Affairs Group meeting on June 21, the Soviets came in for a round of bashing amid promises to prevent any further forward movement in Sino-Soviet relations without progress on the "three obstacles." "We should not create an illusion for the Soviet Union that they are doing us a favor," Li Xiannian argued. The meeting resolved for the time being to continue work on the visit, because improvement of Sino-Soviet relations was deemed a strategic goal.[170] But it was not until December 1984 that Arkhipov, after a delay of six months, finally turned up in Beijing, bringing proposals for economic cooperation.[171]

The last Soviet official of somewhat comparable rank to visit China was Prime Minister Aleksei Kosygin, in September 1969. Then, following bloody border skirmishes, Sino-Soviet relations were so tense that the talks were held in the Beijing airport, not in the city. By contrast, Arkhipov's reception was warm and cordial. In the breaks between official sessions, he attended a song and dance pageant called "Song of the Chinese Revolutionary," viewed Beijing from the twenty-sixth-story revolving restaurant of Xiyuan Hotel, squeezed in a visit to a Chinese worker's family, and even managed a side trip to a Soviet-built steel plant in Wuhan and the special economic zone in Shenzhen. Arkhipov's meetings with his Chinese counterpart, Yao Yilin, yielded three agreements: on economic and technical cooperation, scientific and technological exchange, and the establishment of a Sino-Soviet committee on economic, trade, scientific, and technological cooperation.[172]

The real highlight of the trip was Arkhipov's meeting with his old-time acquaintances, now the "elders" of China, especially economic mastermind Chen Yun, who was Arkhipov's chief counterpart in the Chinese government during his work in China in the 1950s. On Christmas Eve, Arkhipov visited Chen Yun at the leadership compound in Zhongnanhai. Chen, who could no longer walk without assistance, insisted on greeting Arkhipov at the door. They embraced tearfully, and Chen Yun said, "You are an old friend of ours ...we worked swimmingly together,"[173] before pulling out a piece of paper to read out the standard Chinese position on the "three obstacles," which Deng had ordered him to read lest Chen, with his well-known sympathies, say something that "might cause confusion on foreign policy."[174] A Russian participant in the meeting recalled, "One could tell that Chen Yun was reading this paper unwillingly, carrying out an unpleasant instruction."[175]

Even what Chen Yun said in his "official" comments was a world apart from Deng's conventional anti-Soviet talk. "Whether during the years of revolutionary struggle, or during the years of peaceful construction, the Soviet government and the Soviet people helped us. The Chinese government and the Chinese people have not forgotten about it." Chen paused for a fraction of a second, then added: "nor can they ever forget."[176] Shunning words like "hegemony" that were for the Soviets like a red flag and registering his disbelief with the idea that China, as a socialist country concerned first and foremost with "further development of socialism," would ever attack the USSR, Chen Yun went on to talk about the "great, untapped reserves" for Sino-Soviet economic and technical cooperation in spite of the "three obstacles."[177]

Arkhipov's visit did not lead to a political breakthrough on the "three obstacles." Here, both sides maintained "principled" positions. On the Chinese side, coming as it did in the same year as highly successful visits by Premier Zhao Ziyang to Washington and by Ronald Reagan to Beijing, Arkhipov's mission was anticlimatic. The least the Chinese could do was appear even-handed in foreign policy. On the Soviet side, despite the death that December of Defense Minister Dmitrii Ustinov, there still remained opponents of normalization—especially Rakhmanin—who minimized the importance of what had just happened.

At a meeting in Moscow on February 18, 1985—almost two months after Arkhipov's visit—Rakhmanin informed his colleagues from the bloc that the Soviet assessment of the visit was "strongly negative." He said:

"The People's Republic of China does not want a true normalization of relations with the USSR. The PRC also cooperates with the imperialist powers on a global scale.... The CC CPSU concludes that the present anti-socialist line in the PRC's foreign policy is long-term and [includes] strategic cooperation with American imperialism. Beijing thinks that by weakening the USSR and the entire socialist commonwealth it will be able to carry out its own great power and hegemonic ambitions. Objectively speaking, there is a dangerous resemblance between China's strategy and that of US imperialism: Reagan wants to open the Eastern front against the USSR; Beijing aspires to strengthen its military potential for hegemonic purposes and also seeks a military cooperation with the U.S. in this respect. Together, this is a joint aspiration of Beijing and U.S. imperialism in order to change a global system to the disadvantage of the USSR and the entire socialist commonwealth."[178]

This was Rakhmanin's personal opinion, even if it was packaged as a position of the Soviet Politburo. Just as Deng had to yield to pressures, not least from Chen Yun, to move forward toward Sino-Soviet normalization despite the "three obstacles," so Rakhmanin, who had since the beginning opposed the Tashkent line, found it impossible to hold back the winds of rapprochement. Dry economic agreements settled in Beijing—spiced up by Arkhipov's "moving reunions with ... old friends"—accomplished what political consultations could not do in the previous two years: created a sense of forward movement in Sino-Soviet relations, even warmth barely remembered after twenty-five years of bitterness and confrontation.[179] "We could not help but think of the happy years of friendship between our two countries," Arkhipov said as his visit drew to a close.[180]

This sort of friendship was no longer in the cards as policy makers in China and the Soviet Union pondered the future of Sino-Soviet relations. Still, by early 1985, conditions were in place for a major breakthrough on the road to normalization. What happened in Sino-Soviet relations after 1982 was somewhat comparable to the changes in Sino-American relations the week Richard Nixon visited China, except that these changes happened over the span of three years, and so did not seem shocking to most observers. Yet what used to be unthinkable—meetings, exchanges, embracing of old friends—was now accepted as the norm. Such were the consequences of the process that was launched by, of all people, the symbol of Soviet decay Leonid Il'ich Brezhnev, in Tashkent, on March 24, 1982.

CONCLUSION

The meaning of China's "independent foreign policy," noted Zhao Ziyang shortly after it was officially proclaimed at the 12th Party Congress in September 1982, was not that China would now be "equidistant" from the United States and the Soviet Union, but that the Chinese leaders would look at current "international circumstances" before deciding whether to oppose American or Soviet "hegemonism." This allowed Beijing a measure of flexibility in dealing with the "bullying" on the part of either superpower.[181] Deng Xiaoping insisted that he was not "playing cards" and that this policy was based on "principles," including China's opposition of hegemony everywhere in the world. The reality was more complex. In the short term, this policy opened up possibilities for playing the Soviet Union and the United States against each other, and so directly led to the beginning of the Sino-Soviet normalization. In the long term it set up China as a challenger to the international status quo.

Whether this was entirely unavoidable—as Kapitsa and Oksenberg would have us believe—is another question. Deng Xiaoping saw China's relationship with the United States as second to none in importance, a sine qua non for the country's modernization effort. He invested himself heavily into building this relationship, even in the face of skepticism among other senior leaders. The lesson Deng learned in the early 1980s was that this relationship was hostage to US domestic politics, and that it was dangerous to over-rely on Washington. "We must not be too naïve," Deng concluded by early 1982, implying that he, too, had been naïve in the past about what the United States would and would not do for China.[182] Disputes over technology transfers and Taiwan arms sales fed Deng Xiaoping's resentment of and disillusionment with Washington, puncturing big holes in Deng's once-upon-a-time vision of "standing on the side of the United States." Get-tough policies of the early Reagan Administration helped turn predictions of pundits like Kapitsa and Oksenberg into self-fulfilling prophecies.

The beginning of the Sino-Soviet normalization process, it has been argued, was inevitable because Deng "de-ideologized" China's foreign policy and prioritized economic reform, which made the continuation of conflict with the USSR unnecessary and even harmful for China.[183] Although this explanation seems logical, it is not borne out by facts. "De-ideologization" of Chinese foreign policy was something that Mao Zedong had accomplished much earlier, for such was the real meaning of the Sino-American rapprochement in the early 1970s. Deng's anti-Soviet feelings had no ideological component; instead, they were underpinned by real security concerns and fears of Soviet expansionism that were rooted not in Marxism-Leninism but in China's historical experience with Russia since the 19th century. Moreover, tensions with the USSR helped rather than hampered Deng's policy of opening to the outside world, because this policy targeted the West, not the socialist bloc. For China, the beginning of Sino-Soviet normalization was intricately linked to the deterioration of Sino-American relations and the need to bring pressure to bear on the United States. Reevaluation of the intensity of the Soviet threat was another important factor in the process.

Likewise, the Soviet Union was initially interested in rapprochement with China for tactical reasons. Indeed, the Tashkent initiative was a direct consequence of President Reagan's tough rhetoric in his early years in power, and a sense of international isolation engendered by Moscow's misadventures overseas, followed by a robust response from the West. The Soviets were card players, just like the Chinese, and it was immediately apparent to each what the other side was doing. Nevertheless, there were voices in both the Soviet and the Chinese policy circles that saw rapprochement as less of a tactical ploy and more as a strategic imperative underscored by common ideological legacy of the two countries. It was this shared socialist identity, conspicuously absent in Sino-US relations, that propelled the dialogue between Beijing and Moscow beyond mere platitudes toward constructive engagement.

It was a very slow process because neither side trusted the other. Deng's lack of trust in Soviet intentions was the reason he insisted on the resolution of the "three obstacles" to normalization—Soviet troops at the Sino-Soviet border and in Mongolia, the Soviet invasion of Afghanistan, and Soviet support of Vietnam's occupation of Cambodia. The same lack of trust also haunted the Soviet leadership. "I don't believe them.... These people are ruthless"—for many years this had been Brezhnev's assessment of the Chinese.[184] Lowering one's guard by satisfying Deng Xiaoping on any of these obstacles was deemed suicidal. The only guarantee against perfidy was toughness and military force. Yet what happened between 1982 and 1985 was that little practical steps the two sides had agreed upon—exchange of visits and increase in trade—helped to build up a certain reserve of trust that made further movement toward normalization possible. This was a valuable lesson in how even most tangled knots can be untangled one thread at a time.

CHAPTER 2

Lost Opportunities: Japan and the Soviet Union, 1982–87

From snow-capped Kamchatka to the milder latitudes of northern Japan stretches a seven-hundred-mile-long island chain, the Kuriles. Rising steeply from the depth of the Pacific, these forbidding reminders of the earth's violent tectonic past are home to thriving colonies of sea birds and seals. Their human population is insignificant and dwindling—summers are too short, winters are too harsh, and the mainland is too far away. The few Russian settlers, who have weathered typhoons and braved earthquakes, service the islands' economy, the fisheries. Fish (especially salmon), crabs, sea urchins, and valuable seaweed are in abundance in the rough territorial waters. The land holds untold and mostly untapped treasures, including gold and rare metals. Majestic sceneries are meant to inspire tourists but formidable difficulties of access keep all but a handful of enthusiasts from enjoying this desolate and inhospitable edge of the world.

The Kuriles were once inhabited by peoples of the Ainu stock who had spent centuries in scattered fishing villages. The history of early "exploration" of the Kuriles by the Russians and the Japanese is murky and heavily politicized, as each side claims they were there first. The Russians reached the Kuriles from the north in 1697; this was followed by decades of haphazard colonization by fur hunters and traders as the empire's interests extended further and further down the island chain. The native Ainus were sporadically declared Russian subjects and forced to pay taxes. By contrast, the concept of sovereignty was alien to Tokugawa Japan. While the

Japanese certainly knew of the Kuriles before the Russians did and their contacts with the Ainus predated Russia's colonization efforts, these contacts did not lead to Japan's administration of the islands or the natives' acceptance as Japanese subjects.

Indeed, Japan's national boundaries were not truly defined in conceptual terms until the 19th century; encounter with Russia in the north played a crucial role in this conceptualization. In 1855, by a Russo-Japanese treaty, the Kurile Islands were divided between Russia and Japan. The Shogunate obtained the southern Kuriles: the relatively large Iturup and Kunashir, and the lesser isles of Shikotan and Habomai.[1] The Russians swallowed the rest of the archipelago. This was followed by another treaty in 1875, which assigned the nearby Sakhalin Island to Russia's sovereignty while Japan obtained the rest of the Kuriles chain all the way to Kamchatka. With the Russo-Japanese War of 1904–5 (ending in Russia's ignominious defeat), Japan annexed southern Sakhalin. Following the Russian Revolution it also briefly occupied northern Sakhalin and even sent forces to Siberia to protect Japanese interests. From the time of the Russo-Japanese War until the closing chapter of the Pacific War, Japan presented the greatest security challenge to Russia and the Soviet Union in the Far East.

On August 8, 1945, the Soviet Union declared war on Japan (in violation of the 1941 Soviet-Japanese neutrality pact), and in the following weeks southern Sakhalin and all of the Kuriles were occupied by the Soviet forces. Stalin seriously considered landing on the major Japanese island of Hokkaido but changed his mind in the face of strong US opposition to this prospect. But the Kuriles and Sakhalin remained in Soviet hands after the war, indispensable as both were, in Stalin's view, to Moscow's security interests. In 1951 the Soviet Union missed its chance to conclude a peace treaty with Japan, dismissing the US draft circulated at the San Francisco Peace Conference as an anti-Soviet ploy. Moscow-Tokyo relations were normalized in 1956 but a peace treaty between them was never signed, despite rounds of discussions between 1955 and 1956. The key obstacle was the continued Soviet occupation of the Kuriles. The Japanese wanted the islands back—not all of them but only the southern four islands, symbolically declared the "northern territories."

In 1956 the Soviet government and Japan issued a joint declaration by which the Soviet Union promised to return to Japan two of the four islands in question (namely, Shikotan and the Habomai isles), subject to the conclusion of a peace treaty. However, the renewal of the US-Japan security treaty in 1960 prompted the Soviets to denounce the promise of the 1956 Declaration—the return of the two islands.

Occupied and re-occupied, colonized, and re-colonized, fortified and re-fortified—the Kurile archipelago boasts a nasty history. This history is important to the broader story of Soviet-Japanese relations because the territorial dispute over the "northern territories" has dominated postwar Soviet-Japanese relations to an improbably absurd extent. The Kuriles problem was symptomatic of deeply running Soviet-Japanese antagonisms and the most visible expression of a complex foreign policy dynamic, which was closely tied in with the Soviet Union's and Japan's regional policies and their relationship with the United States.

By the late 1960s the Soviets faced two fundamental problems in the Far East, and looked to Japan as part of the solution. The first was the security dilemma amid heightening tensions with China. A rapprochement with Japan could in some ways compensate for the disastrous demise of the Sino-Soviet alliance—a possibility that the Chinese leaders were very aware of and anxiously sought to preempt. There was also the need to sabotage improvement in Sino-Japanese relations, for in the imagination of the Soviet policy makers, these relations were based on "racial principles" and so had the potential for casting the USSR in the role of an outsider in a Sino-Japanese Asia.[2] The other problem was the economic backwardness of the Soviet Far East. The Soviets were attracted to a mostly self-induced illusion that the Japanese entrepreneurs would rush to invest their cash in the extraction of natural resources in Siberia.

The anticipated windfall did not materialize. Efforts to enlist Japan as an anti-Chinese sympathizer also led nowhere. In fact, in August 1978 Japan and the People's Republic of China concluded a treaty with an anti-Soviet clause (at Beijing's insistence). The Soviet invasion of Afghanistan in December 1979 brought Soviet-Japanese relations to a new low as Tokyo firmly backed American sanctions against the USSR. Soviet-Japanese trade—a trickle in either country's external trade balance—actually declined by over 20 percent between 1983 and 1984 from its 1982 high of 3.7 billion rubles. This decline was a byproduct of worsening Soviet-US relations—the collapse of détente and the onset of the Second Cold War. The Soviets complained of Japan's support for American imperialism and supposed revival of Japanese militarism. In Japan, the ruling Liberal Democratic Party (LDP) had few kind words for the menacing northern neighbor, even fewer once Nakasone Yasuhiro, who openly advertised his close relationship with Ronald Reagan, was selected to be Prime Minister in November 1982.

This chapter recounts Soviet-Japanese relations from 1982 to 1987. It shows that the internal dynamics of policy making in the Soviet Union and in Japan were very different from what transpired on the surface. Certain political forces in both countries favored a compromise solution to the territorial problem. In Japan, Nakasone, for all his hawkish anti-Soviet rhetoric, was willing to stake his political reputation on achieving a breakthrough in relations with Moscow. This was to be an act of statesmanship on his part, something that history would remember him for. But, a canny political operator, he eventually sacrificed that pie in the sky for concrete gains in the relationship with the United States, which he always thought was more important to Japan and to him personally. Unbeknownst to Nakasone, there was in fact an internal debate in Moscow on the issue of the islands, with even ostensible conservatives like Foreign Minister Andrei Gromyko—the Mr. No of Soviet-Japanese relations—being in favor at one point of giving in to at least some of the Japanese demands.

There was no breakthrough. In Tokyo, the Foreign Ministry clung to the unrealistic and unproductive position of all or nothing, making it difficult even for statesmen like Nakasone to show flexibility. In Moscow, proponents of compromise faced resistance from the military and the party hardliners. There were, however, a few moments of lost opportunity: between 1982 and 1983, when the Soviet Union faced international isolation and really needed improvement of relations with Japan, and between 1986 and 1987, when Mikhail Gorbachev was at the peak of his power to make drastic steps in foreign policy. The first opportunity slipped away because of unfortunate domestic political situations in both countries: General Secretary Yurii Andropov's illness—which took the wind out of the sails of his efforts to steer a more active foreign policy course—and the public outrage in Japan over the downing of the Korean airliner off the island of Sakhalin. The second opportunity never materialized, because Gorbachev, upon assumption of office, did not understand Japan's crucial role in the Asia Pacific, and because Nakasone sacrificed improvement in Soviet-Japanese relations to the imperative of appeasing Washington. At an important turning point, key players in Moscow and in Tokyo prioritized their relationship with the United States at each other's expense. Both sides thought that the other side needed them more, and would therefore make all the concessions.

"UNSINKABLE AIRCRAFT CARRIER"

Nakasone boasted a truly charismatic personality in a political culture where charisma is a rare gift. A son of a timber entrepreneur from Gunma prefecture, he served in the Imperial Navy and then in the police force before being elected a member of the Japanese Diet in 1947 at age twenty-eight. Over the next thirty-five years Nakasone held a number of cabinet positions. In the meantime, he built up a loyal faction within the ruling LDP and acquired a reputation as a "leaf in the wind" and a "weathervane" within the Japanese political establishment for his propensity to adapt his views to the changing circumstances.[3] His years as Prime Minister were marked by contentious tax reform and privatization initiatives. In foreign policy, he acted with boldness and resolve uncharacteristic of Japan's postwar political leadership.[4]

Nakasone became the Prime Minister at a difficult time for US-Japanese relations. The American economy was in the middle of a severe recession, and the unemployment rate exceeded 10 percent. As the US automakers laid off thousands of workers, protectionist sentiments swelled up in Congress, and Japan was singled out as the scapegoat. The Democrats were indignant over the Toyotization of America and lambasted the Reagan Administration for not doing enough to protect US manufacturers from Japanese competition, while turning a blind eye to Japan's own protectionist policies that had hurt US exports, especially tobacco, beef, and oranges. The media predicted a coming trade war between Washington and Tokyo.[5]

Fuelling congressional and public discontent, the Japanese were not very responsive to Washington's prodding to raise defense expenditures. The United States had long complained about Tokyo's unwillingness to share the defense burden and had called on its reluctant ally to assume a greater degree of responsibility for peace and security in Northeast Asia. By the early 1980s even Deng Xiaoping was urging Japan to rearm.[6] These entreaties did not have the desired effect: Tokyo cited constitutional constraints and maintained the budgetary allocations for the Self Defense Force within 1 percent of the GNP, at a time when Washington was spending six times as much. Nakasone promised to redress US grievances, but for all his hawkish rhetoric the spending increase for 1983 was only 6.5 percent, even less than what Japan spent in the previous two years.[7] The Prime Minister argued that it was "the maximum we could do," but the lawmakers on Capitol Hill were unconvinced.[8]

Still, when Nakasone turned up in Washington in January 1983, Reagan was highly hospitable. The Japanese Premier was treated to a private unscheduled breakfast meeting at the White House, where Reagan proposed that his guest call him simply "Ron." Not to be outdone, Nakasone (who boasted "fluency in basic English") offered to be called "Yas."[9] Later, perhaps because he did not want to be ridiculed as Reagan's "yas-man," he changed that to "Yasu."[10] Thus the "Ron-Yasu" relationship was born, as Nakasone wasted no time reporting to the Japanese media.[11] The Prime Minister also pulled off a public relations coup when he met with the family of retired steelmaker Mort Winski, with whom Nakasone's daughter Mieko stayed when she was an exchange student. "At that time," wrote Nakasone in a letter to the Winskis, which was promptly handed over to the journalists, "I was hoping and dreaming that one day they [his daughters] would become of big help to me in my future state visits to the United States as prime minister of Japan. Today my long-term dream has come true."[12]

Nakasone's most impressive feat in Washington, however, was his interview with the *Washington Post*. He explained his views on defense in the following terms: "My own view...is that the whole Japanese archipelago or the Japanese islands should be like an unsinkable aircraft carrier," a bulwark against penetration by the Soviet Backfire bomber, surface ships, and submarines.[13] The remark caused a storm of controversy back in Japan, as it was evocative of Japanese wartime propaganda about the unsinkable Imperial Navy, which after all proved very much sinkable.

Stung by domestic criticism, the Prime Minister claimed he never said anything about unsinkable carriers. Upon inspecting the interview tapes, Don Oberdorfer of the *Washington Post* discovered that Nakasone had been mistranslated and had actually said "big aircraft carrier" rather than "unsinkable aircraft carrier."[14] It turned out to be a lucky mistranslation. Nakasone recalled later: "the one term 'unsinkable aircraft carrier' was worth more than one million words: its outcome was immediate and effective."[15] "[W]ith this one shot, all of Washington's pent up feelings of mistrust at Japan's negative attitude toward defense, were blown away. It was an enormously effective shock treatment that changed the gloomy atmosphere between Japan and America completely."[16] "Yasu" Nakasone now stood high in glory as a captain of the great aircraft carrier in the treacherous waters off the Soviet coast—such was the public image the Japanese Prime Minister hoped, and to a certain extent managed, to project in Washington. US officials were reported as "impressed" by Nakasone's statesmanship.[17] What he did in Washington—and not for the last time—was to play the Soviet card to distract the Americans from Japan's record on trade and defense and to improve relations at Soviet expense. Nakasone was doing what Deng Xiaoping had done during 1978 and 1980 in his instrumental use of the Soviet threat to manipulate the Americans.

By contrast, no one in Moscow was impressed. The Soviet news agency TASS denounced Nakasone's remarks and hinted at the prospect of nuclear retaliation: "for such a densely populated, insular country as Japan, this [a Soviet nuclear strike] could spell a national disaster more serious than the one that befell it 37 years ago [at Hiroshima and Nagasaki]."[18] Soviet saber rattling stirred uproar in Japan. Ambassador Vladimir Pavlov was given a verbal note of protest.[19] In his turn, Japanese Ambassador Takashima Masuo was received in Moscow by Gromyko, who complained that "remarks like Nakasone's statement...reveal Japan's intention to damage Soviet-Japanese relations and to re-militarize." Gromyko added that "concern in Japan over the 'Soviet threat' was being 'artificially created.'"[20]

In reality, however, it was not. Soviet policy toward Japan bordered on plain bullying. In addition to verbal threats, which showed complete Soviet insensitivity toward Japan's nuclear allergies, Moscow was also formulating plans for moving a part of its missile force—the highly mobile SS-20s—to Asia as a part of the disarmament process in Europe. Andropov reportedly said that the missiles would target "a new military base in Japan" (this was a reference to the Misawa airbase in the northern part of Japan). In the context of the TASS insinuations about turning Japan into a nuclear battlefield, such plans appeared particularly menacing. The Soviet Ambassador was called in for an "acrimonious" session at the Foreign Ministry. "Frustration just really boiled over," a Japanese official was reported as saying after meeting. "Things have mounted up with the Russians and we let them have it this time."[21]

This Japanese reaction was entirely predictable. But why did the Soviet policy makers think they could achieve anything through a strategy of intimidation and threats, and what was it, exactly, that they were trying to achieve? The answer connects to the long-standing Soviet conviction that there were serious exploitable contradictions in the American "camp," and that the policy of brutal threats could force Japan to distance itself from the United States because, presumably, Japanese public opinion would not allow Nakasone to steer the country toward a confrontation with the powerful northern neighbor. The useful precedent for this was the upheaval of 1960, when Japan descended into a sea of protest following the renewal of the Security Treaty with the United States and President Dwight D. Eisenhower memorably even had to cancel his visit for fear of being confronted with the protesters.

Yet nothing like that happened this time around. It is true that Nakasone came under serious domestic criticism for provoking the Soviets with his militant talk. But the public opinion on the whole rallied behind the government in the face of the mounting Soviet threat. In addition, clumsy Soviet arm-twisting helped forge a consensus within the Japanese government (between the Cabinet and the Foreign Ministry) to the effect that "this is not a time for Japan to undertake initiatives or make any major moves vis-à-vis the USSR, but rather is simply a time to wait until Soviet intransigence moderates."[22] All of this was a matter of deep satisfaction to the American policy makers, who were, in fact, initially concerned that—as George Shultz put it—the Soviets could "use arms control talks to drive a wedge between our European and Asian friends."[23] He should not have worried. Soviet saber rattling only drove the wedge between themselves and everyone else. The row over Nakasone's "unsinkable aircraft carrier" remark vividly demonstrated Moscow's self-defeating policy.

THE LOST CHANCE

Did anyone in Moscow recognize that promising to rain atomic destruction on Japan was a counterproductive policy? The declassified record shows that there was more to the Soviet thinking on the subject than met the eye and that at one point, realizing their inability to sow discord in the US-Japan alliance, the Soviet leadership considered making unthinkable concessions on the territorial problem. This point was reached in late spring 1983, after a very bumpy ride in Soviet-Japanese relations. In the end, internal deliberations failed to translate into political concessions. This was due to entrenched resistance on the part of the military, and because Yurii Andropov's prolonged illness effectively incapacitated decision making in the Soviet Union. In early September 1983 the uproar over the downing of the Korean airliner off the coast of Sakhalin buried hopes of significant improvement in Soviet-Japanese relations for the foreseeable future.

By late 1982–early 1983, Soviet policy makers were thinking hard about Japan, to the extent, of course, that their declining mental faculties allowed them to do so. Even Brezhnev, who by then had practically succumbed to senility, realized that not enough was being done to move the Soviet-Japanese relationship forward. "Relations with Japan in the present circumstances [i.e., growing Soviet international isolation] are extremely important to us," Brezhnev mumbled at a Politburo meeting on September 9, 1982, "but they are not improving, on the contrary—[they are] worsening." He went on to criticize existing Soviet proposals, such as that Gromyko should visit Tokyo, foreign ministry consultations, "reinvigoration" of exchanges with the ruling LDP, and the big political notion of "moving forward" with the Soviet draft of the Treaty of Good Neighborliness and Cooperation. The latter treaty had been on offer since 1975 but was repeatedly vetoed by the Japanese because it implied a de facto dismantling of the US-Japan alliance and completely ignored the territorial problem.[24]

"Probably," Brezhnev continued, "it is not easy [for us] to think of something else. However, honestly speaking, I do not believe that simply repetition of a position, which we have been offering for five years, will lead to any kind of a move in our relations with Japan. Probably, the Foreign Ministry, the Ministry of Defense, and the KGB should all continue to think about this problem, look for ways out of a political dead end in our relations with this country, which is very important to the interests of the USSR."[25] Brezhnev himself had neither the energy nor the imagination to offer any new ideas for a breakthrough; the only thing he proposed at the Politburo meeting was improving Soviet coverage of Japan, so that positive things would also be reported in the Soviet media, rather than merely endless reproach of Japanese "militarism." Brezhnev's criticism did not have any immediate results. Two months later he died, and in the following months, relations with Japan went from bad to worse amid hostile rhetoric on both sides.

But when the dust began to settle over Nakasone's scandalous "aircraft carrier" remarks, and Andropov's equally scandalous plans to target Japan with SS-20s, the Soviet leaders realized that their hopes of splitting Japan from the United States had led nowhere and that Nakasone, far from having been intimidated into a more friendly attitude or undermined in the eyes of Japanese public opinion, was as strong as ever. Nothing demonstrated this as well as the Prime Minister's performance at the G7 summit in Williamsburg in May 1983. Even as the French and the Canadians had second thoughts about Reagan's Evil Empire–busting foreign policy— Canada's Pierre Elliot Trudeau aptly summarized the doves' sentiments with his memorable "we should be busting our asses for peace"—Nakasone called for Pershing deployments in Europe and for continued US presence in Asia, while reiterating that any nuclear arms control negotiations with the USSR must include Asian SS-20s.[26]

During his meetings at the summit, Nakasone went out of his way to persuade America's disgruntled allies to put up a united front "in the face of Soviet attempts to divide [them]." As he explained to Prime Minister Margaret Thatcher, "he wished Williamsburg to demonstrate Western solidarity so that President Reagan felt that all his allies were behind him in the [nuclear arms control] negotiations."[27] Some of his stronger statements again caused commotion in Japan, especially among the opposition parties, but what really impressed the Japanese public was how Nakasone managed, multiple times, to get photographed next to Reagan in the lineup of leaders at the summit. Needless to say, Nakasone's "fast footwork" at photo opportunities—to borrow from the Washington Post's sarcastic comment—had a great symbolic significance for US-Japanese relations.[28]

The Soviet leadership watched these developments with growing concern. Williamsburg followed months of increasingly brazen US military exercises, including the largest-ever naval exercise off the Soviet Pacific coast and psychological operations (PSYOPs) entailing violation of the Soviet airspace to tickle Moscow's nerves and probe its air defenses. Reagan's announcement of the inauguration of the Strategic Defense

Initiative ("Star Wars") in March 1983 added to the Kremlin's apprehensions. Andropov could not understand what the Reagan Administration was driving at. To Averell Harriman, who met with the General Secretary days after Williamsburg, Andropov "seemed to have a real worry that we could come into conflict through miscalculation." He told Harriman that he had no confidence whatsoever in the present US administration; his comments betrayed a sense of desperation, for, in Andropov's view, Reagan simply wanted the Soviet Union to lay down arms unilaterally. "That," he said, "could not be."[29]

What, then, could be done? On May 31 Andropov called a Politburo meeting to discuss the Soviet response to Williamsburg, where he also broached the question of improving relations with China. While half a year earlier Andropov had spoken optimistically about fostering dissent among Reagan's allies, he now offered a much more sober—and, to be sure, a more realistic—assessment of the situation in the Western camp. At last, Andropov admitted that Reagan had successfully forged "an anti-Soviet coalition" among America's allies. The Williamsburg summit showed that despite differences between the United States and its G7 partners, this did not prevent them from closing ranks to deal with the Soviet Union in a coordinated fashion on essentially American terms. Japan was a case to the point. "I am especially concerned by Japan's—in particular, Prime Minister Nakasone's—behavior," Andropov noted. "He is completely on the side of the more aggressive Western countries and fully supports Reagan's actions."[30]

Still determined to woo Nakasone away from his close reliance on the United States, Andropov proposed to "think about a *compromise* [my italics] in relations with Japan." "For example," he added, "one could think of joint exploitation of some of the small islands which have no strategic importance." The transcript of this Politburo meeting then documents the following exchange.

> GROMYKO: About Japan. I am thinking of the following proposal: how about us making a proposal regarding the islands of Habomai, Kunashir and other trivial islands, which in reality are small dots, and to draw the border, or to make a correction to the border. This would really be a prestigious offer.
> ANDROPOV: When I spoke about Japan, I had a different proposal in mind. I spoke about joint exploitation of some of the small islands.
> GROMYKO: One could combine both things. After all, these islands are small dots in the ocean and do not really have a great strategic importance.

Andropov did not respond to that. However, Gromyko's proposal was questioned by Defense Minister Dmitrii Ustinov, who had also warned Gromyko that the Soviet Union should not make concessions to China. Now, Ustinov pointed out that "one could only look at some small islets, but as for the big islands, like Kunashir, we are fairly well settled there."[31] He went on to make the usual strategic argument to the effect that the Soviet Union needed the islands to have a free exit to the Pacific.[32]

To allow the Japanese the right to use the disputed islands alongside the Soviets—for this was what Andropov's idea of "joint exploitation" entailed—was a major departure from the existing Soviet policy; that the General Secretary entertained this idea in itself shows the extent of his exasperation with the evident strengthening of the US-Japanese alliance. The episode suggests that, just as in the case of the Soviet policy toward China, Andropov viewed relations with Japan through the prism of Cold War priorities. Improvement in relations with Japan was desperately needed—not so much for its own sake but as a means to an end—to crack the unity of the Western alliance. At a time when Moscow refused to recognize the existence of the territorial problem, Andropov's proposal clearly amounted to tacit recognition of Tokyo's rights to the islands, although the Soviet leader did not clarify whether he had in mind Shikotan and Habomai or the bigger islands of Kunashir and Iturup.

The most striking aspect of this exchange was Gromyko's reaction: he proposed to give away Habomai, Kunashir, and "other trivial islands." It is possible, of course, that he had in mind Habomai and Shikotan and was referring, specifically, to the promise of the 1956 Declaration, although this still leaves open the question of "other trivial islands." Or it may well be that Gromyko meant what he said—that is, proposing to go beyond the 1956 Declaration by returning all of the "northern territories" to Japan. It is quite remarkable that such a far-reaching proposal came from Gromyko, who was notorious in the West for his stubborn diplomacy, who had denied time and again that the territorial problem existed at all, and who had told the Japanese several times that he would not even visit Tokyo if they attempted to bring up the "northern territories." At the very least, this episode demonstrates that there was more to Gromyko's diplomacy than what one could see on the surface.

Gromyko's half-hearted attempt at the Politburo meeting to portray the "northern territories" as "trivial" islets and insignificant "dots in the ocean" did not go down well with Andropov, but especially not with Ustinov and the defense establishment he represented. Among them, Andropov, Ustinov, and Gromyko held the reins of foreign policy; if they had reached a consensus on the territorial solution, it is inconceivable that the Japanese would not have gotten the islands back. But Ustinov was doggedly opposed. Gromyko, seeing that his "prestigious offer" met with resistance, dropped the matter. Andropov did not follow up on his own proposal of "joint exploitation." After Andropov and Ustinov died in, respectively, February and December 1984, Gromyko did not rehabilitate his idea of territorial concessions to the Japanese. It is difficult to speculate why, but one obvious possibility was that his proposal at the May 31, 1983, Politburo meeting was a reaction to specific events: the strengthening of the anti-Soviet front in the West. By early 1985 the Soviet Union had somewhat maneuvered itself out of the corner, and Japan no longer mattered to Gromyko.

Cutting Gordian knots requires statesmanship, and Gromyko was never much of a statesman. Perhaps if Andropov had not been as ill as he was, he would have been able to override entrenched resistance within the party and the military and to break the ice in Soviet-Japanese relations, for instance by returning to the 1956 Declaration. The timing was right: everyone could see the existing policy was not working; Gromyko supported changes; the Soviet Union badly needed friends in the region, and relations with China had only begun to thaw. And Nakasone, anti-Soviet in appearance, was far from being an American "puppet," as the Soviet media had portrayed him. In 1983 he was charting a new course in relations with Japan's neighbors, including South Korea and China, and working hard to strengthen Tokyo's standing in the Third World, something he was in fact thinking of the very same day the Soviet leaders voiced their worries about his pro-American orientation.[33] If Andropov had gathered enough strength for the exercise of statesmanship, he would have probably seen the Japanese Prime Minister going out on a limb to meet him halfway. But the ailing General Secretary was tightly bound by chains of military-bureaucratic interests, and, from the fall of 1983, connected to an artificial kidney machine. This was a highly disadvantageous position for the conduct of innovative foreign policy.

THE DEEP FREEZE

To the extent that there was a window of opportunity in 1983, it closed shut on September 1 of that year. On that day, a Korean Airlines Boeing 747, en route from New York, via Anchorage, to Seoul, strayed off course into forbidden Soviet airspace. A Soviet SU-15 intercepted the plane and shot it down just off the coast of Sakhalin, killing 269.[34] As the world reacted with disbelief and indignation (although not the Chinese, who abstained in the UN vote), Moscow lamely issued conflicting denials. Almost a week after the tragedy, it admitted taking the plane down but blamed the Korean pilots, who (supposedly) knew they were off course and did not heed the signals of the Soviet interceptors.[35] According to the public Soviet account, KAL 007 was actually a spy plane on a mission to investigate Soviet defenses in the Far East. Some of the Soviet claims were deliberate lies: for example, it has since been revealed that the Soviet interceptors did not contact the plane and did not fire tracer bullets to alert the Boeing crew before downing the plane. On the other hand, Soviet belief in the espionage mission was possibly genuine—"beyond any doubt," in the words of a KGB/Defense Ministry memorandum submitted to Andropov.[36] It cannot be ruled out, however, that the military and the KGB deliberately misinformed Andropov in order to avoid taking responsibility.[37]

Whatever the case, shooting down an unarmed civilian airliner was not the kind of public relations coup that could contribute to the Soviet Union's peace-loving image. "It was an act of barbarism," Reagan declared, "born of a society which wantonly disregards individual rights and [the] value of human life and seeks constantly to expand and dominate other nations."[38] This view gained wide acceptance outside the Soviet bloc. Angry demonstrations swelled up in South Korea, complete with placards and banners denouncing the "Massacre by Cold-blooded Russians" and the burning of Soviet flags.[39] Similar sentiments were expressed across Japan, which lost twenty-eight of its citizens in the tragedy. Rallies were held near the Soviet Embassy in Tokyo and consulates in Sapporo and Osaka. Although the protests were mainly peaceful, in Sapporo someone hurled a Molotov cocktail at the consulate building, and in Tokyo the police arrested five ultra-nationalists who tried to storm the embassy compound.[40]

Grieving relatives of the deceased were taken in boats as close to the site of the tragedy as the Soviets allowed. The Japanese television reported on emotional scenes aboard one ferry: two girls, Mei and Mai, aged eight and eleven, screaming "Otosan! Otosan!" (father, father!); a man shouted "Henji-shite kudasai!" (please answer me!) to the waves.[41] Some of the ferries carrying mourning relatives were harassed by low-flying Soviet military aircraft.[42] The Soviet authorities kept American and Japanese ships from conducting searches in the crash area.[43] Their own search-and-rescue operations, conducted using inadequate equipment, only turned up some pieces of wreckage and personal belongings, which were transferred to the Japanese patrol boat *Tsugaru* at the Soviet port of Nevelsk. It was reported that the Soviets ordered *Tsugaru* stripped of all weapons and its helicopter unloaded before allowing it into the port—"to avoid any possibility of a confrontation."[44] In the meantime, bits and pieces of the airplane and mangled body parts, carried by the currents, washed up on the Hokkaido beaches.[45]

The few months between the KAL 007 incident and Andropov's death in February 1984 were the most difficult period in US-Soviet relations since the Cuban Missile Crisis more than twenty years earlier. Reagan's anti-Soviet rhetoric escalated to new heights. On top of this came the deployment of Pershing missiles in Europe, deepening Moscow's sense of vulnerability as Soviet command centers in Europe were now theoretically five minutes from nuclear obliteration. Tensions came to a head with the NATO command post exercise Able Archer 1983 in November, which imitated a nuclear war with the Soviet Union. Soviet military and intelligence circles were genuinely concerned that the United States was preparing a nuclear strike on the USSR under the guise of this military exercise, a concern Andropov possibly shared. It was anyone's guess whether the Soviet leadership was really capable of sound policy making or whether, under the pressure from trigger-happy generals, the panicking Politburo might order a preemptive action against the West. War by miscalculation loomed.[46]

In the same period, Soviet-Japanese relations took another dive. Nakasone recalled that he wanted to have a "strong mind" and "straighten the Soviet attitude."[47] Japan's Self Defense Force (SDF), in close coordination with the Americans, staged the largest military exercise in years, mobilizing 150 ships, 117 aircraft, and 30,000 troops. Parts of the US 7th Fleet and the 5th Air Force also participated.[48] Moscow issued customary condemnations, although it also called for closing ranks with China in the face of what was described as a common threat to both countries.[49] The reality did not favor Moscow: instead there was evidence of increasing Sino-Japanese cooperation at Soviet expense. Beijing and Tokyo jointly opposed SS-20 deployments in Asia. This opposition was reaffirmed during Hu Yaobang's visit to Japan in November 1983. In his talks with Nakasone, who emphasized the growing Soviet military threat in Northeast Asia, Deng's protégé said that it was "understandable" that Japan would seek to bolster its essential defense capabilities.[50] This was not reported in the Soviet press at the time: TASS tried to put a positive spin on Hu's comments, claiming in a report that the CCP chief dodged "the anti-Soviet aspects that the Japanese side tried to emphasize."[51]

Another aspect of the visit that was necessarily overlooked in the Soviet reports, though trumped up by the Japanese, was the Chinese Foreign Minister Wu Xueqian's endorsement of Tokyo's position in the territorial dispute. Speaking in Sapporo on November 27, Wu declared that the Japanese demand was "a just cause in defending the country's territorial integrity and sovereignty."[52] Hu, for his part, held talks with Yokomichi Takahiro, which not only marked an important achievement for the Japan Socialist Party (JSP) and Hokkaido's socialist governor—who was known in the party ranks as a man of "pro-Chinese" orientation—but also underscored the Soviet failure to make headway with the Japanese socialists.[53] Even low-level exchange between Hokkaido and the Soviet Far East was put on hold after the KAL downing, including a scheduled visit by a delegation of Sakhalin party officials. Explaining the decision to postpone the delegation's visit, JSP officials told General Consul Yu. Rudnev that "because there were Japanese among Hokkaido passengers, there is an emotional reaction, while many Hokkaido residents are simply scared by the fact that the plane had been shot at. Therefore, it will take some time for the emotions to calm."[54]

In the meantime, Nakasone paid a return visit to China in late March 1984. Neither he nor his Chinese hosts spoke kindly of the Soviet Union. Prime Minister Zhao Ziyang even told Nakasone that "the main threat to China's security comes from the Soviet Union."[55] Anti-Soviet themes were also raised in Deng Xiaoping's conversation with Nakasone. The two discussed strengthening of Soviet sea and air forces in the Far East as their "common concern" (Deng's words), with Nakasone complaining specifically about the SS-20s and Deng raising the "three obstacles" to Sino-Soviet normalization.[56] The Soviets responded that the Chinese and the Japanese attempted "to create a distorted image of Soviet policy" and criticized the Chinese for their failure to see that "the Nakasone cabinet is positively engaged in forming a tripartite military alliance between Japan, the USA and South Korea."[57] This was a deliberately measured response; for all their frustration with ever closer relations between Beijing and Tokyo, the Soviets treaded carefully to protect the fragile sprouts of Sino-Soviet normalization. In private, however, Mikhail Kapitsa noted with disappointment that while "recently Hu Yaobang visited Japan and behaved himself with reserve, now both the Chinese and the Japanese sides made fairly insolent anti-Soviet statements. This should not particularly surprise us. These are efforts to put us under pressure."[58]

The Soviet response to this perceived "pressure" was to apply counterpressure. "We will push on Japan," Kapitsa told a visiting Mongolian Foreign Minister on March 29, 1984. "The situation is difficult, militarization of East Asia and the Pacific Ocean is under way.... The crux of the matter is that Imperialism is creating a global military coalition, which has linked three fronts of forward deployment of the first strike: Western Europe, Near East [and] the Indian Ocean, and East Asia [and] the Pacific...Japan is becoming a part of the global system of Imperialism, it is being integrated."[59] Gromyko gave a similar assessment: "We must see the danger in relation to Japan. Before, under Suzuki Zenko, too, but especially now, under Nakasone. Japan considers itself a kind of a NATO member. It kind of moved into the North Atlantic."[60] Rakhmanin's boss in the

Central Committee, Konstantin Rusakov, added: "We are very concerned by the inclusion of Japan into the anti-socialist zone. They don't have the right to do it formally. But it is easy to dispense [with the formality]. The [Japanese] industry is ready for it. And they have enough samurai."[61]

These were exceptionally sober, gloomy assessments of Soviet-Japanese relations by people who made the Soviet foreign policy. The basic premise, rooted in great power disdain for Japan, was to play it tough until the Japanese gave in and adopted a more conciliatory attitude toward Moscow. This policy was fundamentally flawed and self-defeating. As one US intelligence report pointedly summarized, "public opinion polls indicate many Japanese are worried by Nakasone's tough stand on defense, but there has been nearly universal resentment of Moscow's heavy-handed threats. These threats have reinforced Nakasone's firm approach to relations with the USSR, and he has made clear that he will not be bullied."[62] Rather than spoiling US-Japanese relations, military buildup and nuclear threats only amplified the Soviet menace in the eyes of the public, as well as in government circles. The KAL incident reinforced the negative tendencies in Soviet-Japanese relations. Director of Policy Planning at the US State Department Stephen W. Bosworth, who visited Tokyo days after the downing of the South Korean plane, reported that his Japanese colleagues were "unrestrained in manifesting their traditional distaste of the Russians, 'with whom [they] had three wars in this century.'"[63]

But were the Foreign Ministry's anti-Soviet sentiments aligned with the views higher up the chain of command? The bureaucrats liked to think so. As Deputy Director for Soviet Affairs Miyamoto Yuji put it, it would be "political suicide" for either Nakasone or his Foreign Minister Abe to attempt a breakthrough in the face of Soviet unwillingness to relent on the territorial issue. Yet, both the Prime Minister and the Foreign Minister were keen to be seen in search of a dialogue with the Soviet Union with the aim of "bolstering their own political popularity here in view of the upcoming elections."[64]

In fact, the Soviet hands at the Ministry were worried lest Prime Minister Nakasone break ranks to achieve a breakthrough in relations with the Soviet Union. This would be in keeping with his style—an act of statesmanship in blatant disregard of the cautious recommendations of the unimaginative bureaucrats. What could stop him? "Once you have grasped political power," wrote Nakasone, "it is yours; there is only the judgment of history for those who hold public office."[65] Nakasone was no loose cannon, but, as US Ambassador Mike Mansfield pointed out, he was "clearly attracted to a dramatic step by Japan" in relations with the Soviets.[66] But what dramatic step could he take while the Soviet Union was ruled by the dying Andropov, plugged to his kidney machine, or, once he died, by his asthmatic successor, Konstantin Chernenko, who, upon assumption of office, looked more dead than alive? In such adverse circumstances, no act of statesmanship could have revived Soviet-Japanese relations from the state of paralysis.

NAKASONE EYES THE PRIZE

In the memorable third week of March 1985, when Mikhail Gorbachev shone on the world stage as the charming host of Chernenko's funeral, the Soviet General Secretary for the first time shook hands with Prime Minister Nakasone Yasuhiro. Nakasone had proposed to go to Moscow just as soon as he heard of Chernenko's death. At the height of his popularity at home, a prophet of assertive nationalism, and Reagan's comrade-in-arms, Nakasone was well placed to talk to the Russians. Gorbachev was such a stark contrast to his struggling predecessors that Nakasone would have stirred into action even if he had no political acumen. But the Japanese Prime Minister had unparalleled political acumen and an intuitive feeling that he and the youthful General Secretary could succeed where all others had failed. Nakasone instructed the Gaimusho (Japanese Foreign Ministry) to arrange a meeting.[67]

The Gaimusho bureaucrats were disheartened by the prospect, no doubt because Nakasone's initiative went against the grain of entrenched Foreign Ministry conservatism. "There was a fear combined with a suspicion," noted Togo Kazuhiko, one of the old Soviet hands of the Gaimusho, "that the most important principle [that is, the territorial issue] could be bent [for the sake of] a politician's private ego."[68] The Prime Minister was told it was for his sake, because there was no guarantee that a meeting could be arranged between him and Gorbachev, and his reputation would suffer if Gorbachev refused to meet. Nakasone overruled all objections and left for Moscow on the gamble that the General Secretary would agree to a meeting after all.[69] He later explained his motivations: as the Prime Minister, he did not think that foreign affairs was the Gaimusho's business. Gaimusho could never achieve breakthroughs, only leaders. "As a Prime Minister, [I thought] I should grab opportunities."[70]

The gamble paid off, but only because of Nakasone's determination. He saw Gorbachev briefly at a reception, when foreign dignitaries lined up for a chance to shake hands with the new General Secretary. During their two-minute exchange of pleasantries, Nakasone pushed for, and obtained, a vague promise of a meeting. The Japanese delegation was soon informed, however, that they would be received by Prime Minister Nikolai Tikhonov instead. Nakasone was outraged by this slight and threatened to leave for Tokyo right away unless the Soviets delivered Gorbachev. At last, the hosts relented and Nakasone obtained an appointment after most Western leaders. Even then, the meeting was delayed by two hours without any explanations or apologies.[71]

In a sense, the snubbing was not deliberate. It simply reflected Gorbachev's insufficient understanding of Japan's importance for the USSR. Moreover, he had to rely on the advice proffered by the Japan specialists of the Central Committee, led by the orthodox stalwart Ivan Kovalenko, who had no sympathy for Nakasone, the LDP, or Japan. Even as Nakasone was humiliated, Gorbachev found the time to meet with the second-in-charge of the Japanese Communist Party, Fuwa Tetsuzo. Gorbachev's talking points included an anti-American tirade and an appeal to the JCP to develop "fraternal trust" with the Soviet Communist Party.[72]

According to scholar of Soviet-Japanese relations Tsuyoshi Hasegawa, Nakasone's meeting with Gorbachev was very significant, and not simply for the handshake. Nakasone called for a "comprehensive approach" to Soviet-Japanese relations, which allowed for simultaneous discussion of the territorial problem and the expansion of bilateral cooperation in other areas, such as culture, economics, and science and technology. This approach was an early formulation of the policy of "balanced expansion," which was eventually adopted by the Japanese government in late 1988, perhaps a bit too late to make any real difference in Soviet-Japanese relations. At a deep level, probably imperceptible to the Soviet leadership, Nakasone's "comprehensive approach" undercut the Gaimusho's "entry approach," the idea that the territorial problem had to be resolved *before* any improvement in other aspects of mutual relations.

The idea was some months in the making, and in fact, the Soviets had been already informed of it during the October 1984 visit by a high-ranking Soviet delegation to Japan (led by Politburo member Dinmukhamed Kunaev). At the time, Cabinet Secretary Fujinami Takao told the visitors that the Prime Minister did not insist on the final resolution of the territorial question before Soviet-Japanese relations could improve. "There are opportunities for all-sided development of our relations, and one must look into this. As for the territorial question, this is a problem of the future."[73] Chernenko's foreign policy aide, Andrei Aleksandrov-Agentov, a member of the delegation, was said to have been "very impressed" with the Prime Minister.[74] Still, as Hasegawa writes, "it should be emphasized that the initiative for improving Soviet-Japanese relations came from the Japanese side," crediting "Nakasone alone."[75]

The last point does not fully account for the complexity of LDP factional politics. In October 1984 the Liberal Democratic Party confirmed Nakasone as Party President and, therefore, Prime Minister. Although Nakasone's public approval ratings topped 60 percent, his second term did not come easily. This was because Nakasone's LDP faction was merely the fourth strongest in the Diet. He only kept power because he enjoyed the support of former Prime Minister Tanaka Kakuei. Rival factions—those of former prime ministers Suzuki and Fukuda, and a lesser faction led by Komoto Toshio—were not amused by Nakasone's iron grip on the top post. Former Cabinet Minister Miyazawa Kiichi and Nakasone's Foreign Minister, Abe Shintaro, were known contenders for the job, as was Tanaka's right-hand man, Nikaido Susumu.

In the end, an agreement was hammered out and Nakasone was the only one to stand in the election.[76] On October 31 he formed a new cabinet, proving himself yet again an unbeatable political manipulator. Yet under these circumstances, all contenders for power stood to benefit from an act of statesmanship, and improvement of relations with Moscow was highly prized as a public relations coup. It is not surprising, then, that Nakasone's potential rivals were not averse to a dialogue with Moscow.

LDP Vice President Nikaido's conversations with the Soviets serve to underscore this point. Nikaido was among those who met with the Kunaev delegation in October 1984. In his comments Nikaido actually downplayed the territorial problem. "If we keep talking about it [the territorial issue], we will run against a dead end. We must settle all the problems of Japanese-Soviet relations, which I have mentioned [he had talked about economic, cultural and technical-scientific cooperation], developing and improving these relations as a whole. Once we have good relations, then, we could take up the territorial question."[77] These remarks went even beyond Nakasone's "comprehensive approach," and in fact amounted to an "exit approach"—the territorial problem was restated but its solution was postponed until Soviet-Japanese relations had been significantly improved.

Nikaido then proposed that he should go to Moscow to broker a breakthrough. He would do that if it were possible to arrange his reception at the highest level. "I would like to go to Moscow," he said, "in order to exchange opinions with the Soviet leadership on all questions of interest to the two sides. In this case, I can take it as my responsibility that the results of such a trip are properly understood in Japan. I have enough influence and power to achieve this." This was a bit presumptuous on Nikaido's part and one wonders what Nakasone would have said to this if he had overheard the conversation. Certainly, the Gaimusho would not have looked kindly on such one-man missions, something Nikaido knew all too well, which was why he urged the Soviets *not* to contact the government or the Foreign Ministry to arrange his visit. Instead, he proposed a secret channel, through Miura Kineji, the board director of Asahi National Broadcasting (whom the KGB defector Stanislav Levchenko had incidentally identified earlier as one of his "agents" in Japan and who, Nikaido said, "enjoys the trust of the Soviet side" and his own trust).[78]

Nikaido's maneuvers—and he was certainly not the only LDP dietman in search of a role in Soviet-Japanese relations—illustrate the close relationship between foreign policy and domestic politics in Japan. Probably Nikaido, just as Nakasone or Abe or Miyazawa, believed in the importance of returning the "northern territories" to Japan. But unlike the career bureaucrats who strolled the hallways of the Gaimusho, career politicians were less interested in the principled approach to the USSR and by far more interested in being seen in an act of statesmanship. A high-level dialogue with Moscow was for the latter less of a policy imperative than a method of self-advancement in the factional struggle. This sort of personal diplomacy remained a very attractive option for LDP politicians, and was part and parcel of Soviet-Japanese relations for the better part of that turbulent decade and beyond.

As for Gorbachev, Japan was not among his priorities when he assumed office, and his meeting with Nakasone in March 1985 did not change that. Gorbachev was quite disappointed with the "difficult" conversation and complained later that Nakasone immediately brought up the territorial problem. To this, he said, he replied "in a most decisive way, and showed him, on our part, where the Japanese leadership was slowly drifting toward, and how it was getting pulled more and more into military cooperation with the United States." Gorbachev recounted telling Nakasone that Japan stood to lose out should it drag its heels in economic relations with the USSR: "we had a planned economy, and if we plan everything out for the five-year period, then there might be no space left for economic ties with Japan."[79] All of that was read from an old script.

"I have to say," Gorbachev recalled, "that we had not thought through our policy with regard to Japan in light of 'new thinking.' There was a desire to draw a line under the past and 'begin everything anew.' I repeated these words at first to all my Japanese interlocutors without yet feeling the significance—state, political, emotional, traditional, psychological, of any kind—which the Japanese attached to the Southern Kurile problem. In early conversations I did not even want to discuss this question, considering the postwar partition everywhere to have been final and irreversible. I did not recognize the existence of the problem."[80] It took about five years before Gorbachev began to recognize that the existing policy was not working, and that something had to be changed in the Soviet approach to Japan. By the time he realized that he couldn't talk his way toward better Soviet-Japanese relations, Gorbachev had all but run out of time.

ILLUSION OF PROGRESS

Although Japan was not at the top of Gorbachev's priorities, it is fair to say it received some attention in the process of policy formulation during his first year of leadership. There was a range of opinions to consider, from the most orthodox of views to radical proposals, none more radical, perhaps, than Georgii Arbatov's advice to Gorbachev in April 1985 to "give up two, if not all four, islands to the Japanese because otherwise we will not get anywhere with them."[81] Only someone with Arbatov's clout could peddle such a hugely controversial idea with impunity. Yet some thinking along these lines obviously persisted in the broader policy-making circles. Director of the Institute of World Economy and International Relations (IMEMO) Evgenii Primakov, when he was in Tokyo in December 1985, probed the Japanese on the possibility of returning to the 1956 Declaration. But news of the probe leaked out into the Japanese press, in what, Hasegawa argues, was possibly a preemptive strike by the Gaimusho conservatives against a two-island solution. Primakov was very unhappy about such a breach of confidence.[82]

Views such as these remained fairly uncommon within Soviet policy circles, however. There is no evidence that Gorbachev gave serious thought to a two-island solution until 1990 or 1991. His initial idea was to seek a broad political and economic dialogue with Japan in the hope that it would encourage the Japanese to shelve their territorial claims. The Soviet leadership redoubled efforts to win Japanese support for various disarmament and security proposals, including Gorbachev's new idée fixe, the Asian Security Forum. The idea was promoted in a personal letter from Gorbachev to Nakasone in September 1985. Nakasone eventually replied, agreeing to the project in principle so long as Japan could stand by its alliance with the United States. But from the Soviet perspective, this defeated the whole idea. Gorbachev picked up on the theme in his meeting that same month with the JSP Chairman, Ishibashi Masashi, calling for disarmament and confidence-building measures in the Far East while lambasting Washington for military preparations in the region.[83]

Disarmament was a subject of the conversation between the newly appointed Soviet Foreign Minister, Eduard Shevardnadze, and Abe Shintaro when they met for the first time at the United Nations on September 24, 1985. Shevardnadze impressed the Japanese, not least because his style was so different from that of his inscrutable predecessor. He even put out Russian *pirozhki* for Abe's sampling and offered him coffee and tea—unheard of hospitality. Feeling he needed to cultivate what appeared to be a new Soviet attitude, Abe entirely omitted any reference to the territorial problem in his speech at the UN.[84] Nakasone was equally intrigued by what seemed like increased Soviet interest in a dialogue with Japan, and for this reason he, too, took a low-key approach on the "northern territories" issue. He avoided the topic in his letter to Gorbachev in October 1985 and took a soft line on the Russians during his visit to the United States the same month. Nakasone mentioned he would like to visit Moscow again.[85]

"Utterly ridiculous" was the Gaimusho's reaction to Nakasone's mild attitude.[86] Suspecting that Soviet disarmament proposals were simply a ploy to separate Japan from the United States, the Foreign Ministry became even more intransigent in its insistence on the resolution of the territorial problem as a precondition for any serious improvement in Soviet-Japanese relations. Hasegawa writes of the emergence of two policy lines in Tokyo at this time: the Prime Minister's flexible and forward-looking policy, and the Gaimusho's conservative and short-sighted policy. The Foreign Ministry's entrenched conservatism was one of the reasons, in his opinion, that Soviet-Japanese relations stalled and important opportunities were missed, among them, perhaps, the opportunity of solving the territorial problem on the basis of the 1956 Declaration. If the Soviets officially placed this proposal on the agenda, Nakasone could well have accepted a compromise solution; therefore, the Gaimusho had to work hard to preempt and sabotage any such tendencies by ever more rigid adherence to the "entry approach" and the notion of "inseparability of politics and economics."

In fact, the Gaimusho was probably not far off target in some respects. There is little doubt that Soviet disarmament proposals for Northeast Asia in large part aimed at sowing discord in US-Japanese relations, something Moscow had been obsessed with for many years but never quite worked out. Before his meeting with Abe, Shevardnadze privately spoke of "a US-Japan-South Korean triangle" in Asia and the imperative for the USSR to "use their mutual contradictions."[87] Gorbachev evidently shared these sentiments; for example, one of his speech drafts for a Warsaw Pact conference in October 1985 referred to certain "influential forces in Japan, which resent one-sided reliance on the USA."[88] By this logic, the Soviet Union had to exploit these friendly feelings while stonewalling the territorial problem.

There was a degree of misperception in Soviet-Japanese relations, leading each side to think that the other was more prone to concessions than it actually was. This impression was to a large extent caused by incoherent and divergent policies on both sides. Moscow's increased interest in improved relations suggested a high degree of Soviet economic desperation. Unclear feelers about a two-island solution must have convinced Gaimusho officials that Japan held all the cards and that if they only maintained a tough negotiating position, the Soviets would give in. This impression was mirrored for the Soviet leadership. Nakasone's "comprehensive approach" appeared to signal Japanese willingness to deemphasize the territorial problem, and if so, it was best to ignore the problem altogether to discourage the Japanese from bringing it up in the first place. These misperceptions played out during Eduard Shevardnadze's visit to Japan in January 1986.

The last time Japanese shores welcomed a Soviet foreign minister was in 1976, so Shevardnadze's appearance in Tokyo was bound to cause a commotion. Six thousand uniformed and plainclothes policemen were mobilized to stave off the protesters. Hundreds of rightist activists cruised the streets of downtown Tokyo in vans, some decorated with Imperial Navy flags, shouting anti-Soviet slogans to military music. Several protesters attempted to break through the gates of the Soviet Embassy; one threw a smoke bomb, while "another was seized as he waved a toy sword outside the mission."[89] "Armed policemen stand on rooftops around our Embassy," wrote Teimuraz Stepanov-Mamaladze of Shevardnadze's entourage. "Unwavering, reliable, but also full of reproach. Work is work but hearts scream in unison with the loudspeakers: Thief! Return Sakhalin and the Kuriles right away!"[90] It was an unpleasant experience for the Soviet delegation but it served the Gaimusho's purposes to have the militant rightists on hand, to loudly remind Shevardnadze what mattered most to the Japanese.

He was also reminded of what the Soviet Union was missing, what could be in store if relations improved. Shevardnadze toured a Nissan factory and walked away infinitely impressed by the state-of-the-art technology of the production process (especially the robots), promising to buy a Nissan upon retirement. There were more sighs of astonishment at the Sony exhibition pavilion in central Tokyo, as Shevardnadze inspected new models of TVs and video cameras. He filmed his wife Nanuli and a crowd of reporters and "broke into a broad smile when the film he had just made was projected onto a screen."[91]

Shevardnadze pushed hard for upgrading Soviet-Japanese economic relations but faced mixed signals. The Gaimusho sternly insisted on having the islands back before all else but the business circles were enthusiastic about selling a little technology to the communist foe, although decidedly less so when it came to buying unneeded Soviet natural resources in return.[92] In short, Shevardnadze fell far short of what Deng Xiaoping had managed to accomplish when he visited Japan eight years earlier: there was neither a boom in Japanese investment in the USSR, nor any significant transfer of technology. In 1978 Deng's opening to Japan became immensely important in driving China's modernization effort. But Shevardnadze's trip became simply another lost opportunity.[93]

Other than shopping for a bigger share of Japanese trade, Shevardnadze came bearing disarmament plans, which included a proposal to eliminate nuclear weapons in three stages. The Russians had peddled these sorts of proposals for the better part of forty years, but that, Shevardnadze said, was "propaganda." Now was the real thing. "A historic step has been made to save life on earth," he timidly told Nakasone.[94] He did not get very far. The Prime Minister complained about Soviet military buildup in the Far East, and when Shevardnadze leaned on Abe to resist Reagan's Star Wars program, he was effectively told to mind his own business.[95] A few days later, Shevardnadze attempted to explain this reluctance in a way that was perhaps not entirely off the mark: "The Americans are irritated by Japanese economic activities, by their penetration of the US internal market, and by a big surplus in Japan's favor in [US-Japanese] trade.... The Japanese want to dull America's irritation by politically supporting the United States on the international arena."[96]

One thing Shevardnadze did not want to discuss in Japan was the territorial problem. But it crept in nonetheless. The Soviet Foreign Minister reportedly "turned red with anger" when Abe attempted to slip a tricky formulation into their joint communiqué that made it sound as if the Soviet Union was willing to discuss the territorial problem in the context of peace treaty negotiations.[97] The least Abe expected was to return to the oblique formulation of the October 1973 Brezhnev-Tanaka summit (about there being "unresolved questions" in Soviet-Japanese relations). Shevardnadze locked horns with his counterpart: "You should not raise unrealistic questions. If I were you, I would not raise it.... This is a way of sowing hate and hostility."[98] In the end, Shevardnadze and Abe agreed on this formulation: "The two foreign ministers conducted negotiations on the conclusion of a peace treaty, including the problems which might constitute the content of said treaty, on the basis of the agreement affirmed in the joint communiqué of 10th October 1973."[99]

This unclear formulation inevitably caused misunderstanding.[100] Abe thought that it was "a step in the right direction" and that it reflected a "softening of the Soviet attitudes."[101] Shevardnadze, however, had no intention of negotiating on the future of the four islands and thought he would not have to, as his experience in Tokyo (especially his conversation with Nakasone, who barely mentioned the "northern territories") suggested that it was the Japanese who had softened and that relations would improve irrespective of the territorial problem. "They understand"—he explained at an internal ministerial meeting—"that the territorial question cannot be solved in their favor; however, they are willing to work with us, including in the sphere of scientific-cultural cooperation. The Japanese are men of business."[102] Discussing results of his visit at a Politburo session on January 30, 1986, the Foreign Minister recognized that the problem would not go away and proposed to "maintain consistency while showing certain flexibility. Of course, we are not talking about changing our position."[103] The slippery formulation of the Soviet-Japanese communique was, in Shevardnadze's view, a practical manifestation of this sort of "flexibility."[104]

Shevardnadze was very pleased with himself for widening the presumable gap between Japan and the United States. He believed that Gorbachev's disarmament proposals won wide acclaim among the Japanese public. "Taking Japanese 'nuclear allergy' into consideration, Soviet initiatives kind of grew a fertile layer for improving our relations with Japan," he claimed at the Politburo.[105] Although Tokyo, in Shevardnadze's view, continued to follow the US lead in foreign policy, Japan was increasingly unhappy with the role of America's "younger brother" and aspired to claim "leading positions" in world affairs, and especially in Asia.[106] "Contradictions are obvious" in US-Japanese relations, argued Shevardnadze, and the Japanese already understood that "the policy of isolating the USSR does them no good."[107] All of this provided the needed opening for the Soviet Union, he said, calling for renewed efforts to improve relations with Japan "today" because "tomorrow Japan may become different."[108]

Beyond the economic component in the Soviet approach to Japan, Moscow's interest in better relations stemmed from an increasing realization of the country's "huge potential"—in Shevardnadze's words—not only as an economic superpower but also as a political heavyweight.[109] The idea, heavily colored by traditional Russian conceptions of realpolitik, as well as Marxist-Leninist notions, was that tensions in the US-Japanese alliance would eventually bring it to ruin, driving Japan toward neutrality and possibly transforming the Cold War outlook in East Asia. At that stage, the territorial problem would no longer matter, as in the Soviet view it was just a function of Japan's pro-American orientation. By then, it was hoped, Sino-Soviet relations would also improve, and Moscow would then need good relations with Japan "for balance with China," so that the Soviets would be in a position to play Japan and China against one another, and both of them against the United States.[110] For the time being, Shevardnadze told his subordinates, "we should deal with the Japanese calmly, without showing too much interest," with an eye toward "weakening the American factor on the basis of US-Japanese contradictions."[111]

After his sparring with Shevardnadze, Abe walked away with an altogether different impression. If Shevardnadze agreed to something that smelled of the 1973 formulation, obviously the Soviets were beginning to back away from their intransigent position, which had negated the very existence of the territorial problem. Although he granted that "no dramatic advances could be expected," Abe was evidently pleased that "the Soviet Union had changed its policy of ignoring Japan."[112] Togo Kazuhiko, one of the leading Soviet hands at the Gaimusho, recalled that the difference between Gromyko and Shevardnadze was that when the Japanese raised the territorial question, Gromyko would answer that there was nothing to discuss. But Shevardnadze's position was, if you want to say anything, then say it. We can agree or oppose but let us talk! In retrospect, it seems that the Japanese were carried away by what after all was more of a change of style than of substance. But after the "hopeless feeling of entrapment" of Soviet-Japanese relations in the early 1980s, even a change of style would have looked like considerable progress to Abe.[113]

There was also an element of wishful thinking here. Of course, Abe, as one of the main contenders to succeed Nakasone in the premier's seat, wanted to be the one to deliver a breakthrough. After his talks with Shevardnadze in Tokyo, he went to Moscow in May 1986 for another round, hoping to make a dent in the Soviet position on the territorial problem. Abe even met with Gorbachev, but the latter remained steadfast: "You are raising a question that should not be raised at all. This question is concerned with the inviolability of borders that were legitimated by the results of World War II. So long as the Japanese take this approach, there will not be any prospect for resolution."[114] Kapitsa recalled that Abe "visibly soured" when he heard Gorbachev's categorical answer.[115]

Abe Shintaro's catchphrase, as Foreign Minister, was "creative diplomacy." What exactly it meant no one could say, probably not even Abe himself.[116] Creative diplomacy was sorely needed in Soviet-Japanese relations—this much at least was clear from the modest results of Abe's visit to Moscow. The most creative outcome of this visit was the Soviet agreement to allow Japanese nationals to visit the disputed islands visa-free to pay respects to deceased relatives. Gorbachev demanded reciprocity for these graveside visits, and the Japanese hurried to identify a number of long-neglected Russian graves, mainly near Matsuyama City on Shikoku, from the Russo-Japanese War of 1904–5.[117] Abe had to pay for these Soviet concessions with a cultural agreement and the reestablishment of the committee for scientific and technical cooperation, suspended since 1981. These were meager results for Japan, as Abe knew all too well. After his return to Tokyo, the Foreign Minister vowed to "tenaciously negotiate with the Soviet Union" for the return of the four islands.[118]

The Soviets had mixed feelings. The press played up the vastly improved atmosphere of Soviet-Japanese relations, and new agreements, however limited in scope, were an indication that something was moving, at however slow a pace. Soviet Ambassador Nikolai Solov'ev noted at the time that although Abe had raised the territorial question in his conversations in Moscow, it was "not with the same emphasis as before." He pointed out that although in public the Japanese Foreign Minister closely followed cues from Washington, his private comments on issues like nuclear disarmament and SALT II betrayed subtly different views.[119] Such subtleties provided a measure of reassurance to the Soviet leadership that improvement of relations was possible despite the territorial problem, if only the Japanese were brought around to recognize where their true interests lay. The trick was to think up a way to get them to do that.

One of the reasons Gorbachev did not at first think very hard about the causes of persistent stalemate in Soviet-Japanese relations was that he was completely carried away by global schemes. Particular ailments of Soviet-Japanese relations were to him but a local consequence of the Cold War. There was merit to this top-down approach, but it also meant that problems of specifically bilateral nature—especially thorny problems like the territorial question—were shelved as Gorbachev pursued holistic solutions to peace and security in Asia. In 1986 he was just beginning to piece together a major Asia outreach; the highlight was his July 28, 1986, Vladivostok speech, with its sweeping proposals for ending regional conflicts, breaking up military blocs, and achieving thorough denuclearization and disarmament. Only after the dust of Vladivostok settled did the General Secretary realize that the Soviet-Japanese relationship was still on the rocks.

As months passed, Gorbachev kept Japan in the corner of his mind. "We must think, and think more, about relations with Japan," he concluded vaguely at the Politburo, after seeing Abe in May.[120] In August he returned to the problem: "What we had up to now with Japan satisfied both China and the US. But we have to move....We need Japan. Something needs to be done."[121] Just as in Brezhnev's times, however, no one could think of anything useful. There were, of course, various proposals floating in the broader policy community; the Institute of USA and Canada Studies and the Institute of World Economy and International Relations (known by their Russian acronyms ISKAN and IMEMO) peddled new (and not so new) ideas. The Vladivostok initiative itself was in part inspired by a report Arbatov had submitted to Gorbachev in mid-summer 1986.[122] What exactly Arbatov had to say we do not know, but Gorbachev called upon him (and ISKAN) to write parts of his Vladivostok speech. Arbatov passed the assignment to Vladimir Lukin, who drafted the "Japanese" section of the speech. This was just a paragraph or two on "economic diplomacy"—the idea of improving relations step by step through regional economic cooperation—creation of joint ventures, and the like. In the context of earth-shaking ambitions of the Vladivostok initiative, these sounded like timid platitudes.[123]

It goes without saying that Gorbachev did not mention the "northern territories." The Gaimusho immediately advertised this omission and dismissed Gorbachev's economic diplomacy out of hand.[124] But even without the disputed islands, the Vladivostok proposals simply did not go far enough to make a strong impression in Japan, especially where it mattered—within the LDP. For example, Gorbachev did not say anything new about the Asian SS-20s, the Soviet military buildup on the Kuriles, or the naval exercises. In response to Tokyo's pleas to show "political courage," the Soviets reiterated that it was "unrealistic to count on the Soviet Union's unilateral disarmament in the face of existing threats to its own security."[125] As if to underscore this point, days after Vladivostok, the Soviet Pacific Fleet held its largest naval exercises in years, soon followed by the largest-ever US-Japanese-South Korean naval exercise.[126] It was truly business as usual for Soviet-Japanese relations, and that was hardly reassuring.[127]

Gorbachev did not think about Vladivostok in those terms. He believed the Soviet Asia outreach was turning out to be immensely successful, and argued so at the Politburo on September 25, 1986: "After [my] visit there [to Vladivostok], there has been movement of minds in the Asia Pacific. They want to rely on us, against American dominance. This is the beginning. The road is difficult. It is more difficult than in Europe. It is a serious matter. Everyone has got excited. Especially the big countries."[128] A lot of that was hot air, but not all. Soviet-Indian relations were on a sharp upward curve; Gorbachev's maiden voyage to New Delhi in November 1986 added new impetus to their development. In February and March 1987 Eduard Shevardnadze hopped across Southeast Asia all the way down to Australia and New Zealand, selling Gorbachev's proposals to faraway audiences, and he was well received. Sino-Soviet normalization was edging forward, and things were improving in the Soviet-US global disarmament dialogue, despite the partial setback of Reykjavik.

The Japanese did not know what to make of Gorbachev's Asia outreach. On the one hand, Nakasone had to admit that "the Soviets have great interest in Asia and the Pacific, and also appeared to wish to adjust relations with Japan."[129] On the other hand, it was far from certain that such adjustment contained any promise whatsoever of territorial concessions. The Japanese government therefore concentrated all efforts on the imperative of bringing Gorbachev to Japan on the premise that the General Secretary would not come empty-handed, and even if he did, he would have to face the territorial problem in his discussions in Tokyo. The visit was on the agenda from at least December 1985, and the General Secretary seemed quite willing to accept the standing invitation, even mentioning the possibility in his Vladivostok speech.

In the absence of progress in political relations, Gorbachev's visit to Japan appeared as a panacea of a kind. So long as this visit was on the agenda, policy makers in both Tokyo and Moscow could look forward to it in the expectation that it would serve as a stepping stone to whatever each side thought was important to Soviet-Japanese relations. Preparations for the visit were to begin in April 1987.[130] Unfortunately, these plans were derailed by a scandal that rocked Soviet-Japanese relations. This time the chief culprit was Toshiba Corporation, accused by the Americans of selling sensitive naval technology to the Soviet Union. This scandal placed an unexpected obstacle in the way of Soviet-Japanese rapprochement at a time of breakthroughs for Soviet relations in the West (with the United States and Western Europe) and in the East (with China).

TOSHIBA FOR SUBMARINES

In 1984 American author Tom Clancy published *The Hunt for Red October* to instant acclaim. Even President Reagan claimed to have enjoyed the bestseller. In the novel, Soviet ballistic missile submarine captain Marko Ramius, fed up with the system, decides to defect to the United States. He takes the *Red October* on a desperate dash across the Atlantic in the hope of avoiding detection by Soviet attack boats sent to intercept and sink the stray missile sub. Ramius feels he can succeed because his sub is equipped with a new and virtually silent propulsion system, allowing it to approach enemy shores undetected and launch its nuclear payload. In the end, both the Russians and the Americans track down the *Red October*, but brave captain Ramius and his officers escape to freedom. For most readers, *The Hunt for Red October* was just a gripping work of fiction; for those in the know in the Navy, the military intelligence, and the CIA, the problem posed in Clancy's novel hit a sensitive chord. Indeed, it had become more and more difficult for the Americans to detect Soviet submarines, ever quieter, ever stealthier.

In late 1979 Igor A. Osipov, Deputy Director General of the Soviet import organization Tekhmashimport and, reportedly, a KGB officer, approached Kumagai Hitori, the Moscow representative of Japanese trading firm Wako

Koeki. He wondered whether any Japanese company made robots for milling ship screws, and what it might cost to purchase such technology. Kumagai brought the Soviets in contact with Toshiba Machine, a wholly owned subsidiary of the Japanese heavyweight Toshiba Corporation. Toshiba Machine manufactured a piece of equipment called MBP-110, capable of milling screws as large as 11 meters in diameter, weighing up to 130 tons, with the remarkable precision of 0.01 millimeters. Most importantly, MBP-110 could be operated in nine different axes and had two rotating cutters, which allowed the end-user to carve a surface to practically any shape. In other words, with MBP-110 the Soviets gained the capability to mill highly sophisticated and extra-quiet ship screws, needed, according to the Soviet explanation, for tankers and cargo ships. In reality, the machines were intended for milling screws for a new generation of Soviet aircraft carriers and submarines at a top secret facility in Leningrad.[131]

It was clear to both Wako Koeki and Toshiba Machine that export of MBP-110 to the Soviet Union was against the law, as Japan was bound by COCOM restrictions not to supply the communist bloc with sensitive technology that could have military applications. Toshiba Machine's asking price was one billion yen (or five million dollars) for each MBP-110. When it turned out that the price was ten times what it would cost to buy the same machine on Japan's domestic market, the Soviets were told that "export of this kind of machinery is in violation of export restrictions, and when one considers the costs and the risks involved if something were to go wrong, one billion yen is not high at all, but rather an appropriate price, and if the Soviet Union thinks it is too high, they can refuse the deal." But the Soviets agreed and negotiations went ahead. Four MBP-110s were purchased for a reported 17.430 million US dollars. Moscow opted to buy numerical controllers and software from Norwegian firm Kongsberg Vaapenfabrikk (the deal was secretly arranged with Kongsberg's Moscow representative, British citizen Bernhard John Green). This made it easier for Toshiba to obtain an export license from Ministry of International Trade and Industry (MITI) and clear the shipment with the Japanese customs. Wako Koeki received a handsome commission and bowed out. The equipment was delivered through a trading firm, Itochu, and installed in Leningrad between 1983 and 1984.[132]

This would have been the end of the story but for Kumagai's decision to blow the whistle on his superiors in Tokyo. Why would he do something like this? As he later explained, "I am a typical Japanese businessman, not a Rambo but an ordinary man. I was tired with the Russian way of doing business and made up my mind to get out of this small world." He also quarreled with the Wako Koeki management, who, Kumagai said, "treated me as a kind of servant."[133] The less flattering version was that Kumagai wanted to be paid for his silence—and he wasn't.[134] In December 1985 Kumagai wrote a letter to COCOM (headquartered in Paris), detailing various transgressions committed by Wako Koeki and its suppliers in Japan. The Toshiba MBP-110 deal was first on the list, though it also included other restricted items obtained by the Soviet Union from Japanese companies through Wako Koeki's efforts.[135] Kumagai's exposé was forwarded to MITI in Japan, which conducted its own investigation in early 1986, holding ten meetings with Toshiba and Itochu. Both firms denied any wrongdoing. According to MITI's later explanation, the National Police Agency declined their request to interview Kumagai in person regarding these allegations because "it is impossible to follow-up on every letter of complaint received." By March 1986, Kumagai's evidence was quietly swept under the rug, an inter-ministerial committee being told that nothing could or would be done.[136]

A year passed before the Japanese government brought itself to reconsider the Toshiba case—and then only because the Americans forcefully intervened. First, in June 1986, the Japanese were informed through diplomatic channels of the substance of Kumagai's allegations. There was no discernible reaction in Tokyo, although supposedly in December 1986 MITI restarted its investigation of the Toshiba case. Then, in March 1987, the Japanese were reminded—in no uncertain terms—that the United States expected action on Toshiba. On the 24th, Undersecretary of State Ed Derwinski (on his very first day in office) called in Sato Yoshiyasu, Minister at the Japanese Embassy in Washington, to underscore the "gravity" of the Toshiba diversion and to express "serious concern over this Soviet acquisition, which affects not only United States and NATO security, but also Japanese strategic interests."[137]

The reaction was not what Washington would have expected: Japanese officials merely explained that they had already looked into the allegations by a "disgruntled ex-employee of Wako trading" and had found that "no prosecution was possible."[138] American diplomats on the ground in Tokyo pleaded with the State Department not to jump to conclusions, but the mood was darkening in Washington.[139] The quickest to lose patience with the Japanese were those in the Pentagon. Stephen Bryen, who was responsible for COCOM-related matters at the Department of Defense, noted that "everyone in the Pentagon, [Defense Secretary Caspar] Weinberger included, were appalled" by what he called "provocative and dangerous" Japanese actions.[140] Above all, there was frustration with the Japanese reluctance to admit that a COCOM violation had in fact taken place and their insistence that the United States furnish photographic evidence. "I recall a fruitless discussion in Tokyo," Bryen wrote, "in which I said that while we had very good satellites, seeing through buildings or under water from outer space was not one of our better skills."[141] One of his staffers hammered the point home: "The Japanese have the luxury of poking holes in our position and 'sucking' the entire case into an Asian quagmire."[142]

The Toshiba affair became public knowledge at a very sensitive time in US-Japanese relations. By the spring of 1987 perennial tensions over Tokyo's unfair (from the US perspective) trade practices had boiled over and on March 27, 1987, Reagan announced the imposition of penalty tariffs on Japanese electronic products (such as TVs and pocket calculators) in retaliation for Japan's failure to abide by the September 1986 semiconductor agreement with the United States. These were, as the *New York Times* was quick to note, "the most sweeping trade sanctions against Japan since World War II," a serious blow to US-Japanese relations and personally to Prime Minister Nakasone, who was just about to leave for Washington for another summit with "Ron."[143] This time, his friendship with Reagan was not enough to bail him out: he was coming under growing pressure in Japan for his inability to placate the Americans. Nakasone's political base was wearing thin.

The Toshiba diversion and the unexpected US resilience in demands for a proper investigation could not help but add to the Prime Minister's headaches. But, ever the manipulator, he would have realized that strong action on Toshiba could improve the chances that the United States would lift the semiconductor sanctions. It was under these circumstances that on April 9, 1987, Nakasone was "informed" (for the first time, according to a Japanese account) that a diversion had taken place. The Prime Minister reportedly found it "incredible" and "inexcusable."[144] The investigation, hitherto buried deep in red tape, began to gain momentum. On April 30, 1987, the Japanese police raided the headquarters of Toshiba Machine and the homes of key employees, seizing enough evidence "to fill two rooms."[145] Two weeks later the Japanese government slapped sanctions on Toshiba Machine and Itochu, barring both from trade with the USSR for one year and three months, respectively—an unprecedented move, which, according to a dramatic Japanese government interpretation, could even cause suicides within the firm.[146]

Fortunately, no one went to this extreme. On May 27 the police arrested two executives at Toshiba Machine responsible for the sale of MBP-110s to the USSR, Hayashi Yuzo and Tanimura Hiroaki.[147] There were some high-profile resignations, including those of Toshiba President Watari Sugiichiro and Chairman Saba Shoichi. The latter explained to US Ambassador Mike Mansfield on July 2 that his resignation was a way to take responsibility for the misdeeds of a subsidiary but was in no way an admission of guilt. Mansfield replied that he understood the Chairman's reasons and that "we must substitute reasons for emotions" and "get on with the job."[148] But sentiment was very different back in Washington, especially on Capitol Hill. As Republican congressman Duncan Hunter put it, "In light of what's occurred, resignations are expected. But they hardly meet the severity of the crime."[149] A short time later Hunter led half a dozen congressmen to the lawn in front of the Capitol, where they smashed a Toshiba radio with sledgehammers.[150]

Congress was talking sanctions. On June 30, 1987, the Senate voted overwhelmingly to prohibit the sale of Toshiba products—*any* Toshiba products—in the United States for at least two and possibly five years. The House was heading in that direction, looking at proposals like one peddled by Hunter, who wanted to "ban the import of Toshiba goods forever."[151] On July 7 the Japanese Ambassador in Japan, Matsunaga Nobuo, was summoned to the State Department and upbraided for what he was told was his government's insufficient reaction to the Toshiba diversion. The State's senior representative for strategic technology policy, Allan Wendt, said to the Ambassador that when he had reported to Congress that Itochu merely received a three-month export ban, "he had been laughed at." Undersecretary of State for Political Affairs Michael Armacost warned that punitive legislation against Japan was virtually certain—"and you won't like it."[152]

The Japanese, who had up to then acted most apologetically, were shocked by the battle cries on Capitol Hill. There was a backlash in Tokyo as prominent academics, defense experts, and even government officials publicly questioned the connection between the export of Toshiba milling machines and the fact that Soviet submarines had become increasingly quiet.[153] There was a growing sense across broad segments of the Japanese public opinion that Toshiba was simply a scapegoat and that the Americans were in fact intent on undermining Japan's industrial might.[154]

This conspiracy theory was present even in the Japanese Diet. During a luncheon with Komeito Chairman Yano Junya, Ambassador Mansfield was told that Toshiba sanctions were simply a part of "a USG plan to destroy the Japanese economy."[155] In a conversation with Mansfield a fortnight later, Japanese dietman (and later Prime Minister) Kan Naoto said that he and many others in the Diet thought there was "some merit" to the theory that "the real USG intention was to check the growth of Japanese industries in advanced technologies by limiting Japanese access to markets."[156] In the meantime, senior Japanese Foreign Ministry officials privately pressed the State Department to furnish evidence linking Toshiba with quiet Soviet submarines: it was badly needed by Prime Minister Nakasone, who had to defend his government's handling of the Toshiba case before an increasingly skeptical public.[157]

Fortunately for Toshiba, the worst did not come to pass. Congress ultimately adopted punitive legislation, but in a much-watered-down version (Toshiba Machine was banned from the US market for three years, but Toshiba Corporation as a whole escaped relatively unscathed).[158] Yet the Toshiba diversion case had very damaging ripple effects for Soviet-Japanese relations. The dialogue between Moscow and Tokyo, which, it briefly seemed, began to pick up in early 1987, sank in the wake of the Toshiba scandal. On March 6, 1987, Nakasone was rather upbeat on where the Soviets were heading, telling visiting US Secretary of State George Shultz that he thought Moscow wanted to improve relations with Japan.[159] But weeks later Nakasone was thrust to the forefront of the struggle against devious Soviet efforts to undermine NATO security.

Vigilance became the order of the day. Four Japanese citizens were arrested in May 1987 on charges of spying for the Soviet Union and China, specifically selling information on US military aircraft. Four Soviet diplomats were implicated in the case and slipped out of Japan to avoid being deported. The Soviets retaliated in August, ordering two Japanese—the naval attaché Takeshima Tobuhiro and the Mitsubishi representative in Moscow, Otani Takeo—out of the country. The former was accused of "intelligence activity" in Odessa, the latter of trying to obtain commercial secrets and engaging in "currency speculation." Within hours of this announcement, the Japanese expelled Yurii Pokrovskii, the Soviet Union's Deputy Trade Representative, for nothing less than "purchasing stolen documents on sophisticated aviation systems."[160]

Senior Japanese officials suspected that the diehard Japan hand in the Central Committee, Ivan Kovalenko, had something to do with the tough Soviet measures. "He still treats Japanese as war prisoners," one official explained in an interview.[161] Certainly the KGB was deeply involved in the decision making on the Soviet side, but Gorbachev was likely not on top of the situation. In fact, these Soviet expulsions coincided with Gorbachev's attempt to reformulate his policy toward Japan in order to achieve a "breakthrough" in relations.[162] In a Politburo meeting on August 6, 1987, Gorbachev pointed out: "What we have had with Japan has satisfied both China and the USA. But we have to move forward. We'll have to return to this question taking into account the development of events. Something must be done."[163] Expelling Japanese citizens—for the first time since World War II—was not exactly what he had in mind. He was clearly overtaken by events and by the KGB's zeal. Gorbachev's "breakthrough" never materialized in anything like a workable policy.

The mood in Soviet diplomatic circles was quite gloomy but also distinctively realistic. Foreign Ministry experts realized that relations with

Moscow was a problem of the second order for Nakasone: those with the United States were just that much more important, not least in terms of security. Also, in economic terms, trade with the socialist bloc was just a negligible bit of Japan's international commerce. The bottom line was that the USSR could easily be sacrificed if this is what it took for Japan (and Nakasone personally) to strengthen relations with Washington, then under strain. Big Japanese companies, which would have stood to gain from trade with the Soviets under normal circumstances, learned lessons from the Toshiba scandal: stay well clear of the Soviets. Toshiba not only imposed stricter export controls but in fact broadened export prohibitions to items that were not even on the COCOM list. "For the concerned Japanese companies, the government's policy is disadvantageous," said the Soviet Charge d'affaires in Japan, Yurii Kuznetsov, "but because of their interest in the American market and because of intimidation, they do not offer any active resistance."[164]

The Soviets were pleased to see lesser Japanese companies attempt to fill the void left by the multinational heavyweights. Another hopeful sign was that regional authorities in Japan appeared more inclined to cooperate with the USSR than the central government. For example, in July 1987, Governor of Osaka prefecture Kishi Sakae toured Siberia; in August, Governor of Hokkaido Yokomichi went to the USSR. Both men talked up smoke for the Soviet pipe dream of Siberian development. As for the central government, by mid-1987 the Soviets had basically lost hope in Nakasone. As Kuznetsov had put it, "We do not expect significant improvement of Soviet-Japanese relations until the establishment of a new government [in Japan]. It is the American government that stands behind the aggravation of tensions [as] it seizes every opportunity to restrain Japan from economic, technical and scientific cooperation with the Soviet Union for the remaining duration of the Nakasone cabinet."[165] This was not far off the mark, although it was a bit premature of the Soviets to think that things would turn for better once Nakasone bowed out. If anything, foolhardy Nakasone, for all his great love for "Ron," was the best candidate in years to broker a breakthrough in Soviet-Japanese relations. As he surrendered the highest office to his successor, Takeshita Noboru, in November 1987, the prospects for a breakthrough appeared bleak.

CONCLUSION

Mikhail Gorbachev had been in office for just a little over half a year when he met with Ronald Reagan in Geneva. This was an important step in the building of a reserve of trust between the two leaders that would prove indispensable for making further progress at Reykjavik, Washington, and Moscow, and ultimately bringing the Cold War to a peaceful end. Gorbachev was willing to meet with Reagan face to face despite their various disagreements. Could Gorbachev have achieved comparable breakthroughs in relations with Japan if he had opted for an early engagement with Nakasone? There were certainly opportunities at hand. In fact, despite the cold winds that battered Soviet-Japanese relations between 1982 and 1987, there were multiple unrealized opportunities, even before Gorbachev came to power, and more so after he did.

All this time there were voices in the policy-making circles in Moscow and in Tokyo calling for a breakthrough in relations. There were plenty of takers among Japanese politicians, despite the risks: rapprochement with Moscow was the ultimate act of statesmanship, and Nakasone was only one among many who fancied himself wearing that set of laurels. On the Soviet side, some of Gorbachev's key advisers on foreign policy urged a compromise with Japan, and, with hardliners like Ustinov already out of the way, the Soviet leader could have taken that road, or at least he could have put the ball back into Nakasone's court by returning to the promise of the 1956 Declaration. Who was to stop him? By the mid-1980s, the most senior voice at the Politburo was Andrei Gromyko, who, we have seen, had also favored compromise. Gorbachev and Nakasone, both at the height of their political power, could have solved the problem that eluded generations of policy makers before and after. But they didn't. The question is why.

Part of the answer is that for both leaders, their relationship with the United States was much more important than their relationship with each other. Although Gorbachev realized Japan's economic potential, Soviet-Japanese relations were far down the list of priorities. In the global view of things, he was more interested in the ambitious goal of mending fences with the United States, the prospect that would bring peace to the world and glory to Gorbachev. Even in the context of Gorbachev's Asia outreach, Japan was a rather insignificant sideshow. Here, he worried first and foremost about China and India. There was no place for the territorial problem with Japan in Gorbachev's grand strategy; the whole problem rather seemed like a petty diversion from the greater task at hand. In the sense that Japan even mattered, it was not so much as a player in its own right but mainly as a potential weak link in the US-led Cold War front in the Far East. The idea was to split Japan from Washington either by brutal intimidation or by enticing economic schemes, which the Japanese capitalists—by their very nature—would have to fall for.

Both tactics proved demonstrably ineffective, as much for Gorbachev as for his predecessors. Threats and intimidation only worsened Soviet standing in the eyes of the Japanese public opinion, while capitalist appetites proved less insatiable than Moscow had imagined. Furthermore, Nakasone would not "split" from the United States because he valued US-Japanese relations above all other aspects of Japan's foreign policy. This does not mean that he was a US "puppet" in any sense. Nakasone was an astute politician with a good sense of where Japan's national interests lay, which was why he actively engaged with South Korea and China, and also kept his eye on a potential rapprochement with Moscow. Still, the Prime Minister found it quite acceptable to risk the fallout in Soviet-Japanese relations for the sake of smoothing the dialogue with the Americans. The "aircraft carrier" episode and the Toshiba controversy were the most convincing illustrations of where his priorities lay.

Washington's role at this juncture was decisively one of a spoiler. It was not the first time. For the better part of the Cold War, in fact, the Americans torpedoed moves toward Soviet-Japanese rapprochement, most famously in 1956 to sabotage a two-island solution. This time the United States did not apply naked pressure on the Japanese to keep their distance from the Soviet Union. There was certainly no strategy to this effect. But it was clear to the Japanese that improvement in Soviet-Japanese relations would not be greeted with understanding in Washington, not while the Cold War raged on. Ironically, just as the Japanese bravely stood by their ally amid mounting tensions with the northern neighbor, Ronald Reagan, acting sometimes against the best advice of the hardliners, began to engage seriously in a dialogue with his Soviet counterpart. This dialogue sharply diverged from the road taken by the Japanese over the same period. Frightened by the Toshiba allegations, the Japanese jumped way ahead of the curve in their anti-communist struggle. This meant that later on they had to cover a much longer distance just to keep up with the changing winds of history. For once, "weathervane" Nakasone missed the right moment to make his turn.

CHAPTER 3

The Rise and Fall of Gorbachev's Vision for Asia, 1985–89

On August 10, 1992, the Russian Ambassador in India, Anatolii Dryukov, sent his superiors in Moscow an alarming letter. After the Soviet collapse, he wrote, the Embassy found itself in an impossible financial situation. Funding from home dried up and there was hardly any money left for paying the diplomats' salaries or water and electricity bills, or for buying petrol for the Embassy's car. Despite cost-cutting measures and massive downsizing, lamented Dryukov, the Embassy was practically unable to make ends meet and had to rely on private lending by sympathetic Indians just to stay open. All of that, he concluded, made a bad impression on Indian public opinion and "did little to facilitate the upholding of Russia's prestige."[1]

Dryukov's plea struck a chord with Russia's second most powerful politician, head of the Supreme Soviet Ruslan Khasbulatov, who criticized the government for "political myopia" of one-sided orientation toward the West on the premise that Russia allegedly had no business in the East. The "loss of India," Khasbulatov argued in a lengthy internal memorandum, undermined Russia's economic and geopolitical interests in the context of the "Russia-India-[China] triangle" with its potential to create a more equitable international economy and "counteract the unipolar world led by the USA." How did it happen, Khasbulatov wondered, that Russia had lost overnight all that the Soviet Union had achieved after four decades of courting India?[2]

This chapter helps to answer Khasbulatov's question. India was crucial to Mikhail Gorbachev's Asia policy as he assumed the reins of leadership in 1985. It was the centerpiece of his vision for the Soviet Union's Asian outreach. Gorbachev saw India as a potential ally in projecting Soviet influence in South Asia, a key Cold War theater, and he treasured the Soviet-Indian relationship as one of the pillars of the new global order that he had set out to create. This chapter shows how the Soviet Union and the United States competed for India's loyalties, and how the Indian leadership played on this competition. As Sino-Soviet relations began to improve, Gorbachev became attracted to the idea of a strategic triangle, bringing together the Soviet Union, India, and China under his implicit leadership, something that few Russian politicians, from Khasbulatov to Putin, had given him credit for. But the triangle that he had invested his hopes in failed to materialize and even bilateral Soviet-Indian relations stagnated and declined.

This was partly a function of Soviet retrenchment occasioned by mounting domestic problems and increasing economic difficulties, and partly a result of changing Soviet foreign policy priorities. One of Gorbachev's most urgent tasks was to find a solution to the war in Afghanistan, something that required Pakistan's cooperation. This chapter recounts the story of Gorbachev's painful disengagement from Afghanistan and what it meant for Moscow's regional policy. India proved more of an obstacle than a helper in this task, and so it soon found itself on the sidelines of the discussions that paved the way to the Soviet withdrawal in 1989. At the same time, general improvement of the international situation in the late 1980s left Soviet-Indian relations without a clear direction. Instrumentalized as a Cold War pawn, India suddenly became irrelevant as the Cold War came to an end and Gorbachev embraced the West. India, which had been central to Gorbachev's vision for Asia, was "lost" because this vision had, quite literally, gone bankrupt.

SOVIET-AMERICAN COMPETITION FOR INDIA

For the better part of the Cold War, India had a close, even intimate, relationship with the USSR. By extension, New Delhi was on strained terms with the United States. That the world's two largest democracies would be at odds even as Washington managed to get along with Pakistan and China suggests that Indo-American relations were shaped less by intrinsic incompatibilities than by the tides of the global Cold War. For US policy makers, India mattered less than the imperative of containing the communist threat. Political and military backing of Pakistan seemed like a sine qua non of checking Soviet encroachment in South Asia; that such policy strengthened India's principal foe was something that successive US administrations could live with. The same logic worked for the US rapprochement with the People's Republic of China in 1972, an uncomfortable development for the Indians, who were weighted down by their own viciously adversarial relationship with Beijing. US support for India's enemies was a consequence of Washington's Cold War strategy, but this support had an unintended consequence of forcing India to rely more on the USSR, which, in turn, reinforced US apprehension of the growing Soviet menace in the subcontinent.

More by coincidence than by design, India was caught up between the hammer of US strategic interests and the sickle of Soviet efforts to "save India from the arms of the imperialists." The latter cliché was a favorite of the self-proclaimed pioneer of Soviet-Indian friendship, Nikita Khrushchev. Khrushchev had berated his predecessor, Joseph Stalin, for neglecting India's vast potential. From the mid-1950s the Soviet Union offered both economic and military assistance to India. In the course of the thirty years between 1954 and 1983, Soviet credits to India (according to CIA estimates) exceeded 3.2 billon US dollars, much of it spent on industrial construction, in particular steel mills and oil refineries.[3] In addition, Moscow offered extensive military aid, helping India maintain a large margin of military superiority over Pakistan. Soviet arms deliveries to India topped ten billion dollars by 1987.[4]

The Soviet-Indian relations were raised to a new level with the conclusion of the 1971 Treaty of Friendship and Cooperation between Moscow and New Delhi. The Soviet leadership, despite continued disagreements on issues like collective security in Asia and nuclear non-proliferation, saw India as a de facto ally and a vehicle of Soviet influence in the Third World.[5] By contrast, relations between India and the United States worsened in the wake of the 1971 Indo-Pakistani War and were further aggravated by a difficult personal relationship between the Nixon/Kissinger duet and Prime Minister Indira Gandhi. Gandhi's fall from power in 1977, a brief reign of the opposition under Morarji Desai, and an interregnum under Charan Singh did not occasion any monumental shifts in India's foreign policy, although Desai's (and his foreign minister Atal Bihari Vajpayee's) relatively pro-Western views initially encouraged speculations of a foreseeable improvement in Indo-American relations. It also helped that under Jimmy Carter, Washington suspended aid to Pakistan because of Islamabad's covert efforts to develop nuclear weapons.[6]

The Soviet invasion of Afghanistan in December 1979 upset the delicate balance of power in the subcontinent. President Reagan's extensive—2.5

billion US dollars—military aid program to Pakistan (including provision of advanced F-16 fighter aircraft) triggered strong protests in New Delhi, which were characteristically brushed aside by the Undersecretary of State, James Buckley: "I am not an international psychologist. I honestly do not understand the Indian reaction."[7] This reaction was confidentially elaborated by the one-time head of the Indian Foreign Ministry's Policy Planning Division, M. L. Trivedi: China and the United States, he said, are supplying Pakistan with weapons, including F-16s, that can strike India's oil-producing regions, the bombing of which could set India back by a hundred years.[8] On top of this, New Delhi was increasingly concerned by the developments in Pakistan's nuclear program. The Indian military reportedly considered a strike against Pakistani nuclear facilities patterned after Israel's preemptive bombing of an Iraqi reactor in June 1981.[9] Subsequently, India's fear of the prospects of a nuclear-armed Pakistan remained "the most insurmountable of the barriers" to better relations between the two countries.[10]

The Indians were worried not only by the prospect of a rearmed Pakistan but also by the symbolism of US weapons transfers for the balance of American priorities in South Asia. Indira Gandhi, for all her supposedly pro-Soviet inclinations, repeatedly voiced her reservations about the Soviet invasion. Yet her reluctance to be publicly more critical of the Soviet occupation raised ire in Washington, adding new grievances to a difficult relationship. India's refusal to permit implementation of IAEA safeguards at its nuclear facilities and a row over two US companies—Coca-Cola and IBM—quitting the country in protest of government regulations added to tensions between Washington and New Delhi.[11]

However, Indira Gandhi made a conscious effort to steer India toward a more balanced relationship between the Soviet Union and the United States. Her July 1982 visit to Washington proved to be a public relations success, resulting in a personal rapport with Reagan, who—contrary to expectations—found her "shy," "warm," and "generous."[12] Gandhi told Reagan that "Indians as a whole are neither communist nor pro-communist" and that "friendship with one country [the USSR] does not preclude friendship with any other." The Prime Minister was assured of US support for India's "independent foreign policy."[13] She reached an agreement to resolve the long-standing deadlock over US supplies of fuel for the Tarapur nuclear power plant and to develop science and technology cooperation between India and the United States.

In May 1984 US Vice President George Bush visited New Delhi in a bid to take the relationship forward despite continued disagreements over the arming of Pakistan. The Indians found it particularly difficult to accept that the US program of assisting Pakistan's navy was directed against the Soviet intervention in Afghanistan, a landlocked country.[14] Nevertheless, Bush's visit helped advance the cause of US technology transfers to India despite resistance to this prospect from the Defense Department and the CIA, which feared leakage of sensitive technologies to the Soviets.[15] In October 1984 the National Security Council issued new decision directives for US policy toward India (NSDD-147), with the proclaimed purpose being to "weaken Soviet influence in South Asia." This was to be achieved by fostering Indo-Pakistani dialogue, promoting better Sino-Indian relations, and, crucially, selling weapons and technology to India in order "to reduce [its] military supply and economic dependence on the USSR."[16]

A lot of what transpired between New Delhi and Washington between 1982 and 1984 was atmospherics, but that was enough to cause serious apprehension in the Soviet Union. Lamenting India's increasing interest in developing ties with the West and especially gaining access to Western technology, the Soviet Ambassador in New Delhi, Vasilii Rykov, complained in May 1982 that "India is not actively supporting our [Soviet] proposals; they only express regret over the severance of links between the USSR and the USA, without saying who is at fault."[17] This was an exaggeration—a US State Department study concluded in 1983 that in the UN, India sided with the USSR 80 percent of the time and with the United States only 20 percent of the time.[18] Nevertheless, the Soviets worked hard to prevent what in their imagination was already a rapprochement in the making. In view of India's increasing disillusionment with the prospect for Soviet-Indian economic cooperation, Moscow did not have that much leverage with the Indians, save for oil shipments and military aid. Indeed, oil and oil products constituted more than half of all Soviet exports to India after 1977 (peaking at 78 percent in 1982), while the bill for Soviet arms transfers to India just for 1982 through 1987 reached an estimated 6.8 billion US dollars.[19]

Of course, there was no shortage of harebrained schemes in the Kremlin, not when the war in Afghanistan assumed an ominously protracted character. In 1982, for example, the Soviet Ambassador in Kabul, Fikryat Tabeev, reportedly proposed to his Indian colleague that India should take advantage of the Soviet Union's presence in Afghanistan to assert control over all of Jammu and Kashmir at Pakistan's expense. The idea was immensely provocative and exceptionally dangerous for regional stability. It may have been inspired by Tabeev's belief that India was on a collision course with Pakistan and that it would strike as soon as international conditions permitted.[20] However, Indira Gandhi's foreign policy confidant G. Parthasarathy thought that Tabeev had made an "adventurous" proposal, which, if implemented, would not only heighten Indo-Pakistani tensions and cause widespread condemnation of India in the West but also possibly trigger China's military intervention in Kashmir. Unsurprisingly, the civilian Indian leadership vetoed the idea.[21] Other Soviet probes had better luck: the KGB, for example, was relatively successful in feeding Gandhi disinformation about CIA and ISI (Pakistani intelligence) plots against her and her government.[22]

In the early 1980s India's relations with both superpowers effectively stagnated. Divergent US and Indian strategic interests precluded New Delhi from moving toward qualitatively better relations with Washington. Indian and Soviet regional interests were, by contrast, relatively compatible, but Indo-Soviet relations had lost momentum, certainly in large part because Soviet party leaders died one after another at embarrassingly short intervals, leaving no scope for long-term policy planning. In the meantime, India's domestic problems—especially unrest in the Punjab—increasingly commanded Gandhi's attention at the expense of foreign policy, which had basically succumbed to inertia. It was under these circumstances that Rajiv Gandhi assumed power in November 1984 upon his mother's death at the hands of her Sikh bodyguards.

Rajiv Gandhi's emergence as India's leader coincided with Mikhail Gorbachev's assumption of power in the USSR in March 1985. The two first met at Chernenko's funeral, the same occasion at which Gorbachev snubbed Nakasone. Rajiv, by contrast, was at the center of attention. Indeed, Gorbachev looked to India before he looked anywhere else. Closer Soviet-Indian relations were central to his efforts to imbue Soviet foreign policy with a new sense of dynamism and vitality. India, unlike Japan, would be a part of a new international order he had set out to create at America's expense.

The key questions for Gorbachev were whether Gandhi was a reliable partner and how close a partnership he could count upon. The subject came up at a Politburo meeting on March 20, 1986, after the Soviet leader received an invitation from Gandhi to make an official visit to India. "A trip to India," Gorbachev said, "is a good thing…but a very careful analysis of the situation is needed. So that we don't leave something out or simplify anything." Gorbachev spoke of Rajiv Gandhi's efforts to determine the direction of India's foreign policy. He believed that "Rajiv will not begin to dismantle what had been built by his mother unless we, of course, do something stupid." In Gorbachev's view, the new Prime Minister realized very well that he was being courted by the United States and the USSR at the same time and he will "use both us and the West in the country's interest." But there was no room for complacency: "there will be a big misbalance if India turned to the West." The bottom line for Soviet policy was therefore to act "without imposing ourselves," because "relations with India cannot depend on anyone's disposition. They have a strategic character."

Gorbachev resolved that he had to visit India before the year was out to keep the momentum of Soviet-Indian relations.[23]

Competition for Gandhi's loyalty was thus most clearly present in Gorbachev's early approaches to India. In fact, this element came out all the more clearly at the first Indian-Soviet summit in Moscow in May 1985. Gorbachev's talking points for his meeting with Gandhi on May 21 narrow down to a nasty anti-American tirade with a few jabs in the Chinese direction.[24] Washington was condemned for its efforts to control Asia, not so much to oppose socialism, but to secure the region's enormous resources. "The American ruling circles," Gorbachev said, "would like to turn history backwards, to take 'social revenge.' Therefore, they bid on the arms race, on the military machine, on imposing their will on those countries, which do not want that."[25] Gandhi won Soviet appreciation by criticizing Washington for the deployment of Pershings in Europe and (unsurprisingly) US military aid to Pakistan. He also reportedly told Gorbachev that while the Indians were no doubt interested in Western technology, they would "never sacrifice their principles for this end."[26]

Gandhi's assurances convinced Gorbachev of the importance of increasing Soviet commitment to India. "The US and China will not recognize India as a great power," he explained at a Politburo meeting. "But there [in India] the question is: either we are a great power or we are doomed. We [the Soviets] came in at the right time. Rajiv has not succeeded in the West." Moreover, in Gorbachev's view, the Indian Premier faced problems with the British Commonwealth and with the Non-Aligned Movement, where he competed with Yugoslavia for leadership. "All the mechanisms are in operation against Gandhi," Gorbachev argued, which gave the Soviet Union a "unique chance." "We cannot under any circumstances lose the chance that has opened up. We must support Rajiv Gandhi with all possible means. The struggle will be really tough."[27]

Traditional "support" for India included help in the construction of heavy industry and weapons sales. But Gorbachev thought that there was considerable scope for improvement both in economic and military cooperation with India. In the 1970s and the early 1980s, he complained, the Soviet Union had lost many of its gains with India from the 1950s and the 1960s—not only because Moscow had not committed its best effort to building up solid relations with India but also because the Soviet Union was "unattractive" to India. "What is Russian business?" Gorbachev joked at a Politburo meeting on December 4, 1986 "To buy a boxful of vodka bottles, drink it all, sell the bottles [to the recycling center], [buy more vodka], drink it all again." Moscow had to do better than that in relations with India. Gorbachev looked to the future of mutually profitable cooperation in science and technology and hoped to direct this cooperation toward the private sector. In other words, Gorbachev came back from India with the idea that the Soviet Union could well supplant the United States as a supplier of high technology. "If we limit ourselves to the old mechanism of relations—to repair [the old] and not to build anything anew, if we do not create new mechanisms for work in India, [we will achieve] nothing."[28]

The other key sphere was that of military relations. Here Gorbachev followed the logic of his predecessors: nothing brought the Soviet Union more friends in the developing world than the sale of weapons. When the matter came up for discussion at the Politburo, Central Committee Secretary Lev Zaikov was bitterly critical of the existing patterns of cooperation. "We give [them] outdated technology, and it compromises itself there, and [compromises] us as well." Gorbachev concurred: "I agree with Zaikov: one must never export anything outdated."[29] The Soviet leader was also willing to increase the volume of military sales to India, doubling it between 1986 and 1990 over that of the previous five years, to the total of 7.2 billion rubles. If this amount was realized, Soviet arms supplies to India would have exceeded what Moscow provided to any of its other allies.[30]

The Indian Prime Minister, like his Soviet counterpart, did not so much have a strategy for what he wanted to accomplish as enthusiasm for what seemed like endless possibilities for remaking India's foreign relations. In global terms, this meant a qualitative improvement in relations with both the USSR and the United States. Evident willingness of both superpowers to compete for India's loyalty created a positive environment for raising India's international profile, extending its foreign influence, and winning the best terms from all contenders. During the banquet at the end of Gandhi's visit in May 1985, Gorbachev said that "in all spheres of cooperation with India, we, as a friend, share the best of what we have with it."[31] Rajiv's talks in Moscow proved that much. General Secretary of the Congress Party Srikant Verma commented in the wake of the Prime Minister's visit that India "got practically everything from the USSR it asked for."[32]

It is interesting to compare these statements to what Rajiv Gandhi heard from US President Ronald Reagan, whom he saw only a few weeks after that meeting with Gorbachev. The President went into great detail about Soviet savagery in Afghanistan, recounting the story of an arrested doctor who was "subjected to numerous tortures, including being made to watch as the eyes of a captured Afghanistan freedom-fighter were plucked out and set on the table in front of her." Gandhi responded that he was appalled by the report and Reagan pressed on, relating how Soviet soldiers were being instructed "to kill women and children." The President went on to discuss Soviet resistance to disarmament, how they have been "deeply suspicious throughout their history. They have had an abiding fear of foreign domination, and yet it's the Soviets who dominate in so many places." Then, responding to Gandhi's complaints about Pakistan, Reagan promised to do everything possible "to ease those strains."[33] For his part, Gandhi reportedly assured Reagan that "India does not want the Soviet U[nion] to have a foothold anywhere in S[outh] Asia" (of course, he could well say the same thing about the United States—in both cases, with complete sincerity).[34]

Nevertheless, between 1985 and 1986 Indo-American relations were on an upward curve. Reagan was ready to capitalize on Rajiv's obvious interest in expanding economic and military cooperation with the United States. In May 1985 the United States indicated willingness to work with India in the production of light combat aircraft. Up to then, military cooperation between India and the United States had been virtually nonexistent, in part because Washington felt uneasy about leakage of sensitive equipment to the USSR and in part because the Indians themselves felt uncomfortable about US weaponry, since "sooner or later it would end in blackmail."[35] Now, despite Rajiv Gandhi's reservations—"We'll have to see exactly what the small print is"—India and the United States concluded an agreement on the provision of eleven General Electric jet engines for the aircraft-in-the-making, an agreement widely heralded as a breakthrough for Indo-American military relations.[36]

In May 1985 Washington and New Delhi agreed on an implementation of the memorandum of understanding on technical cooperation, opening the way for US computer exports to India. The highlight of this arrangement was the proposed US sale of a supercomputer Cray XMP-24 to India for weather-related research. That such a sale was discussed at all was a sign of American eagerness to woo India away from the Soviets, who were not in a position to provide anything remotely as powerful. In fact, XMP-24 was so powerful that, other than being used for weather forecasting, it could well help the Indians with nuclear and ballistic missile research and with cryptography.[37] In addition to selling their own high-tech equipment, by 1986 the Americans were even considering upgrading and maintaining old equipment that India had obtained from the USSR / East Bloc countries.[38] What could be more symbolic of their technological edge over the backward Soviets?

Looking back at this brief flare of American enthusiasm for Indian-US relations, it is easy to see that it was a result of Cold War imperatives. Much as in the case of China, this was a policy that instrumentalized India as a "card" in the regional struggle with the USSR. The United States needed India not for its own sake, not because it was the largest democracy in the world, not for the sake of better relations with one of the world's most populous nations, but because it could play a useful role in undercutting Soviet strategic maneuvering in South Asia. Indeed, the strategy of the Reagan Administration at this juncture, both State and the NSC agreed, was to "exploit the early period of Rajiv Gandhi's rule for strategic gain."[39] This strategy required transfers of military equipment and technologies, as well as Washington's prodding in improving India's relations with China and Pakistan (including, for instance, by advising China to give up on some of its territorial claims) and for support for a greater regional role for India. As one participant in the State/NSC internal discussion put it: "The Indians seek to be world actors; their egos can be massaged to good effect."[40] This was a very short-sighted strategy, but it was not unique. The Soviets were doing the very same thing.

Soviet-Indian relations were at their very best from late 1986 through 1987, if, perhaps, not in economic terms (Gorbachev complained incessantly of the Soviet inability to stimulate India's interest), then certainly in political terms. By late 1986 India loomed largest on the Soviet General Secretary's agenda. That November Gorbachev made his first and much celebrated visit to India. Meetings with Rajiv Gandhi contributed to a buildup of trust in the leaders' relationship. Gorbachev's interpreter, Pavel Palazhchenko, recalled:

> Gorbachev found it much easier to talk with Gandhi than with Reagan or some other leaders. Their rapport was total and their discussions were genuinely frank.... Gorbachev's talks with Rajiv Gandhi were long and for the most part very private. The trust between them continued to grow. Some of Gandhi's proposals, if fully accepted, would have meant a tilt in policy, so Gorbachev had to react cautiously. Gandhi seemed to understand that Gorbachev could not be forthcoming on some matters, and it did not hinder their developing relationship, which, I thought then and later, could become an important moral factor in the world for years to come.[41]

We are not told what proposals Gorbachev was unwilling to accept but his joint press conference with the Indian Premier at the end of the visit suggests that Gorbachev had to fend off pressure from India on relations with China. The Soviet leader was asked—not once but several times—whose side he took in the Sino-Indian border conflict and even what the Soviet Union would do if China and India went to war again, as they had in 1962. Gorbachev dodged the question, sticking to generalities like "I am sure that your forecast will not come true."[42] Weeks later he recounted details to a visiting functionary from the Portuguese Communist Party: "They asked what position the Soviet Union will take if India and China go to war. That's a hell of a question!"[43]

One notable achievement of the summit between Gandhi and Gorbachev was the joint declaration, signed by the two leaders—the Delhi Declaration. The Declaration was unusual for its emphasis on universal human values in connection with the pledge to rid the world of nuclear weapons by 2000. Gorbachev later cited this Declaration, time and again, as one of the first statements of his policy of new thinking for the world. It is significant, although perhaps not surprising, that the concepts of new thinking were applied to Soviet-Indian relations before Gorbachev managed to make any headway with Reagan. In fact, the Delhi Declaration filled in the vacuum left in the wake of the failure of the Soviet-US summit in Reykjavik. It was a substitute for Reykjavik, a testament to Gorbachev's ability to sell new thinking to an international audience, even if there were no buyers in the West for the time being.

THE TRIANGLE

Gorbachev returned from his summit with Gandhi fascinated by India and the prospects for Soviet-Indian relations. The Soviet leader later claimed in his memoirs that India offered a testing ground for his ideas about the "new international world order," but that was a case of reading history backwards. In reality, the Soviet General Secretary continued to look at India squarely in bloc terms, as a potential Soviet ally in the global struggle against the United States. His early excitement about India was really an outcome of a growing conviction that he would win the struggle for India, that he would help it "free itself from imperialist pressure." At a Politburo meeting on December 4, 1986, days after his return from India, Gorbachev outlined various "strategic" and "geopolitical" reasons for why closer ties with India were all-important for the USSR. "The Indian Ocean,..." Gorbachev said, "the US has settled here." Then, there was Pakistan—US ally. "Here India is our natural ally. India is a key link in our Asia policy." "In a word," Gorbachev summarized, "[we] cannot say aloud the word 'ally' with regard to India but [we] should take the matters in that direction."[44]

Those were remarkable revelations but perhaps not all was reflected in the meeting transcript. Politburo member Vitalii Vorotnikov wrote in his diary that Gorbachev went so far as to consider strengthening Soviet relations with India at the expense of other countries: "Perhaps, we will have to sacrifice ties with other countries in India's favor," the Soviet leader was heard to say.[45] It is not clear what Gorbachev could have meant by this, except, perhaps, that at the time he ranked India ahead of China on the list of Soviet foreign policy priorities. The ideal was of course to keep both nations onboard, a scenario that would give the Soviet Union maximum flexibility. This was something that Gorbachev had hoped to achieve when he first took office as the General Secretary.

More precisely, Gorbachev's idea entailed the notion of "collective security" for Asia, an idea he first raised at the banquet in Gandhi's honor in May 1985. Reflecting on previous initiatives pertaining to Asian security—namely, the proposal to turn the Indian Ocean into a "zone of peace" and pledges, by the Soviet Union and China, agreeing not to use nuclear weapons in a first strike—Gorbachev said:

> Now a question arises: taking into account all of these initiatives and also, to a certain extent, Europe's experience, should one not think about a general, complex approach to the problem of security in Asia and possible joint efforts by Asian countries in this direction? Of course, the road to this is difficult. But the road to Helsinki was not smooth and straight. Different methods are probably possible here: bilateral talks and multilateral consultations—to the extent of holding, in the prospect, of some general pan-Asian forum for exchange of opinions and joint search for constructive decisions.[46]

The Soviet leader repeated his call for such a conference several times in 1985 and 1986, most prominently in his speech in Vladivostok in July 1986. Indeed, "collective security" was one of the cornerstones of Gorbachev's new thinking in Asia. The idea, however, was not new by any means. Leonid Brezhnev first called for such a conference in 1969, although the Soviet proposal of Asian "security" then had a clear anti-Chinese tint. It was predictably rejected as a propaganda ploy by all but a handful of Soviet allies.

The recycled version of Asian collective security also met an unenthusiastic reception. Nakasone was only willing to subscribe if Japan could maintain its alliance with the United States. Gorbachev could have expected this from Nakasone, but he was disappointed that the Indians would not buy the concept, either. Privately, Indian officials were skeptical that there was any scope for transplanting an essentially European concept onto Asian soil: "In Europe there are two clear-cut blocs, territorial disputes are basically settled and the issues are fairly limited," one official told the *Washington Post*. "In Asia, it is more difficult, territorial disputes are still alive. You can't compare the situations."[47]

Western analysts suspected that Gandhi was unhappy with superpowers meddling in regional affairs, where India should run the show.[48] Gorbachev had a similar impression. As he said after his return from Delhi, "India...at first met our idea of creating a system of security in Asia with caution; then, it felt that it was clearly falling out of step with our policy. Subsequently the Indians started saying that the USSR must do better to take into account India's interests in the region and award an appropriate role to it."[49] In his memoirs, Gorbachev explained the problem in even more personal terms: "At one stage I got a feeling that Rajiv was oversensitive about the Vladivostok speech. And I thought to what extent one must be attentive and careful in putting forward all-embracing initiatives. Perhaps, there was a certain amount of jealousy on the part of my young friend, a leader of a huge country, which belonged to this exact region."[50]

One way or another, the grand concept of collective security—Gorbachev's first effort at conceptualizing new thinking in the Asian context—foundered upon the Soviet inability to sell this concept to anyone else in the region, including Gandhi. But as Gorbachev was moving away from collective security, he began to piece together another conceptual framework for Soviet policy in Asia, rooted in the notion of a "triangle," comprising the Soviet Union, India, and China. By the mid-1980s, Sino-Soviet relations were noticeably improving. If, at the same time, the Indians also managed to mend fences with their foes to the east of the Himalayas, all pieces would be in place for a powerful anti-American entente. As Gorbachev explained to the Portuguese leader Alvaro Cunhal, the Americans "are carefully watching what is happening in the Asia Pacific. They are literally shaking over the signs of improvement in Sino-Soviet relations and rapprochement between the USSR and India. They are doing everything possible to prevent the creation of such a triangle in Asia. Indeed, over two billion people live in these three countries—the USSR, India and China. They have a huge potential."[51]

During his visit to India in November 1986 Gorbachev raised the prospect of the "triangle" with Gandhi, but without success. At the Politburo the Soviet leader concluded, with disappointment, "the triangle (USSR-India-China) will not work for now. The main resistance is from India. There, China is an obsessive idea. It's not for nothing that we are improving relations with the PRC. We are prodding India to do the same."[52] At this time, the best position the Soviet Union could adopt was that "we must not knock them (China and India) head to head."[53] But could Moscow avoid taking sides in the bitter feud between the two nations and improve relations with both? The alternative was to improve relations with India irrespective of the pace of Sino-Soviet normalization, even perhaps, to return to Vorotnikov's oblique comments, at China's expense. Perhaps Rajiv offered this alternative to the Soviet leader during their talks in Delhi. We can be relatively confident, however, that the "triangle" idea did not inspire the Indians at a time of a new deterioration of Sino-Indian relations between 1986 and 1987 over their disputed border in Arunachal Pradesh.

The idea of a "triangle" continued to haunt the Soviet leader over the following months. He returned to it during his next visit to India, in November 1988. Gandhi was more open to the idea on this occasion, seeing in it a means for opposing "the challenge of the US-EEC-Japan grouping."[54] Gorbachev, after his recent meetings with the Brazilian President, enthused to Gandhi: "You know, Brazil is striving to join this USSR-India-China triangle. It is literally knocking at the door."[55] But the early prototype of the Brazil-Russia-India-China (BRIC) grouping continued to suffer from Sino-Indian disagreements. Discussing the results of his visit at the Politburo on November 24, 1988, Gorbachev said: "China is a problem for Rajiv. I told him about the 'triangle': India-China-USSR. It seemed like he met [this idea] with applause. But...I asked him about the border with the PRC. His response was: it seems as if it was settled but we did not become friends."[56]

The Soviet leader also tried to sell the triangle to Chinese Foreign Minister Qian Qichen when he came to Moscow in December 1988, a step that signaled a serious upgrade of Sino-Soviet contacts. The selling point was again subtly anti-Western. According to Gorbachev, "when Gandhi became the head of the Indian government, he had the intention to make the society more dynamic by means of cooperation with the West. Now one can see that this calculation did not bear fruit.... The West has no intention to develop cooperation in those areas, which could lead India to the road of technical-scientific progress; they would like to keep India at a distance. In any case, Gandhi is now convinced that the interests of his country would be best served by more intensive cooperation with the Soviet Union and China."[57] Rajiv Gandhi did go to China a few days later, in what became a crucial step toward Sino-Indian normalization. This visit was seen in some quarters as the result of Gorbachev's encouragement.[58] However, Deng Xiaoping, in his own meeting with Rajiv, did not touch on the "triangle," criticizing "bloc politics" and only mentioning the Soviet Union to stress its insignificance compared to the combined might of China and India.[59]

Gorbachev, however, persisted with "the triangle." The project, he thought, was helped by the Chinese crackdown on student protesters in Tiananmen Square. "As far as the USSR and India are concerned," he told Gandhi during their very last meeting on July 15, 1989—"I think China will not distance itself from us and from you as a consequence of the latest events. They were grateful for our measured response, and, perhaps, now they will value more their relations with us and with you.... Do you remember how we talked about a 'triangle'—trilateral cooperation?... We made a good forecast. Perhaps now is that exact moment when they are truly interested in ties with us and with you."[60] All of these revelations were accompanied by remarkably severe criticism of the Bush Administration—how the White House wished them all ill, something "even worse" than Tiananmen.[61]

The triangle theme featured again in Gorbachev's conversation with a Mongolian delegation in May 1990 and in July with the new Indian Premier, V. P. Singh: "It seems to me that our common efforts allow us to attain a new level of relations in an exceptionally important triangle: the Soviet Union, India, China. I think this great process has only now begun to unfold. If we show a responsible approach, patience and friendly disposition to each other, new hopeful perspectives will open here, which will have a beneficial influence on the development of the situation not only in Asia but everywhere in the world." Singh agreed for once, saying that India was "deeply interested in the development of a dialogue and trilateral cooperation with China."[62] By that time, however, Gorbachev was in no position to sponsor any more "triangles."

Karen Brutents, who served as the Deputy Head of the International Department of the Central Committee, observes in his memoirs that Gorbachev's return, time and again in his conversations, to the USSR-India-China triangle indicates that it was a serious, well-thought-out observation on the part of the Soviet leader.[63] It was a part of Gorbachev's vision for Asia, a framework for his foreign policy, a kind of counterpart to his "Common European Home" approach in Europe. Both approaches were essentially exclusive of the United States, and both attempted to place the Soviet Union in a position of leadership among equals—the French, the Germans, and the British in Europe, and the Indians and the Chinese in Asia. Both approaches failed, primarily because Soviet leadership was not wanted in either Europe or Asia, but also because, in the case of the Asian "triangle," China and India had their own serious contradictions. It is also ironic that just as Gorbachev was trying to bring China and India closer together in a kind of anti-American entente, policy planners in Washington were promoting the idea of Sino-Indian rapprochement as an anti-Soviet ploy. Gorbachev, however, was much more committed to the idea than Carter, Reagan, or Bush had been. Over a decade after Gorbachev floated the concept of the Soviet-Indo-Chinese triangle, Russian leaders returned to this idea: Putin and Primakov are now credited with the authorship.[64] As the Russian saying goes, everything new is well-forgotten old.

SOVIET WITHDRAWAL FROM AFGHANISTAN

When Gorbachev became the General Secretary in March 1985, the Soviets had already been embroiled in a war in neighboring Afghanistan for almost six years. The decision to invade stemmed from ideological blind spots, fears that Afghanistan could be turned into a US platform, and the inertia and mustiness of senior decision making. It was soon regretted even by the diehards who forced it through, a decision so absurd and incomprehensible in retrospect that it was immortalized in the infamous Soviet joke: "Why did the Soviet Union invade Afghanistan?" "They decided to begin with the first letter of the alphabet."[65] By 1985, withdrawal from Afghanistan had already become a topic of backroom conversations in the Kremlin's corridors of power. Andropov and even Defense Minister Ustinov had privately alluded to the prospect of a political settlement in 1981; by 1983 Andropov was considering the possibility of UN involvement in finding a solution to what had by then become the Soviet Union's Vietnam: a human tragedy, a financial drag, and a factor contributing to the USSR's international isolation and to stalemated Sino-Soviet relations.[66] Consequently, when Gorbachev privately declared Afghanistan an issue of "first-rate importance" in 1985, he met with the approval of much of the policy establishment and of his own Politburo colleagues.[67] The question of withdrawal was not whether but when and how.

It was quite another matter to face the probable consequence of the Soviet withdrawal, the collapse of the Soviet-sponsored Democratic Republic of Afghanistan and the triumph of the anti-Soviet, likely fundamentalist, mujahedeen.[68] Simply leaving was not an option. This was not because Gorbachev cared for the fate of the Soviet client in Kabul, Babrak Karmal. Nor did he think that Afghanistan was geopolitically indispensable to the Soviets as one of those strategic platforms that Dmitrii Ustinov, in his time, liked to talk about. Gorbachev did occasionally voice concerns about the possibility that the void left by the Soviet withdrawal would be filled by the Americans, but it was not an immediate concern. He did not believe the United States would counter-invade Afghanistan.[69]

The biggest obstacle to withdrawal was the issue of credibility, both international and domestic. Internationally, Gorbachev was most worried about the reaction of other Soviet clients in the Third World should Moscow "betray" an ally in need. He returned to the subject repeatedly: "you, they say, 'abandon' Afghanistan; therefore, you will 'abandon' us" was how, in Gorbachev's view, the prospects of the Soviet withdrawal looked from the Third World.[70] When the topic turned to Afghanistan at Politburo meetings, the Soviet leaders appeared at pains to prove to themselves and their colleagues that the withdrawal would not look like the Soviet version of America's defeat in Vietnam. There was also the issue of the domestic reaction. By the mid-1980s, there was—in the words of one insider—a "torrent" of letters coming to the party authorities from mothers, soldiers, and even generals, which could be summarized with one phrase: "why are we there?"[71] But a withdrawal would raise an even more painful question: "what was it all for?" In the Vietnam case, Lyndon B. Johnson accepted some of the blame, choosing not to run for reelection in 1968. Gorbachev, though, was not prepared to follow this pattern.

As a consequence, his early policy toward Afghanistan was to win the war through a combination of nation-building, military pressure, and diplomatic maneuvering. Nation-building was to be accomplished through the process of "national reconciliation," by which Gorbachev meant broadening the social base of the Afghan regime, curbing socialist policies, especially in the countryside, allowing a measure of Islamic revival, and engaging with some of the more moderate opposition in an effort to foster disunity among the mujahedeen. For all of these, Karmal was utterly unsuitable, so Gorbachev had him purged in 1986. His replacement, Muhammad Najib, who later changed his last name to the more Muslim-sounding Najibullah, tried to reverse the fortunes of the regime through "national reconciliation," but it was a case of too little, too late. The mujahedeen attacks intensified; by 1987 the government had little actual control outside the major cities; the Afghan army was rendered ineffective through constant desertions and mixed loyalties of the servicemen; and the ruling elites were unable to overcome the long-running feud between the two main factions of the People's Democratic Party of Afghanistan (PDPA), the Parcham and the Khalq.[72]

By early 1987 it was also clear that the Soviet efforts to defeat the mujahedeen militarily would not bear fruit. There were a hundred thousand Soviet soldiers in the country, but they were poorly equipped for counter-insurgency warfare. The Soviets could take but not hold territory; the moment Soviet soldiers left the latest "liberated" area, the mujahedeen would return and reassert control, taking advantage of the anti-Soviet sentiments of the local people. "Little remains of the friendly feeling towards the Soviet people that had existed for decades," Shevardnadze reported at the Politburo in January 1987 after returning from talks with Najibullah in Afghanistan. "Too many people died, and they were not all bandits."[73] Afghanistan's economy was in free fall. Soviet aid—in billions of rubles— never reached the intended recipients, having been looted by the government officials in the process. Furthermore, it proved impossible to prevent smuggling of weapons and supplies to the mujahedeen from neighboring Pakistan. In October 1985 Gorbachev vowed to "put an end to it all" in Afghanistan; two years later he was no closer to that goal.[74]

In 1987 Gorbachev expended a lot of effort on finding a political solution to the Afghanistan problem in a way that would secure a fairly loyal regime in Kabul and would allow for the Soviet forces to leave with dignity.

To achieve this goal, he intensified his campaign for reaching "national reconciliation" in Afghanistan, which entailed, as he explained to Najib during their meeting on July 20, 1987, creating "real pluralism" in the Afghan society and in the government.[75] This meant offering government positions to two or three insurgents—"but these must be real proposals and not political game."[76] Najib played along, promising to talk to his enemies, although Gorbachev's political concepts were just as alien to Afghanistan as socialist modernity, which his Kremlin predecessors had tried in vain to plant in this inhospitable soil. Unbeknownst to the Afghan leader, Gorbachev was even considering giving as many as 50 percent of government portfolios to the opposition. He thought that, without making Najib "No. 1," he would somehow preserve the Communist Party (PDPA) as a player in the political settlement.[77] There was a wide gap between this sort of wishful thinking and the much more brutal logic of the Pakistanis and the Iranians who responded to Soviet pleas for "national reconciliation" with the pragmatic observation that some things just could not be reconciled. "It is unrealistic to think," Ali Khamenei told Shevardnadze shortly before he was appointed the Supreme Leader of Iran, "that one can sit yesterday's enemies at one table. Too much blood was spilled between them."[78]

Najibullah never accepted the idea of the political settlement Gorbachev had in mind. For instance, he sabotaged the Soviet military's efforts to negotiate with the Tajik leader Ahmad Shah Massoud, one of the strongest players in the Afghan resistance.[79] Najibullah was fairly successful in this because he enjoyed the support of the KGB and of Eduard Shevardnadze, who, as the head of the Politburo's Afghanistan Commission, carried a lot of weight in defining Soviet policy. In general, he proved remarkably apt at exploiting Soviet intra-bureaucratic rivalries to stay in power and to derail Gorbachev's efforts to achieve a political solution. The Afghan Foreign Minister, Abdul Wakil, had to be arm-twisted into signing the Geneva Accords of April 14, 1988, with Pakistan, which paved way to the withdrawal of Soviet forces.

Najibullah had a different idea for dealing with Pakistan, which he had elaborated to Gorbachev the previous July: "what do you think, if Pakistan and the USA refused to agree to a political settlement, would it not be worth to develop, jointly with India, a coordinated plan?" The essence of this plan was to carry out a preemptive strike against Pakistan together with the Indians, who suffered from Pakistan's meddling with the Sikhs, just as the Afghans suffered from Pakistan's sponsorship of the Afghan resistance. Gorbachev gave a sour response to this proposal.[80] Najibullah raised the subject again in June 1988, proposing "to organize a joint war: USSR-India-Afghanistan against Pakistan." This time, however, "M. S. [Gorbachev] rebuffed him pretty bluntly."[81] Given that only a few years earlier a similar proposal came from the Soviet Ambassador in Afghanistan the dramatic turn-about in the Soviet Union's South Asia policy was obvious.

Rather than fight a joint war against the Pakistanis, the Soviets were thinking hard about improving relations with them, seeing such rapprochement as a sine qua non of a dignified withdrawal. Like Richard Nixon, who mended fences with China in part to find a way out of Vietnam, Gorbachev hoped that the Pakistani President Zia ul-Haq would help the Soviets leave Afghanistan on acceptable terms. This thinking in fact predated Gorbachev. Already in 1984 the Soviet Ambassador in Pakistan, Vitalii Smirnov, whom Zia thought "crude and rude" although "his predecessor was even worse," offered Islamabad "total security" and "guarantees of freedom"—something that the Pakistani President wasted no time advertising to the United States, no doubt to extract more American aid.[82] In March 1985 Gorbachev dangled the prospect of better Soviet-Pakistani relations before Zia in person, at Chernenko's funeral. However, this prospect was interlaced with implicit threats should the Pakistanis persist in arming the mujahedeen. Zia, according to Gorbachev's recollections, "left the room clearly unhappy," while the Soviet leader soon received a letter from Reagan, who warned him of the "great danger" of threatening "a trusted US ally."[83]

A real breakthrough in Soviet-Pakistani relations did not occur until the Soviets had firmly decided on withdrawing from Afghanistan. The decision was made in December 1987, after Gorbachev returned from a very successful visit to the United States. By December 30, everyone on the Afghanistan Commission was resigned to the inevitable: "we are leaving."[84] Then, on February 8, Gorbachev made a television announcement— the Soviet forces would begin their withdrawal on May 15. This dramatic gesture, in the absence of any agreement with the United States or the Pakistanis, and in the face of Najibullah's resistance, was aimed at forcing Islamabad and Kabul to make mutual concessions.[85]

Soviet deputy foreign minister Georgii Kornienko (who claimed credit for the withdrawal announcement) wrote that he expected the US to put pressure on Pakistan, just as Moscow could put pressure on Najibullah.[86] Separately, the Soviets also appealed to China to "exert appropriate influence" on Islamabad.[87] But neither the White House nor the Chinese showed much interest in putting Pakistan under any kind of pressure. There was another rationale behind Gorbachev's decision: it was a signal to Islamabad that the USSR would not threaten Pakistan. Gorbachev was convinced that there were people in the fractious Pakistani leadership who were not averse to mending fences. As his close ally Aleksandr Yakovlev commented on February 22, they "understand that they cannot live under the American wing forever, especially that there is India here on one side, and the Soviet Union on the other, and they [the Pakistanis] need a buffer state, well disposed towards them, and they do not want a regime hostile to them."[88]

The problem was finding the right people to talk to. In June 1988 Zia ul-Haq sent Gorbachev a letter in which (according to the latter's account) he "open[ed] the embrace of friendship and shed the tears of affection." In Gorbachev's view, this letter showed that he, Zia, "ha[d] to take into account what could happen to Afghanistan if the Soviet Union, India, and Afghanistan squeezed it on three sides."[89] Zia invited Gorbachev to come to Islamabad, but the Soviet leader was not yet prepared for such a dramatic step, not least because he thought Zia "a political bastard" who "could not be trusted."[90] Zia's death in a plane crash in August 1988 and the election of Benazir Bhutto as the Prime Minister later that year created new opportunities for a rapprochement between the USSR and Pakistan, a task that fell to Eduard Shevardnadze when he arrived in Islamabad in February 1989.

Shevardnadze met with Bhutto on February 5. The Soviet delegation was charmed by her looks. (Shevardnadze's aide spent a full page of his diary describing the "seductive strength of her thighs"). What she had to say was less attractive: Bhutto was reluctant to include the PDPA in any kind of a political settlement. The PDPA, she told Shevardnadze, "has weapons but it has no will. And if this is so, it can expect nothing." One positive element was Bhutto's apparent willingness to tolerate a "moderate" government in Afghanistan, with the former king, Zahir Shah, playing a central role (here she agreed with Gorbachev, who also sought a role for the king).[91] However, Bhutto's assurances proved short-lived. The very next month, she approved ISI's heavy involvement in the Battle of Jalalabad, an effort by the mujahedeen to force a quick military solution to the war. Bhutto later admitted that she could not refuse her intelligence chiefs the pleasure of victory on the battlefield when it was within reach.[92]

Shevardnadze, however, had reasons to be optimistic about his visit. On the plane trip back from Islamabad, he explained that he had not counted on "super-results" from this trip. What he wanted was: to win time and to spoil relations between Pakistan and the loose alliance of the mujahedeen, the Peshawar Seven—in other words, "to put the Pakistani leadership before a choice: either they improve relations with us, which Pakistan undoubtedly needs, or strengthen [their] unity with the alliance [the Peshawar Seven] on the basis of the Muslim kinship." Shevardnadze wanted to have the benefit of better Soviet-Pakistani relations even if the situation in Afghanistan went completely out of control. He sought to weaken Iran with its pretensions of leadership in the Muslim world and to prevent India and China from exploiting Soviet-Pakistani differences in their interest. The main thing, Shevardnadze explained, was to "restore the regional balance."[93] This meant abandoning the old Soviet attachments in the region, including reliance on India, in favor of a much more nuanced policy with uncertain payback. This was all part of Gorbachev's idea that, even losing in Afghanistan, the Soviets could still "win in the world."[94]

Another country affected by this policy in a direct and immediate way was Iran. Soviet interest in engagement with the radical regime, after Moscow spent the better part of the decade and some billions of rubles on neighboring Iraq, was, as with the Pakistanis, a result of the urgency of finding a way out of the war in Afghanistan. Iran sponsored Shiite insurgents who fought the Soviet forces in the country. Although these insurgents were not as numerous or well-armed as the ISI/CIA-backed mujahedeen of the Peshawar Seven, they added to Soviet problems in Afghanistan. Tehran also refused to be drawn into the Geneva process of finding a political settlement. Nonetheless, from 1988, the Iranian leadership opened a dialogue with the Soviets. In the opinion of Soviet policy makers Tehran was wary of the prospect of Afghanistan becoming a US platform in South Asia, and sought to benefit from economic and technological cooperation with the USSR at a time when Iran had few other options.[95]

The rapprochement between xenophobic and fanatical Iran and the USSR was both swift and bizarre. In January 1989 Ayatollah Khomeini sent a messenger for improved relations, Abdollah Javadi-Amoli, with a personal letter for Gorbachev. In this letter Khomeini urged Gorbachev to abandon communism, and "questioned the value of the Marxist teachings." To his credit, Gorbachev saw the letter as an invitation to "continue exchange of opinions on philosophical, political and, of course, practical questions of life."[96] The dialogue was continued during Shevardnadze's visit to Tehran in February. Shevardnadze was taken to a poor house somewhere in the northern part of Tehran, to a room with "boring surroundings," where he treated Khomeini to the standard Gorbachev fare about "common human values," including interest in nuclear disarmament; the Soviets' respect for the "great" Iranian revolution; and great prospects for Soviet-Iranian cooperation on the basis of equality and mutual non-interference. After listening to Shevardnadze's lengthy monologue, Khomeini declared that he was "not interested in this worldly life, but in the afterlife." "If one pays no attention to it [the afterlife], worldly tasks cannot be brought into order. But I did not receive the answers to the questions I raised in my message [to Gorbachev]. I wanted to speak to him about something else—about the spiritual, eternal, non-material." Shevardnadze countered with a prepared formula: "spirituality is our main task!" "No, after all, I did not receive the answers," responded Khomeini, after which he got up and exited the room, leaving Shevardnadze dumbfounded.[97]

Fortunately, other Iranian leaders proved more pragmatic than their ailing Imam. The meeting was publicly spun as a success, and Shevardnadze's other talks in Tehran—including with Khomeini's imminent successor, Ali Khamenei—showed that the Iranians were just as keen as the Soviets to rid their relationship of the ideological ballast of the Cold War years.[98] There was a clear demonstration of this during Akbar Hashemi Rafsanjani's visit to Moscow in June 1989, shortly before he succeeded Khamenei as the President of Iran. Rafsanjani brought with him a long list of requests for economic cooperation (draft agreements added up to five billion dollars): Soviet help in building a hydropower plant, in increasing the production output of a steel plant in Isfahan, and in constructing an atomic power station. "Good" was Gorbachev's short reply, which opened a new era for nuclear cooperation between Iran and Russia.[99]

Soviet withdrawal from Afghanistan was completed on schedule, on February 15, 1989. There was some last-minute hesitation in late January, as Shevardnadze argued for leaving ten to fifteen thousand troops behind to protect communications, especially the road that supplied Kabul.[100] Shevardnadze, who had been deeply involved in Afghan affairs and had frequently met with Najibullah, returned from Kabul on January 16, convinced that the city should be defended "at all costs."[101] But leaving forces was not an option Gorbachev was willing to entertain at this late stage. On January 24, at a Politburo meeting, he dismissed the Foreign Minister's pleas as "baby talk," deciding instead to supply the Afghan forces to let them hold out on their own.[102]

Thus, after the last Soviet soldiers crossed the border, Najibullah was left to face the mujahedeen alone. The forces clashed in March, when the opposition assaulted the major city of Jalalabad. On March 9 Najibullah, desperate, called Moscow all day in an effort to get the Soviets to carry out an airstrike against the mujahedeen. The following day, the Politburo decided to reject his appeal. "E. A. [Shevardnadze] is darker than the clouds," wrote his aide on the following day. "No one from those who had to take this decision sat in Kabul one-on-one with doomed Najib, looked into his eyes and entreated him. . . . I understand E. A. After all these frequent trips to Kabul and talks with Najib, he has some internal, personal obligations before him. He, as a man, 'got along' with him and, as a human being, sympathizes."[103] But there was no reversal of the Soviet decision to leave.

The Battle of Jalalabad unexpectedly ended with Najibullah's victory. His regime fell only when the Yeltsin government refused to provide aid to Afghanistan. Amid the ensuing chaos, the Taliban came to power. On September 27, 1996, Taliban thugs captured Najibullah at the UN compound in Kabul, where he had sought refuge, and on the following day the former President was castrated, dragged through the streets, and hanged on a lamppost. Such was the sad postscript to the failed story of national reconciliation once championed by Gorbachev.

Other than the long-suffering people of Afghanistan, the real losers in this dramatic story were the Americans. US support for the mujahedeen made it more difficult for the Soviets to withdraw. Gorbachev, fearful of the Vietnam parallels, sought an acceptable political settlement before ending Soviet involvement in this war that neither he nor, indeed, his predecessors, really wanted. US and Pakistani reluctance to endorse any settlement that would leave Karmal or Najibullah in power delayed the Soviet decision to withdraw until the winter of 1988, three years after Gorbachev had decided to pull out. In the meantime, by aiding the mujahedeen, the Americans and the Pakistanis ultimately contributed to the anarchic conditions that would provide a fertile soil in the 1990s for the emergence of the Taliban movement.

Furthermore, by providing support to Islamabad in the 1980s, the White House contributed to India's fears of a stronger, menacing, and aggressive Pakistan and undermined the chances for the genuine US-Indian rapprochement Rajiv Gandhi so hoped to achieve. Despite moderate improvement of bilateral relations in the mid-1980s, it was a lost decade for US relations with South Asia's most powerful nation. On the balance, Gorbachev gained more from the Afghan endgame than just about anyone else in the region. The withdrawal was a notable success of his foreign policy and, but for the short-sighted US policy, it could have well contributed to what Shevardnadze called restoration of the regional balance. In the 1990s, Russia's economic collapse and ideological handicaps of the early Yeltsin government precluded active involvement in the region. Only recently has this involvement manifested itself in new ways, with none of the goodwill that Gorbachev had for solving regional problems through Soviet-American cooperation and compromise.

CONTRADICTIONS

Between 1985 and 1987 Gorbachev made a major effort to upgrade Soviet relations with India by supporting Rajiv's regional policies. The circumstances were favorable for Soviet posturing as the true friend of India, especially with regard to the intractable problem of Sri Lanka. Moscow had a problem-free record in Sri Lanka, unlike the United States, whom the Indians suspected of duplicity and subversion. In the early 1980s, New Delhi, which viewed Sri Lanka as lying squarely within its sphere of influence, watched Colombo's foreign policy with increasing unease as Sri Lankan President J. R. Jayewardene extended friendly feelers to the United States, China, Pakistan, and even Israel. Indian-Sri Lankan tensions came to a head after the July 1983 ethnic riots in Sri Lanka, which set in motion the island's rapid decline into a brutal civil war. New Delhi, under pressure from Tamil constituencies in the southeast, looked the other way when the Tamil Tigers sought shelter and support in India's province of Tamil Nadu. Nevertheless, India tried to mediate in the conflict, no doubt with an eye to excluding any other potential mediators or foreign supporters to whom Colombo may have turned. In fact, the Indians exaggerated Jayewardene's chances of finding reliable friends in faraway quarters.[104]

The Soviet leader predictably blamed the problems in Sri Lanka on the United States. "Look at the conglomerate of countries, which has been pulled into the Sri Lanka's problems," he told the Indian Foreign Minister Shiv Shankar on June 14, 1986. "And the spring here is the United States. Neither Pakistan, nor Israel, nor South Africa could do anything without encouragement on the part of the United States. The political conductor here is the United States, and the helper to the conductor is Great Britain." The conflagration in Sri Lanka, Gorbachev reasoned, was a US ploy intended to "put India under political pressure, create tension in the Indian society, undermine the Prime Minister's personal authority." By contrast, the Soviet Union had great respect for India: "such a huge and ancient country as India, which has a huge experience of struggle for independence, which enjoys universal recognition as an influential force in world politics, [cannot] become someone's satellite. This is reality and this is the point of departure for us."[105]

These views rang true to Rajiv Gandhi, especially when the Sri Lankan situation worsened in early 1987, as the government launched a new offensive against the Tamil rebels in the north. By June 1987 the Tamils seemed to be on the verge of annihilation. Faced with the prospect of the collapse of the insurgency, Rajiv Gandhi unwisely authorized an airdrop of supplies to the Jaffna peninsula. Colombo protested bitterly—as did all of India's neighbors, who, far from appreciating Rajiv's proclaimed humanitarian motives (the Sri Lankan offensive had left the population of Jaffna in desperate straits), claimed that India's action was an act of blatant gunboat diplomacy. Gandhi's standing in the eyes of US policy makers slipped considerably. The New York Times lamented: "Where is the calm, good-humored and conciliatory Rajiv Gandhi who so impressed the world a year ago?"[106]

Under these circumstances, Soviet support was essential to the Indian Prime Minister. On July 2, 1987, Gandhi and Gorbachev had a most telling exchange:

RAJIV GANDHI: ...[Sri Lanka] has long been friends with the Americans. I have in mind calls by the American Navy, visits by highly placed American military officials. Sri Lankans have relations of military character with Pakistan. We suppose that the Americans want to obtain a base in Trinkomali. So far we have been able to apply sufficient pressure so that Sri Lanka does not agree to this. But in recent months, the leadership of Sri Lanka has come closer and closer to Pakistan and the USA. They may even sign treaties with these two countries. I have an impression that the United States will not want to act in too obvious a manner there. Perhaps, under some exceptional circumstances they will send ships from the 6th or the 7th fleet. But if they see that the conflict gets worse, the United States will not want to be pulled into military action.

M. S. GORBACHEV: Yes, the Americans are afraid of this.

RAJIV GANDHI: The US does not like when Americans get killed.[107]

For the time being, Rajiv thought that his gamble paid off. In July 1987, Sri Lanka and India reached an agreement for a peaceful settlement of the ethnic conflict on the island. This agreement resulted in the deployment of the Indian Peace Keeping Force in Sri Lanka, which before long found itself embroiled in counter-insurgency warfare against the Tamils. Rajiv, who was increasingly bogged down by domestic unrest and corruption allegations, found himself stuck in a quagmire in a neighboring nation that would last more than two years. Reflecting upon his woes in Sri Lanka in March 1989, Gandhi criticized the United States, Pakistan, Israel, and South Africa for meddling in the island's affairs, but defended his decision to send troops. "It was an expensive measure on our part to send troops to Sri Lanka. Even so, if we think about the danger from the gathering of the evil forces, which had threatened our security [in Sri Lanka?], the decision to send troops was a correct one."[108] There was a tinge of paranoia in Rajiv's words about the evil forces; in any case, India's military intervention in Sri Lanka was one of the worst foreign policy blunders of his administration. It ultimately cost Rajiv his life—in May 1991 he was killed by a Tamil Tiger suicide bomber for his role in the intervention.

If in relations with Sri Lanka Gandhi could count on unequivocal Soviet support, with regard to Pakistan he found himself outpaced by events and practically abandoned by the Soviets by 1988 and 1989. Common Indian and Soviet interests with regard to Pakistan had been one of the strategic pillars of their relationship, especially after the Soviet invasion of Afghanistan. As Gorbachev put it, "in our actions, we will take as our point of departure our common interests, common striving towards ruining Pakistan's plans, directed against the Soviet Union and India." This was a far stronger message to the Indians than Reagan's vague promise to "ease strains" in Indo-Pakistani relations. As long as tensions plagued Soviet relations with Pakistan (with no improvement expected as long as Soviet troops remained in Afghanistan), Gandhi could count on Gorbachev's unwavering support, something he could never expect to get from the Americans.[109]

The big question was whether the quasi alliance with India envisioned by Gorbachev could put undesirable constraints on the foreign policy of the USSR or possibly commit it to support India to the detriment of Soviet interests in the region. Anatolii Dobrynin, former Soviet Ambassador in the United States, who had taken over the International Department in the Central Committee in 1986, cautioned Gorbachev to keep an eye on Indo-Pakistani relations: "India is preparing its own nuclear bomb.... Some circles do not rule out a preventive strike against Pakistan." Gorbachev responded that Gandhi "understands the consequences."[110] Yet what would the Soviet Union do about another Indo-Pakistani conflict, especially at a time when Gorbachev tried hard to project a peace-loving image in foreign affairs in the context of "new thinking"? The contradiction between a Soviet-Indian alliance and the broader goals of Gorbachev's foreign policy were already present, if not yet fully evident to all, including the Soviet leader. Indeed, his hope for closer relations with India was premised on the understanding that Rajiv Gandhi would opt for compromise and negotiations with his neighbors, first and foremost Pakistan.

It did not take long before this theoretical dilemma created complications for day-to-day Soviet policy. The occasion was a new flare-up along the Indo-Pakistani border in January 1987. Tensions had been growing since November 1986, when the Indian army carried out exercises along the border with Pakistan. In December Islamabad responded with a buildup of its own and on January 23 Rajiv Gandhi placed the Indian army on highest alert and closed the border with Pakistan as the Indian press forecast an inevitable war. Observers disagreed about the causes of the latest crisis, with some speculating that Gandhi meant to put pressure on Pakistan to dissuade it from procuring the latest military technology from the United States, and others suggesting that he was responding to mounting domestic pressures over unrest in the province of Punjab.[111]

Gandhi later explained his actions with reference to Pakistan's intentions in the Punjab. "It is quite possible that if we did not deploy our forces, the

Pakistanis would be able to quickly grab a piece of our territory, proclaim 'Khalistan' there, and hand it over to the Sikhs," he said, pointing out that the Indian army was "itching" to turn the situation to its advantage and "cut Sindh from Punjab." According to Rajiv, only New Delhi's peace-loving attitude prevented this scenario.[112] In any case, the state of Soviet-Indian relations left Moscow with few options but to support India's cause in cautiously phrased TASS reports.

There was much more to the Soviet reaction than TASS reports could tell. On January 24 Gorbachev's foreign policy aide Anatolii Chernyaev addressed the problem in a memorandum to Gorbachev. He had the impression that

> R. Gandhi (or his circle) want to "make a little war" or something like this in order to "unite the nation" and fix domestic problems. Willingly or unwillingly on his part, but it turns out that India is exploiting its friendship with us for this purpose. We can end up in an awkward situation because the whole world will see that it was not Pakistan that unleashed a military clash.

Chernyaev added that sending a protest to Pakistan was a "necessary measure." However, he felt that it was also necessary to send an intelligence report to New Delhi to the effect that "our information on the military activities and intentions in the ruling circles of Pakistan do not lead to a conclusion that [they are] preparing an invasion of India's territory."[113] One-sided condemnation of Pakistan, Chernyaev argued, was "not profitable" to the Soviet Union from the perspective of achieving a settlement in Afghanistan, where, as Gorbachev recognized, Pakistan was bound to play a major role.[114] Such, then, was the "interconnection" of things, to use Gorbachev's favorite word: Soviet regional priorities—in particular, withdrawal from Afghanistan, which was really the key priority—required careful maneuvering to win over Pakistan, the United States, even the Chinese.

Unequivocal support for India in its long-running feud with Pakistan did nothing to help the Soviet situation. Gorbachev saw the contradiction and urged the Politburo on February 26 to "remove Rajiv Gandhi's concern about Pakistan," mirroring in this respect US efforts to bring India and Pakistan together. Whereas the White House urged reconciliation to keep the Soviets out, Gorbachev wanted reconciliation at US expense.[115] In his own meeting with the Indian leader in July 1987 (Rajiv's third visit to Moscow in just over two years), Gorbachev dwelled on the prospect of peace talks between India and Pakistan: "At one moment, in a concrete historical situation [in 1966] such a trilateral meeting of the leaders of the Soviet Union, India and Pakistan was held. Perhaps, time will come when it will be appropriate to repeat such a meeting, keeping in mind, of course, other, new tasks. I think we should not discount this idea." Gandhi said he tried to improve relations with Pakistan, "but the problem is that they talk a lot and when it comes to doing something, [they] don't do anything good."[116] But in the following months the Soviet Union moved a long way toward a better relationship with Pakistan.

Rajiv's own efforts to match Soviet achievements with Pakistan by and large failed. After the 1987 war scare, Indo-Pakistani relations appeared to improve in 1988, in large part because of the visible democratic advance in Pakistan occasioned by the death of President Zia ul-Haq and the beginning of Bhutto's premiership. In July 1989 Rajiv went to Islamabad on his first and last official visit amid high expectations in both countries that Gandhi and Bhutto, a new generation of leaders who had no direct experience of the partition, could somehow end decades of rivalry. In particular, Bhutto expected Indian concessions on Jammu and Kashmir, but Rajiv took a hard line. As Indian diplomat J. N. Dixit argues, "Benazir was bitterly disappointed and took great umbrage at being thwarted in her expectations which, in any case, were unrealistic."[117]

Rajiv was equally disappointed. Although Bhutto may have been well-intentioned, Rajiv noted in March 1989, "in order to become the Prime Minister she made a lot of concessions to the Americans, the Pakistan military and the President, and to the intelligence. All of this limits her ability to work freely."[118] In a meeting with Gorbachev a few months later, Rajiv illustrated his views about Bhutto with a specific example: "By the way, when in December [1988] I talked to her in Islamabad, and the conversation touched on sensitive subjects, she did not speak but wrote notes and handed them to me. I answered her in a similar manner. And all of this was in her office."[119] Soon after his return from the July 1989 summit with Bhutto, Rajiv Gandhi was swept up in the electoral frenzy, which took the wind out of his Pakistan policy. In the meantime, the situation in Kashmir seriously deteriorated, marked by an increase of secessionist activities and terrorism, mostly—the Indians claimed—inspired by the Pakistani intelligence with Bhutto's quiet agreement. Rajiv's appraisal of the situation in December 1989 was that India had not done enough to crush separatism in Kashmir and Punjab. It was a fitting, if ironic, postscript to five years of Gandhi's futile efforts to arrive at a settlement with Pakistan.[120]

Nothing demonstrates better Rajiv's loss of touch in relations with India's neighbors between 1988 and 1989 than his approach to the settlement in Afghanistan. Although New Delhi disliked the Soviet invasion, Gorbachev's resolve in seeking a political settlement sank the Indians into a dilemma. The biggest problem was that India was not a part of a major international settlement within its sphere of interest, while Pakistan was.

The exclusive nature of the April 1988 Geneva Accords dealt a serious blow to Rajiv Gandhi's efforts to project the image of India's regional and global indispensability as a great power and a broker between the East and the West. The other major problem with the Soviet military withdrawal, from New Delhi's perspective, was that its most likely result was the creation of a fundamentalist Afghanistan, courtesy of the ISI. This was also unacceptable to Rajiv.

In a conversation with Gorbachev in July 1987, Rajiv argued that "if Afghanistan becomes a fundamentalist country or if the Americans have a strong influence there, like in Pakistan, Afghanistan will not be a truly independent country, and this will create problems for us."[121] Reflecting on these comments days later, Gorbachev told Najibullah that, in his view, Indians did not truly want a Soviet withdrawal from Afghanistan. "The Indians are concerned that a normalization of the situation in Afghanistan will result in Pakistan directing its subversive activities against India." But, he added, Rajiv's position took only the Indian interest into account at the expense of the Soviet interests.[122]

Seeing that a political settlement was inevitable, New Delhi lobbied the Soviets to at least include provisions for constraining Pakistan, for example by forcing Islamabad to scrap the stockpiles of weapons intended for the mujahedeen (but certainly usable against India). India's Defense Minister, K. Ch. Pant, worried that if terrorists got their hands on the US-supplied "stingers" and used them against civilian (presumably Indian) aircraft, "there would be chaos."[123] The Soviet leader rejected this, however, because he feared that Soviet insistence on the disarmament of Pakistan would come back to haunt the Soviets in the form of US demands that they do the same with respect to Najibullah's government in Kabul. By early 1989, Rajiv, having been sidelined in the Afghanistan settlement, was at pains to come up with a way to seize initiative in the solution of outstanding problems on the subcontinent. Yet he did not appear to have an overall strategy, save for fantasizing about the prospects of a joint Afghan-Indian war on Pakistan, which would be unleashed in case Islamabad dared to use force to topple the Najibullah regime. Mongolia's President, Jambyn Batmunkh, with whom Rajiv shared his views, was so taken aback that he even asked the Prime Minister to repeat himself, thinking that something had been lost in translation. Rajiv Gandhi reiterated his readiness to intervene to save Najibullah from a Pakistani aggression.[124]

By 1988 Gorbachev's policy toward India became more nuanced. Remarkable breakthroughs in economic cooperation, expected between 1986 and 1987, had not materialized. Gorbachev blamed "a contemptuous attitude of some of our bureaucracies: they think that India is at 'an early stage of civilization' and we, allegedly, are prepared to teach it. In the meantime, it would not do us harm to learn something from them—banking, services and many other things."[125] After coming back from his second visit to New Delhi in November 1988, Gorbachev again called for pooling scientific research with India because "it has brains, and good ones."[126] But these calls were beginning to sound hollow after two years of unrealized expectations. The bigger problem was that both the Soviets and India were in need of modern technology; unable to get it from each other, they both had to look to the West.

Gorbachev's political love affair with Gandhi also showed signs of strain, as he formed a more sober assessment of Rajiv's policies: "In India, we are faced with a great power policy. At the same time, [they] understand that they cannot implement it without us and that we do not want 'to give them the leading role.' There is a nuance here, and we sense it. India wants for everyone to 'rotate' around it: Burma, Bangladesh, Sri Lanka, Maldives, etc. In other words, it wants to have a 'patrimony' with vassals in this region. That's why it is not reacting well to our initiatives about naval disarmament in the Indian Ocean."[127] Gorbachev's personal rapport with Gandhi could no longer paper over growing divergences between India's regional interests and the Soviet leader's pursuit of "new thinking." Indeed, the more Gorbachev pushed his agenda of disarmament and his reconciliation with the West, and the more dividends he enjoyed from his increasingly successful policy vis-à-vis the West, the less India mattered in Gorbachev's global calculations.

THE SUBMARINE

One issue that demonstrated as nothing else the deepening contradictions between broader goals of Soviet foreign policy and some aspects of Soviet-Indian relations was Moscow's involvement in India's atomic submarine program. Over the years the Soviets had provided New Delhi with diesel submarines. On October 31, 1986, the Soviet leadership decided to upgrade the level of military cooperation with India, confirming in principle an earlier idea of renting a nuclear submarine to the Indians. This decision was taken only days after Gorbachev's return from his meeting with Reagan in Reykjavik, subsequently hailed as a breakthrough in ending of the Cold War, and it shows to what extent the General Secretary still kept his eggs in different baskets at this crucial turning point.[128]

That transfer—the first time any country had given another a nuclear submarine, even temporarily, and even, as in this case, for "training purposes"—was a potential bombshell, and Soviet experts recognized it as such. An internal memorandum drawn up at the time spelled out some of the possible negative consequences of such a decision. Thus, it could violate Soviet obligations under the Nuclear Non-Proliferation Treaty, in particular because the SS-N-7 missiles, which the sub could theoretically carry, could be equipped with 10-kiloton nuclear warheads. Although the Soviets would not supply the nukes, there was no escaping the negative publicity or "malicious rumors." The United States could well retaliate by providing nuclear subs to Pakistan, armed with real Tomahawk cruise missiles.[129]

There was also another issue. The Soviet leadership could be accused of "inconsistency": on the one hand peddling the proposal to turn the Indian Ocean into a "zone of peace" (one of Gorbachev's pet projects announced in the 1986 Vladivostok speech), while on the other hand upgrading India's military capabilities. The experts also feared leakage of Soviet technologies to US intelligence (in the past the Soviet Union had acquired US technologies by way of India). The authors of the memorandum proposed to "discuss one more time the far-reaching consequences" of the transfer with Gandhi to see if he could be persuaded to give up on the training sub.[130]

There is no indication that Gorbachev followed this advice in his conversations with Rajiv Gandhi when they met that November. By contrast, the Soviet leader was at the high point of his enthusiasm for the Soviet-Indian relationship, and military transfers were one effective way of strengthening the alliance. The lease agreement was signed on December 12, 1986, with the transfer of the submarine scheduled for mid-1987. A hundred Indian navy men were dispatched to the (then still closed) port of Vladivostok, where they were trained in the operation of the submarine.

By late 1987 the Indians were getting nervous, especially after the Soviets proposed that the Indian personnel be sent home from Vladivostok until the transfer was actually implemented. India's Ambassador in Moscow, T. K. Kaul, called on Premier Nikolai Ryzhkov to ask "if there had been any change in the policy of the Soviet government," in which case the Indians "would have to reconsider the whole thing." Ryzhkov gave a "perfectly frank" answer: "There is absolutely no change in our policy."[131]

He then explained the delay:

We made the request only for a short postponement because delicate matters were being discussed with the Americans who were already suspicious of India's plans and attributing motives to both India and the Soviet Union. They were looking at each Indo-Soviet deal as if through a microscope and magnifying glasses. It was for this reason that the Soviet government had proposed that there be a short postponement in the project.[132]

Ryzhkov kept his word. The next month, the Soviets publicly announced the decision to lease the atomic submarine to India. The news was an international bombshell. One Pentagon official commented that obtaining this submarine was "a real boost for [India's] effort to build a world-class, blue-water fleet that can project power throughout the Indian Ocean region."[133] The submarine, christened the INS *Chakra*, began patrolling the Indian Ocean in early February 1988. As Mark Kramer has argued, "despite being warned that the transfer of a nuclear submarine to a potential combatant in a volatile region of the Third World would set an ominous precedent, the Soviet Politburo concluded that the political-military benefits outweighed the risks."[134] Gorbachev the pragmatist again won the contest of wills with Gorbachev the idealist.

The December 12, 1986, agreement provided for Soviet aid to India in building its own nuclear submarine. The Indians were not told about it at the time, but as early as January 13, 1982, the Soviet Council of Ministers had adopted a resolution that proscribed export of nuclear reactors for submarines or technical documentation for their construction. This ban could be violated when circumstances required and, in fact, when it turned out that the Indians were unable to manufacture their own nuclear reactor for the sub, the Soviets—on March 11, 1988—decided in principle that they could supply the necessary technology. However, this decision was not disclosed to the Indians at the time, and by the end of that year the Soviet outlook on weapons transfers changed the equation in a direction distinctly unfavorable for the Indians.[135]

Gorbachev's advisers—people like Anatolii Chernyaev and Georgii Shakhnazarov, both the staunchest liberals in the General Secretary's entourage—were voicing frustration with the practice of military transfers to Soviet clients in the Third World, a practice incompatible with "new thinking" in Soviet foreign policy. The use of these weapons "in eyes of the world community identified . . . with our intentions in this or that region," the two argued in a memorandum for Gorbachev on September 30, 1988, concluding that the time had come for the Soviet Union to cut off the weapons lifeline. It had been "provided by a kind of inertia, as a result of promises given in the past, or mainly in response to unending requests of those who speculate on our internationalism contrary to the interests of peace, about which they generally do not care."[136] In another memo to Gorbachev on December 13, 1988, Chernyaev argued against uncritical support of Soviet clients by what he called "inertia of proletarian internationalism."[137]

Although what Chernyaev and Shakhnazarov had in mind was the traditional Soviet support of militant clients like Cuba, North

Korea, and Ethiopia, the logic of "new thinking" increasingly undercut Soviet-Indian military cooperation. The issue of the submarine reactor was broached in a special study coauthored by Shevardnadze, Defense Minister Dmitrii Yazov, and Vladimir Kamentsev for Gorbachev. Noting that Soviet weapons transfers could "facilitate dangerous development of the military-strategic situation in this or that region," the trio specifically argued against helping the Indians with the submarine business, because such cooperation could undermine Soviet peace initiatives and strategic situation in South Asia.[138] Soon enough, on August 28, 1989, the Central Committee and the Council of Ministers passed a joint resolution banning any aid to India in the way of building nuclear propulsion systems for its submarines.[139]

Characteristically, this decision was not conveyed to the Indians—and no wonder, for only a few weeks earlier Gorbachev, in his meeting with Rajiv, bent over backwards to emphasize the common purpose in Soviet-Indian relations and talked up the theme of hastening the tempo of bilateral cooperation. Unaware that a decision had already been made, Rajiv sent Gorbachev a letter on October 27, 1989, reminding him of the importance of moving the project forward and asking for his "personal intervention."[140] The matter resulted in yet another study by a high-powered commission in the Soviet leadership with the recommendation—confirmed in a Politburo decision on November 18—that because the supply of reactors could have "rather unfortunate international consequences" and in effect "undermine the Soviet prestige," the answer to Rajiv's letter would have to be "no."[141]

However, seeing that it was difficult to give a cold shoulder to Rajiv, who, after all, was Gorbachev's first love on the world stage, the Soviets chose the path of procrastination. Gorbachev's response mentioned that the matter was being "carefully studied" with an eye to finding "positive solutions."[142] The ploy in this case was to wait it out until the Indian elections, which, the Soviets accurately expected, would end in Gandhi's defeat. The reactor was never transferred. And Gandhi's replacement by V. P. Singh as Prime Minister in December 1989 removed the personal aspect in Indo-Soviet relations, which, for better or worse, had contributed to their improvement since Gorbachev first shook hands with charismatic Rajiv.

CONCLUSION

Although in 1990 Moscow and New Delhi still maintained an appearance of close cooperation, negative tendencies were already making themselves felt. The enthusiasm of the mid-1980s was gone for good. Soviet-Indian relations were limping along, rapidly losing momentum. Anatolii Chernyaev captured the spirit of the times in a thoughtful observation in his diary (July 1990): "How many solemn words were uttered! And M. S. [Gorbachev] sincerely believed that things will go forward with 'great India.' Nothing happened. In economic relations—everything is as it was, and we are cutting back military [ties]. . . . This was not the main direction."[143] Much worse was to come. By 1991 trade relations between the USSR and India shrank from 5 billion dollars to 3.4 billion, further reduced to 1.2 billion by 1992. Military cooperation reached a dismal level. Political relations were plagued by a series of scandals—from the Russian leadership implicitly endorsing Pakistan's territorial claims against India to bitter disagreements over exchange rates and who owed what to whom.[144]

Days before he was swept aside by the political forces he had helped unleash, Gorbachev tried his best to salvage whatever pieces he could of the crumbling façade of Soviet-Indian cooperation. In his meeting with the Indian Foreign Minister, Madhavsinh Solanki, on November 15, 1991, he argued that "current temporary difficulties are not at all a reason to weigh anew the policy of the Soviet leadership, to doubt the developed and tested course of Soviet-Indian relations."[145] He promised that, for as long as he was in charge of the country, Soviet policy toward India would not change.[146] That was little comfort for the Indians, since Gorbachev's days were clearly numbered. Solanki's meeting with Yeltsin was hardly more reassuring. According to Chernyaev, the Russian leader urged New Delhi to abandon the Soviet leadership and build direct relations with him: "[Gorbachev] has nothing, and I have everything: oil, machines, weapons for export. And I will take from you what Russia needs. Make a political alliance with us and everything will be good between us. . . . No? You don't want this? Then go to hell together with your Gorbachev!"[147]

Between 1985 and 1991 Soviet-Indian relations were caught up in global changes. Who could have predicted that Moscow and New Delhi would drift apart by 1991? Gorbachev, for one, had altogether different expectations. His Indian breakthrough in 1986 was the first major victory of his foreign policy, supposedly a triumph for "new thinking." How much of this thinking was genuinely new and how much was rooted in traditional geopolitical concepts is debatable. What cannot be contested is that Gorbachev saw a de facto alliance with India as a cornerstone of his entire Asian policy. His early approach toward India was inevitably anti-American in essence, if not in form. But Gorbachev's Asian vision went beyond the narrow confines of an Indo-Soviet alliance. Speedy rapprochement with Beijing very much on his mind, Gorbachev looked forward to a possibility of a strategic triangle in Asia, involving the Soviet Union, India, and China in a potent combination, which would shame all US efforts to exert influence in the region. This grand vision had a fatal defect: neither India nor China was keen on the "triangle" idea. Each saw the other as a rival, and even where they chose to agree and cooperate, they hardly required any Soviet input. Both India and China were in fact interested in limiting Soviet influence in the region, India in its backyard—the Indian Ocean—and China in Southeast Asia.

For all the momentum in Soviet-Indian relations in 1986 and 1987, Moscow and New Delhi pursued increasingly different agendas. Gandhi was interested in developing India's regional hegemony, primarily at Pakistan's expense. He needed Soviet political endorsement in this task, as well as Soviet weapons. But Moscow's key interest was in ending hostilities in Afghanistan, which in turn required improvement in Soviet-Pakistani relations. Provided that Rajiv Gandhi was also moving toward rapprochement with Islamabad, Soviet policy toward Pakistan need not have caused any friction for Soviet-Indian relations. However, in practice, policy trajectories in Moscow and in New Delhi frequently diverged. At a more fundamental level, shifts in Soviet foreign policy since Reykjavik—Gorbachev's peace offensive and his increasing engagement with the West—soon began to contradict the logic of closer Soviet-Indian relations. After all, these relations were originally premised on basically anti-American assumptions.

As Gorbachev's foreign policy became more "Western" and less "Eastern," Soviet interest in India began to wane. Between 1989 and 1991 Gorbachev traveled extensively abroad but mainly in the West. He did not return to India. He treasured his relationship with George Bush, Helmut Kohl, and Margaret Thatcher rather than with Gandhi, Gorbachev's first foreign love. One time that Gorbachev did remember the former Indian Premier was on February 23, 1991, when he called him on the occasion of the US War in the Gulf.[148] A brief spell of anti-Americanism in the increasingly gloomy Gorbachev brought back the memories of the former alliance with India. By that time, whatever was left of Soviet foreign policy was rapidly disintegrating in the chaos of domestic problems—India was only one of many victims of this chaos. One should not overlook such a seemingly odd aspect of Gorbachev's foreign policy in 1990 and 1991 as money collection. At meetings with Western leaders, Gorbachev often asked for credits to save the Soviet economy from collapse. He had even put this question to the Indian Foreign Minister, Solanki, but India's abilities in this respect were very limited; India itself owed money to the USSR.[149]

When Rajiv Gandhi formed his government in 1984, improvement of relations with the United States was high on his agenda. Access to US technology was an important consideration underpinning his policy, but the bigger idea was to increase India's international leverage by projecting an image of true non-alignment. This effort appeared to bear fruit, but New Delhi and Washington failed to achieve a genuine rapprochement. This was not Rajiv's fault even though Gorbachev, for his part, tried hard to fuel Gandhi's resentment of the United States by means of occasional disinformation about CIA plots against him. The key obstacle to better relations was in Washington, where strategic imperatives of anti-Soviet character and deeply felt, if misplaced, suspicions that India was merely a Soviet pawn continued to influence policy making in ways highly unfavorable to India. Moreover, by the late 1980s, with the Afghanistan problem out of the way, India lost relevance for Washington, as it had lost relevance for Moscow; the White House set its sights upon events in Europe and, to a lesser degree, on China.

Rajiv Gandhi set out to chart anew India's foreign policy course: to improve its battered standing in the eyes of other regional players, to reshape India's relations with the superpowers, to recast the international order itself—a moral imperative to which, in his view, India had much to contribute. Unfortunately, his great hopes were not realized. As he stood down from power in late 1989, India's relations with its neighbors (with the important exception of China) were as bad as ever. India was sidelined and marginalized as the bitter competition between the two superpowers died away at last. The international order changed, but in spite of, rather than because of, India's efforts, and these changes were not at all what Rajiv had had in mind. Much of India's familiar world crumbled around it as the Cold War came to an end.

CHAPTER 4

Vietnam's Vietnam: Ending the Cambodian Quagmire, 1979–89

Between March 1982, when Leonid Brezhnev made his memorable appearance in Tashkent, and May 1989, when Mikhail Gorbachev shook hands with Deng Xiaoping in Beijing, no single issue exercised a greater influence on the Sino-Soviet relationship than that of the Vietnamese occupation of neighboring Cambodia. Deng Xiaoping never tired of repeating that this issue was one of the three obstacles to normalization with the USSR; in fact, he identified it as the main obstacle.[1] Yet there was much more to Sino-Soviet relations, even in the years before Gorbachev, than the futile sparring over the Cambodian problem in the seemingly endless biannual consultations. Contrary to the claims of mainstream Chinese historiography, Sino-Soviet normalization was not achieved because Gorbachev removed this "obstacle" by making Vietnam pull out from Cambodia, but, rather, in spite of what happened or failed to happen in that war-torn country.

In the course of the 1980s the Cambodian problem was demoted from a theater of the global Cold War to merely a regional conflict, especially for purposes of Chinese foreign policy. Deng Xiaoping finally gave up on his grand theory about Soviet encirclement of China, and while he continued to link the Sino-Soviet rapprochement with progress in Cambodia, his reasons for doing so changed from containing perceived Soviet aggression to constraining Vietnam's regional ambitions. He abandoned this linkage in 1989, when Sino-Soviet relations were normalized, although the Cambodian problem had not yet been resolved to Deng's satisfaction. The myth of Soviet concessions on Cambodia allowed Beijing to save face and maintain the air of moral superiority vis-à-vis the Soviet Union. In fact, neither China's pressure nor Soviet urging proved sufficient to force Vietnam out of Cambodia. Its withdrawal was a consequence of realization among the Vietnamese leaders that leaving Cambodia would allow them to focus meager resources on economic reconstruction and open the road to engagement with other regional powers.

This chapter recounts Soviet policy toward Southeast Asia from active support of Vietnamese policy in the early 1980s to careful urging of Vietnam's withdrawal from Cambodia after 1986. While Gorbachev was interested in removing the Cambodian conflict from the list of irritants in Soviet relations with China and with the West, his policy was influenced less by new thinking than by financial imperatives. The costs of Vietnam's occupation of Cambodia were passed on to the Soviet Union in the form of endless requests for credits and economic aid, a heavy burden on the struggling Soviet economy and a constant headache for Gorbachev, who struggled to lower the costs of maintaining a far-flung empire without antagonizing his overseas clients. Keeping the Vietnamese content was especially important for the Soviet leader, as he saw this country as an important geopolitical platform for Soviet influence in Southeast Asia.

THE LESSON

On April 17, 1975, after weeks of ferocious battles, government troops of the Republic of Cambodia surrendered the capital city of Phnom Penh to black-uniformed "forest people," the communist guerrillas, the Khmer Rouge. The end was anticlimatic. The population welcomed the victors, for the Khmer Rouge promised an end to the deprivations of war, which in the space of just a few years had left hundreds of thousands dead and millions homeless. After receiving independence from France in 1953, Cambodia lived in relative peace under Prince Norodom Sihanouk, who maneuvered desperately to maintain Cambodia's neutrality in the zero-sum game of Southeast Asia, juggling friendship with China and North Vietnam against an increasingly difficult relationship with the United States. By the early 1960s Sihanouk's balancing act became impossible to maintain. Cambodia broke relations with the United States in 1965 and allied with Communist China and North Vietnam. At the same time, Sihanouk unleashed anti-leftist repressions, forcing communists underground.

In April 1970, while on a trip abroad, Sihanouk was overthrown by his own Prime Minister, Lon Nol, who reallied Cambodia with the United States. Sihanouk found asylum in China.[2] He also struck up a friendship with North Korea's Kim Il-sung and split his time between Beijing and Pyongyang. Pragmatically, he closed ranks against Lon Nol's right-wing government with his former enemies, the Khmer Rouge, giving them diplomatic support from exile as the communist guerrillas, relying in part on Vietnam's support, made steady gains against Lon Nol in the countryside. Massive bombing of Cambodia by the United States added to the misery of the rural population and swelled the ranks of the Khmer Rouge sympathizers. In 1975, after defeating Lon Nol, the revolutionaries proclaimed the establishment of Democratic Kampuchea and declared themselves allied to Beijing and Hanoi.

Cambodia was reborn in the flames of the revolution, and the capture of Phnom Penh by the Khmer Rouge was just the beginning. Pol Pot, "Brother Number One," ordered everyone in the capital to leave. Millions of people were forced into the countryside, to be reeducated in labor cooperatives, where thousands died. Anyone with an education, intellectuals, doctors, lawyers—the elites of former Cambodia—were singled out for the "killing fields." Perhaps as many as 1.7 million people were murdered or starved to death.

Prince Sihanouk witnessed the bloodbath inside Cambodia. The wary ally of the Khmer Rouge was confined to his palace, powerless and in great uncertainty. As it happened, the hapless monarch was spared. Instead, Pol Pot turned his attention to the former ally Vietnam. Resentment of the Vietnamese great power arrogance and Hanoi's efforts to mold the communist movement in all of Indochina to its liking, supported by ancient hatreds and memories of Vietnam's past domination of the Cambodian kingdom, turned into violence against neighboring communist Vietnam. Between 1977 and 1978, border skirmishes between Cambodia and Vietnam occurred with increasing frequency.

On Christmas Day 1978, Vietnam invaded Cambodia and within weeks overthrew the Khmer Rouge. In place of Pol Pot, who, with the retreating troops of Democratic Kampuchea, fled to the Cambodia-Thailand border, the Vietnamese installed a former Khmer Rouge, Heng Samrin. Hanoi justified its action on humanitarian grounds—to stop Pol Pot's genocide in Cambodia. In reality, Vietnam would have lived with a genocidal regime across the border if it recognized the proper hierarchy in Indochina: the revolutionary movements in Cambodia and neighboring Laos were the sons of the Vietnamese revolution, and sons had to be obedient to the father. For Vietnam, invading Cambodia was an attempt to reassert its preeminence in Southeast Asia.

In China's view, the Vietnamese invasion of Cambodia was the latest example of Hanoi's unacceptable behavior. Vietnam was for China what Cambodia had been for Vietnam—a "son," a revolutionary appendage and a vassal in the traditional East Asian tributary system. The relationship was not without hidden tensions in the 1960s, as China resented Vietnam's reliance on the Soviet weapons and aid, but the façade of amity did not crumble until after the American defeat in Vietnam. Hanoi, euphoric after defeating the world's greatest military power, became increasingly resentful of any kind of a Chinese tutelage or Chinese meddling in the affairs of Indochina. In the meantime, Hanoi deepened its ties with the Soviet Union, which did not mind Vietnam's regional ambitions and provided badly needed economic aid to the economy of the war-torn nation.

On November 3, 1978, the Soviet Union and Vietnam concluded a treaty of friendship and cooperation with a clause that provided for mutual consultations "to safeguard peace and the security of the two countries."[3] This formulation impressed the Chinese, who realized that they were the target of the treaty. An alliance between "social-imperialist" Soviet Union and Vietnam marked a new stage in the Soviet encirclement of China, a major strategic coup in the Sino-Soviet confrontation. Nothing symbolized the new realities better than Vietnam's decision in 1979 to lease a former US military base at Cam Ranh Bay to the Soviet navy.

The Chinese had good reason for their security concerns. And yet the assumption that the Soviet Union blessed or even encouraged Vietnam's invasion of Cambodia had no factual basis. The balance of evidence indicates that the Vietnamese leaders did not share their plans with Moscow.[4] The Soviet hand behind the overthrow of Pol Pot was more likely than not an imagined threat, seeming to the Chinese, at the time, much bigger than it really was. Of course Sino-Soviet relations were full of bloated menace and mutual hysteria, so one should not underestimate the impact of the Soviet-Vietnamese alliance on the Chinese leaders' feeling of insecurity. To do so would understate the importance of the conflict in Indochina for China's strategic calculations in the Sino-Soviet rapprochement.

China reacted to Vietnam's invasion of Cambodia with a show of force: in February 1979 the Chinese army invaded Vietnam in what became one of the most bizarre conflicts of the Cold War. Facing determined resistance from the battle-tried Vietnamese forces, the Chinese army made slow advance. Deng Xiaoping then ordered the withdrawal of China's forces, claiming that a victory had been won and "a lesson had been taught." "In reality," pronounced the Vietnamese Premier Pham Van Dong later that year, "it was not they who gave us a 'lesson,' but it was we who gave them a 'lesson.'"[5]

The war entailed a careful calculation on Deng's part: the attack had to be powerful enough to impress the Soviet Union and not so powerful as to bring the Soviets into the war. The last thing Deng wanted was for China to fight a two-front war. On the other hand, he probably calculated that the Soviet Union would not want to be drawn into a war with China over Vietnam. "The Soviet Union would not dare to engage China in a big way," Deng told Prime Minister Lee Kuan-Yew two months before China's attack on Vietnam.[6]

Nevertheless, in response to China's invasion, the Soviet Union staged a massive military exercise at the Sino-Soviet border, in Mongolia and in the Pacific, involving an astonishing 20 divisions—200,000 troops, 2,600 tanks, 900 planes, and 80 ships. Within two days, forces were brought in from as far away as the Soviet Union's European frontier. It took the Soviet Ministry of Defense two years before it could fully restore the gasoline reserves depleted in the course of this single military exercise. The Soviets also stepped up supplies to Vietnam: before the end of March, they shipped more than 400 tanks and armored personnel carriers, 400 artillery pieces, 50 "Grad" multiple rocket launchers, and 20 jet fighters. Soviet transport planes were involved in moving troops and equipment inside Vietnam. The Chinese kept a cool nerve, and did not mobilize forces in the north, probably to avert unwanted escalation of the conflict, although Chinese residents of the border areas were alarmed, and many fled inland.[7]

If the war against Vietnam was China's effort to frustrate Soviet "hegemony," it served another, more subtle purpose: to bring China into a close alignment with the West. Deng had been very sensitive to US criticism that China had only talked about being tough on the Soviet Union but had not acted accordingly. When confronted with the question in his conversation with Gerald Ford in December 1975, Deng found little to say, but the US note taker observed "visible tension in his face."[8] It was not easy to counter Zbigniew Brzezinski in May 1978 when he made the point that "for the last thirty years it has been the US which has opposed Soviet hegemony designs and this is roughly twice as long as you have been doing it."[9] With China having gone to war with Vietnam, these embarrassing questions could no longer be plausibly asked of the Chinese. Thereafter, Deng did his best to show that China had been at the forefront of struggling with the Soviet menace even as the West clung on to the last shreds of détente.[10]

This war served the same purpose for Deng as the Korean War had served for Mao; both addressed a real security threat and also proved China's worth: in Korea, as a stalwart Soviet ally; in Vietnam, as America's reliable partner in the Cold War and, ironically enough, a bulwark against communist expansion in Southeast Asia. Both were a means of reasserting China's moral superiority over the two superpowers, first the Soviet Union, then the United States. China was poor and backward—so the logic went—but it was paying the heaviest price to defend the world against the American (in 1950) and the Soviet (in 1979) evil designs. In this sense, the war was an instrument of diplomacy, an effort to strengthen China's hand in negotiating a partnership of equals with the United States, and an instrument of engagement with the very rich—but still suspicious—non-communist Asia.

China's invasion failed to force the Vietnamese out of Cambodia. The ousted dictator Pol Pot and the remnants of the Khmer Rouge continued resisting the Vietnam-installed government of Heng Samrin from their bases along the Cambodian-Thai border, supplied and armed by the Chinese. At China's behest, Prince Norodom Sihanouk lent his clout to the beleaguered Khmer Rouge, and a government-in-exile was organized—a trilateral coalition with Sihanouk as the head and with the participation of the Khmer Rouge and another Cambodian faction of formerly right-wing orientation, led by Son Sann. This unlikely combination of the leftists, the rightists, and the monarchists not only represented Cambodia in the UN but also enjoyed broad international support from China, the United States, and the Association of Southeast Asian Nations (ASEAN).

The Cambodian internal situation was infinitely complicated, with four factions vying for power, but with the Vietnam angle, the China angle, and the ASEAN angle added, a picture emerges of such complexity that it is hard to see how a solution was ever found. Deng Xiaoping believed the situation had been cooked up by the Soviets. Heng Samrin was propped up by the force of the Vietnamese arms and would fall if Vietnam withdrew its forces from Cambodia. Vietnam would not withdraw its forces from Cambodia unless pressured to do so. China's pressure obviously proved insufficient. As the Soviet Union provided economic and military aid to Hanoi, it had the necessary levers to make Vietnam pull out of Cambodia and so resolve the Cambodian problem and, with it, China's daunting security dilemma in Indochina. This was how Cambodia became an obstacle to Sino-Soviet normalization.

Neither the crisis in Sino-American relations between 1981 and 1982 nor the beginning of talks with the Soviets resulted in China's strategic reorientation or a change of position on the Vietnam problem. Deng continued to insist that the Soviets should "make" Vietnam pull out from Cambodia. Deng Xiaoping continued to cling to strategic concepts from the late 1970s, which assumed a Soviet intention to control the Malacca Straits and all of Southeast Asia. This perception began to change in the mid-1980s.

By the time Gorbachev assumed power in the USSR, there had been no movement on the three obstacles; on Cambodia, the stated policy was that

Sino-Soviet normalization must not "harm" the interests of third parties (i.e., Vietnam and Cambodia—both Soviet allies).[11] When Gromyko brought up the issue at a Politburo meeting on May 31, 1983, Andropov refused to discuss it. Hardliner Dmitrii Ustinov added his opinion, in predictably stark quasi-imperial terms: "we have talked about Kampuchea [Cambodia] and Vietnam more than once. I suppose we should not lose the bridgeheads [sic] won in these battles; we should maintain the positions we have taken there."[12] It was hard to expect much Soviet movement on the Cambodian problem because the Soviet leaders were exceptionally reluctant to pressure Hanoi. This would surely upset the fragile Soviet-Vietnamese alliance and one could not be sure that the Vietnamese would pull out from Cambodia even under Soviet pressure.

Gorbachev's rise to power did not dissuade Deng Xiaoping from dropping the obstacle. In fact, in 1985 he returned to it time and again, even though he downplayed the other two obstacles, militarization of the Sino-Soviet border and the Soviet occupation of Afghanistan. However, this is not to say that his position was completely inflexible. In April 1985, for instance, Deng offered incentives to Moscow, telling a Belgian correspondent that the Soviets "can still maintain its relations with Vietnam and can still obtain bases provided by Vietnam."[13]

Deng's offer to the Soviets to stay at Cam Ranh Bay was indicative of the changes in his strategic outlook, increasingly evident from the mid-1980s. The subtle process of Sino-Soviet normalization had already made an impact on perceptions in both Moscow and Beijing, and the theory about Soviet encirclement of China that Deng had espoused just a few years earlier had begun to lose its edge. The problem was not so much that the Soviets acquired a strategic platform in Southeast Asia and menaced the Malacca Straits but that Vietnam's continued occupation of Cambodia created a source of instability on China's southern frontier and in the broader region. Therefore, while Deng continued to insist on the removal of the Cambodian obstacle, he was now much less concerned about potential Soviet encirclement of China and more about using improved Sino-Soviet relations as a lever to resolve one of China's most daunting regional security challenges. China's foreign policy was becoming "regionalized"—that is, China was exiting the Cold War.[14]

THE DRAG

Moscow continued to insist that it could not "make" Vietnam withdraw from Cambodia. In truth, the resolution of the Cambodian problem was in Vietnam's, not Soviet, hands. Vietnam was in a difficult situation. On the face of it, Hanoi had won in Cambodia: Pol Pot had been ousted, and Phnom Penh was in the hands of a loyal regime. China's "lesson" had been rebuffed. On the other hand, the Khmer Rouge and other opposition forces continued to harass the government forces on the border with Thailand. They stood no chance against the Vietnamese troops, but it was also exceptionally difficult for the government forces to rout and extinguish these isolated pockets of resistance, and constant skirmishes were a huge drain on Cambodia's and—by extension—on Vietnam's economy.

Then there were the Chinese. The enormous army sitting just north of Vietnam's border forced Vietnam to keep an army of its own at the border with the attendant economic costs for a country already on the brink of economic collapse. Vadim Medvedev, who was in Vietnam in December 1986 for the party congress, recalled the unspeakable poverty, runaway inflation, and lack of basic necessities even among the more affluent government officials. "In a conversation with us, the First Secretary of the Ho Chi Minh City's Party Committee said that he was compelled to breed pigs in his household in order to receive additional income."[15] Half the state budget went to defense-related tasks, and even as late as 1989 Vietnam's military expenditures exceeded the state's investment in the economy.[16] Witty Vietnamese joked that of Ho Chi Minh's famous statement—"There is nothing more valuable than freedom and independence"—only the first part was borne out by the situation in socialist Vietnam: "there is nothing."[17]

It was not the Cambodian problem that worried Gorbachev but the problem of Vietnam. His foremost concern was that billions of rubles in Soviet subsidies went into the bottomless pit of Vietnam's economy. Relatively early in his tenure Gorbachev registered his growing annoyance at Vietnam's chronic economic woes. Inasmuch as Vietnam's economic crisis was in part a function of the Cambodian problem and the need to maintain a huge army, starting Vietnam on the road of reforms indirectly contributed to Hanoi's willingness to leave Cambodia. The Chinese reinforced that the Soviets must "make" Hanoi leave Cambodia, the obvious lever being Soviet economic aid.

Even before Gorbachev, the Soviets sensed that their Vietnamese comrades were megalomaniacs, that their emphasis on the development of heavy industry was basically misplaced, and that they were wasting Soviet aid.[18] But, rather than curbing commitments, Moscow extended further aid to make the Vietnamese happy. In the 1980s the Soviet Union built a hydroelectric plant at Hoa Binh, with a projected power capacity five times greater than all available electricity produced in North Vietnam in 1979.[19]

Other Soviet contributions to Vietnam's great industrial future included Pha Lai Thermal Power station, the Bim Son cement factory, the Cao Son coal mine, the Ha Bac nitrogenous fertilizer factory, and the Thang Long bridge in Hanoi, which, the Vietnamese were keen to point out, had been left unfinished by China when relations soured.[20] All of these and dozens of other projects had cost the Soviet Union 16.4 billion rubles since 1955. Of that, as of 1990, 2.2 billion had been refinanced and 1.1 billion had been written off, while the remainder was never to be repaid.[21]

This heavy burden worried Gorbachev. Vietnam was a recurrent subject in the Politburo discussions. "It's upsetting that we spend so much, take it away from our own people, and there is no result," Gorbachev grumbled in June 1986. "One should look for approaches to encourage their development with their own forces. The main emphasis is the agrarian sector. The country is hungry and one should find clothes and shoes for millions [of people].... But [we] must not yield to their ambitions. And hammer their brains, against dependency."[22] A year later he was still complaining: "the Vietnamese comrades tried to build the heavy industry as quickly as possible. How many discussions and conversations have we had with them on this subject!"[23] In March 1987 he ordered to develop new concepts for Soviet-Vietnamese cooperation: "half the Politburo had been there—and then what? The Politburo has been 'vietnamized,' we are being pulled by their leash.... It's enough. Now, the stress should be on light industry and food processing."[24]

Was it that simple, just telling the Vietnamese enough is enough? Why didn't Gorbachev speak to the Vietnamese with greater resolve born of new thinking? One problem was inertia at every level. It was one thing to want Vietnam to reform and quite another to restructure the existing pattern of economic relations with the USSR. Not only did the Vietnamese resist reform but also the Soviet bureaucrats, and advisers in Indochina, who had grown accustomed to the status quo and did not like the smell of change.

The vast amplitude of Soviet views on the problem of Vietnam showed in a meeting Medvedev hosted at his department in April 1988. Participants included functionaries from the State Planning Committee (Gosplan) and the advisers' corps in Vietnam, the Ministry of Defense, the KGB, the Foreign Ministry, and academia. The Deputy Head of Gosplan, Petr Paskar, blamed the United States and China for the dreadful economic situation: the billions of dollars that used to come Vietnam's way were now nowhere to be found. Chief Adviser V. S. Orlov called for greater centralization of state resources and for a state monopoly on trade in rice and tobacco. A representative of the General Staff, V. A. Kharitonov, played up the Chinese threat and justified Vietnam's army expenditures. And Vladimir Kryuchkov of the

KGB ranted about the "imperialist ploys" in Indochina and the falling Soviet prestige. The academics, including Georgii Kim and Oleg Bogomolov, criticized Vietnam's failures and called for new approaches.[25]

Where, then, were Gorbachev's sympathies—with the military, the KGB, and the bureaucrats, or with the liberal academics? There is no easy answer. It is true that Gorbachev was concerned with Vietnam's wasteful economic practices; nay, he raved at the Politburo about the money ill-spent. But he was also keenly aware of the Soviet Union's strategic interests in Vietnam and Indochina, which could not be dispensed with lightly. Even when he criticized Vietnam at the Politburo, as on June 26, 1986, it was carefully framed: "Here is a problem: we cannot invest as much there as before, but we cannot abandon everything. After all, who knows how much more it would cost us if we lost [the Cam Ranh] military base there? We need them no less than they need us. . . . Vietnam can get away from us if we do not help them put into operation what we have begun to build for them."[26] If Gorbachev had tried forceful levers, if he had tried to pressure Vietnam by withholding aid, he would have risked Hanoi's wrath and the prospect of losing influence. China's own experience with Vietnam in the 1960s spoke to this.

Nothing illustrates Gorbachev's strategic thinking about Vietnam better than the problem of the Soviet withdrawal from the Cam Ranh naval base. This prospect was mentioned in Gorbachev's Vladivostok speech in 1986. But Gorbachev phrased his offer in such oblique terms that the prospects of it actually happening were slim at the outset: "I would like to say that if the United States gave up its military presence, say, in the Philippines, we would not leave this step unanswered."[27] This was simply a propaganda move.

But the idea of a Soviet withdrawal received support in unexpected quarters—in Hanoi. Gorbachev cornered himself: the Soviets had a base in Vietnam, ostensibly to protect a loyal ally from imperialist (and Chinese) ploys, but with time the Vietnamese grew weary of the Soviet military presence, which did not really square with the image of a fearless Vietnam, and they diplomatically hinted that they wanted the base closed. The problem was discussed by Mikhail Gorbachev and General Secretary Nguyen Van Linh on July 20, 1988. Medvedev, who was present at the meeting, recalled: "The Vietnamese leader spoke in favor of the Soviet proposal to eliminate our presence in Cam Ranh in exchange for the liquidation of US naval bases in the Philippines. But at the same time he let it be known that if such an exchange does not take place, they are prepared to solve this question without connecting it to the American bases in the Philippines."[28]

Medvedev suspected "Chinese-like" cunning on Nguyen's part: "when Gorbachev pointed out the undesirability of unilateral steps in this question, Nguyen Van Linh pretended that he was happy to hear that."[29] In the same month, the Vietnamese Foreign Ministry put out a carefully phrased feeler to the Russians about the possibility of a "unilateral statement" on Cam Ranh.[30] None of these tricks had much effect on Gorbachev. In September he readvertised his idea of the Philippines/Cam Ranh exchange in a speech in Krasnoyarsk, by which means he ostensibly intended "to put [the Americans] on the defensive, to force them to justify themselves before the world opinion."[31]

The Vietnamese resented Gorbachev's bargaining with the Americans at their expense; rumors had reached Gorbachev that his proposal was interpreted in Hanoi as an arrogant attempt to dispose of their country's territory as he liked. In a meeting with the Vietnamese Politburo member Vo Chi Cong on September 21, 1988, Gorbachev could but register his disbelief: "Has the Soviet Union ever had this kind of attitude towards Vietnam?" He went on to denounce the "many people in the world who would like to harm our relations" and pledged to maintain a full measure of Soviet support to his comrades in Hanoi.[32] The status of the Cam Ranh Base remained a source of tensions in bilateral relations, and the Soviet (and later Russian) presence was wound down and eventually eliminated, though not until 2002. Still, the base controversy reflected Gorbachev's keen awareness of Soviet strategic interests in Vietnam, which he wanted preserved even as the Vietnamese hinted that the Soviet presence was no longer necessary.

Gorbachev's policy toward Vietnam was much more sophisticated than his myth would allow: If there was new thinking, there was also a good deal of old thinking geared toward sustaining the client relationships of a truly global superpower. Raw figures illustrate this point: Soviet aid to Vietnam during the 12th Five-Year Plan (1986–90) amounted to 8.22 billion rubles, that is, a half of all of Soviet aid to Vietnam since 1955. To be sure, about two billion of this was spent on rescheduling Vietnam's previous debts, and another two billion on paying for "technical assistance," that is, conceivably Soviet projects in Vietnam, of which many were begun before Gorbachev. However, there was also a gratis category "special cooperation," that is, military aid, which cost the Soviet Union over 2 billion rubles between 1986 and 1990, as opposed to 1.8 billion rubles spent on the same between 1981 and 1985.[33]

The bottom line of Vietnamese reform was not that the Soviet Union induced Vietnam to reform, but that the desperate economic situation left the Vietnamese leadership with no other options. After a long period of hesitation, Hanoi embraced full-fledged economic reforms in 1988, and the results quickly appeared: inflation dropped to 7–8 percent in July 1988 from 18 percent at the start of the year. Agricultural production increased, thanks to government deregulation, which allowed farmers to keep a larger share of their harvest.[34] In 1988 Vietnam raked in a record harvest, enough to feed its own people and even export rice abroad.[35] In July 1988, for the first time in years, Nguyen Van Linh did not ask for emergency food aid from the Soviet Union.[36] Price liberalization brought goods to the empty shelves.[37]

Indeed, by 1989 Gorbachev was struggling to keep up with the pace and the depth of the Vietnamese reforms. He was at pains to find similarities between Hanoi's and his own economic policies, to link the Vietnamese *doi moi* (renovation) to the Soviet perestroika. For example, when Nguyen Van Linh told Gorbachev that his government substituted food tax for brutal food requisition—and that the policy was a great success—Gorbachev hurried to christen the policy *Lenin's prodnalog* (food tax) to show that it had been tried long ago in Russia. The minute Nguyen mentioned the development of the wholesale market in Vietnam, Gorbachev remarked that he had been doing the same in the Soviet Union. Just when Nguyen said that some in Vietnam were complaining that he was steering the country toward capitalism, Gorbachev replied that some people had said the same thing about him but that they were dogmatists lacking a "Leninist, creative understanding of socialism."[38]

The "Leninist, creative understanding of socialism" bore an imprint "made by Gorbachev," and the Soviet leader wanted to make sure that the Vietnamese gave him the credit for the success of *their* reforms. It was a point of pride. Recalling his feelings about the Vietnamese "miracle" years later, Gorbachev wrote: "Frankly speaking, I had a bitter, nagging sense of frustration—it turned out that the Vietnamese who lived half a world away from Moscow listened to my good advice and reached tangible results in their country, but our [officials] are so pig-headed—they keep talking, even agree, but the cartload of…problems remains where it was."[39]

Clearly Gorbachev felt bitter about Vietnam's reforms, but in large part because he envied their success amid his own persistent failures. The latter he explained by inept Soviet bureaucracy, the former by Vietnamese heeding his "good advice." In fact, Hanoi's reforms owed a great deal to observing the Southeast Asian experience, in particular, Thailand's policies.[40] Indeed, it was Vietnam's good fortune that it did not learn from the Soviet model. In the words of one high-ranking Vietnamese official, "the greatest benefit of perestroika was that they [the Vietnamese] no longer felt bound by the doctrines of Communist (i.e. Soviet) ideology. Vietnam … should decide by itself how it wanted to overcome its difficulties."[41]

What can one conclude from all of this? The Chinese wanted the Soviet Union to stop economic aid to Vietnam, thinking that without it, Vietnam would have to leave Cambodia. This was the meaning of the "obstacle" to Sino-Soviet normalization. Gorbachev, too, wanted to stop economic aid to Vietnam, because it was just too expensive. But doing so risked undesirable consequences for the Soviet geopolitical position. Vietnam might even be "lost," perhaps to China again. For this reason, Gorbachev hoped to induce Vietnam to reform its economy. Sure enough, by 1988 Vietnam embarked on the path of genuine economic reform. But this owed mainly to Hanoi's reappraisal of its endemic poverty and its performance vis-à-vis the relative prosperity and dynamism elsewhere in Southeast Asia.

OVERCOMING THE IMPASSE

If Gorbachev took an early, direct, and personal interest in curbing Soviet aid to Vietnam, the resolution of the Cambodian problem was for him a matter of lesser importance. Still, from the mid-1980s, the Soviets became increasingly impatient with the ongoing war in Cambodia, which harmed Soviet interests. For one, it was a financial burden. At a time when the Soviet Union underwrote the Vietnamese economy, the Vietnamese were sinking money into the Cambodian quagmire. And still Cambodia required aid; by early 1987 the Cambodian Prime Minister, Hun Sen, effectively admitted to the Soviets that his Vietnamese patrons were bankrupt, and appealed for direct subsidies, at a time when Gorbachev was at pains to work out a way to reduce Soviet aid to Vietnam.[42]

Second, Cambodia was of secondary—and diminishing—strategic importance to the USSR. In the late 1970s and early 1980s, when the Soviet Union and China were at each other's throats, Vietnam's adventures in Cambodia were like Moscow's second front, and even as late July 1987 Gorbachev (manifesting some of the same strategic thinking that underpinned his interest in maintaining military outposts in Indochina) was still concerned about what would happen if Vietnam pulled out from Cambodia: "the Chinese will turn up there [in Cambodia] three days after Vietnam leaves."[43] However, this rationale began to lose its importance with the gradual improvement in Sino-Soviet relations. Cambodia was already becoming a distraction from what really mattered to the Soviets: full rapprochement with China.

The negative impact of this "obstacle" was felt keenly by the Soviets in the latter part of 1986 from the sour Chinese reaction to Gorbachev's Vladivostok speech. The speech itself was full of positive comments on

Sino-Soviet relations, so the Soviets might have hoped for a more enthusiastic reply than Deng Xiaoping's cautious comment that he saw "something new" in the outreach.[44] The shortcoming was immediately identified by the Chinese: on August 13, 1986, Foreign Minister Wu Xueqian explained to the Soviet Charge d'affaires in Beijing, Vladimir Fedotov, that while the speech was "appreciated," "he regretted that Mr. Gorbachev had not mentioned Kampuchea." Recounting his frustration to the UN General Secretary some weeks later, Wu said that "if it did not do something more positive the Soviet Union could not expect to play a positive role in the Asian area."[45] The Soviet leadership was beginning to realize the truth of this statement, which was another reason to rethink their involvement with Vietnam and Cambodia.

Indeed, not only was it a supposed obstacle to normalization with China but also a blemish on Soviet relations with many other countries, in Asia and beyond. It certainly did not help Soviet relations with the ASEAN member states, which were very important for the Soviet great dash to the East. Gorbachev wishfully hoped the Soviet Union stood a chance there against a much more dynamic China and Japan: "why, the ASEAN countries also do not want to end up in the paws of China or Japan, they are reaching out to socialist countries which offer them a point of support, and this must be used."[46] Gorbachev also thought that the Soviets could fill the void left by imaginary US setbacks; in his words, some regional players "had enough of their [American] insolence and unceremoniousness.... No one wants to be a vassal and the countries there [in Southeast Asia] are moving in the right direction."[47]

Gorbachev was perhaps unduly optimistic about ASEAN moving in the Soviet direction. This talk did not square with the reality well summarized by *Christian Science Monitor* correspondent Geoffrey Murray: "the Soviet Union is being told bluntly in most ASEAN capitals that its diplomatic courtship doesn't stand a chance until Moscow exerts its influence to get Vietnam to the negotiating table for talks on Cambodian independence."[48] None was blunter than the self-proclaimed ASEAN spokesman, Indonesian Foreign Minister Mochtar Kusumaatmadja, who, in a meeting with Shevardnadze in September 1986, argued that "something would have to be done to facilitate a solution for Kampuchea, if it [the Soviet Union] really wanted good relations with ASEAN." According to Mochtar, he would himself remain "skeptical" of Gorbachev's Vladivostok speech until the three Chinese "obstacles" were overcome, of which Mochtar singled out Cambodia as the key obstacle. Shevardnadze reportedly "listened without denying or protesting."[49]

Cambodia was not one of the main problems of Soviet-American relations, but even here Gorbachev could well do without Ronald Reagan's lectures about how Vietnam "now rules Cambodia" and how "we should put an end to this and together supervise establishment of a government chosen by the Cambodian people."[50] When Gorbachev asked the French Premier, Jacques Chirac, why there was a "surge of anti-Sovietism" in France, Chirac listed Cambodia alongside Afghanistan. "Of course, it is understandable that Cambodia is not one of the Soviet Union's problems. Rather, it is Vietnam's problem. But you must know about historical and, I would say even more, sentimental relations between France and Cambodia. Therefore, the 'Cambodian affair' was very poorly received in France."[51] The Cambodian problem repeatedly popped up—sometimes predictably, sometimes unexpectedly—at different points in Soviet policy making.

Given that Gorbachev did not need a war in Cambodia, why did he not simply tell the Vietnamese enough is enough? This was a question Teimuraz Stepanov-Mamaladze, Foreign Minister Shevardnadze's aide, was asking himself in March 1987, when his boss embarked upon the first-ever (for a Soviet foreign minister) tour of the Pacific and Southeast Asia, itself a telling indication of how far the Soviets had gone down the road of reappraising Asia's global importance. After visiting Thailand, Indonesia, and Australia (where the Soviets heard endless complaints about Vietnam's occupation of Cambodia), and after seeing first-hand the devastation in Indochina, Stepanov was probably not the only man to think, "The logic is elementary. If we feed and clothe Vietnam, then it must obey us. And if it obeys us, why can't we tell it: leave Cambodia?"[52]

Added Stepanov: "It turns out, we can't. It turns out, it does not obey us that much after all. It turns out that our aid does not weigh so much on the scales of its security." So, Shevardnadze had to play a skillful game, prodding the Vietnamese toward a solution, but gently. Igor Rogachev, top Soviet expert on the Far East, called this "flogging" the Vietnamese "without having them lower their pants." But this was perhaps too generous an assessment of Shevardnadze's performance. His key argument was to draw a parallel between Cambodia and Afghanistan and urge the Vietnamese to bring about "national reconciliation" in the former, much as the Soviets had tried to do in the latter. This meant a dialogue with the opposition, including the Khmer Rouge. The Vietnamese were noncommittal. They talked about "a long struggle" ahead, paid for with Soviet economic aid, to which the Vietnamese comrades felt completely entitled as a Soviet "platform" in Asia.[53]

The Vietnamese were courteous but inscrutable. "Pham Van Dong is sitting in front of me with an absent appearance," wrote Stepanov-Mamaladze of the long-time Vietnamese Prime Minister who had served a pro-Soviet

Vietnam every bit as well as he had earlier served a pro-Chinese Vietnam. "One cannot see the expression of his eyes behind the dark glasses. Lips are extended in a stern thread. Perhaps, he sees a revisionist in E.A. [Shevardnadze] and regrets that he can't kill him?" No direct threats were made. Indirectly, the Soviets sensed a message: insufficient Soviet attention could lead the Vietnamese to look elsewhere for support. Where elsewhere—China? Or ASEAN? Or perhaps the so-called triangle of "three I's"—Indochina (meaning Vietnam, Cambodia, and Laos), Indonesia, and India—which the harebrained strategists in Hanoi unsuccessfully labored to bring about. If the Vietnamese thought the world was dying to save their ruined economy from collapse, they were unduly optimistic. But the Soviets took the threat seriously, which was why neither Shevardnadze nor, indeed, Gorbachev, could directly tell Hanoi to leave Cambodia.[54]

Fortunately, the Soviet cause was not hopeless—Vietnam's decision makers gradually realized that the war had to be brought to an end. It took time before such thinking became mainstream: Vietnam had more than its fair share of diehard generals and the party orthodox. But, the party was undergoing a generational change: the old guard was dying, critically Le Duan, who had been the Party's General Secretary since the 1950s. Slots were being opened for the likes of Nguyen Van Linh, the reform-oriented General Secretary of the party, and Nguyen Co Thach, the Foreign Minister, who believed that "Vietnam's economic crisis could not be solved without improving Hanoi's relations with the Western countries and China."[55]

The military dragged their feet, personified by the Minister of Defense, Van Tien Dung, who had directed the 1978 invasion of Cambodia and was least inclined to cooperate with China.[56] But in 1986 Dung was sent into retirement, as a part of the leadership shake-up. It was becoming obvious that the war was being lost, even as Hanoi made claims of ever greater successes in the struggle against the rebels, predicting impending marginalization of Pol Pot.[57] By the time Shevardnadze arrived in Hanoi to flog the Vietnamese, they realized, according to a contemporary assessment of Anatolii Dryukov (a Soviet expert on Southeast Asia and Ambassador to India), that they had been "trapped" in Cambodia: "they are thinking how to leave with minimal losses."[58]

There was more to Hanoi's foreign policy than met the eye. The Vietnamese were probing the Americans, the Japanese, and their ASEAN neighbors (especially Indonesia) to break out of diplomatic isolation.[59] When Indonesia's Foreign Minister, Mochtar Kusumaatmadja, visited Hanoi in March 1985, he was struck to find not only Nguyen Co Thach but even Pham Van Dong very receptive to the idea of inviting the United States back into the region as means to counterbalance both the Soviets and the Chinese.

Pham Van Dong told Mochtar that if his concept of "strategic balancing" could be achieved, it would be a "turning point in the history of Southeast Asia." The next month, as a signal to the United States, the Vietnamese released Bill Mathers, a US yachtsman who had been detained in Vietnam for months for having violated Vietnam's territorial waters. Clearly, policy makers like Nguyen Co Thach were hoping that by improving relations with the United States and its allies, Vietnam would not only escape international isolation but also lessen its political and economic reliance on the USSR. When Mochtar told Thach that Vietnam's alliance with the USSR was "not leading anywhere" while China was "building its economy," the latter reportedly replied that "Vietnam had no choice in this regard."[60] In fact, though, as Thach and like-minded thinkers in the Vietnamese leadership realized, there was a choice: to develop broader regional engagement.

Cambodia remained the sticking point. The Vietnamese increasingly pinned their hopes on Prince Sihanouk: if only the monarch could be brought around to break with the Khmer Rouge, it would be much more difficult for China and ASEAN to insist on including Pol Pot or his followers in any kind of a coalition government. Phnom Penh, with the Vietnamese approval, probed Sihanouk through the French. Initially, the prince agreed to talk, saying that he was a "man of dialogue."[61] But when Cambodia's Foreign Minister, Hun Sen, tried to secretly meet with the Prince in Paris in December 1984, Sihanouk refused to see Phnom Penh's envoy and leaked the story to the media.[62] The Vietnamese blamed China for ruining the probe but vowed to continue their work with Sihanouk, hoping to entice him into meeting with a representative of the Phnom Penh government.[63]

Pol Pot's participation in the settlement remained the stumbling block. Vietnam was vehemently opposed to his involvement and refused to recognize the Khmer Rouge as negotiating partners. Failing to lure Sihanouk away from the "forest people," Hanoi conceded an important point: in November 1986 the Prince was told, through the Austrians, that the Khmer Rouge would be acceptable to Vietnam but without Pol Pot. The Prince leaked the news and the Vietnamese publicly disclaimed this. An opportunity for negotiation was squandered in part because Sihanouk wanted to negotiate directly with Vietnam, not with the Phnom Penh regime. That was unacceptable to the Vietnamese, who argued that they were not party to the Cambodian problem.[64]

The Vietnamese offer was allegedly renewed in January 1987, through the Romanians. Prince Sihanouk, after his talks with Romania's leader, Nicolae Ceauşescu, claimed that Vietnam offered for the four factions—including the Khmer Rouge—to negotiate a peace settlement. The Prince refused and the Vietnamese denounced the rumor as a "Western fabrication."[65] There is no doubt that something was going on below the surface of public statements. By July 1987, evidence shows, Phnom Penh (and so the Vietnamese) favored peace talks over military action and agreed to the participation of the Khmer Rouge. Such was the Soviet impression after talks with the Vietnamese and the Cambodians in late spring and early summer of 1987.

Of the two Cambodian leaders, Heng Samrin impressed the Soviets the least. Medvedev, who met him for the first time in December 1986, remembered him as a "very narrow-minded, dependent and even spineless person" who repeated diehard formulations "framed exclusively by the struggle against the Polpotists and the necessity of pushing them out of the country."[66] Discussions with Hun Sen turned out much better. In a meeting with Shevardnadze and Medvedev on July 1, 1987, he signaled Cambodia's readiness for peace talks: "Despite our military advantages, we cannot win the war with our own forces for the opponent receives support from China, USA, Thailand. But the enemy also cannot destroy our rule by military means. Therefore, the Cambodian problem can be solved only by political means."[67]

Then Hun Sen outlined Phnom Penh's position on the Khmer Rouge. In words borrowed from Gorbachev's vocabulary, and certainly designed to emphasize similarities between the Cambodian problem and Afghanistan, the Prime Minister spoke of "national reconciliation" in Cambodia and his readiness to talk to the Khmer Rouge, but without "Pol Pot and his closest followers."[68] Pieces of this platform leaked into the public domain over the next two months in the form of hints in the Soviet media and leaks from "Eastern European sources" before Phnom Penh officially launched the policy of "national reconciliation" on August 27, 1987.[69] These developments were unfolding amid persistent rumors that Pol Pot was seriously ill, even that he had cancer and had less than a year to live.[70] Although such rumors were inaccurate, they underscored Pol Pot's gradual marginalization and his growing irrelevance to the Cambodian settlement.

Finally, China, a long-time supporter of Pol Pot, signaled a policy change. On May 11, 1987, in a conversation with the UN Secretary General, Javier Pérez de Cuéllar, Deng Xiaoping said that any future coalition government "should not be based on one faction alone. The Pol Pot forces should be only one part of a future government, headed by Sihanouk. China will not support a government headed by Pol Pot, but rather one led by Sihanouk."[71] Deng probably expected Pérez de Cuéllar to pass on this signal to the Soviet Union and their allies in Indochina. Whether through Pérez de Cuéllar or by other means, Moscow learned of the content of the Chinese proposals.

According to the Soviet records, Deng told Pérez de Cuéllar that he was firmly against Pol Pot's participation in the talks, much less the coalition government, and the same went for his brother-in-law, Ieng Sary. In their place the Chinese patriarch supported Pol Pot's former Head of State Khieu Samphan, a leftist intellectual and a "moderate" Khmer Rouge of long standing.[72]

Beijing's willingness to dump Brother Number One did not result from Deng Xiaoping's belated realization of Pol Pot's horrendous crimes; Deng only said that Pol Pot "made many mistakes, by no means small ones."[73] The bottom line was that with Vietnam putting Sihanouk under pressure to negotiate, the rebels' tripartite coalition, weakened by internal disagreements and in-fighting, could crumble any day. This would leave China on the sidelines of the Cambodian settlement. Deng Xiaoping did not want to lose Sihanouk. The Prince had called China his "second motherland" but he was famously unpredictable. Keeping him happy required some maneuvering, including China's concessions on the setup of the eventual coalition government. By the spring of 1987 the sights of great powers tied up in the Cambodian knot were all on the intentions and actions of the maverick Prince.

STRUGGLE FOR SIHANOUK'S SOUL

It was difficult to fathom what Sihanouk had on his mind. There were indications in unlikely places, like *Playboy* magazine. The May 1987 issue featured a lengthy interview with the Prince, in which he recounted his dreams: "[S]ometimes I see the Vietnamese. They come in a car, a luxury car. And I am standing there, half dressed, with bare chest, bare feet. And the Vietnamese, they come and say to me, 'Please come with us.' I say, 'I cannot go outside my house; I have no clothes. I have just a sarong around my waist.'"

Sihanouk said that he felt like a naked man, a king who had lost his kingdom. How could he be friends with the Vietnamese unless his lost kingdom were restored to him, unless the Vietnamese were willing to give him more than a figurehead position in the Heng Samrin regime? Was this Sihanouk's message for those who could read between the lines? For everyone else he presented an uncompromising façade: "I know that China and Thailand fear that I could change sides. But no, I am a man of loyalty."[74]

By mid-1987 it seemed that Vietnam's efforts to woo Sihanouk were beginning to pay off. That May the Prince announced from Pyongyang that he would resign as the head of the coalition to protest the Khmer Rouge attacks on his forces in Cambodia. The move had a bombshell effect on regional players. The Thais and others in ASEAN were alarmed that Sihanouk's moves "could shake the delicate alliance against Hanoi and complicate efforts to draw Vietnamese into talks."[75] The Indonesians were so concerned with Sihanouk's "fatal" decision to "go it alone" that Mochtar flew to Pyongyang in July to dissuade the Prince from meeting with Hun Sen, because being drawn over to Phnom Penh's side "would not lead to a durable solution."[76] The Chinese were privately exasperated, seeing that "there was no sign that either the Soviets or Vietnamese were relaxing their efforts."[77] Although Sihanouk was not entirely persuaded by all this commotion, he did stay on as the head of the coalition. Even the most informed observers were unsure what the Prince had on his mind, though many would have agreed with the Indian Foreign Secretary, K. Natwar Singh, who commented, after his own meeting with Sihanouk on October 5, that he "had a lot of balls in the air."[78]

Unquestionably, for much of 1987 Prince Sihanouk drifted in the direction of talks with the Phnom Penh regime despite the best efforts of his coalition partners—the Khmer Rouge—to ruin his personal diplomacy. On the other hand, there was reciprocal movement from both Cambodia and Vietnam. Both sides were making compromises. Some of the biggest concessions came from Phnom Penh in the form of a five-point statement issued on October 8, a fresh call for four-party talks including the Khmer Rouge (but excluding Pol Pot), and an offer for Sihanouk to take "a high position in the leading state organ." Perhaps of greatest significance was Phnom Penh's willingness to hold elections with UN observers, organize a coalition government, and "build a peaceful, independent, democratic, neutral and non-aligned Cambodia, maintaining friendly relations with neighboring countries and all countries the world over." The last formulation was an explicit olive branch to China and ASEAN and a sign of Cambodia moving away from the Vietnam-centered regional order.[79]

On November 26, 1987, Barbara Crossette of the *New York Times* reported from Phnom Penh that "according to foreign residents in this isolated capital...the Soviet Union has apparently played a major role in persuading Cambodia's Communist leaders to begin negotiating with Prince Norodom Sihanouk."[80] This was easy to believe; it squared well with Gorbachev's emphasis on broad engagement and international dialogue. In fact, such speculations were misleading. The Soviet Union was not interested in perpetuating the Cambodian conflict and therefore consistently supported a peace settlement. But Cambodia and Vietnam needed that peace settlement even more than their Soviet comrades. For this reason they had danced rounds with Sihanouk for months on end, enticing him to break with the Khmer Rouge.

To the extent that great powers were important to the Cambodian settlement, it was less through their action than through their inaction. China played a more significant role in this respect than the Soviet Union because of its leverage with Sihanouk. Even so, Li Peng called him "contradictory" and a "strong personality," meaning that he was stubborn and unpredictable.[81] Early contacts between the Prince and Hun Sen failed partly because of China's pressure. However, by the fall of 1987 there was a noticeable change in Beijing's position. The Chinese leaders appeared resigned to a meeting between Sihanouk and representatives of the ruling regime. Foreign Minister Wu Xueqian declared that the Prince would "know what was best" for the Cambodian people. Prominent Austrian politician Leopold Gratz, who was heavily involved in the Cambodian settlement, speculated that such flexibility showed "Beijing was perhaps afraid that Prince Sihanouk would suddenly appear in Phnom Penh."[82] He was probably right, though a bigger change was under way. The Chinese policy makers were increasingly less concerned with dealing a strategic blow to the Vietnam-Soviet alliance and more with solving the Cambodian problem.

Hanoi first announced that it was prepared to withdraw forces as early as 1985. That April, Nguyen Co Thach told *Le Monde* that two thirds of Vietnamese troops would be withdrawn from Cambodia by 1990, with the remainder leaving by 1995 irrespective of the political settlement.[83] In August 1985 a specific date was announced: by 1990 all Vietnamese troops would leave unless someone took advantage of the pullout to "undermine the peace and security of Kampuchea."[84] Commentators in China and in the West were quick to dismiss these pronouncements as ploys and propaganda. Vietnam's limited troop withdrawals were said to be regular rotations. There was no way to verify Hanoi's claims in any case. For a time there was probably more propaganda than substance to Vietnam's moves—that is, until the political stalemate in Hanoi was resolved in 1987 in favor of the reformers.

But from 1987 this kind of counter-propaganda became more difficult to square with what appeared to be Vietnam's genuine withdrawals and a clear intention to adhere to the 1990 deadline. In November 1987 Vietnam not only pulled 20,000 troops from Cambodia (the largest single withdrawal since the beginning of the occupation) but invited foreign observers to see for themselves that the troops actually left.[85] The Thai military soon confirmed that the Vietnamese troops had been leaving their positions.[86] The United States agreed that the pullout was for real.[87] By the spring of 1988 Western diplomats in the region had come around to believing that "Vietnam has now embarked on a genuine time-table to pull out of Cambodia by its promised deadline of 1990."[88]

On May 25, 1988, Vietnam announced yet another major cut: 50,000 troops, half of the original deployment, would leave Cambodia in 1988. The remaining forces would leave by the end of 1990. Vietnam's initiatives "pull[ed] the rug from under their [Chinese] feet," commented one Asian diplomat.[89] The Vietnamese intended to solve the problem of their presence in Cambodia on their own schedule, ruling out outside involvement. Shevardnadze explained this much to his US counterpart, George Shultz: "As for Vietnam, its course was clear. By 1990 it would have withdrawn its troops. The process was already underway; a substantial number was already out. The Vietnamese had their own plan. There was no reason for anyone else to interfere."[90] The Americans concurred. Cambodia was no longer a stumbling block in Soviet-US relations. It was barely even mentioned at the Gorbachev-Reagan summit in May 1988.[91] To keep the initiative in their hands, the Vietnamese privately informed Beijing and Moscow in July 1988 that they would complete their withdrawal by late 1989 or early 1990.[92]

In the meantime, the internal Cambodian dialogue was edging forward, though very, very painfully. In December 1987 Sihanouk and Hun Sen held their first series of meetings at a small French village sixty-five miles from Paris. Hun Sen offered Sihanouk a "high position" in the Cambodian government. The Prince refused. He was more interested in a dialogue with Moscow or Hanoi, suggesting to Hun Sen, with characteristic self-importance, that he wanted to negotiate with Soviet or Vietnamese "high figures," and not anywhere but "at [his] residence" in France.[93] For the time being, the Prince fell short of this ambition, although, after talks with Hun Sen, at least he received a letter from Pham Van Dong with such assurances of "des sentiments d'amitié" for "Samdech respecté," the Princess, and their "honorable famille" that one could think few people in the world treasured the Prince more than the Vietnamese communist leadership.[94]

Several weeks later Hun Sen and Sihanouk met once more, with the latter's coalition partners again boycotting the talks. The second round went no further than the first: Sihanouk insisted on self-liquidation of the Phnom Penh regime *before* national elections were held. He wanted it replaced with a quadripartite coalition government. An international peace keeping force would monitor Vietnam's complete withdrawal. Hun Sen, for his part, vetoed all these demands.[95]

China took an officially polite line on the Sihanouk–Hun Sen talks, but acidic Chinese news commentaries left no doubt that Beijing would rather the talks fail than risk the prospect of Sihanouk being lured into Phnom Penh on unsatisfactory terms. Qian Qichen spelled out China's terms to Soviet Ambassador Oleg Troyanovskii just as the first round of Sihanouk–Hun Sen talks wound up in Paris: "There is a very important point that must be emphasized. It is useless to look for a solution on the basis of Heng Samrin's government."[96] Later, Qian, presumably on the basis of what the Chinese heard first-hand from Sihanouk, recounted that Hun Sen "would record their conversations during the day, review the recordings in the evening in the company of his Vietnamese and Soviet partners and decide with their advice what to say to Sihanouk on the following day." According to Qian Qichen, Sihanouk had found those meetings "meaningless."[97] Whether or not this conspiracy theory had any basis in reality, the Chinese thought so and insisted on Vietnam's direct involvement in the talks.

For their part, the Soviets were annoyed and bewildered by Sihanouk's unpredictable maneuvers at the talks with Hun Sen. Deputy Foreign Minister Yulii Vorontsov speculated in February 1988 that "Sihanouk . . . might be making some fancy dance steps to satisfy the Chinese." In any case, "the Soviets were very hopeful about the process and were encouraging it in every way." Asked whether the Soviets tried to take up the matter with the Chinese, Vorontsov responded that they did but that the "discussion . . . had not been very productive. The Soviets understood that internally within the leadership, the Chinese had a more progressive view and were moving away from the old clichés."[98] Interestingly, the Russians at this stage had much more energetic discussions of the Cambodian situation with the Americans than with the Chinese. Of course, both the Soviet Union and the United States were much further away from Cambodia's borders than was China; for them, Cambodia was a small backward country that really did not matter in the greater scheme of things at the time of improving Soviet-American relations. For the Chinese, however, Cambodia was a factor in the regional power struggle, and so it is not surprising that their "old clichés" died slowly. Old clichés for Gorbachev were daily realities for Deng Xiaoping.

The search for Cambodian settlement continued through the spring and summer of 1988. Sihanouk blew hot and cold, to the astonishment of other players. In January he resigned once again "permanently, irrevocably and irreversibly" as the President of the opposition forces but changed his mind a month later in response to pleas from the Chinese, ASEAN, and his coalition partners, Son Sann and Khieu Samphan. Sihanouk's game plan was probably to get the Vietnamese to talk to him directly. There were rumors that a meeting was being planned in Japan; the Japanese even agreed to refurbish the Cambodian Embassy in Tokyo in order to host Sihanouk and his Vietnamese guests. But nothing ever came of these rumors. Instead, the Vietnamese agreed to meet with the Cambodian factions within the framework of a "cocktail party."

The idea of a cocktail party was floated by the Indonesians in July 1987. It entailed an informal meeting of the four Cambodian factions, with Vietnam joining the cocktails at an ill-defined second stage. The idea met with cool reception among most of ASEAN's policy makers, especially the Thais, who were "nervous and upset" about Mochtar's creativity, for it went a long way to legitimizing the government in Phnom Penh.[99] The Chinese were also not happy. It was eventually agreed that a "cocktail party" could proceed only if the Vietnamese agreed to join it immediately after the initial meeting of the four rival factions (they did). The meeting was postponed, in part because Sihanouk's wife had told the Prince that as the "father of the nation," he should not meet with other Cambodian parties in Jakarta on an equal footing.[100] But when Sihanouk's meeting with Hun Sen in Paris led nowhere, and when other parties reached the end of the road, the idea was revived.

At the last moment, however, Sihanouk surprised the world by suddenly resigning—yet again—as the head of the coalition and announcing that he would go into exile in France.[101] By that point no one knew what to make of Sihanouk's erratic behavior; the Thai Prime Minister summed up the feelings of many when he said that he was "fed up" with the Prince.[102] The cocktail party talks opened on July 25 at the green mountain resort of Bogor, near Jakarta. Sihanouk could not resist leaving his exile in France to witness the occasion. He was not a participant in the talks but stayed in Jakarta as a private guest of President Suharto.

As the Cambodian rivals drank cocktails at Bogor, other regional and global players engaged in frantic diplomacy to encourage a settlement. None were more important than China and Vietnam; their rivalry, after all, underpinned the Cambodian conflict. The Chinese relaxed their otherwise inflexible terms on Cambodia; they no longer required a full Vietnamese withdrawal before the establishment of a coalition government in Phnom Penh. Both processes could now develop side by side. It also transpired that the Chinese offered asylum to Pol Pot and his associates, although this rumor was promptly dismissed in Beijing as a fabrication. But, as Don Oberdorfer perceptively remarked in the *Washington Post*, Beijing's overtures "suggested for the first time that China ... is now more interested in ending the long war than in continuing its campaign to 'bleed Vietnam.'"[103] There were reciprocal moves from Vietnam, too. Hanoi announced ahead of the talks that the Vietnamese forces would be withdrawn from Cambodia by early 1990, some months before the original deadline of the end of the year.[104]

In the meantime, the Vietnamese appealed directly to China in an effort to mend fences. The change in attitude began to register in the first half of 1988. In late 1987 the Vietnamese still denounced China, even though such intransigence was by then out of line with Soviet policy. At a regular meeting of socialist diplomats in Beijing on November 10, the First Secretary of the Vietnamese Embassy hammered home the point: "While Deng Xiaoping is alive, Sino-Vietnamese relations will not improve in any case." He was even reprimanded by his Soviet colleague: "Comrade, you are exaggerating. You are talking too tough."[105] But only a few weeks later, on December 30, the Vietnamese Ambassador in Beijing called on Deputy Foreign Minister Liu Shuqing to tell him of Hanoi's interest in ending mutual propaganda and border skirmishes and promoting trade and people-to-people contacts in the Sino-Vietnamese border area.[106]

Keith B. Richburg of the the *Washington Post's* Southeast Asia Bureau, who was in Vietnam on an assignment in early July, heard Vietnamese officials make more open-minded and positive comments about China than the sorry state of Sino-Vietnamese relations would allow. Struggle against Chinese "hegemonism" was nowhere mentioned. The head of the China desk at the Foreign Ministry, Ngo Tat To, endorsed normalization with China in order to "restore our historic solidarity." Gen. Tran Cong Man, editor of the army newspaper *Quan Doi Nhan Dan*, said that the Vietnamese had already begun reducing troops on the border with China. Deputy Minister of Agriculture Nguyen Van Phuoc praised China's reforms and went as far as to say that "We don't consider China as an enemy. We can learn many good things from China."[107]

On July 19, 1988, Foreign Minister Nguyen Co Thach summoned the Chinese Ambassador, Li Shichun, supposedly to tell him about Vietnam's decision to withdraw troops from Cambodia by late 1989 or early 1990.[108] In reality the meeting was an opportunity for Nguyen to explain the essence of Vietnam's new policy toward China. As Nguyen Van Linh recounted a day later in a meeting with Gorbachev, Li Shichun was told that "the leadership of Vietnam considers it necessary to turn to normalization of Vietnamese-Chinese relations. It is China's fault in that these relations have soured, but it is also because of Vietnam's miscalculations, its insufficient flexibility."[109] Nguyen Van Linh said that the Chinese ambassador immediately left Vietnam to report to his superiors but that the Vietnamese had not yet heard anything of China's reaction. "In any case," Nguyen summed up, "we extended our hand to China, we are keeping it extended and we are prepared to wait for a reciprocal step on China's part."[110]

It was a long wait for Vietnam. Sino-Vietnamese relations continued to stagnate in 1988 despite Hanoi's positive attitude. In addition to Cambodia, other irritants worsened prospects for rapprochement, including the intractable territorial dispute over the Spratly Islands in the South China Sea. In March 1988 the Chinese and the Vietnamese navies fought a battle in the vicinity of one of the reefs, causing a fresh crisis in the already over-burdened relationship. Because of improving Sino-Soviet relations, Beijing counted on Moscow's benevolent neutrality, citing the Soviet territorial dispute with Japan as an example where the USSR, like China, refused to negotiate. But the Soviets dismissed the parallel and called for Sino-Vietnamese talks.[111] Indeed, unlike the case of Vietnam's occupation of Cambodia, in the territorial dispute with China, Vietnam was seen as more of a victim than as an aggressor not only by the Soviets but also by Vietnam's neighbors, who had their own problems with China's claims in the South China Sea. As the Malaysian Prime Minister, Mahathir Mohammed, put it, "the best approach to solving the problem was not to shoot at each other but to negotiate."[112] By the end of the year Beijing's refusal to talk to Vietnam risked alienating China's friends in ASEAN, leaving China on the sidelines of the Cambodian settlement and eroding some of the regional support Deng had been able to marshal over the previous decade.

By 1989 China was already far behind some of Vietnam's most stalwart ASEAN opponents, including Thailand. The new Thai Prime Minister, Chatichai Choonhavan, impressed by the views of Thai businessmen who sought new opportunities for economic cooperation with reforming Vietnam, proclaimed his readiness to turn the battlefields of Indochina into a "marketplace" in August 1988. Vietnam's foreign investment legislation made it particularly attractive for eager investors from Bangkok to bring their cash to ostensibly communist countries.[113] Politics followed economics: that very month, Nguyen Co Thach met with Choonhavan, and between January 9 and 12, 1989, the Thai Foreign Minister led a ninety-person delegation to Hanoi (including a cohort of businessmen), resulting in a "greater meeting of minds" between the former enemies, according to a confidential Thai assessment.[114]

The significance of these developments was not lost on Beijing. At last, on January 16, 1989, the Sino-Vietnamese dialogue got off to a promising start when the Vietnamese Deputy Foreign Minister, Dinh Nho Liem, held talks with his counterpart, Liu Shuqing (and, briefly, with Qian Qichen), which the Chinese later privately characterized as "having been good and very constructive."[115] Although Deng Xiaoping still complained bitterly about his unwillingness to trust the Vietnamese, relations gradually improved over the following months, especially after socialist regimes began to tumble in Eastern Europe and Soviet reforms assumed a more menacing form. Soon, the Chinese and Vietnamese policy makers began to see that they had a lot in common, and, for all the lingering mistrust, the two sides mended fences.

Improving Sino-Soviet relations became an important factor in the eventual Sino-Vietnamese normalization. But it was not the only factor, or even the defining factor. What made the real difference was that Hanoi was anxious to normalize relations with China and took calculated steps to defuse tensions. Gorbachev helped, of course, but it would be simplistic to give Gorbachev, or the Soviet Union, credit for the end of the Cold War in Southeast Asia. The process was much more sophisticated and multilayered than that. It was ultimately—and properly—a Southeast Asian game.

QIAN QICHEN IN MOSCOW

The cocktail party—or Jakarta Informal Meeting—held from July 24–28, 1988, did not result in a breakthrough. Sihanouk wanted a quadripartite government put in place of the Heng Samrin regime—with four ministers in each government post—and only then to organize the general elections. Hun Sen resisted demands to have his government prematurely dismantled. Khieu Samphan of the Khmer Rouge lambasted the Vietnamese for holding on to Cambodia and demanded complete withdrawal before any progress. Son Sann found himself a middleman: "They don't agree on anything yet, so why put them together?"[116] While no progress was achieved, the rivals at least agreed to continue discussions at another round of talks while Hun Sen made a separate arrangement for a meeting with Sihanouk in Paris in October 1988. All things considered, Phnom Penh had reasons to be satisfied with the cocktail party. It had won the right to talk directly to the other three factions, and that alone went a long way toward endowing the Heng Samrin regime with badly needed international legitimacy.

A month after the end of the first round of the cocktail party talks, on August 27, 1988, China's Deputy Foreign Minister, Tian Zengpei, hosted his Soviet counterpart, Igor Rogachev, for a round of special talks on the Cambodian problem. The announcement of the meeting stirred up a lot of excitement in the international media. For the first time the Soviet Union had agreed to discuss a solution to the problem with the Chinese; if a solution were found, the clients would have to fall in line, or so it was thought. "Meeting of the masters," the *Economist* called it.[117]

The meeting was held in strict secrecy. Foreign Minister Qian Qichen would only say that the two sides "reached a certain confidential understanding," occasioned by the "loosening" of the Soviet position.[118] He exaggerated. They only agreed about the desirability of Vietnam's pullout from Cambodia—by then even Vietnam deemed it desirable. They could not agree about the outline of the political settlement or about the schedule of Vietnamese withdrawal. The Chinese, making the parallel with the nine-month schedule of the Soviet withdrawal from Afghanistan, then under way, insisted on getting the Vietnamese out in nine months, or by the end of June 1989. The Soviets went as far as to propose a deadline of the end of 1989, which partially overlapped with what the Vietnamese said they would do.[119]

By the fall of 1988 the Chinese found themselves in a difficult position. The logic of Sino-Soviet normalization required expansion of contacts at the senior level, which meant the exchange of foreign ministers. Could this really happen while the Vietnamese forces still occupied Cambodia? There were signs of China backing down when, in late September 1988, Foreign Minister Qian Qichen announced his forthcoming visit to Moscow, the first such visit since Sino-Soviet foreign minister exchanges stopped in the late 1950s. The meeting was widely expected to result in the agreement on the final summit between Gorbachev and Deng Xiaoping—the symbolic endpoint of normalization. "After years of showing caution and even coolness toward the idea of a Sino-Soviet summit," reported the *Washington Post*, "the Chinese now appear to be the ones who are forcing the pace."[120]

Qian Qichen arrived in Moscow on December 1, 1988. Fittingly for the first day of winter, it was icy and snowing in the Soviet capital. Memories of a bitter winter still haunted Sino-Soviet relations. Qian with his delegation, put up at a government residence at Leninskie Gory, feared being overheard and strategized outside, in the courtyard, puffing cold air and treading on the snow.[121] They struggled over how to wrestle a Soviet concession on Cambodia. With Beijing and Moscow mending fences at last, perhaps they feared China would lose its only real lever over Vietnam. Who could then guarantee that Vietnam would abide by all of its promises rather than attempt to maintain tutelage over Cambodia in disguise? The Chinese had no faith in Vietnam.

There was another reason for Qian's preoccupation with the problem: it was a matter of face for the Chinese to say that the Soviets had removed obstacles to normalization, so painstakingly maintained for so many years. Otherwise, it would seem that China had capitulated with the loss of moral superiority. Nothing mattered to the Chinese more than keeping a sense of moral superiority over their neighbors. There already was movement on some of the obstacles. Soviet forces had partially been withdrawn from Mongolia, leaving Ulaanbaatar bewildered, since they did not want to be left alone with the Chinese.[122] The Soviets were on schedule to leave Afghanistan (although it was then unclear whether they would adhere to the schedule or invent a pretext to stay). But the most important obstacle—Vietnamese occupation of Cambodia—was still there. How, then, could the Chinese pretend that it had been overcome?

The Soviet position at the talks can be deciphered with relative precision because of the extensive documentary record. The Soviets consulted with Hanoi ahead of Qian Qichen's arrival. Apparently, they probed tacitly whether there was flexibility in the pullout schedule, and the Vietnamese insisted on the existing schedule (late 1989, with a political settlement, or early 1990, without). However, there was a nuance in their position. If, Nguyen Co Thach told the Soviets, the Chinese engaged in direct dialogue with Vietnam, "we can promise something else."[123] Given this sort of attitude, the only thing the Soviets could plausibly do in talks with Qian Qichen was to encourage a direct dialogue between China and Vietnam, and resist the Chinese pressure to commit to an early schedule of troop withdrawals.

This was what Shevardnadze did in talks with Qian Qichen. One of the participants noted:

> Immediately after the ritual prologue about the new quality of Sino-Soviet relations, the guest takes the "Cambodian-Vietnamese" bull by the horns, conditioning the normalization of Sino-Soviet relations upon the achievement of an internal understanding about the withdrawal of Vietnamese forces from Cambodia in the course of 1989 [in fact, by summer 1989]. The Vietnamese have their own reasons and conditions [lists conditions]. Qian Qichen laughs: "Too many conditions."...E. A. [Shevardnadze] tried to persuade Qian that the Vietnamese have moved away from their "dead positions," but the Chinese said politely-unequivocally: "No they have not changed their positions. They are as insincere as before."

The first round of talks ended in complete disagreement. Shevardnadze stuck to his guns:

> I believe that the Sino-Vietnamese dialogue is an important factor of the settlement. [We] used to think: the more contradictions the better. [Now, things are different.] For example, the better your relations with the USA, the better for us! (Tries to persuade them to make up with Vietnam). Our ability to influence Vietnam has limits. We can't even [influence] the Estonians . . . (laughter).

Qian Qichen insisted, and Shevardnadze reiterated: "Our relations do not allow us to put the SRV [Socialist Republic of Vietnam] under pressure."

The exchange ended with Qian offering to relegate the issue to a special working group, which could then report to the two foreign ministers. The Russian record is silent as to whether this working group achieved any kind of agreement.[124] Yet Qian claimed in his memoirs that the Soviets, after resisting the Chinese schedule, in the end agreed that Vietnam would have to withdraw completely in the second half of 1989 and, in any case, no later than the end of December 1989. This understanding was fixed in the "common notes."[125] Days after his meetings in Moscow, Qian Qichen publicly insisted that "the Soviet Union had for the first time agreed to intervene in the matter of the withdrawal of Vietnamese troops from Kampuchea."[126]

The Soviets remained tight-lipped on the subject, and the question of whether Shevardnadze caved at the eleventh hour remains open. It is possible that the Soviets agreed to an earlier withdrawal date and, a few weeks later, the Vietnamese announced a revised schedule: all troops would leave by September 1989, if a political settlement were found (or 1990, if not). It is possible that the Vietnamese announcement was a product of the Soviet urging. By the same token, the Vietnamese, who were about to host a high-level delegation from Thailand, had their own reasons for appearing constructive. But for the time being, the Soviet concession, real or imagined, allowed the Chinese to save face. The Chinese leaders could claim, as Wu Xueqian did in a meeting with US Congressman Tom Lantos, that "as a result of the agreement reached with the Soviets, the Soviet Union was urging Vietnam to withdraw its troops from Cambodia."[127] Now, Gorbachev could come to China in 1989. Qian passed on this invitation in a meeting with the Soviet leader on December 2, in what became something of a surprise for the Soviets. Shevardnadze had thought that the Chinese were not yet prepared for this decisive step.

SHEVARDNADZE IN CHINA

Eduard Shevardnadze paid a return visit to Beijing on February 1, 1989, thirty years since a Soviet Foreign Minister had last visited China. His objective was to obtain an exact summit date from the Chinese while giving away as little as possible on the Cambodian problem. The Chinese strategy, by contrast, was to make use of whatever leverage they still had on the summit date in order to squeeze a face-saving concession from Shevardnadze on Cambodia. The trade-off was simple. All Shevardnadze was asked to do was sign a joint statement with China, making public the two ministers' alleged private agreement on the outlines of the Cambodian settlement. Qian Qichen recalled that it was a Soviet idea to begin with—to have a statement on Cambodia and a statement on the summit date as a package. He was surprised when "the Soviet side went back on its promise."[128] The sticking point was Soviet unwillingness to endorse the Chinese view of a Sihanouk-led quadripartite government, which would undermine Hun Sen's position. The Chinese leaders argued that a prompt agreement on such a government was important so as to avoid an Afghan-type civil war in Cambodia following the withdrawal of the Vietnamese forces. Fortunately, unlike the situation in Afghanistan, in Cambodia all factions accepted Sihanouk.[129]

Shevardnadze was not convinced. His refusal to sign a statement on Cambodia sparked a mini-crisis. Qian threatened that China would not announce the date of the summit. He told Deng Xiaoping about Soviet intransigence. But Deng's options were limited. Gorbachev had been invited already, and for a host of reasons he could not be uninvited for the sake of Cambodia: the summit would take place. Deng confirmed this in a meeting with Shevardnadze on February 4 but declined to agree to a specific date, throwing the ball back to Qian and Shevardnadze: "I will listen to your directions."[130]

Deng, for his part, spent much of his time with Shevardnadze driving home his point about the importance of the Cambodian problem to China. Smoking one cigarette after another, "talking expansively, gesturing, his fingers trembling," he dismissed Shevardnadze's claims that one could rely on Hanoi's promise to withdraw forces from Cambodia. "Even when we were hungry, we gave the Vietnamese food, clothes and ammunition. We helped them a lot. But they tricked us. We know the Vietnamese better than you do. I am telling you: one cannot believe them completely." Instead of withdrawal, Deng told Shevardnadze, the Vietnamese "will disguise their forces," dressing them up as Cambodians and hiding them in the mountains.[131] Deng added that Hanoi had not yet given up the idea of creating an "Indochinese federation."[132] "I admit, I was too naïve with the Vietnamese [in the past]. I advise you: do not be like that."[133]

The patriarch's protestations were to no avail. Shevardnadze dug in his heels: talks continued on the plane back from Shanghai to Beijing.[134] The Soviet Foreign Minister was already overdue in Pakistan for crucial talks with Bhutto. And yet there was no agreement. A Chinese Foreign Ministry official called the Soviet Embassy, telling Shevardnadze not to announce the date of the summit until the statement on Cambodia had been agreed upon. Rogachev thought the Chinese were simply playing a "game" to "squeeze" as much as possible from the USSR.[135] "This was petty blackmail," he recalled a few days later. "What could be done?"[136] Shevardnadze gambled. In a packed press conference in Beijing the Soviet Foreign Minister announced that the summit would take place in mid-May.[137] Immediately after the press conference, Shevardnadze and his party went to the airport, to be seen off by a "very grave, unhappy Qian Qichen," who "must have watched the press-conference on television."[138]

With a "strained smile," Qian told Shevardnadze that the Soviets were violating an earlier, internal agreement on Cambodia: "We need relations that will be free of elements of inconsistency and changeability." Shevardnadze, turning "purple," angrily rebutted Qian's allegations of inconsistency.[139] He departed China without agreement, leaving Georgii Kireev to work out a solution. Several hours later, in a separate press conference, Chinese Deputy Foreign Minister Tian Zengpei insisted that mid-May was only a Soviet proposal, which would still have to be discussed.[140] As the media speculated that "negotiations had hit a last minute snag," the Chinese and the Soviets had another go at resolving their differences.[141] Eventually Kireev called Shevardnadze with the welcome news: they managed to agree with the Chinese on the Cambodian statement, and the compromise "was closer to the Soviet version in its content."[142] On the following day—more than twenty-four hours after Shevardnadze left Beijing—the Chinese confirmed the summit date and at the same time published the joint Sino-Soviet statement on Cambodia.[143] "This was a small battle of nerves," Igor Rogachev explained several days later, thinking, no doubt, that Shevardnadze had won the battle.[144]

The statement had stains of blood and tears from days of painful negotiations. The Soviets, in the end, did not say what the Chinese wanted them to say—endorse the Chinese view on the internal political settlement and on Vietnam's early withdrawal. Shevardnadze carefully dodged the question of dismantling the existing Phnom Penh regime before holding elections, a long-time Chinese demand. On the question of Vietnam's withdrawal, the statement said that China and the Soviet Union took note of the decision announced by Vietnam to withdraw all its troops from Cambodia by the end of September 1989 at the latest, and hoped that this would facilitate the process of negotiations on settling other aspects of the Cambodian question.[145] This was the much dreaded part about "making" Vietnam pull out of Cambodia—and it meant that the "obstacle" had been overcome.

Deng Xiaoping knew that he had made serious concessions ahead of the summit. "So far, I don't know how many gifts [Gorbachev] will bring.... I don't even know what will happen regarding Vietnamese troop withdrawal from Cambodia," he told US President George Bush soon after the summit date was announced.[146] In all truth, Deng Xiaoping raised the Cambodian obstacle, and it was Deng Xiaoping who removed it when he agreed to a summit with Gorbachev. Lack of progress on Cambodia was no longer allowed to impede full Sino-Soviet normalization. When Deng and Gorbachev met in Beijing—at last—in May 1989, lingering differences over Cambodia did not prevent the two from opening a new page in Sino-Soviet relations.[147]

CONCLUSION

The Cambodian quagmire continued for several more years. Sino-Soviet normalization did not put an end to this conflict. While Cold War logic helped perpetuate the Cambodian conflict, the logic of regional and national struggle for power and influence was equally important. It was a struggle with a momentum of its own quite irrespective of the great schemes worked out in Moscow, Washington, or Beijing. In this sense, it is hard to disagree with Vietnamese Politburo member Tran Xuan Bach, who told a Soviet counterpart in December 1988: "If you look at the surface of the situation [in Cambodia], it could appear relatively calm. But there are strong waves under this surface. After a possible conclusion of agreements, the struggle will continue in other, mainly in political, forms."[148]

From 1989 onward the Cambodian problem no longer affected Sino-Soviet relations. On April 5, 1989, Vietnam announced that it would withdraw forces from Cambodia by the end of September—unconditionally. There was some speculation in the media that the pullout decision was a result of Soviet "arm-twisting."[149] But the available evidence suggests that it was Hanoi's decision. Explaining the reasons for the announcement to Gorbachev, Nguyen Van Linh said: "We carefully analyzed the situation, considered whether or not the Kampuchean revolution would be sustained if the Vietnamese forces left, and came to a confident conclusion that it will not be weakened. The correlation of forces is favoring our comrades."[150]

The real problem for the Vietnamese was how to use the goodwill accrued in the wake of their withdrawal to jumpstart relations with Beijing and reach out to the capitalist powers of East Asia and to ASEAN. Vietnam's withdrawal was a necessary and inevitable component of *doi moi*, and it would have happened with or without Soviet urging. It helped that Gorbachev appreciated Vietnam's new philosophy.

Vietnam withdrew forces from Cambodia on schedule. The internal bickering continued. A long-hoped-for conference of the Cambodian factions—urged on by the entire international community—took place in Paris in August 1989 but did not result in an agreement. It would take another two years before a comprehensive settlement for Cambodia was worked out. Sihanouk returned as King. Hun Sen stayed on as Prime Minister, now wearing a capitalist's hat. The UN administration came and went. It did little to change the traditional political patterns of Cambodia. The undisputable loser of the eventual settlement was the Khmer Rouge, which disintegrated as a political force.

Deng could have held fast to the Cambodian obstacle. After all, the Vietnamese were still in Cambodia and the pro-Vietnamese Cambodian government remained in place, with little hope that it would be replaced anytime soon with a combination favored by the Chinese. Most important, the Soviet Union never "made" Vietnam withdraw from Cambodia in the sense that Deng Xiaoping expected when the obstacle was initially announced. Since then, the world had changed. China was ripe for full normalization of relations with the Soviet Union whatever happened or did not happen in Cambodia. For this reason, the Cambodian obstacle was quietly forgotten by the Chinese. Deng wanted to go down in history as the man who "closed the past and opened the future."

China's policy toward Indochina underwent a complete change after the early 1980s. Then, fresh after the Vietnamese invasion of Cambodia and China's own brief war against Vietnam, Deng Xiaoping adopted the policy of "bleeding Vietnam white." This policy was a product of the Cold War. For one thing, Deng was genuinely apprehensive of the Soviet "encirclement." China's confrontation with Vietnam, and support for the Khmer Rouge in Cambodia, were aimed at addressing Beijing's pervading sense of insecurity. Also, Deng consistently used Vietnam to signal his reliability to the United States, the key partner in China's modernization. Finally, Vietnam, as an "obstacle" to Sino-Soviet normalization, allowed the Chinese leader to control the pace of rapprochement with Moscow, cooling the enthusiasm of some of his own colleagues.

By the late 1980s, this strategy was no longer sustainable. Gradual improvement in Sino-Soviet relations made the problem of Soviet "encirclement" of China a lot less pressing. Meanwhile, by 1987 there was clear progress in the Soviet-US rapprochement—something that had increasing influence on the regional problems. By being inflexible on the issue of the Cambodian settlement, China risked being left on the wrong side of history. Thus, by 1987 Beijing softened its position by dropping support for Pol Pot and giving Prince Sihanouk more room for maneuver in his negotiations with the other Cambodian factions. The Chinese still pressed the Soviets to "make" Vietnam pull out from Cambodia, but now Beijing's policy was informed not so much by Cold War priorities as by a genuine concern about Vietnam's regional hegemony and a realization that China had very few effective instruments to influence Hanoi except for outright military pressure, which was no longer a plausible option.

As a result of the Sino-Soviet normalization, the Chinese lost a lever for finding a solution to one of their most difficult foreign policy problems of the 1980s. Over the course of the decade, however, this issue dropped from the rank of a global problem to merely a regional one. Difficult as it may have been for Deng Xiaoping to decouple this problem from China's broader foreign policy outlook, it was the only sensible decision. But, as a regional problem, it was not resolved in China's favor. Vietnam withdrew from Cambodia on Vietnam's terms. Beijing continued to criticize this "un-genuine withdrawal" and even called on its partners to "exert maximum pressure on Vietnam" but it ultimately had to settle for much less than Deng Xiaoping had hoped for when, in 1979, he decided to teach Vietnam a "lesson."[151] China's ten years of involvement in the Cambodian conflict left the Sino-Vietnamese relationship a legacy of mutual suspicion and mistrust. This is one of the poignant consequences of the Cold War in Southeast Asia that may yet lead to unpredictable consequences for China and Vietnam.

CHAPTER 5

Sino-Soviet Normalization, 1989–91

In the 1950s the Chinese and the Russians stood shoulder to shoulder in a communist alliance, built upon allegedly immutable principles of Marxism-Leninism and proletarian internationalism. It was not a marriage of convenience—or was not meant to be. The Sino-Soviet alliance was a scientific project, an experiment in communist diplomacy, meant to last. But from the time the alliance was conceived in 1950, it took less than a decade before the façade of solidarity crumbled. In the early 1960s there were a barrage of mutual accusations and a bitter competition for influence in the communist movement and the Third World, bloody border skirmishes, and the menace of a nuclear war. How did things get so badly out of hand?

The problem was that it was a partnership of a superpower—the Soviet Union—with an economically underdeveloped and militarily weak China. The Soviets regarded this inequality as entirely natural: Russia was the first country to have a communist revolution; it had defeated Germany; it had built the atomic bomb and launched Sputnik; and it had confronted the United States in the global Cold War. In the Soviet-invented system of coordinates, China could only be second best, and that role clearly did not suit the ambitious and intensely nationalistic Chinese leadership. The Sino-Soviet split was about China's efforts to escape the inequality of the alliance. This is not to say that the Chinese bear the main responsibility for the ensuing confrontation. The Soviet leaders have an equal share of responsibility for their persistent unwillingness to recognize that China could not and would not be the Soviet Union's "younger brother."[1]

When the ice began to melt in Sino-Soviet relations in the 1980s, the Chinese were quick to point out that if there were to be a rapprochement, it would have to be on the basis of complete equality; there would be no return to the 1950s. Equality meant for Deng Xiaoping that "there is no father party." "A father-son relationship in fact denies independence," argued the Chinese patriarch on one occasion in early 1983.[2] Echoing these sentiments in September 1984, Li Peng told a visiting Japanese delegation: "The Soviet Union wants to control China ... China is a great country. It cannot accept Soviet control and it cannot accept American control." In turn he praised Sino-Japanese relations for their "equality."[3] When Li Peng and Gorbachev met in December 1985, Li made the point in no uncertain terms. "China will not become [the Soviet Union's] younger brother."[4] Gorbachev recounted his response: "I said it would just be difficult to imagine China in the role of a younger brother. At the 27th Congress we clearly told the whole world of our willingness to develop equal relations with all countries."[5] But did he really mean it?

Gorbachev belonged to a younger generation of Soviet policy makers. He was only twenty-five at the time of the 20th CPSU Congress, at which Nikita Khrushchev delivered the famous condemnation of Stalin that caused a great upheaval in the socialist camp, an upheaval from which that camp never fully recovered. Intellectually, Gorbachev owed much more to the "shestidesyatniki"—the intelligentsia of the 1960s—than to the Stalinist diehards who preceded them.[6] By the time Gorbachev reached political maturity, China and the Soviet Union were at each other's throats. Long gone were the days of great solidarity and fraternity. Gorbachev did not take China for granted. He knew it as a hostile power, eyeing the Soviet Union ominously from across the border. The Chinese were never "younger brothers" for Gorbachev.

Although Sino-Soviet relations began to improve before Gorbachev came to power, it would have been so much more difficult to achieve genuine rapprochement had Gorbachev not recognized that China was a great power in its own right and that a rapprochement would not have to mean subordination of one side to the other. While Sino-US rapprochement in the early 1970s alerted the Soviet leadership that a whole different game was under way, it is easy to detect in some of the late Brezhnev-era calls for normalization with China the notion that relations would improve when the Chinese abandoned their "chauvinist" policies and returned to the fold.

Gorbachev was sufficiently removed from such Stalinist sentiments to make a difference with China. He embraced the Soviet role in the socialist camp and while he readily agreed to some democratization of allied relations, Gorbachev insisted that "one cannot allow that democratization of relations turns into anarchy."[7] But that did not apply to China, not for Gorbachev. As he put it at a Politburo meeting, "One has to understand the Chinese. They have a right to become a great power, we should not call it 'chauvinism.'"[8] Speaking to the same group a few weeks later, Gorbachev called on his colleagues to talk "respectfully" about China.[9] He was impressed with China's economic progress and believed that, like India, it was "getting stronger—everyone can see it."[10]

How Gorbachev came to these conclusions is a matter for debate; there is no doubt that such sentiments about China were prominent in his close circle, among the likes of Chernyaev, Arbatov, and Yakovlev. For example, in early 1988 Aleksandr Yakovlev explained: "Of course, we will not restore such relations as we [thought we would] have 'forever.' They never do anything but harm. One has to be a realist. [China] is a great power.... If we talk about foreign policy, one must get rid of imperialist pretensions. This concerns us as well. One has to get used to living as equals among equals."[11] This is not to say that Yakovlev coached Gorbachev or the other way around. Yet there was a growing understanding in Gorbachev's circle that it would take the Soviet recognition of China's right to be a great power to normalize relations on the basis of real equality. Gorbachev was not the only prophet in the land. He was, however, the one in the position to make the big difference, and thus has the Soviet part of the credit for normalization with China.

MEETING WITH DENG

At around midday on May 15, 1989, Gorbachev landed in the old Beijing airport to begin his historic visit to China. He arrived in a city gripped by political unrest. In April students at Beijing's universities and across China took to the streets to mourn the passing of Hu Yaobang, the former General Secretary of the CCP who had the reputation of a reformer. The occasion offered an opportunity to fan built-up resentment with what many students—and for this matter, many ordinary Chinese—perceived as the authorities' unwillingness and inability to redress growing social inequality, nepotism, and corruption. As the political leadership lingered in uncertainty, what began as a law-abiding protest swelled into a radical movement. Students in their thousands filled Tiananmen Square, calling for democratic reforms. On April 26 the *People's Daily* imprudently characterized the protests as "turmoil," escalating stakes for both sides. On May 13 several hundred students declared a hunger strike in the square. Things were heading toward a showdown.[12]

Gorbachev's visit was a pivotal moment in the unfolding crisis. For many Chinese students, Gorbachev represented all that the Chinese leaders were not: he was a democrat, a reformer, and a force for change. The summit offered the protesters a rare opportunity to take their case to Gorbachev over the heads of the Chinese authorities and embarrass the leadership into making concessions. Days before Gorbachev's arrival, student activists launched an appeal to get him to speak to them. On May 13 six thousand signatures were delivered to the Soviet Embassy in Beijing, attached to a letter praising Gorbachev's "amazing courage and intelligence" and called on him to share with the students his "valuable experience of conducting socialist reform."[13] The Soviet response was pointedly cautious: spokesman Gennadii Gerasimov told the journalists that Gorbachev would meet with members of the public, adding: "it is not us compiling the list of who will be attending."[14] At the very least, the protesters expected a glimpse of the Soviet leader as he arrived in Tiananmen Square for the planned welcoming ceremony. To make space for Gorbachev, students moved to the far side of the square and even "used their banners to sweep up some of the litter from the protests."[15]

The Chinese leaders faced a difficult situation. There had been meticulous preparation for the Sino-Soviet summit for weeks before Gorbachev's arrival. Igor Rogachev arrived early with his team to work out a joint communiqué. Then, as Ambassador Oleg Troyanovskii put it, there was a "real invasion" of Soviet personnel—from protocol specialists, to communications staff, to medics who literally "tested water, meals and anything that the President might touch," to a small army of bodyguards.[16] These people worked closely with their Chinese colleagues to fine-tune every little detail, so that, in the words of PRC Chairman Yang Shangkun, the "summit meeting with Gorbachev comes off without a hitch."[17] Student demonstrations were an embarrassment on a staggering scale, especially since the Chinese government had allowed hundreds of foreign journalists and TV crews into Beijing to cover the summit. Now these foreign journalists were all over Tiananmen Square, interviewing student protesters and broadcasting live images to the world. The last thing Deng Xiaoping wanted was to have Gorbachev mingle with this crowd: "When Gorbachev's here, we have to have order at Tiananmen. Our international image depends on it. What do we look like if the Square's a mess?"[18]

Seeing that appeals to students' patriotic feelings were not enough to clear the Square, the Chinese authorities hastily moved the "red carpet welcome" to the old Beijing airport.[19] Except there was no proper red carpet. It was stored at the Great Hall of the People, next to Tiananmen Square, and the protocol officials figured there was no way they could get it out without the protesting students taking notice.[20] From the airport, to avoid the pro-testers, Gorbachev was taken through back streets and dark alleys to a side entrance of the National People's Congress. There, Yang Shangkun hosted a welcoming banquet for the Soviet leader in a great chamber the size of a "train station," featuring shark fins and abalone, among other delicacies.[21] To improve digestion, the People's Liberation Army orchestra entertained the guests with nostalgic Soviet songs and classical music.[22] Just a few hundred meters away, in Tiananmen, Chinese students were on the third day of their hunger strike.

From the Soviet viewpoint, the only appropriate thing to do was pretend that everything was normal. "We didn't want to offend the Chinese hosts," recalled Soviet spokesman Gennadii Gerasimov, "so we didn't discuss it—in any detail at least. We just discussed it as you would discuss something which is there[,] just like 'Today it is raining'—so 'today this square is not available'—but no judgment."[23] Gorbachev proposed to stick to the pro-gram—"so that one does not get the impression that the visit is falling apart."[24] But privately the Soviet visitors wondered whether China itself was falling apart. "This is a revolution," concluded Evgenii Primakov, eyeing stu-dent crowds. "Could it not be," another Soviet official noted in private, "that we have normalized relations with political dead men?"[25] Ambassador Oleg Troyanovskii recalled that there were "one or two radicals" in Gorbachev's entourage (including, apparently, Shevardnadze)[26] who urged him to go to Tiananmen and address the students, but Gorbachev was clearly unwill-ing to cross that line.[27] "We tried to act with reserve and judiciousness," the General Secretary recalled two months after the travails—"although I, frankly speaking, thought that we should leave [for home] as quickly as possible."[28]

At his press conference on May 17 Gorbachev was repeatedly asked about the student protesters. He answered, vaguely, "I wouldn't take it upon myself to be the judge, and I wouldn't take it upon myself to perform the mission of assessing what is happening here today." Asked what he would do if students assembled to protest in Red Square, Gorbachev responded that he was for political dialogue on the basis of democracy and glasnost. But he was at pains to emphasize that each country had a different situation and that he was in no position to become China's Gorbachev.[29] In private, Gorbachev was relieved that he was not in Deng Xiaoping's shoes. "Some of those present here," he told the Soviet delegation at the Embassy on May 15, "have promoted the idea of taking the Chinese road. We saw today where this road leads. I do not want Red Square to look like Tiananmen Square."[30]

A fortnight later, on June 4, 1989, government forces turned on the demonstrators in Tiananmen Square with appalling ferocity: hundreds of students were killed in the bloodbath. CCP General Secretary Zhao Ziyang, a supporter of a dialogue with the students, was ousted from power. The crackdown was loudly condemned around the world but not in the Soviet Union. Gorbachev was privately "dismayed" by the situation but abstained from public criticism, as he explained to Helmut Kohl.[31] The Congress of People's Deputies—the new Soviet parliament, convened after the first competitive elections in decades—issued a mellow statement calling for "wisdom, reason and weighted approach" in dealing with the crisis and decrying outside pressure on China.[32] Not all the deputies agreed. Human rights advocate Andrei Sakharov took the podium to demand recall of the Soviet Ambassador from China but Gorbachev switched off his microphone.[33] "We regret some aspects of what happened" was all Gorbachev could say in public.[34] It was a far cry from comments made by some of the Russian radicals, including Boris Yeltsin, who called the crackdown a "crime against the people."[35]

Gorbachev's reaction to the Tiananmen Square massacre points to the wide gap between Gorbachev the ideologue and Gorbachev the politician. His zealous advocacy of peace and democracy inspired respect and admiration; for millions of people around the world Gorbachev became the symbol of change. He certainly was for the desperate and idealistic protesters in Tiananmen Square who held up portraits of him naïvely hoping their hero would answer their pleas for help. One foreign journalist, unable to bike through the crowds of protesters on his way to Gorbachev's press conference, pulled out the Soviet leader's photo and waved it before students. The crowds gave way and the reporter got through.[36] This was the power of the amulet that Gorbachev had become.

Often the magic of Gorbachev and the myth of Gorbachev did not square with political realities. The first political reality was that China was too important to the Soviet Union to risk alienating this country by what could only be interpreted as Soviet interference in Beijing's internal affairs. "Politicians," Gorbachev told Rajiv Gandhi when they met in November 1989, "must be careful in these matters. Especially when we are talking about a country like China. A country with more than a billion people. This is a whole civilization!"[37]

Another political reality weighed strongly against criticizing China for what happened in Tiananmen. In 1989 Gorbachev was in serious trouble. His economic reforms were failing. His foreign policy encountered backlash among home-grown conservatives. He was attacked from the right and from the left.[38] Against this lamentable background, Gorbachev's rapprochement with China was a notable success. Unsurprisingly, he did not want to do anything to upset the fragile relationship, even when awkward silence squared poorly with moral principles.[39]

It is possible that Gorbachev sympathized with the students. Deng Xiaoping may have sympathized with the students, too, but that did not stop him from ordering Tiananmen Square to be cleared by force when political expediency so required. Gorbachev recognized Deng's predicament. As he put it at a Politburo meeting on October 4, 1989, when Anatolii Luk'yanov reported that the number of casualties at Tiananmen topped three thousand: "We must be realists. They, like us, have to hold on. Three thousand ... So what? Sometimes one has to retreat. This is what strategy and tactics are for. If one has adopted a general policy, one may have different maneuvers within its framework."[40] This willingness on Gorbachev's part to condone a massacre of unarmed demonstrators as a tactical measure reflects the General Secretary's moral relativism, which has sometimes been overlooked in uncritical commentaries on Gorbachev's single-minded advocacy of universal human values.

Perhaps Gorbachev also sympathized with his Chinese counterpart, General Secretary Zhao Ziyang, who was purged in the wake of the crackdown. Zhao was often called "China's Gorbachev." When Gorbachev was in Beijing, he and Zhao engaged in an interesting (and, for Zhao, fatal)[41] conversation about reforms. Speaking of the student protesters, Gorbachev told Zhao Ziyang:

> [GORBACHEV:] ... On the whole we face the same problems; we also have hot heads. Many of them are good people, committed to the task of the renewal of socialism. People are concerned about the process of perestroika, by the fact that someone is obstructing this process, putting obstacles in our way. And we see that they are correct in many aspects. The forces of inertia, orthodoxy and conservatism turned out to be very resilient in our [country].
>
> ZHAO ZIYANG: Here we speak one language with you. I think currently the socialist movement has really entered the decisive stage. Many young people ask: who has the advantage now—socialism or capitalism? ... The advantages of socialism can show only through reforms. Only they can show its attractive force. We must respond to the challenge of capitalism. We have no other way out but to follow on the road of reforms.[42]

Gorbachev fondly remembered reformer Zhao Ziyang as a kindred spirit and recalled a "feeling of openness and mutual sympathy" in their dialogue.[43] But soon after his departure from China, Gorbachev reportedly remarked that Zhao Ziyang was purged because of his—and his children's—corruption and because the CIA took advantage of his pro-American sentiments to foment political unrest in China.[44] This does not mean that Gorbachev was insincere when he wrote of his sympathy for Zhao Ziyang, but clearly there was much more to Gorbachev's thinking on the Tiananmen tragedy than what met the eye.

Let us not repeat the mistake, however, of foreign reporters who were so carried away by the student unrest in Beijing that they lost interest in the first Sino-Soviet summit in thirty years. The highlight of the visit was Gorbachev's meeting with Deng Xiaoping on May 16, 1989. Previous Sino-Soviet summits went down in history as serious protocol disasters. During Mao Zedong's first visit to Moscow, in the winter of 1949–50, when the Chinese delegation were at Stalin's dacha, the host put on a record and asked the visitors and his own Politburo colleagues—a strictly male company—to dance to the tunes. As Molotov waltzed with Zhou Enlai, Chairman Mao looked on in awkward silence.[45] Mao matched the embarrassment in 1958. He hosted Khrushchev in his swimming pool in Zhongnanhai, taking evident delight in the clumsy performance of the Soviet Chairman.[46] There was no scope for this kind of intimacy this time around.

The main question of protocol, mulled over by the media, was whether Deng would bear-hug Gorbachev or offer him a handshake.[47] This came under careful scrutiny of policy makers at the highest level. "Embracing might shock the world," Deng said with an eye to the West's reaction.[48] Therefore, the Chinese protocol specifically provided for "handshake, no embrace" to highlight the new character of Sino-Soviet relations.[49] Gorbachev, too, prepared well for his meeting with Deng. He told his entourage that he would conduct the conversation as a younger person would with his elder: "This is valued in the East."[50] So Gorbachev let Deng do most of the talking. The Chinese leader (who had no prepared notes) turned to questions of philosophy and history. "This was fairly unexpected for me," recalled Gorbachev. "The conversation was [supposed to be] about changes in the present-day world, about our relations with China, and then suddenly there was a turn like this."[51]

After a brief lecture about Marxism-Leninism and how it could be applied differently in different countries, in ways neither Marx nor, indeed, Lenin, could have predicted, Deng spoke of China's encounter with modernity. In Deng's opinion, it was not a pleasant encounter. "China was subjected to aggression and enslavement by foreign powers."[52] Deng talked about China's bitter experiences with Japan and with tsarist Russia, which in his view annexed 1.5 million square kilometers of China's territory. Far from redressing Russia's misdeeds, the Soviet Union annexed more territory and ultimately severed Outer Mongolia from China.[53] Then there was the ideological quarrel, though Deng Xiaoping did not think it was the root of the problem. "The question was not in the ideological disagreements. We were also wrong. . . . The Soviet Union incorrectly perceived China's place in the world. . . . The essence of all problems was that we were unequal, that we were subjected to coercion and pressure."[54] Gorbachev wisely refrained from contradicting Deng. After all, the whole point of the meeting was, in Deng's words, to "close the past and open the future."[55]

The Gorbachev-Deng summit represented a symbolic turning point in Sino-Soviet relations. For all intents and purposes, the relationship was already "normal" before the summit. Since late 1982, year by year, relations improved: increasing trade, scientific, and cultural exchange, annual meetings and consultations on many levels. Outstanding problems were being solved, although some problems remained. This was true even after the summit. In this sense, it is clearly inappropriate to say that Sino-Soviet relations were "normalized" in 1989. At another level, there was much symbolism in Gorbachev's visit to China. There was symbolism in his conversation with Deng Xiaoping. Every little detail was thought through to underscore this symbolism: that China and the Soviet Union were now equal partners—not brothers-in-arms, not allies, but partners. For this reason, Deng offered his lecture on philosophy and history, and to Gorbachev's credit he understood what the Chinese were driving at. The year 1989 inaugurated equality in Sino-Soviet relations, equality registered by that warm handshake—"but no embrace."

AMERICA'S RESPONSE

Since the beginning of the Sino-Soviet rapprochement in 1982, Deng Xiaoping was exceptionally careful to reassure Washington that such rapprochement would in no way undermine China's relations with the United States. Although he was not above playing the Soviet "card" to scare the Americans into being a little more forthcoming on issues like technology transfers and Taiwan, Deng was, on the whole, sincere in his assurances. He just did not attach the kind of importance to the USSR as did some of his comrades, not least Chen Yun.

When Gorbachev's forthcoming visit to China was publicly announced in February 1989, President Bush was still trying to work out what shape his Soviet policy should take, a review that would continue for months, to general detriment of Soviet-American relations and Gorbachev's considerable frustration. For one thing, the President knew already that he did not want to be upstaged by Gorbachev in developing relations with China. Former Ambassador in the US James Lilley recalled: "Both Gorbachev and Deng were ballyhooing [Gorbachev's] visit as a 'big deal.' They were sort of saying: 'In your face, America.' The old Kissingerites in Washington, the old "triangular pole" people, were saying: 'This is bad news. The Soviet Union and communist China are getting back together.'"[56] On the heels of Shevardnadze's departure from China, Bush visited Beijing to find out where the Sino-Soviet relationship was going and to prevent the Soviets from claiming new ground at American expense.

In China, Bush was reassured by all leaders from Deng down that Gorbachev's visit would not become the dramatic breakthrough that the Americans were worried it would. Deng was especially emphatic, spending most of his time with Bush on complaints about the Soviet aggressiveness, and how, historically, the Soviet Union and Russia had been China's worst enemy, worse even than Japan, because the Russians helped themselves to three million square kilometers of Chinese territory, including Outer Mongolia. "Those over 50 in China remember that the shape of China was like a maple leaf," Deng said. "Now, if you look at the map, you see a huge chunk in the north cut away; the maple leaf has been nibbled away."[57] The Soviet Union had encircled China, creating an unfavorable strategic situation, which was the reason Mao Zedong had sought rapprochement with the United States in the first place. Deng said he was not sure that the situation would change after Gorbachev's visit. Even if it did, this did not mean that China and the USSR would become allies. "Nor is this possible. There are current and future reasons for this not to happen. The historical reasons are the most important ones."[58]

Bush has been criticized for being so absorbed in the geopolitical manipulations that he missed the significance of much more important events that were then unfolding in China: the buildup of tensions that would lead to the Tiananmen tragedy.[59] Certainly, in his meetings with the Chinese leaders in February, Bush steered clear of the human rights theme, although he did say, in general terms, that he would like for China's reforms to continue. It was actually the Chinese who brought up the theme repeatedly, criticizing the domestic opponents of the regime and linking the future of reforms with the Chinese government's ability to keep democratic sentiments in check.

Most vocal in this respect was Zhao Ziyang. Zhao spent a lot of time in his conversation with Bush criticizing the views of those people in China who had called for a multi-party democracy. "The above proposition [democracy] does not tally with the realities of China. If it is carried out, chaos will result, and reform will be disrupted." Zhao pleaded with Bush to turn a deaf ear to the advocates of political reform: "Mr. President, you know well China's history and its realities. I know you understand the above analysis. I hope the US government will pay attention to this question for the sake of

Sino-US friendship, the stability of China, and the success of the reform." "That was a fascinating exposition" was all that Bush could bring himself to say.[60] Contrary to Zhao, he was much more reserved and much less willing to explain where he actually stood on the issue of human rights in China. Bush's preferred method was to sweep the discussion under the rug, which did not help the White House when weeks later it came to dominate the bilateral agenda in Sino-American relations.

Bush's visit to China was overshadowed by an embarrassing incident involving the astrophysicist and prominent Chinese dissident Fang Lizhi. Fang, who had criticized the government's handling of student unrest in 1986 and since then had emerged as the most vocal proponent of democratic reform in China, was invited to attend a large banquet that President Bush would hold on the occasion of his visit. The idea originated with the US Embassy in Beijing. On February 18, Ambassador Winston Lord cabled Washington that he would invite "the noted dissidents" Fang and his wife.[61] Lord had encouraged Bush to keep human rights on the agenda with the Chinese, suggesting he raise issues like treatment of prisoners in Tibet, something Bush safely avoided.[62] Perhaps Fang Lizhi's presence in the banquet was meant as a reminder for the Chinese officials that US willingness to strengthen the strategic dialogue would not mean compromise on human rights. But the method chosen was remarkably short-sighted. It is hard to see how Lord expected the high-ranking Chinese officials would tolerate the idea of being in the same room as Fang Lizhi. While undoubtedly his views resonated with the hopes of some of the reformers in the leadership, such a snub could not be allowed. Lord had badly miscalculated.

Even more shocking, his blunder went unnoticed in Washington, and Fang Lizhi was invited to attend. It therefore was down to the Chinese officials to save their own face—this was done successfully when the authorities physically prevented the dissident from coming to the banquet, pulling his car over for traffic violations. The incident exploded in the media and caused back-and-forth recriminations between the US Embassy and Washington. As a result, Bush's visit failed to make the sort of impression he had hoped to convey to the Chinese leaders; instead, Bush came across as someone who had no clear policy toward China other than preempting closer Sino-Soviet relationship. It was lucky for Bush that Deng proved to be so deeply antagonistic toward the USSR that even an unimaginative policy sufficed for the time being for Bush to muddle through. However, this policy was soon outpaced by the events in Beijing.

Gorbachev's visit to Beijing saw Bush still struggling to contain what in some circles in Washington appeared—despite all assurances to the contrary—like an act of major reorientation of Chinese foreign policy. The

White House took comfort in the fact that just when Gorbachev was scheduled to appear in Beijing, three ships from the US navy would make a port call at Shanghai. This would serve to reinforce the impression of the strategic depth of Sino-American relations.

The worsening situation in Tiananmen spoiled all this and the ships left China hastily and prematurely. The US Embassy in Beijing was aware of the seriousness of the situation and predicted the crackdown days before it took place. Nonetheless, the White House was still at a loss about what to do. Unlike Gorbachev, Bush could not switch off the microphones of his congressional critics, who demanded a prompt and severe response. While the realities of policy making in Washington made it impossible to avoid reacting in some ways to what had happened in Tiananmen, Bush lacked a firm policy, and his administration was sending mixed signals to China. Early cautious response was followed by tougher sanctions, including suspension of developmental aid, after the Chinese government resorted to repressions, arresting and executing a number of leading activists.

Overnight, US relations with China were thrown back to lows unseen since the 1960s. This was very useful from Gorbachev's perspective, giving him the much-needed opening. Just as the White House angrily denounced the Tiananmen atrocity, Gorbachev quietly schemed for building up closer relations with China and bringing India in to make a strategic "triangle" of a subtly anti-American orientation.

It was ironic that the United States, which had so much to offer to China and, from Deng's perspective, was the most crucial partner in China's modernization, would lose out to the USSR and India (until then despised and feared in Beijing)—all because of Bush's inability to dispense with the human rights agenda. Just as in February Fang Lizhi's invitation had been counterproductive, so US sanctions accomplished very little, except for pushing China toward a better relationship with the USSR, something Bush had painstakingly tried to avoid. Even if such a response was unavoidable for domestic political reasons, it revealed US diplomacy as poorly coordinated, given to extremes, self-contradictory, and in many ways self-defeating. Needless to say, it did not have any impact on China's domestic situation, except for further undermining the reformist faction in the leadership.

Bush realized this very well, which was one reason why he proceeded, promptly if secretly, to reestablish contact with the Chinese leadership. In July National Security Adviser Brent Scowcroft famously smuggled himself into China aboard an unmarked airplane for talks with Deng Xiaoping and Li Peng: both resented US "interference" in China's affairs. Deng went into a lengthy account of China's struggle with modernity: "I think that one must understand history; we have won the victory represented by the founding of the People's Republic of China by fighting a twenty-two-year war with the cost of more than twenty million lives, a war fought by the Chinese people under the leadership of the Communist Party.... [P]eople must come to understand that China is an independent country, which means no interference by foreigners."[63] Scowcroft recalled feeling that the "clash of cultures" created a wide gap between China and the United States, but the purpose of his trip was to keep channels open for communication.

Scowcroft was back in China in December in an effort to arrange for the safe exit of Fang Lizhi. While no breakthrough was achieved, relations continued to improve gradually. The Chinese leaders took every opportunity to demonstrate that the relationship was back on track, reaching out to every US delegation that turned up in China in early 1990. In a meeting with former US congressmen, the new General Secretary of the CCP, Jiang Zemin, stressed that "there were no fundamental, irreconcilable differences" between the United States and China, and that "the future would be bright." Reporting on this trip to the White House, one of the members of the delegation, Lawrence Hogan, noted: "I would like to see their economy fail to accelerate popular unrest and a concomitant blossoming of democracy which I feel will inevitably come. But, a strong Chinese economy would help the Chinese people whose lot, if improved by a higher standard of living and more contacts with the free world, might result in an evolution toward democracy after Deng Xiaoping's death." "Your ambivalence about the situation in China is felt by many of us," responded Brent Scowcroft; "the state of our relations is not good and, for the short term, not hopeful."[64]

In assessing the handling of the Tiananmen massacre by the Bush Administration, it is useful to consider what could have been done differently. The White House was under immense pressure from Congress to react firmly to the crackdown. The media used every opportunity to criticize Bush for appeasing the "butchers of Tiananmen." There were enormous political risks for the Administration in moving too quickly to restore normal relations with China. In this sense, the very structure of US domestic policy making made it difficult for the Americans to build the kind of positive relationship with China that Bush had hoped to achieve at the start of his term. There is little doubt, on the other hand, that the Chinese went to greater lengths in 1989 to appease the United States. Yet the White House, in the euphoria of 1989, saw no reason for being unduly flexible with China. There was an expectation of collapse, which made Bush all the more reluctant to extend a hand to the Chinese communists, especially when doing so entailed political risks. Compared to the Russians, who (for all of Gorbachev's alleged pro-Western sentiments and his political weakness notwithstanding) immediately seized the opportunity to build firmer bridges to China, the Bush Administration proved fairly short-sighted in not seeking deeper engagement with China at a crucial time in the reform and opening process.

TWO ROADS

One of the fascinating elements of the relationship between Moscow and Beijing since the establishment of the PRC was their shared adherence to vaguely defined principles of economic development, which, given time, would lead both countries toward a common socialist destiny. The means of getting there, however, was never spelled out precisely. In the early 1950s the Soviet leaders held the seniority: the Chinese listened to the advice of "elder brothers" offered by thousands of Soviet specialists working in China on countless development projects, and brought back by thousands of Chinese students who experienced the Soviet economic model first hand. China imported machines, entire plants, know-how, and technologies, but most important, Soviet managerial approaches. The Chinese planned economy of the early 1950s was not as well planned, perhaps, as the Soviet model would permit, but it bore the imprint of "made in the USSR." In retrospect, the Soviet economy serves as a textbook example of disastrous mismanagement and wasteful inefficiency, but in the 1950s, the Soviet Union was home to an economic miracle, deemed worthy of admiration and emulation not only in China but, indeed, in the emerging postcolonial world.[65]

But by the mid-1950s China's policy makers began to question the Soviet economic model. Mao Zedong, disappointed that Soviet-style development failed to harness the enthusiasm of the Chinese masses, unleashed radical policies under the banner of the Great Leap Forward. Radicalism misfired: rosy targets were missed, China succumbed to famine, and the leadership was forced to return to Soviet-inspired economic practices. Mao may not have known much about economics, but he was an economic reformer. Like Deng Xiaoping after him, Mao sought to replace the inefficient Soviet model with a model that would allow China to achieve more impressive results in a shorter time. The failure of the "Leap" discredited leftist radicalism as a viable development strategy. But the search continued, as Deng Xiaoping embraced economic reforms. As for Mao in the 1950s so for Deng in the 1980s: the Soviet economic model provided an important reference point against which to judge the success or failure of the Chinese reforms. Endemic failures of the "ossified" Soviet economy at least made clear to Deng what he did not want to see in China.[66]

From their inception in 1985, Gorbachev's reforms were intently observed in China. Soviet-watchers published studies of new tendencies in the USSR in scholarly journals like *Sulian Dong'ou Wenti*, some even finding fault with Gorbachev for moving ahead too slowly. On the whole, Soviet reforms were favorably assessed, and inevitable parallels between Soviet and Chinese experience gave impetus to the development of comparative studies of socialism in China. For a time such scholarly exercise enjoyed tacit endorsement or at least benevolent neutrality of the Chinese leadership.[67] That changed in 1987 for two reasons: political unrest in China and political reforms in the USSR.

Deng's economic reforms, for all their positive impact on China, contributed to growing income inequality, unemployment, inflation, and rampant corruption. Social tensions offered a fertile environment for public protest. In December 1986 student demonstrations erupted in Hefei, home to the prestigious University of Science and Technology. Students' demands for democratic reforms met with sympathy in the ranks of China's intelligentsia and in the reformist faction of the party elite, supposedly represented at the top by Deng Xiaoping's protégé Hu Yaobang. These connections may have encouraged demonstrators; by late December the movement's ranks swelled: 50,000 protested in Shanghai on December 20. Concerned about political instability, Deng Xiaoping ordered repressive measures. By early January, key activists were arrested and others were frightened into submission. Demonstrations died out. Then there was blood-letting at the top. Hu Yaobang was designated the scapegoat for the unrest and lost his position as General Secretary. Deng Xiaoping unleashed a campaign against "bourgeois liberalization."[68]

Just days after the Chinese authorities clamped down on the student democratic movement, Gorbachev, at a specially convened party plenum, announced unheard-of democratic reforms in the USSR. These included competitive elections of regional (and eventually national) officials by secret ballot and allowing workers a greater say in the running of state enterprises. "We need democracy like air," Gorbachev said in his three-hour speech to the stunned plenum delegates.[69] There was enormous international fallout, too. Western media published commentaries under titles like "An uncanny sound of dissidence at the top" and "Gorbachev urges more democracy, openness."[70] Soviet allies in Eastern Europe were visibly nervous: "Your Khrushchev ... caused 1956 in Hungary with his reforms. And now Gorbachev is destabilizing the socialist commonwealth."[71] Gorbachev, however, was determined to push ahead: "We will not quiver. And if we make a mistake somewhere—don't panic. The main thing now is to involve the people."[72]

Thus, by early 1987 China and the Soviet Union found themselves on two different reform trajectories. The irreconcilable differences of the two approaches were not yet manifest; for a time, rare Chinese comments on Gorbachev's reforms projected a sense of caution rather than disapproval. For example, when on March 3 the Central Committee called a special meeting of scholars and officials to discuss the situation in the Soviet Union, opinion split between those who thought that Soviet reforms could be successful and those who cautioned against unrealistic optimism. Yet others insisted that the Soviet reform attempt demonstrated that "all socialist countries need to reform" and thus in this sense if Gorbachev succeeded "it would be a good thing."[73] Deng Xiaoping himself, in comments to a Canadian visitor on March 19, erred on the side of caution and emphasized, with subtle assertion of reformist leadership, that whatever Gorbachev did, China was still at the forefront: "As to the outcome of Gorbachev's reforms, we still have to see. We are now doing what no man before us has done; we are feeling our way forward. If China is successful, it can show example to three quarters of the world's population, to the poor and backward nations."[74]

Gorbachev steamed ahead. In meeting after meeting at the Politburo, he criticized, demanded, advised, promised, threatened: "perestroika is skidding, comrades"... "if things go like they did before, the people will see that we have no hands, and that we only babble"... "remember, comrades ministers: if you restructure yourselves like you did before, nothing will come out of perestroika. No one needs this kind of perestroika."[75] In June 1987 Gorbachev announced far-reaching economic reforms: henceforth, the government was to reduce its intervention in economic matters; enterprises would obtain greater autonomy to manufacture, market, and sell their products at a profit; peasants were promised land and incentives; and all of that would happen alongside greater openness and democratization. To show good example, Gorbachev publicly named several ministers and regional party secretaries who, in his opinion, were failing perestroika and the people's hopes. This could not inspire bureaucratic confidence.

By late 1987 it was obvious to all that Gorbachev faced a serious conservative backlash, as well as liberal prodding. Tensions came to a head on October 21, 1987, at a party plenum. After Gorbachev delivered his plenum report, Boris Yeltsin, the Moscow party boss, criticized the slow pace of reforms: nothing had been done in two years, he said. The people were losing faith in the party proclamations. Yeltsin took a personal jab at conservative Politburo member Yegor Ligachev for suppressing criticism, and at Gorbachev for tolerating an incipient personality cult. These remarks caused uproar. Gorbachev counterattacked. Yeltsin was cowed into admitting his mistakes, but there was no hiding the obvious: Gorbachev faced an unprecedented affront.[76] Within days, details of the standoff went public, setting the foreign press abuzz with speculations.[77]

The Chinese were watching these developments intently. They coincided with the 13th Congress of the Chinese Communist Party, which was everywhere hailed as a victory for China's reformers. Deng Xiaoping orchestrated the retirement of the old guard. They were replaced in the Politburo and in the Central Committee by relatively young technocrats—"Mr. Deng's new boys," the *Guardian* called them—pragmatists, "untrammeled by dogma."[78] "Deng went far beyond anything previously attempted in China or the Soviet Union," echoed the *Washington Post*, praising the "triumph for Deng ... that goes beyond what most diplomats and analysts expected in terms of the power struggle between the conservatives and reformers."[79] Zhao Ziyang, the new General Secretary, would lead China on the path of reforms. The question on many observers' minds in November was how China's reforms would compare to developments in the USSR: how fast and how far the Chinese were willing to go in matching the Soviet experience of democratization and glasnost.

These kinds of questions were put to Zhao Ziyang in his meeting with journalists on November 2, 1987. Asked whether China was progressing faster than the Soviet Union in its reforms, Zhao stressed, painstakingly, the differences between China and the Soviet Union. In his view, any comparison was out of place: "We have not started a competition with the Soviet Union in terms of carrying out reform. And we are not preparing to emulate the Soviet Union in this regard."[80] However, off limits to reporters, the Chinese leaders sounded alarm. At a special meeting called at the Central Committee on November 19 to consider the Soviet situation, criticism of Gorbachev's reforms was noticeably sharper. Li Peng penned in his diary: "some comrades thought: we formerly had a high appraisal of Soviet reforms; in reality, Gorbachev shouts a lot and does little. Other comrades thought that Gorbachev, by his methods, created an opposition to himself, whereas the Chinese [methods] have united the great majority of officials."[81]

The next few months proved crucial for making judgments. In February 1988 ethnic strife flared up in Nagorno-Karabakh between the Armenians and the Azeris. The rigidity of the multinational Soviet state was suddenly put to a violent test. Those were ominous warnings for the Chinese, who had their own thorny nationalism problem, especially in Xinjiang and Tibet. By July 1988, conservatives like Li Peng privately voiced disdain for Gorbachev's policies: "Gorbachev's nationalities policy can lead to the break-up of the USSR. If all the republics, which constitute the union, become independent, the Soviet Union will be reduced only to Russia and it will no longer be a great power."

Speaking at a special closed meeting called on July 14, 1988, to consider Soviet reforms, Li Peng, now the Prime Minister, vowed that China would "advance gradually, preserving stability and unity," unlike Gorbachev, whom he criticized for "ingratiating the West."[82] Soviet bloc intelligence reports suggested that by early 1989 Li Peng was personally inclined to put the Chinese reforms on hold "until the reform processes in the Eastern European countries and in the Soviet Union reach some kind of an equilibrium, [so that], taking into consideration the experience of these countries, one could then . . . implement reforms in China."[83]

"In contacts with the Soviet leaders, he acts with reserve and correctness"—so Li Peng was characterized in an internal Soviet assessment. "He takes active interest in the Soviet reality, but has not registered open sympathy towards the Soviet *perestroika*, especially in the political [sphere]." In fact, Li Peng, the darling of conservative elders like Chen Yun and Bo Yibo, was a staunch opponent of Gorbachev-style reforms. But it would be unfair to take his self-serving diary at face value and assume everyone else in the Chinese leadership reacted to the perestroika as Li Peng had.

There is evidence that Zhao Ziyang was more open to the Soviet experience. Reportedly, during a Politburo meeting in December 1988, he unveiled a proposal for political reforms in China and—interestingly, with Deng Xiaoping's support—managed to get them approved. This proposal included an idea of "activation" of the political parties other than the CCP, and, after 1990, bringing them on board in the form of a coalition government. Zhao argued that the existing political structure was too rigid for economic reforms, that the CCP monopoly on power obstructed integration with Macao and Hong Kong and reunification with Taiwan, and, most unusually, that "it was unacceptable that in the sphere of political reforms China would 'tread' behind the Soviet Union."[84]

Unfortunately for him, Zhao was soon ousted as a result of student protests. It is rather ironic that the student movement, with its emphasis on Gorbachev-style reforms in China, indirectly contributed to the demise of "China's Gorbachev." But whether it met with Li Peng's skepticism or Zhao Ziyang's sympathy, Gorbachev's reforms project caused intense debate in the Chinese leadership. For better or worse, the outcome of that particular debate decided China's fate.

Gorbachev did not make the same sort of comparisons. The failure of the "ossified" Soviet model was an important reference point for Deng Xiaoping's reform strategy, but the opposite was not true. When he set out on the path of reform, Gorbachev did not pay attention to the Chinese experience. In his *Perestroika and New Thinking*, published in late 1987, Gorbachev wrote that the Chinese had "very interesting and in many respects productive ideas" about modernization. That was it—just one line in 270 pages.[85] It was a curious thing to say after nearly ten years of China's breathtaking economic reforms, of which many were immediately relevant to the Soviet situation. China was an example, a precedent, a textbook for reform; she had in store innumerable lessons for Gorbachev if he cared to look her way.

It was not that Gorbachev ignored Chinese reforms altogether. For example, he followed fairly closely what the Chinese attempted in agriculture—and he was full of praise, for there was no hiding that China managed to feed itself when the Soviet Union had to import grain to cover chronic shortfalls. He occasionally cited from the Chinese experience at Politburo meetings and in meetings with foreign leaders.[86] On the whole, however, Gorbachev was scathingly critical of the "four modernizations"—but only in private encounters. Most of the times he brought up Chinese reforms, he downplayed them and prophesied their failure. His message was: perestroika was made in the USSR. Others were imitators. "They all now claim they started perestroika before us."[87]

One obvious problem with Chinese reforms, from Gorbachev's perspective, was that they were confined to economic matters, leaving politics out of the picture. Gorbachev was convinced that glasnost and democratization at the grassroots level were a sine qua non for successful decentralization and effective operation of the Soviet economy. His democratic innovations at the January 1987 party plenum, which had far-reaching effects for the entire Soviet system, were in fact aimed at giving workers a greater voice in economic decision making—for example, by means of electing their own factory managers. The entire economic system had to be opened up to scrutiny and democratized, Gorbachev decreed, or else the armchair apparatchiks would put a break on any reform effort. In other words, political democratization from the outset was not an end in itself but an indispensable means to the restructuring of the economy. How could the Chinese put the cart before the horse? By putting economics first, Gorbachev told Bulgaria's Todor Zhivkov in May 1987, the Chinese "disturbed the dialectic between the base and the superstructure, and that created difficulties."[88] "Gorbachev is an idiot," was Deng's comment on such order of priorities: "he won't have the power to fix the economic problems and the people will remove him."[89] Time proved Deng right on that score.

In the meantime, it was clear to Gorbachev that the Chinese were running into serious problems in their economic reforms. "China has almost used up its foreign currency reserves. Of course, there are now radio receivers, TVs, cars and maybe something else on the country's market. But on the whole these are prestigious goods, for the elites. The main capacities of equipment China had purchased do not work. For its work depends on the West, and they [the Chinese] have no money to pay for the supplies."[90] All of that naturally made the Chinese look to the Soviet Union for clues about how to make reforms work. "In practice they are adopting our approaches."[91] "Now they are carefully analyzing the course of their reforms. They are thinking about conclusions, which have to be made in terms of the political leadership and the state system. And one should say that they are very carefully, intently like no one else, watching our perestroika."[92] On his last point Gorbachev was certainly right.

Economic tribulations of the late 1980s took some steam out of Gorbachev's confidence about the great relevance of the Soviet experience. But concerns about China's problems remained. First, Gorbachev saw problems with the Chinese "family responsibility system," which allowed private production in agriculture. As he told Fidel Castro in April 1989, "A peasant household has its limitations—one needs agricultural technologies, biotechnologies, etc., and the house responsibility system does not correspond to this well. The growth of output stopped." Compared to this pathetic performance, Soviet agricultural reforms held a much greater promise because peasants were free to lease equipment and enter into contract relations with collective farms.[93] A few weeks later Gorbachev repeated this view to James Baker: "Look at what happened in China. First, they attained great successes in the economy but now they have stumbled over the inadequate level of scientific-technical progress, especially in the agrarian sector."[94]

Second, Gorbachev perceived serious problems with the Chinese special economic zones, usually celebrated as a remarkable achievement of Deng's policy of reform and opening. The Chinese, in his view,

> expected, with the help of foreigners, to build factories and earn foreign currency but their product turned out to be uncompetitive, and they had to repay their loans using their own gold reserves. They went quite far in the economic liberalization.... This made the economy more dynamic but also led to increase in prices, inflation and certain social tensions.[95]

These woes made the Chinese leaders abandon some of the more liberal economic practices, leading Gorbachev to believe—in the wake of the post-1988 Chinese austerity measures—that "in essence, there is a restoration of the Maoist [sic] model [in China], strengthening of state regulations and centralization.... Therefore, China will have to travel a very long way even to raise the question of moving to the market [economy]."[96] In other words, by the turn of the decade Gorbachev concluded that he was ahead of China not only in political reforms but also in the move toward a market economy.

Why was Gorbachev so unwilling to learn from the Chinese experience? A Central Committee functionary, Karen Brutents, offers an uncomfortable but fair reason—Gorbachev's "personal ambitions, jealous view of China as a competitor in his messianic path-breaking pretensions [and] a kind of arrogance, which hindered [Gorbachev] from a correct appraisal of anything which was being done *differently from us*."[97] The point was to engineer a perestroika not solely for the Soviet Union, but—to cite the subtitle of his 1987 book—"for our country and for the entire world." "The entire world" was a far-reaching claim to make for a Soviet General Secretary. Perestroika opened new vistas for Gorbachev. His ideas would save the East and the West, the North and the South. He was the new Lenin, designated by fate to transform the world in accordance with his own blurry vision. At the very least, he was the prophet of reformed socialism. How could the Chinese match Gorbachev's credentials?

Gorbachev was not alone in his sense of exceptionalism amid pragmatic, sober-minded Kremlin policy makers. It was a sense that permeated the elites, especially Gorbachev's circle of close friends and advisers. Here is, for example, what Georgii Shakhnazarov had to say of the relative importance of Chinese and Soviet reforms in August 1987:

> The question of priority is being raised. One should say that some people are already raising these questions and even consciously try to prove [their] priority. One can hear insinuations of this kind in the Chinese press.... Probably, there are countries, where leaders, even if they do not say so directly, suggest that they are in the vanguard. They want to reserve, as it were, their leadership in this respect. I think that this is not the main thing. We'll be paid back in glory, as they say.... Let's say the Chinese started several years ago, the Hungarians started their own reforms even earlier, the Polish had them, and so on. If we leave these disagreements aside, I think everyone will agree that perestroika in the Soviet Union has, of course, the decisive significance. It has it because the Soviet Union is the leading state of the socialist system... this is one of the greatest powers or superpowers of the modern day, upon which depends the fate of the world more than on anyone else.[98]

These statements should be understood in the context of "traditionally dismissive" stereotyping of China, to which Gorbachev and other Soviet leaders may have subconsciously succumbed despite being "internationalist" in appearance. They found it difficult to stomach China's remarkable rise from poverty and backwardness.[99] Indeed, Moscow had always sought recognition in the West, seeing it in a reference point against which to judge their own country's successes and failures.[100] China's experience was irrelevant to the Soviet quest for recognition. If this is kept in mind, the seemingly perplexing question—why Gorbachev turned a blind eye to the Chinese experience—acquires unexpected clarity.

CHINA AND THE COLLAPSE OF THE SOVIET BLOC

The year 1989 was a turning point in the Chinese assessment of Soviet reforms. The crackdown in Tiananmen was no doubt inspired by Gorbachev's failures in the USSR. The Chinese leaders cited the chaotic Soviet situation to justify their use of force in the weeks and months after Tiananmen. The fall of the Berlin Wall convinced policy makers in Beijing that Gorbachev was no longer a Marxist-Leninist. Despite rapid changes inside the USSR, the Chinese took care to maintain and improve Sino-Soviet relations, and to emphasize that Gorbachev's reforms were his own problem—that his unpredictable twists and turns would not affect the fortunes of the Sino-Soviet rapprochement. Yet when Gorbachev was locked up at his Black Sea villa in an attempted coup d'état, there were no regrets or protests from the Chinese. On the contrary, Beijing cautiously probed the intentions of the coup leaders. The coup attempt collapsed, and Gorbachev was temporarily rescued. No tears were shed in Beijing.

In 1989 communist regimes in Eastern Europe tumbled like a deck of cards. On June 4, the day of the Tiananmen crackdown, Solidarity swept the first genuinely democratic elections in Poland. In the spring of 1989 the opposition steadily gained ground in Hungary. Soviet forces began a phased withdrawal in April 1989; Gorbachev promised not to intervene. In October, Hungary ceased to be a "People's Republic." In the meantime, thousands of East Germans fled to the West through the border between Austria and Hungary, putting enormous pressure on the communist regime in Berlin. Hardliner Erich Honecker was ousted in October, but there was no stemming the tide of public protest: the Berlin Wall fell on November 9, 1989. At the same time, revolutionary changes transformed Czechoslovakia, Bulgaria, and Romania, ending with the execution of Romania's long-time leader and friend of China Nicolae Ceaușescu. That was as violent as it got in Eastern Europe: everywhere, communism collapsed swiftly and unexpectedly, with barely a hint of hardliner resistance.

What did the Chinese think of this remarkable transformation? None of the Eastern European scenarios were to their liking. What happened there, in Deng Xiaoping's view, was a case of US-sponsored turmoil: "Capitalism wants to defeat socialism in the long run. In the past they used weapons, atomic bombs and hydrogen bombs, but they were opposed by the peoples of the world. Now they are trying peaceful evolution."[101] Eastern Europe was particularly vulnerable to these schemes because "socialism [there] had been imposed by the Soviet Army and the end of World War II so it was not so deep rooted," according to Qian Qichen. But the fundamental reason was economics. "The main thing," argued the new CCP General Secretary Jiang Zemin, "is that they did not improve the economy and people's lives." Moreover, there had been, in Jiang's words, "all kinds of unhealthy tendencies and decadence," and the parties had been "separated from the masses."[102]

Jiang could have said the same thing about the Chinese Communist Party. The parallels were staggering. Of course, the Soviet Red Army did not impose communism on China as it had on Eastern Europe, but this was a small comfort. Who could give guarantees that China would not succumb to turmoil as did Eastern Europe? China's own recent history was full of turmoil. "You see," Li Peng told Brent Scowcroft in December, "when China was in the Cultural Revolution we had a similar case—that is, chaos emerged in just a few days' time. Had we not adopted the resolute measures on June 4, the present situation in China would be even more turbulent today.... Similar events as in Eastern Europe will not occur in China." Yet Li Peng was a politician and not a prophet.

Naturally, the Chinese leaders were worried about the consequences of Eastern European revolutions for China's communist regime. Perhaps nothing frightened them more than the gruesome death of Nicolae Ceaușescu and his wife, Elena, on December 25. Deng Xiaoping supposedly played a VCR tape of their execution to the senior leaders. "We'll be like this if we don't strengthen our proletarian dictatorship and repress the reactionaries," said one of the viewers. "Yes, we'll be like this," Deng replied, "if we don't carry out reforms and bring about benefits to the people."[103] The shock was all the greater because only days before Ceaușescu met his fate, he had received the Chinese envoy, Politburo member, and security czar Qiao Shi, who shared with the Romanian dictator China's experience of crushing public protests. Qiao Shi came back convinced that Ceaușescu would keep the situation under control.[104] He got it wrong.

There was a flurry of discussions in the Politburo. Provincial leaders were invited for some of the meetings. On December 27 General Secretary Jiang Zemin talked about the importance of checking Western ideological subversion: "Not only should one prevent the Western infiltration and corruption but one must take the initiative—strengthen the Marxism-Leninist and Mao Zedong thought education of the officials and the masses."[105] To make sure these points were not lost on the lower ranks of Chinese party officials, a special circular about the situation in Romania was sent down to the provincial and municipal levels.[106] In Beijing, the army, armed police, and public security personnel were put on high alert and told to be ready for all eventualities.[107] In internal meetings the Chinese leaders emphasized the need to "strengthen the unity of the army, and to ensure that the army is absolutely under the leadership of the party."[108] Ceaușescu had paid too dearly for neglecting this simple rule.

What happened in Eastern Europe did not endear Gorbachev to the Chinese leaders. At Politburo meetings in the fall of 1989, Gorbachev was described "in unflattering terms."[109] At a meeting on December 5, Li Peng, predicting Gorbachev's downfall, concluded that he was no longer "a Marxist-Leninist" but "in essence a social democrat."[110] At a farewell dinner with Soviet Ambassador Oleg Troyanovskii, Li Peng put it with diplomatic politeness: "the views of comrade Gorbachev evolve so quickly that we cannot keep up with them."[111] Several leaders, including Wang Zhen and Deng Liqun, called for public denunciation of Gorbachev.[112] Critical pieces appeared in the internal press.

To complement his political short-sightedness, Gorbachev was accused of economic incompetence. "The Soviets [do] not grasp the economy well," Qian Qichen told Brent Scowcroft in December 1990, "and Gorbachev often [does] not grasp what he [is] asking of it..., I have not seen Gorbachev taking any measures."[113] During his trip to Moscow in April 1990, Li Peng was surprised to see a lack of agreement among Soviet leaders about basic issues of economic development. Gorbachev called for a "state-regulated market economy" and Nikolai Ryzhkov spoke about a "market-regulated planned economy." Li Peng returned to Beijing convinced that there was factional struggle in Moscow among conservatives, liberals, and moderates.[114]

Whatever Gorbachev's economic agenda, the Chinese were dumbfounded when the Soviets turned to China for "commodity loans." "We were quite taken aback when they first raised this," Qian Qichen said; "We have agreed to extend some money to them."[115] At least two agreements were signed—one worth five hundred million Swiss francs (in early 1990) and one for a billion francs (in March 1991).[116] The latter was reportedly intended as "support" for Gorbachev, who had, some weeks earlier, gone along with a crackdown against secessionism in the Baltics, and had become noticeably cooler with the West.[117] China would provide grain, meat, peanuts, tea, silk, tobacco, cigarettes, textiles, and light industrial products to stock up the Soviet shelves.[118] Li Peng apologized for offering this "rather limited" aid: China, he said, is "a developing country faced with problems caused by its huge population." "The irony must be bitter to the diehards of the Kremlin," commented the *Economist*. If it was, no one said a thing: the Soviets were too desperate at this point in time to look a gift horse in the mouth.[119]

Why all this charity for the sake of a man whom the Chinese blamed for the ruin of socialism in Eastern Europe? The answer is, China needed Gorbachev. China needed the Soviet Union. The collapse of the birthplace of the socialist revolution would have very serious, potentially disastrous consequences for the stability of the Chinese communist regime, weakened and isolated as it already was following the Tiananmen massacre and the revolutions of 1989. The overnight freeze in China's relations with the West after June 4 had been a heavy blow. "After taking Eastern Europe in its hands," argued Li Peng in February 1990, "the US can put China under greater pressure." However, he added, "different kinds of international contradictions still give us room to maneuver."[120]

In the early 1970s, Mao was the master strategist of contradictions, using them to position China at its most advantageous vis-à-vis the superpowers. So now, Deng Xiaoping and other Chinese leaders were not taken in by Gorbachev's embrace of one big world. They kept their eyes open for signs of Soviet-American tensions. Li Peng insisted that despite the East-West détente, "the Soviet-American contradictions still remain"; indeed, contradictions between socialism and capitalism, alongside the North-South contradictions, were "intensifying."[121] Deng Xiaoping thought that the bipolar world was falling apart, but "in the future, whether the world becomes three-polar, four-polar or five-polar, the Soviet Union will be one of the poles, no matter how weakened it may be and even if some of its republics withdraw from it."[122] Deng was also under the impression that following the collapse of Eastern Europe, the US attitude toward the Soviet Union "stiffened."[123] This gave an opening to China to engage with the Soviets as a way of decreasing Beijing's international isolation. The Soviets, for once, stayed well clear of criticizing China after Tiananmen. What would have happened if people like Boris Yeltsin took power? For this reason alone, China needed Gorbachev.

Then, of course there was the issue of the legitimacy of the Chinese communist regime if the Soviet Union disintegrated. Beijing might find it difficult to maintain territorial unity when a neighboring multinational empire was falling to pieces in the whirlwind of ethnic nationalism. Tibet, Xinjiang, and, to a lesser extent, Inner Mongolia were all potential trouble spots. In Tibet pro-independence protests were brutally put down in

March 1989, but Lhasa remained under martial law. Trouble was brooding in Xinjiang: there were reports of "separatist activities" in early 1990.[124] The democratic revolution in Mongolia (between the winter and spring of 1990), and its strong undercurrent of Mongolian nationalism, added to Beijing's concerns. No wonder it was reported in February 1990 that the Chinese government decided to increase the number of troops in the three regions, train riot police, and intensify intelligence work among minorities.[125] Ismail Amat, a senior Chinese official in charge of minority affairs, explicitly blamed nationalist unrest on, among other things, the bad Soviet example.[126]

The second problem was the legitimacy of communism itself. Soviet collapse would leave only China as a major power under a communist regime. The banner of the leading communist power—something Mao had coveted—was now falling into China's hands. Would the Chinese leadership be able to carry the burden of the flagship of socialism? These were all questions Deng Xiaoping and his comrades were asking themselves as they pondered the fate of Soviet socialism. Much has been written about the existence of a hardliner faction in the CCP leadership, including Wang Zhen and Chen Yun as well as Beijing Mayor Chen Xitong. The hardliners' response to the prospect of Soviet collapse was to intensify class struggle inside China and roll back economic reforms. But Deng thought that the lessons for the Chinese Communist Party were precisely the opposite: economic reforms had to be continued. "If, while these countries are in turmoil, China, according to the plan, really doubles [its economy] for the second time, that will be a success for socialism."[127]

Yet for both the hardliners and the reformers, there was nothing to be gained for China from Soviet collapse—and much to be lost. Whatever they thought of Gorbachev and his policies, the Chinese leaders pragmatically decided that it was in their interest to maintain good relations with the USSR and do whatever they could—given their modest means—to strengthen its stability. Gorbachev, too, tried to use China's post-Tiananmen international isolation to improve his standing with the Chinese leaders. This became especially visible in early 1991, when Gorbachev began to tilt to the right in his domestic politics in response to the escalating crisis in the Baltics.

This period in fact witnessed a brief renaissance of Sino-Soviet relations, especially in the military sphere. The hardliner Minister of Defense, Dmitrii Yazov, visited Beijing in May 1991, reportedly promising his Chinese colleagues that the Soviet armed forces would "defend the gains of socialism," and even proposing to form a Sino-Soviet alliance aimed against the West.[128] That same month Jiang Zemin went to Moscow to meet with Gorbachev.

In their long exchanges Jiang talked about the importance of preserving political stability. "If there is no stability, it is difficult to advance reform, not to mention development. Only if you have political stability can you promote economic development, and economic development, on the other hand, can promote political stability."[129] But it was too late for Gorbachev to heed China's advice: he was already in a free fall, taking with him political stability and the Soviet economy.

CHINA AND THE SOVIET COUP D'ÉTAT, AUGUST 1991

On August 19, 1991, Gorbachev was placed under virtual house arrest in the Crimea by his comrades-in-leadership: Vice President Gennadii Yanaev, KGB Chief Vladimir Kryuchkov, Minister of Defense Dmitrii Yazov, Interior Minister Boris Pugo, Prime Minister Valentin Pavlov, and several other conspirators. The coup leaders formed the State Emergency Committee (Russian acronym: GKChP). Yanaev was declared the Acting President on account of Gorbachev's "illness." In the meantime, the conspirators negotiated with Gorbachev to get his blessing for their declaring emergency. Gorbachev refused. In Moscow, GKChP forces moved downtown to take control of the Russian "White House," defended by the supporters of Russia's President, Boris Yeltsin. After a brief stand-off, the coup attempt collapsed, and Yeltsin triumphed in Moscow. It is amazing, in hindsight, how incompetent the GKChP leaders turned out to be: despite representing the army and the security apparatus, at the crucial moment they were unable to take decisive action against Yeltsin and Gorbachev. They hesitated, negotiated, and ultimately failed. All were arrested, with the exception of Pugo, who committed suicide. Gorbachev emerged from the ordeal politically weakened; he literally owed his survival to Yeltsin.

The Chinese leadership may have known more about the coming coup d'état than their cool public reaction revealed. The week before the coup the Soviet Ministry of Defense hosted a Chinese military delegation, headed by PLA Chief of Staff Chi Haotian. During the talks, Defense Minister Yazov and Chief of the General Staff Mikhail Moiseev "talked about [their] strictly positive attitude towards the Chinese 'experience' of military suppression of the movement for democracy, and spoke about their own resolve to use military force to 'stop the chaos in the country.'" According to Chinese sources, Chi Haotian left Moscow convinced that the Soviet military would "take decisive measures in the nearest future." The coup d'état came as no surprise.[130]

Contemporary Russian analyses suggested that the instigators of the coup counted on a strategic partnership with China and did not fear Western sanctions: China's own experience in Tiananmen suggested that one could weather Washington's wrath.[131] The coup collapsed before the conspirators had a chance to develop their foreign policy priorities. That being said, already on August 20 Gennadii Yanaev met with Chinese Ambassador to the USSR Yu Hongliang, perhaps to receive assurances of China's support for the coup. The details of their conversation, as so much else in this murky story, remain unknown, although the initiative allegedly came from the Soviet side, and Yu Hongliang only agreed to the meeting after insistent requests to this effect from the Soviet Foreign Ministry.[132] It turned out to be a fatal misstep on Yu's part; he was discredited by his association with the perpetrators of the coup and soon left for China, lamenting the "squabbles" inside the USSR and comparing the mess of the Soviet disintegration to the cultural revolution in China.[133]

But Yu cannot be blamed for his failure to predict the future, nor was he alone in putting his bet on the wrong horse. Back in Beijing, on the night of August 19, as soon as the news came in of what was happening in the USSR, Jiang Zemin held a Politburo meeting. The Chinese leaders felt that the coup was a "good thing," not least for China, because "the West will exert pressure on the Soviet Union, and lessen the pressure on us." The meeting decided that the Chinese media would report on the developments with a bias in favor of the instigators of the coup.[134]

The Politburo's views were immediately circulated to top-ranking officials in a secret document entitled "The Victory of the Soviet People Is a Victory for the Chinese People."[135] When the leadership realized that the Soviet coup was failing, the document was hastily withdrawn, but it had already caused confusion and disarray in the party ranks.[136] In the following days, Beijing scrambled to minimize the coup's potential consequences for China. Reportedly, decisions were made to subject bilateral exchange with the Soviet Union to greater control and to minimize publication of Soviet news in the Chinese newspapers. PLA forces in Xinjiang were put on alert, to watch for signs of possible unrest spreading across the border from Soviet Central Asia.[137]

The failure of the coup put tremendous pressure on Deng. He had to defend his policies against conservatives of the Chen Yun faction, who argued that China, too, was heading toward apocalypse under the banner of reforms. They criticized people like the reformist-minded Vice Premier Zhu Rongji, Deng's recent appointee, whom Chen Yun reportedly labeled a "Yeltsin-like figure."[138] Deng fought back at his eighty-seventh birthday party on August 22, telling those assembled that Gorbachev, although he may look "intelligent," is in reality "very stupid." "Having first disposed of the Communist Party, what will he rely on in reforms?" However, Deng continued, "Soviet conditions are different from China's. He [Gorbachev] did not place economic construction at the center. His reform strategy was erroneous, he did not focus the energies on grasping economic construction. The Soviet lesson demonstrates that China's road of socialism with [Chinese] characteristics is the correct one. The crux of these characteristics is the placing of economic construction at the center."[139] In the months ahead, the patriarch of the Chinese reforms summoned his waning strength to trump up support for reforms in China even as the collapse of the USSR signaled that reforms could lead to lamentable outcomes. He did so by emphasizing the difference between Gorbachev's "stupid" policies and China's pragmatic path of economic reform.

In the meantime, in the days and weeks after the coup, the central authorities put out several circulars. One, sent to the Chinese party officials in late August, stated that the Soviet Union had just had a "bourgeois coup." The letter called for strengthening of "absolute leadership" of the CCP over the public sphere and for raising vigilance in the face of internal and external enemies.[140] A month later, the Politburo circulated yet another document about the lessons of the failed Soviet coup. It blamed Gorbachev for implementing "completely erroneous policies," causing "deep discontent inside and outside the party." The document accused Gorbachev and Yeltsin of leading a "mad counterattack against progressive forces that support socialism and national unity" and unleashing "white terror." The lesson for China was to oppose any bourgeois tendencies and rely for guidance on the "old comrades who have experienced the test of long revolutionary struggle."[141]

Despite the shock of the failed Soviet coup, Beijing maintained Deng Xiaoping's policy of developing Sino-Soviet relations irrespective of what happened, or failed to happen, in the USSR. To this end, the August circular pointed out that the Chinese leadership would stay out of open polemics with the Soviet Union that could only weaken China's international position and negatively impact the internal Chinese situation.[142] The Chinese leadership showed itself at its most pragmatic: great as Yeltsin's or Gorbachev's sins may have been in China's eyes, there was nothing else on offer. Much as two years earlier Beijing quickly moved to secure good relations with transformed Eastern Europe, so the Chinese took care to distance themselves from the events in the USSR and proclaim development of relations with the Soviets based on the Five Principles of Peaceful Coexistence. The Chinese leaders emphasized how history winds up a circuitous road and hundreds of years may pass before there is a definite transit from one social system to another. Jiang Zemin elaborated this view on December 7 at a meeting of the Central Military Commission: feudalism, he said, took thousands of years to replace slavery; capitalism, in turn, took hundreds of years to replace feudalism: "Looking [at events] from the point of view of the long river of history, some of the current setbacks [suffered by socialism] are nothing to be surprised about."[143]

On December 26, 1991, the Soviet Union ceased to exist. China recognized the Russian Federation on December 27, 1991, alongside eleven other former Soviet republics.[144] For a few weeks Sino-Russian relations were in complete disarray. On the Chinese side, the problem was not so much their antipathy for Yeltsin and his team, although there was no love lost between the Chinese and Yeltsin. But things were changing so fast that the Chinese policy makers were simply at a loss about what was actually happening and who was in charge. Charge d'affairs Zhang Zheng conceded on January 10 that the Chinese were putting some contacts on hold, simply because it was unclear whom the Chinese should deal with and whom various Russian delegations actually represented. In addition, there were political uncertainties. Zhang wondered whether the newly formed Commonwealth of Independent States was a sustainable organization, or whether it would fall apart under the pressure of "contradictions and conflicts." Indeed, he did not rule out that Russia itself would further split into "sovereign states."[145]

Despite these uncertainties, the Chinese policy makers acted quickly to achieve an understanding with Russia. Deputy Foreign Minister (and veteran of the Sino-Soviet rapprochement) Tian Zengpei was promptly dispatched to Moscow to work out what the Russians were up to. On December 29, Tian and his Russian counterpart Georgii Kunadze signed a memorandum on Sino-Russian relations, reiterating that these relations would be developed on the basis of the Five Principles of Peaceful Coexistence.[146] Although tensions back home raged between the conservative and the reformist factions in the CCP leadership, the Chinese did not think twice about embracing the Russian democrats. Who else was there to embrace? As Zhang Zheng succinctly put it a few days later, "We are against the ideologization of inter-state relations. Everyone has a right to have their own assessment of the changes which are taking place in your country. But politics is a different thing. China's relations with former Soviet republics will, of course, develop."[147]

HUMAN RIGHTS AND TAIWAN

Russian policy toward China also underwent a transformation. Yeltsin had been at the forefront among China's critics since 1989 and no doubt knew about China's sympathies during the attempted coup in August 1991. "Early" Yeltsin was more pro-Western than just about any other Russian policy maker before or after. With so much communist-bashing at home, it was difficult to see how Yeltsin would accommodate communists in Beijing, especially when there was an ideological alternative to Sino-Russian relations—development of ties with democratic Taiwan. Despite initial leanings in this direction, Yeltsin changed his mind once he assumed real responsibilities as President of independent Russia. In December 1992 he was already in Beijing on a journey that would take the Sino-Russian relationship on a path toward "strategic partnership."

If anyone could take credit for such turnaround, it was Vladimir Lukin, who had been involved in the drafting of Gorbachev's Vladivostok speech of 1986. Lukin, who then worked under Georgii Arbatov at the Institute of USA and Canada Studies, took a direct and early interest in China and was one of the foremost advocates of Sino-Soviet rapprochement. In the late 1980s he briefly worked in the Soviet Foreign Ministry before drifting into Yeltsin's camp, becoming, as the head of the International Affairs committee of the Russian Parliament, something of a counterweight to Yeltsin's much more "pro-Western" Foreign Minister, Andrei Kozyrev.

Yeltsin valued Lukin's insight, which was why in December 1991 he sent him to Beijing with a letter to the Chinese leadership explaining that the turmoil in the USSR would not affect Sino-Russian relations and that Russia would stand by all bilateral agreements.[148] The Chinese received Lukin at an unexpectedly high level, stressing at every opportunity their interest in continuing the development of Sino-Russian relations on the basis of the Five Principles. They were, however, concerned about two things. First, Yeltsin made defense of human rights one of his foreign policy preferences, in contrast to Gorbachev, who, Lukin felt, did not care about human rights and maintained relations with various evil regimes. These policy preferences were especially manifest in relations with countries like North Korea, Cuba, and Afghanistan, which experienced overnight collapse of their relationships with Moscow. The big question was whether Yeltsin might try to peddle a human rights agenda in relations with Beijing.

Upon his return from China, Lukin reported on these concerns: "in the PRC, they have certain worries that Russia will build its approach to China in linkage with its understanding of the problem of human rights, market economy, etc. Thus, there will be ideologization of bilateral relations but, this time, with a minus sign." Lukin cautioned against that: "It seems that the strategic interests of Russia require a pragmatic approach to relations with China, free from any ideologization."[149] Such views increasingly gained ground in the Russian policy establishment; indeed, they were always current among Moscow's China experts and in the general policy community, under Gorbachev or under Yeltsin.

What really took human rights off Moscow's agenda in relations with China, however, was the rapidly escalating socio-economic crisis in Russia itself, with the attendant resurgence of nationalism and a political confrontation that would lead, in 1993, to a standoff between the Parliament and the President. As Russia found itself broke, marginalized, and effectively abandoned by the West, a partnership with China looked more appealing than ever; human rights no longer seemed as important if they meant chaos and misery on a national scale.

Yeltsin's thinking on this score is less apparent than that of his rival in power, Ruslan Khasbulatov. Khasbulatov explained his views to Chinese Ambassador to Russia Wang Jinqing in March 1992: "We simply admire how you implemented your economic reform. What a tragedy would it be for the whole [of] humanity if you did not implement your reform and did not feed your billion people.... In my view, you took a very wise road. Let them reproach you for lack of democracy but, you know, to feed a billion people! What a burden would the humanity have had!" Wang agreed: "you see, many people want to impose their vision that, allegedly, we have it this way, and why don't you have it the same way, etc. The thing is, every country should select what suits it best." "Yes," retorted Khasbulatov, "you are right. We have 157 million [people]. I can imagine if you began your movement towards democracy like we did. You could blow up the entire world."[150] This exchange between Wang and Khasbulatov summarizes the consensus that emerged in Russia's policy community in the early 1990s, a consensus that continues to characterize Moscow's approach to China, to the clear satisfaction of the Chinese leaders.

The other big question mark from Beijing's perspective—as Lukin learned during his visit—was whether Yeltsin would move away from the long-standing Soviet policy of non-engagement with Taiwan. Problems started on this front in the late 1980s. Jealous of arch-competitor South Korea's suspicious economic activities in the USSR, the Taiwanese businessmen eyed opportunities for a breakthrough in the Soviet direction. In October 1988 the first trade delegation from Taiwan visited the USSR and held meetings with Soviet foreign trade officials.[151] Lin Chih-ching, the head of the delegation, came back convinced that Soviet citizens were "seriously undernourished" in their access to foreign-made consumer goods. Taiwan had to act quickly to fill the gap before the South Koreans or the Japanese did. Other members of the delegation lamented that Taiwan was losing out to competitors because of the restrictions on indirect trade.[152]

Business delegations from Taiwan toured the Soviet Union in May and August 1989.[153] The Soviets were also beginning to make reciprocal steps. Coinciding with Gorbachev's trip to China, two Soviet observers, Yurii Akhremenko and Vladimir Ivanov, attended the annual conference of the Pacific Basin Economic Council in Taipei. Although they were "very cautious" and "deliberately kept a low profile," the two became instant celebrities in the Taiwanese press, being the first "trade officials" to visit the Republic of China in forty years.[154] They were not *really* trade officials: Akhremenko was the Executive Secretary of the Soviet National Committee for Asia Pacific Economic Cooperation and Ivanov was the head of the Pacific Region Research Department at the IMEMO. But this did not decrease the Russians' importance in the Taiwanese eyes: their invitation was approved by a special decision of the cabinet.[155]

Little by little, the ice was melting in Soviet-Taiwanese relations. Indirect Soviet-Taiwanese trade alone grew a staggering 868 percent in 1989.[156] All of that boded well for what one correspondent called Taiwan's "guerrilla diplomatic offensive." The idea was that Taipei, with its economic leverage, could well capitalize on the PRC's international isolation following the Tiananmen crackdown to score diplomatic victories in the camp of Beijing's long-time supporters—Eastern Europe and even the Soviet Union.[157] The odds were not in Taiwan's favor, but apparently the Chinese leaders were concerned enough about this "guerrilla diplomacy" that Jiang Zemin wrote a letter to Gorbachev in 1989 asking him to be vigilant in the face of Taipei's courting.[158] However, Soviet-Taiwanese contacts continued to expand and deepen between 1990 and 1991. These contacts were regarded with great suspicion by the Chinese policy makers, who issued warnings about Taipei's "silver bullet diplomacy." To address these concerns, the Soviet Foreign Ministry on occasion reiterated Moscow's commitment to the "One China" principle. Taiwan was not allowed to become a major issue in Sino-Soviet relations—that is, not until October 1990.

On October 27, Gavriil Popov, Moscow's first democratically elected Mayor, arrived in Taipei for a two-day visit. It was technically a "private visit" (the mayor was invited by Chung Shing Textile Co.), but in fact Popov held talks with highly placed Taiwanese officials, including Foreign Minister Chien Fu and Taipei Mayor Huang Ta-chou, from whom he received a set of "keys" to the city as a symbolic gesture of goodwill. Popov's statements to the press were nothing if not sensational. He said he was "going to immediately arrange" Boris Yeltsin's visit to Taiwan and even speculated about political contacts with the breakaway province: "Different kinds of vegetables are in season at different times."[159]

Perhaps the biggest bombshell was Popov's meeting with Wu'er Kaixi, a student activist from Tiananmen who managed to flee China after the crackdown and was sentenced to death in absentia for his role in the unrest. In October 1990 Wu'er Kaixi was in a hospital in Taiwan, undergoing post-traumatic treatment. Popov took the initiative and visited Wu'er Kaixi at the hospital, with the press corps on his heels. "I was very happy and flattered [by] his presence," recalled Wu'er Kaixi. "We had 10 minutes meeting in front of [the] press corps: ...salute and support from one democracy activist [and] reform[er] to another."[160] According to press reports, Popov told Wu'er Kaixi that "he supported and was concerned about the mainland's pro-democracy movement. He said the efforts of the mainland students bore permanent witness to the meaning and value of democracy."[161] Newspapers bore photos of Popov shaking hands with the Chinese dissident.

All of this was a huge affront to Beijing. Yu Hongliang turned to Soviet officials for explanations. He was assured at all levels that the Soviet Union firmly adhered to the "One China principle." There followed some internal squabbles and finger-pointing in Moscow. As a result, after consultations among the Soviet Foreign Ministry, Soviet diplomatic missions, and the Russian Foreign Ministry, the latter prepared guidance (February 1991) proscribing any official exchanges with Taiwan and warning of a fallout for Sino-Soviet relations should Popov-type initiatives continue: "one may suppose that the Chinese leadership is capable of certain steps with regard to the USSR and the RSFSR [i.e. Russia], in particular, of sharp reduction or termination of border and regional ties.... The Chinese like to repeat: 'If you chase after a seed you may lose the watermelon.'"[162] The big question, however, was: how much clout did the Russian (or, for that matter, Soviet) Foreign Ministry actually have, and what could it do to constrain actions of radical democrats like Popov who had their separate channels to Yeltsin, or of businessmen who itched to strike it rich with Taiwanese contracts?

The Chinese made the situation even more difficult by demanding that the Soviet Union curb not only official but even most unofficial contacts with Taipei. During Foreign Ministry consultations in April 1991, the Soviet negotiators pointed to the discrepancies in the Chinese attitude toward Japan's or America's relations with Taiwan and the much tougher restrictions imposed on the Soviet dealings with the province. The Chinese representative Ni Yaoli agreed that the Soviets were being held to a much higher standard: "the Chinese," he said, "count on a 'special approach' of the Soviet Union to the Taiwan question in light of the currently friendly character of Soviet-Chinese relations." This kind of approach could work in a different setting, but in the context of the great changes of 1991 the Chinese had clearly overplayed their hand: Ni Yaoli was told to "take into account the new realities in the Soviet Union." The internal Soviet report highlighted Moscow's frustration with the diehard attitude of the PRC representatives: "the Chinese side is interested in...controlling our actions with regard to Taiwan, sanctioning or, more probably, prohibiting Soviet initiatives in this sphere."[163]

Gradual improvement in Soviet-Taiwanese relations continued, to Beijing's chagrin, especially after the coup. Unlike Beijing, Taipei welcomed Gorbachev's return: Foreign Minister Chien Fu said that the coup's defeat was a "monumental victory in the Soviet people's fight for freedom and democracy" and promised to help the Soviets "tidy up their economic mess."[164] Already in July 1991 Taipei offered to extend economic and financial aid to the Soviet Union and to promote Soviet development projects.[165] In September, Taiwan pledged ten million dollars to a special fund of the European Bank for Reconstruction and Development to finance various projects in Eastern Europe and the Soviet Union.[166] Finally, in early 1992, Taiwan agreed to supply food aid—one hundred thousand tons of rice—to help the Russians cope with serious food shortages.[167]

Despite its huge stocks of foreign reserves, Taiwan was really in no position to compete in these efforts with other potential sponsors of the Soviet Union such as Japan or South Korea. This was partly because massive investments in the Soviet economy were politically risky for Taiwan, and partly since the Soviet government, fearful of the Chinese wrath, could not approach Taipei with requests for economic assistance. Even when Gorbachev was desperate for foreign cash, as he was in the spring of 1991, he turned to Japan and South Korea, but not Taiwan—this was simply inconceivable given the Soviet Union's investment in relations with the PRC. But with Gorbachev out of the way, all bets were off as to where Yeltsin might take Russia's relations with Taiwan. By the time Lukin went to Beijing in December 1991, the Chinese had already dropped opposition to all forms of Russian contacts with Taiwan, barring just government-to-government contacts. Lukin, who had long urged caution in relations with Taipei, found that the Chinese demands "corresponded" with Russia's position.[168]

Things got more difficult in 1992 due to a new scandal, this time connected to exploits of Yeltsin's long-time associate, First Deputy Prime Minister and Chairman of the "Experts' Council" Oleg Lobov. According to scholar and diplomat Evgenii Bazhanov, "during this period [early 1990s], Lobov frequently traveled to Taiwan, and met with its high-ranking representatives.... There were rumors that the Taiwanese provided Lobov with generous financial inducements."[169] If true, this would by no means be unusual in the Russian context of the early 1990s. The Taiwanese, Lobov recalled, "needed a person fairly close to the governmental circles, but not from the government; fairly close to the President, but not from his administration.... Probably, at the time I was the person who most closely corresponded to the delicate character of Moscow-Taipei relations."[170]

Throughout the spring and early summer of 1992, Lobov held at least two meetings with the Taiwanese Vice Foreign Minister (and Jiang Jingguo's illegitimate son), John Chang, first in Moscow and then in Paris. The result was an agreement to establish representative offices in Moscow and Taipei called "Moscow-Taipei (and Taipei-Moscow) coordination commissions on economic and cultural cooperation."[171] These commissions were meant to fulfill consular functions, enjoy diplomatic immunity, and employ official government personnel. What's more, both commissions would be funded by the Taiwanese government. One could only speculate what that would mean personally for Lobov, who would become the Chairman of the Russian commission.[172] Using his personal connections to the Russian President and his chief of staff, Yurii Petrov, Lobov managed to get Yeltsin to sign a decree on the establishment of the Moscow-Taipei commission on September 2, 1992.[173]

A week later, the story leaked to the media, causing a huge stir. Lobov pretended it was business as usual, announcing to the press that Yeltsin "proceeded from reality and Russia's interests." He downplayed the fallout for Sino-Soviet relations: "we don't expect any wrath on the part of Beijing."[174] On that last point, he was certainly mistaken: there was a sharp and predictably negative Chinese reaction to what in fact appeared like a major Russian step toward diplomatic recognition of Taipei. On September 12, Ambassador Wang Jinqing called on Foreign Minister Andrei Kozyrev to demand explanations. The situation was particularly awkward because the Russians and the Chinese had been working on preparing Yeltsin's first visit to the PRC, scheduled for December 1992. Wang Jinqing pointed out that the Taiwan decree was out of step with the Sino-Soviet understanding on the Taiwan problem. Although Kozyrev tried to calm the Ambassador's fears, this was obviously an embarrassing situation for the Russians.[175]

Yeltsin's decree prompted serious objections not only from the Russian Foreign Ministry but also from other ministries and agencies, including the Ministry of Defense and the Foreign Intelligence Service. On September 15, faced with these unexpected developments, Yeltsin issued a follow-up decree, "On Relations between the Russian Federation and Taiwan," which stated that Russia abided by the "One China" principle and did not contemplate anything but strictly non-governmental relations with Taiwan. Moreover, Yeltsin's decree passed the ball to the Russian Foreign Ministry: it was charged with monitoring that all contacts with Taiwan would fall under the non-governmental category, closing down inappropriate organizations and even punishing private individuals who violated these regulations.[176] This was a slap in the face for Lobov, who was on his way to Taiwan to participate in the grand opening of the Taipei-Moscow commission.[177] The honeymoon between Russia and Taiwan was over.

Indeed, in spite of bitterness in Sino-Russian relations between 1991 and 1992, there was never much of a chance that Moscow would stray too far from the road of "two Chinas." Of course, some radically minded democrats in Yeltsin's circle were very bitter about 1991 and, for that matter, 1989, and looked to China with contempt and antipathy. The swiftness of Soviet collapse spoke to unseen fragility in China's communist edifice—who could vouch for Chinese communism in the days of tumultuous transformation of the world? Even Lukin, China's best friend in Yeltsin's circle, predicted in 1989 that the situation in China would change in two to four years, that the "old men" would leave the scene, and that China would undergo transformation "in the Soviet spirit." Even Chinese diplomats in Moscow were privately saying this.[178] Such predictions proved premature; by 1992, Lukin and many others had become "de-ideologized" in their approach to China. People like Lobov of course played their role, but their influence on the course of events was quite limited.

It remains to be determined just what Yeltsin had in mind when he signed Lobov's decree, or what he was led to believe. Undoubtedly Yeltsin recognized his mistake fairly quickly; if he was influenced in his decisions by the likes of Lobov, he also listened to people like Lukin and to the Foreign Ministry and the intelligence chiefs. In the end, the story with the Taiwan decree showed Yeltsin's policy making at its most erratic and inconsistent. However, as the Taiwan episode suggests, there were strict limits to Yeltsin's unpredictability, defined by a fairly traditional interpretation of Russia's "national interests," which, through all the changes between 1982 and 1992, remained essentially unchanged. It is fair to say that the same set of principles guided policy makers in Beijing. Yes, they sided with the coup d'état in 1991. Yes, they had hoped that "dangerous scum" and "reactionary" Yeltsin would be overthrown.[179] Yet when faced with a fait accompli in Russia, the Chinese pragmatically embraced their ideological foe. It was in China's long-term interest to be on friendly terms with its northern neighbor.

CONCLUSION

Normalization of relations in May 1989 was a new milestone for Moscow and Beijing. It took seven years before seeds sown in Brezhnev's Tashkent overture produced a harvest. The road to the Beijing summit was long and arduous. It required domestic policy consensus in both countries, something that was especially slow in coming on the Chinese side. Deng Xiaoping, despite his instrumental use of Sino-Soviet rapprochement for gains with the United States, eventually came around to endorsing full normalization, removing some of the obstacles that he himself had placed in its way. Other obstacles fell by the wayside, such as the Soviet withdrawal from Afghanistan. Throughout, the biggest obstacle to normalization was in fact the Soviet leaders: would they, or wouldn't they, see China for a great power and mend fences on the basis of real (not hypocritical) equality? Gorbachev proved that he was up to the task, achieving what evaded previous Soviet policy makers. This was the biggest success of Soviet *ostpolitik* since 1949, when the Sino-Soviet alliance was born, and one of the few real achievements of Gorbachev's Asian policy. Ironically, this achievement was only possible thanks to the failure of Gorbachev's grand vision for Asia. Pragmatic concessions and simple show of respect for China as an equal helped bring the two countries together in a way that geopolitical ploys like Gorbachev's treasured "triangle" never would have.

Deng was at pains to explain to the world that the normalization of relations did not mean that the defunct alliance would be restored. To "close the past and open the future" meant to rid Sino-Soviet relationship of the ideological vestiges of the bygone days. Beijing and Moscow would build their ties on the basis of the Five Principles of Peaceful Coexistence. But the two countries, despite decades of confrontation, still shared common ideological heritage. This heritage was especially reflected in the interconnection of the Soviet and the Chinese reform experiences. Gorbachev proved less attentive to the Chinese experience than the other way around, yet what the Chinese reformers learned from Gorbachev strengthened their resolve to resist any manner of political reform in China. Gorbachev was satisfied that he did not follow the Chinese road that could have led to another Tiananmen; still, his failure to follow that road in itself contributed to the standoff at Tiananmen.

After Tiananmen, the Soviets and the Chinese actually moved closer to each other in ways that Deng did not anticipate. There was again an element of shared "ideology" to this renewed friendship. The Chinese were taken aback by the extent of hostility in the West following the crackdown in suppression of student demonstrations. Gorbachev, for his part, sought to exploit China's insecurity to build up relations with Beijing at US expense. Thus, Washington's fears of a renewed Sino-Soviet alliance were partially borne out by events, although only because of policies the Bush Administration itself adopted. Like Gorbachev, who had previously overestimated the appeal of his ideas in Asia, Bush was carried away with a vision of a new world that rang hollow with the Chinese policy makers. By the time of the coup, the Chinese leaders were clearly sympathetic toward the Soviet hardliners, and, had the coup succeeded, China would have lent support to the USSR in the face of adverse Western reaction. Yeltsin's triumph buried all hopes of socialist solidarity. By 1991/92 the Sino-Russian relationship was at a crossroads, with the possibility that all gains of the previous decade could be wiped out if Yeltsin embraced the West and turned his back to the East. In the event, he did not. His attachment to the human rights agenda proved short-lived. Instead, Beijing and Moscow jointly set out on a road toward strategic partnership informed by a shared sense of resentment of the United States, which, in Gorbachev's words, had wished them both ill.

CHAPTER 6

Moscow and Seoul Mend Fences, 1986–90

In 1945, following Japan's surrender, the Korean peninsula was occupied by the Soviet Union and the United States and temporarily divided along the 38th parallel. The arrival of the Cold War in Korea precluded its unification. Moscow and Washington sponsored viciously adversarial regimes— the Democratic People's Republic of Korea (DPRK) in the North and the Republic of Korea (ROK) in the South, respectively. In June 1950 the leader of North Korea, Kim Il-sung, with Joseph Stalin's blessing, launched an invasion of the South. The ensuing war brought in the United States, China, and the Soviet Union and resulted in terrible destruction and loss of life. It ended in a stalemate in 1953. In the late 1950s Kim Il-sung consolidated his power and proclaimed *juche* (often translated as self-reliance) as the guiding ideology of his regime. In reality, Kim continued to rely on political, economic, and military support from the Soviet Union and China.

Soviet alliance with North Korea carried an exorbitant price tag. But it was a price Moscow was willing to pay, even though the Soviet leadership did not necessarily subscribe to Kim Il-sung's views about the heinous plans of the United States and its puppet allies in Northeast Asia. Beating war drums was part of Kim's tactic for procuring aid on favorable terms. He was not always successful in these questionable pursuits, however. For example, Nikita Khrushchev was unenthusiastic about North Korea's militant policies and in 1962 refused to supply weapons to Kim Il-sung. The result: dramatic deterioration of Soviet–North Korean relations and Pyongyang's support of China in the widening Sino-Soviet rift.[1]

After Khrushchev's fall from power in October 1964, Moscow reverted to a policy of active support for North Korea, though at least some Soviet specialists believed that such aid did not translate into increased influence over Pyongyang's decision making.[2] For example, North Korea's handling of the *Pueblo* crisis in 1968 caused the Kremlin to fear that Kim's warmongering might drag the Soviet Union into a war with the United States.[3] There were no consequences for Kim Il-sung, however, except for a subtle Soviet reprimand. This is because North Korea was far too important to the Soviet Union as a strategic ally in the Cold War context and also in the context of tense relations with the People's Republic of China. Kim Il-sung, for his part, balanced carefully between China and the Soviet Union, taking aid from both and promising little in return.

In the meantime, South Korea experienced rapid economic growth in the 1960s and 1970s, leaving its dysfunctional rival far behind and undermining Kim Il-sung's hopes of a communist revolution in the South followed by unification on his terms. Faced with South Korea's increasing international prominence, Kim worked hard to keep his allies in the socialist camp from developing contacts with Seoul, complaining bitterly every time such contacts, however occasional or unintended, took place. Until the late 1980s, he was successful in this sabotage, but the changing international situation finally led to abrogation of political and ideological taboos and direct engagement between the Soviet bloc and Seoul. This chapter recounts the stories of scholars, journalists, and spies who brokered Soviet–South Korean rapprochement and explores motivations of both sides in bringing it about.

Close investigation of Soviet policy toward North and South Korea in the 1980s discredits simplistic assertions that Soviet recognition of South Korea was an inevitable result of Gorbachev's "new thinking" in Asia. The Soviet leader's vision for Asia hampered a pragmatic approach to Seoul. South Korea, being a close US ally, did not fit in Gorbachev's strategic pivot centered on the Sino-Soviet-Indian triangle. At the same time, he was careful not to compromise Soviet relations with North Korea, an important strategic platform. Only the crash of his grand vision in the late 1980s and the Soviet Union's dire need for credits changed the equation, leading to Moscow and Seoul mending fences. This belated rapprochement left Gorbachev without leverage in South Korea, even as it undermined Soviet influence in the North. The Korean peninsula remained divided and volatile.

TIGER'S LAIR

On a crisp winter day, January 19, 1986, Eduard Shevardnadze arrived in Pyongyang as the head of a delegation of Foreign Ministry functionaries. At the airport, he was greeted by crowds of enthusiasts waving paper flags to the sound of an orchestra. The North Koreans had a special talent for staging propaganda rallies. Whether to celebrate eternal friendship with fellow communist regimes or to condemn "US imperialism" for terrible crimes, thousands of people readily assembled to line the streets with expressions of sympathy or hatred, happiness or anger, but above all with boundless love for the ailing Great Leader lurking in tight security behind palace walls.[4]

Kim Il-sung did not leave his lair to welcome Gorbachev's comrade-in-arms. He would have, if only Gorbachev had come to North Korea in person. Pyongyang repeatedly extended invitations. Foreign Minister Kim Yong-nam reminded Shevardnadze: "The cherished leader already invited comrade Gorbachev to Korea. We know that Nakasone invited comrade Gorbachev to Tokyo, but we would want for his first visit to Asian countries to begin with the DPRK. After all, all US Presidents begin their trips to Asia with South Korea." North Korea was especially deserving of such a high-profile visit because it was at the forefront of struggle against the evil forces. The Foreign Minister elaborated: "The peninsula is the most explosive point on the planet. How can the Middle East and Central America compare with it? South Korea is the nuclear arsenal of the United States. If a war breaks out here, it will inevitably become a world war."[5]

On January 21 Kim Il-sung welcomed Shevardnadze at his palace. The Foreign Minister's aide scribbled in his diary:

> He greets us with a wide smile, dimming the light of TV spotlights and camera flashes. Outwardly youthful, straight and stern; [his] light-blue suit had been tailored to fit a chubby body so that it conceals elderly plumpness. He has a lump on his neck—a lipoma, a benign tumor, and he walks dragging his foot, barely managing the pulling weight of the tumor.

After small talk about his poor health, the "Great Leader" expediently praised Soviet foreign policy, both in relation to Gorbachev's "peace offensive" against the United States, and specifically to the Soviet Union's Asia policy, of which a key element was the effort to improve relations with Tokyo. Shevardnadze in fact flew to Pyongyang on the way back from his maiden trip to Japan, which was at the time hailed as an important milestone for Soviet-Japanese relations. Kim Il-sung characterized Soviet initiatives as "going into the tiger's lair in order to kill the cubs." The Great Leader did not mind Shevardnadze's talks in Japan because, in his strategic calculations, the net result was detrimental to the United States. "The Japanese are crafty people," he said. "First there was the Anglo-Japanese alliance—they swallowed us. Then, Hitler and Mussolini. Now—America. It is very important for us to wrestle Japan away from America."[6]

As Gorbachev toyed with the idea of better relations with the Japanese, Kim Il-sung did not think that North Korean interests would be jeopardized. Whether he really believed so, or—more likely—simply pretended, Kim peddled the proposition that the Soviet Union and North Korea in fact followed the same strategy of "neutralizing" Japan. If so, certainly the Soviets would not spare any effort to support their long-time ally in the Far East. The point was not lost on Shevardnadze's delegation: "Kim's aim is obvious—to squeeze as much moral and material aid from us as possible by means of flattery, promises of support, and invention of horror [scenarios]."[7]

After the Soviet delegation returned home, the North Korean Embassy invited them over to present them with a film of their visit to Pyongyang. At a dinner overflowing with food and drinks, Shevardnadze's deputy, "Mikhstep" Kapitsa, showered praise on the "Great Leader" and the "Dear Leader" and even allowed himself a somewhat undiplomatic toast to the North Koreans: "Let us all have a hard-on like the [ballistic missile] SS-20 . . . with MIRVed heads."[8] Shevardnadze was above such intimacy. Yet he, too, left Pyongyang with the sense that "the Korean comrades now really do need support" because they faced South Korea, "armed to its teeth" and even "more dangerous than Japan."[9] Reporting on the trip at the Politburo, Shevardnadze noted that there was a basis for closer Soviet–North Korean relations—anti-American sentiments in Pyongyang effectively served Soviet regional interests. "In any case," he noted, "we went away with a firm conviction that one can and must work with Kim Il-sung [and] Kim Jong-il. . . . By improving relations with the DPRK we also influence the position of China."[10]

What he evidently meant was that the Chinese would find it more difficult to oppose Soviet global and regional initiatives if Kim Il-sung was on the Soviets' side. North Korea could thus not only become an important Soviet platform in opposing US presence in East Asia but also a lever in the process of Sino-Soviet rapprochement. This strategy required that Moscow forgo contacts with South Korea, even though doing so went against basic Soviet economic interests. But the contradiction was not yet evident to the top Soviet leadership, including Gorbachev.

Kim Il-sung's friendly attitude toward the Soviet Union in the mid-1980s was in pleasing contrast to his pro-Chinese position in the 1970s. The reasons for this change of direction can be identified with a fair degree of confidence simply by taking account of the international circumstances at the time. Two key developments of the late 1970s, which made the Great

Leader wonder where his friends' priorities lay, were the Sino-Japanese treaty, concluded in 1978, and the Sino-US normalization on January 1, 1979. These strategic coups were directed in essence against Soviet interests in East Asia, but Kim Il-sung too had much to lose from closer relations between China and North Korea's archenemies—Japan and the United States. China ostensibly represented Pyongyang's interests—for example, by advocating directs talks between North Korea and the United States. Deng Xiaoping and Kim Il-sung met often in official and unofficial capacities: twice in 1982, once in 1983, 1984, and 1985. Each time Deng tried very hard to project China as North Korea's friend in need and as an implacable critic of the US actions in South Korea.[11]

Yet Kim could hardly be sure that his interests would not be sacrificed in the name of Deng Xiaoping's strategic calculus, especially after Sino-US relations improved in 1983–84. For example, Korea was discussed during US President Ronald Reagan's visit to China in April 1984, but what the Chinese had to say on the subject—their willingness to develop contacts with South Korea and even participate in the 1986 Asian Games in Seoul, and their failure to insist on the immediate US troop pullout (a sore point for Pyongyang)—would not have been to Kim Il-sung's liking. Far from putting up a hard fight on behalf of North Korea's struggle for reunification on unrealistic terms, the Chinese "stressed their desire to explore means of reducing tensions in Korea and achieving long-term peace and stability there."[12] China projected an image of a constructive broker and refused to subscribe to the North Korean militant rhetoric.

In the meantime, Deng used his private meetings with Kim Il-sung to dissuade him from military action. As he put it in November 1985, "all international problems may only be resolved through talks. It does not matter whether you are a great power, a medium country or a small country, whoever wants to start a war will himself suffer, and, moreover, no one can achieve victory in such a war."[13] While Kim Il-sung had no intention at the time of starting a war in Korea, Deng's talk struck the wrong note with the Great Leader because it did not square with the imperative of obtaining weapons for North Korea's defense. Even if China was willing to provide weapons, it could hardly match the sophistication of Soviet military technology. Kim Il-sung, realizing how far his country had fallen behind South Korea, would naturally have wanted to gain access to more advanced weapons, which only the Soviets could provide. Whatever the reasons, when in May 1984 Kim Il-sung went on his first trip to the USSR in nearly twenty years, weapons topped his agenda.

The Great Leader brought a long list of requests for airplanes, ships, tanks, surface-to-air missiles, and spare parts.[14] In August 1985 the North

Koreans asked for help in the construction of a helicopter factory.[15] In the following months, the Soviets transferred sixty jet fighters (MiG-23Ps and MiG-23MLs) to replace Pyongyang's aging MiG-21 fleet. The North Koreans also received 10 Mi-2 and 50 Mi-24 helicopters. In 1988 the Soviet Union further supplied thirty MiG-29 and twenty Su-25K jets.[16] In fact, the volume of military cooperation between the USSR and North Korea increased fivefold between 1981–85 and 1986–90.[17] Moscow and Pyongyang upgraded their military coordination with high-profile mutual port calls by the two navies and a series of joint exercises in the Sea of Japan between 1986 and 1990.[18]

Soviet–North Korean economic ties also experienced strong growth. The most important development from North Korea's perspective was the Soviet agreement, in 1985, to build a nuclear power plant for the DPRK. This had long been Kim Il-sung's aspiration, both because North Korea had experienced energy shortages and because South Korea already had a nuclear power plant. The Soviets had been apprehensive in the past about aiding Pyongyang's nuclear energy ambitions, for fear that sensitive technology could be diverted to the North Korean military. In the end, however, Kim Il-sung had his way, although at the expense of joining the Nuclear Non-Proliferation Treaty in December 1985.[19]

The initiative for better Soviet–North Korean relations came from Kim Il-sung. It was a pleasant surprise for the Soviet leadership, who had long regarded the Great Leader as a fence sitter and quite possibly a Trojan horse for Chinese interests in the communist movement. The first clear signals of Kim's changing priorities came in early 1984, just when Sino-US relations also improved, suggesting correlation if not direct causality. In January 1984 Pyongyang articulated a set of proposals for tripartite talks involving itself, the United States, and South Korea, the ostensible aim of which was to conclude a peace treaty with the United States, which would then pave way for the withdrawal of US troops from the peninsula. Moscow was not consulted about this move ahead of time, and the Soviets privately criticized the North Koreans for deemphasizing US withdrawal for the sake of a bilateral treaty, which could, quite possibly, undercut Soviet interests in the region. Faced with Soviet criticism, the North Koreans did something highly unusual: they apologized. Recounting this episode, Soviet Deputy Foreign Minister Mikhail Kapitsa mused: "Something is happening in [North] Korea.... They have become more careful on many questions."[20]

Kim Il-sung also became an ardent supporter of Sino-Soviet normalization. He raised the subject on every suitable occasion—with the Chinese, with the Soviets, with whoever would listen. This included East German leader Erich Honecker, whom he saw in May 1984, on the same trip that took him to the USSR to mend fences: "Kim Il-sung said that he believed that all socialist nations should work toward creating trust between the Soviet Union and China. No new mistrust must be permitted to arise."

Kim's reason for advocating Sino-Soviet unity (when he had formerly profitably exploited their disunity) was that he hoped closer relations with the socialist bloc could forestall China's alignment with the West and Japan: "Because of our position—the length of our border with China, confrontation with the US and Japan—what we are most afraid of is that China will not stick with socialism. There are one billion people in China. We have to make sure that they follow the socialist path rather than some other path. We have to focus on drawing them toward us."[21]

Nevertheless, Sino-North Korean relations evidently worsened in 1985–86, amid evidence of intensified contacts between China and South Korea. Kim did not take lightly China's decision to participate in the 1986 Asian Games in Seoul.[22] Even before that, in November 1985, Deng Xiaoping privately dispelled Kim's illusions that China would boycott the Olympic movement, since it was applying to host the Games in 2000.[23] The Chinese were privately exasperated with the North Korean intransigence and their failure to consult. As top Chinese sports official Li Menghua put it in a serious understatement, "We have solidarity and friendship with [North] Korea. But our opinions often do not coincide."[24] For his part, the Great Leader vented his anger at the Chinese in talks with the Soviets: an internal Soviet report (dated December 10, 1985) noted that "The [North] Korean leadership is rightly furious with Beijing, whose statements in support of the DPRK contradict its behind-the-scenes ties with Seoul."[25]

In his July 1986 Vladivostok speech—a showcase for new thinking in the Asia Pacific context—Gorbachev condemned the Washington-Tokyo-Seoul "militarized triangle" for effectively "evading a serious dialogue which has been proposed by [North Korea]" and called for a nuclear-free Korean peninsula, endorsing Pyongyang's long-standing propaganda ploy. There was perhaps a hint—a shadow of a hint—buried deeply beneath familiar formulations, when Gorbachev proclaimed Soviet readiness to "invigorate its bilateral relations with all countries in the region without exception."[26] Did he really mean South Korea?

When Kim Il-sung visited the Soviet Union in October 1986, he had no reason to think that Gorbachev was anything other than a political reincarnation of his predecessors. On the other hand, Gorbachev was also not in the best mood to talk peace. His summit with Ronald Reagan in Reykjavik, on which Gorbachev staked great hopes, ended in "un-success" in his own words.[27] Gorbachev declined to move forward with disarmament unless the United States gave up Star Wars (its missile defense program), which

Reagan was not prepared to do. Gorbachev returned to Moscow to face yet another crisis in Soviet-US relations: Washington's expulsion of scores of Soviet diplomats from the United States for espionage activities. Commenting on this development at a Politburo session on October 22, Gorbachev said that the Americans "act extremely rudely, behave like bandits."[28]

For his part, Kim Il-sung did not meet with Gorbachev to teach him how to deal with Reagan. On the contrary, the "Great Leader" could, when needed, pose as a foremost fan of Gorbachev's grand foreign policy designs. Days before his meeting with Gorbachev, on October 19, he even found it expedient to praise Soviet initiatives in Vladivostok and Reykjavik as "evidence of a peace-loving foreign policy" and claimed that "progress in relations between the Soviet Union and the US would also help to resolve the Korea problem."[29] In return for his praise, Kim expected the Soviet Union to subscribe to his version of the situation on the Korean peninsula and provide political, economic, and military support.

Kim spelled out his views in a meeting with Gorbachev on October 24. He wanted US forces out of Korea for good. He promised not to invade South Korea. Finally, he was certain that South Korea would soon become communist on its own:

> We do not want to attack South Korea, do not want to make it red.... The population of South Korea would support socialism, though this would meet with resistance in the West. There is a large movement for socialism in the South; work is being carried out to create a national front. A third of South Korean parliamentarians support the North. Not to mention students, many [people] are now speaking out against the American presence....

Before the promise of communism transpired in South Korea, Kim Il-sung was adamantly against admission of both Koreas to the UN, or cross-recognition of North and South Korea by the USSR and China, on the one hand, and by the United States and Japan, on the other. Both of these developments, he said, would make Korea's division permanent.[30]

The Great Leader's scheme was fairly transparent: to bring Soviet pressure to bear on the United States to leave the Korean peninsula, which, he imagined, was the main obstacle to a communist revolution in the South. To this end, he even told Gorbachev that before he left Pyongyang, there was a Politburo meeting, which resolved to "appeal to the USSR to turn to the USA with a proposal to withdraw its forces from the peninsula and turn a united Korea into a neutral non-aligned state."[31] This is exactly what Kim meant when he said that improved Soviet-US relations could help solve the Korean problem.

Gorbachev politely ignored Kim Il-sung's predictions of an imminent revolution in South Korea, though he did support North Korean proposals for a nuclear-free zone on the peninsula (i.e., withdrawal of US nuclear weapons) and for improved relations with the South. Gorbachev also claimed, in a later interview, that he defended the idea of cross-recognition and accession of both Koreas to the UN: "Sounds nice. That's reasonable." Kim was allegedly surprised and offended by Gorbachev's position: "Kim disappointed me and I disappointed Kim," the Soviet leader recalled.[32] Other participants in that conversation remembered a different story. Vadim Tkachenko, the leading Soviet expert on Korea, recalled that after the talks, as Kim and Gorbachev were about to part, the General Secretary "suddenly told him: we have no intention to recognize South Korea. I thought to myself—what a fool! [bolvan!]—who pulled you by your tongue?"[33] As the Soviet Union embarked upon a new course in foreign policy, Gorbachev's promise would prove very hard to keep.

CONTACTS WITH SOUTH KOREA

Soviet rapprochement with South Korea was not Gorbachev's idea. The impetus for better relations originated south of the 38th parallel, years before anyone in Moscow gave serious thought to changing the status quo. The policy was called *nordpolitik*, and it stood for Seoul's willingness to mend fences with the communist world. There were two related yet distinct aspects to nordpolitik. One was strictly a matter of state interests: to isolate the North Korean regime and increase Seoul's international reputation. South Korea's remarkable economic success paved the way to a more assertive foreign policy and lesser reliance on the United States. Improved relations with Moscow would excellently serve the cause of South Korea's self-perception as a major independent player on the international stage.[34]

Nordpolitik also had obvious benefits as a political weapon in South Korea's electoral struggles. In 1987 South Korean President Chun Doo-hwan agreed to step down and allow free presidential elections. Opposition candidates Kim Young-sam, Kim Dae-jung, and Kim Jong-pil quarreled among themselves, and the public vote went to the ruling party nominee, Roh Tae-woo. The ensuing "One Roh, Three Kims" combination, marked by bickering among the three Kims and their common criticism of the Roh regime, remained in place until early 1990. In this inherently treacherous and uncertain political landscape, nordpolitik offered a quick way to winning public support. Roh was particularly vulnerable after his party's surprising defeat in the 1988 parliamentary elections. But the opposition figures, especially "YS" (Kim Young-sam) and "DJ" (Kim Dae-jung), also realized the political dividends of being the first to break the ice with Moscow.

Roh Tae-woo held all the good cards. First of all, the notorious South Korean intelligence agency, the KCIA, was completely at his disposal. The KCIA had a bad reputation under President Chun Doo-hwan, earned by frequent resort to intimidation, arrests, and torture of opposition activists. But the KCIA also had a powerful foreign intelligence apparatus and boasted wide connections in the business world and in academia. KCIA was intimately involved with Roh Tae-woo's nordpolitik initiatives. Yet overall policy coordination was in the hands of Roh's aide for policy development, Park Chul-un. Despite the ambiguous title, Park was a serious player behind the scenes. He was nicknamed "the prince" for his young age, ambition, and power.[35] In early 1988 it was up to him to chart a new path to Moscow.

Park Chul-un did not have direct access to Soviet policy makers. One possibility was to approach a Soviet academic institute through a university in South Korea. The prime target was the Institute of Oriental Studies, the oldest and best known center for Asia studies in the Soviet Union. The Institute, a crumbling building with long, dark corridors a short walk from the KGB headquarters, was de facto headed from 1985 to 1987 by Georgii Kim, a Russian Korean who had worked on Korea-related problems since the 1950s. "De facto" meant that Kim was never officially confirmed as the director. Like thousands of other Koreans in the USSR, Kim suffered from subtle discrimination on the account of his ethnic origins.[36] Nevertheless, he was one of the most highly placed and influential ethnic Koreans in the Soviet Union and a keen student of Korean history and politics.

In the spring of 1988 Georgii Kim received an invitation to visit Seoul from Hannam University, a Christian institution south of Seoul.[37] Needless to say, Hannam could not take such an unprecedented step without prior consultations with the KCIA and Park Chul-un. In Moscow, Hannam University's invitation was taken very seriously: Georgii Shakhnazarov instructed Kim before departure at the Central Committee, along with two other members of his delegation—Nikolai Vasil'ev, Deputy Director of the Institute of Oriental Studies (who also had a KGB affiliation),[38] and Konstantin Sarkisov, a leading Japan specialist of the same Institute.[39] In late May the trio departed for Seoul via Tokyo, although Kim had to return to Moscow after falling ill.

When Vasil'ev and Sarkisov arrived in Seoul on May 29, 1988, the academics who invited them were nowhere to be found. Instead, the two were introduced to Park Chul-un.[40] Park (not unreasonably) believed that Vasil'ev's Institute of Oriental Studies affiliation was only a cover and that the bureaucrat was in reality a ranking KGB officer. Unsurprisingly, the subject of their conversations was not exactly academic.[41] Vasil'ev briefed Park about Soviet plans to establish a free economic zone in the Far East—a Soviet "Shenzhen"—and asked for South Korean investments. Park appeared forthcoming, but he warned that the Soviet Union should change its view of South Korea and pressed Vasil'ev to explain what stood in the way of Soviet-Korean normalization. In the end he offered to establish a secret communication channel between Seoul and Moscow to begin the process of normalization.[42]

The meeting was a major ice-breaker. In retrospect, Vasil'ev regretted the slow pace of change and blamed the Soviet leadership for failing to take full advantage of the opportunity afforded by this first trip: "The subsequent actions of the leadership were unprofessional. We did not make use of their [the Koreans'] disposition and exceptional interest."[43] Yet Roh Tae-woo was optimistic about improving relations with the Soviet Union. The first step had been taken. To move things forward, he wrote a special letter to Gorbachev and ordered Park Chul-un to Moscow to deliver it in person.

This was easier said than done. Park Chul-un now knew at least two Russians, Vasil'ev and Sarkisov, but this was hardly enough to arrange meetings with the country's top leaders. Park resorted to his excellent connections. One of his acquaintances was university professor Joseph Ha (known in Korea as Ha Mangyong), a Korean-born American who had studied at Columbia University's Russian Institute in the 1960s and taught international affairs at Lewis and Clark College in Oregon, publishing widely on subjects dealing with peace and security in the Far East. In 1974 he had helped set up a forum for meeting Soviet international affairs experts, which alternatively convened annually between the United States and in the USSR.[44] Ha's Soviet counterpart was Georgii Arbatov.

Ha's access to Arbatov made it possible to reach out to Gorbachev, bypassing the complicated structures of the Soviet bureaucracy. He also had other acquaintances in Moscow, including Vladimir Lukin, who had worked at Arbatov's Institute for almost twenty years as the head of the Far Eastern policy department before moving to the Foreign Ministry in 1987, where he took charge of Pacific and Southeast Asian affairs. Ha recalled that over the years he discussed the situation on the Korean peninsula with Arbatov, Lukin, and other Soviet experts and that "some of them had a fair knowledge of South Korea."[45] It all sounded too good for Park Chul-un. In late August 1988, accompanied by Joseph Ha and a KCIA operative, Yeom Don-jae, and equipped with women's stockings (allegedly to bribe train conductors), Roe Tae-woo's envoy went to Moscow—the highest ranking South Korean official to do so since the Cold War began.[46]

Park arrived on August 28 and checked in at Mezhdunarodnaya Hotel on the bank of Moscow River—not the best place in town, but a busy one. He wanted to blend in with the crowd to avoid the prying eyes of the North Koreans (he did eventually stumble into North Koreans and pretended, probably unconvincingly, to be a sugar entrepreneur from California).[47]

Two days later, Roh's envoy went to the Institute of Oriental Studies to meet with its director "Mikhstep" Kapitsa, whom he remembered as a "nervous" man, "pretending to be a mogul."[48] Mikhstep ended up at the Institute after Shevardnadze unleashed a shake-up at the Foreign Ministry. Kapitsa was purged, by some accounts because he was too conservative and by others because of frequent drinking binges.[49] Kapitsa's recollections of the meeting with Park were somewhat demeaning: "Minister-aide to the President of SK Park Chul-un showed up at the Institute of Oriental Studies…, said that he had brought a message from President Roh Tae-woo and asked to arrange a meeting with Gorbachev for him. I arranged for him to be seen by the Deputy Foreign Minister, through whom he passed the message."[50] The mogul also told Park that should he come up with good economic proposals, he ought to get back in touch with him.[51]

The same theme came up in Park's meeting on September 1 with the Deputy Head of the State Committee for Foreign Economic Relations, Ivan Ivanov, who made it clear that official Moscow was far more interested in economic relations with Seoul and South Korean investment in the Far East than in exploring general normalization. Ivanov said that he had no authority to discuss political relations, only economic ties. The Soviet Union, he said, wanted to expand trade with South Korea, irrespective of whether or not Seoul's relations with Pyongyang improved. Moreover, South Korea's companies, such as Hyundai Construction, could participate in the development of the Soviet Far East. "Soviet firms know well South Korea's potential," Ivanov said.[52]

On September 8 Park Chul-un met with his most promising contact yet—Joseph Ha's long-time acquaintance Georgii Arbatov. What Park did not know was that Arbatov was one of the foremost advocates of closer relations with South Korea in Gorbachev's inner circle. He had just submitted a lengthy memorandum to the Soviet leader, proposing to "activate the search for ways to widen cooperation with South Korea." The rationale was economic, of course: Arbatov stressed that South Korea needed Soviet ore, coal, oil, and timber, which were no longer in great demand in Japan, and that it could "help us substantially in the development of the Far East, and other regions (in the building of ports, automobile and electronics factories, and in the creation of joint ventures in fishing, etc)."[53] But it wasn't all economics. Indeed,

Arbatov told Park Chul-un that the Soviet Union was "considering political improvement."[54]

Park then announced that the main reason for his visit to the Soviet Union was to meet with Gorbachev and pass him a letter from Roh Tae-woo. Arbatov replied that this was impossible, citing Gorbachev's busy schedule. That very day, Arbatov confided, the General Secretary had a meeting of the Politburo.[55] Perhaps not satisfied with his own explanation, Arbatov added that a secret meeting with Gorbachev was out of the question until relations with South Korea improved. However, he also promised Park that he would personally convey to Gorbachev all the nuances of their conversation. As for the letter, Park agreed to deliver it through Lukin, then Deputy Foreign Minister, with whom he met later that day.[56] Lukin told Park that the Soviet Union was "under pressure"—from North Korea, that is—though he promised a "step-by-step" normalization.[57]

The meeting with Lukin ended Park's official business in Moscow. Results were mixed. On the one hand, Soviet bureaucrats torpedoed Roh Tae-woo's hopes for immediate normalization of relations and did not agree to any practical proposals—for example, establishment of permanent representatives in Moscow and Seoul as a first step toward full diplomatic relations. At best, Park received uncertain promises of eventual normalization. At the same time, it was very clear that Moscow wanted to develop economic relations with South Korea, seeing trade and investment as an important part of the first step in this drawn-out process. Naturally, the South Korean leadership preferred simultaneous expansion of political and economic contacts, and on a much faster scale than what was allowed by the Soviet timetable.

After leaving the Foreign Ministry, Park Chul-un organized a banquet at the hotel's restaurant, Russkii ("The Russian"). Indeed, the Russians outnumbered Park's small delegation. Among others, Lukin, Arbatov, and Kapitsa were in attendance (under strict police surveillance on the outside).[58] Although the South Koreans and the Russians had widely different visions of normalization, different means, and different timetables, something was set in motion. If nothing else, this was the most important outcome of Park Chul-un's exploratory visit to the Soviet Union.

THE SEOUL OLYMPICS

On September 29, 1981, the International Olympic Committee (IOC) voted to award the 1988 Olympic Games to the city of Seoul.[59] It was a daring, if not to say reckless, decision. Seoul, within a short distance of the world's most militarized border, was an easy target for attack from the North. But apart from a strained situation on the Korean peninsula, tensions marred South Korean domestic politics as President Chun Doo-hwan resorted to brutal suppression of the opposition to maintain his hold on power. To add to the IOC's problems, the Soviet bloc did not recognize South Korea and had no diplomatic relations with it. There was a good chance at the outset that the communist and some Third World governments would boycott the Seoul Games out of solidarity with Pyongyang.

The prospects of Soviet participation in the Games did not look good at the outset and worsened after September 1, 1983, when a Soviet interceptor downed a Korean airplane just off Sakhalin Island. Chun Doo-hwan called the incident a "barbarous act, sinning against god and man."[60] In this matter, even the North Koreans failed to endorse Soviet actions, being that most of those killed were ethnic Koreans and Kim Il-sung was ever sensitive to the image he projected among his countrymen north and south of the 38th parallel. Demonstrations erupted across South Korea amid much public outrage. The South Korean government called for a public Soviet apology and restitution to the victims' families.[61]

Despite rather unfavorable circumstances, organizers of the Seoul Olympics bent over backwards to obtain an early Soviet agreement to participate in the Games. To this end Roh Tae-woo asked Adidas President Horst Dassler, a frequent visitor to the Soviet Union, to convey to the Soviet leadership that he, Roh Tae-woo, would do "everything possible for neutralizing the so-called 'plane' incident, which at the present times remains a serious negative factor." Roh expressed Chun Doo-hwan's opinion to the effect that "if the Soviet Union takes part in the Olympic Games in Seoul, all questions, connected with the downing of the Korean plane will be taken off [the agenda], insomuch as he [Chun Doo-hwan] sees here not only a mistake on the part of the USSR, but also another great power's [i.e. US] fault."[62] These views reached the Soviet leadership in late June 1984.[63] A month later, however, the Soviets boycotted the Summer Olympics in Los Angeles, which underscored the possibility of continued boycotts. Cuban leader Fidel Castro even urged Moscow to begin holding "socialist" Olympics.

The bad news for North Korea was that the Soviet leadership from the start was not inclined to boycott Seoul, as IOC President Juan Antonio Samaranch found out, much to his probable relief, on a visit to Moscow in July 1985. There were concerns, of course. "They are not worried about the position of North Korea. But they told me that they were worried regarding the position of Cuba, because Cuba is a very important socialist country for them. USSR thinks that Cuba and North Korea working together can be quite dangerous."[64] The problem was no doubt that Cuba had high prestige in the Non-Aligned Movement and among various "progressive" audiences that mattered a great deal to the Soviets. If Cuba backed Kim Il-sung, Soviet participation in the Games would not only harm Soviet-Cuban relations but also tarnish the Soviet image in the Third World, something that Gorbachev was very worried about. Even so, by January 1986 the Soviets had come to recognize that, as Shevardnadze put it, "a boycott of the Olympic Games is unrealistic. It can bury the entire Olympic movement."[65]

Faced with this attitude of his Soviet comrades, Kim Il-sung decided that North Korea should take part in talks with the South and with the IOC about sharing the Games. These talks began in Lausanne, Switzerland, in October 1985 and went through several inconclusive rounds, adjourning in July 1987. Although the North Koreans displayed characteristic self-defeating stubbornness, it was not as if the South Koreans were inclined to compromise. They only took part in the talks to appear accommodating so that the socialist bloc did not have a pretext for boycotting the Games. President Chun Doo-hwan thought that he held all the cards and that North Korea could do nothing, short of war, to prevent the Games from taking place. "President Kim Il-sung," Chun said, "knows that he cannot attack us and I know it and he knows that I know it." This question was connected to the global politics of the Cold War. "The problem of the danger of war depends on whether the USSR is inclined to fight against the United States in my region. The reply is quite clear: NO. The second [issue] is the position of China.... That country does not want war either."[66]

Kim Il-sung was under no illusion that anyone would go to war over the Games in Seoul. He hoped, however, that the Soviet Union would endorse North Korea's demands at the talks in Lausanne. In May 1986 he dispatched top-ranking North Korean functionary Hwang Jang-yop to Moscow in a bid to win Soviet support so that the Soviets would "put pressure on the enemy."[67] It may be that the North Koreans really hoped to cohost the Games on acceptable terms (more than just token participation) and believed that Soviet pressure would help break the deadlock. The other possibility is that Kim Il-sung had no intention of participating in the Games but wanted to take Soviet policy hostage, so that Moscow committed to support whatever demands the North Koreans made in Lausanne, and then boycotted the Games when these demands were refused.

In either case, what the Great Leader actually received from the USSR was a general expression of support in the form of a letter from the head of the Soviet Olympic Committee, Marat Gramov, to Samaranch on June 5, 1986: "I am not fully familiar with the details of the talks between the

National Olympic Committees of the DPRK and South Korea under the auspices of the IOC...but I firmly believe that the conduct of the Games in the North and in the South is possible."[68] When the Great Leader turned up in Moscow in October of that year, Gorbachev told him that while he was in favor of the North Korean bid to hold a part of the Games in Pyongyang, he was not interested in equitable representation. "I will tell you frankly," Gorbachev said, "that the issue is in the principle, and not in the arithmetic."[69]

The East Europeans were getting the idea. Seeing where the wind was blowing, East Germany's Erich Honecker, Kim Il-sung's "brother and best friend," told Samaranch after meeting with Gorbachev that his country's athletes "were preparing for the 1988 Olympic Games at Seoul."[70] The Czechs and the Hungarians signaled their readiness to participate in the Olympics and provided their flags and anthem recordings to the IOC. The North Koreans were increasingly anxious. In April 1987 socialist ambassadors (other than China's and Cuba's) were summoned to the Foreign Ministry in Pyongyang and given a lecture about how their countries' undue eagerness in the Olympic matters hindered the progress of talks at Lausanne, because, seeing the attitude of the Eastern Europeans, "the other side [the South Koreans] has shifted to a tougher position."[71]

In May Kim Il-sung went to China in a desperate effort to get his other ally to boycott the Seoul games, while also urging China to stem the tide of business ties with South Korea. He was told, however, that business ties would continue—"there is no way to stop or control this"—and that China had firmly decided to participate in the Olympic Games, although "we will not hurry to announce this." The reason for Beijing's attitude, Kim Il-sung learned to his dismay, was that South Korea was doing exceptionally well economically. "We have to try to become closer to them. The people will follow where life is better." These may not have been exactly the terms used in the talks with Kim Il-sung, but this was how the Chinese ambassador in Pyongyang described the encounter in his conversations with fellow diplomats. No doubt, being exposed like this was a huge blow to the "Great Leader."[72]

As for the Soviets, Gorbachev offered the following explanation as to why he could not support Kim Il-sung's demands: the problem was the threat of boycott. "This [the Olympiad] is an enormous channel for cooperation, for influencing [the West] in the needed direction.... If we were to take this road [boycotting the Games] we would hurt ourselves, our policies. This is the interconnection of these elements." This was the first time, perhaps, that Gorbachev discovered "interconnection" of Moscow's policy toward the Korean peninsula and the broader Soviet "peace offensive." Kim Il-sung, according to Gorbachev's account, "met [our position] with...understanding. But he hopes for our firm position, and I promised that we will have a meeting, I promised that we will talk about this."[73] Gorbachev did not keep his promise—he never again met with the "Great Leader." In the meantime, on January 11, 1988, the Soviet Union announced its agreement to participate in the Olympics irrespective of North Korea's intentions.

On September 3, 1988, the massive 144-meter-long cruise liner *Mikhail Sholokhov* became the first Soviet boat to dock in the Pusan harbor since the Korean War. The port authorities played the Soviet national anthem and hoisted the hammer and sickle in a symbolic moment for a fervently anti-communist country.[74] *Sholokhov* brought the first installment of Soviet Olympians and dozens of tourists to an exotic destination. Soviet citizens had come to South Korea before, but never in such numbers. Between those who arrived by boat and those who flew in from Moscow, the Soviet Union fielded 514 athletes—the second-largest contingent after the US delegation.[75] In addition to the athletes, there were officials, their interpreters and support staff, various celebrities—including two Soviet cosmonauts—and several Soviet Koreans who had come to see their relatives after decades of separation occasioned by the Cold War.[76]

The last group became immediately popular with the Korean media. There were emotional reunions, such as that of Kim Sang-yun, a Soviet Korean, with his uncle Yoon Doo-han, whom he had not seen for fifty years. Kim, a fifty-six-year-old doctor, followed his parents to Sakhalin Island (then Japanese Karafuto) when he was only six years old, while his two aunts and four uncles remained behind. When he returned to Korea as an interpreter for the Soviet cycling team, Kim distributed the names of his relatives to the Korean media. Days later, his only surviving uncle showed up outside the Olympic village and tearfully embraced a long-lost nephew in front of flashing cameras:

"Your nose is a carbon copy of my older sister's!"
"You look like my mother!"

These simple but heartening stories of human suffering and joy captivated Korean audiences and helped break down barriers built over many years of political estrangement between South Korea and the Soviet Union.[77]

Moscow also sponsored a remarkably rich cultural program in Seoul to coincide with the Olympiad. Fifty-one ballet dancers, including third-generation Soviet Korean Svetlana Tsoi, performed for three days at the stage of the Sejong Cultural Center in downtown Seoul for an audience of almost nineteen thousand people.[78] The Moscow Philharmonic, performing two weeks later, drew nearly thirteen thousand people to the same center.[79] In addition, two Soviet Koreans, Nelli Li and Lyudmila Nam, held separate recitals that commanded audiences of over 2,300 each time.[80] *The New York Times* reported on October 2 how "curious shoppers flocked to 'Russia Week' at the huge Lotte Department Store, snapping up sets of Russian Olympic pins—including one with the Soviet and South Korean flags side by side—and inspecting Soviet-made porcelain and nested wooden dolls."[81] In the meantime, Soviet athletes handed out Lenin badges and perestroika t-shirts to their "new Korean friends."[82]

By contrast, the American athletes managed to put off the Korean audiences from the day of the opening ceremony, when the US team swept past the stadium stands in a torrent of enthusiasm.

Some athletes left the track momentarily, moving closer to the stands to wave to family members and mug for television cameras. This did not endear them to the Koreans, who construed the American behavior as "rude and arrogant."[83] It did not help that two US gold-winning swimmers, Troy Dalbey and Doug Gjertsen, were detained by the South Korean police for stealing an $830 marble lion head from a bar in a Seoul hotel and parading it in the street. The Koreans were outraged, and radical students of Seoul National University even denounced the prank in a letter to the US Embassy as an example of American "arrogance."[84] Another American athlete was arrested for kicking a taxi.[85] Such unpleasant incidents fed anti-American sentiments in Korea, already very strong at the left side of the political spectrum, especially among students. No wonder, then, that at a preliminary soccer match between US and Soviet teams, some Koreans "cheered for the Soviet side, waving huge hammer-and-sickle red flags." Similar scenes were observed at the US-Soviet basketball match, when Korean fans held up posters with "CCCP" (USSR in Russian) and jeered the Americans.[86] Of course, anti-Americanism in South Korea had its limits, and the sudden passion for the Soviet Union was fuelled by curiosity more than any long-term political imperatives. Yet Soviet charm left its mark on South Korea, noted the *Financial Times*: "after the hysteria has died down, the result should be a far more balanced picture of the world."[87]

If South Korea discovered the USSR during the Olympics, the reverse was equally true. Brought up on dramatic stories of poverty and strife in the "puppet" South Korean state, Soviet visitors discovered a world of futuristic skylines, busy highways, and crowded shopping centers—a modernity that favorably compared with shabby housing, worn down infrastructure, and empty shelves back home. The Olympic Village was itself a high-tech showcase. Four hundred athletes lined up daily to play free video games—"Shooting Master" and "Motorcycle." The latter was so popular that the organizers had to replace parts that broke down from overuse.[88] Athletes received "electric mail" messages from their fans through a prototype "wide network information service."[89] There was a color copier facility on hand, though police permission was required to make copies for fear of money forgery.[90] And the city of Seoul—with its freshly refurbished streets, newly built subway lines, and slim modern buildings—was impressive by all standards, especially so to an unaccustomed Soviet eye.

Olympic broadcasts in the Soviet Union averaged between fourteen and sixteen hours daily, while the opening ceremony attracted about two hundred million Soviet television viewers.[91] Of course, only sports-related facilities were shown on the television, but it was enough to give the Soviet audiences an indirect experience of Seoul—an experience that did not square with the image of South Korea cultivated for years by the Soviet propaganda. In the end, however, it was not the common man in the living room who mattered but the elites—Soviet athletes, officials, journalists, performers, and scholars—those who had seen South Korea first-hand and came back to share their experiences with friends and colleagues in Moscow. Many would agree with an assessment offered by the head of the Soviet press delegation, Vitalii Ignatenko: "Everything I had read before turned out to be outdated; I arrived into the 21st century."[92]

NEW TIMES, NEW FACES

Ignatenko's interests in Seoul extended beyond the Games. He met with and interviewed one of the leaders of the South Korean opposition, Kim Young-sam. The trail of events that had far-reaching political consequences began in Tokyo in August 1988. On August 17 Kim Young-sam arrived in Japan at the invitation of the Foreign Correspondents' Club for a week-long visit. He was playing a tricky political game against the other two opposition Kims, and against Roh Tae-woo as well. The rules of the game became more complicated after April 1988 parliamentary elections, when Roh Tae-woo's Democratic Justice Party lost out to the opposition. Roh moved to shore up his political position by striking a deal with his rivals to abstain from undermining each other, and to restrain the radical demonstrators ahead of the Seoul Olympics. The three Kims also agreed to support Roh's efforts to engage Beijing and Moscow.[93]

For Kim Young-sam the trick was to support nordpolitik in principle, but also to show that *his* nordpolitik was better than anyone else's. He did just that during his press conference in Tokyo on August 18, calling for a meeting of Northeast Asian parliamentarians—from the two Koreas, China, Japan, the Soviet Union, and the United States—to discuss outstanding regional problems and "to promote the flow of exchange and understanding among the people of the region."[94] MPs could succeed, Kim said, where governments had failed: "Just as the Korean peninsula could be transformed from a symbol of war to a symbol of peace, the Northeast Asian region itself could also be changed from an arena of cold war confrontation to an area of international reconciliation."[95]

One of the attendees at Kim Young-sam's talk was Vladimir Ovsyannikov, a Tokyo-based correspondent for the liberal Soviet weekly *Novoe Vremya* (*New Times*). A well-known character in the press corps, Ovsyannikov was fluent in Japanese and appeared on television programs. "I thought he was one of you know who" (implying the KGB), recalled Daniel Sneider, at the time the Tokyo correspondent for the *Christian Science Monitor*—"he seemed to be in places where I wasn't."[96]

After the talk, Ovsyannikov was taken aside by Hwang Byong-tae, YS's fellow party member, who made an unexpected proposal: Kim Young-sam was willing to give an extended interview to the *New Times*. Would the Russian agree?

> I did not doubt—recalled Ovsyannikov—and agreed at once, though the situation was rather complicated at the time. On one hand, there was clear movement in the relations of the Soviet side with South Korea.... On the other hand—there were no official symptoms or instructions regarding rapprochement, and it was necessary to coordinate each "sharp" question with the editor (and therefore, with the Central Committee).[97]

Ovsyannikov contacted Vitalii Ignatenko, then the Editor-in-chief of the *New Times*. In Moscow, Ignatenko approved the interview and promised publication. At the appointed time, Ovsyannikov appeared in Kim Young-sam's presidential suite. In the presence of several people from YS's entourage, who took meticulous notes, he asked between five and six questions, in English, with Hwang Byong-tae translating. When the interview was finished, the note-takers left the room, and only Kim, Hwang, and Ovsyannikov remained.

Now—Kim said, switching to Japanese—let's talk business.... The issue at stake, Kim said, was that the Soviet leadership was on the brink of making a serious mistake in its South Korean policy. Kim Dae-jung had already received an invitation to visit the USSR. But, YS said, if his rival came to Moscow first, President Roh Tae-woo would have to make changes to nordpolitik, because he has already determined that Kim Young-sam should be Roh's successor as President, and therefore the first man in Moscow. Kim then explained that he had already coordinated policy decisions with President Roh and that the latter had instructed him to pave the road to normalization.[98]

The following evening Ovsyannikov took this information to the Soviet Embassy. It was late, but he asked the Soviet Ambassador, Nikolai N. Solov'ev, to receive him. "I remember how past 1 am in the morning we treaded circles in the embassy garden, discussing the situation. In the end Nikolai Nikolaevich suggested that I build my own channel of 'unofficial diplomacy' through my editor in chief V. N. Ignatenko." It was a predictable move on the part of the extra-careful ambassador. Solov'ev would not have been an ambassador had he not taken care to stay well away from risky schemes, Kim Young-sam's scheme being a good example of this. Ovsyannikov was on his own. "I returned to the office and wrote a substantial memorandum addressed to Ignatenko."[99]

Ignatenko judged the matter important enough that he and Ovsyannikov had a follow-up meeting with YS in Seoul, during the Olympic Games.[100] In an interview published in a late September issue of the New Times, Kim Young-sam professed admiration of Gorbachev's "bold leadership," praised Soviet political initiatives, and expressed readiness to "go to Moscow, Beijing or Pyongyang" if that would help to ease tensions in the region. He also dangled the promise of economic cooperation with the Soviet Union—just the kind of juicy prospect that interested the Soviet bureaucrats the most, especially after Gorbachev publicly called for economic ties with South Korea in his speech in Krasnoyarsk on September 16.[101] This was enough to sicken the North Korean officials who would have been reading the New Times. But there was something left out of the published story: Ignatenko and Kim Young-sam discussed the possibility of Kim's visit to the Soviet Union.[102]

The invitation to Kim Young-sam was sent from IMEMO, then headed by Evgenii Primakov. YS, after all, beat his rival Kim Dae-jung to become the first South Korean politician to visit Moscow openly. DJ had all the chances, and he tried hard. Kim Young-sam had not deceived Ovsyannikov—Kim Dae-jung really did receive an invitation to visit the USSR, from none other than Georgii Arbatov, as DJ publicly disclosed on October 22. What happened then? "Well...," Arbatov recalled, "These were Primakov's intrigues of some kind.... We did invite him [Kim Dae-jung], and everything was already agreed, but he [Primakov] somehow managed to persuade [the leadership] that this one [Kim Young-sam] is even more important."[103] It was a brilliantly executed coup on the part of YS, and he did not hide his satisfaction in retrospect: "Umm, by the way, DJ, this guy, is good at lying. He did not even have an invitation from the USSR."[104]

On June 2, 1989, Kim Young-sam, heading a small delegation of party functionaries, arrived in Moscow, "as scary and far-away as the kingdom of the dead."[105] He faced considerable uncertainties. "I felt that I went to the Moon," Kim later recalled.[106] In his memoirs, and in the interview for this book, Kim Young-sam best remembered drinking vodka with Primakov, who, just when YS was in Moscow, soared to political prominence after being elected the Chairman of the Council of the Union, one of the chambers of the newly created Soviet Parliament.[107] According to Kim's recollections, Primakov made it clear that he considered YS to be the future President of South Korea.[108] This explains why YS was invited to Moscow in the first place: it was an opportunity to set up a relationship with Roh's likely successor—a relationship that would become very important if and when Soviet relations with South Korea normalized.

Normalization, however, was not on the Soviet official agenda for now, as Kim Young-sam found out to his chagrin. On June 6 YS met with the deputy head of the Central Committee International Department, Karen Brutents, who "responded coolly to Kim's suggestion that political ties be upgraded along with trade links, noting that 'giving priority to economic exchange is Soviet policy.'"[109]

It would be surprising if Brutents had said something different under the circumstances, but it was beyond doubt that his meeting with YS was in itself a major political demarche. The media hype got worse after Kim Young-sam disclosed that he secretly met in Moscow with ranking North Korean Politburo member Ho Dam. Kim Il-sung dispatched Ho Dam to invite YS to visit Pyongyang; the latter wisely declined the honor of becoming a tool of the North Korean propaganda. Even so, the *Financial Times* concluded, prematurely, that YS's meetings "could lead to a breakthrough in relations between the two Koreas," while the *Boston Globe* perceptively suggested that "Kim's venture at international diplomacy was certain to bolster his own political standing at home."[110]

Thus, by late 1989 the Soviet Union and South Korea were edging closer and closer to normal diplomatic relations. While on the Soviet side economics superseded politics, for the South Koreans politics took precedence over economics, but there were more and more points of agreement in practical areas, and none came too early for the beneficiaries of this piecemeal reconciliation: academics, students, entrepreneurs, and elderly Koreans who shed tears in emotional reunions in Seoul. "Mikhstep" Kapitsa was also in Seoul in September 1989, for a conference. He spoke about the importance of "people's diplomacy," how it "strengthen[s] mutual confidence by concrete common actions, by joint work at non-governmental, public levels."[111] Kapitsa had a point. But there was one lingering uncertainty: where did "people's diplomacy" end and normal diplomacy begin? Kim Young-sam may have been a "people's diplomat" by Kapitsa's measure, but his visit to Moscow was nothing if not a milestone on the road to normalization.

TENSIONS WITH NORTH KOREA

Despite the outward signs of healthy cooperation, tensions were quietly building up in Soviet–North Korean relations, leading to a sense of estrangement by the end of 1987, and even more so in the early months of 1988. The North Koreans proved completely unreceptive to reform. Soviet contacts with North Korean officials in 1987 showed that there was not the slightest interest in Pyongyang in following the Soviet experiment in democratization. In March 1987 Hwang Jang-yop, in his meetings with Vadim Medvedev, expressed "certain understanding" of Gorbachev's reforms and even wished success in their implementation. But it was the limit of Hwang's interest; instead, he praised the North Korean ideology of self-reliance and explained that his country was successfully implementing its seven-year plan and was moving ahead with the birthday celebrations of Kim Il-sung and Kim Jong-il.[112]

Gorbachev's liberal adviser Georgii Shakhnazarov thought that Pyongyang "politely ignored everything that we are doing in the sphere of reforms" and turned a "deaf ear to all impulses, which originate from Moscow, from our politics." He lamented, too, that the government authorities prevented fresh political ideas from reaching the rank-and-file North Koreans.[113] Vadim Medvedev, in a later assessment, wrote: "naturally, the ideas of democratization and glasnost, which lay at the basis of the *perestroika*, turned out to be alien to the North Koreans."[114] Medvedev thought that Pyongyang's failure to follow the Soviet suit in political reforms was one of the reasons for cooling of relations between the two countries, which began sometime after November 1987.

Similar tensions developed in North Korea's relations with China over the same period. The Great Leader had already formed an opinion about the Chinese reforms—it was not a positive opinion, but he kept tight-lipped about his reservations. "The Chinese are saying that they will build 'socialism with Chinese characteristics,'" Kim Il-sung noted in December 1986. "When I meet with the Chinese, I tell them directly that if you think you can build socialism in your own way, well, then go ahead and try. I don't tell them whether it's right or wrong."[115] However, by 1987 he had more reasons to worry because of the expanding Chinese contacts with South Korea. In May of that year he visited China in a bid to persuade Deng Xiaoping to halt these contacts.

After advertising China's policies of reform and opening to Kim Il-sung (Deng even proposed that the Great Leader visit Shenzhen to see the changes for himself), the Chinese leader explained China's position on the question of reunification of Korea: "Our two countries both have the reunification problem. For you, in resolving the problem of relations with South Korea, and for us, in resolving the problem of Taiwan, the key is to advance on our own, to handle [these problems] on our own." He warned Kim against reliance on military force: "One day, our social system will demonstrate its superiority over their social system, the pace of development of our economy will exceed the pace of development of their economy. Current international circumstances demonstrate that no dispute can be resolved with military force."[116]

A few days later, in a meeting with a delegation of the Japan's Komeito party, Deng explained China's basic approach to the problem of Korea, which had remained unchanged: "Our two countries, Japan and China, share one common point: we both hope that the Korean Peninsula has a stable and peaceful environment."[117] In this sense, Deng's policy toward the Korean peninsula shared important traits with his take on Indochina: in both cases, one could sense a shift toward "regionalization" of the problem, as China exited the Cold War.

Worried lest other socialist countries also turn their sights on Seoul, the Great Leader worked hard to avert the budding rapprochement between the Soviet bloc and South Korea. This was in fact the main purpose of the visit by Kim Yong-nam to Moscow in May 1988. The North Korean Foreign Minister appealed to the Soviet leadership to abstain from economic contacts with South Korea and to prevail upon their allies to do the same (Hungary, in particular, had "sinned" in this respect). "How can you doubt our support?" Gorbachev asked. "Of course, we don't doubt it," lied Kim Yong-nam.[118] One day after his meeting with Kim Yong-nam, Gorbachev discussed Soviet policy at the Politburo. He noted that South Korea was sending "signals" about better relations but concluded in the end: "do not change anything, so that they don't accuse us of agreeing to the concept of two Koreas."[119]

Gorbachev's remarkable resilience in supporting North Korea underlies the force of inertia in Soviet policy and a reluctance to broach taboo subjects. South Korea had been vilified for so long that Gorbachev found it psychologically difficult to accept the changing realities on the Korean peninsula. Similar handicaps marked Gorbachev's policy toward other clients in the Third World. Perhaps because Kim Il-sung and his likes had been around for too long, their importance to Soviet foreign policy was taken for granted, even though it was increasingly clear that Gorbachev's "new thinking" in foreign affairs was basically incompatible with continued support for militant regimes like North Korea's. The problem was that Gorbachev was not willing to admit this contradiction—not to the North Koreans and not even to himself. For this reason, he continued to reassure Pyongyang that the Soviet Union would not recognize South Korea, even though clearly the winds were blowing in that direction, and Gorbachev's closest advisers were already privately urging a change of policy to take advantage of the economic opportunities in developing relations with South Korea.

By the fall of 1988 Gorbachev was at last willing to face the reality. His speech on September 16, 1988, in Krasnoyarsk became an important turning point. There, he announced for the first time that "in the context of a general amelioration of the situation on the Korean peninsula, opportunities can also be opened up for arranging economic ties with South Korea."[120] Gorbachev's announcement came after months of a secret dialogue with the South Koreans and marked a breakthrough for the enthusiasts of Soviet–South Korean rapprochement in Gorbachev's own inner circle as well as within the wider policy community. The policy consensus articulated in the Krasnoyarsk speech was that Moscow would welcome economic but not political relations with South Korea.

In October 1988 Hwang Jang-yop visited Moscow to air North Korea's views concerning Gorbachev's Krasnoyarsk speech. The memorandum that Hwang handed over to the Soviets was predictably sharp on this score:

> Esteemed comrade Gorbachev M. S. said in his Krasnoyarsk speech: "I think that, in the context of a general amelioration of the situation on the Korean peninsula, opportunities can also be opened up for arranging economic ties with South Korea." For the amelioration of the situation on the Korean peninsula one must first and foremost evacuate the American troops from South Korea and put an end to the anti-people, treacherous actions of the South Korean regime. With this aim, it is necessary to conclude a peace agreement between the DPRK and the USA, carry out the evacuation of American forces from South Korea, liquidate the American military bases, adopt a declaration on the non-aggression between the North and the South, cut the numbers of the armed forces of each side to 100 thousand and less, and thereby reduce the military confrontation. At the same time, in South Korea, there must be the abolition of the "anti-communist law" and the "state security law," providing thereby for free action of the South Korean people for the unification of the Motherland, and establishing a situation of confidence between the North and the South.... In

this sense we support the statement of comrade Gorbachev M. S. about the ame-lioration of the situation on the Korean peninsula.

This sense, which Hwang's statement mentioned, was certainly not the sense Gorbachev intended in his Krasnoyarsk speech. Kim Il-sung warned Gorbachev that he had come perilously close to heresy and had better take care not to cross the thin line that divided his new thinking from betrayal of Marxism-Leninism. In this connection, Hwang pointed out, "we notice that some of our friends claim that today the existence of two states on the Korean peninsula is an indisputable fact, and therefore the establishment of relations with South Korea corresponds to new thinking, based on real-ity. *However, one must not take as truth everything that exists in reality. This is a basic notion for communists.*" These sorts of passages might have inspired characters from George Orwell's work, but not Gorbachev or his key ally Aleksandr Yakovlev, who motioned to expand Soviet relations with South Korea soon after receiving Kim Il-sung's envoy.[121]

The following year was marked by the collapse of socialism in Europe, and its persistence—after the violent suppression of students in Tiananmen Square—in China. The Soviet Union descended into an economic crisis amid swelling nationalist sentiment in the Baltics and escalating violence in the Caucasus. North Korea was very far from Gorbachev's mind as he faced these daunting obstacles. By contrast, Kim Il-sung was gravely wor-ried about the turn events were taking; Europe in 1989 challenged his entire worldview. He was at pains to come to terms with these changes. Kim's response was to redefine socialism as basically an Asian phenomenon and to call on China to take charge in leading the communist movement.

Two developments contributed to this reassessment. First, Kim Il-sung failed to achieve a breakthrough in relations with South Korea. In particular, he was unable to start up a dialogue with the South Korean presidential hopeful Kim Young-sam during the secret talks between YS and Ho Dam in Moscow in June 1989. The second development was the violent dispersal of demonstra-tors in Beijing on June 4, 1989. By the end of that year, Kim Il-sung secretly visited China for a round of talks with Deng Xiaoping. New General Secretary of the CCP Jiang Zemin paid a return visit to Pyongyang in April 1990 and received Kim's assurances that North Korea will "struggle side by side with China" on the road to socialism, "to carry the revolutionary banner forward."[122]

REAPPRAISAL IN MOSCOW

In Moscow, it was not until October 1988 that the policy makers seri-ously considered the prospects of mending fences with South Korea. The initiative originated on the "liberal" front of Gorbachev's circle, which included Alexander Yakovlev, Gorbachev's advisers, and the International Department of the Central Committee. In September 1988 Yakovlev was appointed Central Committee Secretary in charge of international questions. In this capacity, on October 19, 1988, he wrote to Karen Brutents in the International Department: "Probably, the first proposal that we will introduce [to the Politburo] will be on South Korea."[123] That instruction (which likely resulted from Hwang's dramatic performance in Moscow the previous day) apparently led Valentin Falin, the head of the International Department at the Central Committee, to call a meeting on October 22 with participation of academics and Korea specialists, including Georgii Kim and Evgenii Primakov.[124]

The meeting produced a draft policy paper, "On Our Policy in South Korea," which criticized Moscow's unequivocal support for North Korea, even against the Soviet long-term interests. It pointed out that "without South Korea and at odds with this dynamically developing country, it is more difficult to push forward our initiatives, concerning the Asia-Pacific region, it is more difficult to develop stable and mutually beneficial relations with many countries of [that] region," and proposed to accept "de facto realities." "Soviet policy must not be an assistant to the policy of the DPRK," the paper said.[125] The document was signed by Yakovlev, Shevardnadze, Deputy Premier Vladimir Kamentsev, and KGB Chairman Vladimir Kryuchkov, but Kamentsev was seen as the main author, probably because of the economic emphasis of the recommendations (Kamentsev, among other things, also chaired the Foreign Economic Relations Commission). The Kamentsev report was discussed at a Politburo meeting on November 10, 1988. This time, Gorbachev was much more assertive:

> The memorandum on economic relations with South Korea, provided by Kamentsev, is a very serious one. If we do not react now, we'll be late. We have come to the solution of this question in the context of our present-day interests. For now, we are not talking about political relations. And one must necessarily talk to "friends" [i.e. Warsaw Pact allies]. A channel is opening up for our influence on the entire Korean situation. Contact with South Korea will be our response to North Korea, too, and a signal to the USA.[126]

Gorbachev's change of heart reveals important shifts in his perception of the Korean problem. First, the Soviet leader realized that he could not afford to waste any more time. The Soviet policy toward South Korea had been dormant for months, even as Gorbachev peddled new thinking for Asia Pacific. Indeed, nothing of importance had happened in the Soviet

Korea policy in the two years that had elapsed since Gorbachev's speech in Vladivostok in July 1986, which inaugurated new thinking in Asia. Now, the South Koreans were extremely eager to develop relations. They grabbed every little opportunity to reach out to the Soviets, from the top leaders down to the lowest clerks. And they came bearing gifts. In the absence of the Japanese capital (Japan dragged its heels over the territorial dispute), South Korea was the golden goose. The bottom line was, would the Soviet Union seize the hour or drag it out until the South Koreans lost all interest in cooperation? These thoughts added up to one component of Gorbachev's thinking.

The other component was of strategic character. Talking to only one side in the Korean conflict—to North Korea—limited Moscow's options, reducing the Soviet Union to a tool of Pyongyang's propaganda. On the other hand, developing relations with the South increased Soviet clout in regional problems. There was nothing new in this thinking—similar ideas circulated for months in the wider policy community, certainly in academia, where the notion of the "Washington-Tokyo-Seoul axis" had long been discredited, at least among the more progressive researchers.[127] When Gorbachev finally decided that something had to be changed in his Korea policy, he did not have to go very far to justify those changes. All the arguments were already on the table.

Finally, Gorbachev was simply frustrated with Pyongyang's stubborn unwillingness to embrace reforms. His new Korea policy was thus meant as a reality check for the North Koreans. Even so, he promised to be gentle and unobtrusive: "One should not act by a shock method with North Korea."[128] Thus, the Politburo agreed that changes in the Soviet policy toward South Korea were necessary, recommending, however, establishing contacts with Seoul through non-governmental channels.[129] Within days, the academics were already submitting reports to the authorities for developing contacts with South Korea, with IMEMO being at the forefront. The rationale was to use those contacts to attract South Korean investment.[130]

In comparison with the flurry of activities at the institutes and the economic agencies, the Soviet Foreign Ministry maintained a very reserved, cautious position with regard to South Korea, despite the fact that Shevardnadze's signature appeared on Kamentsev's report, discussed in the Politburo on November 10. Shevardnadze maintained, in retrospect, that the decision to establish diplomatic relations with South Korea had been made "on my initiative."[131] But the archival record easily overturns the Foreign Minister's recollections.

Indeed, as the Politburo came around to rethinking relations with Seoul, the Foreign Ministry produced recommendations of unwavering Soviet support of Pyongyang's policies. In October 1988, in response to reports by the Soviet Embassy in Pyongyang about the North Korean leaders' unhappiness with increasing Soviet–South Korean contacts (probably with the exchange of memoranda on Soviet–South Korean economic cooperation on October 15), the Foreign Ministry proposed to reassure the North Koreans that there was no real intention of a rapprochement with Seoul. In fact, as Yakovlev, Falin, and Brutents discussed how to move forward in relations with South Korea, Soviet diplomats were busy spreading the story that Moscow would not move away from its "principled" positions and "does not have plans of developing official ties with South Korea."[132] The Foreign Ministry's views reached the desk of Gorbachev's aide Georgii Shakhnazarov, who forwarded them to the General Secretary with a damning indictment:

> The Soviet Foreign Ministry's proposal…raises certain doubts. The way we have it is: every time when Pyongyang sounds an angry "warning," we begin assuring them that everything will be as it was and we don't have any serious intentions of having contacts with South Korea. In reality now we are talking precisely about the intention of acting in that direction, which is entirely in accordance with the interests of the Soviet Union, and generally speaking, will contribute to favorable development of events in Asia. Why should we mollify Kim Il-sung and assure [him] that we will not change anything? Wouldn't it be more correct and honest to say directly that further implementation of this line is unreasonable, that everything has shifted in the world, and one should look for new approaches to the settling of the situation also on the Korean peninsula? Otherwise, if we do not show initiative here, the West will win.[133]

Shakhnazarov proposed to send a special envoy to Pyongyang to "explain these new aspects in our Asian policy." He thought that Kim Il-sung might turn out to be "very unhappy but in the end he would have to reconcile himself" to these changes.[134] All of that made sense to Gorbachev, and he agreed to send an envoy to North Korea. Yet, ironically, he decided that Shevardnadze would be the envoy, even though the Foreign Ministry he represented offered much more conservative recommendations regarding South Korea than people like Chernyaev and Shakhnazarov. The visit, which took place in December 1988, turned out to be something rather different from what Shakhnazarov had in mind.

Shevardnadze's first meeting in Pyongyang, on December 23, 1988, was very tense. Foreign Minister Kim Yong-nam told Shevardnadze about a rumor he had heard: that a secret meeting of socialist countries had been held in Moscow, which decided to establish relations with South Korea, using Hungary as the ice-breaker. Kim Yong-nam complained that "this is nothing but betrayal of the interests and ideals of socialism, crawling into the tiger's mouth, capitulation before the power of the capital." Shevardnadze disclaimed any knowledge of such meeting and said that he was insulted by the insinuations.[135]

Soon the clouds dissipated, as the Great Leader played up his appreciation for Gorbachev's policies (he even said that he approved of perestroika). He praised Soviet foreign policy initiatives, referring to them again as "going into the tiger's lair to kill the cubs." Shevardnadze showered pleasantries in return.[136] At last, Kim turned to the most sensitive question. "They are striving for cross recognition of the 'two Koreas.'" Shevardnadze responded, "with passion," as his aide noted, "This will never be!"[137] By some accounts, he actually gave Kim Il-sung a "communist's word" that the Soviet Union would not recognize South Korea.[138] A Soviet report circulated to Moscow's allies after the visit specifically noted that the "Korean comrades…expressed their appreciation for our unaltered approach to the question of diplomatic non-recognition of Seoul."[139] For Kim Il-sung, Shevardnadze's word was worth all the flattery expended: for that word alone, he could praise perestroika to the sky.

How does this reconcile with Shevardnadze's signature on a major policy document that spelled out normalization of relations with South Korea? There is no evidence that Shevardnadze backed the draft paper "On Our Policy in South Korea" wholeheartedly. In fact, head of the Central Committee International Department Valentin Falin recalled that he and Yakovlev had to "break" Shevardnadze to sign the paper, despite his fears of complications in relations with North Korea.[140] Falin, for his part, was thoroughly dissatisfied with the pace of rapprochement with Seoul: "We have already lost economic opportunities in South Korea. Koreans are disappointed with us," he argued on one occasion.[141]

Unlike Falin, who headed one of the most "liberal" departments in the Central Committee, Shevardnadze was in a more complicated position. Although he supported Gorbachev in many of his foreign policy initiatives, Shevardnadze also had the weight of the relatively conservative Foreign Ministry establishment on his back. To some extent he had to juggle ideas from both camps. There may have been a personal aspect to Shevardnadze's actions. He was the face of Soviet foreign policy; he was the one who had to meet with people like Kim Il-sung, Najibullah, and other Soviet clients, and assure them of Moscow's support. It could also be that, as Chernyaev speculated, "He took offense that he was bypassed [in Korean matters], that other people were drawn in—Yakovlev, Primakov.... I don't think he had any ideological considerations.... One way or another, his Georgian character played a role here."[142] Therefore, the pro–South Korean camp (the liberal wing of Gorbachev's circle) had to get Shevardnadze on board with their proposals on normalizing relations with Seoul, in order to present a broader front in the Politburo discussion. Hence, Yakovlev needed to "break" Shevardnadze. The Foreign Minister's weight could sway the General Secretary, who had also been sitting on two chairs. Even as late as May 1989, days before Kim Young-sam's visit to Moscow, Gorbachev argued that he would not allow political contacts with South Korea. "This is ... out of the question."[143]

This uncertainty in the top ranks facilitated a bureaucratic tug-of-war between the Foreign Ministry and Gorbachev's liberal advisers in early 1990. On January 27, 1990, the Foreign Ministry's collegium (council of senior diplomats) held a meeting to discuss the Soviet policy on the Korean peninsula. The meeting produced starkly conservative recommendations. It was said that the Soviet policy would be, "as before, perfection of cooperation on the equal basis with the DPRK, further strengthening of friendly ties with it." The diplomats recommended widening the "political dialogue with the DPRK at all levels" and finding new forms of economic cooperation with North Korea.[144] As for South Korea, the Foreign Ministry vowed to "continue the policy of development various ties ... on *non-governmental basis* without establishment of diplomatic relations, to take necessary measures to neutralize the attempts of the South Korean side to use the economic lever [and] soberly, without euphoria, appraise Seoul's ability and readiness to develop economic ties with us."[145]

In other words, the Foreign Ministry specialists well realized that without full normalization, South Korea would not be willing to make major investments in the Soviet economy. But the point was: economic incentives should not tempt the Soviet Union to turn to Seoul with open arms. Maintaining Soviet alliance with North Korea was by far a higher priority.

The Foreign Ministry's recommendations once again struck Brutents and Chernyaev as conservative, self-contradictory, and overly subordinated to the task of preserving good relations with North Korea: "We should not become hostages to Pyongyang's policy," they advised Gorbachev. "Kim Il-sung did not use the chance to put an end to the Cold War in Korea. The bid is still made on the politics of force. The leadership of the DPRK declared détente harmful for small countries and openly calls for 'overthrowing the fascist clique of Roh Tae-woo.'" Warning that North Korea was pursuing a clandestine nuclear program, a concern that was corroborated in a KGB report in February 1990 that claimed Pyongyang already had the bomb,[146] Brutents and Chernyaev called for distancing Soviet policy from that of the militant ally and for normalization with South Korea. "If this is done too late, we will not win politically or economically, but will only make a forced move."[147]

These recommendations were diametrically opposed to those of the Foreign Ministry. Chenyaev and Brutents were also a gulf apart from the military, whose view, as expressed by Sergei Akhromeev in February 1990, amounted to assertion that rapprochement with Seoul would be tantamount to betrayal of an ally and, moreover, jeopardize Soviet security interests in the Far East.[148] Yet, with characteristic uncertainty, Gorbachev did not fully endorse either the Foreign Ministry's proposals or his advisers' recommendations. Indicative of a mess in the Soviet policy-making circles at the time, the Foreign Ministry actually sent out its recommendations in late May 1990 to the provincial party authorities for implementation. The recommendations were preceded by an instruction to stage a propaganda campaign at the local level "on the occasion of the traditional month of solidarity with the struggle of the Korean people for withdrawal of American forces from South Korea and peaceful reunification of the country."[149] In the meantime, the liberal wing of the Soviet policy-making establishment resorted to more active measures to bring about a sharp change in the Soviet policy on the Korean peninsula.

YS AND THE PRINCE DOUBLE UP FOR A CRUCIAL VISIT

In March 1990 Kim Young-sam once again visited the Soviet Union on the IMEMO invitation. The visit came in the aftermath of a major political realignment in Seoul. Two of the three main opposition parties joined up with President Roh Tae-woo's ruling party to establish the Minjadang, the Democratic Liberal Party. Roh probably calculated that rather than dealing with the noisy opposition, which outdid his own party in the 1988 parliamentary elections, it was better to share power and co-opt key opposition figures—in this case, Kim Young-sam of the Reunification and Democracy Party and Kim Jong-pil of the New Democratic Republican Party. Only one Kim remained on the other side of the barricades—charismatic pro-democracy champion Kim Dae-jung, who led the Party for Peace and Democracy—but he certainly posed a much lesser problem for Roh Tae-woo than the three Kims combined.[150]

Of the two co-opted Kims, Kim Young-sam commanded more political capital, and he expected that the new party would nominate him to stand in the presidential elections when Roh's term expired in 1992. With the backing of the ruling party, YS hoped to beat his former opposition rival Kim Dae-jung—and that's exactly what he did. Responding to critics who were saying that YS had bartered away his political principles, the former opposition leader claimed that he had to "enter a tiger's lair to capture the tiger" (that is, join Roe Tae-woo's regime to undermine it from within).[151] But this particular tiger bit a big chunk out of Kim Young-sam's reputation. For this reason, YS's visit to Moscow had special significance for him personally. This time he needed to show that his talks resulted in a major breakthrough for his nordpolitik.

While Kim Young-sam was widely regarded as the most likely next President, he held no position in Roh Tae-woo's administration at the time of his visit. To beef up the delegation, YS asked Roh to send along his assistant for policy development, Park Chul-un. It was a finely calculated tactical coup. With Park's participation the delegation acquired greater weight than an IMEMO-sponsored visit of party politicians, but YS was older and had more prominent political stature than Park. In a very traditional political milieu of South Korea, Kim Young-sam expected that he would lead the delegation, and Park would follow. But the ambitious minister wanted not to "follow," but to "go together." Even before they left Korea, Kim and Park quarreled about their relative importance in the delegation.[152]

Park had another reason to resent YS's meddling in the normalization process. The minister was very deeply involved in contacts with Moscow, handled by the KCIA through a top secret channel to the Kremlin. The channel was operated by Vladislav Dunaev, a Japan specialist who doubled as Bureau Chief of the Soviet news agency APN in Tokyo. It was not unusual for APN to be a cover for KGB agents, and quite possibly Dunaev worked for the KGB (this was the assumption of his KCIA contacts). But it was Dunaev's personal connections in the Kremlin that made the channel viable. He was a close friend of Anatolii Chernyaev, who since 1986 had immediate access to Gorbachev. By passing information to Dunaev, Park could be sure that it would not simply fall on the deaf ears of a mid-level bureaucrat but reach the highest echelons of Soviet power.[153]

According to Park's recollections, the channel was used to request a meeting for Kim Young-sam with the highest possible Soviet official.[154] By another account, the request for a meeting with Yakovlev was put through IMEMO. Vladlen Martynov, who had replaced Primakov as director, labored to arrange a meeting, and everything seemed to be on track when suddenly, just prior to the arrival of the South Korean delegation, "E[duard] Shevardnadze made a demarche against a meeting between Kim Young-sam and the highest Soviet leadership." Martynov had to plead with Chernyaev to report to Gorbachev that if Shevardnadze persisted, YS's visit would be ruined. In the end, sometime before March 19, Gorbachev called

Yakovlev and told him to go ahead with the meeting despite Shevardnadze's schemes.[155]

This was already a remarkable breakthrough, for Yakovlev ranked No. 2 in the Soviet Politburo. But he was a party, not government, functionary, so in a sense Gorbachev signaled that he was not yet prepared to move ahead with state-to-state relations, though quite willing to explore party-to-party ties. Park Chul-un was a different matter, because he was a high-ranking state official. Far from being content with following YS around, he had an agenda of his own: a confidential meeting with Foreign Minister Shevardnadze.

This request was passed on to Shevardnadze, but the Foreign Minister had left on a tour of Africa and instructed his deputy, Igor Rogachev, not to receive the South Korean envoy. Once again, Chernyaev had to interfere, with a note to Gorbachev on March 19:

> It seems to me that this is after all a question of State policy, and not of institutional-personal sympathies and calculations. Rogachev talked about stage-by-stage process. But isn't the Korean asking for a purely confidential meeting? And one can probably reconcile oneself with hurt feelings of Kim Il-sung and his heir apparent, taking into consideration the irreversible course of events.[156]

This time, however, Chernyaev did not mention a word about "new thinking" in Soviet foreign policy. Rather, he noted that Park's inclusion in Kim Young-sam's delegation was "another proof of serious intentions of President Roh Tae-woo" and that Park would likely use his time in Moscow "for practical and, for us, very profitable economic aims." The shift of emphasis is revealing. In the previous months, economic cooperation with South Korea was clearly on the agenda of Soviet policy makers, but it was only one of the reasons for a rapprochement with Seoul. Political factors mattered to no lesser extent: building up confidence in the Asia Pacific, putting an end to militant ambitions of North Korea, reconciling Soviet propaganda about "new thinking" with actual foreign policy priorities in Asia. As the economic situation in the USSR deteriorated rapidly and Gorbachev sought funds from all possible outside sources, the South Korea problem suddenly acquired unexpected urgency.

Because of the Foreign Ministry's intransigence—"it is not very polite to force any one of Shevardnadze's deputies"—Chernyaev asked Gorbachev to appoint a person from the Central Committee to meet with Park Chul-un.[157] The task fell to Brutents, who was instructed to receive

Roh Tae-woo's envoy on March 22. Park could not be thrilled about that: Brutents was a high-ranking functionary, but his stature was not comparable to Shevardnadze, who was both the Foreign Minister and a member of the Politburo.

Brutents turned up to greet the delegation on their day of arrival (March 20), unaware of the rivalry between Kim Young-sam and Park Chul-un. Had he known, he would have taken better care with the photo-op. On the following day, the *Chosun Ilbo* featured a front-page photo of Kim Young-sam shaking hands with Brutents. Park barely squeezed into the picture. The caption read: "Congressman Kim Young-sam in Moscow."[158]

On the 21st both Kim and Park had a number of meetings. Kim saw Yakovlev that morning, first one-on-one, and then with Park Chul-un and other members of the delegation. YS reportedly asked for three things: establishment of diplomatic relations between the Soviet Union and South Korea, establishment of inter-party ties between the Democratic Liberal Party and the Soviet Communist Party, and a meeting between Gorbachev and Roh Tae-woo. Yakovlev replied that there were "no insurmountable obstacles to the establishment of diplomatic relations," but insisted that other spheres (i.e., economics) should develop first, until eventually "quantity will turn to quality." When that might happen Yakovlev did not say, but he did insist that "the question is the selection of priorities by the two sides," making it clear where the Soviet priorities lay.[159]

Judging from YS's wide smile in the photo-op, the meeting went well enough.[160] After his return to Seoul, Kim dispatched a box of fresh fruit to Yakovlev by the first direct flight from Seoul to Moscow, with a letter—in slightly awkward English—in which YS profusely thanked Yakovlev for his "precious time" and promised to "make my every effort to benefit mutual interests between two countries."[161]

It was all good, but not good enough. The whole point of Kim Young-sam's trip to Moscow was to have a meeting, at any cost, with Gorbachev. Anything less would make it difficult to call the visit a success and would not bode well for YS's political reputation. Before his departure from Seoul, Kim wrote a letter to Gorbachev, with Byzantine praises of "Your Excellency's great ideology" and of "Your impressive might in the shaping of the future of the human history." More to the point, the letter said:

> Your Excellency! Might it not be self-confident or overly demanding to put a modest request to Your Excellency, although You are very busy with affairs of state, to give me an audience, despite the undeveloped diplomatic relations between the USSR and South Korea? This would be the greatest honor personally for me,

in the 40 years of my political career. I dream to receive lessons and inspiration from the charismatic leadership of Your Excellency.

Moreover, Your audience would not only be an honor for me personally. This would be the most important encouragement and hope for the entire population of Korea, passionately desiring the restoration of peace and the reunification of their Motherland.[162]

Gorbachev did not respond.

But Kim Young-sam persisted. After a meeting at the Soviet Academy of Sciences, he took IMEMO director Vladlen Martynov aside and pressed him to arrange a meeting with Gorbachev. "For about twenty minutes near the fountain in front of the building of the Presidium of the USSR A[cademy of] S[ciences] he was telling me insistently, and even firmly that this meeting was not only the main condition for the success of his trip to Moscow but for the further process of [Soviet–South Korean] negotiations." Martynov could not promise anything. But he passed Kim Young-sam's request on to Primakov.[163]

That night, a dinner had been planned on the twelfth floor of Kim Young-sam's hotel, where Karen Brutents would be the host. The Korean delegation had some time to rest; some went to their rooms; YS received a Soviet journalist for an interview in his hotel suite. At around 6:00 pm a government car pulled up to the hotel, whisking Kim Young-sam off to the Kremlin. Events were unfolding at lightning speed, but Kim managed to grab a photographer from his media entourage, who got into the front seat of the car, next to the Soviet-supplied driver. The only other person YS brought along was his interpreter. The car drove straight to the Kremlin.[164] YS and his entourage went up the elevator, but the photographer ploy did not work. "There were many big guys up there, they pushed the photographer away."[165]

YS and the interpreter were taken to Primakov's office in the Kremlin. After a short meeting, the door opened and Gorbachev appeared, as if he was just stopping by after work and "incidentally" bumped into Kim Young-sam. Gorbachev and Kim Young-sam exchanged a few remarks, with the Soviet leader reportedly saying that he saw no obstacles to the establishment of diplomatic relations between Moscow and Seoul in the near future.[166] It was said that Kim emerged from the meeting "smiling like a Cheshire cat."[167]

Soon the news of the unexpected meeting reached Park Chul-un, who was killing time at the hotel. He went over to YS's suite and found him pacing back and forth in excitement: "Minister Park, it's over. Everything is over." Park pressed YS for details and learned that there was no agreement about anything, and no memorandum. That was not important, insisted Kim Young-sam. The important thing was the fact of the meeting itself.[168]

Someone—likely Kim Young-sam himself—leaked the story of the meeting with Gorbachev to the Korean journalists. On the 23rd, the *Chosun Ilbo* published sensational news: "on Gorbachev's request," Kim Young-sam and the General Secretary met alone, in Gorby's office, for fifty minutes! To the side was a large photo of Kim embracing grinning Primakov in his trademark dark glasses. Gorbachev was nowhere to be seen.[169] Still, it was all big news for South Korea, and observers speculated on the importance the Soviet Union attributed to relations with Seoul, if Gorbachev agreed to meet with Kim Young-sam in the very difficult circumstances of unrest in the Baltic republics.

Park Chul-un found himself in a ridiculous situation. Roh Tae-woo had written a letter to Gorbachev and asked Park Chul-un to hand-deliver it. Park assumed that he would meet with the highest-placed person to whom this letter could be delivered, or, at the very least, that he would have such a meeting together with Kim Young-sam. Therefore, he kept the letter to himself.[170] YS's meeting with Gorbachev suddenly made Park and his letter irrelevant. Brutents later recalled that there was no deliberate slight, just an oversight: "sometimes, our one hand does not know what the other is doing."[171] Of their meeting with Park Chul-un on the 22nd, Brutents said: "I went to great pains to calm [Park] down, to convince him that the conversation [between Gorbachev and YS] had a momentary character, and does not indicate the lack of attention to Roh Tae-woo."[172]

Park Chul-un recalled a different story:

> I went to the Communist Party building with Yeom Don-jae. It was the first visit to the Soviet Communist Party building by a high-ranking Korean official since the separation [of Korea]. But I was very uncomfortable. It was difficult to begin the talk because I did not know whether the agreement on rapprochement between Korea and the Soviet Union was a done deal as YS said. Therefore I wanted to test Brutents.

Park pretended that Kim Young-sam and Gorbachev had already reached an "agreement in principle" to normalize relations, and there would be no further difficulties in store. But when Brutents heard this, he frowned. He then criticized the Korean delegation for exaggerating the significance of the meeting: as Gorbachev was leaving work, Brutents explained, he stopped by Primakov's office and there,

> standing, he only shook hands with Chairman Kim and said a few sentences. They even did not drink the tea. They only exchanged very formal greetings. They only talked for five—no, two or three—minutes, and that was all.

Brutents then "strongly complained" about the media hype, and said that the Soviet Union would run into problems with North Korea. Park recalled that he was at pains to assure Brutents that such a situation would not arise again.[173]

Eventually, Park Chul-un agreed to surrender Roh's letter to Brutents. It turned out to be a modest appeal to mend fences:

> In order to improve as soon as possible stability, peace, and mutual relations, I think that the two countries should normalize their relations, and I believe that this opportunity has come. I expect that the wave of reconciliation and cooperation, which has materialized in Europe on Your Excellency's initiative, will spread to the Korean Peninsula and Northeast Asia. March 19, 1990. President of the Republic of Korea. Roh Tae-woo.[174]

The key words were "the opportunity has come"—indicating that Roh Tae-woo was running out of patience.

Park added to this that South Korea was not a US satellite and that it conducted its own independent foreign policy. He even speculated that the US forces would be withdrawn from the Korean peninsula altogether by the mid-1990s. Under these circumstances, putting an end to the arms race in Korea was an important policy goal, more easily attainable if the Soviet Union recognized Seoul, while the United States and Japan established diplomatic relations with the North.[175] Roh's envoy was especially concerned about the information that North Korea had been secretly developing nuclear weapons. He appealed to the Soviets to pressure Kim Il-sung to give up his nuclear ambitions and cooperate with the IAEA inspectors.[176]

North Korea's reaction to even a hint of Moscow-Seoul collusion worried Brutents so much that when Park pushed for a formal reply from Gorbachev to Roh's letter, the envoy was told that things would have to be done a step at a time.[177] Perhaps realizing that Gorbachev's meeting with Kim Young-sam was a signal that there was no turning back the rapprochement with Seoul, Park Chul-un opted for a head-on attack:

> Sympathizing with Gorbachev's philosophy that all of the countries on earth should become friends and normalize relations through talks, I came here for rapprochement two years ago. However, not only are you dragging out the negotiations for rapprochement, but I cannot avoid the impression that you link [rapprochement] with money. After rapprochement we can cooperate in the economic field, but economic support cannot be a condition for rapprochement.... If I do not get an affirmative note with regard to Korea-Soviet rapprochement from President Gorbachev before my departure, please return the letter to me.

According to Park, Brutents met these brazen comments "with wide eyes."[178]

Russian records of the same meeting are not nearly as dramatic, but Park Chul-un's key message undoubtedly came across. Brutents wrote:

> Roh Tae-woo is definitely inclined to support large projects of cooperation of South Korean business with the USSR. South Korean business takes keen interest in the projects of large investments in the Far East and in Siberia. But businessmen will *only* take the large risk connected to this if there are appropriate government guarantees, which requires an adequate level of political relations.[179]

It now became clear—certainly to Brutents and Chernyaev—that Roh Tae-woo was not willing to offer significant economic aid before full normalization of relations; in other words, the step-by-step policy pedaled by the Soviet policy makers was simply not working.

The following day, Brutents informed Gorbachev in a special memorandum about the results of his meeting with Park Chul-un and proposed to reply to Roh Tae-woo's letter. Gorbachev apparently agreed, but, once again, half-heartedly, for he did not want to commit his thoughts to paper. Instead, he had Brutents meet with Roh's envoy once again (on March 26) and pass Gorbachev's reply to Roh Tae-woo orally. Brutents told Park that the Soviet leader agreed to the ideas expressed in Roh's letter, as well as to the concrete economic proposals mentioned by Park Chul-un a few days earlier.[180] The envoy was happy with what he heard, but he wanted it on paper. Brutents initially resisted the idea, citing the Russian proverb "Moscow was not built in one day."[181] Possibly on his own initiative, Chernyaev finally wrote down Gorbachev's oral reply, signed it, and gave it to Park.[182]

Shortly after the Korean visit, Brutents and Chernyaev prepared a memorandum for Gorbachev, in which they argued:

> The policy of stage-by-stage approach to normalization of relations with [South Korea], which has been carried out up to now, does not have the desired effect in political or in economic spheres. In fact we are taking step after step towards recognition of South Korea, without obtaining in exchange any substantial advantages.

Gradual escalation of contacts with Seoul with continued gestures of commitment to North Korea was a policy of fence-sitting that neither endeared

Roh Tae-woo nor really fooled Kim Il-sung. Brutents and Chernyaev therefore recommended a radical approach: immediate recognition of South Korea in return for Seoul's agreement to initiate large-scale economic projects in the USSR. Such a trade-off would be by far preferable to piecemeal efforts of normalization, as it would allow the Soviet leadership to "test seriousness of South Korean intentions."[183]

Perhaps recognizing that their far-reaching recommendations might upset Gorbachev as an explicit money-making scheme, Brutents and Chernyaev also floated ideas of new thinking. The memorandum said that both Koreas had still not renounced the idea of using force for reunification, and therefore "normalization of relations between the USSR and South Korea will lead to a turn from a confrontation on the Korean peninsula to creation of conditions for peaceful reunification."[184]

As for Pyongyang's reaction to this scenario, Chernyaev and Brutents warned not to overdramatize it. Kim Il-sung would do fine as long as Moscow remained "fairly loyal to the North Korean regime." In any case, "our intentions with regard to Seoul must not be unexpected for the leadership of the DPRK."[185] The ideas of being "fairly loyal" to North Korea and not doing anything "unexpected" with Seoul contradicted the substance of the memorandum, which indicated Gorbachev's lingering uncertainties about Korea. If Brutents and Chernyaev were more forceful, their recommendations would be more difficult for the Soviet leader to accept. The escape clause on "loyalty" to North Korea allowed Gorbachev to approve the memorandum.

SAN FRANCISCO ENCOUNTER

At their final meeting in Moscow, Brutents and Park Chul-un, seeing that expanding contacts required something other than their ad hoc arrangement through Dunaev, agreed that routine communication would be handled by one "Nazarov" of the KGB station in Tokyo. Dunaev, with his direct access to Gorbachev, would be reserved strictly for emergency contacts.[186] Before long, there was such an emergency. On April 7, 1990, former US Secretary of State George Shultz informed Roh Tae-woo in confidence that Gorbachev would visit the United States in early June for talks with US President George Bush and that he would also make a stopover in San Francisco to give a lecture at Stanford on Shultz's invitation.[187] Roh decided that he could use this opportunity to arrange a face-to-face meeting with Gorbachev on US soil.

Roh's plan was code-named "five percent," as his advisers initially thought that the chances of a summit with the Soviet leader were that low.[188] To make things worse, the President's chief secret negotiator, Park Chul-un, resigned on April 13 over a bitter conflict with Kim Young-sam. Just when his services were most needed, he was about to leave the country on a prolonged business trip. On April 23 Roh's Foreign Policy Aide, Kim Chong-hwi, summoned Park for a meeting at the downtown Plaza Hotel. There, Kim asked the former Minister to arrange a meeting between Roh, Gorbachev, and Bush on the evening of May 30 through the Dunaev channel. Park agreed. A couple of days later, followed only by Yeom Don-jae, he flew to Japan for a secret meeting with Dunaev.

Shortly after eight o'clock in the morning on April 27, the three conspirators met at the Japanese restaurant of the Akasaka Prince Hotel, a luxurious high-rise west of the government district.[189] Park asked Dunaev to pass on a message that Roh would like to meet with Gorbachev in Washington on May 30 or 31, either alone or in a three-man combination with Bush. Subjects to be discussed were all too familiar: stability and peace in Asia and (needless to say) prospects for economic cooperation. Park supplied Dunaev with a memorandum for the Soviet leadership and paid for his ticket to Moscow. Dunaev departed right away.[190] Yeom Don-jae returned to Seoul.[191] Park proceeded to Cairo for his scheduled business trip.

Dunaev delivered his message as promised. But nothing followed—for weeks. As Roh Tae-woo lingered in uncertainty, Gorbachev had his hands full with more urgent problems. Boris Yeltsin vigorously pushed for Russia's sovereignty; Gorbachev was losing the battle with centrifugal nationalism. Shakhnazarov registered Gorbachev's comments on May 17, 1990: "we should not run around now, should not allow any panic. Everything is under control, we should not let off steam." Shakhnazarov was not persuaded:

> During such moments [Gorbachev] more and more reminds me of a daredevil desperately convinced in his own right, stubbornly breaking through to his aim across all the obstacles in the face of hostile fury.[192]

But obstacles multiplied by the day, and the hostile fury did not abate.

On that same day (Thursday, May 17), Chernyaev pressed Gorbachev to respond positively to Roh Tae-woo's initiative. On Sunday, Gorbachev's Foreign Policy Aide and long-time Ambassador in the United States Anatolii Dobrynin was leaving for Seoul to participate in a conference of the InterAction Council, a group of former heads of state and diplomats, brought together by West Germany's former Chancellor Helmut Schmidt.

Chernyaev wrote that Roh Tae-woo would personally receive everyone in the "Schmidt company" (including Dobrynin):

> In this situation having no answer about his [Roh Tae-woo's] meeting with you implies a negative answer. Perhaps we should make an appointment for Roh Tae-woo in San Francisco after all.[193]

Chernyaev also warned against reliance on Shevardnadze for advice:

> Shevardnadze is not a helper in search of a solution. He was offended that you met with the Korean [Kim Young-sam] despite his opinion, which he left with the Foreign Ministry, before leaving for Namibia.... We are letting billions slip out of hand.[194]

Gorbachev, who evidently shelved Dunaev's message in early May, now had to make a choice between further procrastination and decisive action. The Soviet President resolved to stand in the face of hostile (North Korean) fury. He called in Dobrynin. The latter recalled that Gorbachev greeted him with the words "we need some money" and impressed upon his aide to sound out Roh Tae-woo regarding financial assistance. He then agreed to meet with the South Korean President in the United States.[195] Facing a deepening economic crisis, Gorbachev shed his concerns about North Korea's reaction and decided to commit his efforts to a rapprochement with Seoul. Unsurprisingly, the meeting in San Francisco was to be kept secret from Shevardnadze and the Foreign Ministry; only Gorbachev's closest confidants were aware of the plan.[196]

Gorbachev made his decision in favor of the summit with Roh on May 17. On the same day, Chernyaev urgently called in Dunaev, who was then still in the Soviet capital. Dunaev immediately drove his old Volga to the Kremlin, but got a flat tire on the Greater Stone Bridge across the Moscow River. Desperate, he approached a traffic policeman, explaining to him the importance of his mission and, unexpectedly, received permission to park his Volga at the side of the road. Dunaev walked to the Kremlin; Chernyaev broke the news.[197] Right away, Dunaev requested a meeting with Gong Ro-myung, the head of the consular department of the Korean Trade Promotion Corporation in Moscow. Gong arranged for a staff member to meet with Dunaev, which they did, at one of Moscow's restaurants. Dunaev, reportedly "nervous" for fear of eavesdropping, told the Koreans: "Gorbachev agrees to meet with Roh Tae-woo on June 4."[198] Dunaev would provide further details two days later in Japan. On May 19, in Tokyo, Dunaev told Yeom Don-jae about Dobrynin's mission in South Korea.[199]

Dobrynin arrived in Seoul on the 22nd. Evidently, the South Korean policy-making establishment was oblivious to his special mission in Seoul. The KCIA actually petitioned Roh to use Dobrynin "as an important messenger to convey President Roh's personal letter to Gorbachev for the early improvement of the Seoul-Moscow relations."[200] South Korea's Foreign Ministry was completely clueless. In the meantime, on May 23, Dobrynin was brought to the grounds of the presidential compound, to the traditional Korean reception house Sangchunjae. There, at the foot of the pointed Bukaksan Mountain, which is said to command a certain magnetic field, Dobrynin met for three hours with Roh Tae-woo and Kim Chong-hwi.[201]

It was now time for Dobrynin to practice his magnetic appeal with Roh Tae-woo. He reportedly asked Roh for a "loan of some billions of dollars." Roh recalled that Dobrynin told him of the desperate financial situation in the Soviet Union: "They expected that South Korea could somehow play a role in the success of the *perestroika*. As a model, they were attracted by the Korean economic development. That was their top priority at the time, and they naturally expected that South Korea could contribute to this." Roh promised money, but only after full diplomatic recognition.[202] Dobrynin said that Gorbachev was prepared to meet with the South Korean president but warned not to attempt to confirm anything with the Soviet Foreign Ministry or the KGB for fear of ruining the meeting.

Roh and Gorbachev met in San Francisco on June 4. The site of the meeting became a thorny subject of discussion. The Russians proposed the Soviet consulate in San Francisco, but that was unacceptable to Roh Tae-woo as it suggested an unpleasant historical precedent. In 1896 the Korean King Kojong fled to the Russian legation in Seoul to seek protection from the Japanese. Imperial Russia used Kojong's weakness to obtain special rights for itself in Korea.[203] Korean historians even invented a term for the embarrassing occasion, *Akwan Pachon*, standing for "King's Taking Refuge at the Russian Legation." Roh was unequivocal: "If I see Gorbachev at the Soviet Consul General in San Francisco, then our people would call it the second *Akwan Pachon*. I cannot do it."[204] Roh proposed the luxurious Fairmont Hotel in the heart of old San Francisco. This was also a problematic option, because former US President Ronald Reagan, in town for his own meeting with Gorbachev, was staying at the presidential suite at the Fairmont. George Shultz helped persuade Reagan to vacate his suite to make space for the Gorbachev-Roh summit. It was agreed that the two presidents would meet on the twenty-third floor of the hotel, in Gorbachev's suite, at 4 pm.[205]

Gorbachev failed to show up at the appointed time. After about an hour and a half of nervous anticipation, Roh was finally told that Gorbachev was ready to meet with him. The President and his delegation hurried to the elevator, but the Soviet security men would only allow five advisers to get in. Even the Foreign Minister, Choi Ho-joong, had to say "I am the Foreign Minister of the Republic of Korea" to follow along. Roh's security escort had to be left behind. The Soviet security then took Roh's party to the twenty-second floor and left them in a dark hallway on a sofa for ten minutes. Finally, Dobrynin appeared with a shout of "who guided these gentlemen here?," and Roh was finally taken up to meet Gorbachev, at 5:45 pm, a good hour and forty-five minutes behind schedule.[206]

Despite this embarrassing start, Gorbachev and Roh Tae-woo managed to have a constructive conversation, broaching three main subjects: reform and opening inter-Korean relations, and Soviet-ROK relations. Gorby and Roh agreed that reforms were good for peace and stability and that "the ROK and the Soviet Union should make joint efforts to encourage similar movement on the Korean peninsula." Roh said he hoped that their meeting would "encourage North Korea and the PRC toward reform." Gorbachev agreed, remarking that reforms in Northeast Asia were lagging behind those of Eastern Europe. At the same time, however, Gorby voiced support for some "noteworthy" proposals advanced by North Korea concerning Korean reunification. Roh replied that Kim Il-sung's proposals were nothing but propaganda aimed at maintaining Pyongyang's isolation.

Gorbachev then asked if Roh Tae-woo had a message for Kim Il-sung. Roh listed three points: he wanted Kim to agree to a summit meeting, adopt openness and reforms, and end military and political confrontation. Roh's last two points were quite far-fetched. He probably meant to impress Gorbachev rather than spur Kim Il-sung into openness and reforms. Roh declared that South Korea "would not seek military and political superiority over the North." Gorbachev diplomatically linked North Korea's intransigence and US nuclear weapons in the South. Roh declined to discuss the nuclear issue, though he added that "as a matter of principle, he would like to see the abolition of nuclear weapons."

Finally, Gorbachev and Roh talked about diplomatic normalization. Roh had high expectations for this summit, even though the odds were against immediate recognition. Just in case Gorbachev decided to act on the spur of the moment, the South Korean delegation had prepared protocols on opening diplomatic relations with the USSR.[207] But the Soviet leader merely promised recognition at some future date and suggested that the two sides "proceed gradually, working step by step until the process was completed." He then offered an analogy, "the fruit will be sweet when it ripens," to which Roh replied that he was "well known for his patience."

What about Gorbachev? Did he agree to meet with Roh Tae-woo, knowing full well North Korea's reaction to such a meeting, to exchange pleasantries and talk about peace in the world? When Gorbachev gave a green light to the meeting, he did so with a specific purpose in mind: money. The Soviet economy needed South Korean credits. Gorbachev's own political survival depended on foreign aid. He had traveled from coast to coast calling on US businessmen to invest in the USSR. In San Francisco, too, Gorbachev entertained the local business elites at a luncheon, which was reportedly why he arrived late for his meeting with Roh Tae-woo.

Yet Gorbachev postponed diplomatic recognition, though the South Koreans had stated explicitly that credits would come only *after* recognition, not the other way around. Gorbachev did just what his aides had warned he should not: he failed to reap the benefits of prompt recognition of South Korea, but did enough to ruin the Soviet relationship with North Korea. The reason for his uncertainty in San Francisco was probably psychological: as a great world leader he felt it beneath his dignity to beg for credits from yesterday's "puppet" of the United States, to show Roh Tae-woo that he was interested in South Korea for financial reasons rather than the noble imperative of peace and stability in Northeast Asia.

In any case, if Gorbachev had voiced any more interest in economic cooperation with South Korea, and if he had been willing to pay the price for such economic cooperation (by granting diplomatic recognition or at least setting a deadline for such recognition), he could have left San Francisco with a juicy deal in hand. The South Korean delegation had prepared a memorandum of understanding on economic cooperation before the summit, should it come to it.[208] That moment never arrived. In the end, Roh Tae-woo simply "announced a readiness to grant considerable credit" to the Soviet Union.[209] Of course, the South Korean President had the political tact not to boast about his economic cards, nor did he need to. Gorbachev knew the game.

Before taking his leave of Gorbachev, Roh Tae-woo asked the Soviet leader to pose for a joint photograph. Gorbachev replied that this was impossible. Roh insisted: people's curiosity would have to be appeased. Gorbachev was reluctant: "best things are better cherished in the heart." But Roh showed firmness: "Without a single picture I cannot persuade my people. To me a photograph is necessary." Gorbachev finally gave in: "Is it so important? Then let's take *one* picture," at which point a Blue House photographer was called in.[210] On the following day, South Korean newspapers published the historic photograph of widely smiling Roh Tae-woo holding tight-lipped Gorbachev gently by his elbow. One of the President's aides recalled that "Roh dragged Gorbachev's arm a little bit forcefully to make a friendly pose for the picture."[211]

Three days later, Gorbachev hosted a summit of the Warsaw Pact leaders in Moscow. In his speech he mentioned his meeting with Roh Tae-woo

in passing. Roh once again appeared as an American puppet. He allegedly sought Washington's agreement to the meeting ahead of time and
even asked President George Bush's "permission" before meeting with
Gorbachev. Nevertheless, the Soviet leader welcomed the results of the
meeting, naturally not because of promised credits from Seoul, but because
"this undertaking of ours will in the end contribute to positive changes in
Korea and in the region as a whole."[212] Departing from his prepared text,
he added: "Roh Tae-woo, naturally, endeavored to achieve agreement on
diplomatic recognition as soon as possible. We linked that with the general
process on the Korean peninsula and pushed to find a constructive solution
to the problem."[213] By putting the Korean problem into a wider context of
new thinking, Gorbachev tried to justify improvement of relations with
Seoul to his colleagues from Eastern Europe and—above all—to himself.

THE CRISIS

In 1990 the Soviet–North Korean relationship suffered a sudden breakdown. This did not result from Gorbachev's dissatisfaction with Kim
Il-sung's performance. Dissatisfied he certainly was, but it did not follow that Gorbachev would cut ties and let Kim drift. On the contrary,
Gorbachev was even willing to compromise long-term Soviet interests in
developing better relations with South Korea just to keep Kim happy, and
if it were not for the lure of Seoul's economic aid, who knows how long
the Soviet commitment to North Korea would last? There was no way the
Soviet Union could keep up the supply of aid to North Korea to the same
extent as between 1985 and 1989. But there was a Soviet *political* commitment to the North Korean regime, which would have lasted longer had it
not been for Gorbachev's dire need of South Korean economic aid.

Pyongyang reacted angrily to the news of the Gorbachev–Roh Tae-woo
meeting. The North Koreans rejected the message Gorbachev thought-
lessly volunteered to convey as "an unbelievable concentration of lies and
slander."[214] Not content with leaving the matter at this, North Korean officials in charge of negotiating with the South, Chon Gum-chul and Paek
Nam-jun, on June 13 issued a fierce condemnation of Roh Tae-woo's back-
door tactics: "it diametrically runs counter to our internal efforts for reunification that the person in authority of South Korea, peddling our domestic
affairs abroad, recklessly begged somebody to lead someone to reform and
opening, and help bring North-South summit talks."[215]

It fell to Foreign Minister Eduard Shevardnadze to go to Pyongyang
to persuade the North Koreans that establishment of Soviet–South

Korean diplomatic relations from January 1, 1991, would not undermine Pyongyang's interests. It was ironic in the sense that Shevardnadze had tried to prevent normalization with the South—it was he who had repeatedly met with Kim Il-sung and promised him not to recognize the South Koreans. Now he would blatantly break his promise. Thus, it was bound to be a difficult mission.

On September 2–3 the Soviet Foreign Minister visited Pyongyang for the very last time. Kim Il-sung refused to receive him, so Shevardnadze instead met with Kim Yong-nam. Kim pointed out that the Soviet Union had repeatedly promised not to recognize South Korea. Therefore, such recognition would signal the end of the Soviet–North Korean treaty of alliance. As the Soviet defensive "umbrella" stipulated by this treaty would no longer offer protection to the North Koreans, they would have to pursue their own nuclear deterrent against the American nuclear weapons stationed in South Korea. This meant North Korea would quit the Nuclear Non-Proliferation Treaty, with dire consequences for the Korean Peninsula and for regional stability.

Kim accused the Soviet Union of joining ranks with the United States and South Korea in trying to "open doors" to North Korea. Normalization of relations with Seoul would presumably provide leverage to the South Koreans to pressure Pyongyang to open up in order to "overthrow [the] socialist regime in our country" and annex North Korea as West Germany had done with regard to East Germany. He warned Shevardnadze not to count on North Korea's capitulation a la Eastern Europe: "Frankly speaking, the USSR actively inspired *perestroika* politics in the GDR, as a result of which the situation changed sharply and she was annexed by the FRG.... The situation in Korea will not turn out the way the USA and South Korea want it, and it will not develop the way you [the Soviet leadership] expect."[216] Shevardnadze was also told that now that the Soviets were dumping North Korea like "worn-out shoes," Pyongyang would retaliate by recognizing the independence of Soviet republics. In Asia, the North Koreans intended to improve relations with Japan and to recognize Tokyo's territorial claims to the Soviet-held Kuriles.[217]

Kim Il-sung's reaction to the Soviet recognition of South Korea was unintelligent and, indeed, harmful to the DPRK's national interests, for no sense of betrayal and wounded pride could justify venting rage in front of a Soviet Foreign Minister. This was a foreign policy blunder of first-rate magnitude. Soviet–North Korean relations hit their lowest point ever. But if Kim Il-sung thought the Soviet leadership was bad, he was in for a surprise when Russia replaced the Soviet Union as North Korea's neighbor. In place of mild rebukes and persuasion, and of remarkable tolerance exercised by

Gorbachev in his dealings with Pyongyang, the Russians resorted to blatant threats and ultimatums—a tactic that Kim Il-sung himself had used for years but never before heard from the Russian comrades. Some of the same people who briefly scared the Chinese by seeking engagement with Taiwan sought better relations with South Korea and were only interested in the North as a target of international condemnation.

In September 1991 (even before the Soviet Union collapsed), the Russian Foreign Minister threatened to freeze military contracts and cut fuel supplies to the DPRK, and to halt the construction of the nuclear plant, which Kim Il-sung had wrestled away from Gorbachev at the height of their friendship a mere five years earlier.[218] The reason for Moscow's wrath was Pyongyang's unwillingness to sign the safeguards agreement of the Nuclear Non-Proliferation Treaty. Squabbles over the NPT led to a full-fledged crisis by 1993; unfortunately, Russia was practically marginalized in the resolution of this crisis, with the United States taking the lead.

However, even at the lowest point of North Korean–Russian relations in the early 1990s, there were people in the Russian policy-making circles who called for an alternative approach to the North Korean problem. Some of the same academics who had previously pushed for normalization of relations with South Korea—at the IMEMO, the Institute of Oriental Studies, and the Institute of the Far East—now proposed that Russia should strike a balance in relations with the two Koreas: "Russia must stand on two legs, supporting good neighborly relations with both Korean states." A special report, submitted by the Institute of the Far East to the Russian policy makers, explained Russia's unique position as a country with diplomatic relations with both Koreas: "We will be a useful partner for Pyongyang if our relations with Seoul continue to develop. We will be taken into consideration in Beijing and in Tokyo, in Washington and in Seoul, if we maintain our presence in Pyongyang." As a starting point, the report recommended that the Russian President visit both Seoul and Pyongyang. Yeltsin refused to do that, although Vladimir Putin did in 2000. By then, Russia was trying to play the role of a broker in Korea, although it had a lot less leverage than the USSR had in the 1980s.[219]

CONCLUSION

As the Berlin Wall fell and socialism collapsed in Eastern Europe, few dared to imagine that North Korea would survive as one of the remaining bastions of Stalinism. Yet the North Korean problem persisted, and it was made much worse by Pyongyang's pursuit of nuclear weapons. For the last twenty years, the international community has been at pains to persuade the North Korean leadership to give up their nuclear weapons program, with very little luck so far. The absence of progress of the Six-Party Talks is not surprising. The bomb is the last trump card Pyongyang has left; it translates into considerable leverage for North Korea on the international stage. It is also the ultimate security guarantee for the struggling regime. As the Cold War wound up, North Korea did not yet have this trump card. There also was no firm intention in Pyongyang to pursue a clandestine nuclear program. Then, several things went wrong.

Part of the problem was Moscow's policy toward North and South Korea, which was marred by contradictions and blunders. The Soviet Union should have pursued early normalization with South Korea in a prompt and resolute manner, not dragged it out as Gorbachev did. South Korea should have been one of the pillars of Gorbachev's Asian outreach from the very beginning. Moscow needlessly lost out on a profitable economic relationship. Instead, the mid-1980s saw unprecedented blossoming of Soviet–North Korean ties, a real bonanza for Kim Il-sung, but a drag on the Soviet economy. Gorbachev could not just cut North Korea loose: he was much too worried about Soviet credibility in the Third World—a problem that also complicated Moscow's efforts to solve the Afghan and the Indochina problems. Gorbachev had to prove to himself and to others that he was a true Marxist-Leninist, a proletarian internationalist who would defend clients worldwide, especially such a respected client of long standing as the aged Kim Il-sung. The best Gorbachev thought he could do was to lead by example and hope that Kim would embrace reforms. What he should have done was use the threat of recognition of South Korea as a lever to encourage Pyongyang to compromise but also utilize the prospect of recognition to influence Seoul in the direction of greater engagement with the North. The key years in this respect were 1986 through 1988, which were uselessly squandered in fence-sitting.

In two years, from May 1988 to May 1990, the Soviet leader's Korea policy evolved from his view that "nothing is to be changed" to his agreement to meet with Roh Tae-woo and effectively mend fences. Perceptible changes began to happen in the Soviet Korea policy only when Gorbachev realized the economic benefits of better relations with Seoul. By the fall of 1988 it became clear to Gorbachev that the South Koreans were rich and that they were willing to invest in the Soviet economy without unacceptable preconditions like those put forth by the Japanese. When he finally agreed to political relations, he did so primarily because financial considerations weighted heavily on his mind, not because of abstract attachment to new thinking. As the Soviet Union sank into financial ruin, Gorbachev looked around for helping hands—any hands he could grab, including the South Korean hand. The problem was that by the time Gorbachev recognized the necessity of mending fences with the South, he was in no position to dictate the conditions of normalization, and he was unable to use it as a lever to force South Korea to adopt a more accommodating policy toward the North. Gorbachev's advisers were right to argue against the gradual process through which Gorbachev step-by-stepped himself into the corner until Roh Tae-woo caught him there and, literally, held him by his elbow.

After his meeting with Gorbachev, Roh Tae-woo reportedly left his briefing papers for the visit in the Soviet leader's suite. A little later, a member of Gorbachev's entourage returned the Korean papers, presumably after making photocopies.²²⁰ That's how nervous Roh Tae-woo must have been. After all, Roh staked his personal reputation on that meeting and on the success of his nordpolitik overall. Soviet recognition of South Korea several months later meant that Roh achieved what he had set out to accomplish. In April of the following year, meeting with Gorbachev on the South Korean island of Cheju-do, he even agreed to extend credits to the Soviet economy, much too late to make any difference for the empty Soviet coffers. In effect, Roh got an excellent result and paid a very modest price. So modest, in fact, that the South Koreans did not find enough room to put up Vladislav Dunaev (who had come with Gorbachev) at the hotel in Cheju-do. Poor Dunaev, who had done so much to make normalization happen, crashed for the night in Chernyaev's suite, and the latter, in protest, boycotted Roh Tae-woo's reception.²²¹ Gone were the days when messengers for improved relations received a royal welcome in South Korea.

In a letter to Boris Yeltsin written shortly after Gorbachev's meeting with Roh, Vladimir Lukin, one of the early advocates of rapprochement with South Korea and privy to the secret talks with Park Chul-un, argued that Gorbachev had "lost" by agreeing to meet with Roh in San Francisco. Seoul's position, noted Lukin, was "first, high-level visits, establishment of diplomatic relations in full, etc., and then 'we will shower you with credits.'" The South Koreans were "first-generation dealers—energetic, cynical and pushy. One should deal with them courteously in terms of style and brazenly in terms of content."²²² It was very good advice, and if the Soviets had acted on these recommendations some years earlier, they would have gotten much further with both North and South Korea, and would have maximized their leverage in East Asia.

By the late 1980s, Gorbachev's foreign policy was increasingly disorganized, but he did at least try to be helpful in the resolution of the Korean problem by carrying messages between the North Koreans and their enemies in the late 1980s. Washington's mistakes were of a different nature. The White House never felt the necessity of direct engagement with Kim Il-sung; in fact, as the Cold War came to a close, the expectation in Washington was that the North Korean regime would crumble, so there was no use in compromise. Unlike Gorbachev, who, despite all the backtracking and second thoughts, found the courage to meet with Roh Tae-woo and mend fences with South Korea, President George Bush never even came close to the thought of engaging with North Korea. As he told Roh Tae-woo shortly after the latter's meeting with Gorbachev, "your having met with Gorbachev in no way implies that at this point I'll sit down with Kim."[223] That was terribly short-sighted, although perhaps characteristic of the triumphalist myopia of the Bush Administration. As the Cold War wound up, few were paying attention to North Korea. But a problem forgotten is not a problem solved.

CHAPTER 7

Tokyo's Miscalculation, 1988–89

After the dust from the 1987 Toshiba scandal settled, and the passions of mutual recriminations, protests, and expulsions died out, the Soviet Union and Japan found themselves, if not exactly at square one, then not very far from where they had been when Gorbachev came to power. The Japanese were nowhere close to reclaiming the "northern territories." That they could live without. But could the Soviet Union live without Japanese investment in the broken economy of Soviet Siberia and the Far East? It was a question of first-rate significance for the Japanese Foreign Ministry, which had stuck by the carrot-and-stick policy of inseparability of politics and economics ("seikei fukabun" in Japanese) in the expectation that Gorbachev would give up the islands for the sake of economic development of Soviet Asia. At a time when Japan loomed large as the industrial powerhouse of Asia, policy makers in Tokyo believed they could draw on Japan's economic leverage to force Gorbachev to make all the necessary concessions.

This chapter shows how such thinking backfired on Japan's policy aims. Disturbed by what he perceived as Tokyo's arrogant belief in the might of the yen, Gorbachev refused to budge on the territorial question. Soviet-Japanese relations stagnated, bucking the trend toward general improvement of the international political climate. While Japanese politicians appealed to Gorbachev to mend his ways and return the islands, the Soviet leader reached the apex of his international prestige. As he basked in glory as a prophet of a post–Cold War world, Gorbachev had little patience for Japan's territorial concerns. As before, Soviet policy was based on the assumption that eventually the Japanese would recognize that they needed better relations with the USSR rather than the other way around. At the same time, pragmatic considerations encouraged Moscow to show flexibility in at least agreeing to discuss the territorial issue, without any intention to compromise.

As the Cold War wound up, Soviet policy makers were inspired by the idea of turning the country's Far Eastern region into another California. But they exaggerated the Soviet ability to attract investors from the Asia Pacific and to play Japan against its competitors, including South Korea, China, and the United States. Although there was a brief proliferation of wild schemes that promised billions of dollars worth of foreign investment in the Far East, these either fell through or proved much more complicated than first estimates suggested. In particular, the Soviets failed to tap into private Japanese capital in the face of the government's resistance.

Gorbachev's domestic reforms in the late 1980s confused the situation for the Japanese. As Moscow allowed republican and regional governments a greater measure of autonomy, and as the policy of glasnost opened the way to public expression of widely different views, the Japanese leaders were presented with a multiplicity of negotiators and negotiating positions. Their tendency was to engage in wishful thinking in believing that those positions most in favor of returning the islands would win the day. In reality, decentralization of Soviet decision making became a daunting obstacle in the way of compromise. For the first time in Russia's history, the residents of the Kuriles and the Sakhalin region had a voice, and they were bitterly opposed to territorial concessions.

A MILLIMETER OF PROGRESS

Anatolii Chernyaev writes that it was not until 1988 that Gorbachev began to show flexibility on the territorial problem. Gorbachev finally opened up to a dialogue, elaborating his own views on this question, which meant going beyond oft-repeated clichés like "the Soviet position is well known to the Japanese side" and "the problem was solved by the Second World War." Gorbachev attempted to reason with his Japanese interlocutors instead of simply shutting them out. Yet Gorbachev's changed approach was simply a tactical ploy aimed at attaining improvement of relations through a change of style rather than of essence. Unfortunately, his new tactic was misperceived in Tokyo. The Japanese policy makers began to think that the ice was melting and Soviet concessions were not far off. This mistaken assumption encouraged undue rigidity on the part of the more conservative-minded

Japanese politicians and ultimately impeded progress towards better Soviet-Japanese relations.

Gorbachev's lively encounters with two key Japanese political actors served to underline his changing methods. The first was the elegant spokeswoman for women's rights, Doi Takako, who, as the Chairwoman of Japan's Socialist Party, met with Gorbachev in the Kremlin on May 6, 1988. Doi was careful in her formulations but could not avoid the subject of the 1956 Declaration. In response, Gorbachev talked about the "postwar realities," and the need to take them as the point for departure. "Reality," Doi answered, "is that you think that the question has been solved, that it does not exist. And we think that it exists. This is how we understand reality." She then reminded Gorbachev of the "feelings" of the Japanese people. "These feelings tell us that these are our lands, that our ancestors lived there." "We also have national feelings" was Gorbachev's response.[1]

Something similar happened when on July 21 Gorbachev met with former Prime Minister Nakasone, who had to overcome serious resistance from the Foreign Ministry. Officials were worried lest the retired weathervane strike a bargain with the Soviets, possibly along the lines of the 1956 Declaration. Nakasone had no such intention. His idea was to entice the Soviet leader to soften up: "Even if he cannot say that we would agree to the return of the four islands, it would be better to move ten or fifteen meters forward on this question."[2] He told Gorbachev that as they both were "lawyers" by education, they could "talk about these problems in cold blood, like lawyers." Nakasone then restated the territorial demands. Gorbachev explained his views: "We didn't lose the war to you, and you are trying to dictate to us." He warned Nakasone against using economic levers to win Soviet concessions: "We think there is an opinion in Japan that the Soviet Union is more interested than Japan is in improving relations. I hear the Japanese have concluded: the Soviet Union needs new technology. It will surely come to Japan to bow down. This is a big misperception. If this approach lies at the basis of Japanese policy, we will not get anywhere."[3] The imagery of this last comment was striking: among other things, it indicated that far from making the Soviet leader more pliable, seikei fukabun was an affront to Gorbachev as the leader of a great power, which in the final count did not need Japan.[4]

Nakasone told the Soviet leader that he appeared to be much more interested in Europe than in Asia, despite all that had been said in Vladivostok.[5] In reality, Gorbachev simply did not know what he could do to move forward in the relationship with Japan without giving up the islands. The solution of the territorial problem on Tokyo's terms was still anathema for Gorbachev. As he put it at a Politburo meeting on July 28, 1988: "We have shown much flexibility on our side in the talks [with Nakasone], but on the question of the islands we should not leave the Japanese with any illusions." Gromyko agreed: "One should not keep the count from 1956 but from the postwar realities."[6]

These internal Soviet discussions are both revealing and puzzling. They suggest that the Japanese, looking for signs of a changing Soviet position and thinking they were seeing such signs, were unduly optimistic. The Soviet leadership was not even close to considering territorial concessions. Gorbachev's flexibility instead aimed at talking his way out of an impasse in Soviet-Japanese relations. What is perplexing, however, is why he thought he could succeed in this without giving any ground to Japan and why he, as well as Gromyko, who had called for concessions in the much more rigid political circumstances of the early 1980s, had now become so dogmatically attached to the notion of "postwar realities." Gorbachev himself was challenging those realities through dynamic foreign policy initiatives, which by mid-1988 had led to full-fledged rapprochement with the United States.

It may be simply that Gorbachev did not care about Soviet-Japanese relations as he cared about achieving a breakthrough with the United States.[7] This explanation tallies with his occasional insinuations about Japan's second-rate status, and that the Soviet Union, as a great power, could not be seen "bowing" to the Japanese. Another possibility is that Gorbachev had sacrificed so much of his political capital effecting rapprochement with the West against considerable domestic opposition that he had none left when it came to dealing with Japan. Finally, Gorbachev was an heir to a conceptual framework of his predecessors, both communist and tsarist, that associated greatness with territory and humiliation with territorial loss.

Compared to previous Soviet practice of unequivocal refutations, Gorbachev's readiness to debate the merits of his case with the Japanese seemed like a big step forward, and it raised the question of how Tokyo should respond. It was impossible to ignore the changes in Soviet foreign policy and the winding down of the Cold War they helped bring about. Of all the major powers, Japan alone was stuck in a stalemate with the USSR. All others, including the United States and China, boasted a much better relationship with the Soviet Union. By narrowing down all policy to the territorial problem, the Foreign Ministry risked losing out on a possible rapprochement with the USSR.

Tokyo countered by seeking to shore up support for its territorial claims among the Western allies. To this end, at the Toronto G7 meeting in June 1988, the Japanese peddled the idea that Soviet foreign policy in Asia had remained much the same, even as changes were discernible in Europe and elsewhere. A special LDP delegation toured European capitals in July and

August to remind the Europeans that the four islands should be marked in Japanese color on maps.[8] The Japanese Foreign Ministry resorted to occasional disinformation, as in February 1989, when Deputy Minister Kuriyama Takakazu lied to George Bush that the population of the disputed islands consisted of forty thousand Soviet troops. In fact, there was at most a division (twelve thousand troops), soon dwindling to a mere seven thousand ill-equipped and ill-fed troops on the island chain all the way up to Kamchatka. This was anyhow merely a fraction of what the Japanese had in Hokkaido.[9] Kuriyama altogether forgot to mention the civilian population of the Southern Kuriles. His comments—in the spirit of the "Soviet menace"—were highly misleading. They reflected unwillingness to come to terms with the changing international realities, because doing so required a reappraisal of Japan's own role in the emerging post–Cold War world, which Kuriyama and many other Foreign Ministry conservatives were unable to do.

However, by late 1988, the Japanese Foreign Ministry developed a new policy to replace the rigid entry approach by then seen as unworkable in key respects. Called "balanced expansion," it harked back to the probes of LDP politicians, including Nakasone, in the mid-1980s. The idea was to support development of Soviet-Japanese relations along all fronts (including in the sphere of economics), but only if there were simultaneous advances toward the resolution of the territorial problem. As historian Tsuyoshi Hasegawa argues, the policy was "like walking on a tightrope."

> Although it in essence contradicted the policy of the inseparability of politics and economics—and indeed its adoption was necessitated by the bankruptcy of the earlier principle—the old policy was never repudiated. This contradiction was perhaps necessary to reach a consensus within the Gaimusho [Foreign Ministry]. It was also dictated by the political necessity of satisfying all the disparate factions within the LDP.[10]

As a result, the Japanese Foreign Ministry was saddled with a policy useful only for arguing against those who maintained that the Foreign Ministry did not have a policy. It was a tactical maneuver and not a change of course.

In the meantime, Shevardnadze, after a pause of nearly three years, announced that he would come to Japan in December 1988. In the run-up to the visit, the Japanese received indications from Soviet sources that the Foreign Minister would not try to evade the discussion of the "northern territories" issue. Shevardnadze was expected to recognize that there was an unresolved territorial dispute between Japan and the USSR. This was to be followed by Soviet confirmation of the 1956 Declaration during the long-awaited Gorbachev visit to Japan, and ultimately the solution of the problem with the return of Iturup and Kunashir to Japan during another summit in Moscow.[11] In the short term, the Foreign Ministry was willing to engage in constructive dialogue with the USSR to entice Gorbachev to come to Japan.

The Soviet leaders continued to follow a policy that, according to Shevardnadze's aide Teimuraz Stepanov-Mamaladze, aimed at making it look as if there was progress in Soviet-Japanese relations in the absence of any advancement. As he put it in his diary on December 19, 1988: "We are facing difficult talks. The islands—the four 'northern' islands of Habomai, Shikotan, Urup [sic][12] and Iturup—are the stumbling block in Soviet-Japanese relations. If we do not remove it, we cannot improve relations. But we also have no intention to remove it, that is—to return the islands to Japan. However, if we remain at this dead position, we could be encouraging the Japanese to militarize. Not to allow this is our strategic task."[13] It is interesting that Stepanov did not mention Japanese investment as a strategic task. This was because the Soviet Foreign Ministry, as an institution, was more interested in the high politics of security than in economic questions, which by then loomed large for many regional specialists at the Soviet think tanks and in some of the ministries. In any case, Stepanov's comments are revealing because they indicate that if Shevardnadze had a softer attitude this time around, it was not at all because he was impressed by the policy of seikei fukabun but because he was worried that a resurgent Japan could undermine Soviet security in the Far East. This was completely different from Japanese estimations.

Shevardnadze planned to propose that the Japanese establish a working group composed of officials from the two foreign ministries in order to discuss questions pertaining to the peace treaty between Japan and the USSR. These questions would naturally include the territorial problem. The other "bait" (in Stepanov's apt wording) was to dangle the promise of Gorbachev's visit to Japan. In order to prepare this visit, the two Foreign Ministers would have to meet for consultations. How many times? "Preferably, on a permanent basis," Stepanov noted in his diary. Shevardnadze hoped to exhaust the Japanese by means of countless meetings. He even articulated this ingenious scheme to his Japanese counterpart, Uno Sosuke, in their first meeting on the morning of December 19. "Uno reacted weakly," noted Stepanov. In fact, the Soviets soon learned that "he [Uno] did not understand what Mr. Shevardnadze proposed to him today when he talked about the necessity of frequent meetings."[14]

Shevardnadze's afternoon meeting with Uno offered the latter a chance to talk about Japanese territorial claims in some detail. Uno went into a long-winded historical account, including the frequently cited Japanese story about Brezhnev's response to Tanaka's question of whether unresolved questions in Soviet-Japanese relations included the territorial problem—Brezhnev allegedly said "da, da" (yes, yes). "Brezhnev had this habit, to say 'da' to everyone," Shevardnadze countered, prompting uneasy laughter on the Japanese side. When Uno finished, the Soviet Foreign Minister played his working group card. "I don't know how long the work of this group will last," he said, adding, "With the Swedes we had talks for 17 years." "The main thing," Shevardnadze explained, "is to move forward."[15] Uno promised to look into this matter, and in fact, the relevant working group was soon established. A preliminary meeting was held on December 20, followed by meetings in Tokyo (in March 1989) and in Moscow (in April 1989).[16] These meetings did not bring the two sides closer. If anything, as Hasegawa argues, they "served only to harden disagreements and hostility rather than formulate concessions and compromises."[17]

It could not be otherwise. To begin with, Shevardnadze and his deputy Igor Rogachev, who was responsible for Soviet-Japanese relations at the Foreign Ministry, had no intention of giving up any islands. Their sole rationale for the establishment of the working group was to trick the Japanese into thinking that there was in fact some movement and so ease up on other aspects of Soviet-Japanese cooperation. It is not surprising that the working group meetings ended in failure. It is interesting, however, that the Japanese Foreign Ministry fell for a time for the Soviet plan, in anticipation that the Soviets would make concessions. In the end Shevardnadze's approach backfired because the Soviet unwillingness to budge on the territorial issue provided an argument for those in Tokyo who thought that balanced expansion was a misguided policy.

In early 1989 the Japanese backtracked from "balanced expansion." This was particularly evident during Uno's rather testy meeting with Shevardnadze in Paris in January 1989, when the Japanese Foreign Minister stressed that the Soviets would have to pay for economic cooperation with territorial concessions. Shevardnadze greeted these comments with resentment and told Uno that it was wrong to narrow down Soviet-Japanese relations to only the territorial problem.[18] In fact, Uno's apparent lack of flexibility resulted from a bizarre incident, in which a Japanese diplomat allegedly intimated to the Soviets that Tokyo *was* willing to move forward with bilateral cooperation. The outlines of this murky story, pieced together from several confidential sources, suggest a KGB setup and a homosexual liaison on the part of the Japanese diplomat. In Paris, therefore, Uno had to take a hard line to undo the damage. Japanese experts, including Hasegawa and Togo, point to this instance of Japanese intransigence as a key lost opportunity to hasten Soviet-Japanese dialogue and perhaps advance Gorbachev's visit.[19] Yet this seems unlikely in view of the Soviet strategy of talking for the sake of talking.

Negotiations did not get back on track until half a year later, when in May 1989 Uno promised Gorbachev not to limit Soviet-Japanese relations to the territorial problem. "The Japanese government wants neither the downgrading nor stagnation in our relations; it advocates their movement in the direction of balanced expansion on the basis of solid confidence," he explained.[20] A subsequent Soviet report called this a "significant new element" in the Japanese approach, but that was too generous an assessment. Gorbachev said it better: "their position has moved by [a few] millimeters but no farther than that."[21]

There still was a contradiction between the balanced expansion and continued fixation with the territorial problem, and here Uno did not budge even a millimeter. Gorbachev warned him not to resort to ultimatums, repeating what he had told Nakasone almost a year earlier: it was wrong to think that the Soviet Union needed Japan more than Japan needed the Soviet Union. Gorbachev still had this problem on his mind more than two months later, when he recounted his conversation with Uno to Rajiv Gandhi: "I told them: for as long as you think that we are more interested in improving relations than you are, nothing will work out." "The Japanese are a difficult people," retorted Rajiv.[22]

During his meeting with Uno, Gorbachev said something that Chernyaev later characterized as a new point of departure for the General Secretary. He was in favor, he said, of "moving the process of mutual understanding forward, without leaving any questions aside."[23] This was supposed to mean that he was willing to discuss the territorial question, and that, in turn, meant that he did not rule out territorial concessions, at least according to Chernyaev.[24]

But it seems much more likely that, far from having the prospect of territorial concessions in mind, what Gorbachev did was to continue to appear flexible, just as he did a year earlier with Doi and later with Nakasone, and just as Shevardnadze did in Tokyo. Simply talking to Uno was from his perspective better than not doing anything at all, which was one reason why Gorbachev received the Japanese Foreign Minister, even though Chernyaev, seeing the General Secretary's busy schedule in May, proposed to drop Uno in favor of Greek communist politician Charilaos Florakis. "Uno has been useless so far," Chernyaev wrote to Gorbachev.[25] He could well add that all Soviet effort up to then to jumpstart the dialogue with Japan had proven quite useless as well. The Cold War was practically finished, and yet Moscow and Tokyo were still at loggerheads.

Before the end of the year, there was one more attempt to broker a breakthrough in relations with Japan, this time by Aleksandr Yakovlev, the intellectual pillar of perestroika, who had replaced the more conservative Anatolii Luk'yanov in September 1988 as the Central Committee Secretary in charge of foreign relations. Having played an important role in advancing the schedule of recognition of South Korea, Yakovlev hoped to do the same in relations with Japan, pushing an approach he called "the third way." This "third way" briefly caused speculations in the Japanese media as to whether Yakovlev had in mind a "two-islands-plus-alpha" solution—a return of three or more islands, instead of the two promised by the 1956 Declaration. Tokyo recognized only such creative solutions, which would allow the Japanese to get back the "northern territories," all at once, or one by one.[26]

It turned out, however, that this was not at all what Yakovlev had in mind. When quizzed about the "third way" by Doi Takako in November 1989, he specified that the "third way" was not about the territorial dispute.

If all the doors have been hopelessly blocked, we have to make a new one. This is how it is in this case. Let us take the road of constructive and realistic dialogue. They say, the Japanese public opinion supports a certain position. But the USSR also has a public opinion, and it also takes a certain position. Perestroika raised its role and weight, its activity and quality. At the present time, neither the party nor the government can make even a step without the support of the public opinion, without taking it into account. The governments of the USSR and Japan created a working group to prepare a peace treaty. The work of this group is currently the best way towards a constructive dialogue. We have to give this group the time and the opportunity to do some real work. In general, the "third way" can be defined as a combination of a dialogue, reliance on the public opinion, and on the existing realities.

This was merely a repetition of the Gorbachev position Doi had first heard more than a year earlier. She told Yakovlev that his vision fell short of demolishing "the wall of mistrust" between the two nations. "There is no wall on our side," answered Yakovlev.

DOI: But it was built from the east.
YAKOVLEV: We have no wall in the east. We have to develop bilateral relations in all directions. When big problems are solved, other [problems] become sort of smaller. The ancients thought the Earth was huge. Then it "shrank," and from space it looks very small and helpless. This is how different problems in

Soviet-Japanese relations may look. Time is the best doctor. The main thing is not to lose the sense of reality.[27]

Yakovlev's poetic vagueness suggested that there was a softening of the Soviet position. Such comments could be open to a wide range of interpretations. Was he saying that with a relative shrinking of the territorial problem as Soviet-Japanese relations developed along other tracks, the islands might also lose their significance for the USSR? It is easy to see how such interpretation could reinforce wishful thinking in Tokyo that the return of the islands was just around the corner. In light of global changes—the Berlin Wall fell a week before Yakovlev's visit to Japan—such interpretation was not far-fetched. It appeared even more plausible in view of the crumbling state of the Soviet economy that could benefit greatly from Japanese credits. No wonder Japanese policy makers believed time was on their side.

CALIFORNIA OF THE FAR EAST

Gorbachev was painfully aware of the sorry state of the Soviet economy east of the Urals. He went to Vladivostok in July 1986 to get a sense of what could be done to jumpstart regional development. Gorbachev mentioned a few ideas: developing manufacturing, expanding infrastructure, and investing in agriculture.[28] The Far East of the future, in his imagination, would look a little like California, and Vladivostok perhaps like San Francisco.[29] It would have to have high living standards, intensive industry, self-supporting food production, and formidable export capacities to compete with the emerging dragons of East Asia. To reach these herculean targets, in August 1987 the Soviet government adopted a strategic document called "The Long-Term State Program for Complex Development of the Production Forces of the Far Eastern Economic Region, Buryat ASSR and Chita Oblast Until the Year 2000." According to the planners, this program, if implemented, would have seen industrial production in the Far East increase two and a half times by the end of the century. Machine-building capacity would grow nearly fourfold. The region would become self-sufficient in potatoes, vegetables, and milk.[30]

Although Japan was mentioned in the document, its intended role was that of a market for Soviet timber and other resources. It was also vaguely proposed to get Japan, alongside India, to cooperate in the construction of "joint machine-building ventures" in the Far East. In addition, the fulfillment of the export potential of the Far East, Buryatia, and Chita depended on trade with the socialist countries of Southeast Asia, China, Mongolia, North Korea, and, curiously, Cuba. South Korea, Taiwan, and ASEAN were not even mentioned. Gorbachev, who realized better than most that Asia Pacific was where the future lay, presided over an economic development program that was utterly ill-devised for tapping into Asia's economic potential. The Long-Term State Program was inward-looking in terms of its key aims and means.

Soviet scholars and the more forward-looking policy makers were not very impressed by the Long-Term State Program. It came in for serious bashing at the March 30–31, 1988, special closed-door workshop at the Soviet Foreign Ministry for having been put together "without taking into account the prospective significance of the Soviet Far Eastern regions in the structure of inter-regional ties" and for "leav[ing] this region in the role of a resource appendage of not only developed but also developing countries of the region." In addition to overlooking the potential of ASEAN and the newly industrialized countries of the Asia Pacific, the Program was hopelessly outdated in the part premised on the export of resources to Japan because it failed to account for Japan's shift toward energy-efficient technologies.[31] But what were the alternatives? Unlike before, conservative ideas of the Soviet economic planners were increasingly challenged by people like Primakov and Arbatov, who, through their connection to Gorbachev, were having significant impact on policy making. Suddenly, the Long-Term State Program was no longer *the* program but *a* program, one among many potential approaches to developing Siberia and the Far East, and perhaps not the best.

By far the most exciting alternative program was that offered by Ota Seizo, President of the Japanese insurance company Toho Seimei, for establishing an economic zone in the Soviet Far East with the Japanese capital. Ota recalled that he first raised this issue with Soviet officials as early as June 1987, when he visited Moscow and Leningrad; supposedly, his plans "received a warm welcome of various government agencies."[32] Ota proposed to create a 100-square-kilometer free economic zone at the juncture of the Soviet, North Korean, and Chinese borders; foreign entrepreneurs would invest up to four billion dollars into this zone, building up the infrastructure (including a major port and an airport). When this idea was discussed at the Soviet Foreign Ministry in March 1988, the feeling was that "the implementation of Ota [Seizo]'s proposal, and creation of other special economic zones, could in principle facilitate the realization of the plans of socio-economic development of the Soviet Far East and the active involvement of the USSR in the Asian Pacific economic cooperation."[33]

Ota's baffling plans were public knowledge by late 1988, as he enthusiastically advertised the rosy prospects of the economic zone in various interviews. As Ota put it in one interview in December 1988 (when he visited Moscow again), "In time, there would arise a city here, the biggest in the world, even according to standards of the 21st century." He continued: "If we begin to build an airport, the US concern Boeing will readily take part in the construction. I have a preliminary agreement. There is an intention to create a satellite communication station and other most updated communication means here. A power station will be built, of course. Excellent roads will be built. I provided for creating green belts around residential areas, building cultural and everyday services projects which the World has not seen yet." As for the manpower, presumably the Chinese and the North Koreans would provide the construction workers. Ultimately, however, "as soon as residents of the European part of the USSR learn about the fantastic prospects awaiting the economic zone, they will pour there. Moreover, this place will attract people from all the continents, everyone will want to work and live in the best city of the 21st century."[34]

These were the types of ideas peddled by Mr. Ota, and although many Russian bureaucrats thought him insane, the impact of this kind of proposal on Gorbachev's policy making cannot be underestimated. Evgenii Primakov was among those who took Ota seriously. His institute, IMEMO, was at the time a real generator of ideas with regard to special economic zones.[35] Primakov was an early champion of a breakthrough in relations with Japan and an advocate of Soviet economic cooperation with the Asia Pacific. Indeed, he headed the Soviet National Committee for Economic Cooperation in the Asia Pacific, established in March 1988 and representing a qualitatively new departure for the USSR. Primakov was someone who initially gave a sympathetic ear to Ota.

Another prominent advocate of an economic zone was the Chairman of the Soviet Chamber of Industry, Vladislav Mal'kevich. In March 1988 he went on a research trip to Soviet Siberia and the Far East, visiting Irkutsk, Maritime, Khabarovsk, Kamchatka, and Sakhalin provinces at the head of a delegation that also included officials of the CPSU Economic Department and economic experts.[36] The report of this delegation categorically concluded that the task of turning the Soviet Far East into another California, set out in Gorbachev's speech in Vladivostok in 1986, "faces serious difficulties." Mal'kevich and his team concluded that the Long-Term State Program of August 1987 was no good, at least in the part dealing with foreign economic relations. They proposed a major overhaul of Moscow's developmental policies in the region, with an eye to bringing their businessmen on board joint ventures in the Soviet Far East and getting their banks to finance capital-intensive projects, like Sakhalin's oil and gas development. This approach would not only allow the USSR to avoid COCOM regulations but also "create a counterweight to the economic influence of Japan and to stimulate its [Japanese] companies to develop contacts with the USSR."[37]

The logic behind Mal'kevich's recommendations was that once entrepreneurs from Hong Kong, Singapore, or South Korea began to pump cash into the Soviet Far East, the Japanese would realize that by refusing to participate in the bonanza, they only hurt themselves. Seikei fukabun would have to be abandoned. In the meantime, Mal'kevich urged others to pay attention to the "proposals of Japanese business circles" about the establishment of special economic zones. "It appears," the report went, "that creation of such zones in the Far East would facilitate the intensification of USSR's participation in the regional foreign economic processes, that it would become a kind of a testing range for trying out new forms of economic cooperation. The Soviet side will not be required to expend much in material terms, because one could count the cost of the supplied land as a 'contribution.'" This was perhaps naïve, but these ideas were taken seriously. The report on Mal'kevich's trip was submitted to the Central Committee.[38] In September 1988, in his famous Krasnoyarsk speech, Gorbachev himself addressed the question of the special economic zones in the Far East, saying for the first time: "We are thinking [about it]."[39]

The unclear prospects of a special economic zone in the Maritime Province sparked a discussion in the Soviet press and on television at the turn of 1988/89. Opinions ranged from "I ask to be sent there for any job" (Leonid Mikhailov from Naberezhnye Chelny) to "Can it be that the Soviet Union will let the Japanese in Nakhodka, Vladivostok and Pos'yet? They will crawl away throughout the entire Far East like ants, and finally, will take away our land, which they did not succeed in doing with the help of weapons" (Anna Fedotova from Kochubeevskoe village in Stavropol'skii Krai). During the popular TV program *Rezonans* on February 7, 1989, Ota's proposals were criticized by Ivan Ivanov, the Deputy Chairman of the State Foreign Economic Commission, for their "halo of romanticism" and lack of calculations: "Where will that money come from, what is that zone to be filled with, what enterprises will there be, what markets will they work for and will they find those markets? The question remains open." Vladimir Lukin, who then worked for the Soviet Foreign Ministry and also took part in the program, questioned how Ota would be able to overcome the likely resistance of the Japanese government to the project.[40]

Both Ivanov and Lukin met with Ota when he visited the USSR in late 1988.[41] So did Primakov. By that time, Primakov's enthusiasm began to wane. Like Ivanov and Lukin, he was beginning to wonder whether Ota was for real. After their conversation, Primakov wrote to the Soviet Deputy Premier Vladimir Kamentsev that the Japanese entrepreneur did not go beyond a "philosophical" discussion of the subject. Ota, Primakov noted, was unable to say anything specific about issues like the source of credits for the project, the industrial specialization of the proposed zone (in his public comments Ota had talked about producing cars whose engines could easily start at a temperature of −45 degrees C), or about revenues and profits. "Moreover," Primakov added, "when we asked whether he could obtain the Japanese government's support for such a large-scale project, Ota unequivocally answered in the negative." Under such unclear circumstances, Primakov suggested to continue pressing Ota on the specifics through the Soviet Embassy in Tokyo.[42] In the end, Ota's ambitious proposals were turned down by the unconvinced Soviet bureaucrats. For this the Japanese entrepreneur should have been grateful, since this decision saved his company, Toho Seimei, from a most dreadful investment. Toho Seimei went bankrupt in 1999 for reasons unrelated to the imagined best city of the 21st century.[43]

The discussion of the merits of special economic zones in the Soviet Far East in the late 1980s occurred nearly a decade after the Chinese set up such zones in the coastal areas. The Chinese example no doubt encouraged people like Mal'kevich to do something similar for the country's underdeveloped eastern regions. However, the Soviet Far East was not like China's coastal regions. There was not enough labor, especially cheap labor, to power economic growth. There was also no capital in sight, no overseas Soviets who could play the role of overseas Chinese investors. Siberia and the Far East, dependent on export of raw resources and dominated by unwieldy, rusting state-owned enterprises that produced more for the military than for the civilian economy, were at much greater disadvantage than the Eastern Chinese seaboard, with its untapped reserves of labor force, abundant foreign capital, and wealth of entrepreneurial spirit. This meant that ideas about attracting massive foreign investment to the Far East only by providing "territory" were difficult to put into practice, especially so in the face of Tokyo's resistance.

LOCAL VOICES

As Mikhail Gorbachev relaxed centralized controls, giving a greater voice, if not yet decision-making power, to the regions, he found that local perspectives did not always agree with what the center thought expedient.

In a more open political climate, Gorbachev had to appear accommodating to the local constituencies. The one constituency that mattered most for Soviet-Japanese relations was the population of the Sakhalin region, including the residents of the disputed islands. Local politicians were hostile to the idea of territorial concessions to Japan. At the same time, they were wildly overoptimistic about the economic potential of the region and about their ability to attract foreign investment if only the center gave them more independence. Local Soviet politics showed Tokyo's seikei fukabun at its most ineffective. Instead of putting pressure on Gorbachev to mend fences with Japan in order to extract greater economic benefits, Sakhalin authorities appealed for removal of constraints that prevented them from building closer ties with other regional players. For as sensitive an area as Soviet-Japanese relations, this new degree of regional assertiveness and autonomy opened a Pandora's box of complications.

Although he did not foresee the implications, Gorbachev himself worked to allow greater regional autonomy to the Far East so that the local authorities and companies engaged directly with the foreign entrepreneurs and investors, without having to deal with the red tape of the central Soviet bureaucracy. The local KGB office, asked by the center to devise measures to promote the Long-Term State Program of August 1987, submitted a report in March 1989, which on the whole made it sound as if the Soviets held all the cards in terms of the development of the Far East and that the Japanese were not in a position to sabotage these efforts. The reasons for this optimism were that foreign investors other than the Japanese were supposedly keen to bring their money there, especially the Americans and the South Koreans. The Japanese government would have to keep abreast of these efforts or risk losing ground to competitors.[44]

The Sakhalin directorate of the KGB was quite optimistic about the prospects of attracting US interest to Sakhalin's oil and gas development projects. This is evident from the KGB's reports on their contacts in Sakhalin with Robert Miller, the Vice President for Worldwide Marketing of the energy giant McDermott International, who visited the northern town of Okha for a seminar on oil and gas development in August 1988. The KGB supposedly urged Miller to bring McDermott on board a joint venture with the USSR to develop the offshore deposits. Miller was told that such participation would "allow McDermott to claim the status of one of the leading suppliers of oil in the Asia Pacific." According to the report, Miller not only agreed but even promised to use his personal contacts with President George Bush and US Defense Secretary Frank Carlucci to "evade" COCOM restrictions on the export of drilling equipment to the USSR. After years of fruitless talks with the Japanese about developing Sakhalin's oil and gas, these intimations were a gulp of fresh air for the Soviets and a point of pride for the KGB.[45]

During the summer of 1988, there were press reports that the Americans—specifically, Commerce Secretary William Verity, Jr.—urged the Soviets to allow McDermott to drill for oil and gas off the coast of Sakhalin. *National Security Record*, the monthly of the ultraconservative Heritage Foundation, reported in its June 1988 issue: "The McDermott case is causing confusion in Tokyo and disillusionment about the U.S. as an ally. If the U.S. makes the kind of deals with the Soviets that America's allies are not making, it will undermine the whole Alliance effort and give the Soviet economy the kind of boost it needs the most."[46] But McDermott's contacts with the Soviets continued, and by May 1991 the company submitted an ultimately successful joint bid with Mitsui and Marathon (the MMM Group) to develop oil and gas off the shore of Sakhalin.

Another achievement advertised by the Sakhalin KGB was in retrospect less consequential but at the time seemed like a blow to the Japanese Foreign Ministry's policy of blocking foreign investment in Sakhalin and, in particular, the Kuriles. In view of the ongoing discussion at the policy-making level of the idea of free economic zones, the KGB probed reaction of various foreign visitors to the prospect of such a zone in Sakhalin and the Southern Kuriles. This matter was raised with the Political Officer of the US Embassy in Moscow, Michael Guest, who turned up in Sakhalin in February 1989. Guest aroused great interest on the part of the local KGB officials when he remarked that although the Japanese Foreign Ministry would not look kindly upon American activities in the "northern territories," he thought that "once American businessmen decided to cooperate with the USSR in the 'northern territories,' the Japanese position on this question will not have any substantial influence on the implementation of [this decision]." Guest added that the US Embassy in Moscow already received a number of inquiries from American businesses interested in developing cooperative ties with the Sakhalin region.[47]

Similar views were voiced by a Tokyo-based journalist of the South Korean daily *Joong-Ang Ilbo*, Choi Chul-joo, who was in Sakhalin in January 1989 to report on the progress of Soviet perestroika.[48] According to the KGB, Choi reacted positively to the prospect of having a free economic zone in the Southern Kuriles, even though he recognized that Japan would take exception to the idea and that the Japanese political and business circles would "put the South Korean entrepreneurs under pressure" to prevent their participation in this type of project. However, he thought that some South Korean businessmen would ignore the Japanese pressure. South Korea, Choi said, "is not burdened by any problems with the Soviet Union."

For this reason, it was only reasonable to set up joint ventures in the Southern Kuriles, located relatively near South Korea. This was the kind of analysis the KGB wanted to hear, for it opened up the prospect of breaking out of the Japanese economic blockade of the Southern Kuriles, and thus, undermining the foundations of the seikei fukabun policy. If Japan's neighbors and allies ignored seikei fukabun, then perhaps, in good time, the Japanese would understand the fallacy of this approach and opt for a genuine economic engagement with the Soviet Far East.[49]

This was already happening in Hokkaido, according to the KGB. Supposedly, the socialist governor of Hokkaido, Yokomichi Takahiro, was genuinely concerned about the apparent synergy between the South Koreans and the Soviets, for their cooperation threatened the economic future of Hokkaido. If the South Koreans moved in with force to snatch up business opportunities in the Soviet Far East, Hokkaido would lose out on economic relations with both South Korea and the northern neighbor. For this reason, the KGB reported, Yokomichi, after his trip to South Korea in November 1988, approached the Japanese Foreign Ministry and got it to agree to Hokkaido's more active engagement with the Soviet Far East in light of the South Korean factor.[50]

Already local Hokkaido businessmen were drawn to the prospect of trading with the Soviet Far East and even establishing joint ventures. One such venture was announced in May 1988, in the face of the Gaimusho's fury. Shiiku Tadaichi, the head of the Utari Fisheries Cooperatives run by the Ainu minority in Shibetsu, Hokkaido, signed an agreement with the Sakhalin authorities to set up a salmon-hatching venture on Kunashir, one of the disputed islands.[51] The US Assistant Secretary of State for Intelligence and Research, Morton Abramowitz, speculated that what the Soviets wanted to do with this particular joint venture was "to embarrass the GOJ, which hates to look heavy-handed with the Ainu, into allowing the venture and thereby tacitly accepting Soviet sovereignty over the sea zone concerned." Abramowitz thought that "this approach has got no results so far except to anger Tokyo."[52] He was quite on target with his analysis, except, of course, that the Soviets, especially the KGB on the ground, which was no doubt behind this venture and other similar initiatives, thought they were succeeding. This was not the first time that the Soviets tried to profit by dividing Japan's regions from the center; the hope was that this time such a strategy might succeed because of the changing political and economic atmosphere in the Far East.

Encouraged by presumably strong foreign interest in investing in Sakhalin and the Kuriles, the Sakhalin party authorities lobbied Moscow to allow them greater local autonomy in developing these foreign contacts.

On March 10, 1989, the Secretary of the Sakhalin Oblast Party Committee, Viktor Bondarchuk, sent a memorandum to the Central Committee. Arguing that poverty in the Kuriles was a major liability—indeed, embarrassment—for the Soviet Union in the territorial dispute with Japan, he wrote of the need to raise living standards and jumpstart economic growth. The civilian population of the "northern territories," a mere twenty-four thousand, mostly lived in shabby wooden houses; roads were nonexistent; cultural and social facilities were dreadfully inadequate. "The level of the industry and of the livelihood causes just indignation on the part of the population," the memorandum went. "Opinions are being voiced that the State intentionally is not making serious investments here because of the 'unsolved nature of the territorial question.'"[53]

The salvation lay in setting up joint ventures with foreign capital. Bondarchuk recognized that the Japanese government would prevent their own businessmen from investing in the Southern Kuriles. But in his assessment, other countries were increasingly interested in the Kuriles, with the American, Western European, Chinese, New Zealander, and South Korean businessmen probing investment opportunities. If these foreign partners were brought on board, the Japanese would be forced to be "more loyal and constructive in approaching the problem of the 'northern territories'" because of their "fear of considerable economic losses" in the Southern Kuriles. Bondarchuk wanted two things: first, Sakhalin would need autonomy to set up foreign links directly, without interference on the part of the national authorities. Second, the Southern Kuriles would need to be opened up to visits by foreigners, despite the large-scale Soviet military presence on the islands.[54]

These proposals received a mixed response at the central level. On the one hand, Shevardnadze spoke very much in favor of "taking energetic measures" to develop the Southern Kuriles in economic terms. The Soviet Embassy in Japan backed Bondarchuk's proposals.[55] On the other hand, when the issue was probed at the Politburo level on October 2, 1989, the more ambitious aspects of the March 10 memorandum, particularly Sakhalin's autonomy to develop foreign contacts, were vetoed. The Politburo endorsed the recommendations of a special group, which included Defense Minister Dmitrii Yazov, KGB head Kryuchkov, and Deputy Foreign Minister Aleksandr Bessmertnykh, among others. The key recommendation was not to advertise joint venture opportunities in the Kuriles, as Japan would likely resort to "diplomatic and propagandistic countermeasures." The way to go about the problem was to attract investment to the Sakhalin region as a whole, or, better yet, to the entire Soviet Far East. In any case, this would have to be done under the watchful eye of the central authorities, including the Foreign Ministry. As for the Southern Kuriles, the Sakhalin authorities were told to rely on the "mobilization of internal resources" to pull the islands out of endemic poverty.[56]

In the late 1980s, just as the Japanese government redoubled efforts to encourage Soviet concessions with promises of economic cooperation, the Soviets debated ways of developing Siberia and the Far East. Proponents of more traditional and self-reliant measures, and of orientation toward socialist markets, found their views challenged by academics calling for building closer economic ties with the Asian "dragons" and attracting foreign investments on the Chinese model. These views were echoed by the regional constituencies, which for the first time could air their views at the national level in a bid to influence policy. Both the academics and the local politicians exaggerated Soviet chances of economic revival in Asia. The lack of institutional guarantees, unclear divisions of responsibility between the center and the provinces, infrastructural weaknesses, the lack of a qualified labor force, and the presence of powerful regional competitors all worked to undermine idealistic schemes that promised to turn the region into a paradise in one great stride. But the persistence of such schemes worked against the Japanese, who had put so much emphasis on the inseparability of politics and economics.

CONCLUSION

The years 1988 and 1989 saw some positive movement in Soviet-Japanese relations. Unfortunately, there was no tangible improvement, just better atmospherics. To a large extent, this can be attributed to Gorbachev's newfound willingness to discuss the territorial problem in meetings with various Japanese politicians. This meant that he could hear Japanese arguments, and then offer his counterarguments—in other words, engage in a dialogue. Gorbachev hoped that the dynamic of this dialogue by itself would provide a sufficient boost to lift Soviet-Japanese relations out of stalemate. Shevardnadze had the same purpose in mind when he tried to sell the idea of "permanent meetings" to his Japanese counterpart, Uno Sosuke. A corresponding idea underpinned Yakovlev's fabled "third way." The bottom line was that the Soviet leadership was unprepared to budge on the territorial question.

The Japanese briefly bought into the Soviet tactic, with the Foreign Ministry adopting the policy of "balanced expansion" in late 1988. Balanced expansion was not exactly what Gorbachev had in mind, for he had no intention of expanding any further than he already had with regard to the "northern territories." For this reason, the new policy did not produce any obvious positive results for the Japanese, and soon the conservative voices in Tokyo were calling for a more hardline, traditional approach. Between 1988 and 1989, Japanese policy was shifting back and forth, from broader engagement with the USSR (marked by growing recognition that Japan had missed out on the end of the Cold War) to reaffirmation of entrenched position—the "all or nothing" of the entry approach.

This position could have worked well at the height of the Cold War tensions, but by 1989, it was completely anachronistic. When Bush and Gorbachev announced at their summit in Malta in December 1989 that the Cold War had ended, Tokyo was completely at a loss. In fact, in the run-up to the summit, the Japanese Foreign Ministry worked hard to get the Americans to support the Japanese position on the territorial problem. To this end, Deputy Foreign Minister Owada Hisashi was dispatched to Washington to plead "that the 'northern territories' issue be raised with Moscow as a global (general East-West) rather than merely a Japan-USSR bilateral problem." Tokyo was duly "keenly disappointed" when it turned out that Bush did not push the "northern territories" issue at Malta. Owada castigated the Americans for proposing that the Soviets be given an observer status in General Agreement on Tariffs and Trade (GATT) and for talking about improving ties between the Soviet Union and the Organization for Economic Cooperation and Development (OECD).[57] All of that shows that the Japanese Foreign Ministry was increasingly out of touch with reality and exceedingly concerned with being the last "Cold Warrior" after the Americans and the Soviets mended fences.

In the meantime, the orthodox conservatives within the Foreign Ministry and the broader LDP circles counted on the promise of the Japanese economic carrot that was supposed to seduce the Soviet Union, thought of as badly in need of investments. At one level, these expectations were not without basis. By the late 1980s, the Soviet Union was in dire straits, and Japanese money would have been very welcome, especially in the context of the Soviet plans to jumpstart the ailing economy of Siberia and the Far East. The public debate occasioned by Ota Seizo's abortive proposal to create an economic zone near Vladivostok is one example of keen Soviet interest in economic cooperation with its wealthy Asian neighbor. Yet the appeal of Japanese investments should not be exaggerated. For one thing, aware of the linkage between the territorial problem and economic cooperation, some Soviet policy makers, especially at the local level, looked to other foreign sources, not least South Korea, China, and the United States. The feeling was that the Japanese would recognize the ineffectiveness of seikei fukabun and jump on the bandwagon. It was an incorrect perception. On the other hand, the blatant use of economic leverage against the USSR upset Gorbachev, as it reflected badly on the Soviet Union as a great power. For this reason, the Soviet leader repeatedly told the Japanese not to think that the Soviet Union needed Japan rather than the other way around.

In the meantime, progressive decentralization of political power in the USSR meant that even as Gorbachev was beginning to open up to a dialogue with Japan, his options were increasingly limited. The "northern territories" issue was becoming not simply a foreign policy matter for the USSR, as it had been since the 1950s, but a question of domestic politics. Local politicians—not least the nationalists in Sakhalin—were strongly against territorial concessions. There were, of course, voices in favor of concessions, coming mainly from the liberal camp and academics of various stripes in Moscow. In this pluralism of opinions, one opinion mattered more than others—Boris Yeltsin's. Yeltsin, after initial procrastination indicative of his leaning toward a negotiated solution with Japan, came out hard on the side of those who, like the deputies of the Sakhalin legislature, cautioned against giving up the islands. By 1990—as Gorbachev well realized—any concessions on the territorial issue could cost him in terms of a severe nationalist backlash at home. Yeltsin would be sure to explore these sentiments.

CHAPTER 8

Equation with Many Variables: Soviet-Japanese Relations, 1990–91

On September 27, 1989, during his meeting with Nakayama Taro in New York, Shevardnadze announced what the Japanese had longed to hear: Mikhail Gorbachev would come to Japan in 1991.[1] Although the visit was still more than a year away, Shevardnadze's announcement was a milestone. From the Japanese perspective, if Gorbachev agreed to become the first Soviet (or, for this matter, Russian) leader to come to Japan, surely he would not come empty-handed. The Gaimusho conservatives were unwilling to go out on a limb for the sake of the uncertain promise of a compromise solution, preferring the unworkable but familiar all-or-nothing entry approach and the inconsistently advanced notion of "balanced expansion." But the Gaimusho was not the only player in the game. As the summit date of April 1991 neared, various politicians across the Japanese political spectrum redoubled their efforts to reach an agreement with the Soviets ahead of Gorbachev's visit. Being the first to bring back the good news of Soviet territorial concessions would bring sure political dividends to anyone who could score such a coup.

Few realized this better than Ozawa Ichiro, the Secretary General of the LDP since 1989, known simply as Destroyer for his uncanny ability to stir up trouble for his own party. Ozawa knew that whatever solution was reached with the Soviets, it could not be anything less than the return of the four islands. A compromise on this issue was like political suicide—even calling for a phased return (two plus two) was a recipe for an outrage. No less a battleship than Kanemaru Shin, an old LDP kingmaker, learned that much when he proposed in April 1990 that the Soviet Union return Shikotan and Habomai before the other two islands—otherwise, "we will never get back anything."[2] Kanemaru sank beneath a shower of poisoned arrows. Making these sorts of announcements was tantamount to making concessions to the Soviet Union without any hope that there would be reciprocal flexibility on Moscow's part. But doing nothing—as the Gaimusho liked to do—was also unproductive, for the Soviets had no incentive to give up the islands in this case, save for the uncertain promise of future economic benefits, which underpinned the logic of seikei fukabun. There had to be a solution somewhere to this impossible equation.

"An equation with many variables," Nakasone had called it. The key was to "find the values for all the unknown variables"—and this was something the Japanese Foreign Ministry was just not capable of. In fact, the best idea was to keep the diplomats out of this complicated mathematics. Everything had to be agreed upon in private, in back-channel talks. The Soviets would know exactly what they would get for the islands and when. Then, the package could be announced to the public, hopefully when Gorbachev came to Japan. Then what could the Japanese Foreign Ministry do about it? This was the idea, and Ozawa was the man to make it happen. Throughout 1990 and 1991 there was a flurry of back-channel negotiation, the unsaid purpose of which was to buy the islands for what at the time seemed like a sizable pile of cash.[3]

These negotiations came to nothing because some things just cannot be bought. Gorbachev had enough political acumen to understand that an underhanded deal could cost him his political future. Facing rising nationalist sentiment, skillfully manipulated by his archenemy Boris Yeltsin for his own political purposes, the last thing Gorbachev needed was to face accusations that he was selling Russia down the river. The force of public opinion that he had himself unleashed had come to haunt Gorbachev. The Soviet leader was being pulled away by a powerful historical current. There was little that Ozawa, or anyone else, could do about it.

MIXED SIGNALS

In January 1990 senior LDP leader Abe Shintaro visited Moscow in a bid to broker a breakthrough in Soviet-Japanese relations. The media speculated that it was a carefully planned maneuver to bolster Abe's political reputation ahead of a leadership contest with Prime Minister Kaifu Toshiki.[4]

Soviet foreign policy experts concluded that Abe was trying to "capture the initiative from the opposition in advancing a new foreign policy course."[5] In fact, Abe knew that he did not have much time left because of terminal cancer. The Moscow visit was his swan song, and perhaps he truly hoped that he would go down in history as a man who brokered a breakthrough in Soviet-Japanese relations.

For this reason, Abe tried to exclude the Gaimusho hardliners from his delegation, packing it instead with bureaucrats from MITI and the Ministry of Finance.[6] The Soviets knew perfectly well that Abe and the Foreign Ministry "have serious disagreements" and that the latter "is trying to make Abe put forward the 'territorial question' in the traditional manner." But that meant that Abe was more pliable than the diplomats, and maybe he could be brought onboard the Soviet vision for rapprochement with Japan, which was—according to the Soviet preparatory materials—to let the experts (historians, geographers, and lawyers) "clarify the truth for the politicians"—and before that happened, "not to become hostage to history and geography" and to "take the road of the widest constructive dialogue on other problems."[7]

In his meeting with Gorbachev on January 15 Abe was careful not to refer directly to the "northern territories," saying only that "difficult questions" would have to be "settled with wisdom."[8] Abe also made an eight-point proposal for improving relations, with emphasis on economic and technological cooperation and greater cultural exchange. He made no promise of money, and he could not have done so without causing an outrage. Gorbachev played along, reportedly saying that Japan had an "inherent right to claim the islands." These comments proved controversial in Japan, with many speculating that Gorbachev had "reversed" his position.[9] This was a deliberate effort to trick the Japanese into giving economic aid without giving away the islands—something he had no intention of actually doing. "They will have to be disappointed with [me]," Gorbachev told Chernyaev shortly after the meeting.[10]

Who could blame the Japanese for thinking that in the desperate economic situation, Gorbachev would return the "northern territories" if only Japan would bail him out with credits and aid? This was not some far-fetched proposition, considering that many voices—both Japanese and Soviet—were in fact calling for the resolution of the territorial problem. Not all were as ambitious as the chess champion Garry Kasparov, who, in an interview with *Playboy* during the fall of 1989, blurted out: "Why don't we sell the Kuril Islands to the Japanese? Frankly speaking, I'm not sure the islands belong to us, and the Japanese, who claim them, would give us billions and billions for them! That would keep us going for maybe five or ten years."[11] Nor was everyone as fanatical as the historian-turned-anti-Soviet parliamentarian Yurii Afanas'ev, who, on a visit to Japan in October 1989, openly called for return of the four islands to Japan to overcome the legacy of the bankrupted Yalta system.[12] More and more people took a middle ground, among others the dissident nuclear physicist Andrei Sakharov, who called for a compromise solution to the problem that same month.[13] These comments provoked nationalist backlash in the Soviet Union but on balance they seemed to suggest that the Soviet public opinion was beginning to shift toward the Japanese position.

These were encouraging times for the Japanese. The fall of the Berlin Wall carried unmistakable symbolism for Soviet-Japanese relations, while calls for the islands' return by prominent Soviet political figures—a far cry from the rebuttals and denials of the recent past—invited expectations of more Soviet concessions in the near future, if only enough politicians followed in Afanas'ev's and Sakharov's footsteps. In December 1989 Tokyo Broadcasting Systems (TBS) set its sights high by inviting Boris Yeltsin to visit Tokyo. "We would be very happy," wrote TBS official Ota Hiroshi, "if you spoke to us about this matter [the territorial dispute], because the Japanese people are deeply interested in this subject." Yeltsin was happy to oblige at the TBS's expense. Gorbachev, who had his chance to deny Yeltsin an exit permit to go to Japan, chose not to interfere.[14]

Yeltsin arrived in Japan on January 14, 1990, for a ten-day visit. On January 16 he made a statement at the National Press Club in Tokyo, outlining a five-stage solution to the territorial dispute. Unfortunately for his Japanese hosts, however, Yeltsin fell short of saying anything that approximated Afanas'ev's radical pronouncements. The first four stages (taking between fifteen and twenty years, in Yeltsin's estimates) would see Soviet recognition of the existence of the territorial problem, demilitarization of the four islands, their opening to Japanese investments, and the signing of the peace treaty. As for the fifth stage, Yeltsin said he preferred "not to dot all the i's," "because there will be a new generation instead of us, and in Japan too. The situation on the islands will change, there will be mutual understanding in Soviet-Japanese relations. Un-fixated people will come, and they will find some innovative final solution."[15] As for the shape that "final solution" might take, Yeltsin said it could be joint administration of the islands or even resumption of Japanese sovereignty. Japanese irritation with Yeltsin's multi-stage scheme registered in the remarks of Foreign Minister Nakayama Taro, who told Yeltsin that "Soviet leaders may consider various formulas for resolving the territorial issue but Japan wants all four islands, seized by the Soviets at the close of World War II, returned to Japan, en bloc."[16]

Yeltsin's acute political instincts clearly worked against any public commitment to return the islands, even though he was immensely impressed by the promise of Japanese economic aid in the event of the successful resolution of the territorial issue and tended toward this scenario in private conversations.[17] Yeltsin played his cards well, for he emerged from his visit to Japan as a statesman with a solution to the territorial dispute, upstaging Gorbachev, who had not offered any solution at all. Even Chernyaev remarked, in a grudging acknowledgment, that Yeltsin, for once, "has advanced a reasonable plan."[18] Prominent Japan specialist Konstantin Sarkisov, who at the time was coming to play an increasingly visible role in the internal Soviet debates on the territorial issue, pointedly wrote of Yeltsin's visit: "As a political actor, he was something of a gambler; when engaged in a game he didn't exactly know how to win, he would hope to get a lucky card. Actually he didn't want to lose any territory, and hoped to win the game without ceding any. His 'five-stage resolution' plan was an expression of that. All the controversial aspects of his statements and behavior can be explained by his lack of a clear vision on the matter."[19]

In the following months, Yeltsin's vision cleared up. He was quick to recognize the power of nationalist sentiment. On May 29, 1990, in a new departure for his struggle for leadership, Yeltsin was elected the head of the Russian Supreme Soviet. That summer, he traveled around Russia drumming up support among the local constituencies. In August 1990 he got as far as the Kuriles—it was the first time any Russian or Soviet leader set foot on these islands. While in Kunashir on August 22, Yeltsin told the local residents: "Since I came here, my views on the Kuriles have changed completely.... I had thought it would be a terrible place to visit, but this is a wonderful island which can be developed as a resort. We should not abandon this island. We should rather encourage more people to live here."[20] As he headed back to the airport, dense fog descended on Kunashir. The pilot refused to proceed. The air traffic controller refused to sanction the takeoff. "But the 'tsar' orders to fly. Everyone gets aboard in silence. There is milk outside. Cannot see the ground. We are taking off. God is protecting us.... Yeltsin suddenly says that we will not give the Kuriles to the Japanese."[21]

Yeltsin had seen the Kuriles. The "tsar" defined his position. This was especially important at a time of ambiguity in the ranks of the Soviet leadership. Gorbachev, no less than Yeltsin, was unprepared at that point to give up any territory. He even told a visiting Japanese parliamentarian, Sakurauchi Yoshio, on July 25 that there was no territorial dispute between the two countries, and was later heard "swearing": "if they only talk about the islands, he will not go to Japan at all."[22] But in the eyes of the nationalist pundits, Gorbachev's resolve to defend the islands against encroachment could not be taken for granted. To the contrary, suspicions mounted that an underhanded deal was in the making. Shevardnadze's trip to Japan in September 1990 (his third since 1986) did not allay these suspicions. There were worries in Sakhalin in particular about these visits, with their unclear hints and hidden agendas. This time Shevardnadze publically talked about taking "a larger view" on Soviet-Japanese relations, which, of course, could be interpreted in a variety of ways.[23]

On September 12, 1990, in a sign of local resentment at being bypassed in the big political game, the recently elected Sakhalin Regional Soviet of People's Deputies passed a resolution to "require" that their representative be included in any negotiations with Japan over the fate of the Southern Kuriles.[24] This resolution was a direct consequence of Shevardnadze's visit to Japan and the Deputies' suspicion that the Foreign Minister might give away the islands. The resolution was sent to Shevardnadze, but he just ignored it.[25] The same document was sent to Yeltsin. Sure enough, people in Yeltsin's team had a much better grasp of the tactical side of the game than did Shevardnadze in his high-handed oversight of Sakhalin's concerns. Russian Foreign Minister Andrei Kozyrev responded to the petition of the island legislature, promising to "necessarily consult" with Sakhalin deputies before talking with the Japanese about the territorial issue.[26] Henceforth, opponents of the islands' return could count on the sympathetic ear of Gorbachev's nemesis. In May 1990 Evgenii Primakov urged Gorbachev to challenge Yeltsin to a televised public debate in order to grill him with uncomfortable questions about the Kuriles: "Let him twist like a grass snake in a frying pan."[27] If the Soviet leader had followed that advice, he might well have emerged in the public eye as the protector of the motherland. But by the fall of 1990, that role was Yeltsin's, and it was Gorbachev who had to twist in the frying pan of Russian nationalism.

OZAWA SETS UP A BACK CHANNEL

During the second half of 1990, Gorbachev was preoccupied with efforts to resuscitate the collapsing national economy. In July he had agreed with Boris Yeltsin to join forces in tackling the economic problems. A joint team of experts was assembled at Sosinki, a government resort near Moscow, to prepare a program christened the "500 Days" plan. The team included the economist Stanislav Shatalin, Gorbachev's liberal Economic Adviser Nikolai Petrakov, and younger intellectuals, including Grigorii Yavlinskii. 500 Days offered to turn the Soviet Union into a capitalist country in exactly as many days through radical measures such as price liberalization and privatization. But as Shatalin and others labored away at 500 Days, the Soviet government, headed by Prime Minister Nikolai Ryzhkov, pieced together an altogether different program of much more conservative and long-term economic reforms. In September and October Gorbachev's initial support for 500 Days began to waver. On October 19 the Supreme Soviet passed a watered-down economic program—a major blow for the liberals in Gorbachev's team. Gorbachev increasingly turned against Shatalin and Petrakov, threatening to "kick them out." By November even Yakovlev and Primakov—long-time pillars of support for Gorbachev's reforms—began to feel that they were being neglected.[28]

The more dismal things looked on the inside, the more Gorbachev looked to the outside. Japan drew more and more of his attention, as he remained hopeful that Tokyo would relent and offer much-needed economic aid to the Soviet Union. Gorbachev rarely missed the opportunity to receive a Japanese delegation of any importance, even though he knew that the subject would inevitably turn to the "northern territories." His hope was to inspire the Japanese with his vision of a brave new world so that they could see the bigger picture and invest themselves (morally as well as financially) in that great enterprise of remaking the world order. Only the Buddhist philosopher Ikeda Daisaku (whom Gorbachev received in Moscow on July 27, 1990, in large part due to Vladislav Dunaev's efforts) bought into Gorbachev's enthusiasm.[29] "An interesting figure," noted Chernyaev. "Patted Gorbachev on his shoulder all the time and kept shouting something in Japanese—in admiration of a great man. Gorbachev was inspired by that. And he started philosophizing and 'went far' once again."[30] Unfortunately for Gorbachev, most of his other Japanese interlocutors were less inclined to buy into this sort of rhetoric.

"Each side understands what the other wants," Ozawa told Shevardnadze on September 5, 1990.[31] The LDP kingmaker had been thinking of ways to extract the promise of islands from Gorbachev. The best strategy seemed to be in reaching a secret understanding so that Gorbachev would know exactly what he would get for giving the islands away. This was not something that could be done through the foreign ministry. There had to be a back channel to the Kremlin. In the summer through early fall of 1990, such a back channel was established.

The key players on the Soviet side were Arkadii Volskii, the self-appointed spokesman for the emerging Soviet businesses, who, as the President of the Soviet Union of Science and Industry, was well familiar with Japan's economic prowess; the Central Committee Secretary in charge of relations with Japan, Gennadii Yanaev; and Vasilii Saplin, a Japan expert at the

International Department of the Central Committee.[32] As Saplin recalled in retrospect, "This was the very pinnacle of the Japanese bubble, and it seemed that their abilities were inexhaustible. And we needed credits. The country was falling apart. We could not feed the people. The situation was extremely critical."[33]

Players on the Japanese side included LDP dietmen Yamaguchi Toshio and Kumagai Hiroshi, as well as Sugimori Koji, the General Secretary of the Japanese Association for Cultural Ties with Foreign Countries, and Aso Shigeki, a political commentator for the newspaper *Mainichi*. This diverse cohort of operators shared common political ties with Ozawa. They had a stake in his political rise, and worked hard to advertise him. As Saplin put it, "people in his circle were saying: here is the great Ozawa, the future prime minister. Especially Yamaguchi bustled about. The short guy. He was later jailed for embezzlement. It was he who was a crucial figure in the organization of this channel."[34]

This Yamaguchi was a political wheeler-dealer like no other. He was well known in Moscow from his earlier visits (in the mid-1980s), when he privately (and, as it turned out, misleadingly) urged the Soviets to simply admit the existence of the territorial problem, because this would "seriously advance" Soviet-Japanese relations even if the Soviet Union then refused to do anything about solving this problem.[35] He had previously told the Soviets that he did not think that the territorial problem should be at the forefront and that relations should be improved and expanded across the board, which would in turn facilitate the solution of all unsolved problems, including the territorial problem. But, Yamaguchi thought, "one cannot openly take such a position in the current situation in Japan, because this would mean placing oneself under fire of criticism from those who oppose developing relations with the USSR."[36] This was why he had been looking for a secret channel to the Soviet leadership.

How, exactly, the channel came into existence is unclear. Yamaguchi was in Moscow in September 1990, when some of the early discussions may have taken place. He was a member of a parliamentary delegation, whose visit to the USSR received extensive media coverage. But we have no evidence of Yamaguchi's involvement other than Saplin's recollections. By contrast, Kumagai and Sugimori left a paper trail. In July 1990 they arrived in Moscow, "unofficially" to probe the ground for the establishment of a back channel.

The two had had a very difficult time, especially Kumagai, who ran into a six-month delay in having his paperwork processed at the Soviet Embassy in Tokyo. "Surprising behavior" was what Kumagai had to say about that, given that he expected to have a conversation that could potentially land billions of dollars in the Soviet coffers. His and Sugimori's luck was no better in Moscow, when they did come. The highest-placed official to have received them was Karen Brutents. "Mr. Brutents," fumed Kumagai shortly afterwards, "conducted conversations as if [I am] a director of some Foreign Ministry department, but [I am] a big figure within the LDP. I have not yet changed my views but ..." [three dots in the original].[37]

The purpose of the visit was to clarify how much aid the Soviets wanted and then to set up a back channel bypassing bureaucracies on both sides. Kumagai explained this to Anatolii Milyukov, the head of the department for social and economic development in the Presidential Administration. "The USSR must create a channel as quickly as possible and conduct secret and sincere negotiations in parallel with the official [negotiations].... We are prepared to provide aid in solving any problems." Kumagai did not hide who "we" were. The key players were Ozawa and Kanemaru, he told Milyukov—"[they] will decide." Sugimori added: "In Japan, one must first and foremost have in mind Ozawa. No decisions are possible without him."[38]

Milyukov was quite modest in his assessment of what sort of aid the Soviets would need. "You have to understand that our people cannot beg," he said. The economic situation was difficult enough, but there was going to be an improvement "in the nearest future." For now, he said, the Soviet Union needed between five and five and a half billion dollars "like air." Of this, between two and three billion could come from Japan. Kumagai and Sugimori named figures of Japanese aid to China and to South Korea that were much higher than what Milyukov had requested, and made it clear that such an amount was nothing for Ozawa if only "a political decision" were made. Milyukov's notes of this conversation do not show whether he and the Japanese discussed the possible outlines of this "political decision." Kumagai and Sugimori used very oblique language and did not directly refer to the territorial problem. Milyukov wrote up a memorandum for the Presidential Council after his conversation with Ozawa's messengers.[39]

The trace of the back channel does not again pick up until October, when Vol'skii, Yanaev, and Saplin visited Japan and met with Prime Minister Kaifu and Ozawa himself.[40] Then, in November 1990, Ozawa dispatched Sugimori and Aso to Moscow to continue negotiations. Sugimori, who by now claimed that Ozawa had appointed him a special "coordinator" of Soviet policy, was a curious choice for so sensitive a mission.[41] He was not a member of the LDP, but rather a politician of the rival Socialist Party. Moreover, in the early 1980s, Soviet KGB defector Stanislav Levchenko had identified Sugimori as one of his "agents" in Japan (code name: Sandomir), although these allegations were later refuted by Japanese investigators.[42]

On the other hand, it was well known that Sugimori had "connections in the Kremlin" and his role in arranging for Ozawa's later visit to Moscow was reported in the Japanese press in April 1991.[43] As for Aso Shigeki, he simply introduced himself to the Soviets as Ozawa's "intimate friend."[44]

On November 22, Sugimori and Aso met with Yakovlev. Gorbachev's key liberal ally (known to have sympathies toward Japan's territorial claims) was then a member of the recently created Presidential Council. The idea behind this council was to centralize policy making after Gorbachev's election to the Presidency of the Soviet Union. Unfortunately for the liberals, the Presidential Council was already in decline by late 1990 and was officially disbanded that December. Among the winners were Yanaev, who was promoted to Vice President by the People's Congress of Deputies (only after Gorbachev's desperate plea). Yanaev's meteoric ascent was a huge surprise for Gorbachev's liberal allies, as was the rise of Aleksandr Bessmertnykh, who was picked to replace Eduard Shevardnadze as the new Foreign Minister at a time when Yakovlev was widely expected to take up that role. In August 1991 Bessmertnykh would back the coup against Gorbachev, while Yanaev would emerge as one of its leaders. For now, the result of the palace maneuvers was that Gorbachev moved away from the team of reformers. Those who might have made a difference with regard to Japan (including Yakovlev) found themselves on the sidelines, as their voices were ignored by the increasingly weak and disoriented Gorbachev.

Little of that was known to Sugimori and Aso, who proposed to "establish a direct confidential link between the Presidential Council and the General Secretary of the LDP," where in their belated view "the real political power is being concentrated."[45] Sugimori said that while there were many channels through which the two sides could exchange their opinions, "political decisions must be discussed and prepared between the LDP (Ozawa) and the Presidential Council (Yakovlev)." He went on to outline Ozawa's island-for-cash deal. The plan was to lay the groundwork for Gorbachev's visit by agreeing ahead of time on what the Soviets would get from Japan (in economic terms) for returning the islands. Then, at the time of the visit, the peace treaty would be signed, alongside agreements on long-term economic cooperation. In the meantime, Sugimori explained, "the Japanese side, without waiting for the peace treaty, is ready to take urgent measures for economic and financial cooperation on the same conditions as Germany."[46]

Sugimori's mention of Germany is noteworthy. It served as a model for what Ozawa hoped to achieve. Indeed, from 1989 until 1993, the Soviet Union (and later, Russia) received direct and indirect assistance from the Federal Republic of Germany amounting to perhaps eighty-five billion

Deutschmarks (more than fifty billion US dollars). In 1990, when the Soviet Union had effectively lost any ability to borrow money on the international credit market, German Chancellor Helmut Kohl arranged an aid package for Gorbachev that included provision of food, as well as bank credits and payments for the withdrawal of Soviet troops from East Germany. In addition, the West German government assumed the burden of Moscow's economic obligations toward East Germany. All of this constituted an implicit payment for Gorbachev's decision to accept German reunification and united Germany's membership in NATO.[47] Kohl naturally recognized the trade-off and played his cards well, for the terms of this "payment" were never explicit, which allowed Gorbachev to save face and pretend that his loss of Germany was just an outcome of new thinking and a by-product of the new world he had set out to create.[48]

Kohl believed that the Japanese could be even more helpful if only Gorbachev could be brought around to discuss their territorial issues—he suggested as much to the Soviet leader during their meeting on November 9, 1990: "if there was a basis for a conversation with the Japanese, things would take a different course. Of course, you know what I mean." Gorbachev's immediate response—"Of course!"—spoke to his awareness of the dangers latent in a cash-for-land deal. He went on to tell Kohl that "this is a sharp and sensitive question for us. The moment Yeltsin raised this question, the people began asking directly: Is it true that he [Gorbachev] wants to give away our land?"[49]

Kohl recalled the process of German reunification, saying: "At one time, we put the German question, the problem of unification, to the side, and concentrated all our attention on economic cooperation." Perhaps the Japanese could be asked to do the same—direct all their efforts toward economic aid in order to build up a reserve of trust, and then see what happens. "Historical processes," Kohl added, "have taken their course, sometimes unexpectedly for us."[50] Kohl claimed in retrospect that he made the quid pro quo fairly transparent for Gorbachev as early as their June 1989 meeting in Bonn. In fact, available German and Russian records of Gorbachev's conversations with Kohl suggest that the quid pro quo was quite a bit less than what Kohl later made it out to be; Gorbachev must have even missed the message altogether, even if one was intended.[51] In any case, what Ozawa had in mind was very different from the German model. The trade-off was explicit from the very beginning. Economic aid would only be granted if the Soviets agreed to give up the islands—all four.

The idea behind the establishment of the back channel was precisely to work out all the details of the economic package in order for Gorbachev to have a clear sense of what he would qualify for should he opt to return the islands. Sugimori promised Yakovlev that a business delegation would come to the USSR in early December that would include key players from the most prominent Japanese companies, such as Mitsubishi, Mitsui, Japan Railways, NTT, and Fujitsu. The business heavyweights would come to hear if the Soviets had any "concrete proposals" for cooperation. Aso explained: "It will not be a protocol visit. The leaders of the business world want to have a concrete conversation and hear answers from the Soviet side." Sugimori added that the trip would be sponsored by *Mainichi* (the newspaper) rather than the Foreign Ministry, which "was not inclined to approve this idea." But the economic ministries and the LDP were allegedly in full agreement with these plans.[52]

Yakovlev was clearly interested in these proposals. The record of this meeting suggest that he was personally in favor of reaching an agreement with Japan, although Yakovlev could hardly say so openly. Instead, he offered not-so-subtle hints: "I think urgent aid measures would be duly appreciated." Asked to elaborate, Yakovlev raised the issue of humanitarian aid (including food, medicine, and basic consumer goods) and a loan of "3–4–5 billion dollars." For comparative perspective, Gorbachev had earlier appealed to US Secretary of State James Baker to provide "1–1.5 billion dollars," but Baker demurred. Getting Congress to approve this sort of aid, Baker explained, would require two perestroikas.[53] At a time when a loan of just one billion from the United States was beyond reach, Yakovlev's request for "3–4–5 billion dollars" as a stop-gap measure was a fair indication of the sort of expectations the Soviet leadership had from Japan. Yakovlev explained that it was in Tokyo's interest to come up with the money in order to create what he called "a 'soft pillow' for Soviet public opinion."[54] Sugimori knew what Yakovlev was talking about. "We are prepared, from the position of political significance, to discuss your proposals seriously," he said, even in the face of the Gaimusho's probable wrath. He promised that he would send his (in other words, Ozawa's) answer through another envoy, and Yakovlev suggested that he contact Saplin or Petrakov.

Interestingly, at a time when Ozawa sent messengers to Moscow to probe the possibility of an underhanded deal, former Prime Minister Nakasone was doing something very similar, only through different channels. In November 1990, Vadim Medvedev, a member of Gorbachev's Presidential Council, visited in Seoul in a bid to attract South Korean funding for the resolution of "acute credit and currency problems."[55] While there, he met with the South Korean/Japanese tycoon Shin Kyuk-ho, who conveyed a proposal from Nakasone and another former Prime Minister, Takeshita Noboru, to "arrange" between twenty and thirty billion dollars for the USSR in lieu of payment for the return of the "northern territories."[56] This proposal was also tied to the idea of the Soviet Union sending troops to the Middle East to restrain Saddam Hussein, another "variable" in Nakasone's equation. Medvedev rebuffed linkage of Japanese aid with territorial concessions or with the Middle East, but he did invite Nakasone and Takeshita to visit Moscow. However, this unusual back channel was soon abandoned: the Soviets clearly preferred Ozawa the Destroyer to two retired Prime Ministers.

On the day when Medvedev reported to Gorbachev about his discussions with Shin Kyuk-ho, Yakovlev met with Edamura Sumio, the Japanese Ambassador. Chernyaev had indicated to Edamura that, in his personal opinion, Gorbachev was not ruling out in his mind the prospect of returning the islands to Japan.[57] But the Ambassador was losing patience. "The idea of the Soviet side...comes down to delaying the decision...to delay this question for ten years and to begin economic cooperation in the meantime." Although the decision may be "torturous and difficult" for the Soviet Union, the step had to be made. Simply delaying the question for ten or twenty years was "uncomfortable for the Japanese people.... And one needs a show of political will, which would be stronger than diplomatic procedures and the prerogatives of the Ministry of Foreign Affairs." Yakovlev's notes of his meeting with Edamura merely indicate that he explained "the position of the Soviet side" on the territorial question; yet these notes read like a direct appeal to Gorbachev, laden as they are with Gorbachev's terminology: "political will," "deep steps," and so on. Yakovlev added a cover sheet to the conversation and forwarded it to Gorbachev in an indication of the importance he attached to this meeting with Edamura.[58]

PREPARING FOR THE SUMMIT

In the meantime, Anatolii Chernyaev, charged with making preparations for Gorbachev's trip to Japan, polled the opinions of all the relevant policy constituencies. By December, he received his first feedback. On December 13, a "situational analysis" was held at the Institute of Oriental Studies; the findings were then passed to the Kremlin by Konstantin Sarkisov, who headed the Japan sector at the Institute. The experts recommended recognizing the 1956 Declaration—that is, to return two islands to Japan. As to the question of the other two islands, the Institute proposed to claim that they belonged to the Soviet Union on the basis of the Yalta agreements and the San Francisco Peace Treaty. If, however, the Japanese insisted on having all four islands (as they surely would), the Institute proposed to "form a special mechanism to discuss the question" with Tokyo. This was another way of saying that it was permissible to give up all four islands, if this proved necessary for the conclusion of a peace treaty with Japan.[59] Similar ideas were stated even more explicitly in a report submitted by IMEMO, which, under Vladlen Martynov as its director, took particular interest in developing a dialogue with Japan. IMEMO also proposed to recognize the 1956 Declaration without further delay and did not rule out the transfer of all four islands to the Japanese, "but with a necessary time interval after the transfer of the first [two] and, of course, material compensation."[60]

Gorbachev's economic adviser, Nikolai Petrakov, submitted even more ambitious recommendations, calling for the return of the four islands "unconditionally and immediately," as they were Japanese by the Russo-Japanese treaties of 1855 and 1875 and had unjustly been annexed by Stalin. Once the Soviet Union addressed this terrible historical wrong, "Japan, with its grateful, emotional people will turn its face to us." By this Petrakov meant that Japan would provide "40–70–120 billion" dollars in "real money," which was not procurable from any other source. The islands did not have to be transferred immediately; 2000 was suggested as the target date. For now, Petrakov proposed simply to recognize Japan's sovereignty, leaving the details for later.[61]

One would expect this kind of recommendation from Petrakov. As Gorbachev's Economic Adviser, by late 1990 he understood better than most that the Soviet Union was tottering on the brink of economic collapse. Earlier in October, Petrakov called for a credit of between twelve and sixteen billion US dollars "to finance the import of consumer goods and agricultural products." In November he was reported as saying: "The country does not just need food aid. . . . It needs any sort of assistance, and the sooner the better. Basic consumer goods are also needed. . . . These would help fill the shelves and provide Soviet workers with the incentive to keep on working while the country embarked on its transition to a market economy."[62] Yet the same Petrakov was well aware of the Ozawa back channel and the prospect of obtaining credits from the Japanese. It was only logical from his perspective that the islands should be returned if this is what it took to get the economic aid.

However, Petrakov was no longer in Gorbachev's good graces. Ever since November, when he and Shatalin criticized Gorbachev implicitly for yielding to the conservative pressure, Petrakov had been losing his ground with the President, to the point where he felt the need to submit letters of resignation, just before and shortly after the New Year. These were turned down. Gorbachev raised the matter with Chernyaev on January 2, "swearing." Chernyaev said: "Petrakov is offended, and justly." "Why is that?" "In the days [after December 15] you have not even remembered him once,"

Chernyaev explained, "although Presidential decrees were being issued one after another [in his very sphere]—economic questions.... Why do you have an economic adviser if when these documents were prepared you did not remember him?" "And when did I have the time?" Gorbachev returned.[63] Petrakov had had enough and finally quit on January 17, after he signed his name to a letter that condemned Gorbachev for bowing to the conservatives and instigating a bloody suppression of the Lithuanian protests four days earlier.[64] Gorbachev was duly outraged.[65] Never did Petrakov's advice count for less.

The Foreign Ministry and the International Department of the Central Committee did not go out on a limb like that. The former offered two options: recognize the validity of the 1956 Declaration, or—even less promising for the Japanese—recognize that the territorial problem existed but that it could only be solved in a "new atmosphere of mutual understanding and trust." It is not that the Foreign Ministry was a conservative bastion; simply, it was a vast bureaucracy with logic of its own, and this logic mitigated against any sharp policy changes. The same could be said of the International Department, which submitted a set of even more conservative recommendations, summarized thus: "[T]o take a position, which would not appear frozen and would not close the way to future movement. To declare readiness to discuss the territorial question but to try to limit its place in the course of development of relations."[66] This was an oblique, completely meaningless formulation. It only makes sense in light of Saplin's later explanation: "The whole idea was to pull the wool over the Japanese eyes. We are, allegedly, prepared to discuss the question seriously. Just give us the credits."[67]

CONCRETE PROPOSALS

In the meantime, Ozawa pressed ahead with his effort to reach an under-the-counter deal with Gorbachev. Vol'skii and Saplin went to Japan in December 1990 for further discussions with the kingmaker.[68] Several weeks later, Ozawa once again dispatched Kumagai Hiroshi to Moscow with a specific offer. The terms were as follows: the Soviet Union would first recognize the 1956 Declaration (i.e., Japan's sovereignty over Shikotan and Habomai). These islands would have to be handed over within a few months or, at most, a year from the date of the public announcement. As for the other two islands, Kumagai floated the concept of "potential Japanese sovereignty," which meant that while the Soviet Union would agree that the islands were Japanese, it could take up to ten years before the territories were vacated and returned to Japan. However, the Soviets would have to promise to return the islands when the peace treaty was signed.[69]

In return for the islands, Kumagai offered economic aid, in two stages. The first stage was emergency aid, amounting to between three and four billion dollars of untied credits, which could be used for the purchase of food or consumer goods, "or for other aims and measures, which would lead to the stabilization of the financial and economic situation in the USSR." This stage could begin before the peace treaty was signed, but only "with clear expectation" that it would be signed when Gorbachev came to Japan. The second stage would see Japan provide aid of two kinds. First, private Japanese companies would invest up to eight billion dollars in the Soviet economy in the first five years, of which one billion would come "practically immediately." "Relevant firms," Kumagai explained, "are prepared to begin work immediately after receiving a 'signal' from the Japanese government."

Second, the government would step in with massive thirty-year loans at a 2 to 3 percent interest rate, tantamount, in Kumagai's view, to gratis aid. These loans could come up to about ten billion dollars. In addition, the Japanese would cover Soviet expenses of vacating the islands, which would cost up to four billion dollars. The entire package would amount to twenty-six billion dollars, and that, in Kumagai's estimates, was more than what Helmut Kohl had been able to offer. "Tokyo has carried out fundamental experts' analysis: of all countries, Japan is the only one that can provide the USSR with economic aid. We have enough strength for that: Japan is now financing 50% of the US budget deficit."[70] At a time when the Soviet economy was going under, Ozawa's offer was a real windfall for the Soviets and a serious burden for the Japanese, especially at a time when the Americans were demanding Japanese billions for the Gulf War effort. Even so, it was worth it, if it could advance Ozawa's career. However, secrecy was of topmost importance. "If what I said today were revealed in Japan, there would be a forceful wave of angry denunciation.... But Ozawa I[chiro] is prepared to act.... he has taken everything into account and is confident that he can suppress any resistance." The Soviets would have to give up the islands, however. "Without moving forward on the territorial question, neither Ozawa...nor any other politician can do anything. And if they tried to do something, they would be condemned to political death."[71]

Yakovlev, who received Kumagai, did not record his response to the offer. Yet there was certainly a response. Shortly before Kumagai's arrival, Chernyaev forwarded talking points to Gorbachev with a cover page that read: "We have to tell him [Kumagai] what we are counting on, if Ozawa can really influence the situation."[72] Unfortunately, what *we* counted on was omitted from the copy of a document made available to this author.

It cannot be ruled out that Kumagai received an unclear promise of some territorial transfer, perhaps a promise of Soviet adherence to the 1956 Declaration. It could not have been much more than that, for Gorbachev was in no position politically to agree to the kind of ambitious conditions Ozawa attached to the aid package. In the meantime, Chernyaev proposed to "continue this work" with Ozawa by sending an envoy to Japan in late January or early February, so as to "make the Japanese side understand the extent of our flexibility on the territorial problem and find out the concrete position of the Japanese, especially in the economic sphere."[73]

In January 1991 Gorbachev asked Yanaev to head a special commission in order to prepare his visit to Japan.[74] In fact, it was mainly Chernyaev who did all the work. By mid-January, having received feedback from all the interested institutions, he put together a set of policy recommendations. Chernyaev himself supported the idea of recognizing Japanese sovereignty over the four islands but doing so on the conditions that it would not mean a revision of the results of the Second World War and that the actual reversion of islands to Japanese control would take many years (until 2000). Japan would have to offer a "large material compensation" and, crucially, the Russian Federation would have to agree to the transfer. The last condition was, of course, a loophole. It could not be applied to Shikotan and Habomai, as these fell under the 1956 Declaration and would have to be returned anyway, but with regard to Kunashir and Iturup, "the necessity of a Russian referendum . . . gives the Soviet government an important tactical argument in future negotiations."[75]

In the meantime, Yanaev called a meeting of the commission. This meeting brought together advocates of the positions outlined above. Although Petrakov was absent (he had already resigned), Vol'skii argued vocally in defense of a deal with the Japanese. Sergei Grigor'ev, the Secretary of this commission, later shared his recollections of Vol'skii's arguments:

> This is our last chance. Just think about the food and all sorts of other aid. This is all bad. You are all politicians here. And to hell with all of you. . . . You understand nothing. Economics is more important. That's the only place where they will give us money. . . . I spoke to Ozawa, I am in touch with him. Ozawa said: "You really mean that you don't need this money?!" . . . If we do not need it, well then just give me a hint, and I will stop it. But what shall we do without the money?[76]

Vol'skii's views had little support among those present, with the exception of Konstantin Sarkisov, who spoke of a "2 + 2" solution, meaning: give up two islands now and two later. The head of the International Department, Valentin Falin, wanted to link the question of the islands with the US withdrawal from Japan, which was clearly unrealistic. Vladislav Mal'kevich speculated that "we will achieve nothing and we will only make Gorbachev look bad." Yanaev himself clearly was unwilling to take a position. "The president should be our conductor and conduct the choir. The important thing, and it's the answer that we can get only from him, [is] how far we can go, and what we cannot go for."[77] Predictably, nothing was decided at the meeting, and on January 23 Chernyaev sent Gorbachev a summary of the recommendations and his own thoughts on the subject.

The turbulent times had taken the wind out of Gorbachev's sails. He was sending conflicting signals. For example, in a meeting with the Japanese parliamentarian Tsuchiya Yoshihiko on January 9, Gorbachev spoke in unclear terms about "new era as a result of his Japan visit" and "substantial reforms . . . in bilateral ties in the near future." He also proclaimed his "readiness to discuss with Japanese leaders the conclusion of a peace treaty, involving the territorial dispute," which made it look as though he was leaning toward concessions.[78] But in a meeting with Japanese Foreign Minister Nakayama Taro on January 21, Gorbachev's message was rather less inclined toward compromise. He may have been put off by a letter from Prime Minister Kaifu Toshiki (which Nakayama carried), in which Kaifu emphasized that the territorial problem would have to be at the center of discussions during Gorbachev's upcoming visit. "Let's not hammer nails all the way in, especially nails without heads," Gorbachev said with a whiff of irritation. "Instead, nails should be pulled out."[79]

Gorbachev told Nakayama that he was rather more inclined to leave the territorial question to future generations, "to conserve the question, until it becomes ripe."[80] This characteristic indecisiveness was to mark Gorbachev's preparations for the visit, and if anything, it confused the Japanese, who were looking for a breakthrough just around the corner. Chernyaev remarked on Gorbachev's mood in his diary: "M.S. [Gorbachev] no longer thinks deeply about foreign policy. He is busy with 'structures' and 'little deals,' talks with one or another, whoever is imposed on him. Here he receives [Edgar] Bronfman, there—Japanese parliamentarians, or someone else. He does not prepare for anything, repeats the same thing for the tenth time over."[81] It is easy to see why the Japanese were having such a hard time making out Gorbachev's actual position. Even the President himself had no idea what exactly he would take with him to Tokyo that spring.

Ultimately, a strange coincidence of circumstances forced Gorbachev's hand. On January 26 he approved a decree that gave special power to the KGB to enter the premises of businesses and audit their accounts and cash.[82] The decree targeted shady business ventures and scam artists—that is to say, early Russian entrepreneurs—who, needless to say, denounced these measures as "strangling free-market efforts." Artem Tarasov, a prominent businessman and a self-proclaimed first Soviet millionaire, declared, with characteristic hyperbole, that Gorbachev's decree "virtually liquidated the free market in the Soviet Union."[83] A Russian parliamentarian with relatively close ties to Yeltsin, Tarasov himself became the target of the OMON, the special police, whose squad stormed the office of his company Istok on January 27 and took all the documents.[84] Tarasov struck back in a most unusual fashion. On January 28, during a press conference, he announced that the Soviet Union had agreed to hand over the Kuriles to Japan in return for economic aid.

Tarasov followed up his allegations with more interviews, developing his conception of a major cover-up. Gorbachev, he claimed, was turning away from the West toward the East. Here, the Japanese, hostile to democracy and market (in Tarasov's hare brained interpretation), were much in line with Gorbachev's own authoritarian inclinations. Therefore, as part of a broader policy orientation, Gorbachev had agreed to sell the islands to Japan for two hundred billion dollars. The money would be used to "[roll] back democratic transformations in the USSR, including a ban on emerging private entrepreneurship." This emergent Soviet-Japanese alliance, Tarasov ridiculously predicted, "may result in tragic consequences not only for the democratic movement of Russia, but for the whole world."[85] Tarasov later admitted in his memoirs that he had fabricated these allegations. However, he caused an uproar at the time. "A huge scandal broke out. Gorbachev was beside himself [with] rage. Either I really guessed his secret plans, or this [affair] simply exhausted his patience."[86] There is, of course, the possibility that Tarasov's claims were part of a deliberate plan to weaken Gorbachev, hatched in the camp of his political opponents, on the left or on the right.

Gorbachev refuted the claims and threatened to sue Tarasov for libel. The fallout was significant. Gorbachev even had to respond to queries from concerned party delegates at a Central Committee Plenum.[87] Predictably, Yeltsin seized the opportunity to criticize Gorbachev for lack of patriotism and to defend his own credentials: "We will not make any deals with anybody. We shall not give away the Kurile islands."[88] Voices of outrage were heard from Sakhalin: "Our country is now in a difficult position. But this does not mean anything historically. The current transitional situation does not give us any grounds to relinquish part of our national territory."[89] Public opinion polls were held and their results were widely advertised, all showing, naturally, that the Russians were fiercely opposed to the handover of the Southern Kuriles.[90] This uproar tied Gorbachev's hands in the secret negotiations with Ozawa. Gorbachev's aide Georgii Shakhnazarov said in retrospect that Tarasov's claim "ruined any possibility of maneuver. It caused a real turmoil.... Since it was very fashionable then to criticize our president with and without cause, they did their best."[91]

Gorbachev was under pressure from all sides. He certainly could not give away the Kuriles once the results of a national referendum on the preservation of the USSR (with the large majority voting yes) briefly infused him with optimism that all would be well. Handing over any territory to the Japanese (even two, not to mention four, islands) was a political impossibility for the Soviet leader, for he would become an easy target for Yeltsin and a sitting duck for virulent Russian nationalists. On the other hand, not giving the islands away meant that the visit to Japan was not likely to leave Gorbachev with much more than a memory of wasted opportunities. For this reason, perhaps, Gorbachev stalled and evaded key decisions. Chernyaev registered exasperation in his diary: "[Gorbachev] is constantly changing the [delegation] list, throwing out those who anytime, anywhere, had said even a word against M.S. But the most 'interesting' thing is that we still do not have the 'concept' of the visit: to return the islands or not? And without a 'concept,' one should not even travel in that direction."[92]

OZAWA COMES TO MOSCOW

On March 23, one day before Ozawa was expected in Moscow in a desperate dash to wrestle concessions from the Soviets, Gorbachev made up his mind to deal with the basic issue. He called Yanaev, Yakovlev, Bessmertnykh, Valerii Boldin (his recently appointed Chief of Staff), Falin, Rogachev, Primakov, and Chernyaev, and, in their presence, once again pondered various possibilities. Bessmertnykh and Rogachev urged him to return to the 1956 Declaration. Chernyaev peddled the prospect of a comprehensive settlement. As he described the meeting in his diary on the following day:

> Having studied a pile of analyses and brainstorms, conducted in the institutes, I came to the conclusion that one has to return the islands anyway. The only question is when and how. If you [Gorbachev] don't do it, Yeltsin will. He will become the President of Russia and will hand them over—to the applause of the

Russian people. I recall you used to be afraid that the Russian people will not forgive you even your smallest step, which could be interpreted as destruction of the empire, as they will not forgive this of any other politician. But Yeltsin is insolently and openly dissecting the Empire-Union. And, by the way, he is doing so to the applause of precisely the Russians. M.S. replied: "I would be very glad to give this mission to Yeltsin." He spoke for a long time, tried to persuade, but decided not to give back the islands. He is inclined to obscure the problem in beautiful words and to promise a "process"—his favorite word from his "theory of compromises," which has already led us to ... [three dots in the original] So boring![93]

This was the decision, then. The Japanese would not get the islands. They would instead get a "process." Chernyaev's advice fell on deaf ears and even the moderate recommendations of the Foreign Ministry were brushed aside. Instead, Gorbachev heeded the words of KGB Chairman Vladimir Kryuchkov and Defense Minister Dmitrii Yazov, who warned him not to give in to Japanese demands.[94] This was the end of the Ozawa back channel, although the hapless kingmaker still did not know that. Full of hope, Ozawa arrived in Moscow on March 24.

During their meeting on March 25, Ozawa asked Gorbachev what gifts he would bring to Tokyo. Gorbachev did not answer directly. He talked instead about "cross-fertilization" of "processes" of the growing Soviet-Japanese economic cooperation and negotiations over the peace treaty. "Here history must take care of itself. Perhaps it is very close, and perhaps far away. Look at how rapidly everything happened in Germany." "Well," Ozawa said—"are we to wait 50 to 100 years?" "I think that life will make that clear," Gorbachev answered. "I am proposing what will help to resolve all the issues. And life changes the times. If we want to ennoble our relations in the future, to deepen trust, then this is just what is needed. I am convinced that this is a realistic prospect." Ozawa registered his bewilderment at this exposition: "I do not fully understand what you just said. What concretely stands behind that?" Gorbachev rephrased his ideas in opaque terms, leaving Ozawa "both inspired and puzzled."[95] In a press conference later that day, Ozawa said that Gorbachev made "a statement that goes a step further than what I had heard from him previously."[96]

In light of new evidence, what Gorbachev had in mind is relatively certain. He was probably not against the idea of returning the islands, in principle. Gorbachev obliquely hinted that it could be done in the future, once the Soviet Union and Japan had improved their relations and built up a reserve of trust. In fact, this could only be done in the future because Gorbachev was in no position politically to make such a decisive step at a time when he was under attack from the left and from the right at home. Returning the islands was tantamount to political suicide for Gorbachev. Of course, he suspected that his time was almost up (he even said so to Ozawa), but Gorbachev was unwilling to hand his head on a silver plate to Yeltsin and the Russian nationalists. It did not help Ozawa's cause that shortly before he arrived in Moscow, the outline of his financial package was leaked to major Japanese newspapers. On March 24 the *Yomiuri Shimbun* actually named the exact price of the deal: twenty-six billion dollars, including four billion in emergency aid.[97] These reports were picked up in the Soviet media: "Tarasov, it seems, turned out to be partially correct," wrote *Kommersant* on March 25—"in part" because he wildly overpriced the islands.[98]

Puzzled by Gorbachev's "process," Ozawa asked for a second meeting. "Some kind of bustle began," recalled Chernyaev. "Calls were coming in from [Ozawa] himself, and from his circle, with the request to continue the conversation with Gorbachev."[99] "This surprised me," Gorbachev later wrote, "and I did not like this—it went against all rules. However, I decided 'not to offend' this politician in order to rule out misunderstandings in the process of what seemed to me like the beginning of improvement in Soviet-Japanese relations."[100] Ozawa met with Gorbachev again on March 26, and, after prolonged apologies, set out his proposals. The Soviet Union would recognize the 1956 Declaration, confirm that the territorial problem henceforth would refer to the islands of Kunashir and Iturup, and pledge to complete negotiations about the future of these islands by the fall of 1991.

Ozawa's proposals thus evidenced a number of concessions to the Soviet Union in comparison with Kumagai's package. Still, the essence of the deal remained unchanged. The promise of financial compensation remained, and Ozawa wasted no time restating the benefits of reaching an agreement. "Under the condition that the two sides confirm their agreement in principle to these three points, we intended to begin the implementation of economic aid, starting with the provision of credits so that the Soviet side pays back about 450 million dollars that it owes to Japanese companies."[101] Gorbachev did not like the overt linkage of territorial concessions with economic aid. He said that "he was not inclined to and could not conduct a discussion according to such a plan: you give us something and in turn we will give you what you want. That is not a conversation which we can have with you. You are a politician. You are an energetic person and I understand that you want a concrete result. But the approach: 'you give—I give' is entirely unacceptable not only between Japan and the Soviet Union, but in general terms as well."[102]

Ozawa made the final push, urging Gorbachev to tell him privately what he would bring to Tokyo: "That will remain between us." But Gorbachev refused to budge. On parting, the kingmaker said: "I would like to believe that the Japanese will encounter some hopeful statements during the meetings in Tokyo." "No," Gorbachev responded. "There will be no surprises.... I assure you we have conducted a very responsible and serious analysis."[103] According to Saplin, who interpreted at these meetings, Ozawa left "enraged." For a long time afterwards, so the rumor went, he did not want to hear a word about the Soviet Union or Russia. Saplin thought that the failure of Ozawa's plans to buy the islands played an important role in his subsequent political misfortunes (he resigned as LDP General Secretary shortly after his return from Moscow).[104] Chernyaev, for his part, thought that Ozawa's bulldozer tactics "spoiled Gorbachev's mood" ahead of his visit to Tokyo. "M.S. had been put on his guard. If his other official partners during the visit to Japan were also going to act in this way, he would end up in a very awkward position."[105] For once, Chernyaev misremembered. Whatever Ozawa did in Moscow, Gorbachev had already made up his mind not to return the islands.

GORBACHEV COMES TO JAPAN

The remaining few weeks before Gorbachev's visit to Japan were filled with haggling over the composition of the Soviet delegation. Yeltsin demanded the inclusion of Russia's representatives, promising otherwise to sabotage any agreement reached.[106] Gorbachev resisted, not because he was secretly hoping to reach an agreement on the territorial issue but because the inclusion of Yeltsin's men would underscore Gorbachev's political impotence in one sphere where until then he had enjoyed relative ascendancy—foreign affairs. Actually, key people from Yeltsin's team—Andrei Kozyrev (the Foreign Minister) and Vladimir Lukin (head of the International Affairs committee of the Russian Parliament)—met with Igor Rogachev of the Soviet Foreign Ministry and intimated that they had "no complaints" about Gorbachev's agenda for Tokyo. Lukin (who was playing both sides at this stage) even privately proposed a plan "to take Yeltsin out of the equation," prompting Chernyaev's suggestion to Gorbachev that they should bring him to Tokyo because he would help "neutralize" the Russian leader.[107]

In the end, both Kozyrev and Lukin were brought along. Moreover, in a nod to the greater prominence enjoyed by the regional authorities, Gorbachev took the head of the Khabarovsk Soviet, Nikolai Danilyuk ("brash and primitive," in Chernyaev's assessment, but in theory a

Gorbachev supporter),[108] his colleague from Yakutiya, Mikhail Nikolaev (because he had an "Asian appearance"),[109] and the Governor of Sakhalin, Valentin Fedorov (a bitter opponent of territorial concessions). Fedorov, however, was not admitted to the official talks between Gorbachev and Kaifu and left Japan fuming just as Gorbachev's visit began.[110] Back in the USSR, military spokesmen issued dire warnings not to give up any territory.[111] Chernyaev scribbled dejectedly on April 2: "Green melancholy ...I have to write speeches for Japan. But there is no more 'inspiration,' no thought.... The 'talent' dried up because policy dried up. There is only the verbal husk."[112] He added a week later: "I am enraged by the lack of talent, lack of professionalism, the squalor of the materials, provided by the Foreign Ministry for the visit to Japan."[113]

The Japanese Foreign Ministry labored at the same time to furnish Kaifu with all the relevant materials for the summit. Owada Hisashi (counselor), Hyodo Nagao (chief of the European-Asian division), and Togo Kazuhiko (chief of the Soviet section) visited the Prime Minister at his official residence in Nagatacho almost daily, and Kaifu was reported to have studied their papers closely, for he no doubt hoped that he would win where Ozawa had lost by wrestling a major concession from Gorbachev. This would help Kaifu's own waning political fortunes. Owada reportedly believed that Gorbachev would at the very least recognize the validity of the 1956 Declaration and potentially even promise to negotiate on the sovereignty of the other two islands. An affirmation of the 1956 Declaration was thus the bare minimum Kaifu expected to achieve at the summit.[114]

One has to wonder why Tokyo expected Gorbachev to make concessions when he had made it so clear that there would be none. Somehow, the Japanese counted on a fairly improbable outcome. But, as a Japanese Foreign Ministry official put it at the time, "The most important aspects (in Soviet negotiating style) appear only at the end. There is not a single hint about what the Soviet side is going to do. It may be the situation that Gorbachev is still thinking (about it)."[115] Those who missed all the hints must have also missed the significance of Gorbachev's performance in Khabarovsk on his way to Tokyo. In a widely televised impromptu exchange, Gorbachev said: "Everybody asks how many islands I am going to give them." A woman in the crowd shouted: "Don't give them a single one!" Gorbachev replied: "I shall act as you want me to, and I know your opinion."[116] Although all indications were that Gorbachev would not give in, the Gaimusho's position was: so what? "Japan is a prosperous nation," said Foreign Minister Nakayama, "thanks to its democracy and free market system, and it has no security worries, thanks to its ties to the United States. If the Soviet Union is interested in increasing its engagement in the Asia-Pacific region, then we would like them to proceed through their dialogue with Japan."[117]

On April 16 Gorbachev arrived in Tokyo. "The first impression," wrote Chernyaev—"the unnatural [appearance] of an ultra-modern city, something like un-inhabitedness."[118] Actually, traffic was stopped downtown on the occasion of Gorbachev's visit, and twenty thousand police were dispatched to guard against all kinds of incidents. There was only one mishap: a man in kimono with an eleven-inch knife was arrested somewhere along Gorbachev's route. The police said he wanted to commit suicide in protest. In the meantime, about three thousand right-wing marchers assembled in a central Tokyo park armed with loudspeakers blaring: "Gorbachev should get down on his hands and knees and apologize to the emperor."[119] Gorbachev was indeed promptly taken to the Emperor Akihito's presence, although nothing nearly as dramatic transpired. The two discussed the beauty of sakura blooms, the one conversation where the islands issue did not come up.[120] Then, sending his wife Raisa to explore the Ginza shopping district, Gorbachev went into a meeting with Prime Minister Kaifu.

Conversations between Gorbachev and Kaifu were among the strangest the Soviet leader had ever had with his foreign counterparts. Seven sessions were held over the next few days, as the President and the Prime Minister struggled to square the circle of the "northern territories." During the first session on April 16, Gorbachev refused to acknowledge even the 1956 Declaration, much less the Japanese sovereignty over the remaining two islands, and brushed aside Kaifu's hints that Soviet cooperation would be economically rewarded: "We will not trade principles for dollars. If we offered this to Japan, it would consider this insulting." For a while, the two leaders played around with different metaphors: Kaifu offered an Ikebana option for Soviet-Japanese relations, saying that they have to be firmly rooted in a peace treaty (with the territorial issue resolved), or they would wilt like flowers in a vase. Gorbachev countered that political relations would have to have an economic basis first. "What kind of relations are these, if they do not have an economic basis? I don't know about Buddha, but, among us, only Christ could walk on water and not drown. But we, mere mortals, need a firm ground."[121]

The haggling continued on the following day: Gorbachev obstinately refused to discuss the inclusion of the 1956 Declaration in the Joint Statement at the end of the visit. Nevertheless, he offered a number of positive steps that, in his view, would contribute to a better atmosphere for Soviet-Japanese relations in the long run: reduction of Soviet troops on the disputed islands, development of joint economic enterprises, and establishment of a visa-free regime for Japanese citizens wishing to visit the "northern territories." He promised that the "process will continue" and pleaded with Kaifu to observe the "balance of interests." "Christ and Buddha can see that my proposals have a lot of realism in the search of a solution, which accords with mutual interests," Gorbachev said with exasperation. This appeal to the deities, however, did not soften Kaifu's position, for the session had to be continued the next day.[122]

In the meantime, Kaifu held council with LDP heavyweights; their advice was not to issue a Joint Statement if Gorbachev did not budge on the 1956 Declaration. Nishioka Takeo, the head of General Affairs at the LDP, even urged the cancellation of the fifteen agreements (on various practical issues) prepared in advance of the summit by Soviet and Japanese experts. But Gorbachev did not give in. At the next session, he proposed to refer to "all positive factors that have been accumulated through bilateral negotiations over the years since 1956," but resisted Kaifu's pressure to mention the 1956 Declaration by name.[123] It became as bad as negotiating specific words, with Gorbachev agreeing at one point to use the verb "declare" and refusing to use the noun "declaration."[124] Chernyaev recalled a few days later: "It felt very 'uncomfortable' when the President of a superpower and the Prime Minister of Japan argued for hours—whether they should use a verb or a noun. And this is at a time when everything is about to come crashing down back home! But, on the other hand, maybe it is good to 'pretend' that the President is 'busy with his work in spite of everything.'"[125]

Kaifu ultimately agreed to drop his demand for the mention of the 1956 Declaration, pretending that the vague terminology of the good things that happened since 1956 included the Soviet promise to return the islands (while Gorbachev, of course, pretended the reverse). The fifteen minor agreements were signed, and Gorbachev received a little money to repay overdue loans to Japanese companies. But the Soviet leader's appeal for large-scale investments in the USSR fell on deaf ears: Japanese businessmen were far from keen on the recycled versions of the Brezhnev-era resource projects. The basic reality was that there was insufficient Japanese interest in economic cooperation, whatever happened to the islands. The *Economist* was quite on target, writing in the wake of the summit: "the islands would not be such an obstacle if the sides had stronger reason to overcome it and reach an agreement."[126]

Still, Gorbachev did not make the best of the opportunity to get the much-needed government credits, even though $1.6 billion dollars in emergency aid were reportedly his for the taking. Hasegawa argues that the Soviet leader simply did not know what to ask from the Japanese and, moreover, he did not want to give the impression to the public back home that he was begging for Japanese aid. In fact, he would have certainly taken the credits had he been offered, but he did not suspect the Japanese would be so generous. Gorbachev explained his rationale in a telephone conversation with Vadim Medvedev on April 21: "they did not give any money, naturally.... I did not ask them, knowing that it would be useless. [Their] expectations that I would beg for money were not realized."[127] Instead, Gorbachev asked for credits from President Roh Tae-woo, whom he met several days later on the South Korean island of Cheju-do, and received three billion US dollars (some of which was later frozen)—a far cry from the more substantial sums once discussed behind the scenes in the Ozawa back channel.

If there was a positive side to this summit, it was in the atmospherics. Apart from a small number of banner-carrying rightists, Gorbachev elicited an enthusiastic welcome in Japan: crowds poured into the streets in the imperial capital of Kyoto and in Nagasaki, where Gorbachev went very much against the wishes of the Japanese Foreign Ministry, which did not want to offend American sensibilities.[128] Some weeks later, Gorbachev told Kaifu in London: "I know that the Japanese leaders are realists, and they are hardened realists. I felt it when I was in Japan. But I also felt the Japanese people. Honestly speaking, I did not expect that I would meet with so much warmth and sincerity. And the meeting in Nagasaki simply overwhelmed me." "The ice has been broken," he told Kaifu.[129] In the weeks and months after he returned from Japan, Gorbachev continued to receive Japanese visitors, and each time played up the positive aspects of the relationship. "Everyone had a feeling," wrote Chernyaev of Gorbachev and his Japanese visitors, "that 'ice has been broken' and that our relations have reached some kind of a new level."[130]

ON A DOWNWARD SLOPE

Gorbachev's trip to Japan was his last official visit as the President of the USSR to any country. Although his faded glory still commanded admiration on the world stage, Gorbachev was but a shadow of his former self. Domestic developments had left him overboard, and foreign policy was also slipping through his fingers as his erstwhile Western partners probed the unfamiliar outlines of a world without Gorbachev, the more so now that the failure of the August coup left no doubts as to who really held the reins of power amid chaotic disintegration of the Soviet state. Kaifu hesitated momentarily as the coup unfolded, giving the impression that Japan could live with a hardline Soviet government as long as it returned the islands. But once it became clear that Yeltsin had triumphed, Kaifu called him up to express support.[131] Policy makers in Tokyo thereafter switched the focus of their attention to Yeltsin's team. Here, they found much greater willingness to discuss the territorial issue in a positive vein than Yeltsin's previous announcements would have suggested. It briefly appeared in Tokyo that the solution to the "northern territories" dispute was within grasp.

The most encouraging sign of the changes to come was Ruslan Khasbulatov's trip to Japan in September 1991. Khasbulatov had been Yeltsin's deputy when the latter was the head of the Russian Supreme Soviet, and in the summer of 1991 he succeeded Yeltsin as Russia's top parliamentarian. At the time, he was widely regarded as Yeltsin's close associate and Russia's No. 2 power broker. In September 1991 militant liberal Khasbulatov was seen as a voice for Yeltsin's policies, so when he turned up in Japan, he was received with open arms and with much greater attention than Yeltsin himself had seen more than a year earlier. Between September 9 and 12 he had lengthy meetings with Kaifu, Nakayama, and MITI head Nakao Eiichi, as well as with LDP politicians, including Ozawa, Watanabe Michio, Kanemaru Shin, Miyazawa Kiichi, and Obuchi Keizo—Japan's most powerful men.

Khasbulatov delivered the same message in all of his conversations: Russia needed "large-scale emergency economic aid" from Japan— "not on the order of hundreds of millions but *billions* of US dollars."[132] As he told Kanemaru, Russia expected nothing less than "a Japanese version of the 'Marshall Plan.'"[133] Khasbulatov knew that the Japanese would raise the subject of the four islands; his answer was to propose a modified version of Yeltsin's five-stage solution: now the waiting time between the stages could be shortened considerably, so that the Japanese would not have to wait until future generations to resolve the problem. Moreover, Khasbulatov promised that Russia would no longer go by the idea that it was the victor and Japan was the vanquished, but seek to build up relations on the basis of law and justice. Thoughts to this effect were included in a letter from Yeltsin that Khasbulatov delivered to Kaifu, and they elicited a cautiously positive response from the Japanese. Khasbulatov needed much more than that.

In a bid to bring the Japanese around to abandon seikei fukabun and dole out the cash, Khasbulatov went as far as to promise that the islands would be returned. Gone were the days of ambiguity. Russia's No. 2 told Ozawa: "We are prepared to realize the dream of the Japanese people."[134] Kanemaru heard an even more straightforward admission: "In the end the islands must be returned to Japan. The opinion of the [Russian] people is primitive but it was formed under the influence of party workers. They convinced the people that Japan is a vanquished country, which was handled the way it deserved.... Therefore, the important task is to change the public opinion, to show that these were unfair treaties, and one must respect the international law. One cannot live without a peace treaty. This is the position of the President, the Parliament and the government of Russia."[135] Japanese aid was needed to help change Russian public opinion and to stabilize the Russian government, which was then still under the threat of "fascism" perpetrated by the authors of the August coup.

Khasbulatov's postfacto report on his trip (intended for internal consumption) deemphasized the connection between Japanese aid and the return of the islands, but played up that latter motive of saving young Russian democracy. In this interpretation, it was actually Japan's responsibility to pay up: "Russia, which in fact saved the whole world from the resurgence of dictatorship, does not consider it humiliating to ask for large-scale, and not for symbolic, international aid. Especially since Russia, as one of the richest countries in the world, can pay back any loans."[136]

Such was the message delivered by the new Russian leadership in those uncertain weeks after the coup, and it was nothing if not exceptionally promising for the Japanese. No one gave Khasbulatov any aid right away (except for Ozawa, who even here managed to outdo his party colleagues by handing the Russian a certificate of aid for 1.1 million US dollars, extended by private Japanese companies on the Destroyer's personal initiative).[137] Clearly, however, Khasbulatov's message registered in the highest quarters, not least with the powerful Watanabe, Minister of International Trade and Industry Nakao, and the old kingmaker Kanemaru Shin. All seemed quite upbeat on de-linking islands from aid. Nakao even inadvertently fumbled something that sounded like a refutation of the age-old seikei fukabun: "I agree with you that there should be no linkage between the territorial question and Japan's economic aid to the Soviet Union. We are neighbors, and neighbors are supposed to help each other during the difficult times." Realizing his mistake, Nakao added: "as for the principle of inseparability of politics and economics, this is a fundamental principle of the Japanese government."[138] Several weeks later, this fundamental principle was blatantly ignored when Tokyo at last agreed to extend a hefty untied credit—2.5 billion dollars—to the Soviet Union.

There was a strong lobby close to Russia's levers of power that was essentially resigned to surrendering the "northern territories" to Japan. Khasbulatov was no doubt in favor of returning the islands, partly for ideological reasons (anything the communists did must have been wrong and criminal) and partly for financial reasons. In a report that was soon leaked to the press, inflaming tensions, he proposed to deal with the territorial problem "without delay," for fear of losing out on the economic aid and wasting Japanese trust. "It is also extremely important," read Khasbulatov's report, "to inform the people's deputies and the entire Russian public about the real essence of the territorial question, with an objective, not biased, interpretation."[139] Similar sentiments were shared at the Russian Foreign Ministry, first and foremost by the former IMEMO analyst-turned-Deputy-Foreign-Minister Georgii Kunadze. The "Kunadze option"—as Hasegawa termed it—entailed the immediate surrender of two, followed by the discussion of the fate of the other two, islands.[140]

Kunadze went out of his way to change the public opinion of Russia in a direction more favorable to Japan. To this end, the Deputy Foreign Minister, accompanied by the former KGB General Oleg Kalugin and a Russian legislator, Sergei Sirotkin, bravely ventured out to Sakhalin and the Kuriles in September 1991, only to face the rage of the local residents. Governor Fedorov unleashed a personal attack on the visitor, saying that someone named Georgii Fridrikhovich Kunadze (German patronimic and Georgian last name) had no business discussing the future of the "indigenous Russian lands."[141] On September 30 Fedorov fired off a telegram to Yeltsin, demanding the dismissal of the "odious" Kunadze, who "with his capitulatinist views, had compromised himself in the public eye long before he was appointed deputy foreign minister."[142]

In October an internal policy document of the Russian Foreign Ministry (probably written by Kunadze) blamed the Kuriles visit fiasco on the local residents' worries about what would happen to their houses and work if the islands were returned. The recommendation was to let the people "know the truth," to make them understand that returning the islands would "not be a defeat for our country but the triumph of law and justice." Returning the islands was said to be an important measure for the improvement of Soviet-American relations. The key issue, highlighted in the policy document, was the need to avoid any impression that the islands were being sold to Japan. "Unfortunately, one has to state that certain political leaders intentionally put the problem in this light, evidently hoping to make use of the patriotic sentiments inflated upon false premises."[143] That was, of course, exactly what Yeltsin had been doing only months earlier. Now he was seemingly coming around to a different point of view, no doubt because Japanese aid obtained in exchange for Russia's law and justice would benefit his rather than Gorbachev's coffers.

In the meantime, Chernyaev steered what remained of the Soviet Union's foreign policy toward some form of accommodation with Japan. One of the last occasions to do so was Nakayama's visit to Moscow in October 1991. Chernyaev noted on the 12th:

[I looked at the] backgrounds for Nakayama from the Foreign Ministry—dead, just words. I improved them, "Gorbachevized" them, but there is still no position. [Gorbachev's aide Aleksandr] Veber showed up.... I dumped the "memo" on him, asking to obtain the dossier on Khasbulatov's trip to Japan, on the demonstrations and on the media coverage against the transfer of the islands.... Veber showed what he did after me. I called [the new Soviet Foreign Minister Boris] Pankin: "we" don't have a position, what are we taking to the President's level? He began to blabber something. [I said:] Borya! Enough of stalling. All of what was in the stalling has been said already, now one has to choose: either we give up the islands and go to the people (to the Supreme Soviet or Russia or the USSR) and explain this decision, or we tell the Japanese: you will never see them and you can go to hell with your good intentions towards us, with "friendship" and with your billions! And to tell the people honestly: is this what you wanted? I did not hear anything sensible in response.... And M.S. will again paper over the problem: "history wil judge," "let's create the atmosphere."...Pitiful and pointless. No policy. Just blabber left.[144]

Chernyaev sent the "blabber" memo to Gorbachev on the following day, but he prefaced it with a short note, laying out his arguments in favor of a "policy." "I wrote it in a sharp tone. I thought he would get angry but, no, he just called. He says: I exchanged [opinions] with Pankin, tomorrow I will speak with Yeltsin. Indeed, we have to make up our minds."[145] Gorbachev received Nakayama on October 15, and, in his remarks, seemed to edge forward in comparison with his former position: "I am confident that the process will go faster than we thought during my visit to your country. Quantitative changes will inevitably lead to qualitative moves." When Nakayama asked Gorbachev to elaborate on these hints, the Soviet President suggested that he reread the memorandum of their conversation: "You will find an answer to your question in what I said today. I am confident, I will be able to say something new next time. And in general my intuition suggests to me that Soviet-Japanese relations will soon exceed all others in their dynamism."[146] A few days later Chernyaev added to the diary: "[Gorbachev] received the Japanese, basically promised the islands, although it is now absolutely not in his power to hand them back."[147]

Indeed, Gorbachev was on his way out. He was no longer a statesman but a part of history. Gorbachev was still meeting with various Japanese delegations and agreeing to interviews; he had one scheduled for the morning of December 26 with the editor of *Yomiuri Shimbun*, one day after he resigned as the Soviet President. Chernyaev jotted down the details: "M.S. went to his office at the Kremlin at 11am, in order to meet with the Japanese.... But an hour before that his office was occupied by Yeltsin. And M.S. received the Japanese in the office of [his former head of staff Grigorii] Revenko! Why does he have to humiliate himself like this? Why does he come to the Kremlin?!!…What a nightmare!"[148] On December 28 Chernyaev noted that he had talked Gorbachev out of giving yet another interview to the Japanese TV company NHK: "It is shameful to come to the Kremlin, where Yeltsin is 'partying' in his office…. Revenko later reproached me: the Japanese promised a million dollars for that interview."[149] Such was the surreal closure of Gorbachev's arduous search for rapprochement with Japan.

CONCLUSION

When it comes to evaluating Gorbachev's policy toward Japan from late 1990 through early 1991—if there indeed was a policy—it may be summarized as Gorbachev wanting to have his cake and eat it, too. The Soviet leader was completely desperate for Japanese economic aid. With the reins of power slipping out of his hands, and the whole Soviet economy heading toward an apocalypse, how could he remain calm at the thought of some billions of dollars sitting idly in the Tokyo vaults, when they could be had right here where they were most needed, provided Gorbachev was willing to make that political sacrifice? But then he would have to face the full force of public opinion, accusations of betrayal and selling out at a time when he was already blamed for losing Eastern Europe and letting the Baltic republics break away. At least no one could plausibly claim that he had sold Soviet territory until then; with Japan, a sellout was the first explanation that would spring up in the enflamed minds of the swelling crowds of Gorbachev-haters and political opportunists. Faced with this impossible dilemma, Gorbachev chose procrastination.

In the opinion of one of his most critical biographers, Gorbachev had a fundamental leadership flaw—"indecisiveness, propensity towards half-steps."[150] There is some truth to this view, although "indecisive" is perhaps not the right word for the Soviet leader. He had embarked on the road to reforms and carried them through in the face of adversity and mounting opposition. He had achieved tremendous breakthroughs in his foreign policy and played the decisive role in the peaceful ending of the Cold War. "Indecisiveness" simply fails to account for the full complexity of the Gorbachev phenomenon. A more convincing interpretation is that Gorbachev was a politician through and through, but, while a master of behind-the-scenes intrigue, he was unfortunately less skilled at the art of public politics. In spite of all his charisma, the public Gorbachev was— again to borrow Primakov's evocative image—"a grass snake in a frying pan." He could not ignore public opinion, but he also did not know how to make use of it. Yeltsin was much better at that game.

Japanese scholar Shimotomai Nobuo argues that by the time Ozawa came up with the offer of cash for the "northern territories," it was already too late for Gorbachev. The year 1990 could be taken as the turning point. In January of that year, Yeltsin announced his "five-stage plan," but within a few months the Russian leader's position hardened visibly, as he realized that the territorial question was a potent weapon in his struggle against Gorbachev. Moreover, proclamation of Russia's sovereignty in June 1990 placed a formidable obstacle in the path of a settlement with Japan: Yeltsin would have to agree to any deal that Gorbachev would have reached, and what incentive did he have to do so when Tokyo's credits would only serve to bolster Gorbachev's political position at his own expense? In this sense, Ozawa simply placed his bets on the wrong horse. The islands-for-cash deal came too late for Gorbachev and left Yeltsin out in the cold.

Could there be other reasons for the failure of the back channel? Scholar Tuomas Forsberg claimed that the Germans were successful where the Japanese failed because Helmut Kohl knew better than to explicitly offer cash for territorial concessions, and Gorbachev kept his face.[151] In retrospect, Nakasone criticized Ozawa for acting "inelegantly," like a "trader," although the former Prime Minister had also been in favor of an underhanded deal.[152] But Gorbachev did not like these sorts of trades. He was proud—immensely, almost pathologically proud. How easily he took offense when Ozawa barely broached the question of money. How he refused to "beg" in Tokyo for the economic aid that was already set aside for him. Trapped in superpower delusions, Gorbachev found it painful to depend on the good graces of the upstart Japanese. Do not think that we need you more than you need us, he said time and again, even though it was so blatantly clear to any objective observer that precisely the opposite was the case.

Even if the Japanese had followed in Kohl's footsteps, could Gorbachev have acted very differently? In fact, there was a huge dissimilarity between what happened in Germany and what happened in the case of the "northern territories." In Germany, Gorbachev became a victim of events; his agreement to German reunification in 1990 was to a large extent a function of his recognition that it was already happening. There was nothing he could do about it unless he was willing to resort to force, and that would destroy the hard-won trust he had built with the West. The Kuriles were not about to break away. It would take a conscious policy choice to give them away. Gorbachev would not have made that conscious policy choice with either the Kuriles, or with East Germany, for that matter. By drawing comparisons between Germany and the "northern territories," Japanese politicians mistook unexpected outcomes for conscious policy choices. No wonder they had inflated expectations. They were bound to be disappointed, just as Gorbachev had predicted they would be.

Although Gorbachev's meeting with Kaifu in April 1991 failed to produce a breakthrough on the issue of the islands, the Soviet leader was pleased by the dynamic of the Soviet-Japanese relationship in the following months. The intensification of contacts and Tokyo's apparent willingness to expand ties even in the absence of progress on the islands both suggested improvement of relations, which was what Gorbachev set out to achieve in the first place. Who could compare what was happening in Soviet-Japanese relations in 1991 with the frigid climate of the early 1980s? Gorbachev kept reminding the Japanese that a better atmosphere would lead to the final resolution of the territorial problem in time, but he was less than completely honest. In fact, better political relations eroded the incentives for the Soviets to return the islands. As for better economic relations, the much-hoped-for bonanza failed to materialize, but this had little to do with the "northern territories": Japanese capital feared the uncertainties of the crumbling Soviet market. For all his influence in the business circles, even Ozawa was powerless to turn the situation around.

Perhaps, Ozawa was also a bit unlucky. Just as he was working on building up contacts with the liberals in Gorbachev's circle—Yakovlev, Chernyaev, Vol'skii, Petrakov, and others—the Soviet leader was moving away from them. Gorbachev's noticeable turn to the right in late 1990 through early 1991, and the departure or marginalization of the reformers in his circle, strengthened the voices of people like Vladimir Kryuchkov or Dmitrii Yazov, who were strongly against any talk of territorial concessions. Both of these hardliners were purged after the aborted coup of August 1991, when Gorbachev broke decisively with the conservatives. By the fall of 1991, the Soviet leader appeared more optimistic than ever about returning the islands to Japan. Chernyaev thought that "if Gorbachev was not forced to leave and if the Soviet Union did not fall apart, [the territorial] question...would now be close to final resolution."[153] In fact, it seems much more likely that the reason for Gorbachev's apparent change of heart was that he had already effectively lost power, so he could speak more freely about the bright future of Soviet-Japanese relations without taking responsibility for the painful concessions that somebody else would have to make in the end.

Epilogue

Today, Russia's presence in Asia is insignificant and dwindling. The total population of Russia's entire Far Eastern Federal District is a mere 6.69 million people, almost imperceptible in the midst of the billions of Asia and less than 5 percent of Russia's overall population. Although in terms of nominal GDP Russia is among the biggest Asian economies, in reality most of this GDP originates in European Russia. Moscow alone, for example, contributes four times as much to Russia's GDP as the entire Far Eastern Federal District, and twice as much as the entire Siberian District. The combined GDP of Siberia and the Far East is less than that of Hong Kong, and most of it comes down to the extraction of oil, gas, and minerals. Up to a quarter of Russia's foreign trade is with Asia Pacific (with China as the largest trading partner, East or West). But none of the APEC member states count Russia among their top five trading partners. Economically, Russia is a dwarf in Asia. Its regional role is mainly that of China's resource appendage.[1] Despite centuries of expansion toward the East, Russia of today is for all intents and purposes a European, not an Asian, power. It has been left on the sidelines of the "Pacific century."

How does Russia's standing in Asia compare to where it was thirty years ago? In some ways, it is better off. One obvious improvement is that Russia is more secure in the East than the Soviet Union had been. The end of the Cold War and the Sino-Soviet normalization changed the equation for Russia's relations with Asia from mainly adversarial to mainly cooperative. Russia enjoys much better bilateral relations with key regional players, including Japan, South Korea, and ASEAN countries. Its relationship with China has evolved toward a "strategic partnership," something that seemed distinctly improbable, if not inconceivable, in the early 1980s. In other ways, however, Russia is worse off. It is clearly much less influential in Asia than the Soviet Union was. During the Cold War, few regional problems could be resolved without Soviet involvement in one way or another, while today most regional problems do not require Russia's participation.

Russia simply does not possess the military might that had made the Soviets feared but also respected in Asia. Another difference is that the Soviet Union commanded a certain appeal—soft power, if you will—as a developmental model. That appeal began to wear off from the 1950s, but it only vanished completely with the disappearance of the Soviet Union itself. Without hard or soft power to rely upon, Russia has no effective levers for asserting influence in Asia.

Traditionally, the "Asian" dimension of Russia's (and Soviet) foreign policy was closely interrelated with, and, indeed, subordinate to, the "European" dimension. Russia turned to Asia when it was stonewalled or stalemated in Europe. It was always easier to make gains in "backward" Asia than in the West, where Russia itself appeared backward, though often menacing. For example, Russia's defeat in the Crimean War (1853–56) spurred St. Petersburg to seek new opportunities in Central Asia and the Far East, taking advantage of China's internal weakness. In the 1920s, when communist revolutions failed to take off in Europe, the Bolsheviks turned their attention to Asia. Stalin played by the same rules in the late 1940s, when the Cold War sharply curtailed opportunities for making headway in Europe, prompting the Soviet dictator to play his cards in China and Korea. Khrushchev, too, turned to Asia as his first love in foreign policy; this love affair produced nasty offspring in the form of Soviet involvement in various Third World conflicts that continued well into the 1980s. Even senile Brezhnev, ailing Andropov, and dull Chernenko looked to Asia to overcome the challenge of the Soviet Union's international isolation. This was also the starting point for Gorbachev's foreign policy.

The implicit idea that underpinned Russian and Soviet involvement in the East was that Asia was Moscow's for the taking and that it had unlimited reserves, which Russians could exploit, to the detriment of all their Western competitors. In this analysis, Russia was better positioned to understand Asia because Russia was half-Asian, something that no other Western power could boast. Its role was to represent Asia to the West, and, indeed, to lead in Asia. There was a patronizing element in Moscow's policy toward Asia, a need to be recognized as "superior" even as in relations with the West the Soviets longed for recognition of their equality. Gorbachev inherited general belief in the Soviet Union's natural leadership in Asia, and his Asian outreach was in fact premised on the idea that the Soviets could lead by proposing a grand vision for Asia, which everyone else would follow.

Unlike the earlier Soviet initiatives on Asia, which were either piecemeal or stillborn, Gorbachev began with big gestures. The most important of these was his initiative in Vladivostok in July 1986, the opening salvo of the Soviet charm offensive in Asia Pacific. The problem was that no one wanted to follow the Soviet lead in Asia. Most regional players wanted something specific from the Soviet Union: China sought the removal of the "three obstacles"; Japan wanted the islands; Vietnam desired developmental aid, as well as international support for its struggle for hegemony in Indochina; India, too, wanted Moscow's backing for its regional great power ambitions. Asia turned out to be too diverse and too contradictory to be instrumentalized for the purposes of Gorbachev's vision. His failure in this respect is not particularly surprising. The vision of a Soviet-led Asia was only one of many similar visions, sponsored at one time or another by the Japanese, by the Americans, by the Chinese, and even by lesser players. Visions are hard to sell, and ideas, meant to inspire, may frighten instead. One person's dream may be another's nightmare. Gorbachev failed to lead in Asia, and his failure is only a reminder that no one can, a lesson that should not be lost on contemporary policy makers.

This does not mean that Gorbachev's Asian outreach was completely futile or counterproductive. His one major achievement in the region was to complete the process of the Sino-Soviet normalization. Gorbachev's initiatives picked up where Brezhnev's, Andropov's, and Chernenko's had left off—something that the myth of Gorbachev the ice-breaker tends to overlook. Gorbachev made a difference in one crucial respect: he was willing to speak to China on equal terms to a greater extent than his predecessors, who still expected the repentant Chinese to reclaim their vacant position under the Soviet wing. Gorbachev, to the probable relief of the Chinese, was very clear from the start that he would not pretend to be China's elder brother. He had the common sense to see what eluded several generations of Soviet policy makers before him: that China was a great power in its own right, not a Soviet client.

Improvement of Sino-Soviet relations was facilitated by the actions of successive American administrations. Ronald Reagan's tough rhetoric and robust anti-Soviet policies prompted Moscow to rethink its antagonism toward China. Deng Xiaoping reciprocated Soviet feelers in response to Washington's perceived failure to deal with China on equal terms. For both countries, rapprochement was at first a tactical ploy. Yet the beginning of this process tended to strengthen supporters of better relations in both China and the Soviet Union, leading in the longer term to strategic rapprochement. This tendency was reinforced in the wake of the Western sanctions against China after the Tiananmen massacre, despite Beijing's growing frustration with Gorbachev. Both Moscow and Beijing perceived—and continue to perceive—each other largely through the prism of their relations with the United States.

Nevertheless, Sino-Soviet rapprochement was more than just an act of triangular diplomacy void of ideological content. The Soviet and the Chinese leaders were aware of their shared socialist heritage and this awareness at crucial points provided an additional impetus to improving relations. The awareness was greater on the part of the Chinese, who paid much closer attention to what was happening in the USSR and in Eastern Europe than the other way around. Gorbachev believed that he was sailing uncharted waters, and in many ways he was. But it is still remarkable to what extent he ignored, or even dismissed, the Chinese reform experience. This can be explained to a certain extent by entrenched perceptions on the part of the Soviet leadership of the hierarchies of the socialist world, which placed the USSR ahead of other communist countries, especially the seemingly "backward" Asian ones. Gorbachev's failure in Asia in the 1980s was also a failure of learning that the Soviet Union, like China, was not quite ready for radical democratization.

Today, China remains an authoritarian country. So is Russia. They are authoritarian for different reasons. Many Russians have looked on, unconcerned, as Vladimir Putin dismantled the foundations of a democratic order laid down in the late 1980s. They were unconcerned because of the dramatic experiences of the 1990s, which made Russians associate democracy with chaos, crime, economic ruin, and impotence in foreign policy. They longed for a "strong hand"—and they got it. The Chinese, too, learned from the Soviet chaos and economic collapse. The lesson they learned was that any political reform leads to chaos. In other words, where Gorbachev refused to learn from the Chinese, the Chinese learned the wrong lesson from Gorbachev. The net result of this learning experience was that both countries are still very far from democracy and openness. In 1989 Gorbachev congratulated himself on having avoided a Soviet Tiananmen. In a fateful way, however, his own reckless domestic policies spilled over into China and precipitated the standoff between the students and the authorities in Tiananmen Square.

Gorbachev's Asian outreach did not square with the existing Soviet commitments, from Afghanistan, to Indochina, to Northeast Asia. This gap between the propaganda of the "peace offensive" and the reality of Soviet military presence was one reason that Gorbachev's Vladivostok initiative met with skepticism and disbelief among many of the audiences this initiative was supposed to impress. Curbing commitments to militant clients, like North Korea or Vietnam, and pulling back from endless quagmires, like Afghanistan, was a difficult proposition even for a visionary like Gorbachev. After all, upon assuming office, he took upon his shoulders the responsibility for steering a superpower in uncertain seas where each hasty move threatened loss of influence for the state and loss of his own prestige as the leader of that superpower. The main reason for Gorbachev's hesitation in healing various "bleeding wounds" was his fear of losing credibility—both domestically, where he could be blamed for breaking up the empire, and internationally, among various Third World audiences that mattered a great deal to the Soviet leader. By acting too cautiously and too gradually, he lost out on opportunities for maximizing Soviet leverage.

The contradiction between Gorbachev's interest in maintaining the Soviet position in the Third World and reinventing the Soviet Union in Asia was particularly evident in the case of Afghanistan. It is, of course, clearer now than it was back then. With the benefit of hindsight, it is easy to say that the war in Afghanistan was unwinnable. But at the time, Gorbachev was determined to win that war so as to allow the Soviet Union to leave on respectable terms. It took at least two years before Gorbachev realized that the war could not be won and that national reconciliation was not working; it took another two years before the last Soviet troops left Afghanistan. The Soviet withdrawal was a political victory for Gorbachev, but a Pyrrhic one for having taken so long. What in 1985–86 could have still been salvaged as a "victory" by 1989 had become a defeat, contributing to the image of Soviet weakness, and so to Gorbachev's political downfall. Instead of becoming a showcase of new Soviet policy in Asia, this "long goodbye" (as historian Artemy Kalinovsky aptly called it) came to symbolize Soviet retrenchment from Asia, and, indeed, demise of the Soviet imperial enterprise. In the meantime, Soviet hesitation discouraged the regime in Kabul from genuine reforms and intensified anti-Soviet sentiments among the local population.

The same contradiction plagued Soviet efforts to reposition itself on the Korean peninsula. In particular, Gorbachev was much too late with his decision to engage with South Korea. Instead, Soviet relations with North Korea in the mid-1980s reached their best point in decades, helped by a torrent of economic and military aid that, unfortunately, did not translate into Moscow's increased influence over Kim Il-sung's dictatorship. Gorbachev made room in his Vladivostok initiative for North Korean propaganda while entirely ignoring South Korea. Only in 1988 did he come to see the need for changing the Soviet policy, and even then he acted with characteristic hesitation, fearful of being accused of betraying North Korea's interests, and so losing credibility. Soviet recognition of South Korea did not take place until 1990, and when it did happen, it looked more like a financial transaction—far more profitable for the South Koreans than for the Soviets—than an act of statesmanship born of Gorbachev's brave new vision for the world. By then, as in the case of Afghanistan, Soviet concessions appeared forced, and

Moscow had lost leverage for playing a positive role in the reconciliation on the Korean peninsula.

Gorbachev's most notable failure in Asia was his inability to achieve a breakthrough with Japan. The thorniest problem in relations between Moscow and Tokyo was, and remains, the territorial dispute. What went wrong in the 1980s that did not allow Japan and the Soviet Union to find a mutually acceptable solution to this issue when equally intractable matters were being resolved in Europe? Historians, especially Japanese ones, have tried to address the issue of lost opportunities: perhaps if the COCOM scandal and Nakasone's agreement to be involved in Reagan's Star Wars program had not derailed the pace of Soviet-Japanese rapprochement in 1987, it would have been possible to achieve a breakthrough while Gorbachev still had power to act. Or if the Japanese policy makers had not shifted to a hardline attitude in early 1989, Gorbachev would have likely paid closer attention to Japan for the rest of that crucial year, when everything seemed possible. Finally, as a last resort, if Artem Tarasov had not sabotaged Gorbachev's trip to Japan with his sensationalist claims about a secret agreement to sell the islands for cash, the Soviet leader would have probably been more forthcoming in Tokyo. All of these claims are true to an extent, but they miss the bigger picture.

In the negotiations with Moscow, the Japanese had long insisted on an all-or-nothing solution, and even historians have debated the possibilities, or lost opportunities, for resolving the issue on Japan's terms. Yet the question should not be why or how Tokyo failed to trick Gorbachev into signing away all four islands, but why or how the all-or-nothing solution achieved its present status as the unassailable dogma of Japanese foreign policy. Indeed, even questioning its rationale, as some Japanese scholars occasionally do, has led to controversy, backlash, and accusations of selling out Japan's national interests. In recent years Japanese policy makers have begun to move away from this rigid position. Better late than never! Anything must be better than a policy that has never worked.

This book has argued that the territorial problem is more a symptom than a source of Russian-Japanese antagonisms. Japan weathered the Cold War in the comfortable American embrace. The US-Japanese alliance defined foreign policy priorities even in the 1980s. Part of the reason there was no breakthrough in Soviet-Japanese relations with the end of the Cold War was that the Japanese did not want any such breakthrough if it required deep changes to the familiar context of Japanese foreign policy. Like Deng Xiaoping, who raised the three obstacles to slow the pace of Sino-Soviet rapprochement, Japanese policy makers raised the territorial issue. But if Deng Xiaoping found it possible to compromise and achieve rapprochement for less than a complete Soviet capitulation, the Japanese insisted on precisely such a capitulation. No wonder the results proved so different. No amount of sympathy for Japanese national feelings should blind us to this serious defect in Tokyo's foreign policy.

For their part, Soviet policy makers also failed to see the importance of compromise. In the early 1980s, Moscow briefly entertained the possibility of territorial concessions. With Japan, as with China, the Soviets regarded rapprochement as a tactic aimed at weakening the United States in the Cold War. Japan was viewed as a Cold War pawn. The Chinese had much better reasons to dislike Japan, and yet in the 1970s and the early 1980s, Japan became a source of technology and know-how. No sooner had Deng Xiaoping returned to political prominence in 1978 than he flew to Japan. Deng, who had first-hand experience fighting against Japanese imperialism in China, attached huge importance to improvement of relations with Japan. He bear-hugged Japanese politicians, toured Japanese factories, and sought to convince the Japanese government and Japanese businessmen to invest in China. Thus, while Japan proved crucial to China's modernization, the Soviets were too slow and too bureaucratic to take advantage of this country's potential.

Gorbachev ignored Japan until relatively late in his tenure. It was relegated to margins in the Vladivostok initiative. He did not consider that Japan was important enough to warrant serious Soviet concessions, such as those involving the transfer of territory. The Japanese, Gorbachev liked to say, should not think that the Soviet Union was more interested in better relations with Japan than the other way around. A similar attitude underpinned Tokyo's approach to the Soviet Union. Japanese politicians overestimated their ability to win Soviet cooperation through economic incentives. Great power sentiments and illusions of self-importance led both sides into a dead end. An early agreement to resolve the dispute along the lines of the 1956 Declaration would have contributed to a better relationship between Moscow and Tokyo, not only giving a major boost to Gorbachev's Asian outreach but also allowing Japan to rebalance its foreign policy away from Cold War alignments.

The failure of the Soviet-Japanese dialogue holds lessons for the present. Russia's one-sided orientation toward China—still a pillar of Moscow's Asian policy—leaves it with little leverage in regional affairs. Japan, too, needs Russia, especially since the worsening of the Sino-Japanese territorial dispute. The one thing that all three powers should have learned but have unfortunately neglected is that the postures of moral superiority and unwillingness to make concessions in the final count benefit no one.

Gorbachev's core concept for Asia was the Soviet-Indian-Chinese strategic triangle. He is not widely remembered for this idea, even though it was the precursor to the so-called BRICS (Brazil, Russia, India, China, South Africa) of today. It did not work at the time, for many reasons. One was that neither China nor India wanted the Soviet Union to lead in the triangle, but Gorbachev's point was exactly to put the Soviet Union in charge. In common with Russia's traditional approach to Asia as a lever for making gains in the West, Gorbachev overrated the extent of Soviet appeal in and influence over Asia. Another reason was that despite his criticism of bloc thinking, Gorbachev still thought in terms of blocs, and his triangle excluded the United States. Today, Russia is again attempting to exert its influence in Asia through BRICS-style arrangements. As before, Moscow is preoccupied with working out a grand design (now called multipolar world), which, as before, features subtle anti-American themes and basically serves as a means for maximizing Russian leverage in relations with the West.

When Gorbachev came to power in 1985, he realized that, weighted down by Third World entanglements and the growing liabilities of the dysfunctional socialist commonwealth, Moscow was losing the Cold War. Gorbachev's answer was to reinvent the Soviet Union as an Asian power, strategically aligned with the region's two heavyweights, China and India. This was his method of waging the Cold War. Is this the Gorbachev we know? What about that other Gorbachev who turned the Soviet Union toward engagement with the West, championed universal human values, and stood by as the Berlin Wall came down? Gorbachev the idealist was also there, and he was often in conflict with the other, more geopolitically-inclined Gorbachev. The two Gorbachevs coexisted in one person until the hour of the Soviet collapse, although by 1988 Gorbachev the idealist was winning the contest of wills with Gorbachev the Cold Warrior. Both had visions to sell and both ultimately failed. Yet, it is the latter Gorbachev that left by far the greater legacy for contemporary Russian policy makers.

Under Putin, Russia's standing in Asia saw a modest recovery from the dismal depths of the 1990s. Russia's relationship with China is strong, if economically unbalanced. Russia is on decent terms with both South and North Korea, and even with Japan, despite the deadlocked territorial dispute. The Kremlin wrote off Vietnam's debts and, even as it folded up its military presence, has tried to come back to Indochina in the guise of oil and gas multinationals. Russia's position in India is a gulf apart from where it was at the height of the Soviet-Indian cooperation, but it is not as bad as during the early 1990s. Russia may have lost positions in Afghanistan, but this is more than made up for by a better relationship with Iran. It continues to claim leadership in Asia, dismissing skeptical views that it is merely a resource appendage. In this sense, there is a lot in common between the Russia of today and the Soviet Union of the 1980s. This is bad news.

The Soviet outreach in Asia in the 1980s failed because it was based on several flawed premises: that the Soviet Union could lead in Asia; that the Soviet Union could take advantage of anti-American sentiments in Asia to undermine US influence; and that it could maintain its geopolitical presence in Asia and yet make headway in relations with China, India, Japan, South Korea, ASEAN countries, Pakistan, and Iran. These contradictions were eventually recognized, after considerable bureaucratic wrangling, but then, Gorbachev's great dash toward the East had already fizzled out. Like so many other initiatives of Gorbachev's tenure, his grand vision for the Soviet return in Asia proved too grand to be practically workable.

In place of geopolitical manipulation, rooted in 19th-century conceptions of great power politics, Moscow should have adopted low-key solutions for finding a place in Asia. This is not a question of building up military power, of exporting ever larger amounts of oil and gas across the border, or of tireless proclamations of a "multipolar world." These sorts of solutions are self-defeating in the long run. This is rather a question of opening borders, of removing barriers to the flow of goods and capital but also people, of encouraging cross-border communities that would tie Russia to this region linguistically and culturally in ways that would support a notion of an Asian identity. It is only then that Russia can claim, credibly, that it is not just a European but also an Asian power.

NOTE ON SOURCES

Writing this book was a challenge as much of the archival record pertinent to the end of the Cold War is still inaccessible to historians even in the West, much less in Russia and Asia. Nevertheless, more has become available than one would assume. This note, in lieu of a bibliography, is intended as a guide for scholars.

This book relies heavily on the Russian archives. Since the mid-1990s, the archival situation in Russia has worsened and once-sweeping declassification initiatives have all but ground to a halt. At a time when millions of files from the Stalin era remain secret, it was surprising to see how much was available for the 1980s and the early 1990s. One of the most important sources for the book was the Archive of the Gorbachev Foundation, a private facility that stores documents that Gorbachev and his advisers carried away when the Soviet Union collapsed. These include Politburo records, records of conversations and speeches, and internal memoranda, of which many are available for consultation in the Archive's reading room.

Unfortunately, instead of making all of the documents available, the Foundation censored its own archive, withdrawing the key records from open access. This author collected his research materials both from the Archive's reading room and from other sources within the Foundation who could be persuaded to share their materials. The Gorbachev Foundation has also published many of these materials in the form of Gorbachev's collected works (*Sobranie Sochinenii*) and other documentary collections, cited in this book with caution, since the editors often tampered with their documents in a bid to put the best spin on Gorbachev's actions.

Another archive that proved exceptionally useful for researching this topic was the State Archive of the Russian Federation (GARF). By far the most interesting materials were those of Fond 10026, the Russian Supreme Soviet. Until the late 1980s this Soviet (or Parliament) was just a rubber stamp. But by 1990 the centrifugal tendencies that afflicted the

USSR turned it into an important center of political power, one opposed to Gorbachev. Its committees were deeply involved in formulating Russia's foreign and security policies, leaving a documentary trace that is now completely open to scholars. Another useful source from GARF are the papers of Aleksandr Yakovlev, the intellectual father of perestroika. These, too, contain a wealth of records on Soviet foreign policy in the 1980s.

The Archive of the Foreign Ministry of the Russian Federation (AVPRF), a treasure trove for historians of Soviet foreign policy, proved only marginally useful for this book, because documents for the 1980s have not yet been declassified. Nevertheless, unclassified documents were occasionally illuminating. A much better source on internal policy discussions are the diaries of Foreign Minister Eduard Shevardnadze's aide Teimuraz Stepanov-Mamaladze, which ended up at the Archive of the Hoover Institution in Stanford, CA. He not only recorded Shevardnadze's meetings with foreign leaders but often made notes of his own conversations with the Foreign Minister, and of internal discussions, which shed light on how Soviet foreign policy was made. Another important source at Hoover are the papers of Valentin Kataev, who was in charge of defense-related matters at the CPSU Central Committee.

Scholars of Soviet foreign policy in the 1980s may also consult holdings of the National Security Archive and the Dmitrii Volkogonov papers at the Library of Congress in Washington, DC. Both places hold a vast volume of materials, many of which have been withdrawn from access in Moscow. Additional archival documents on Soviet foreign policy making are available for download from the website of the Cold War international History Project's Digital Archive.

A discussion of the Russian archival research would be incomplete without a mention of the regional archives. For much of the Soviet era, regional party and government organs were under strict instructions to return confidential documents to the Center. However, the system began to break down in the late 1980s. One of the most important archives used in this book is the Sakhalin State Archive. Its holdings not only contain records of local deliberations on Soviet-Japanese relations but also lengthy and often bitter exchanges with Moscow concerning policy choices.

In line with the now well-known methodology of international historians, this author filled the gap in the documentary record by drawing on archival materials of the Soviet Union's former satellite states and communist parties. While Polish, Czechoslovak, Bulgarian, Romanian, and Italian Communist Party archives yielded interesting evidence, only the former East German, Hungarian, and Mongolian archives were used extensively in the course of writing this book. The first two countries are popular destinations for Cold War scholars, but Mongolia has been virtually neglected. It turned out, however, that the Soviets kept the Mongols well appraised of their Asian policies and often briefed them during stop-overs in Ulaanbaatar on the way to or from Asia. These records, stored at the Mongolian Foreign Ministry Archive, are completely open to scholars all the way through the early 1990s, and they offer a new and unique angle on the Cold War in Asia.

This book takes advantage of declassified Chinese materials. Regrettably, the Chinese authorities have largely ignored historians' pleas for archival access. Central archives are completely inaccessible and even the Chinese Foreign Ministry Archive, opened some years ago to much fanfare, has recently curbed whatever limited access it had allowed. However, a careful scholar may still be able to obtain excellent materials by working in the regional archives. In this case, the Shanghai Municipal Archive, one of China's most open, became an excellent source of materials on the early 1980s, making this book probably the first one to recount Deng Xiaoping's foreign policy on the basis of the Chinese archival record.

Unfortunately, the same is not true for South Korea, where declassification, though orderly and commendable, has not yet reached the 1980s. But as so much South Korean policy making during that decade had to do with the holding of the Olympic Games, the author relied on the Archive of the International Olympic Committee in Lausanne, Switzerland, to clarify important details. This archive, it turned out, contains much more than simply sports-related documentation, confirming the observation that politics and sport are inseparable.

Formerly completely closed to historians, the Indian archives have now cracked open. This book relied on the materials of the Nehru Memorial Library and Museum, which holds papers of several senior Indian diplomats still active in the 1980s. In the meantime, Rajiv Gandhi's papers continue to be tightly held by his family, forcing historians to rely on third-party materials, in this case, American and Soviet, to account for India's foreign policy.

The Japanese are among Asia's most reluctant declassifiers, so, apart from papers procured from former politicians, the author had to rely on third-party documents to analyze Tokyo's foreign policy, including documents held by the Reagan and Bush Presidential Libraries, and those obtained by the National Security Archive in Washington, DC, by relentless filing of requests under the Freedom of Information Act. This author, too, contributed to the FOIA process not only in the United States but also in the United Kingdom. The results, records of conversations between Ronald

Reagan, George Bush, and Margaret Thatcher with Asian leaders, are highly useful, if inevitably one-sided.

The book drew extensively on the Archive of the United Nations, located in New York. The rumor mill of world politics, the UN Secretariat holds thousands of pages of documents on international problems of the Cold War era. Among the most pertinent for the purposes of this book were the UN files on the Cambodian and the Afghan conflicts, especially the Secretary General's conversations with the regional players. The author also benefited from the papers of the former Cambodian leader Norodom Sihanouk, which ended up at the French National Archives.

While archival research was very important for this book, no less important were the contemporary periodicals—newspapers like the *New York Times*, *Washington Post*, and *Guardian*, and agency newswires, including those of the BBC, Japan Economic Newswire, TASS, and Xinhua. Most of these sources were accessed through the LexisNexis database.

Finally, many of the policy makers in all the countries discussed in this book authored memoirs or published diaries. Though often unreliable, these books nevertheless fill gaps and offer important insights into policy making. In Russia, some of the best accounts were written by Mikhail Gorbachev, his Foreign Policy Aide Anatolii Chernyaev, whose diary is perhaps the best single source on Soviet policy making in the 1980s, Vitalii Vorotnikov, Georgii Shakhnazarov, Vadim Medvedev, Karen Brutents, Andrei Grachev, and Georgii Arbatov. The Chinese memoir literature is less convincing; still, books by Foreign Ministers Huang Hua and Qian Qichen, by Prime Minister Li Peng, and by the purged General Secretary Zhao Ziyang all shed light on matters of Chinese foreign policy. Like the Russians, though with even greater tampering, the Chinese have released a number of useful "chronologies" (*nianpu*) and collected works (*wenxuan*) of leaders like Deng Xiaoping, Chen Yun, and Li Xiannian. Indian, Japanese, and Korean memoirs, including those by J. N. Dixit, Nakasone Yasuhiro, Togo Kazuhiko, Kim Young-sam, and Park Chul-un, made up for the relative dearth of archival materials from these countries.

NOTES

INTRODUCTION

1. Alison Smale, "The Soviet Union bade solemn farewell ...," *Associated Press*, March 13, 1985.
2. Martin Walker, "Gorbachev keeps Thatcher waiting / Soviet leader holds reception for world leaders following Chernenko funeral," *Guardian*, March 14, 1985.
3. Anatolii Chernyaev et al. (eds.), *V Politbyuro TsK KPSS* ... (Moscow: Al'pina Biznes Buks, 2006), pp. 37, 72, 114.

CHAPTER 1

1. "Kak Brezhnev ne stal generalissimusom," *Versiya*, No. 11, March 22, 2004, p. 22. Author's interview with Alisher Vakhidov, November 25, 2010. Tashkent, Uzbekistan.
2. Brezhnev was given pain relief injections but he did deliver his speech. Author's interview with Alisher Vakhidov, November 25, 2010. Tashkent, Uzbekistan.
3. Serge Schmemann, "Brezhnev presses overtures to the Chinese leaders," *New York Times*, March 25, 1982, Section A, p. 8.
4. For an interesting account of Brezhnev's medical condition, see Evgenii Chazov, *Zdorov'e i Vlast': Vospominaniya "Kremlevskogo Vracha"* (Moscow: Novosti, 1992).
5. Odd Arne Westad, "Concerning the Situation in 'A': New Evidence on the Soviet Intervention in Afghanistan," *Cold War International History Project Bulletin*, Issues 8–9, pp. 128–32.
6. Zbigniew Brzezinski, *Power and Principle: Memoirs of the National Security Advisor, 1977–1981* (New York, NY: Farrar Straus Giroux, 1985), p. 189.
7. Patrick Tyler, *A Great Wall: Six Presidents and China, An Investigative History* (New York, NY: Public Affairs, 2000), pp. 229–285.
8. Memorandum of conversation between Jimmy Carter and Thomas J. Watson, June 4, 1980. Jimmy Carter Presidential Library, Atlanta, GA (hereafter, JCPL), NLC-126-21-40-1-3.
9. Ibid.
10. James Hershberg, Sergey Radchenko, Péter Vámos, and David Wolff, "The Interkit Story: A Window into the Final Decades of the Sino-Soviet Relationship," *Cold War International History Project Working Paper*, No. 63 (February 2011).
11. O provedenii dopolnitel'noi raboty v tselyakh protivodeistviya amerikano-kitaiskomu voennomu sotrudnichestvu, October 2, 1980. Russian State Archive of Recent History, Moscow, Russia (hereafter, RGANI): fond 89, opis 34, delo 10, list 5.

12. Cable from the US Embassy in Moscow to the Secretary of State, February 16, 1979. JCPL: NLC-16-15-2-12-3.
13. On Gromyko "bleating" about isolation, see Memorandum from Marshall Brement to Zbigniew Brzezinski, September 26, 1980. JCPL: NLC-8-19-2-1-0. On Brezhnev's addiction to sleeping pills, see Evgenii Chazov, *Zdorov'e i Vlast'*, p. 76.
14. Cited in Sergey Radchenko, *Two Suns in the Heavens: The Sino-Soviet Struggle for Supremacy, 1962–1967* (Washington, DC, and Stanford, CA: Woodrow Wilson Center Press and Stanford University Press, 2009), p. 204.
15. Conversation between Henry Kissinger and Leonid Brezhnev, April 21, 1972, The National Archive, Nixon Presidential Materials Project, National Security Council Files, HAK Office Files, Country Files Europe-USSR, Box 72, HAK Moscow trip, April 1972 memcons.
16. Memorandum from Michel Oksenberg to Zbigniew Brzezinski, August 21, 1978. JCPL: NLC-26-56-8-2-2.
17. Memorandum from Michel Oksenberg to Zbigniew Brzezinski, May 25, 1978. Ronald Reagan Presidential Library (hereafter, RRPL): Douglas Paal Files, China-US Meetings/Trips 5/78–9/82, binder 1 of 7.
18. For an interesting portrait of Mikhail Kapitsa, see Anatolii Zaitsev, *Vspominaya V'etnam* (Moscow: RFK-Imidzh Lab, 2010), pp. 54–62; see also Kapitsa's memoirs, *Na Raznykh Parallelyakh: Zapiski Diplomata* (Moscow: Kniga i Biznes, 1996).
19. Conversation between D. Yondon and Mikhail Kapitsa, June 9, 1982. Mongolian Foreign Ministry Archive, Ulaanbaatar, Mongolia (hereafter, MFMA): fond 2, dans 1, kh/n 467, khuu 38-39.
20. Memorandum from Michel Oksenberg to Zbigniew Brzezinski, May 25, 1978. RRPL: Douglas Paal Files, China-US Meetings/Trips 5/78–9/82, binder 1 of 7.
21. Conversation between D. Yondon and Mikhail Kapitsa, June 8, 1982. MFMA: fond 2, dans 1, kh/n 467, khuu 38.
22. Cited in Péter Vámos, "Only a handshake but no embrace: Sino-Soviet normalization in the 1980s," in Thomas P. Bernstein and Hua-Yu Li (eds.), *China Learns from the Soviet Union, 1949–Present* (Plymouth: Lexington Books, 2010), p. 84.
23. Conversation between D. Yondon and Mikhail Kapitsa, June 8, 1982. MFMA: fond 2, dans 1, kh/n 467, khuu 38-39.
24. Péter Vámos, "Only a handshake but no embrace: Sino-Soviet normalization in the 1980s," p. 111; "Soviet specialist leaves Peking," *BBC Summary of World Broadcasts*, March 29, 1980.
25. "Soviet sinologist in China for talks," *New York Times*, May 22, 1982, Section 1, p. 4.
26. Anatolii Chernyaev, *Sovmestnyi Iskhod: Dnevnik Dvukh Epokh, 1972–1991* (Moscow: Rosspen, 2008), p. 506.
27. Anatolii Chernyaev, *Sovmestnyi Iskhod*, p. 505.
28. Alexander Lukin, *The Bear Watches the Dragon: Russia's Perceptions of China and the Evolution of Russian-Chinese Relations since the Eighteenth Century* (Armonk, NY: M. E. Sharpe, 2003), p. 343.
29. Aleksandr Bovin, *XX Vek Kak Zhizn': Vospominaniya* (Moscow: Zakharov, 2003), p. 387.
30. Alexander Lukin, *Medved' nablyudaet za drakonom: Obraz Kitaya v Rossii v XVII–XXI Vekakh* (Moscow: AST Vostok-Zapad, 2007), p. 266.
31. Oleg Rakhmanin, *Stranitsy Perezhitogo* (Moscow: Pamyatniki Istoricheskoi Mysli, 2005), p. 3–6. Rakhmanin published under several *noms de plume*, most often as Oleg Borisov.

32. Evgenii Bazhanov, "Policy by fiat: Inside story: Kremlin twisted its facts on China," *Far Eastern Economic Review*, Vol. 155, No. 23, June 11, 1992, p. 16. The author of this anonymous article is identified as Bazhanov in Elizabeth Wishnick, *Mending Fences: The Evolution of Moscow's China Policy, From Brezhnev to Yeltsin* (Seattle, WA: University of Washington Press, 2001), p. 249.

33. On the Interkit, see James Hershberg et al., "The Interkit Story"; also David Wolff, "Interkit: Soviet sinology and the Sino-Soviet rift," *Russian History*, Vol. 30, No. 4 (2003), pp. 433–456.

34. See Oleg Borisov and Boris Koloskov, *Sovetsko-Kitaiskie Otnosheniya* (Moscow: Mysl', 1971) for a sample.

35. Author's interview with Romulus Budura, Freiburg, Germany, May 13, 2011.

36. Letter from Vladimir Rakhmanin to the author, May 31, 2011.

37. Author's interview with Georgii Arbatov, Moscow, March 24, 2008.

38. Cited in Alexander Lukin, *Medved' Nablyudaet Za Drakonom*, pp. 266–267.

39. Malgorzata Gnoinska, "Sino-Polish Relations in Light of Sino-Soviet Interactions, 1949–1989," paper presented at conference "Interkit: An International Against China?," May 12–13, 2011, University of Freiburg.

40. Jordan Baev, "Bulgaria and the Coordination of the East European Policy Toward China after the Soviet-Chinese Discord (1960–1989)," paper presented at conference "Interkit: An International Against China?," May 12–13, 2011, University of Freiburg.

41. Claudie Gardet, *Les Relations de la République Populaire de Chine et de la République Démocratique Allemande (1949–1989)* (Bern: Peter Lang, 2000), pp. 456–457.

42. Chen Zhongzhong, "Between political pragmatism and Moscow's watchful eye: East German-Chinese relations in the 1980s," Ph.D dissertation in progress.

43. Claudie Gardet, *Les Relations de la République Populaire de Chine et de la République Démocratique Allemande*, pp. 456–457.

44. The Chinese Commission of the Politburo of the CC CPSU included Yurii Andropov, Konstantin Chernenko, Andrei Gromyko, Boris Ponomarev, Mikhail Zimyanin, Leonid Zamyatin, Andrei Kirilenko, and Rakhmanin himself as its secretary. Anatolii Chernyaev, *Sovmestnyi Iskhod*, p. 487.

45. Ibid., pp. 486–487.

46. This was Chernyaev's guess at the time. See ibid., p. 486.

47. "Pravda: Soviet-Chinese differences 'will have to be removed,'" *BBC Summary of World Broadcasts*, May 21, 1982. Section: Part 1, The USSR; A. International Affairs; 3. The Far East; SU/7032/A3/1.

48. Not to be confused with the Department for Relations with Socialist Countries (The Department), where Rakhmanin was the first Deputy Head.

49. Anatolii Chernyaev, *Sovmestnyi Iskhod*, pp. 486–487.

50. Ibid., p. 487.

51. Cable from the Hungarian Embassy in Moscow to the Hungarian Foreign Ministry, July 7, 1982. Magyar Országos Levéltár, Budapest, Hungary (hereafter, MOL): XIX-J-1-j-Kína-103-004774-1982. Obtained by Péter Vámos, translated by Gwenyth A. Jones and Péter Vámos. See also James Hershberg et al., "The Interkit Story."

52. Letter from CC CPSU to Erich Honecker, July 14, 1982. Foundation Archive of Parties and Mass Organizations at the Federal Archives, Berlin, Germany (hereafter, SAPMO-Barch), DY30/13932, s. 25–28.

53. Ibid.

54. Ibid.

55. Ibid.

56. Bernd Schaefer, "The GDR and China during the 'Interkit Period,'" paper presented at conference "Interkit: An International Against China?," May 12–13, 2011, University of Freiburg.

57. "Protokol No. 27 zasedaniya redaktsionnoi kollegii zhurnala 'Kommunist,'" June 27, 1982. Rossiiskii Gosudarstvennyi Arkhiv Sotsial'noi i Politicheskoi Istorii (hereafter, RGASPI): fond 599, opis 1, delo 799, listy 71–82.

58. Ibid. The last statement came from Yu. L. Molchanov, member of the editorial board. On Salychev's KGB affiliation see Petr Cherkasov, *IMEMO: Portret na fone epokhi* (Moscow: Ves' Mir, 2006), p. 328.

59. Ibid.

60. Anatolii Chernyaev, *Sovmestnyi Iskhod*, pp. 494–495.

61. Ibid.

62. Ibid., pp. 496–498.

63. Ibid., p. 498.

64. Ibid., pp. 498–499.

65. Ibid., p. 507.

66. Niederschrift über das Treffen des Genossen Erich Honecker mit Genossen Leonid Iljitsch Breshnew auf der Krim, August 11, 1982. SAPMO-BArch: DY30-11854, s. 32–33. The author is grateful to Lorenz M. Lüthi for providing a copy of this document.

67. Kapitsa's remarks at a meal hosted by the Mongolian Embassy in Moscow in honor of the Soviet Ambassador in Ulaanbaatar S. P. Pavlov, February 25, 1983. MFMA: fond 2, dans 1, kh/n 473, khuu 47.

68. Niederschrift über das Treffen des Genossen Erich Honecker mit Genossen Leonid Il'jitsch Breshnew auf der Krim, August 11, 1982. SAPMO-BArch: DY30-11854, s. 24.

69. The circumstances of this Politburo meeting are recounted in Information über aktuelle Fragen der Außenpolitik der VR China unter besonderer Berücksichtigung der chinesisch-sowjetischen Beziehungen, April 9, 1982. Federal Commissioner for the Stasi Archives, Berlin, Germany (hereafter, BStU): MfS—Hauptverwaltung Aufklärung, No. 16, s. 272–273.

70. 黄花, 亲历与见闻:黄花回忆录 (北京: 世界知识出版社, 2007), p. 358.

71. "Chinese spokesman on Soviet president Brezhnev's recent remarks," Xinhua General News Service, March 26, 1982.

72. Tony Walker, "Brezhnev overture rebuffed by China," *Financial Times*, March 27, 1982, Section 1, 28; "Peking denounces Brezhnev," Associated Press, March 26, 1982.

73. Information über aktuelle Entwicklungstendenzen im außenpolitischen Vorgehen der VR China, May 27, 1982. BStU, MfS—Hauptverwaltung Aufklärung, No. 16, s. 165–166.

74. 钱其琛, 外交十记 (北京: 世界知识出版社, 2003), p. 5.

75. 郭德宏, 张湛彬, 张树军 (主编), 党和国家重大决策的历程, 第6卷 (北京: 红旗出版社, 1997), p. 185; 冷溶, 汪作玲 (主编), 邓小平年谱, 下 (北京: 中央文献出版社, 2004), p. 815.

76. 邓小平年谱, 下, p. 818.

77. Excerpts from Conversation between Deng Xiaoping and a delegation of Japan's Komeito party, October 14, 1982. Shanghai Municipal Archive (hereafter, SMA): B1-9-798-61, p. 62.

78. On Deng the ass-kicker, see Memorandum from Michel Oksenberg to Zbigniew Brzezinski, May 25, 1978. RRPL: Douglas Paal Files, China-US Meetings/Trips 5/78–9/82, binder 1 of 7.

79. Chen Jian, "China, the Third World and the End of the Cold War," in Artemy Kalinovsky and Sergey Radchenko, *The End of the Cold War and the Third World: New Perspectives on Regional Conflict* (London and New York: Routledge, 2011), p. 112.

80. See, for example, materials pertaining to Harold Brown's visit to Beijing in January 1980, especially conversations between Gerald Dinneen and Liu Huaqing, in RRPL: Douglas Paal Files, China-US Meetings/Trips 5/78–9/82, binders 5 of 7 and 6 of 7.

81. See, for example, Memorandum from Cyrus Vance to Jimmy Carter, December 9, 1979. RRPL: Douglas Paal Files, China-US Meetings/Trips 5/78–9/82, binder 4 of 7. Also, Cable from US Embassy in Moscow to the Secretary of State, February 5, 1980. JCPL: NLC-15-61-1-13-3.

82. Memorandum from David McGiffert to Harold Brown, April 8, 1980. US Department of Defense FOIA reading room.

83. Cable from US Embassy in Beijing to the White House, August 27, 1979. JCPL: Zbigniew Brzezinski Collection, China [People's Republic of], President's Meeting with [Vice Premier] Deng Xiaoping: 12/19/78–10/3/79.

84. For the best analysis, see 戴超武，"美国'贸易自由化'政策与中国'开放改革' (1969–1975)"，史学月刊，2010 (2), pp. 83–104.

85. Undated policy paper. RRPL: Edwin Meese Files, China-General 05/07/1981–06/03/1981, CF0160.

86. Conversation between Harold Brown and Deng Xiaoping, January 8, 1980. RRPL: Paal, Douglas Files, China-US Meetings/Trips 5/78–9/82, binder 5 of 7.

87. Cable from the US Embassy in Beijing to Secretary of State, November 19, 1981. RRPL: Paal, Douglas Files, China-US Meetings/Trips 5/78–9/82, binder 6 of 7.

88. Memorandum from Richard Nixon to Ronald Reagan, undated (before September 23, 1982). RRPL: Douglas Paal Files, China-US Meetings/Trips 5/78–9/82, binder 7 of 7.

89. Deng repeated this phrase on many occasions with slight variations. This quote is from Conversation between Jimmy Carter and Deng Xiaoping, January 30, 1979. RRPL: Douglas Paal Files, China-US Meetings/Trips 5/78–9/82, binder 2 of 7.

90. This was Michel Oksenberg's impression at the time. See Memorandum from Michel Oksenberg to Zbigniew Brzezinski, January 24, 1979. JCPL: NLC-26-38-4-11-6.

91. "An interview with Teng Hsiao-p'ing," *Time*, February 5, 1979, pp. 32–35.

92. Memorandum from Michel Oksenberg to Zbigniew Brzezinski, May 29, 1979. JCPL: NLC-26-51-10-15-0. Oksenberg specifically identified the failure to achieve progress on Taiwan, and China's disappointment with technology transfers, as the reasons for apparent policy debate in Beijing.

93. Memorandum from Warren Christopher to Jimmy Carter, August 27, 1980. JCPL: NLC-128-15-8-16-8. On Deng's continued insistence on the cancellation of the Taiwan Relations Act, see Excerpts from Deng Xiaoping's conversation with a US delegation, June 1, 1982. SMA: B1-9-798-22, p. 25.

94. E.g., see "China's view of the Sino-US relationship" (undated, after April 1980), NIO/EA memorandum. JCPL: NLC-4-29-3-19-3.

95. Cable from US Embassy in Beijing to Secretary of State, November 23, 1981. RRPL: Douglas Paal Files, China-US Meetings/Trips 5/78–9/82, binder 6 of 7.

96. Cable from Secretary of State to Air Force Two, May 9, 1982. RRPL: Douglas Paal Files, China-US Meetings/Trips 5/78–9/82, binder 7 of 7.

97. 邓小平年谱, 下, p. 748.

98. Ibid., p. 778.

99. Ibid., p. 829.

100. "Points from Hu Yaobang's report," *BBC Summary of World Broadcasts*, September 6, 1982.

101. For expositions of Deng's theory of the Soviet policy, alternatively called "southern policy" (nanxia zhengce) and "barbell policy" (yaling zhengce), see Conversation between Walter Mondale and Deng Xiaoping, August 28, 1979. RRPL: Douglas Paal Files, China-US Meetings/Trips 5/78–9/82, binder 3 of 7; excerpts from Conversation between Deng Xiaoping and Javier Pérez de Cuéllar, August 21, 1982. SMA: B1-9-798-30 and 国际形势报告 (November 1982), in the author's possession.

102. 邓小平年谱, 下, p. 851.

103. Excerpts of Conversation between Deng Xiaoping and Zia ul-Haq, October 19, 1982. SMA: B1-9-798-73, p. 74.

104. E.g., Excerpts of Conversation between Hu Yaobang and a French Communist Party delegation, November 1982. SMA: B1-9-798-69, p. 70.

105. Excerpts of Conversation between Peng Zhen and a West German delegation, October 11, 1982. SMA: B1-9-798-37, pp. 47–48.

106. 黄花, 亲历与见闻, p. 357.

107. Information über aktuelle Entwicklungstendenzen im außenpolitischen Vorgehen der VR China, May 27, 1982. BStU, MfS—Hauptverwaltung Aufklärung, No. 16, s. 166.

108. Memorandum from Richard Nixon to Ronald Reagan, undated (before September 23, 1982). RRPL: Douglas Paal Files, China-US Meetings/Trips 5/78–9/82, binder 7. Emphasis in the original.

109. Memorandum from William P. Clark to Ronald Reagan, undated (c. July 20, 1982). RRPL: David Laux Files, Taiwan Arms Sales, Vol. II, 1982, binder 7. See also Ezra Vogel, *Deng Xiaoping and the Transformation of China* (Cambridge, MA: Belknap Press of Harvard University Press, 2011), pp. 478–487.

110. Conversation between Javier Pérez de Cuéllar and Deng Xiaoping, August 21, 1982. United Nations Archive, New York, USA (hereafter, UNA): Series S-1033, Box 1, File 4.

111. On Deng's reluctance to receive US Ambassador Arthur Hummel see Cable from US Embassy in Beijing to the Secretary of State, July 11, 1982. RRPL: David Laux Files, Taiwan Arms Sales, Vol. II, 1982, binder 4.

112. "我为小平当特使-莒县籍原驻苏大使于洪亮访谈录,"日照市情网, February 28, 2005, http://www.rz.gov.cn/wtyl/rwrz/rzmr/20050228085719 .htm (accessed on July 22, 2012). Most of Yu Hongliang's "memoir" appeared to have been copied, word for word, from Qian Qichen's account, but not this point. On the meeting between Deng Xiaoping, Chen Yun, Li Xiannian, and others, see 李先念传编写组和鄂豫边区革命史编辑部, 李先念年谱, 第六卷, (北京: 中央文献出版社, 2011), p. 166.

113. This paragraph is based on several memoir sources, which contradict on a number of details. I tried to emphasize those points where all accounts agree. 钱其琛, 外交十记, pp. 8–9; "我为小平当特使-莒县籍原驻苏大使于洪亮访谈录"; 黄花, 亲历与见闻, p. 359; Mikhail Kapitsa, *Na Raznykh Parallelyakh*, p. 112.

114. 钱其琛, 外交十记, p. 10; 黄花, 亲历与见闻, pp. 359–360.

115. Minutes of a Politburo meeting, September 9, 1982. The Library of Congress, Washington, DC, USA: Volkogonov Collection (hereafter, VC): Reel 16, containers 23–24.
116. Anatolii Chernyaev, *Sovmestnyi Iskhod*, p. 503.
117. Mikhail Kapitsa, *Na Raznykh Parallelyakh*, p. 112.
118. 钱其琛, 外交十记, pp. 11–16.
119. 黄花, 亲历与见闻, pp. 359–360.
120. Letter from the Central Committee of the CC CPSU to the Italian Communist Party, undated (probably November 1982). Italian Communist Party Archive, Rome, Italy: file 8302, pp. 53–62.
121. Excerpts of Conversation between Deng Xiaoping and Zia ul-Haq, October 19, 1982. SMA: B1-9-798-73, p. 74.
122. Vystoupení ministra zahraničních věcí Svazu sovětských socialistických republik A. A. Gromyka, October 21, 1982, Archive of the Ministry of Foreign Affairs, Prague, Czech Republic (AMZV): C.j. 015.971/82, s. 13. Courtesy of the Parallel History Project.
123. 邓小平年谱, 下, p. 863.
124. Xinhua General News Service, November 14, 1982.
125. 黄花, 亲历与见闻, pp. 362–363.
126. "China urges Andropov to mend rift," United Press International, November 15, 1982.
127. 黄花, 亲历与见闻, pp. 364–365.
128. "Bush, Brezhnev's successor say countries ready for better ties," Associated Press, November 15, 1982.
129. Marc Rosenwasser, "New Soviet leader Yuri V. Andropov . . . ," Associated Press, November 15, 1982.
130. 黄花, 亲历与见闻, pp. 365–366.
131. Ibid., 368.
132. Minutes of a Politburo meeting, November 18, 1982. VC: Reel 16, containers 23–24.
133. Vystuplenie General'nogo Sekretarya Tsentral'nogo Komiteta Kommunisticheskoi Partii Sovetskogo Soyuza tov. Yu. V. Andropova, January 4, 1983. SAPMO-Barch: DC/20/I/3/1908, s. 54.
134. Ibid., s. 54–55.
135. Minutes of a Politburo meeting, May 31, 1983. *Cold War International History Project Bulletin*, Issue 4 (Fall 1993), p. 79.
136. For an account of the June 28 Moscow meeting, see Memorandum from P. Mladenov to the Politburo of the Bulgarian Communist Party, July 5, 1983. Provided to the author by Jordan Baev. There is also an East German account, which coincides in the main details: Bericht über das Moskauer Treffen der Repräsentaten der Parteien und Staaten der VRB, UVR, DDR, VRP, SRR, UdSSR und CSSR am 28 Juni 1983, SAPMO-BArch: DC/20/I/3/1950.
137. Memorandum of conversation between Ts. Gombosuren and Igor Rogachev, September 27, 1983. MFMA: fond 2, dans 1, kh/n 476, khuu 4. It is not clear whether the Chinese rejected the appeal or simply failed to respond. The document cited here does not in fact say that the appeal was sent to China (only North Korea is mentioned); however, this goes without saying.
138. "Nuclear missiles and relations with China," *BBC Summary of World Broadcasts*, August 29, 1983.
139. 邓小平年谱, 下, p. 936.

140. Boris Vereshchagin, *V Starom i Novom Kitae: Iz Vospominanii Diplomata* (Moscow: IDV-RAN, 1999), p. 195. Fedotov stresses that the initiative to invite Kapitsa came from the Chinese side—an important indication of the dynamic of Sino-Soviet relations. Vladimir Fedotov, *Polveka Vmeste s Kitaem: Vospominaniya, Zapisi, Razmyshleniya* (Moscow: Rosspen, 2005), pp. 471–472.

141. Projev ministra zahraničních věcí Svazu sovětských socialistických republik A. A. Gromyka, October 13, 1983. AMZV: C.j. 016.091/83, s. 13. Courtesy of the Parallel History Project.

142. Memorandum from Kenneth W. Dam to Ronald Reagan, October 6, 1983. RRPL: Edwin Meese Files, China-1983, CF0219.

143. Minutes of a National Security Council meeting, September 20, 1983. RRPL: David Laux Files, China-Foreign Relations-Reagan Trip, Minutes of NSC meetings (1).

144. Memorandum from David Aaron and Michel Oksenberg to Walter Mondale, August 18, 1979. RRPL: Douglas Paal Files, China-US Meetings/Trips 5/78–9/82, binder 3 of 7.

145. Conversation between Henry A. Kissinger and Deng Xiaoping, October 20, 1975. *Foreign Relations of the United States, 1969–1976*, Vol. XVIII, China, 1973–1976 (Washington, DC: United States Government Printing Office, 2007), p. 771.

146. Memorandum from Richard Nixon to Ronald Reagan, undated (before September 23, 1982). RRPL: Douglas Paal Files, China-US Meetings/Trips 5/78–9/82, binder 7 of 7.

147. Ibid.

148. Interne Haltung chinesischer Politiker zu den Konsultationen mit der Sowjetunion, Aktuelle Informationsubersicht, No. 43/82, November 1, 1982. BStU Zentralarchiv, MfS—Hauptverwaltung Aufklärung, No. 19, s. 81.

149. Information über aktuelle Entwicklungstendenzen im außenpolitischen Vorgehen der VR China, May 27, 1982. BStU, MfS—Hauptverwaltung Aufklärung, No. 16, s. 166.

150. Information über interne Ausinandersetzungen in der Führung der VR China zu den Beziehungen mit der UdSSR, December 8, 1982. BStU, MfS—Hauptverwaltung Aufklärung, No. 25, s. 283.

151. Information über aktuelle Entwicklungstendenzen der Außenpolitik der VR China, 1983. BStU, MfS—Hauptverwaltung Aufklärung, No. 25, s. 174.

152. 张宁，吴少京（主编，陈云年谱，下（北京：中央文献出版社，2000），pp. 322–323.

153. Ezra Vogel, *Deng Xiaoping and the Transformation of China*, pp. 561–562.

154. Ibid.

155. See, for instance, Chen Yun's letter to Zhao Ziyang, September 13, 1983. In 陈云年谱，下, pp. 337–338.

156. Broadly, on Chen Yun's conservative economic policies, see Ezra Vogel, *Deng Xiaoping and the Transformation of China*, 450–476. For more on the differences between Chen Yun and Zhao Ziyang, see Zhao Ziyang, *Prisoner of the State: The Secret Journal of Premier Zhao Ziyang* (New York: Simon and Schuster, 2009), pp. 91–110.

157. On the consequences of Reagan's June 9, 1983, decision, see Memorandum from William P. Clark to Secretary of State and others, August 30, 1983. RRPL: Douglas Paal Files, China-Tech. transfer, Vol. 1, binder 4 of 5. On Jesse Helms's opposition to these measures, see Letter from Jesse Helms to William

P. Clark, July 19, 1983. RRPL: Gaston Sigur Files, China-1983, Box 5, Folder 17 of 23.

158. 陈云年谱, 下, p. 339.

159. Zhao Ziyang, *Prisoner of the State*, p. 120.

160. Vladimir Fedotov, *Polveka Vmeste s Kitaem*, pp. 527–528. Fedotov, then in Beijing, wrote about "rumors" of disagreements between Deng and Chen Yun. There is as yet little documentary evidence to account for these disagreements in detail.

161. 邓小平年谱, 下, p. 831.

162. Ibid., p. 877.

163. Minutes of a Politburo meeting, May 31, 1983. *Cold War International History Project Bulletin*, issue 4 (Fall 1993), pp. 78–79.

164. 陈云年谱, 下, p. 340.

165. Vladimir Fedotov, *Polveka Vmeste s Kitaem*, p. 497.

166. Mikhail Kapitsa, *Na Raznykh Parallelyakh*, p. 115.

167. "Ivan Vasil'evich Arkhipov—general'nyi sovetnik po ekonomicheskim voprosam Politicheskogo Soveta Kitaya," September 15, 2009. http://russian.china. org.cn/international/archive/chinarussian60/2009-09/15/content_18530367. htm.

168. 李先念年谱, 第六卷, p. 228.

169. Mikhail Kapitsa, *Na Raznykh Parallelyakh*, p. 115; Boris Vereshchagin, *V Starom i Novom Kitae*, p. 199; Vladimir Fedotov, *Polveka Vmeste s Kitaem*, p. 500.

170. 李先念年谱, 第六卷, pp. 251–252.

171. Boris Vereshchagin, *V Starom i Novom Kitae*, 200; "Soviet vice-premier arrives in Beijing," Japan Economic Newswire, December 21, 1984.

172. "China, Soviet Union sign economic, scientific agreements," Xinhua General News Service, December 28, 1984.

173. "Chen Yun meets Arkhipov," Xinhua General News Service, December 24, 1984. 吴振兴, "陈云和阿尔希波夫的友谊," 世纪, Vol. 3 (2006).

174. 朱佳木, "追忆陈云同志与阿尔希波夫交往的一段往事," 当代中国史研究, Vol. 14, No. 3 (2007), p. 97. On Deng's instructions to Chen Yun, see Zhao Ziyang, *Prisoner of the State*, p. 120.

175. Boris Vereshchagin, *V Starom i Novom Kitae*, p. 202.

176. There are several accounts of Chen Yun's words to Arkhipov, which differ in minor details. I used the following: 朱佳木, "追忆陈云同志与阿尔希波夫交往的一段往事," p. 97; 吴振兴, "陈云和阿尔希波夫的友谊"and Information über Ausführungen chinesischer Spitzenfunktionäre gegenüber Gen. Archipow während seines Besuches in der VR China (21–29.12.1984), February 15, 1985. BStU, MfS—Hauptverwaltung Aufklärung, No. 35, s. 172–174.

177. Information über Ausführungen chinesischer Spitzenfunktionäre gegenüber Gen. Archipow während seines Besuches in der VR China (21–29.12.1984), February 15, 1985. BStU, MfS—Hauptverwaltung Aufklärung, No. 35, s. 172–174.

178. James Hershberg et al., "The Interkit story."

179. Jeff Bradley, "Chinese vice premier says at Arkhipov banquet much to be done," Associated Press, December 28, 1984.

180. Ibid.

181. On equidistance, see Excerpts from Conversation between Zhao Ziyang and a Japan-China friendship delegation, October 23, 1982. SMA: B1-9-798-61, p. 64.

On "bullying," which Deng Xiaoping associated with "lack of development," see Excerpts of Conversation between Deng Xiaoping and Brazilian Foreign Minister Ramiro Saraiva Guerreiro, March 15, 1982. SMA: B1-9-798-105, p. 106.

182. Conversation between Deng Xiaoping and Norodom Sihanouk, February 18, 1982. SMA: B1-9-798-5, p. 116.

183. E.g., see Boris Kulik, *Sovetsko-Kitaiskii Raskol: Prichiny i Posledstviya* (Moscow: IDV, 2000), pp. 592–596.

184. Conversation between Richard Nixon and Leonid Brezhnev, June 23, 1973, The National Archive, Nixon Presidential Materials Project, National Security Council Files, HAK Office Files, Country Files Europe-USSR, Box 75, Brezhnev visit memcons.

CHAPTER 2

1. Habomai is actually a group of islands, not an individual island.

2. As absurd as it appears in retrospect, this was the wording of a policy document adopted at a Soviet-organized meeting in Moscow in May 1973 (Interkit). The Central Archive of Modern Records, Warsaw, Poland (AAN): KC PZPR, LXXVI—1027; obtained and translated by Malgorzata K. Gnoinska.

3. "The fog-clearer," *Economist*, February 26, 1983, p. 15; George Ringwald, "Tokyo's waning faith in US military might," *Business Weekly*, December 31, 1979, p. 54.

4. See Nakasone Yasuhiro, *The Making of the New Japan: Reclaiming the Political Mainstream*, trans. by Lesley Connors (Surrey: Curzon, 1999).

5. See, for example, Julia Malone, "House 'buy America' mood focuses on auto imports," *Christian Science Monitor*, December 13, 1982, p. 3.

6. Memorandum from Richard Nixon to Ronald Reagan, undated (before September 23, 1982). RRPL: Douglas Paal Files, China-US Meetings/Trips 5/78–9/82, binder 7 of 7.

7. "Japan: Nakasone Pushes Defense Budget," *Defense and Foreign Affairs*, January-February 1983, p. i.

8. "Japan defense budget is less than US pushed for," *Christian Science Monitor*, December 31, 1982, p. 2.

9. "Prime Minister Yasuhiro Nakasone" (undated, January 1986), Canada-Japan; official visit of Prime Minister Nakasone, January 1986. Canadian National Archives, Ottawa, Canada: MF-16803, file No. 20-JPN-9, p. 65. I am grateful to James Hershberg for obtaining this file from Ottawa.

10. "Yas" was how Nakasone signed his name—in his own hand—on a letter to Reagan on January 19, 1982, before changing his name to "Yasu" for the media a few days later. The subtle change was lost on Reagan, who called Nakasone "Yas" in their correspondence as late as June 1983. For both letters, see RRPL: NSC, Executive Secretariat, Heads of State, Japan: Prime Minister Nakasone, folders 17 and 18.

11. Don Oberdorfer, "U.S.-Japanese alliance reaches a new stage; Nakasone's visit eases pressure and raises some expectations," *Washington Post*, January 23, 1983, p. A11.

12. Marianna Ohe, "Japan's prime minister meets California friends," United Press International, January 18, 1983.

13. "Because of expansion [we risk] being isolated," *Washington Post*, January 19, 1983, p. A12.

14. Don Oberdorfer, "How to make a Japanese brouhaha: The prime minister's words got hyped in translation," *Washington Post*, March 20, 1983. See also Kumiko

Torikai, *Voices of the Invisible Presence: Diplomatic Interpreters in Post–World War II Japan* (Amsterdam: John Benhamins, 2009) for a very detailed account of this episode.

15. Cited from Kumiko Torikai, *Voices of the Invisible Presence*, p. 132.

16. Nakasone Yasuhiro, *The Making of New Japan*, p. 221.

17. Don Oberdorfer, "U.S.-Japanese alliance reaches a new stage: Nakasone's visit eases pressure and raises some expectations," *Washington Post*, January 23, 1983, p. A11.

18. Don Oberdorfer, "Japanese statements on defense draw warning by Soviets," *Washington Post*, January 20, 1983, p. A1.

19. John Needman, "Japan protests Soviet threat, media attacks," United Press International, January 25, 1983.

20. "Telegram from the US Embassy in Moscow to the State Department," February 28, 1983. Digital National Security Archive (hereafter, DNSA): US-Japanese relations, 1977–1992, Document 01137.

21. Henry Scott Stokes, "Japan sharply protests Soviet proposal on shifting missiles to Asia," *New York Times*, Section A, p. 17. See also Kimura Hiroshi, *Distant Neighbors: Japanese-Russian Relations under Brezhnev and Andropov* (Armonk, NY: M. E. Sharpe, 2000), Vol. 1, pp. 248–249.

22. Cable from US Embassy in Tokyo to the US Department of State, April 27, 1983. DNSA: US-Japan relations, 1977–1992. Document No. 01152.

23. "Summary talker," undated (c. February 11, 1983), DNSA: US-Japan relations, 1977–1992, Document 01132; Cable from US Embassy in Tokyo to the Secretary of State, April 1, 1983. DNSA: US-Japan relations, 1977–1992, Document 01146.

24. Excerpts from Politburo meeting, September 9, 1982. VC: Reel 16, Container 23 through 24.

25. Ibid.

26. On Trudeau's comment, see Barry Schweid, "'Strong statements...strong feelings' at the summit," Associated Press, May 31, 1983. On Nakasone's agenda, see "Nakasone's call for global approach to INF talks endorsed at VA summit," *Jiji Press Ticker Service*, May 30, 1983.

27. Conversation between Margaret Thatcher and Nakasone Yasuhiro, May 28, 1983. Obtained by the author from the UK Cabinet Office in accordance with the Freedom of Information Act (request ref. 272–816).

28. "Fast footwork by Nakasone at photo time," *Washington Post*, May 31, 1983, p. A9.

29. Memorandum of conversation between W. Averell Harriman and Yurii Andropov, June 2, 1983. Library of Congress. W. Averell Harriman Papers: Box 1088, folder: trips USSR 1983. I am grateful to James Hershberg for obtaining this file.

30. Excerpts from Politburo meeting, May 31, 1983. RGANI: fond 89, opis 42, delo 53, listy 1–14.

31. Ibid.

32. Probably, this is what Ustinov wanted to say. His exact words were: "For example, we can only exit the Sea of Japan through the La Perouse Strait and, one could say, we have squeezed ourselves here." The meaning of this is not entirely clear, not least because the La Perouse Strait, which divides Sakhalin and Hokkaido, is a good distance from the nearest island of the Kurile chain.

33. See, for instance, Conversation between Javier Pérez de Cuéllar and Nakasone Yasuhiro, May 31, 1983. UNA: Series S-1033, Box 2, File 3.

34. One of the best accounts is David Hoffman, *The Dead Hand: The Untold Story of the Cold War Arms Race and Its Dangerous Legacy* (New York: Doubleday, 2009).

35. Andrew Rosenthal, "Admission came six days after plane downed," Associated Press, September 6, 1983.

36. Memorandum from Dmitrii Ustinov and Viktor Chebrikov to Yurii Andropov, December 1983. Translation provided at http://www.rescue007.org/docs/Top SecretMemos.pdf.

37. The Politburo meeting on September 2, 1983, which discussed the incident, is reproduced in part in Dmitrii Volkogonov, *Sem' Vozhdei: Gallereya Liderov SSSR*, Vol. 2 (Moskva: Novosti, 1995), pp. 168–171.

38. "Soviets still refuse to tell the truth," *Washington Post*, September 6, 1983, p. A6.

39. Edwin Q. White, "Citizens demonstrate, president mourns over downing of airliner," Associated Press, September 3, 1983.

40. Antonio Kamiya, "Soviet searchers find 'signs' of plane," United Press International, September 2, 1983; K. P. Hong, "Soviet plane buzzes about mourners at sea," Associated Press, September 6, 1983.

41. J. L. Battenfeld, "'Please answer me' victim's relative shouts," United Press International, September 4, 1983.

42. K. P. Hong, "Soviet plane buzzes about mourners at sea," Associated Press, September 6, 1983.

43. "Report that Soviets ignore requests to search waters," Associated Press, September 1, 1983.

44. Antonio Kamiya, "The Soviet Union today turned over . . . ," United Press International, September 26, 1983.

45. Clyde Haberman, "Seas off Japan yielding grim flight 7 debris," *New York Times*, September 12, 1983, p. A1.

46. There is a wide body of literature on the Able Archer 1983, and the nuclear war scare. I have relied mainly on the following accounts: David Hoffman, *The Dead Hand*; Christopher M. Andrew and Oleg Gordievsky, *Comrade Kryuchkov's Instructions: KGB Foreign Operations, 1975–1985* (Stanford: Stanford University Press, 1993), pp. 67–90; Benjamin B. Fischer, *A Cold War Conundrum: The 1983 Soviet War Scare* (History Staff Center for the Study of Intelligence, 1997), https://www.cia.gov/library/center-for-the-study-of-intelligence/csi-publications/books-and-monographs/a-cold-war-conundrum/source.htm#HEADING1-07; Nathan Jones, "Operation RYAN, Able Archer 83, and Miscalculation: The War Scare of 1983," paper presented at the International Graduate Student Conference on the Cold War, UCSB, Santa Barbara, April 2008; Beatrice Heuser, "The Soviet response to the euromissile crisis," in Leopoldo Nuti (ed.), *The Crisis of Détente in Europe: From Helsinki to Gorbachev, 1975–1985* (London: Routledge, 2009), pp. 137–149.

47. Interview, Izumikawa Yasuhiro, Sergey Radchenko and David Wolff, with Prime Minister Nakasone Yasuhiro, Tokyo, Japan, April 12, 2012.

48. P. Y. Chen, "US-Japan launch naval maneuvers," United Press International, September 25, 1983.

49. "Weinberger's visit to Japan: 'Latest instructions' on militarization," *BBC Summary of World Broadcasts*, September 27, 1983.

50. "Hu Yaobang concludes historic visit to Japan," Xinhua General News Service, November 30, 1983.

51. "Sino-Japanese talks: Relations with the USSR," *BBC Summary of World Broadcasts*, November 30, 1983.

52. "Other reports on Hu Yaobang's visit to Japan: PRC foreign minister on northern islands and relations with USSR," *BBC Summary of World Broadcasts*, November 28, 1983.

53. "Chinese party general secretary goes sight-seeing in Hokkaido," Xinhua General News Service, November 27, 1983. On Yokomichi's "pro-Chinese" orientation, the author's interview with Arai Nobuo, Sapporo, March 11, 2010.

54. Conversation between Yu. Rudnev and Nishimoto Yoshitsugu, September 9, 1983. Sakhalin State Archive (hereafter, GASO): fond 4, opis 136, delo 172, listy 91–92.

55. "Zhao Ziyang and Nakasone discuss international relations and co-operation," *BBC Summary of World Broadcasts*, March 26, 1984.

56. Conversation between Nakasone Yasuhiro and Deng Xiaoping, March 25, 1984. Kindly provided to the author by former Prime Minister Nakasone. "Nakasone, Deng share concern about Soviet arms build-up in Far East," Jiji Press Ticker Service, March 26, 1984.

57. "Sino-Japanese talks: 'Distorted image' of Soviet policy," *BBC Summary of World Broadcasts*, March 29, 1984.

58. Conversation between Mangalyn Dugersuren and Mikhail Kapitsa, March 29, 1984. MFMA: fond 2, dans 2, kh/n 489, khuu 58–59.

59. Ibid., khuu 61.

60. "Conversation between Mangalyn Dugersuren and Andrei Gromyko," March 28, 1984. MFMA: fond 2, dans 2, kh/n 489, khuu 49.

61. "Conversation between Mangalyn Dugersuren and Konstantin Rusakov," March 28, 1984. MFMA: fond 2, dans 2, kh/n 489, khuu 43.

62. "USSR-Japan: Increased Acrimony," c. March 1983, DNSA: US-Japan relations, 1977–1992. Document No. 01139.

63. Information memorandum from Stephen W. Bosworth to the US Secretary of State, George Shultz, October 3, 1983. DNSA: US-Japan relations, 1977–1992. Document No. 01177.

64. Cable from US Embassy in Tokyo to the Secretary of State, April 20, 1984. DNSA: US-Japan relations, 1977–1992. Document No. 01216.

65. Nakasone Yasuhiro, *The Making of the New Japan*, p. 208.

66. Cable from US Embassy in Tokyo to the Secretary of State, November 10, 1984. DNSA: US-Japan relations, 1977–1992. Document No. 01245.

67. Tsuyoshi Hasegawa, *The Northern Territories Dispute and Russo-Japanese Relations*, Vol. 2 (Berkeley, CA: University of California, International and Area Studies, 1998), p. 225. "Nakasone calls new leader 'bright, modern man,'" Japan Economic Newswire, March 12, 1985.

68. The author's interview with Togo Kazuhiko (by phone), August 11, 2012.

69. Tsuyoshi Hasegawa, *The Northern Territories Dispute and Russo-Japanese Relations*, Vol. 2, p. 225.

70. Interview, Izumikawa Yasuhiro, Sergey Radchenko and David Wolff, with Prime Minister Nakasone Yasuhiro, Tokyo, Japan, April 12, 2012.

71. Tsuyoshi Hasegawa, *The Northern Territories Dispute and Russo-Japanese Relations*, Vol. 2, p. 225–226. "Nakasone, Gorbachev agree to work for better ties," *Japan Economic Newswire*, March 15, 1985.

72. Gorbachev's talking points for a meeting with the Chairman of the JCP Presidium Fuwa Tetsuzo, March 15, 1985. Archive of the Gorbachev Foundation, Moscow, Russia (hereafter, AGF): fond 3, dokument 4495.

73. Information by Vadim Zagladin on the statements of the Deputy President of the LDP S. Nikaido and General Secretary of the Cabinet of Ministers K. Fujinami, October 1984. AGF: fond 3, dokument 15134.

74. Tsuyoshi Hasegawa, *The Northern Territories Dispute and Russo-Japanese Relations*, Vol. 2, pp. 224–226.

75. Ibid., p. 227.

76. Harubimi Kozawa, "Nikaido has few chances of winning top post," *Japan Economic Journal*, December 18, 1984, p. 6. Jim Abrams, "Emperor Hirohito sworn in …," Associated Press, October 31, 1984.

77. Information by Vadim Zagladin on the statements of the Deputy President of the LDP S. Nikaido and General Secretary of the Cabinet of Ministers K. Fujinami, October 1984. AGF: fond 3, dokument 15134.

78. Ibid. Also, "Levchenko identifies 8 Japanese as his agents," Jiji Press Ticker Service, April 13, 1983.

79. Conference of Secretaries of CC CPSU, March 15, 1985. VC: Reel 17, Container 25. Translated by Svetlana Savranskaya.

80. Mikhail Gorbachev, *Zhizn' i Reformy*, Vol. 2 (Moscow: Novosti, 1995), pp. 258–259. This particular passage coincides almost verbatim with unpublished excerpts from Anatolii Chernyaev's memoirs (provided to the author by David Wolff), which means that the passage was likely written by Chernyaev, not by Gorbachev. Still, it probably reflects Gorbachev's state of mind.

81. Anatolii Chernyaev, *Sovmestnyi Iskhod*, p. 619.

82. Tsuyoshi Hasegawa, *The Northern Territories Dispute and Russo-Japanese Relations*, Vol. 2, p. 234.

83. Ibid., p. 229. Gorbachev's speaking notes for a meeting with Ishibashi Masashi, September 16, 1985. AGF: fond 3, dokument 4786.

84. Tsuyoshi Hasegawa, *The Northern Territories Dispute and Russo-Japanese Relations*, Vol. 2, pp. 229, 570.

85. Ibid., pp. 230–231.

86. Ibid., p. 231.

87. Conversation between Mangalyn Dugersuren and Eduard Shevardnadze, September 13, 1985. MFMA: fond 2, dans 1, kh/n 504, khuu 3.

88. Mikhail Gorbachev's draft speech for the October 22, 1985, PCC meeting of the Warsaw Pact, October 1985. AGF: fond 5, dokument 20677. Gorbachev did not exactly follow this speech in his presentation at the PCC on October 22, omitting the question of Japan, perhaps because it was not deemed important enough. See Mikhail Gorbachev's speech to the Political Consultative Conference of the Warsaw Pact, October 22, 1985. Central State Archives (TsDA), Sofia; 1-B, 35, 1025-85, pp. 1–17. Courtesy of the Parallel History Project.

89. "Tokyo banquet turns frosty after Soviet-Japanese clash," *Globe and Mail*, January 16, 1986, p. A12.

90. Hoover Institution Archive, Stanford, CA (hereafter, HIA): Teimuraz Stepanov-Mamaladze Papers (hereafter, TSP), Diary No. 4, pp. 8–9.

91. "Shevardnadze turns tables on pressmen," Japan Economic Newswire, January 18, 1986.

92. "Industries pleased with outcome of Abe-Shevardnadze talks," Jiji Press Ticker Service, January 20, 1986; James Tyson, "Soviet Union aims at improving relations with Japan," Associated Press, January 10, 1986.

93. On Deng Xiaoping's 1978 trip to Japan, see Ezra Vogel, *Deng Xiaoping and the Transformation of China*, pp. 297–310.

94. HIA/TSP: Notepad 15.1.1986.

95. Tsuyoshi Hasegawa, *The Northern Territories Dispute and Russo-Japanese Relations*, Vol. 2, p. 236.

96. Conversation between Jambyn Batmunkh and Eduard Shevardnadze, January 24, 1986. MFMA: fond 2, dans 1, kh/n 504, khuu 116–117.

97. Tsuyoshi Hasegawa, *The Northern Territories Dispute and Russo-Japanese Relations*, Vol. 2, p. 237.

98. HIA/TSP: Notepad 15.1.1986.

99. "Communiqué on Shevardnadze's visit to Japan," *BBC Summary of World Broadcasts*, January 20, 1986.

100. Tsuyoshi Hasegawa, *The Northern Territories Dispute and Russo-Japanese Relations*, Vol. 2, p. 238.

101. Conversation between Sir Geoffrey Howe and Abe Shintaro, January 21, 1986. Obtained by the author from the UK Foreign and Commonwealth Office in accordance with the Freedom of Information Act (request ref. 0443-10).

102. HIA/TSP: Diary No. 4 (February 7, 1986), p. 66.

103. Record of a Politburo Meeting, January 30, 1986. VC: Reel 17.

104. It is not obvious what Shevardnadze meant by this "flexibility," and whether it included, for example, the possibility of a two-island solution. There is inconclusive evidence to the effect that Shevardnadze briefly supported the idea of returning to the 1956 Declaration but that he was rebuffed by Gromyko, with Gorbachev taking Gromyko's side. See Tsuyoshi Hasegawa, *The Northern Territories Dispute and Russo-Japanese Relations*, Vol. 2, p. 238; Mikhail Kapitsa, *Na Raznykh Parallelyakh*, p. 175.

105. Record of a Politburo Meeting, January 30, 1986. VC: Reel 17.

106. Ibid.

107. Conversation between Jambyn Batmunkh and Eduard Shevardnadze, January 24, 1986. MFMA: fond 2, dans 1, kh/n 504, khuu 117.

108. Record of a Politburo Meeting, January 30, 1986. VC: Reel 17.

109. Conversation between Jambyn Batmunkh and Eduard Shevardnadze, January 24, 1986. MFMA: fond 2, dans 1, kh/n 504, khuu 116.

110. Record of a Politburo Meeting, January 30, 1986. VC: Reel 17.

111. HIA/TSP: Diary No. 4 (February 7, 1986), pp. 66–67.

112. Conversation between Sir Geoffrey Howe and Abe Shintaro, January 21, 1986. Obtained by the author from the UK Foreign and Commonwealth Office in accordance with the Freedom of Information Act (request ref. 0443-10).

113. 東郷和彦, 北方領土交渉秘録—失われた五度の機会 (新潮社, 2007), pp. 148, 143.

114. Cited in Tsuyoshi Hasegawa, *The Northern Territories Dispute and Russo-Japanese Relations*, Vol. 2, p. 240.

115. Mikhail Kapitsa, *Na Raznykh Parallelyakh*, p. 175.

116. "All there is not to know about Abe," *Economist*, June 28, 1986, p. 46.

117. "Soviet request to locate Russian graves in Japan unveiled," Japan Economic Newswire, June 12, 1986.

118. "Abe vows Japan's efforts to seek return of the Northern Territories," Japan Economic Newswire, June 3, 1986.

119. Cable from the Hungarian Embassy in Tokyo to the Hungarian Foreign Ministry, June 27, 1986. MOL: XIX-J-1-j-Japán-002108/1-1986.

120. Mikhail Gorbachev, *Sobranie Sochinenii*, Vol. 4 (Moscow: Ves' Mir, 2008), p. 140.

121. Mikhail Gorbachev, *Otvechaya Na Vyzov Vremeni* (Moscow: Ves' Mir, 2010), p. 844.

122. Mikhail Gorbachev, *Sobranie Sochinenii*, Vol. 4, p. 326.

123. Early draft of the speech, from Vladimir Lukin's personal archive, was kindly provided to the author by Alexander Lukin. Comparison with Mikhail Gorbachev, *Sobranie Sochinenii*, Vol. 4, pp. 370–371 leaves no doubt as to Lukin's considerable contribution to the content of the speech.

124. "Foreign minister [*sic*] rebuts Gorbachev speech," Japan Economic Newswire, August 2, 1986.

125. Conversation between Georgii Komarovskii and Kujiraoka H., September 11, 1986. State Archive of the Russian Federation (hereafter, GARF): fond R-7523, opis 145, delo 4028, listy 184–185.

126. "Soviets undertake military exercise off Japan," Associated Press, August 14, 1986. "Largest US-Japanese military maneuver ends," Xinhua General Overseas News Service, November 1, 1986.

127. Interestingly, at about that time, IMEMO researchers Shaskol'skii and Ivanov circulated a report to the Central Committee and the Foreign Ministry, in which they claimed, among other things, that Japan posed no security threat whatsoever to the Soviet Union, so it was unnecessary to maintain a large military force on the Southern Kuriles, and it was likewise inadvisable to conduct large-scale naval exercises. But such opinions failed to make an impact for the time being. See Nikolai Shaskolskii and [?] Ivanov, "Perspektivy Politiki SSSR v Tikho-Okeanskom Regione i Faktor Voennoi Sily" (undated, but after July 1986), IMEMO RAN Archive.

128. Mikhail Gorbachev, *Sobranie Sochinenii*, Vol. 4, p. 497.

129. Cable from US Embassy in Tokyo to the Secretary of State, March 7, 1987. DNSA: US-Japan relations, 1977–1992. Document No. 01361.

130. Ibid.

131. Cable from the State Department to US Embassy in Tokyo, May 16, 1987. DNSA: US-Japan relations, 1977–1992. Document No. 01403.

132. Ibid.; Cable from the State Department to US Embassy in Tokyo, June 21, 1987. DNSA: US-Japan relations, 1977–1992. Document No. 01313.

133. Cable from US Embassy in Tokyo to the State Department, September 22, 1987. DNSA: US-Japan relations, 1977–1992. Document No. 01443.

134. David E. Sanger, "A bizarre deal diverts vital tools to Russians," *New York Times*, June 12, 1987, p. A1.

135. Including emulsion plant by Konishiroku that produced plates usable in satellite photography. Kumagai's letter to COCOM is reproduced in Cable from US Embassy in Paris to the State Department, September 22, 1987. DNSA: US-Japan relations, 1977–1992. Document No. 01444.

136. Cable from US Embassy in Tokyo to the State Department, September 22, 1987. DNSA: US-Japan relations, 1977–1992. Document No. 01443.

137. Cable from the State Department to US Embassy in Tokyo, March 26, 1987. DNSA: US-Japan relations, 1977–1992. Document No. 01372.

138. Cable from US Embassy in Tokyo to the State Department, April 7, 1987. DNSA: US-Japan relations, 1977–1992. Document No. 01381.

139. Cable from US Embassy in Tokyo to the State Department, March 31, 1987. DNSA: US-Japan relations, 1977–1992. Document No. 01377.

140. Communication from Stephen Bryen to the author, September 21, 2010.

141. Ibid.

142. Memorandum for Stephen Bryen, April 17, 1987. DNSA: US-Japan relations, 1977–1992. Document No. 01386.

143. "Trade shocks, protectionist fevers," *New York Times*, March 28, 1987, p. 26.
144. Cable from the State Department to US Embassy in Tokyo, May 7, 1987. DNSA: US-Japan relations, 1977–1992. Document No. 01397.
145. Cable from the State Department to US Embassy in Tokyo, May 7, 1987. DNSA: US-Japan relations, 1977–1992. Document No. 01396.
146. Cable from US Embassy in Tokyo to the State Department, May 11, 1987. DNSA: US-Japan relations, 1977–1992. Document No. 01402.
147. "Police arrest two Toshiba executives on charges linked to technology sales to Soviets," United Press International, May 27, 1987.
148. Cable from US Embassy in Tokyo to the State Department, July 2, 1987. DNSA: US-Japan relations, 1977–1992. Document No. 01420.
149. Monika Jain, "Japanese say resignations almost as drastic as hara-kiri," Associated Press, July 4, 1987.
150. "Lawmakers hammer Toshiba," United Press International, July 1, 1987.
151. Gerry Braun, "Hunter broadens attack on Toshiba: Congressman calls for permanent boycott of all company's products," *San Diego Tribune*, July 8, 1987, p. A6.
152. Cable from the State Department to US Embassy in Tokyo, July 9, 1987. DNSA: US-Japan relations, 1977–1992. Document No. 01422.
153. Daniel Sneider, "Japan disputes US view of damage done by Toshiba sale," *Christian Science Monitor*, July 20, 1987, p. 11.
154. Masahiko Ishizuka, "Stepping on tiger's tail," *Japan Economic Journal*, July 11, 1987, p. 6.
155. Cable from US Embassy in Tokyo to the State Department, August 8, 1987. DNSA: US-Japan relations, 1977–1992. Document No. 01433.
156. Cable from US Embassy in Tokyo to the State Department, August 28, 1987. DNSA: US-Japan relations, 1977–1992. Document No. 01435.
157. Letter from Allen Wendt (State Department) to Stephen Bryen (Defense Department), September 8, 1987. DNSA: US-Japan relations, 1977–1992. Document No. 01438.
158. Toshiba Corporation was disallowed from entering into contracts with the US government for three years. Barnaby J. Feder, "New trade law: Wide spectrum," *New York Times*, August 24, 1988, p. D1.
159. Cable from US Embassy in Tokyo to the State Department, March 7, 1987. DNSA: US-Japan relations, 1977–1992. Document No. 01361.
160. Bill Keller, "Soviet expels 2 Japanese as spies: Tokyo reacts by ousting Russian," *New York Times*, August 21, 1987; "Moscow, Tokyo expulsions strain relations: Nakasone plays down rift," *Facts on File World News Digest*, September 4, 1987.
161. Bill Keller, "Soviet expels 2 Japanese as spies: Tokyo reacts by ousting Russian," *New York Times*, August 21, 1987.
162. Memo from Anatolii Chernyaev to Mikhail Gorbachev, August 14, 1987. AGF: fond 2, dokument 890.
163. Extract from Politburo meeting, August 6, 1987. Anatolii Chernyaev et al. (eds.), *V Politbyuro TsK KPSS*, 217.
164. Cable from the Hungarian Embassy in Tokyo the Hungarian Foreign Ministry, August 12, 1987. MOL: XIX-J-1-j-Japán-00771/2-1987.
165. Ibid.

CHAPTER 3

This chapter partially draws on Sergey Radchenko, "India and the end of the Cold War," in Artemy Kalinovsky and Sergey Radchenko (eds.), *The End of the Cold War and the Third World: New Perspectives on Regional Conflict* (London: Routledge, 2011), pp. 173–191.

1. Letter from Anatolii Dryukov (Russian Ambassador in India) to Ruslan Khasbulatov, August 10, 1992. GARF: fond 10026, opis 5, delo 159, list 154.
2. O razvitii sotrudnichestva Rossii i Indii, August 1992. GARF: fond 10026, opis 5, delo 159, listy 125–134.
3. "Communist military transfers and economic aid to non-communist less developed countries, 1984," May 1, 1985, p. 89. CIA FOIA online reading room.
4. DCI, "Soviet Foreign Military Assistance," Interagency Intelligence Memorandum, May 1, 1987, p. 42. CIA FOIA online reading room.
5. Nixon's and Kissinger's derisive comments about Indira Gandhi are well known. See, for instance, Jussi M. Hanhimäki, *The Flawed Architect: Henry Kissinger and American Foreign Policy* (New York: Oxford University Press, 2004), p. 175.
6. Dennis Kux, *India and the United States: Estranged Democracies* (Washington, DC: National Defense University Press, 1993), pp. 347–362.
7. Cited in ibid., p. 383.
8. "The Hungarian Embassy in Ulan Bator to the Foreign Ministry: Indian Diplomat on Indo-Soviet relations," August 17, 1983. MOL: Küm, India tük 1983 60. doboz, 004736. Obtained and translated by László Borhi. Courtesy of the Parallel History Project.
9. "Report by the Hungarian Embassy in New Delhi—Confidential Soviet Information on India's Plan to Attack Pakistan's Nuclear Facilities," January 19, 1982. MOL: Küm, India tük 1982 60. doboz, 00599. Obtained and translated by László Borhi. Courtesy of the Parallel History Project.
10. Cable from US Embassy New Delhi to the Secretary of State, December 23, 1985. RRPL: Near East and South Asia Affairs Directorate, NSC records, India, 1985 (1).
11. Dennis Kux, *India and the United States*, pp. 363–374.
12. Douglas Brinkley (ed.), *The Reagan Diaries* (New York: HarperCollins, 2007), p. 97.
13. "Visit of Indian Prime Minister Indira Gandhi," Cable from Secretary of State to select US embassies overseas, August 1982. National Security Archive, Washington, DC.
14. Conversation between George Bush and Zia ul-Haq, May 16, 1984. RRPL: Near East and South Asia Affairs Directorate, NSC records, Pakistan, 1984 (2).
15. Dennis Kux, *India and the United States*, 391–398. See also "India: A Growing Role in Technology Transfer," paper of the Directorate of Intelligence, Central Intelligence Agency, June 7, 1985. RRPL: Near East and South Asia Affairs Directorate, NSC: records, India, 1985 (2).
16. "US policy towards India and Pakistan," National Security Decision Directive 147, October 11, 1984. Copy available at: http://www.fas.org/irp/offdocs/nsdd/nsdd-147.pdf.
17. Sotsialist orny elchin said naryn zuvulguunii tukhai, June 13, 1984. MFMA: fond 13, kh/n 197, khuu 85.
18. Dennis Kux, *India and the United States*, p. 397.
19. Peter J. S. Duncan, *The Soviet Union and India* (London: Routledge, 1989), 74. P. DCI, "Soviet Foreign Military Assistance," Interagency Intelligence Memorandum, May 1, 1987, p. 42. CIA FOIA online reading room.
20. Report by the Hungarian Embassy in New Delhi—Confidential Soviet Information on India's Plan to Attack Pakistan's Nuclear Facilities, January 19,

1982. MOL: Küm, India tük 1982 60. doboz, 00599. Obtained and translated by László Borhi. Courtesy of the Parallel History Project.

21. J. N. Dixit, *Across Borders: 50 Years of India's Foreign Policy* (New Delhi: Picus Books, 1998), pp. 156–157. According to Soviet information, the idea of going to war with Pakistan appealed in particular to the Indian military; the Foreign Ministry had a different opinion. Report by the Hungarian Embassy in New Delhi—Confidential Soviet Information on India's Plan to Attack Pakistan's Nuclear Facilities, January 19, 1982.

22. Christopher Andrew and Vasili Mitrokhin, *The World Was Going Our Way: the KGB and the Battle for the Third World* (London: Penguin Books, 2005), pp. 336–339.

23. Mikhail Gorbachev, *Sobranie Sochinenii*, Vol. 3 (Moscow: Ves' Mir, 2008), p. 463.

24. In fact, there are very strong indications that these "talking points" (called thus for convenience in this paper) were a part of Gorbachev's verbatim statement to Rajiv Gandhi; on later occasions, Gorbachev referred to specific phrases, which appear on the talking points, as to what he had actually told Gandhi.

25. Sovetsko-Indiiskie otnosheniya…, May 21, 1985. AGF: fond, 3, dokument 4766.

26. "The Hungarian Embassy in New Delhi to the Foreign Ministry: Soviet Appraisal of Gandhi's Visit to Moscow," June 18, 1985. MOL Küm, India tük 198567. doboz, 003197. Obtained and translated by László Borhi. Courtesy of the Parallel History Project.

27. Mikhail Gorbachev, *Sobranie Sochinenii*, Vol. 5 (Moscow: Ves' Mir, 2008), pp. 276–279.

28. Ibid.

29. For first Zaikov quote, see Anatolii Chernyaev et al., *V Politbyuro TsK KPSS*, pp. 114–116. For Gorbachev quote, see Mikhail Gorbachev, *Sobranie Sochinenii*, Vol. 5, p. 278.

30. Memorandum from K. Katushev to Mikhail Gorbachev, July 15, 1991. AGF: fond 2, dokument 8897. For comparison: Iraq 5.4 billion, Syria 3.3 billion, Libya 1.9 billion, North Korea 1.6 billion, Vietnam 2.2 billion, Cuba 3.9 billion.

31. Mikhail Gorbachev, *Sobranie Sochinenii*, Vol. 2 (Moscow: Ves' Mir, 2008), p. 278.

32. The Hungarian Embassy in New Delhi to the Foreign Ministry: The General Secretary of the Congress Party (Srikant Verma) on Indo-Soviet Relations, June 28, 1985. MOL: Küm, India tük 198567. doboz, 001411/2. Obtained and translated by László Borhi. Courtesy of the Parallel History Project.

33. Conversation between Ronald Reagan and Rajiv Gandhi, June 12, 1985. National Security Archive, Washington, DC.

34. Rajiv Gandhi's comments in the conversation with Reagan were heavily redacted from the available transcript. Reagan made the latter observation in his diary following his meeting with Gandhi. Douglas Brinkley (ed.), *The Reagan Diaries*, p. 334.

35. The Hungarian Embassy in New Delhi to the Foreign Ministry: The General Secretary of the Congress Party (Srikan Verma) on Indo-Soviet Relations, June 28, 1985.

36. Stuart Auerbach, "Gandhi hits US 'soft line' on Pakistan," *Washington Post*, June 5, 1985, p. A25; Stuart Auerbach, "India signs agreement for US jet engines," *Washington Post*, January 7, 1987, p. A16.

37. Concerned that US confidence in India had exceeded comfortable levels thanks to the enthusiasm of the State and the Commerce Departments, Reagan backed out from the XMP-24 sale, proposing instead to sell a weaker XMP-14 supercomputer. The Indians were not happy.

38. This idea was raised in "Military-to-military initiatives," talking paper for Caspar Weinberger's October 1986 trip to India (undated), RRPL: Shirin Tahir-Kheli Files, South Asia Weinberger Trip, October 7–18, 1986, China-India-Pakistan (2).

39. Letter from Richard Murphy to Michael Armacost, March 1, 1985. RRPL: Near East and South Asia Affairs Directorate, NSC records, India, 1985 (1).

40. Ibid.

41. Pavel Palazhchenko and Don Oberdorfer, *My Years with Gorbachev and Shevardnadze: The Memoir of a Soviet Interpreter* (University Park, PA: Pennsylvania State University Press, 1997), p. 59.

42. "Gorbachev-Gandhi joint news conference on 28th November," *BBC Summary of World Broadcasts*, Part 3, The Far East; C.1 Gorbachev in India; FE/8430/C1/1.

43. Conversation between Mikhail Gorbachev and Alvaro Cunhal, December 29, 1986, National Security Archive, Washington, DC, Russian and Eastern European Archive Document Database (hereafter, REEADD): Box 15. "Nichego sebe vopros!" in the original.

44. Mikhail Gorbachev, *Sobranie Sochinenii*, Vol. 5, 275.

45. Vitalii Vorotnikov, *A bylo eto tak: …iz dnevnika chlena Politbyuro TsK KPSS*, 2nd edition (Moscow: Kniga i Biznes, 2003), p. 136.

46. Mikhail Gorbachev, *Sobranie Sochinenii*, Vol. 5, p. 280.

47. Celestine Bohlen, "Gorbachev's Asian initiative receives cool response from India," *Washington Post*, November 29, 1986, p. A18.

48. Ibid.

49. Conversation between Mikhail Gorbachev and Alvaro Cunhal, December 29, 1986, REEADD: Box 15.

50. Mikhail Gorbachev, *Zhizn' i Reformy*, Vol. 2, p. 111.

51. Conversation between Mikhail Gorbachev and Alvaro Cunhal, December 29, 1986, REEADD: Box 15.

52. Mikhail Gorbachev, *Sobranie Sochinenii*, Vol. 5, p. 276.

53. Anatolii Chernyaev et al., *V Politbyuro TsK KPSS*, p. 116.

54. The acronym stands for European Economic Community, later the European Union.

55. Conversation between Mikhail Gorbachev and Rajiv Gandhi, November 18, 1988. Mikhail Gorbachev, *Otvechaya Na Vyzov Vremeni*, p. 869.

56. Anatolii Chernyaev et al., *V Politbyuro TsK KPSS*, p. 421.

57. Mikhail Gorbachev, *Sobranie Sochinenii*, Vol. 12 (Moscow: Ves' Mir, 2009), p. 484.

58. Mira Sinha Bhattacharjea, *China, the World and India* (Sàmskŗiti, 2001), p. 382. However, the Americans had been equally encouraging of Sino-Indian rapprochement, with the sole difference that it would ostensibly undermine Soviet-Indian relations.

59. 邓小平, 邓小平文选, 第三卷 (北京: 人民出版社, 1993), pp. 281–282.

60. Mikhail Gorbachev, *Sobranie Sochinenii*, Vol. 15 (Moscow: Ves' Mir, 2010), p. 258.

61. Ibid., pp. 262–264.

62. Cited in Karen Brutents, *Nesbyvsheesya: Neravnodushnye Zametki o Perestroike* (Moscow: Mezhdunarodnye Otnosheniya, 2005), p. 465.

63. Ibid., pp. 464–465.

64. See, for example, Waheguru Pal Singh Sidhu and Jing Dong Yuan, *China and India: Cooperation and Conflict* (Boulder, CO: Lynne Rienner Publishers, 2003), p. 81.

65. For extensive documentation of the Soviet decision to intervene in Afghanistan (which, alas, does not include the above-mentioned rationale), see *Cold War*

International History Project E-Dossier No. 4 (November 2001), http://wilsoncenter.org/sites/default/files/e-dossier_4.pdf.

66. Karen Brutents, *Nesbyvsheesya*, p. 141.
67. Anatolii Chernyaev, *Sovmestnyi Iskhod*, p. 635.
68. Conference of Secretaries of the CC CPSU, Held in the Office of CC CPSU General Secretary Comrade M.S. Gorbachev, March 15, 1985. National Security Archive.
69. Mikhail Gorbachev, *Otvechaya Na Vyzovy Vremeni*, pp. 605–606.
70. Conversation between Mikhail Gorbachev and Alessandro Natta, March 29, 1988. REEADD: Box 15.
71. Anatolii Chernyaev, *Sovmestnyi Iskhod*, p. 617.
72. On national reconciliation, see Artemy M. Kalinovsky, *A Long Goodbye: The Soviet Withdrawal from Afghanistan* (Cambridge, MA: Harvard University Press, 2011), pp. 93–121.
73. Anatolii Chernyaev et al., *V Politbyuro TsK KPSS*, p. 136.
74. Anatolii Chernyaev, *Sovmestnyi Iskhod*, p. 649.
75. Conversation between Mikhail Gorbachev and Mohammad Najibullah, July 20, 1987. REEADD: Box 15.
76. Ibid.
77. Mikhail Gorbachev, *Otvechaya Na Vyzov Vremeni*, pp. 615–618.
78. HIA/TSP: Diary 8, p. 339.
79. Artemy Kalinovsky, *A Long Goodbye*, pp. 159–162.
80. Conversation between Mikhail Gorbachev and Mohammad Najibullah, July 20, 1987. REEADD: Box 15.
81. Anatolii Chernyaev's diary, June 19, 1988. National Security Archive. Translated by Svetlana Savranskaya.
82. Conversation between George Bush and Zia ul-Haq, May 16, 1984. RRPL: Near East and South Asia Affairs Directorate, NSC records, Pakistan, 1984 (2).
83. On Zia's "unhappy" exit, see "Conference of Secretaries of the CC CPSU, Held in the Office of CC CPSU General Secretary Comrade M.S. Gorbachev," March 15, 1985. National Security Archive; also, Letter from Ronald Reagan to Mikhail Gorbachev, April 30, 1985. National Security Archive.
84. HIA/TSP: Diary 6, p. 295.
85. Artemy Kalinovsky, *A Long Goodbye*, p. 134.
86. Ibid.
87. Conversation between Yurii Fadeev and Li Fenglin, June 22, 1988. Archive of Foreign Policy of the Russian Federation, Moscow, Russia (hereafter, AVPRF): fond 100, opis 75, delo 3, list 20.
88. Aleksandr Yakovlev (ed.), *Aleksandr Yakovlev. Perestroika: 1985–1991* (Moscow: Mezhdunarodnyi Fond Demokratiya, 2008), p. 180.
89. Conversation between Mikhail Gorbachev and Mohammad Najibullah, June 13, 1988. REEADD: Box 15.
90. Mikhail Gorbachev, *Otvechaya Na Vyzov Vremeni*, pp. 642–644.
91. HIA/TSP: Diary 8, pp. 257–261.
92. Brutents, *Nesbyvsheesya*, p. 145.
93. HIA/TSP: Diary 8, pp. 264–265.
94. Karen Brutents, *Nesbyvsheesya*, p. 144.
95. Otnoshenie Irana k uregulirovaniyu problem Afganistana, undated. GARF: fond 10026, opis 4, delo 2868, listy 1-6.
96. Mikhail Gorbachev, *Otvechaya Na Vyzov Vremeni*, pp. 703–704. This meeting took place on January 4, 1989.

97. HIA/TSP: Diary 8, pp. 328–330.

98. Ibid.

99. Mikhail Gorbachev, *Sobranie Sochinenii*, Vol. 15, pp. 513–514. Also, Svetlana Savranskaya, "Gorbachev and the Third World" in Artemy M. Kalinovsky and Sergey Radchenko (eds.), *The End of the Cold War and the Third World: New Perspectives on Regional Conflict* (London: Routledge, 2011), p. 32.

100. Vypiska iz protokola No. 146 zasedaniya Politbyuro TsK KPSS, January 24, 1989. REEADD: Box 16.

101. HIA/TSP: Diary 8, pp. 196–197.

102. Mikhail Gorbachev, *Otvechaya Na Vyzov Vremeni*, p. 653.

103. HIA/TSP: Diary 8, pp. 364–365.

104. For a useful overview, see John Gooneratne, *A Decade of Confrontation: Sri Lanka and India in the 1980s* (Pannipitiya: Stamford Lake, 2000), and Alan J. Bullion, *India, Sri Lanka and the Tamil Crisis, 1976–1994: An International Perspective* (London: Pinter, 1995).

105. Mikhail Gorbachev, *Sobranie Sochinenii*, Vol. 4 (Moscow: Ves' Mir, 2008), pp. 167–168.

106. "Mr. Gandhi, on four fronts," *New York Times*, June 7, 1987, p. 28.

107. Conversation between Mikhail Gorbachev and Rajiv Gandhi, July 3, 1987, REEADD: Box 15.

108. Conversation between Rajiv Gandhi and Jambyn Batmunkh, March 7, 1989. MFMA: fond 13, kh/n 219, khuu 48.

109. Mikhail Gorbachev, *Sobranie Sochinenii*, Vol. 4, pp. 169–170.

110. Anatolii Chernyaev et al. (eds.), *V Politbyuro TsK KPSS*, pp. 114–116.

111. Sanjoy Hazarika, "India puts military on full alert, citing a Pakistani troop buildup," *New York Times*, January 24, 1987, p. 4; Gordon Barthos, "India, Pakistan troop buildup climaxes months of hostility," *Toronto Star*, January 27, 1987, p. A13.

112. Conversation between Mikhail Gorbachev and Rajiv Gandhi, July 3, 1987. REEADD: Box 15.

113. Memorandum from Anatolii Chernyaev to Mikhail Gorbachev, January 24, 1987. AGF: fond 2, dokument 503.

114. Anatolii Chernyaev et al. (eds.), *V Politbyuro TsK KPSS*, p. 138.

115. Ibid., 152.

116. Conversation between Mikhail Gorbachev and Rajiv Gandhi, July 2–3, 1987. REEADD: Box 15.

117. J. N. Dixit, *Across Borders*, p. 199.

118. Conversation between Rajiv Gandhi and Jambyn Batmunkh, March 7, 1989. MFMA: fond 13, kh/n 219, khuu 48.

119. Conversation between Mikhail Gorbachev and Rajiv Gandhi, July 15, 1989. REEADD: Box 16.

120. Conversation between D. Chuluundorj and Rajiv Gandhi, December 19, 1989. MFMA: fond 13, kh/n 223, khuu 48.

121. Conversation between Mikhail Gorbachev and Rajiv Gandhi, July 3, 1987. REEADD: Box 15.

122. Conversation between Mikhail Gorbachev and Najibullah, July 20, 1987. REEADD: Box 15.

123. Conversation between Mikhail Gorbachev and K. Ch. Pant, February 11, 1988. REEADD: Box 15.

124. Conversation between Rajiv Gandhi and Jambyn Batmunkh, March 7, 1989, MFMA: fond 13, kh/n 219, khuu 48.
125. Anatolii Chernyaev et al. (eds.), *V Politbyuro TsK KPSS*, p. 422.
126. Ibid., p. 421.
127. Ibid., pp. 420–422.
128. Spravka k voprosu o peredache v arendu Indii sovetskoi atomnoi podvodnoi lodki, undated (November 1986), HIA, Kataev papers: 13–14.
129. Ibid.
130. Ibid.
131. T. N. Kaul's report on his conversation with Nikolai Ryzhkov, November 11, 1987. Nehru Memorial Museum and Library (New Delhi): Papers of T. N. Kaul, Subject File (part ii), File No. 10, 1987 (As Ambassador to the USSR, 1986–89), p. 379.
132. Ibid., p. 380.
133. Norman Black, "Nuclear-powered sub now heading toward home port in India," Associated Press, January 22, 1988; a detailed account of India's lease of the nuclear submarine *Chakra* can be found in G. V. C. Naidu, *Indian Navy and Southeast Asia* (New Delhi: Knowledge World, 2000), pp. 54–57.
134. Mark Kramer, "The decline in Soviet arms transfers to the Third World, 1986–1991," in Artemy M. Kalinovsky and Sergey Radchenko (eds.), *The End of the Cold War and the Third World*, p. 69.
135. Ob otvete na poslanie R. Gandi t. Gorbachevu M. S., November 1989. RGANI: fond 89, opis 10, delo 47, list 2.
136. Memorandum from Anatolii Chernyaev and Georgii Shakhnazarov to Mikhail Gorbachev, September 30, 1988, AGF, fond 2, dokument 1547, listy 1–3. This document is also reprinted by Anatolii Chernyaev, *Shest' let s Gorbachevym: Po dnevnikovym zapisyam* (Moscow: Progress, 1993), pp. 259–260.
137. O vizite na Kubu, December 13, 1988. AGF: fond 2, dokument 1592, list 1. This document is also reprinted by Chernyaev, *Shest' let s Gorbachevym*, pp. 196–197.
138. Tovarishchu Gorbachevu, March 25, 1989. HIA, Kataev papers: 13–14.
139. Ob otvete na poslanie R. Gandhi t. Gorbachevu M. S., November 1989. RGANI: fond 89, opis 10, delo 47, list 2.
140. Letter from Rajiv Gandhi to Mikhail Gorbachev, October 27, 1989, HIA, Kataev papers: 13–14.
141. Ob otvete na poslanie R. Gandi t. Gorbachevu M. S., RGANI: fond 89, opis 10, delo 47, list 3.
142. Ibid., list 5.
143. Anatolii Chernyaev, *Sovmestnyi Iskhod*, p. 865.
144. S. Lunev, "Rossiisko-Indiiskie otnosheniya v 90-e gody," in A. Kutsenkov and F. Yurlov (eds.), *Rossiya i Indiya na Poroge Tret'ego Tysyacheletiya* (Moscow: IV RAN, 1998), pp. 30–32.
145. Cited in Karen Brutents, *Nesbyvsheesya*, p. 464.
146. Andrei Grachev, *Dal'she Bez Menya* (Moscow: Progress-Kul'tura, 1994), p. 153.
147. Anatolii Chernyaev, *Sovmestnyi Iskhod*, p. 1021.
148. Gorbachev Foundation, *Kak Delalas' Politika Perestroiki, 1985–1991* (internal publication), p. 88.
149. Andrei Grachev, *Dal'she Bez Menya*, p. 153.

CHAPTER 4

1. He did so as early as his conversation with Nakasone Yasuhiro on March 25, 1984. Kindly provided to the author by former Prime Minister Nakasone.

2. Philip Short, *Pol Pot: Anatomy of a Nightmare* (New York: Henry Holt, 2005).

3. Stephen J. Morris, *Why Vietnam Invaded Cambodia: Political Culture and the Causes of War* (Stanford, CA: Stanford University Press, 1999), p. 214.

4. Ibid., p. 215.

5. Conversation between Jambyn Batmunkh and Pham Van Dong, December 1–2, 1979. Mongolian Government Archive, Ulaanbaatar, Mongolia: fond 1, dans 28, kh/n 19, khuu 21-55.

6. Lee Kuan-Yew, *From Third World to First: the Singapore Story, 1965–2000* (New York: HarperCollins Publishers, 2000), 601. The Chinese took only minor precautions at the northern border ahead of the strike against Vietnam. See National Security Council Meeting, February 16, 1979. JCPL: NCL-132-56-9-1-3.

7. Vladimir Sumarokov, "Kak v 1979 godu SSSR ostanovil napadenie Kitaya na V'etnam (istoricheskie uroki)," January 2007. http://www.centrasia.ru/newsA.php4?st=1167745980. See also Patrick Tyler, *A Great Wall*, p. 281.

8. William Burr (ed.), *The Kissinger Transcripts: The Top-Secret Talks with Beijing and Moscow* (New York: The New Press, 1999), p. 403.

9. Conversation between Zbigniew Brzezinski and Deng Xiaoping, May 21, 1978. RPPL: Paal, Douglas Files, China-US Meetings/Trips 5/78–9/82, binder 1 of 7.

10. Conversation between George Bush and Deng Xiaoping, May 8, 1982. RPPL: Paal, Douglas Files, China-US Meetings/Trips 5/78–9/82, binder 7 of 7.

11. 邓小平年谱, 下, p. 936.

12. Minutes of a Politburo meeting, May 31, 1983, RGANI: fond 89, opis 42, delo 53, listy 7-8.

13. "Deng Xiaoping on Sino-Soviet relations and Soviet bases in Vietnam," *BBC Summary of World Broadcasts*, April 19, 1985. Deng restated this thesis on the following day in a conversation with former British Prime Minister Edward Heath; see 邓小平年谱, 下, p. 1041.

14. Here I owe an intellectual debt to Niu Jun. See 牛军, "'回归亚洲'—中苏关系正常化与中国印度支那政策的演变(1979–1989)," 国际政治研究, 2011/2.

15. Vadim Medvedev, *Raspad: Kak on Nazreval v Mirovoi Sisteme Sotsializma* (Moscow: Mezhdunarodnye Otnosheniya, 1994), p. 289.

16. Balazs Szalontai, "The Diplomacy of economic reform in Vietnam: The genesis of Doi Moi, 1986–1989," *Asia Research*, Vol. 15, No. 2 (2008), p. 242.

17. HIA/TSP: Diary No. 5, p. 300.

18. Balazs Szalontai, "The diplomacy of economic reform in Vietnam," pp. 203–204.

19. "International relations: USSR—Hoa Binh Hydroelectric Station," *BBC Summary of World Broadcasts*, November 19, 1980.

20. "USSR—aid and trade," *BBC Summary of World Broadcasts*, July 16, 1980.

21. Memorandum from K. Katushev to Mikhail Gorbachev, July 15, 1991. AGF: fond 2, dokument 8997. Most of Vietnam's Soviet era debt was written off in 2000.

22. Anatolii Chernyaev et al. (eds.), *V Politbyuro TsK KPSS*, p. 59.

23. Conversation between Mikhail Gorbachev and Mengistu Haile Mariam, April 17, 1987. REEADD: Box 15.

24. Anatolii Chernyaev et al. (eds.), *V Politbyuro TsK KPSS*, pp. 161–162.

25. Ibid., pp. 299–305.

26. Gorbachev's comments at a Politburo meeting, June 26, 1986. Mikhail Gorbachev, *Sobranie Sochinenii*, Vol. 4, p. 249.
27. Gorbachev's Vladivostok speech, July 28, 1986. Ibid., p. 375.
28. Vadim Medvedev, *Raspad*, p. 307.
29. Ibid.
30. Memorandum from Anatolii Chernyaev to Mikhail Gorbachev, September 9, 1988. AGF: Fond 2, dokument 1390.
31. Mikhail Gorbachev's speech in Krasnoyarsk, September 16, 1988. Mikhail Gorbachev, *Sobranie Sochinenii*, Vol. 12, p. 68. Gorbachev's rationale for this exchange is in Conversation between Mikhail Gorbachev and Vo Chi Cong, September 21, 1988. Ibid., p. 79.
32. Ibid.
33. Memorandum from K. Katushev to Mikhail Gorbachev, July 15, 1991. AGF: fond 2, dokument 8997.
34. Balazs Szalontai, "The Diplomacy of Economic Reform in Vietnam: The Genesis of Doi Moi, 1986–1989," p. 242.
35. Conversation between Mikhail Gorbachev and Nguyen Van Linh, May 3, 1989. AGF: fond 5, dokument 20701.
36. Vadim Medvedev, *Raspad*, p. 305.
37. Balazs Szalontai, "The Diplomacy of Economic Reform in Vietnam: The Genesis of Doi Moi, 1986–1989," p. 242.
38. Conversation between Mikhail Gorbachev and Nguyen Van Linh, May 3, 1989. AGF: fond 5, dokument 20701.
39. Mikhail Gorbachev, *Zhizn' i Reformy*, Vol. 2, p. 462.
40. Balazs Szalontai, "From battlefield into marketplace: The end of the Cold War in Indochina, 1985–1989," in Artemy M. Kalinovsky and Sergey Radchenko (eds.), *The End of the Cold War and the Third World: New Perspectives on Regional Conflict*, pp. 155–169.
41. Balazs Szalontai, "The diplomacy of economic reform in Vietnam: The genesis of Doi Moi, 1986–1989," pp. 241–242.
42. HIA/TSP: Diary No. 5, p. 276.
43. Mikhail Gorbachev's comments at a Politburo meeting, July 30, 1987. Mikhail Gorbachev, *Otvechaya Na Vyzov Vremeni*, p. 843.
44. Deng Xiaoping's comments to Mike Wallace, September 2, 1986, 邓小平文选, 第三卷, p. 167.
45. Conversation between Javier Pérez de Cuéllar and Wu Xueqian, September 18, 1986. UNA: Series S-1033, Box 5, File 5. Vladimir Fedotov, *Polveka Vmeste s Kitaem*, p. 593.
46. Record of conversation between Mikhail Gorbachev and Kaysone Phomvihane, September 27, 1988. AGF: fond 5, dokument 20692.
47. Mikhail Gorbachev's comments at a Politburo meeting, August 6, 1986. Mikhail Gorbachev, *Otvechaya Na Vyzov Vremeni*, p. 844.
48. Geoffrey Murray, "Chinese and Soviets, eager for stronger ties, court Southeast Asia," *Christian Science Monitor*, October 24, 1986, p. 11.
49. Conversation between Javier Pérez de Cuéllar and Mochtar Kusumaatmadja, October 1, 1986. UNA: Series S-1033, Box 5, File 6.
50. Record of conversation between Ronald Reagan and Mikhail Gorbachev, November 19, 1985. The National Security Archive.
51. Record of conversation between Mikhail Gorbachev and Jacques Chirac, May 15, 1987. The National Security Archive.

52. HIA/TSP: Diary No. 5, p. 287.
53. Ibid., p. 297.
54. Ibid., p. 302.
55. Record of conversation between Mikhail Gorbachev and Jacques Chirac, May 15, 1987. The National Security Archive.
56. See discussion to this effect in Balazs Szalontai, "The diplomacy of economic reform in Vietnam: The genesis of Doi Moi, 1986–1989."
57. Ibid.
58. HIA/TSP: Diary No. 5, p. 305.
59. Memorandum of conversation between Richard Childress and Nguyen Co Thach, October 17, 1984. Reproduced in Declassified Documents Reference System (Farmington Hills, MI: Gale, 2008) (hereafter, DDRS).
60. Conversation between Javier Pérez de Cuéllar and Mochtar Kusumaatmadja, March 27, 1985. UNA: Series S-1033, Box 4, File 3, Acc 92/154.
61. Javier Pérez de Cuéllar, *Pilgrimage for Peace: A Secretary General's Memoir* (New York, NY: St. Martin's Press, 1997), p. 451.
62. "Sihanouk rejects meeting with 'foreign minister' of Phnom Penh regime," Xinhua General Overseas News Service, January 7, 1985.
63. Conversation between Vadim Zagladin and Nguyen Co Thach, August 1985. AGF: fond 3, dokument 4776. On subsequent Vietnamese attempts to arrange a meeting between Sihanouk and/or Son Sann with Phnom Penh representatives, see Conversation between Javier Pérez de Cuéllar and Ling Qing, February 25, 1985. UNA: Series S-1033, Box 4, File 2, Acc 92/154.
64. "Vietnam seeking Kampuchean talks, say rebels," *Sydney Morning Herald*, November 28, 1986, p. 17.
65. "Vietnam rejects Western 'fabrication' on Cambodian talks stance," *BBC Summary of World Broadcasts*, January 24, 1987.
66. Vadim Medvedev, *Raspad*, p. 312.
67. Ibid., pp. 313–314.
68. Ibid., p. 314.
69. "Gorbachev receives Heng Samrin," BBC Summary of World Broadcasts, July 31, 1987, SU/8634/A3/1; "PRK: Only Pol Pot and nearest aides not welcome at talks on Cambodia," *BBC Summary of World Broadcasts*, August 15, 1987, FE/8647/A3/1; "PRK issues 'policy on national reconciliation,'" BBC Summary of World Broadcasts, August 28, 1987, FE/8658/A3/1.
70. "Vietnam seeking Kampuchean talks, say rebels," *Sydney Morning Herald*, November 28, 1986, p. 17.
71. Record of conversation between Javier Pérez de Cuéllar and Deng Xiaoping, May 11, 1987. Yale University Library (hereafter, YUL): Javier Pérez de Cuéllar Papers (hereafter, JPCP).
72. O podkhodakh stran Indokitaya i Kitaya k Kampuchiiskoi probleme, spravka upravleniya sotsialisticheskikh stran Azii MID SSSR, May 4, 1988. GARF: fond 10026, opis 4, delo 2802, list 168.
73. Record of conversation between Javier Pérez de Cuéllar and Deng Xiaoping, May 11, 1987. YUL/JPCP.
74. Debra Weiner, "Prince Norodom Sihanouk," *Playboy*, May 1, 1987, p. 61.
75. Seth Mydans, "Sihanouk quits Cambodian resistance for a year," *New York Times*, Section 1; Part 1, Page 14, Column 1.
76. Conversation between Javier Pérez de Cuéllar and Ali Alatas, August 28, 1987. UNA: Series S-1033, Box 6, File 7.

77. Cable from the US Embassy in Beijing to the Secretary of State, June 17, 1987. RRPL: Douglas Paal Files, Box 91321, China-Military January-June 1987, April-July 1987.

78. Conversation between Javier Pérez de Cuéllar and K. Natwar Singh, October 7, 1987. UNA: Series S-1033, Box 7, File 1.

79. "PRK ready to offer Sihanouk 'High Position' in the leading state organ," *BBC Summary of World Broadcasts*, October 9, 1987, Part 3, The Far East; A. International Affairs; 3 Far Eastern Relations; FE/8694/A3/1.

80. Barbara Crossette, "Soviet spur seen in Cambodia talks," *New York Times*, November 27, 1987, Section A; Page 5, Column 1.

81. HIA/TSP: Notepad 03.02.1989, p. 3.

82. Conversation between Javier Pérez de Cuéllar and Leopold Gratz, September 28, 1987. UNA: Series S-1033, Box 6, File 7.

83. "Vietnam plans withdrawal of troops from Cambodia," *Globe and Mail*, April 15, 1985.

84. Peter Eng, "Vietnam pledges withdrawal from Cambodia by 1990," Associated Press, August 16, 1985.

85. "China: SRV troops withdrawal 'another falsehood that has greatly disappointed the whole world,'" *BBC Summary of World Broadcasts*, December 5, 1987, FE/0018/A3/1.

86. Nick Cumming-Bruce, "Vietnam pulls back as talks loom," *Guardian*, January 13, 1988.

87. "United States revises estimate of Vietnamese occupation troops," Associated Press, May 5, 1988.

88. M. Baker, "Vietnam says it will double troop withdrawal from Cambodia," *Herald*, March 11, 1988.

89. Jasper Becker, "Hanoi retreat opens door on Sino-Soviet summit: China thrust into awkward position as Vietnam announces withdrawal," *Guardian*, May 26, 1988.

90. Record of conversation between George Shultz and Eduard Shevardnadze, March 23, 1988. DDRS.

91. Record of conversation between Ronald Reagan and Mikhail Gorbachev, June 1, 1988. National Security Archive. On the other hand, we may not yet have all the records. Igor Rogachev mentioned at a press conference in June 1988 that "the USSR and USA had discussed Cambodia 'in quite a lot of detail' at the Moscow summit." He may have referred to the experts' meeting, not to the meetings of the top leaders. "USSR deputy foreign minister on Cambodia and Sino-Soviet relations," *BBC Summary of World Broadcasts*, June 9, 1988, FE/0173/i.

92. 李鹏, 和平, 发展, 合作: 李鹏外事日记 (北京: 新华出版社, 2008), p. 27, for China; AGF: fond 5, dokument 20696 for the USSR.

93. Note pour la presse (Summary of discussions between Norodom Sihanouk and Hun Sen), December 2, 1987. Archives Nationales, Paris, France: 665 AP 342.

94. Lettre de Pham Van Dong à Norodom Sihanouk, January 6, 1988. Archives Nationales, Paris, France: 665 AP 342.

95. "Sihanouk's representative issues communiqué on talks with Hun Sen," *BBC Summary of World Broadcasts*, February 1, 1988, FE/0063/A3/1; Amitav Achrya, Pierre Lizée, and Soprong Peou (eds.), *Cambodia—The 1989 Paris Peace Conference: Background Analysis and Documents* (Milwood, NY: Kraus International Publications, 1991), p. xxxix.

96. O podkhodakh stran Indokitaya i Kitaya, May 4, 1988. GARF: fond 10026, opis 4, delo 2802, listy 169, 175.

97. As recounted in Conversation between Javier Pérez de Cuéllar and Qian Qichen, June 3, 1988. UNA: Series S-1033, Box 7, File 5.

98. Summary of a conversation between US and Soviet officials regarding: Soviet occupation of Afghanistan; the Gulf war; Arab-Israeli peace process; US-Soviet relations, February 21, 1988. DDRS.

99. Conversation between Javier Pérez de Cuéllar and Ali Alatas, August 28, 1987. UNA: Series S-1033, Box 6, File 7.

100. Conversation between Javier Pérez de Cuéllar and Mochtar Kusumaatmadja, October 2, 1987. UNA: Series S-1033, Box 7, File 1.

101. "Sihanouk, in unexplained move, resigns from resistance coalition," Associated Press, July 11, 1988.

102. "Cambodian 'cocktail party' goes on even without Sihanouk," United Press International, July 18, 1988.

103. Don Oberdorfer, "China offers asylum for Pol Pot, aides: Plan might facilitate Cambodia settlement," *Washington Post*, July 18, 1988, p. A1.

104. "Beijing, Moscow to meet on Kampuchea," *Herald*, July 22, 1990.

105. Sotsialist ornuudyn gadaad bodlogyn asuudal erkhelsen zuvlukh naryn eeljit uulzalt, November 10, 1987. MFMA: fond 5, dans 2, kh/n 575, khuu 105.

106. Sotsialist ornuudyn gadaad bodlogyn asuudal erkhelsen zuvlukh naryn eeljit uulzalt, January 4, 1988. MFMA: fond 5, dans 2, kh/n 581, khuu 1.

107. Keith B. Richburg, "Vietnam making overtures to China; Turnabout parallels Gorbachev's effort to improve ties with Beijing," *Washington Post*, July 15, 1988, p. A15. Communication from Keith B. Richburg to the author, August 27, 2008.

108. 李鹏, 和平, 发展, 合作, p. 27.

109. Vadim Medvedev, *Raspad*, p. 306.

110. Ibid., p. 317.

111. Conversation between V. Ya. Vorob'yov and Li Fenglin, March 30, 1988. AVPRF: fond 100, opis 75, delo 3, listy 53–55.

112. Conversation between Javier Pérez de Cuéllar and Mahathir Mohammed, October 4, 1988. UNA: Series S-1033, Box 8, File 2.

113. For a good analysis, see Balazs Szalontai, "From battlefield into marketplace: the end of the Cold War in Indochina, 1985–1989."

114. Conversation between Javier Pérez de Cuéllar and Nitya Pibulsonggram, January 19, 1989. UNA: Series S-1033, Box 8, File 4.

115. Conversation between Javier Pérez de Cuéllar and Li Luye, January 25, 1989. UNA: Series S-1033, Box 8, File 4.

116. Elaine Sciolino, "Cambodia peace talks change with positions unchanged," *New York Times*, July 28, 1988, Section A; Page 3, Column 5.

117. "Kampuchea: Meeting of the masters," *Economist*, September 3, 1988, p. 29.

118. 钱其琛, 外交十记, p. 28.

119. The details of the Tian-Rogachev meeting were spelled out in the talking points for Mikhail Gorbachev's meeting with Kaysone Phomvihane, undated (probably September 1988). AGF: fond 5, dokument 20696. The same deadline is referred to in HIA/TSP, notebook 28.11.1988 and in Conversation between Javier Pérez de Cuéllar and Li Luye, January 25, 1989. UNA: Series S-1033, Box 8, File 4.

120. Daniel Southerland, "Chinese aide to Moscow to set stage for summit: Foreign minister seeks pact on Cambodia," *Washington Post*, December 1, 1988, p. A56.
121. 钱其琛, 外交十记, pp. 29–30.
122. Sergey Radchenko, "Soviet withdrawal from Mongolia, 1986–92: a Reassessment," *Journal of Slavic Military Studies*, Vol. 25, Issue 2 (2012), pp. 1–21.
123. HIA/TSP: Notebook 28.11.1988.
124. HNA XIX-J-1-j-Kína-135-004674/1-1988 (57. d.). See also HIA/TSP: Notebook 28.11.1988 and Diary No. 8.
125. 钱其琛, 外交十记, pp. 32–33.
126. "Asian news—China, Soviet Union, Kampuchea; Qian says Sino-Soviet gap closing on Kampuchea problem," *Japan Economic Newswire*, December 5, 1988.
127. Record of conversation between Tom Lantos and Wu Xueqian, December 21, 1988. US Department of State FOIA reading room.
128. 钱其琛, 外交十记, p. 34.
129. According to Li Peng's comments to Shevardnadze. HIA/TSP: notepad 03.02.1989, p. 3.
130. 钱其琛, 外交十记, p. 35.
131. Conversation between Igor Rogachev and Ts. Gombosuren, February 11, 1989. MFMA: fond 2, dans 1, kh/n 239, khuu 11.
132. As recounted in the Conversation between Javier Pérez de Cuéllar and Li Luye, February 14, 1989. UNA: Series S-1033, Box 8, File 5.
133. Detailed account of Deng-Shevardnadze talks, including various "colorful" details is in HIA/TSP: Diary No. 8, pp. 236–249.
134. 钱其琛, 外交十记, p. 35.
135. HIA/TSP: Diary No. 8, p. 250.
136. Conversation between Igor Rogachev and Ts. Gombosuren, February 11, 1989. MFMA: fond 2, dans 1, kh/n 239, khuu 11.
137. "Shevardnadze speaks on Sino-Soviet 'normalization' at a Peking press conference," *BBC Summary of World Broadcasts*, February 6, 1989, FE/0377/A2/1.
138. Conversation between Igor Rogachev and Ts. Gombosuren, February 11, 1989. MFMA: fond 2, dans 1, kh/n 239, khuu 12.
139. HIA/TSP: Diary No. 8, p. 251.
140. Daniel Southerland, "Summit set for mid-May, Soviets say; Chinese deny date has been confirmed," *Washington Post*, February 5, 1989, p. A29.
141. Jan Wong, "Cambodia deal struck in Beijing," *Globe and Mail*, February 6, 1989.
142. Georgii Kireev, *Rossiya-Kitai: Neizvestnye Stranitsy Pogranichnykh Peregovorov* (Moscow: Rosspen, 2006), p. 197.
143. "Gorbachev to visit China May 15–18," Associated Press, February 5, 1989.
144. Conversation between Igor Rogachev and Ts. Gombosuren, February 11, 1989. MFMA: fond 2, dans 1, kh/n 239, khuu 12.
145. "Chinese and Soviet foreign ministers issue statement on Cambodia," *BBC Summary of World Broadcasts*, February 7, 1989, FE/0378/C2/1.
146. George Bush and Brent Scowcroft, *A World Transformed* (New York: Knopf, 1998), p. 94.

147. Cable from the US Embassy in Beijing to the State Department, April 24, 1989. National Security Archive, http://www.gwu.edu/~nsarchiv/NSAEBB/NSAEBB47/doc7.pdf.

148. O besedakh, provedennykh v khode raboty XII s'ezda Portugal'skoi kompartii, December 1–4, 1988, report by Vadim Medvedev. AGF: fond 4, dokument 7791.

149. "Vietnam's September Song," *Economist*, April 7, 1989, p. 63.

150. Conversation between Mikhail Gorbachev and Nguyen Van Linh, May 3, 1989. AGF: Fond 5, dokument 20701.

151. Conversation between Javier Pérez de Cuéllar and Ambassador Li, September 19, 1989. UNA: Series S-1033, Box 9, File 2.

CHAPTER 5

1. Sergey Radchenko, *Two Suns in the Heavens: The Sino-Soviet Struggle for Supremacy, 1962–1967*.

2. 邓小平, 下, p. 881.

3. 李鹏, 和平, 发展, 合作, p. 6.

4. Czechoslovak Translation of the Soviet Summary of Conversations Between Mikhail Gorbachev and Li Peng in Moscow, January 8, 1986, Central State Archives (SÚA), Prague: UV KSC. Courtesy of the Parallel History Project.

5. Conversation between Mikhail Gorbachev and Alvaro Cunhal, December 29, 1986. REEADD: Box 15.

6. Vladislav Zubok, *A Failed Empire: The Soviet Union in the Cold War from Stalin to Gorbachev* (Chapel Hill: University of North Carolina Press, 2007).

7. Conversation between Mikhail Gorbachev and Alvaro Cunhal, December 29, 1986. REEADD: Box 15.

8. Anatolii Chernyaev et al. (eds.), *V Politbyuro TsK KPSS*, p. 72.

9. Ibid., p. 115.

10. Ibid., p. 420.

11. Aleksandr Yakovlev's statement before the staff of the Soviet Embassy in Ulaanbaatar, March 17, 1988. GARF: fond 10063, opis 2, delo 115, list 44.

12. For an in-depth account of these events, see Zhang Liang (comp.), and Andrew J. Nathan and Perry Link (eds.), *The Tiananmen Papers* (London: Abacus, 2007).

13. The invitation to Gorbachev, dated May 12, 1989, is partially reproduced in Mikhail Gorbachev, *Zhizn' i Reformy*, Vol. 2, p. 448. Gorbachev recalled that there were approximately three thousand signatures.

14. Jim Abrams, "Students continue protests: Officials change Gorbachev welcoming ceremony," Associated Press, May 15, 1989.

15. Michael Putzel, "Gorbachev arrives for first Sino-Soviet summit in thirty years," Associated Press, May 15, 1989.

16. Oleg Troyanovskii, *Cherez Gody i Rasstoyaniya* (Moscow: Vagrius, 1997), p. 370.

17. Andrew Nathan (ed.), *Tiananmen Papers*, 189. I fully realize that the authenticity of some of the documents included in the *Tiananmen Papers* collection has been questioned. I believe, however, that the collection is generally trustworthy.

18. Ibid. Also, see an almost identical remark on p. 196.

19. Or so Xinhua claimed: "Soviet leader receives red-carpet welcome at airport," Xinhua General Overseas News Service, May 15, 1989.

20. 马保奉, "1989年戈氏访华留下的外交遗憾," 党史纵横, No. 7 (2009), p. 43.

21. HIA/TSP: Diary No. 9, p. 51.

22. "杨尚昆主席举行宴会," May 15, 1989. GARF: 10063, opis 2, delo 126, list 30.

23. Gennady Gerasimov at the Foreign Ministry of the USSR. Interview with N. Percy, M. Anderson and OJ, LSE Archives, Second Russian Revolution files, 1/1/25.
24. HIA/TSP: Notepad 15.09.89.
25. HIA/TSP: Diary No. 9, p. 55.
26. Stepanov-Mamaladze included in his notepad on May 16 a cryptic reference to a "proposal by E. A. Shevardnadze to go and talk to the students." HIA/TSP: Notepad 15.09.89.
27. Oleg Troyanovskii, *Cherez Gody i Rasstoyaniya*, p. 372.
28. Mikhail Gorbachev, *Sobranie Sochinenii*, Vol. 15, p. 261.
29. "Press conference by Soviet General Secretary Mikhail Gorbachev," Federal News Service, May 17, 1989.
30. Cited in Roi Medvedev, "Vizit M. S. Gorbacheva v Pekin v 1989 godu," *Novaya i noveishaya istoriya*, No. 3 (2011), pp. 93–101.
31. Telephone call from Helmut Kohl to George Bush, June 15, 1989. DDRS.
32. "New Congress neutral on China bloodshed," Associated Press, June 6, 1989.
33. Bill Keller, "Soviet Congress ends with one last spat," New York Times, June 10, 1989, p. 1. Aleksandr Lukin, *Medved' Nablyudaet Za Drakonom*, p. 280.
34. Alison Smale, "Gorbachev says reforms in China crucial to world peace," Associated Press, June 15, 1989.
35. "New Congress neutral on China bloodshed," Associated Press, June 6, 1989.
36. Rupert Cornwell, "Bedraggled press survive a chaotic odyssey," *Independent*, May 18, 1989.
37. Conversation between Mikhail Gorbachev and Rajiv Gandhi, November 15, 1989. REEADD: Box 16.
38. Aleksandr Lukin, *Medved' Nablyudaet Za Drakonom*, p. 274.
39. See ibid. for further discussion of this point.
40. Record of a Politburo meeting, October 4, 1989. Courtesy of Pavel Stroilov, who had obtained the record of the Gorbachev Foundation. This passage was omitted in the publications of the Gorbachev Foundation until 2010, when it was included in Mikhail Gorbachev, *Sobranie Sochinenii*, Vol. 16 (Moscow: Ves' Mir, 2010), p. 193, but without the incriminating "so what." Three dots are in the original.
41. In the aftermath of the June 4 events, Zhao Ziyang was accused of revealing state secrets during his conversation with Gorbachev, by claiming that Deng still exercised ultimate authority in China. In fact, Li Peng, Zhao Ziyang's mortal enemy, could well be accused of the same crime, because he told exactly that much to Shevardnadze during their meeting in February 1989. See HIA/TSP: Notepad 03.02.1989, p. 4. The real reason, of course, was that Zhao Ziyang ostensibly attempted to shift responsibility for unrest on Deng.
42. Mikhail Gorbachev, *Zhizn' i Reformy*, Vol. 2, p. 442. See also Zhao Ziyang, *Prisoner of the State*, pp. 45–49.
43. Mikhail Gorbachev, *Zhizn' i Reformy*, Vol. 2, p. 445.
44. Aleksandr Lukin, *Medved' Nablyudaet Za Drakonom*, p. 275. Lukin does not reference this statement. It is likely that he refers to Gorbachev's conversations with Rezso Nyers and Karoly Grosz in Moscow on July 24–25, 1989. Available records do not list China as one of the subjects (e.g., see *Cold War International History Project Bulletin*, Issue 12/13, p. 83). This need not mean that Gorbachev did not raise the subject (the record is abridged).
45. 师哲, 在历史巨人身边: 师哲回忆录 (北京: 中央文献出版社, 1995), p. 458.

46. Li Zhisui, *The Private Life of Chairman Mao* (New York: Random House, 1994), p. 261.

47. Dan Biers, "Summit stumper: Will Deng hug Gorbachev?," Associated Press, May 15, 1989.

48. Deng's comments were passed to Li Peng's office as early as October 28, 1988. See 马保奉, "1989 年戈氏访华留下的外交遗憾," 党史纵横, No. 7 (2009), p. 42.

49. 钱其琛, 外交十记, p. 36.

50. Oleg Troyanovskii, *Cherez gody i rasstoyaniya*, p. 373.

51. Mikhail Gorbachev, *Zhizn' i Reformy*, Vol. 2, p. 436.

52. 邓小平文选, 第三卷, p. 292.

53. Mikhail Gorbachev, *Zhizn' i Reformy*, Vol. 2, p. 438. Note that Deng's point about Mongolia was omitted from the Chinese published version of the same conversation. 邓小平文选, 第三卷, pp. 293–295.

54. Mikhail Gorbachev, *Zhizn' i Reformy*, Vol. 2, p. 439.

55. Ibid.

56. James R. Lilley, interview with Charles Stuart Kennedy, May 21, 1998. The Association for Diplomatic Studies and Training Foreign Affairs Oral History Project, Library of Congress.

57. Conversation between George Bush and Deng Xiaoping, February 26, 1989. George Bush Presidential Library, College Station, TX (hereafter, GBPL). Obtained by the author through FOIA request.

58. Ibid.

59. Patrick Tyler, *A Great Wall*, p. 347.

60. Conversation between George Bush and Zhao Ziyang, February 26, 1989. GBPL. Obtained by the author through a FOIA request.

61. US Embassy Beijing Cable, President's Banquet—Chinese Guest List, February 18, 1989. Michael L. Evans (ed.), "The US 'Tiananmen papers,'" National Security Archive Electronic Briefing Book (June 4, 2001).

62. US Embassy Beijing Cable, The President's Visit to China: Suggestions Regarding What We and the Chinese Hope to Accomplish, February 6, 1989. Ibid.

63. George Bush and Brent Scowcroft, *A World Transformed*, p. 109.

64. Letter from Brent Scowcroft to Lawrence Hogan, March 24, 1990. GBPL: NSC, Paal, Douglas 1989–1990 China file, China-US March–April 1990 (3).

65. For discussion, see Odd Arne Westad, "Struggles for modernity: The golden years of the Sino-Soviet alliance," in Tsuyoshi Hasegawa (ed.), *The Cold War in East Asia, 1945–1991* (Washington, DC, and Stanford, CA: Woodrow Wilson Center Press and Stanford University Press, 2011), pp. 35–62. More generally, on the relevance of the Soviet experience for China, see Thomas P. Bernstein and Hua-Yu Li (eds.), *China Learns from the Soviet Union, 1949–Present* (Lanham, MD: Lexington Books, 2010).

66. On Deng's views regarding Soviet economy, see, for instance, 邓小平文选, 第三卷, p. 139.

67. Gilbert Rozman, "China's concurrent debate and the Gorbachev era," in Thomas P. Bernstein and Hua-Yu Li (eds.), *China Learns from the Soviet Union, 1949–Present* (Lanham, MD: Lexington Books, 2010), pp. 449–476. See also Rozman's pioneering *The Chinese Debate about Soviet Socialism, 1978–1985* (Princeton, NJ: Princeton University Press, 1987).

68. Maurice Meisner, *The Deng Xiaoping Era* (New York: Hill and Wang, 1996), pp. 361–363.

69. Jack Redden, "Gorbachev urges more democracy, openness," United Press International, January 29, 1987.

70. Martin Walker, "An uncanny sound of dissidence at the top," *Guardian*, January 29, 1987; Jack Redden, "Gorbachev urges more democracy, openness," United Press International, January 29, 1987.

71. Anatolii Chernyaev et al. (eds.), *V Politbyuro TsK KPSS*, p. 141.

72. Ibid., p. 140.

73. 李鹏, 和平, 发展, 合作, p. 232.

74. 邓小平年谱, 下, p. 1173. For Beijing's self-perception as the "avant-garde of socialist reforms" see also Péter Vámos, "The Rise and Demise of a 'Reform Community': The Role of Tiananmen and the Systemic Change in Sino-Hungarian Relations," paper presented at the conference "Nexus Years in the Cold War," October 16–17, 2009. McGill University. Montreal, Canada.

75. Anatolii Chernyaev et al. (eds.), *V Politbyuro TsK KPSS*, pp. 157, 159, 179.

76. Ibid., pp. 258–265.

77. See, for example, Gary Lee, "Kremlin dispute publicly confirmed," *Washington Post*, November 1, 1987, p. A1.

78. "Mr. Deng's boys," *Guardian*, November 3, 1987.

79. Daniel Southerland, "Deng quits key posts in party; Old guard leaves; Reformers seen gaining strength," *Washington Post*, November 2, 1987, p. A1.

80. "New Chinese leadership meets the press," *BBC Summary of World Broadcasts*, November 4, 1987, Part 3, The Far East; C.1 Thirteenth CCP National Congress; FE/8716/C1/1.

81. 李鹏, 和平, 发展, 合作, p. 233.

82. Ibid.

83. BStU: MFS-Abt X, Nr. 264, s. 292

84. BStU: MFS-Abt X, Nr. 264, s. 374.

85. Mikhail Gorbachev, *Perestroika i Novoe Myshlenie Dlya Nashei Strany i Dlya Vsego Mira* (Moscow: Politizdat, 1987), p. 175.

86. Anatolii Chenyaev et al. (eds.), *V Politbyuro TsK KPSS*, pp. 211, 342, 390; Karen Brutents, *Nesbyvsheesya*, p. 229.

87. Anatolii Chernyaev et al. (eds.), *V Politbyuro TsK KPSS*, p. 208.

88. Conversation between Todor Zhivkov and Mikhail Gorbachev, May 11, 1987. Bulgarian Central State Archives, Sofia (hereafter, BCSA): Fond 1b, Opis 35, a.e. 387; also Karen Brutents, *Nesbyvsheesya*, p. 228.

89. Ezra Vogel, *Deng Xiaoping and the Transformation of China*, p. 423.

90. Karen Brutents, *Nesbyvsheesya*, p. 228.

91. Conversation between Todor Zhivkov and Mikhail Gorbachev, May 11, 1987. BCSA: Fond 1b, Opis 35, a.e. 387.

92. Conversation between Mikhail Gorbachev and Rajiv Gandhi, July 2, 1987. REEADD: Box 15.

93. Conversation between Mikhail Gorbachev and Fidel Castro, April 4, 1989. AGF: fond 5, dokument 20500.

94. Karen Brutents, *Nesbyvsheesya*, p. 228.

95. Conversation between Mikhail Gorbachev and Fidel Castro, April 4, 1989. AGF: fond 5, dokument 20500.

96. Karen Brutents, *Nesbyvsheesya*, p. 229.

97. Karen Brutents, *Nesbyvsheesya*, pp. 228–229. Emphasis in the original.

98. Vystuplenie t. Shakhnazarova G. Kh. na vstreche v Otdele TsK KPSS s predstavi-telyami sovetskikh sredstv massovoi informatsii, August 14, 1987. AGF: fond 5, dokument 17693.

99. Ibid.

100. This point is explored in greater depth in recent work by Deborah Larson and Aleksei Shevchenko.

101. 邓小平文选, 第三卷, p. 326.

102. 钟之成, 为了世界更美好: 江泽民出访纪实(北京: 世界知识出版社, 2006), p. 6.

103. Benjamin Yang, *Deng: A Political Biography* (New York: Sharpe, 1998), p. 257. One should note, however, that Yang's information is based on hearsay and cannot be considered reliable.

104. David Shambaugh, "Europe's Relations with China: Forging Closer Ties," in Susan Maybaumwisniewski and Mary Sommerville (eds.), *Blue Horizon: United States—Japan—PRC Tripartite Relations* (Washington, DC: National Defense University Press, 1997).

105. 李鹏, 和平, 发展, 合作, p. 238.

106. Ibid.

107. "'Ming Pao' Peking on 'Top-grade alert,'" *BBC Summary of World Broadcasts*, January 3, 1990. Part 3, The Far East; B. Internal Affairs; 2. China; FE/0652/B2/1.

108. Ibid.

109. Steven Erlanger, "China's lonely press tries to look the other way," *New York Times*, December 24, 1989.

110. 李鹏, 和平, 发展, 合作, p. 236.

111. Oleg Troyanovskii, *Cherez Gody i Rasstoyaniya*, p. 379. This meeting likely took place in the evening of September 10, 1990: "Li Peng meets outgoing Soviet Ambassador," Xinhua General News Service, September 10, 1990.

112. Jeanne L. Wilson, "The impact of the demise of state socialism on China," in David Lane (ed.), *The Transformation of State Socialism: System Change, Capitalism, or Something Else?* (London: Palgrave Macmillan, 2007), pp. 269–285.

113. Qian Qichen cited in George Bush and Brent Scowcroft, *A World Transformed*, p. 177.

114. 李鹏, 和平, 发展, 合作, pp. 244, 247.

115. Cited in George Bush and Brent Scowcroft, *A World Transformed*, p. 177.

116. "China extends a friendly loan to Moscow," *New York Times*, March 16, 1991, p. 6.

117. Sergei Goncharov, K voprosu o sovremennoi situatsii v otnosheniyakh mezhdu Rossiei i Kitaem, report, September 5, 1991. GARF: fond 10026, opis 4, delo 2805, list 82.

118. Simon Long, "China bails out elder brother," *Guardian*, March 16, 1991.

119. "China and the Soviet Union: A friend in need," *Economist*, March 23, 1991, p. 37.

120. 李鹏, 和平, 发展, 合作, p. 241.

121. Ibid., p. 236.

122. 邓小平文选, 第三卷, p. 353.

123. 李鹏, 和平, 发展, 合作, p. 243.

124. "Xinjiang official tells of separatist Agitation," *Washington Times*, March 26, 1990, p. A2.

125. Yojana Sharma, "China: Fears of separatism Sharpen," IPS—Inter Press Service, February 21, 1990; "Chinese premier asks vigilance against ethnic strife," Associated Press, February 19, 1990.

126. Simon Long, "Chinese fear spread of ethnic turmoil: Border unrest will meet 'simple and brutal' response," *Guardian*, February 15, 1990. The two other

reasons mentioned were: Eastern European revolutions and the decision to award the Nobel Prize to the Dalai Lama.

127. 邓小平文选, 第三卷, p. 320.
128. Hung P. Nguyen, "Russia and China: The genesis of an Eastern Rapallo," *Asian Survey*, Vol. 33, No. 3 (March 1993), p. 295.
129. 钟之成, 为了世界更美好, p. 8.
130. Sergei Goncharov, K voprosu o sovremennoi situatsii v otnosheniyakh mezhdu Rossiei i Kitaem, report, September 5, 1991. GARF: fond 10026, opis 4, delo 2805, listy 79–110. Of course, one should be very careful in the assessment of these "Chinese sources," even though in this case I am convinced of their reliability. The story of the Chinese awareness of the coup is at best sketchy, and, given the sensitivity of the topic, is likely to remain so for a long time.
131. Ibid., list 75.
132. Ibid., list 81. Oleg Rakhmanin, *Stranitsy Perezhitogo*, p. 101.
133. Conversation between I. D. Laptev and Yu Hongliang, September 27, 1991. GARF: fond P9654, opis 10, delo 339, listy 183-184.
134. 杨继绳, 中国改革年代的政治斗争 (Hong Kong: Excellent Culture Press, 2004), p. 483. It should be noted that Yang's account does not meet the standards of Western scholarship due to the lack of references, so it must be used with caution.
135. James A. R. Miles, *The Legacy of Tiananmen: China in Disarray* (Ann Arbor, MI: University of Michigan Press, 1996), p. 71.
136. Ibid., p. 72.
137. Sergei Goncharov, K voprosu o sovremennoi situatsii v otnosheniyakh mezhdu Rossiei i Kitaem, report, September 5, 1991. GARF: fond 10026, opis 4, delo 2805, listy 79–110.
138. Roderick MacFarquhar, *The Politics of China: The Eras of Mao and Deng* (New York: Cambridge University Press, 1997), p. 493.
139. 杨继绳, 中国改革年代的政治斗争.
140. Sergei Goncharov, K voprosu o sovremennoi situatsii v otnosheniyakh mezhdu Rossiei i Kitaem, report, September 5, 1991. GARF: fond 10026, opis 4, delo 2805, list 83.
141. James A. R. Miles, *The Legacy of Tiananmen*, pp. 73–74.
142. Sergei Goncharov, K voprosu o sovremennoi situatsii v otnosheniyakh mezhdu Rossiei i Kitaem, report, September 5, 1991. GARF: fond 10026, opis 4, delo 2805, listy 82–83.
143. 马云飞, 孙翊 (主编), 江泽民思想年谱 (北京:中央文献出版社, 2012), pp. 72–73.
144. "China recognizes Russia, 11 other republics," Japan Economic Newswire, December 27, 1991.
145. Conversation between Mikhail Titarenko and Zhang Zheng, January 10, 1992. GARF: fond 10026, opis 1, delo 2290, list 76.
146. "China, Russia sign memorandum on future ties," Xinhua General News Service, December 29, 1991.
147. Conversation between Mikhail Titarenko and Zhang Zheng, January 10, 1992. GARF: fond 10026, opis 1, delo 2290, list 78.
148. Hung P. Nguyen, "Russia and China: The genesis of an Eastern Rapallo," p. 297.
149. O vizite delegatsii Verkhovnogo soveta RSFSR v KNR, 6–13 dekabrya 1991 goda, undated. GARF: fond 10026, opis 5, delo 1253, list 56.

150. Conversation between Ruslan Khasbulatov and Wang Jinqing, March 16, 1992. GARF: fond 10026, opis 5, delo 458, list 51.

151. "Asia report: Funds flowing from Taiwan to Soviets," Jiji Press Ticker Service, October 21, 1988.

152. "Commentary," Central News Agency (Taiwan), October 23, 1988.

153. "CETRA dispatches fact-finding trade mission to USSR," Central News Agency (Taiwan), May 19, 1989; "ROC delegation to leave for Siberia for trade promotion," Central News Agency (Taiwan), August 9, 1989. It is worthwhile to note that at this time Taiwan made impressive progress in relations with East European countries. On January 1, 1990, for example, Taipei opened a trade office in Hungary. For an interesting account of Hungary's relations with Taiwan in 1989, see Péter Vámos, "The Rise and Demise of a 'Reform Community': The Role of Tiananmen and the Systemic Change in Sino-Hungarian Relations," paper presented at the conference "Nexus Years in the Cold War," October 16–17, 2009. McGill University. Montreal, Canada.

154. Mark Magnier, "Soviets attend Taiwan meeting of Pacific Rim economic forum," Journal of Commerce, May 31, 1989, p. 4A; "First Soviet officials arrive in Taiwan," Associated Press, May 14, 1989.

155. "Taiwan cabinet approves visit by Soviet representative," BBC Summary of World Broadcasts, April 22, 1989. Part 3, The Far East; A. International Affairs; 2. The USSR and Eastern Europe; FE/0441/A2/1.

156. Czeslaw Tubilewicz, "The Little Dragon and the Bear: Russian-Taiwanese Relations in the Post–Cold War Period," Russian Review, Vol. 61, No. 2 (April 2002), p. 286.

157. John Pomfret, "Taiwan's diplomatic offensive showing results," Associated Press, July 31, 1989.

158. Czeslaw Tubilewicz, "The Little Dragon and the Bear," p. 289.

159. "Soviet mayor Feted in Taiwan," Free China Journal, November 1, 1990.

160. Communication from Wu'er Kaixi to the author, January 6, 2009.

161. "Soviet mayor Feted in Taiwan," Free China Journal, November 1, 1990.

162. Ob otnosheniyakh s Taivanem, February 1991. GARF: fond 10026, opis 4, delo 2805, list 3.

163. O konsul'tatsiyakh po taivan'skomu voprosu (April [2?]5, 1991). GARF: fond 10026, opis 4, delo 2805, listy 34–39.

164. "ROC should help Soviets: Chien," Central News Agency—Taiwan, August 24, 1991.

165. "Taipei ready to finance Soviet development projects," Central News Agency—Taiwan, July 20, 1991.

166. "Taiwan to aid East Europe through special fund," Central News Agency, October 9, 1991.

167. "ROC rejects claims of tainted rice," Central News Agency—Taiwan, April 19, 1993.

168. O vizite delegatsii Verkhovnogo soveta RSFSR v KNR, 6–13 dekabrya 1991 goda, undated. GARF: fond 10026, opis 5, delo 1253, list 56.

169. Evgenii Bazhanov, Kitai: Ot Sredinnoi Imperii do Sverkhderzhavy XXI Veka (Moscow: Izvestiya, 2007), p. 301.

170. Yurii Lepskii, "Moskva i Moskvichi: Vernetsya li Lobov v pravitel'stvo?," Trud, November 28, 1997.

171. "Russia approves pact with Taiwan," Central News Agency—Taiwan, September 10, 1992.

172. For a detailed account, see Alexander Lukin, *Medved' Nablyudaet Za Drakonom*, p. 431.
173. Ibid., 430. "Rasporyazhenie Prezidenta Rossiiskoi Federatsii o Moskovsko-Taipeiskoi Koordinatsionnoi Kommissii po Ekonomicheskomu i Kul'turnomu Sotrudnichestvu," September 2, 1992, *KonsultantPlus*, Database "Expert-Prilozhenie," http://www.consultant.ru/about/software/systems/expert.
174. "A thing has just happened …," *Official Kremlin International News Broadcast*, September 10, 1992.
175. Alexander Lukin, *Medved' Nablyudaet Za Drakonom*, 431; Ivan Shomov, "Vostok Vsegda Manil Olega Lobova," *Segodnya*, April 26, 1997. According to Shomov, Yeltsin's original decree was torn to pieces in front of the Chinese Ambassador.
176. "Ukaz Prezidenta Rossiiskoi Federatsii ob Otnosheniyakh mezhdu Rossiiskoi Federatsiei i Taivanem," September 15, 1992, *KonsultantPlus*, Database "Expert-Prilozhenie."
177. "Taipei-Moscow Commission to open first meeting in September," *Central News Agency—Taiwan*, September 15, 1992.
178. Memorandum by Vladimir Lukin on the current state of Sino-Soviet relations, August 22, 1989. GARF: fond 10026, opis 10026, delo 2870, listy 75-78.
179. These epithets were allegedly used to describe Yeltsin in Chinese internal publications in late 1991. See W. Laplam, "Blundering Beijing puzzled by the changing bear," *Courier-Mail*, January 2, 1992.

CHAPTER 6
1. For details of the Soviet–North Korean estrangement in the early 1960s, see Sergey Radchenko, "The Soviet Union and the North Korean Seizure of the USS Pueblo, Evidence from Russian Archives," *Cold War International History Project Working Paper*, No. 47 (March 2005).
2. For statements by Soviet diplomats to this effect, see Report of the Soviet Embassy in the DPRK on some new aspects in the Korean-Chinese relations in the first half of 1965, June 4, 1965. AVPRF: fond 0102, opis 21, delo 20, list 26.
3. Sergey Radchenko, "The Soviet Union and the North Korean Seizure of the USS Pueblo, Evidence from Russian Archives."
4. "Bezzhiznennaya strana: O yadernoi voine v Severnoi Koree dumali eshche pri Kim Ir Sene," *Izvestiya*, No. 039, March 3, 2003, p. 4. For more details on Shevardnadze's visit, see Seung Ho Joo, *Gorbachev's Foreign Policy Toward the Korean Peninsula, 1985–1991* (New York: The Edwin Mellen Press, 2000), pp. 125–126.
5. HIA/TSP: Diary No. 4, p. 40.
6. Teimuraz Stepanov-Mamaladze's handwritten notes of Eduard Shevardnadze's meeting with Kim Il-sung, January 21, 1986. HIA/TSP: Notepad 15.01.86.
7. HIA/TSP: Diary No. 4, pp. 64–66.
8. Ibid.
9. Conversation between Mangalyn Dugersuren and Eduard Shevardnadze, January 24, 1986. MFMA: Fond 2, dans 1, kh/n 504, khuu 142.
10. Record of a Politburo Meeting, January 30, 1986. VC: Reel 17.
11. E.g., 邓小平年谱, 下, p. 935.
12. Cable from the US Embassy in Seoul to the Secretary of State, May 1, 1984. Ronald Reagan Presidential Library, Laux, David Files, China—Foreign Relations, Reagan Trip, The Issues (3).
13. 邓小平年谱, 下, p. 1097.

14. For an account of 1984 Kim Il-sung-Chernenko talks, see Mikhail Kapitsa, *Na Raznykh Parallelyakh*, and Dmitrii Volkogonov, *Sem' Vozhdei*, Vol. 2, pp. 253–254.
15. Dmitrii Volkogonov, *Sem' Vozhdei*, p. 254.
16. Aleksandr Rozin, "Sovetskii flot i VMS Severnoi Korei (KNDR)," available online: http://alerozin.narod.ru/KNDRiUSSR.htm.
17. Memorandum from Konstantin Katushev to Anatolii Chernyaev, July 15, 1991. AGF: Fond 2, Dokument 8997.
18. Aleksandr Rozin, "Sovetskii flot i VMS Severnoi Korei (KNDR)."
19. For the Soviet decision to build a nuclear plant in North Korea, see MOL: XIX-J-1-k Korea, 1985, 76. doboz, 81-532, 2745/1985. Obtained and translated for CWIHP by Balazs Szalontai. See also "North Korea: Potential for Nuclear Weapon Development," CIA Intelligence Assessment, September 1986, p. 19. CIA FOIA Online Reading Room.
20. Conversation between Mangalyn Dugersuren and Mikhail Kapitsa, March 19, 1984. MFMA: fond 2, dans 1, kh/n 489, khuu 59–60.
21. Conversation between Erich Honecker and Kim Il-sung, May 31, 1984. *Cold War International History Project Bulletin*, Issues 14/15 (Winter 2003–Spring 2004), p. 60.
22. "China says it will take part in Seoul Asian Games," Japanese Economic Newswire, June 30, 1986.
23. 邓小平年谱, 下, p. 1097. Although the broader context of his conversation with Kim Il-sung is missing, it is not difficult to surmise that Deng's comments were a response to Kim's request to boycott the Seoul Olympics. The Chinese privately confirmed their attendance at Seoul to visiting Japanese Prime Minister Nakasone Yasuhiro, in the spring of 1984. See Conversation between Javier Pérez de Cuéllar and Kim Kyung-won, April 12, 1984. UNA: Series S-1033, Box 3, File 3.
24. Conversation between Juan Antonio Samaranch and Li Menghua, April 30, 1986. International Olympic Committee Archive, Lausanne, Switzerland (hereafter, IOCA): JAS/Voyages 1986, Paris, Portugal, Pekin etc., JAS Voyage Pekin 27/04-01/05/86.
25. Cited in Natalia Bazhanova, "North Korea and Seoul-Moscow Relations," in Il Yung Chung (ed.), *Korea and Russia: Towards the 21st Century* (Seoul: Sejong Institute, 1992), p. 327.
26. Gorbachev's Vladivostok speech, July 28, 1986. Mikhail Gorbachev, *Sobranie Sochinenii*, Vol. 4, p. 369.
27. Anatolii Chernyaev et al. (eds.), *V Politbyuro TsK KPSS*, p. 88.
28. Politburo session, October 22, 1986. VC: reel 17, containers 24 through 26. The above passage appears as translated by Svetlana Savranskaya.
29. Bernd Schaefer, "Weathering the Sino-Soviet Conflict: The GDR and North Korea, 1949–1989," *Cold War International History Project Bulletin*, Issue 14/15 (Winter 2003–Spring 2004), pp. 66–67. Document translated by Grace Leonard.
30. Cited in Vadim Medvedev, *Raspad*, pp. 324–325.
31. Cited in ibid., p. 324.
32. Gorbachev's quotes are from his interview with Kim Hakjoon in February 1995, see Kim Hakjoon, "The process leading to the establishment of diplomatic relations between South Korea and the Soviet Union," *Asian Survey*, Vol. 37, No. 7 (July 1997), pp. 641–642.
33. Author's interview with Vadim Tkachenko, Moscow, March 27, 2008. On Gorbachev's promise not to recognize Seoul, also see Vladimir Li, *Rossiya i Koreya*

v Geopolitike Evraziiskogo Vostoka (XX vek) (Moskva: Nauchnaya Kniga, 2000), p. 237.

34. For a more detailed discussion, see Don Oberdorfer, *The Two Koreas: A Contemporary History* (Indianapolis, IN: Basic Books, 2002), pp. 186–189.

35. I confirmed this nickname with several knowledgeable Koreans.

36. Vladimir Li, *Rossiya i Koreya*, p. 463; communication to the author from Konstantin Sarkisov, August 27, 2007; the author's interview with Nikolai Vasil'ev, Moscow, March 21, 2008.

37. Account based on a written communication from Konstantin Sarkisov, August 7, 2007.

38. On Nikolai Vasil'ev's KGB affiliation, see, for example, Cable from US Embassy in Moscow to the Secretary of State, February 21, 1979. JCPL: NLC 16-15-6-7-5.

39. Account based on a written communication from Konstantin Sarkisov, August 7, 2007.

40. Author's interview with Nikolai Vasil'ev, March 21, 2008, Moscow.

41. 박철언, 바른역사를위한증언: 5공, 6공, 3김시대의정치비사 (서울: 랜덤하우스중앙, 2005), p. 125.

42. 박철언, 바른역사를위한증언, p. 125.

43. The author's interview with Nikolai Vasil'ev, Moscow, March 21, 2008.

44. Harriman Institute Alumni Newsletter, June 7, 2005, online: http://www.sipa. columbia.edu/hi/hi-alums.html, date accessed: September 1, 2007.

45. Communication to the author from Joseph M. Ha, August 8, 2007.

46. On the visit, see 박철언, 바른역사를위한증언, pp. 126–143. Park and Yeom traveled to Moscow on ordinary (not diplomatic) passports, with cultural exchange visas—on the Soviet insistence. Letter to the author from Yeom Don-jae, September 19, 2007.

47. 박철언, 바른역사를위한증언, pp. 126, 135.

48. Ibid., 128.

49. Author's interview at IMEMO.

50. Mikhail Kapitsa, *Na Raznykh Parallelyakh*, p. 252.

51. 박철언, 바른역사를위한증언, pp. 128–129.

52. 박철언, 바른역사를위한증언, p. 132.

53. Georgii Arbatov to Anatolii Chernyaev, April–June 1988. AGF: Fond 2, Document 1168.

54. 박철언, 바른역사를위한증언, p. 137.

55. Ibid., p. 138, for Arbatov quote and Anatolii Chernyaev et al. (eds.), *V Politbyuro TsK KPSS*, pp. 401–403, for subjects of the Politburo discussion. The complementary nature of Korean and Russian sources offers a useful way of testing (and, in this case) confirming, Park Chul-un's recollections.

56. 박철언, 바른역사를위한증언, pp. 138–139.

57. Ibid., pp. 140–141.

58. Letter from Yeom Don-jae, September 17, 2007.

59. For a detailed discussion, see Sergey Radchenko, "It's not enough to win: The Seoul Olympics and the roots of North Korea's isolation," *International Journal of the History of Sport*, Vol. 29, No. 9 (June 2012), pp. 1243–1262 and Sergey Radchenko, "Sport and Politics on the Korean Peninsula—North Korea and the 1988 Seoul Olympics," *North Korea International Documentation Project e-dossier*, No. 3 (December 2011).

60. Edwin Q. White, "At least 51 Americans...," Associated Press, September 2, 1983.

61. Steve Lohr, "Koreans Demand Apology and Money from Russians," *New York Times*, September 3rd, 1983, Section 1, p. 5.

62. Cited in Mikhail Prozumenshchikov, *Bolshoi Sport i Bolshaya Politika* (Moscow: Rosspen, 2004), p. 131.

63. Letter from Mikhail Prozumenshchikov to the author, November 19, 2007.

64. Samaranch's comments were drawn up by the South Korean Ambassador in Geneva, Kun Park, in a special memorandum, which he sent to Seoul and to Samaranch, for his information, on July 31, 1985. IOCA: Seoul 88/Political matters, de 1982 a Mai 1986.

65. Conversation between Mangalyn Dugersuren and Eduard Shevardnadze, January 24, 1986. MFMA: fond 2, dans 1, kh/n 504, khuu 142.

66. Conversation between Juan Antonio Samaranch and Chun Doo-hwan, April 19, 1986. IOCA: Seoul 88/Political matters, de 1982 a Mai 1986.

67. Conversation between Aleksandr Yakovlev and Hwang Jang-yop, May 16, 1986. GARF: fond 10063, opis 2, delo 55, list 5.

68. Letter from Marat Gramov to Juan Antonio Samaranch, June 6, 1986. IOCA: URSS, sommet Reagan-Gorbatchev 1986–1987.

69. Vadim Medvedev, *Raspad*, p. 326.

70. "Erich Honecker, East Germany's Communist Party chief and head of state...," Associated Press, November 14, 1986.

71. Cable from the Mongolian Embassy in Pyongyang to the Mongolian Foreign Ministry, April 29, 1987. MFMA: fond 3, dans 1, kh/n 178 (irsen shifr medeenii no. 61).

72. Cable from the Mongolian Embassy in Pyongyang to the Mongolian Foreign Ministry, June 6, 1987. MFMA: fond 3, dans 1, kh/n 178 (irsen shifr medeenii no. 80).

73. Vystuplenie M. S. Gorbacheva: Ozdorovlenie mezhdunarodnoi obstanovki, ukreplenie mira (po vtoromu voprosu), November 11, 1986. AGF: Fond 5, Dokument 20669, listy 31–32.

74. *Games of the XXIVth Olympiad in Seoul 1988: Official Report* (Seoul: SLOOC, 1989), Vol. 1, p. 486.

75. Ibid., p. 830.

76. Evgenii Ivanov, "Olympics: Soviet cosmonauts as popular as Soviet athletes," TASS, September 21st, 1988.

77. This story is taken from "Korean-Russian's tearful reunion with his uncle," *Seoul Olympic Villager*, September 27, 1988, p. 7. *Seoul Olympic Villager* was a newspaper published by the SLOOC for distribution to athletes in the Olympic Village. Copies are now obtainable from the Olympic Research Center, 2nd floor of the Velodrome, Olympic Park, Seoul.

78. *Games of the XXIVth Olympiad in Seoul 1988: Official Report* (Seoul: SLOOC, 1989), Vol. 1, p. 436.

79. Ibid., p. 440.

80. Ibid.

81. Susan Chira, "Anti-U.S. Feelings: Amid glamor of the games, Korea sees warts on an ally," *New York Times*, October 2, 1988, Section 4, p. 2.

82. "Let's meet in Moscow or in Seoul Again," *Seoul Olympic Villager*, September 29, 1988, p. 7. For an excellent account of the Soviet cultural program in Seoul, and its significance, see James Riordan, "The tiger and the bear: Korean-Soviet relationship in the light of the Olympic Games," in Seoul Olympic Sports Promotion

Foundation, *Toward One World Beyond All Barriers, The Seoul Olympiad Anniversary Conference*, Vol. 1 (Seoul: Poong Nam Publishing Company, 1990), pp. 338–339.

83. "Rude or Just Exuberant? US Delegation Branded for Less Than Golden Behavior," *Sunday Oregonian*, September 18, 1988; Barry Renfrew, "Government Tries to Stop Anti-American Outbursts," Associated Press, September 29, 1988.

84. "Charges dropped against two US swimmers accused of theft," *Oregonian*, October 1, 1988.

85. Ruth Youngblood, "Soviets sweep Americans in Olympic diplomacy as well as medals," United Press International, October 2, 1988.

86. "Soviets work to create good impression," Associated Press, September 29, 1988.

87. "Koreans succumb to Moscow charm," *Financial Times*, October 3, 1988.

88. "Seeking magic to victory," *Seoul Olympic Villager*, September 17, 1988, p. 7.

89. "Ha gets message through electric mail," *Seoul Olympic Villager*, September 16, 1988, p. 2.

90. "Ban on copying," *Seoul Olympic Villager*, September 16, 1988, p. 3.

91. Don Oberdorfer, *The Two Koreas: A Contemporary History*, pp. 200–201.

92. Cited in ibid., p. 200.

93. "Three Kims pledge to end confrontation," *Sydney Morning Herald*, May 30, 1988, p. 11.

94. P. Wilson, "Opposition calls for world talks on Korea," *Herald*, August 19, 1988, p. 29.

95. Janice Fuhrman, "Korean opposition leader in Japan," United Press International, August 18, 1988.

96. Author's interview with Daniel Sneider, May 24, 2008, Washington, DC.

97. Letter from Vladimir Ovsyannikov to the author, December 12, 2007. Interview with Hwang Byong-tae, August 29, 2007. Hwang Byong-tae recalled a slightly different order of events. He claimed it was Ovsyannikov who approached Hwang with a request for an interview with Kim Young-sam. I adopted Ovsyannikov's recollection in this instance, because he is the most disinterested participant in the episode.

98. Letter from Vladimir Ovsyannikov to the author, December 12, 2007.

99. Ibid.

100. Interview with Hwang Byong-tae, August 29, 2007. Hwang Byong-tae accompanied Kim Young-sam to Tokyo in August 1988, and later to Moscow in 1989 and 1990. Also, 김영삼, 김영삼회고록: 민주주의를위한나의투쟁, Vol. 3 (서울: 백산서당, 2000), p. 152.

101. "Possibilities for dialogue," *New Times*, No. 40 (September 1988), pp. 8–9. See also "Speech in Krasnoyarsk," *BBC Summary of World Broadcasts*, September 19, 1988.

102. The author's interview with Hwang Byong-tae, Seoul, August 29, 2007; the author's interview with Kim Young-sam, Seoul, September 19, 2007.

103. The author's interview with Georgii Arbatov, Moscow, March 24, 2008.

104. The author's interview with Kim Young-sam, Seoul, September 19, 2008.

105. This account is based on Chon Dzhe-mun, *Rossiya: Dalekaya i Blizkaya: Moi Peregovory v Moskve* (Moscow: IDV RAN, 2004), 19–20.

106. The author's interview with Kim Young-sam, Seoul, September 19, 2007.

107. On drinking vodka with Primakov, see 김영삼, 김영삼회고록, Vol. 3, p. 183. The author's interview with Kim Young-sam, Seoul, September 19, 2007. On Primakov's appointment, see, for instance, "Economist to head Soviet body," *Toronto Star*, June 4, 1989, p. A22.

108. The author's interview with Kim Young-sam, Seoul, September 19, 2007.

109. "Kim's emphasis on political not shared by Moscow official," Japan Economic Newswire, June 7, 1989.

110. "Moscow hosts meeting of the two Koreas," *Financial Times*, June 15, 1989, p. 4 and "Soviets try to bolster Korean peace talks," *Boston Globe*, June 18, 1989, p. 19.

111. Mikhail Kapitsa, "Changing East-West relations and the situation in the Asian-Pacific region (Soviet evaluation)," in Koh Byong-ik et al. (eds.), *Toward One World beyond All Barriers*, p. 42.

112. Vadim Medvedev, *Raspad*, pp. 327–328.

113. Vystuplenie t. Shakhnazarova G. Kh. na vstreche v Otdele TsK KPSS s predstavitelyami sovetskikh sredstv massovoi informatsii, August 14, 1987. AGF: Fond 5, Dokument 17693, list 8.

114. Vadim Medvedev, *Raspad*, p. 329.

115. Conversation between Jambyn Batmunkh and Kim Il-sung, November 20, 1986. MFMA: fond 3, dans 1, kh/n 173, khuu 162.

116. 邓小平年谱, 下, p. 1190.

117. Ibid., p. 1192.

118. Conversation between Mikhail Gorbachev and Kim Yong-nam, May 4, 1988. *Otvechaya Na Vyzov Vremeni*, 848. See also About Kim Yong-nam's visit to Moscow (April 28–May 5, 1988). MOL: XIXJ/j-1988-t-Korea/135-002437.

119. Excerpts from a Politburo meeting, May 5, 1988. Provided to the author by the Gorbachev Foundation. It is interesting that Gorbachev's comments in the unpublished document acquired by this author are radically different from the version published in *Otvechaya Na Vyzov Vremeni*, p. 848. It is, of course, possible that there are two versions of that Politburo meeting.

120. "Speech in Krasnoyarsk," *BBC Summary of World Broadcasts*, September 19, 1988.

121. Conversation between Aleksandr Yakovlev and Hwang Jang-yop, October 18, 1988. GARF: fond 10063, opis 2, delo 126, listy 1–13. My italics.

122. 钟之成, 为了世界更美好, p. 6.

123. Karen Brutents, *Nesbyvsheesya*, p. 216.

124. Author's interview with Yurii Vanin, Moscow, March 28, 2008.

125. Cited in Vladimir Li, *Rossiya i Koreya*, p. 235.

126. CC CPSU Politburo minutes, November 10, 1988. AGF.

127. Nikolai Shaskolskii and Vladimir Khlynov, O merakh po sozdaniyu obstanovki dobrososedstva v sovetsko-kitaiskikh otnosheniyakh, September 4, 1986, IMEMO RAN archive. Also, Nikolai Shaskolskii and Ivanov, Perspektivy politiki SSSR v Tikhookeanskom regione i faktor voennoi sily, undated, probably 1986, IMEMO RAN archive.

128. CC CPSU Politburo minutes, November 10, 1988. AGF.

129. "Rossiya i Mezhkoreiskie Otnosheniya," April 17, 2003, available at http://www.gorby.ru/rubrs.asp?rubr_id=124&art_id=13119.

130. K voprosu ob ustanovlenii i razvertyvanii ekonomicheskikh svyazei s Yuzhnoi Koreei, November 1988, IMEMO RAN archive.

131. The author's and Artemy M. Kalinovsky's interview with Eduard Shevardnadze, Tbilisi, May 7, 2008.

132. Conversation between V. I. Trifonov and Chen Di, October 20, 1988. AVPRF: fond 100, opis 75, delo 3, list 92.

133. Dokladnaya Zapiska M. S. Gorbachevu k Spets N. 696 iz Pkhen'yana, October 26, 1988, AGF: Fond 5, Dokument 18169, list 1.

134. Ibid.

135. HIA/TSP: Diary No. 8, p. 152.

136. HIA/TSP: Notepad 20.12.88.

137. HIA/TSP: Diary No. 8, p. 155.

138. Don Oberdorfer, *The Two Koreas*, p. 213.

139. "Information on the main results of Eduard Shevardnadze's visit to Japan, the Philippines and the DPRK," January 2, 1989. SAPMO-BArch: DY 30/J IV 2/2A/3185.

140. "Reagan Provotsiroval Nas Khlopnut Dver'yu," *Vlast*, No. 14 (March 11, 2005).

141. Cited in Evgenii Bazhanov, "Soviet policy towards South Korea under Gorbachev," in Il Yung Chung (ed.), *Korea and Russia: Toward the 21st Century* (Seoul: Sejong Institute, 1992), p. 98.

142. The author's interview with Anatolii Chernyaev, Moscow, April 1, 2008.

143. Cited in Evgenii Bazhanov, "Soviet policy towards South Korea under Gorbachev," p. 98.

144. Informatsiya o vyvodakh, sdelannykh kollegiei Ministerstva inostrannykh del SSSR 27 yanvarya s.g. po voprosu o nashei politike v otnoshenii Korei, undated (January–February 1990). GASO: fond 4, opis 159, delo 145, list 3.

145. Ibid., list 4, my italics.

146. Evgeniya Albats, "Eshche v 1990 godu KGB SSSR dokladyval: V KNDR zaversh-ena razrabotka atomnogo vzryvnogo ustroistva," *Izvestiya*, No. 118 (June 24, 1994), pp. 1, 4.

147. Cited in Karen Brutents, *Nesbyvsheesya*, p. 217.

148. Cited in Evgenii Bazhanov, "Soviet policy towards South Korea under Gorbachev," 102.

149. Informatsiya o vyvodakh, sdelannykh kollegiei Ministerstva inostrannykh del SSSR 27 yanvarya s.g. po voprosu o nashei politike v otnoshenii Korei, undated (January-February 1990). GASO: fond 4, opis 159, delo 145, list 3.

150. For detailed discussion of the three-party merger, see, for instance, John Kie-chiang Oh, *Korean Politics: the Quest for Democratization and Economic Development* (Ithaca, NY: Cornell University Press, 1999), p. 117; Young Whan Kihl, "South Korea in 1990: Diplomatic activism and a partisan quagmire," *Asian Survey*, Vol. 31, No. 1, pp. 64–70.

151. John Kie-chiang Oh, *Korean Politics*, p. 117.

152. *Chosun Ilbo*, March 11, 1990, p. 2; 박철언, 바른역사를위한증언, Vol. 2, pp. 232–234.

153. On details of the Dunaev channel, see박철언, 바른역사를위한증언, pp. 143, 228, 230, 234, 242, 246. According to Park's recollections, messages were also passed through "Nazarov" in Tokyo. I have been unable to find any further details. On Dunaev's friendship with Chernyaev, author's interview with Anatolii Chernyaev, April 1, 2008, Moscow. Also see Anatolii Chernyaev, *1991 god: Dnevnik pomoshchnika prezidenta SSSR* (Moskva: Terra-Terra, 1997); also, personal correspondence to the author from Konstantin Sarkisov, August 3, 2007.

154. 박철언, 바른역사를위한증언, p. 228.
155. This account is based on Vladlen Martynov's recollections, published in the Russian version of Jeong Jae-mun's memoirs, Chon Dzhe-mun, *Rossiya: Dalekaya i Blizkaya: Moi Peregovory v Moskve* (Moscow: IDV RAN, 2004), pp. 173–174. The date of Gorbachev's approval of Yakovlev's meeting with YS has been inferred from Memorandum from Anatolii Chernyaev to Mikhail Gorbachev, March 19, 1990. AGF: Fond 2, Opis 1, Dokument 8240, list 1.
156. Memorandum from Anatolii Chernyaev to Mikhail Gorbachev, March 19, 1990. AGF: Fond 2, Dokument 8240, list 1.
157. Memorandum from Anatolii Chernyaev to Mikhail Gorbachev, March 19, 1990. AGF: Fond 2, Dokument 8240, list 1.
158. *Chosun Ilbo*, March 21, 1990, p. 1.
159. Chon Dzhe-mun, *Rossiya: Dalekaya i Blizkaya*, pp. 209–210.
160. *Chosun Ilbo*, March 22, 1990, p. 2.
161. Letter from Kim Young-sam to Alexander Yakovlev, March 31, 1990. GARF: fond 10063, opis 2, delo 570, list 3.
162. Chon Dzhe-mun, *Rossiya: Dalekaya i Blizkaya*, p. 208.
163. Ibid., 174.
164. Chon Dzhe-mun, *Rossiya: Dalekaya i Blizkaya*, pp. 89–90. The author's interview with Kim Young-sam, Seoul, September 19, 2007.
165. The author's interview with Kim Young-sam, Seoul, September 19, 2007.
166. Kim Hakjoon, "The process leading to the establishment of diplomatic relations between South Korea and the Soviet Union," *Asian Survey*, Vol. 37, No. 7 (July 1997), p. 645.
167. "South Korea and Russia: Cream for the Cat," *Economist*, March 31, 1990, p. 50.
168. 박철언, 바른역사를위한증언, p. 243.
169. *Chosun Ilbo*, March 23, 1990, p. 1.
170. 박철언, 바른역사를위한증언, pp. 244–245.
171. Karen Brutents, *Nesbyvsheesya*, p. 217.
172. Ibid., p. 218.
173. 박철언, 바른역사를위한증언.
174. Ibid., 157. Russian translation in Karen Brutents, *Nesbyvsheesya*, p. 218 slightly differs from the above, but not in the substance of the message.
175. Karen Brutents, *Nesbyvsheesya*, p. 218.
176. Ibid.
177. 박철언, 바른역사를위한증언, p. 157.
178. Ibid.
179. Karen Brutents, *Nesbyvsheesya*, p. 218. My italics. It appears that the cited passage is actually a direct quote from Brutents's own memorandum of the meeting, though Brutents did not mark it as such by quotation marks.
180. Ibid., p. 219.
181. 박철언, 바른역사를위한증언, p. 158.
182. Ibid., p. 247.
183. Cited Karen Brutents, *Nesbyvsheesya*, p. 219.
184. Cited in ibid., p. 220.
185. Cited in ibid.
186. 박철언, 바른역사를위한증언, p. 160.

187. Kim Hakjoon, "The process leading to the establishment of diplomatic relations between South Korea and the Soviet Union," pp. 645–646.
188. Ibid., p. 646.
189. 박철언, 바른역사를위한증언, p. 163. By Kim Hakjoon's account, the meeting actually took place outside of Tokyo in the hot springs town of Atami, to avoid media speculation. Kim Hakjoon, "The process leading to the establishment of diplomatic relations between South Korea and the Soviet Union," 646. Park's account takes precedence here, because he was actually present at the meeting and might remember best. Park's account is also confirmed in Vladislav Dunaev's memoir. Vladislav Dunaev, Dostovernyi Tom (Moscow: Klyuch-S, 2010), p. 416.
190. 박철언, 바른역사를위한증언, p. 164. The author's interview with Park Chul-un, Seoul, August 7, 2007.
191. Letter to the author from Yeom Don-jae, September 19, 2007. By Kim Hakjoon's account, Yeom actually followed Dunaev to Moscow. Kim Hakjoon, "The process leading to the establishment of diplomatic relations between South Korea and the Soviet Union," p. 646.
192. Cited in Anatolii Chernyaev et al. (eds.), V Politbyuro TsK KPSS, p. 595.
193. Memorandum from Anatolii Chernyaev to Mikhail Gorbachev, May 17, 1990. AGF: Fond 2, Dokument 8315, list 1.
194. Ibid.
195. Don Oberdorfer, The Two Koreas, p. 209.
196. Ibid., pp. 209–210. Despite these precautions, it was already an open secret that the Soviet Union was moving toward diplomatic recognition of South Korea. Hyun Hong-choo, the new South Korean permanent observer at the United Nations who arrived in New York in May 1990 via Beijing and Moscow, told the Secretary General on May 21 that in Moscow "he had picked up many encouraging signals. He was of the impression that the USSR would be prepared to respond to ROK's desire for the establishment of bilateral diplomatic relations. The related technical questions, he suspected, could be worked out even before the end of the current year." Conversation between Javier Pérez de Cuéllar and Hyun Hong-choo, May 21, 1990. UNA: Series S-1033, Box 10, File 5.
197. Vladislav Dunaev, Dostovernyi Tom, p. 418.
198. Communication to the author from Gong Ro-myung, December 18, 2007.
199. Communication to the author from Yeom Don-jae, September 19, 2007. Also, Interview with Park Chul-un, Seoul, August 7, 2007. The information that it was Gong Ro-myung who first received the news of Gorbachev's willingness to meet with Roh Tae-woo was confirmed in a telegram dated June 12, 1990, from the US Embassy in Seoul to the Secretary of State (Seoul 06576), National Security Archive, Don Oberdorfer Files. I am grateful to Izumikawa Yasuhiro for pointing my attention to these documents, and to Don Oberdorfer and the National Security Archive for making them available.
200. Kim Hakjoon, "The Process Leading to the Establishment of Diplomatic Relations Between South Korea and the Soviet Union," p. 646.
201. Ibid., p. 646.
202. Don Oberdorfer, The Two Koreas, p. 210.
203. Ibid., p. 211.
204. Kim Hakjoon, "The process leading to the establishment of diplomatic relations between South Korea and the Soviet Union," p. 647.
205. Ibid., p. 648.
206. All information has been taken from ibid., p. 648.

207. Embassy in Seoul to the Secretary of State, June 2, 1990 (Seoul 06215), National Security Archive, Don Oberdorfer Files. For a summary of the conversation, see Mikhail Gorbachev, *Otvechaya Na Vyzov Vremeni*, pp. 899–900.

208. Interview with Sun Joun-yung, Seoul, July 27, 2007.

209. Don Oberdorfer, *The Two Koreas*, p. 212.

210. Kim Hakjoon, "The process leading to the establishment of diplomatic relations between South Korea and the Soviet Union," p. 649. Don Oberdorfer, *The Two Koreas*, p. 212. At least two photos were taken: see *Chosun Ilbo*, June 6, 1990, p. 1 and p. 2.

211. Communication to the author from Yeom Donjae, September 19, 2007.

212. Materialy k zasedaniyu Politicheskogo Konsul'tativnogo Komiteta gosudarstv-uchastnikov Varshavskogo Dogovora (PKK) v Moskve, June 7, 1990. AGF: Fond 5, Dokument 15354, list 2.

213. Rede des Präsidenten der Union der Sozialistischen Sowjetrepubliken M. S. Gorbatschow, June 7, 1990. SAPMO-Barch: DC20/I/3/3000, s. 125. Courtesy of the Parallel History Project.

214. Cited in Natalia Bazhanova, "North Korea and Seoul-Moscow relations," p. 338.

215. "N. Korea refuses to resume dialogue with S. Korea," Japan Economic Newswire, June 13, 1990.

216. Ibid.

217. Cited in Aleksandr Kapto, *Na Perekrestkakh Zhizni: Politicheskie Memuary* (Moskva: Sotsialno-Politicheskii Zhurnal, 1996), pp. 432–436.

218. Conversation between Georgii Kunadze and Song Sen-pil, September 20, 1991. GARF: fond 10026, opis 4, delo 2803, listy 1–3.

219. On our policy in Korea, IDV report, February 1992. GARF, fond 10026, opis 4, delo 2803, listy 96–98.

220. The author's interview with a member of Roh Tae-woo's entourage, Seoul, July 2007.

221. Anatolii Chernyaev, *Sovmestnyi Iskhod*, p. 936.

222. Letter from Vladimir Lukin to Boris Yeltsin, undated, but contains Yeltsin's endorsement dated August 16, 1990. GARF: fond 10026, opis 1, delo 2423, list 299.

223. Conversation between George Bush and Roh Tae-woo, June 6, 1990. GBPL. Obtained by the author through FOIA request.

CHAPTER 7

1. Anatolii Chernyaev, "Poslednii zarubezhnyi ofitsial'nyi visit M. S. Gorbacheva v kachestve prezidenta SSSR," manuscript. The author is grateful to David Wolff for sharing this manuscript.

2. Tsuyoshi Hasegawa, *The Northern Territories*, Vol. 2, p. 280.

3. Anatolii Chernyaev, "Poslednii zarubezhnyi ofitsial'nyi visit M. S. Gorbacheva."

4. During a conversation with Kohl, he put the point even more starkly: "The Japanese do not have more grey matter than the Europeans: they understand only what they buy." Hanns Jürgen Küsters and Daniel Hofmann (eds.), *Deutsche Einheit: Sonderedition aus den Akten des Bundeskanzleramtes 1989/90* (München: R. Oldenbourg, 1998), p. 807.

5. Anatolii Chernyaev, "Poslednii zarubezhnyi ofitsial'nyi visit M. S. Gorbacheva."

6. Mikhail Gorbachev, *Otvechaya Na Vyzov Vremeni*, p. 859.

7. Tsuyoshi Hasegawa, *The Northern Territories*, Vol. 2, p. 283.

8. Ibid., pp. 278–279.

9. Zaklyuchenie general'nogo shtaba vooruzhennykh sil Rossiiskoi Federatsii po probleme territorial'nogo razmezhevaniya mezhdu Rossiei i Yaponiei, July 24, 1992. GARF: fond 10026, opis 4, delo 2612, listy 21–26.

10. Tsuyoshi Hasegawa, *The Northern Territories*, Vol. 2, p. 288.

11. Ibid.

12. That is to say, Shevardnadze's aide did not know for sure which islands were being disputed—another example of Soviet neglect for this subject.

13. HIA/TSP: Diary No. 8, pp. 123–124.

14. Ibid., pp. 125, 142.

15. Ibid., p. 134.

16. Tsuyoshi Hasegawa provides a very detailed account of these meetings in *The Northern Territories Dispute*, Vol. 2, pp. 291–294 and 303–314. English translations of the meeting transcripts can be found in David Wolff (ed.), *Cold War International History Project Bulletin*, No. 10, pp. 203–210.

17. Tsuyoshi Hasegawa, "Stalemate in an era of change: New sources and questions on Gorbachev, Yeltsin, and Soviet/Russian-Japanese relations," in David Wolff (ed.), *Cold War International History Project Bulletin*, issue 10 (March 1998), p. 194.

18. Tsuyoshi Hasegawa, *The Northern Territories Dispute*, Vol. 2, p. 298.

19. Ibid. The author's interview with Togo Kazuhiko (by phone), August 11, 2012.

20. "Szovjet tájékoztatás Uno japán külügyminiszter moszkvai látogatásáról," May 18, 1989. MOL: XIX-J-1-j-Japán-68-10-002370-1989.

21. Meeting between Mikhail Gorbachev and Rajiv Gandhi, July 15, 1989. REEADD: Box 16.

22. Ibid.

23. Anatolii Chernyaev, "Poslednii zarubezhnyi ofitsial'nyi visit M.S. Gorbacheva v kachestve prezidenta SSSR."

24. Ibid.

25. Hand-written note from Anatolii Chernyaev to Mikhail Gorbachev, April 15, 1989. AGF: fond 2, dokument 7457.

26. Tsuyoshi Hasegawa, *The Northern Territories Dispute*, Vol. 2, p. 342.

27. Conversation between Aleksandr Yakovlev and Doi Takako, November 15, 1989. GARF: fond 10063, opis 2, delo 198, listy 7–8.

28. See materials pertaining to Mikhail Gorbachev's visit to the Soviet Far East on July 25–31, 1986 (mainly public speeches) in Mikhail Gorbachev, *Sobranie Sochinenii*, Vol. 4, pp. 342–419.

29. This was Nikita Khrushchev's idea, which Gorbachev recalled and endorsed in a Politburo meeting on August 14, 1986. See ibid., p. 416.

30. See Resolution of the Council of Ministers of the USSR No. 958, August 19, 1987, on "Complex Development of the Production Forces of the Far Eastern Economic Region, Buriat ASSR and Chita Oblast Until Year 2000." Available: http://www.worklib.ru/laws/ussr/10005538.php.

31. O nekotorykh problemakh i vozmozhnykh napravleniyakh rasshireniya ekonomicheskogo sotrudnichestva SSSR v aziatsko-tikhookeanskom regione, June 6, 1988. GARF: fond 10026, opis 4, delo 2867, listy 2–11.

32. Ota Seizo, "東アジア開発計画プロジェクト案," blog entry, October 26, 2008. http://blog.goo.ne.jp/otaseizo/e/a63fd7f976382477273ea2fcbe18ce7e.

33. O nekotorykh problemakh i vozmozhnykh napravleniyakh rasshireniya ekonomicheskogo sotrudnichestva SSSR v aziatsko-tikhookeanskom regione, June 6, 1988. GARF: fond 10026, opis 4, delo 2867, listy 2–11.

34. "Today in the world," *Official Kremlin International News Broadcast*, December 5, 1988.
35. For example, Opyt KNR v razvitii vneshneekonomicheskikh svyazei, April 6, 1988. IMEMO RAN Archive. There are other similar reports at the same location.
36. The report on the travels of this delegation was retrieved by the author from the IMEMO archives, and since in the Soviet bureaucracy reports such as this traveled upwards and not sideways, it is very likely that it was written by someone from the IMEMO who participated in the trip. See K voprosu ob intensifikatsii vneshne-ekonomicheskikh svyazei dal'nevostochnogo ekonomicheskogo rai'ona so stranami aziatsko-tikhookeanskogo regiona, undated, first half of 1988. IMEMO RAN Archive.
37. Ibid.
38. Ibid.
39. Mikhail Gorbachev, *Sobranie Sochinenii*, Vol. 12, p. 71.
40. Transcript of *Rezonans*, *Official Kremlin International News Broadcast*, February 7, 1989.
41. Ibid.
42. Letter from Evgenii Primakov to Vladimir Kamentsev, December 29, 1988. IMEMO RAN Archive.
43. "Toho Mutual sues 2 former executives," *Daily Yomiuri*, July 22, 2000, p. 4. It should be said that this lawsuit alleged that Ota Seizo made illegal loans from Toho Seimei to companies controlled by his relatives; 6.4 billion yen were never recovered.
44. O merakh po sodeistviyu realizatsii programmy razvitiya Dal'nevostochnogo ekonomicheskogo rai'ona, letter from the head of the Sakhalin KGB Directorate A. V. Selikh to the First Secretary of the Sakhalin Oblast Party Committee V. S. Bondarchuk, March 7, 1989. GASO: fond p-4, opis 152, delo 67, listy 1–4.
45. Ibid.
46. "Verity boosting Soviet oil industry," *National Security Record*, Vol. 114 (June 1, 1988), p. 5.
47. O merakh po sodeistviyu realizatsii programmy razvitiya Dal'nevostochnogo ekonomicheskogo rai'ona, letter from the head of the Sakhalin KGB Directorate A. V. Selikh to the First Secretary of the Sakhalin Oblast Party Committee V. S. Bondarchuk, March 7, 1989. GASO: fond p-4, opis 152, delo 67, listy 1–4.
48. Letter from Georgii Fedyashin (APN) to Viktor Bondarchuk, December 12, 1988. GASO: fond P4, opis 150, delo 94, list 145.
49. O merakh po sodeistviyu realizatsii programmy razvitiya Dal'nevostochnogo ekonomicheskogo rai'ona, letter from the head of the Sakhalin KGB Directorate A. V. Selikh to the First Secretary of the Sakhalin Oblast Party Committee V. S. Bondarchuk, March 7, 1989. GASO: fond p-4, opis 152, delo 67, listy 1-4.
50. Ibid. See also Tsuyoshi Hasegawa, *The Northern Territories*, Vol. 2, pp. 275–276.
51. "Joint venture puts government in quandary," *Japan Economic Newswire*, June 4, 1988.
52. Memorandum from Morton I. Abramowitz to the Acting Secretary of State, September 30, 1988. DNSA: US-Japan relations, 1977–1992. Document No. 01560.
53. Letter from V. Bondarchuk to the CC CPSU, March 10, 1989. GASO: fond p-4, opis 159, delo 115, listy 2–5.
54. Ibid.
55. Letter from Vladimir Lukin to Igor Rogachev, August 1989. GARF: fond 10026, opis 4, delo 2868, listy 1–2.

56. O voprosakh postavlennykh Sakhalinskim obkomom KPSS (joint memorandum by D. Yazov, V. Bakatin, K. Katushev, V. Kryuchkov, A. Bessmertnykh), September 1, 1989. GASO: fond p-4, opis 159, delo 115, listy 7–10.
57. Memorandum from Desaix Anderson to the Deputy Secretary of State. December 7, 1989. DNSA: Japan and the US, 1977–1992. Document 01612.

CHAPTER 8

1. This chapter draws on Sergey Radchenko and Lisbeth Tarlow, "Gorbachev, Ozawa, and the failed back-channel negotiations of 1989–1990," *Journal of Cold War Studies*, Vol. 15, No. 2 (Spring 2013), pp. 104–130, © 2013 by the President and Fellows of Harvard College and the Massachusetts Institute of Technology.
2. Raisuke Honda, "Kanemaru blundered on N. Isles issue," *Daily Yomiuri*, April 30, 1990, p. 1.
3. Ozawa, in a later recollection, thought that the price was "cheap." He also claimed the initiative to purchase the islands came from the Soviets, but the record suggests otherwise. See Ozawa's interview in *Asahi-online*, May 5, 2013. The author is grateful to Izumikawa Yasuhiro and David Wolff for bringing this to his attention.
4. Kevin Sullivan, "Moscow shifts in dispute on Japan's claim to islands," *Guardian*, January 17, 1990.
5. K besede s S. Abe, undated. GARF: fond P9654, opis 10-X, listy 21–32.
6. Shimotomai Nobuo, "Japan-Soviet Relations under perestroika," p. 115.
7. K beside s S. Abe, undated. GARF: fond P9654, opis 10-X, list 32.
8. Tsuyoshi Hasegawa, *The Northern Territories Dispute*, Vol. 2, p. 344.
9. Terril Jones, "Soviets seen more willing to solve territorial dispute," Associated Press, January 16, 1990. The Gorbachev Foundation published excerpts from the memorandum of conversation between Abe and Gorbachev. However, none of the above points are mentioned in the excerpts. Mikhail Gorbachev, *Otvechaya Na Vyzov Vremeni*, pp. 905–906.
10. Anatolii Chernyaev, *Sovmestnyi Iskhod*, p. 836.
11. In the same interview, Kasparov also proposed to sell Mongolia to China, which did not go over well with the Mongolians, who sent in hundreds of letters of protest to the Soviet Embassy in Ulaanbaatar.
12. "Soviet historian supports return of northern territories," Japan Economic Newswire, October 20, 1989.
13. "Sakharov urges compromise on island issue," Jiji Press Ticker Service, October 26, 1989.
14. Letter from Ota Hiroshi to Boris Yeltsin, December 5, 1989. RGANI: fond 89, opis 30, delo 17, listy 1–4.
15. Yeltsin's press conference remarks are reproduced in Igor Latyshev, *Yaponiya, Yapontsy i Yaponovedy* (Moscow: Algoritm, 2001), pp. 690–691.
16. "Nakayama dismisses compromise on northern territories," Japan Economic Newswire, January 19, 1990.
17. Igor Latyshev, *Yaponiya, Yapontsy i Yaponovedy*, p. 694.
18. Anatolii Chernyaev, *Sovmestnyi Iskhod*, p. 836.
19. Konstantin Sarkisov, "The territorial dispute between Japan and Russia: The 'two-island solution' and Putin's last year as President," in Kimie Hara and Geoffrey Jukes (eds.), *Northern Territories, Asia-Pacific Regional Conflicts and the Aland Experience: Untying the Kurillian Knot* (London: Routledge, 2009), p. 41.
20. Koichi Hamazaki, "Yeltsin says n.[orthern] isles should remain under Soviet control," *Daily Yomiuri*, August 24, 1990.

21. Diary of Viktor Ilyushin, entry for August 22, 1990. Published in "Boris Yeltsin: Ot narodnogo do svyatogo," *Argumenty i Fakty*, January 12, 2000.

22. "Gorbachev and Japanese visitor discuss Kurils," *BBC Summary of World Broadcasts*, July 27, 1990. Part 1, The USSR; 1. THE USSR; SU/0827/i; Anatolii Chernyaev, *Sovmestnyi Iskhod*, p. 866.

23. "Shevardnadze says no blocks to friendly ties with Japan," Japan Economic Newswire, September 5, 1990.

24. Resolution of the Sakhalin Regional Soviet of People's Deputies, September 12, 1990. GARF: fond 10026, opis 1, delo 2422, list 65.

25. Letter from A. P. Aksenov to Boris Yeltsin, October 5, 1990. GARF: fond 10026, opis 1, delo 2422, listy 63–64.

26. Letter from Andrei Kozyrev to Viktor Ilyushin, November 6, 1990. GARF: fond 10026, opis 1, delo 2422, listy 66–67.

27. Anatolii Chernyaev et al. (eds.), *V Politbyuro TsK KPSS*, p. 594.

28. Anatolii Chernyaev, *Sovmestnyi Iskhod*, p. 891.

29. Anatolii Chernyaev, "Poslednii vizit," pp. 20–22.

30. Anatolii Chernyaev, *Sovmestnyi Iskhod*, p. 866.

31. "One step needed for normal Japan-Soviet ties: Ozawa," Jiji Press Ticker Service, September 5, 1990.

32. Lisbeth Tarlow Bernstein, "On the Rocks: Gorbachev and the Kurile Islands," Ph.D diss. (Fletcher School of Law and Diplomacy, 1997), pp. 190–193.

33. Author's interview with Vasilii Saplin, Sapporo, March 11, 2011.

34. Ibid.

35. Conversation between Petr Demichev and a Japanese parliamentary delegation led by Yamaguchi Toshio, August 27, 1986. GARF: fond R-7523, opis 145, delo 4016, listy 222–223.

36. Conversation between Nikolai Solov'ev and Yamaguchi Toshio, September 24, 1986. GARF: fond R-7523, opis 145, delo 4028, list 195.

37. Anatolii Milyukov's handwritten notes on his meeting with Kumagai Hiroshi and Sugimori Koji, July 24, 2990. GARF: fond 10026, opis 5, delo 1438, listy 1–9.

38. Ibid.

39. Ibid.

40. O poezdke t. Yanaeva v Yaponiyu, October 4, 1990. RGANI: fond 89, opis 20, delo 10, listy 1–3.

41. Conversation between Aleksandr Yakovlev and Ozawa Ichiro's representatives, November 22, 1990. GARF: fond 10063, opis 2, delo 209, list 2.

42. John Barron, *KGB Today: The Hidden Hand* (New York: Berkley, 1987), p. 142.

43. Akihiro Tamiya, "Gorbachev playing isle cards close; Moscow keeps Tokyo guessing in upcoming territory-for-aid talks," *Japan Economic Journal*, April 13, 1991.

44. Conversation between Aleksandr Yakovlev and Ozawa Ichiro's representatives, November 22, 1990. GARF: fond 10063, opis 2, delo 209, list 2.

45. Ibid., list 3.

46. Ibid., list 4.

47. Randall Newnham, "The price of German unity: The role of economic aid in the German-Soviet negotiations," *German Studies Review*, Vol. 22, No. 3 (October 1999), pp. 421–446.

48. Mary Sarotte, *1989: The Struggle to Create Post–Cold War Europe* (Princeton, NJ: Princeton University Press, 2009), pp. 152–160.

49. Aleksandr Galkin and Anatolii Chernyaev (eds.), *Gorbachev i Germanskii Vopros* (Moscow: Ves' Mir, 2006), p. 605.

50. Ibid.

51. The implicit message of the "talk along the Rhine" has been played up by a number of authors, among others, Randall Newnham, "The price of German unity: The role of economic aid in the German-Soviet negotiations," *German Studies Review*, Vol. 22, No. 3 (Oct. 1999), p. 427. There is little doubt that Kohl himself was sure there was an unspoken agreement. See, however, "Conversation between Mikhail Gorbachev and Helmut Kohl (one on one)," June 12, 1989, in Aleksandr Galkin and Anatolii Chernyaev (eds.), *Gorbachev i Germanskii Vopros*, pp. 162–163, and "Conversation between Kohl and Gorbachev," June 12, 1989, in Hanns Jürgen Küsters and Daniel Hofmann (eds.), *Deutsche Einheit*, pp. 284–285.

52. Conversation between Aleksandr Yakovlev and Ozawa Ichiro's representatives, November 22, 1990. GARF: fond 10063, opis 2, delo 209, list 5.

53. Anatolii Chernyaev, *Sovmestnyi Iskhod*, p. 873.

54. Conversation between Aleksandr Yakovlev and Ozawa Ichiro's representatives, November 22, 1990. GARF: fond 10063, opis 2, delo 209, list 7.

55. Letter from Vadim Medvedev to Mikhail Gorbachev, November 1, 1990. GARF: fond 10026, opis 5, delo 1424, list 24.

56. Pavel Stroilov, *Behind the Desert Storm* (Chicago, IL: Price World Pub., 2011), pp. 253–255 for full text of Medvedev's letter. While Stroilov's analysis is completely unconvincing, his sources are generally reliable.

57. Anatolii Chernyaev, "Poslednii vizit," p. 18.

58. Conversation between Aleksandr Yakovlev and Edamura Sumio, November 24, 1990. GARF: fond 10063, opis 2, delo 210, listy 1–6.

59. Skhema podgotovki i provedeniya vizita prezidenta SSSR v Yaponiyu, January 1991, p. 4. Kindly provided to the author by Lis Tarlow.

60. Ibid., p. 3.

61. Ibid.

62. Paul Quinn-Judge, "As plight at home worsens, Gorbachev seeks charity abroad," *Boston Globe*, November 21, 1990, p. 10.

63. Anatolii Chernyaev, *Sovmestnyi Iskhod*, p. 898.

64. Bryan Brumley, "Another top Gorbachev reformer leaves Soviet post," Associated Press, January 18, 1991.

65. Anatolii Chernyaev, *Sovmestnyi Iskhod*, p. 907.

66. Skhema podgotovki i provedeniya vizita prezidenta SSSR v Yaponiyu, p. 2.

67. The author's interview with Vasilii Saplin, Sapporo, March 11, 2010.

68. Lisbeth Tarlow, "Russian decision-making on Japan in the Gorbachev era," in Gilbert Rozman (ed.), *Japan and Russia: The Tortuous Path to Normalization* (New York: St. Martin's Press, 2000), 130.

69. Conversation between Aleksandr Yakovlev and Kumagai Hiroshi, January 9, 1991. GARF: fond 10063, opis 2, delo 8765, listy 1–7.

70. Ibid.

71. Ibid.

72. Cover note from Anatolii Chernyaev to Mikhail Gorbachev, January 4, 1991. AGF: fond 2, dokument 8765.

73. Skhema podgotovki i provedeniya vizita prezidenta SSSR v Yaponiyu, p. 13.

74. Note from Anatolii Chernyaev to Gennadii Yanaev, January 9, 1991. AGF: fond 2, dokument 8775.

75. Skhema podgotovki i provedeniya vizita prezidenta SSSR v Yaponiyu, p. 7. On the other hand, Chernyaev's reservation about approval by the Russian Federation and Kurile residents had already been agreed to by Ozawa's people—in fact, it was put forward by Sugimori in the aforementioned meeting with Yakovlev on November 22, 1990. Perhaps Sugimori did not realize, as Chernyaev clearly did, that this provision offered a loophole for the Russians. Conversation between Aleksandr Yakovlev and Ozawa Ichiro's representatives, November 22, 1990. GARF: fond 10063, opis 2, delo 209, list 2.

76. Lisbeth Tarlow's interview with Sergei Grigor'ev, May 13, 1995. Kindly shared with the author by Lisbeth Tarlow.

77. Ibid.

78. "Gorbachev says he is ready to discuss territorial issue," Japan Economic Newswire, January 9, 1991.

79. Mikhail Gorbachev, Otvechaya Na Vyzov Vremeni, p. 907.

80. Ibid.

81. Anatolii Chernyaev, Sovmestnyi Iskhod, pp. 898–899.

82. "Soviet troops get new powers to keep order," Toronto Star, January 27, 1991, p. A2.

83. "Soviet firms reeling Gorbachev decrees decried as strangling free-market efforts," Globe and Mail (Canada), January 29, 1991.

84. "Tarasov 'case' again?," Russian Press Digest, February 2, 1991.

85. "Correspondent report; Chairman of Russia's innovation council Artem Tarasov: I am ready to assume that a secret protocol on the transfer of Kuril islands has been signed," Official Kremlin International News Broadcast, February 1, 1991.

86. Artem Tarasov, Millioner (Moscow: Vagrius, 2004), p. 211.

87. "Correspondent report; Chairman of Russia's innovation council Artem Tarasov: I am ready to assume that a secret protocol on the transfer of Kuril islands has been signed," Official Kremlin International News Broadcast, February 1, 1991.

88. Mary Dejevsky, "Yeltsin woos Kaliningrad Russians," Times, February 11, 1991.

89. Yevgeni Belovitsky, "Soviet economist on prospects for Kuriles issue settlement," TASS, March 15, 1991.

90. Yevgeni Belovitsky, "Kurile population objects to the transfer of islands," TASS, March 18, 1991; "Opinion of Soviet Far East residents on the Kuriles," TASS, February 13, 1991.

91. Lisbeth Tarlow's interview with Georgii Shakhnazarov, October 1994. Kindly shared with the author by Lisbeth Tarlow.

92. Anatolii Chernyaev, Sovmestnyi Iskhod, p. 930.

93. Ibid.

94. Lisbeth Bernstein, On the Rocks: Gorbachev and the Kurile Islands, p. 259.

95. Anatolii Chernyaev, "The last official foreign visit by M. S. Gorbachev as president of the USSR: The road to Tokyo," Cold War International History Project Bulletin, Issue 10 (March 1998), p. 201.

96. Ann Imse, "Japanese politician discusses disputed islands with Gorbachev," Associated Press, March 25, 1991.

97. "LDP's Ozawa may propose signing treaty by the end of the year," Japan Economic Newswire, March 24, 1991.

98. "Gorbachev i Kurily," Vlast', March 25, 1991.

99. Anatolii Chernyaev, "Poslednii vizit," p. 29.

100. See a detailed account of the Gorbachev-Ozawa meeting in Mikhail Gorbachev, *Zhizn' i Reformy*, Vol. 2, pp. 264–266.

101. Mikhail Gorbachev, *Otvechaya Na Vyzov Vremeni*, p. 911.

102. Anatolii Chernyaev, "The last official foreign visit by M. S. Gorbachev as president of the USSR: The road to Tokyo," p. 202.

103. Mikhail Gorbachev, *Otvechaya Na Vyzov Vremeni*, p. 912.

104. Author's interview with Vasilii Saplin, Sapporo, March 11, 2010. The main reason for Ozawa's resignation was said to be the failure of a candidate he backed to win the Tokyo gubernatorial election.

105. Anatolii Chernyaev, "Poslednii vizit," p. 32.

106. Tsuyoshi Hasegawa, "The Gorbachev-Kaifu summit: Domestic and foreign policy linkages," in Tsuyoshi Hasegawa et al (eds.), *Russia and Japan: An unresolved dilemma between distant neighbors* (University of California at Berkeley, 1993), p. 61.

107. Memorandum from Anatolii Chernyaev to Mikhail Gorbachev, March 28, 1991. AGF: opis 2, dokument 8844.

108. Anatolii Chernyaev, *Sovmestnyi Iskhod*, p. 935.

109. Memorandum from Anatolii Chernyaev to Mikhail Gorbachev, April 1, 1991. AGF: opis 2, dokument 8848.

110. "Sakhalin governor leaves Japan," Japan Economic Newswire, April 17, 1991.

111. Igor Latyshev, *Yaponiya, Yapontsy i Yaponovedy*, pp. 705–706.

112. Anatolii Chernyaev, *Sovmestnyi Iskhod*, p. 935.

113. Ibid.

114. Tsuyoshi Hasegawa, "The Gorbachev-Kaifu summit," pp. 64–65.

115. Michael Nol, "All signs point to a stalemate …," United Press International, April 15, 1991.

116. David Butts, "Gorbachev arrives in Japan to smooth icy relations," United Press International, April 15, 1991.

117. "Secretary Baker's March 21 meeting with Japanese Foreign Minister Nakayama," March 21, 1991. DNSA: Japan and the US, 1977–1992. Document 01682.

118. Anatolii Chernyaev, *Sovmestnyi Iskhod*, p. 936.

119. Elaine Kurtenbach, "Gorbachev, Kaifu meet, but both sides mum on island dispute," Associated Press, April 16, 1991.

120. Gorbachev brought this up in his first conversation with Kaifu.

121. "Zapis' peregovorov Mikhaila Gorbacheva s prem'er-ministrom Yaponii Tosiki Kaifu. Tokio, 16–18 aprelya 1991 goda," *Politicheskii klass*, January 2007, pp. 102–109.

122. Ibid., pp. 104–110.

123. Tsuyoshi Hasegawa, "The Gorbachev-Kaifu summit," pp. 68–70.

124. "Zapis' peregovorov Mikhaila Gorbacheva s prem'er-ministrom Yaponii Tosiki Kaifu. Tokio, 16–18 aprelya 1991 goda," p. 110.

125. Anatolii Chernyaev, *Sovmestnyi Iskhod*, p. 936.

126. "A visit dashed against the rocks," *Economist*, April 20, 1991, p. 31.

127. Conversation between Vadim Medvedev and Mikhail Gorbachev (by phone), April 21, 1991. AGF.

128. Memorandum from Anatolii Chernyaev to Mikhail Gorbachev, April 10, 1991. AGF: opis 2, dokument 8857.

129. Conversation between Mikhail Gorbachev and Kaifu Toshiki, July 17, 1991. AGF.

130. Anatolii Chernyaev, "Poslednii vizit," p. 48.

131. Tsuyoshi Hasegawa, *The Northern Territories Dispute*, Vol. 2, pp. 417–418.
132. Record of the main content of conversation between Ruslan Khasbulatov and Deputy Foreign Minister of Japan Saito, September 11, 1991. GARF: fond 10026, opis 5, delo 418, list 58. My italics.
133. Conversation between Ruslan Khasbulatov and Kanemaru Shin, September 10, 1991. GARF: fond 10026, opis 5, delo 418, list 37.
134. Conversation between Ruslan Khasbulatov and Ozawa Ichiro, September 10, 1991. GARF: fond 10026, opis 5, delo 418, list 18.
135. Conversation between Ruslan Khasbulatov and Kanemaru Shin, September 10, 1991. GARF: fond 10026, opis 5, delo 418, list 36.
136. O vizite delegatsii Verkhovnogo Soveta RSFSR v Yaponiyu, September 1991. GARF: fond 10026, opis 5, delo 418, list 100.
137. Conversation between Ruslan Khasbulatov and Ozawa Ichiro, September 10, 1991. GARF: fond 10026, opis 5, delo 418, list 20.
138. Conversation between Ruslan Khasbularov and Nakao Eiichi, September 10, 1991. GARF: fond 10026, opis 5, delo 418, list 44.
139. O vizite delegatsii Verkhovnogo Soveta RSFSR v Yaponiyu, September 1991. GARF: fond 10026, opis 5, delo 418, list 102; Evgenii Belovitskii, "Kurile transfer to Japan will cause outcry, paper says," TASS, September 28, 1991.
140. Tsuyoshi Hasegawa, *The Northern Territories Dispute*, Vol. 2, p. 421.
141. Ibid., p. 427; S. Sokolov, "Leave half-Kuriles, buddy," *Russian Press Digest*, October 2, 1991. Interestingly, only a few weeks after Kunadze's confrontation with the governor of Sakhalin, Soviet Deputy Foreign Minister Igor Rogachev (formerly a well-known opponent of territorial concessions to Japan) spoke optimistically about the prospects of resolving the territorial problem, telling the visiting governor of Hokkaido, Yokomichi, that the extension of 2.5 billion dollars in aid "helps to change the conscience of the Soviet people." Conversation between Igor Rogachev and Yokomichi, November 19, 1991. GARF: fond 10026, opis 4, delo 2809, list 17.
142. Telegram from Valentin Fedorov to Boris Yeltsin, September 30, 1991. GASO: fond P-4690, opis 1, delo 22, list 1.
143. Russian Foreign Ministry, Ob itogakh rabochego vizita ministra inostrannykh del Yaponii T. Nakayama, undated (probably late October 1991). GARF: fond 10026, opis 4, delo 2809, listy 19–30.
144. Anatolii Chernyaev, *Sovmestnyi Iskhod*, p. 998.
145. Ibid., p. 999.
146. Andrei Grachev, *Dal'she bez menya*, p. 59.
147. Anatolii Chernyaev, *Sovmestnyi Iskhod*, p. 1001.
148. Ibid., p. 1043.
149. Ibid., p. 1044.
150. Dmitrii Volkogonov, *Sem' Vozhdei*, Vol. 2, p. 312.
151. Tuomas Forsberg, "Economic incentives, ideas, and the end of the Cold War: Gorbachev and German unification," *Journal of Cold War Studies*, Vol. 7, No. 2 (Spring 2005), pp. 142–164.
152. Interview, Izumikawa Yasuhiro, Sergey Radchenko, and David Wolff, with Prime Minister Nakasone Yasuhiro, Tokyo, Japan, April 12, 2012.
153. Anatolii Chernyaev, "Poslednii vizit," p. 55.

EPILOGUE

1. Statistics come from Russia's Goskomstat (gks.ru), Customs (customs.ru), and WTO (wto.org).

INDEX

Fedorov, Valentin, 293, 299
Fedotov, Vladimir, 137, 324–325
Florakis, Charilaos, 256
Ford, Gerald, 128
Forsberg, Tuomas, 302
France, 59, 102, 125, 138, 140, 145, 147
Fujinami Takao, 68
Fukuda Takeo, 69
Fuwa Tetsuzo, 68

G7
  Toronto summit of 1988, 252
  Williamsburg summit of 1983, 59-60
Gaimusho (Japanese Foreign Ministry)
  and "balanced expansion," 68,
    255–256, 267, 270
  negative impact on Soviet-Japanese
    relations on the part of, 54,
    66–67, 70–73, 78, 249, 253, 268,
    270–271, 281
  and "seikei fukabun" see "seikei
    fukabun"
Gandhi, Indira
  her death, 93
  policy towards the US, 90–92
Gandhi, Rajiv, 120, 256
  and China, 101
  and India's grand strategy, 122–123
  and Pakistan, 213–215
  response to Gorbachev's Asian
    initiatives, 99–102
  and the Soviet Union, 2, 5, 93–95,
    97–100, 102, 117–118, 164
  and Sri Lanka, 111–112
  and the United States, 96, 110
  and the war in Afghanistan, 6, 116
Gang of Four, 17, 42
Geng Biao, 27
Gerasimov, Gennadii, 162–163
German Democratic Republic (GDR) see
    Germany (East)
Germany (East), 17–21, 23, 180, 213, 244
Germany (West), 102, 238, 244
  and the Russo-Japanese territorial
    dispute, 279–280, 302–303
Gjertsen, Doug, 215
Golikov, Viktor, 16–17, 22
Gong Ro-myung, 239, 361
Gorbachev, Mikhail, 119, 189–190,
    193, 218

becomes General Secretary, 1, 4, 38,
  67, 129
and Chinese reforms, 7, 173–184, 307
coup d'etat against, 185–187, 298
and Iran, 109
and Japan, 8, 54, 68, 70–72, 75–76,
  79, 84–87, 249–258, 267–276,
  279–296, 299–303, 309–310
loses grip on policy making, 238, 279,
  287, 289, 293, 296, 300–301
and North Korea, 200–202, 204–206,
  212–214, 220–223, 245–246
relationship with Nakasone
  Yasuhiro, 67, 86
relationship with Rajiv Gandhi, 93–95,
  97, 110–118, 120
relationship with Ronald Reagan see
  Ronald Reagan, relationship with
  Gorbachev
seeks to develop Siberia and the Far
  East, 259–263
and the Seoul Olympics see Seoul
  Olympics, Soviet position regarding
and the Sino-Soviet normalization,
  151, 153–155, 160–170, 172
and the Sino-Soviet summit of 1989
  see Sino-Soviet summit of 1989
and South Korea, 199, 208–210, 218,
  224–243, 247–248
and the Soviet rapprochement with
  Pakistan, 106–108
and the Soviet withdrawal from
  Afghanistan, 103–105, 308
and the Soviet strategy in Asia, 2–3, 5,
  9, 77–78, 88–89, 98–102, 121–123,
  196–197, 305–306, 311
and Taiwan, 191, 193
and Vietnam, 124–129, 130–146, 148,
  150, 156
Guomindang, 29
Gratz, Leopold, 144
Green, John Bernhard, 80
Grigor'ev, Sergei, 286
Gromyko, Andrei
  and China, 13, 18, 35, 37–38,
    40, 45
  and Japan, 54, 56–58, 60–62, 65, 76,
    86, 252
  and Vietnam, 130
Guest, Michael, 264

Ha, Joseph, 208–209
Harriman, Averell, 60
Hasegawa, Tsuyoshi, 68, 71–72, 253, 255, 295, 299
Hayashi Yuzo, 82
Helms, Jesse, 43
Hiroshima and Nagasaki, 56, 296
Hitler, Adolf, 201
Ho Dam, 219, 223
Hogan, Lawrence, 171
Honecker, Erich, 18–21, 23–24, 180, 203, 213
Hu Yaobang, 31, 36, 161
   views on foreign policy, 42, 64–65
   criticized for pro-Western leanings, 43
   and anti-government protests, 173
Hua Guofeng, 26
Huang Hua, 25, 28–29, 32, 35–37
Huang Ta-chou, 191
Hun Sen, 136, 141, 143–147, 150, 154, 156
Hungary, 12, 19, 173, 179–180, 213, 221, 227, 314
Hunter, Duncan, 82
Hussein, Saddam, 282
Hwang Byong-tae, 217, 357
Hwang Jang-yop, 212, 220, 222–224
Hyodo, Nagao, 293
Hyun Hong-choo, 361
Hyundai (company), 209

IBM (company), 91
Ieng Sary, 142
Ignatenko, Vitalii, 216–218
Ikeda Daisaku, 276
Il'ichev, Leonid 33–36
IMEMO (Institute of World Economy and International Relations)
   and development of Siberia and the Far East, 260, 364
   and Japan, 71, 77, 283, 299, 332
   role in the Soviet-South Korean rapprochement, 218, 225, 229–230, 233, 245
   and Taiwan, 191
"Independent foreign policy" (China's), 4, 31, 48
India, 28, 139, 143, 161, 258, 306,
   abandoned by Russia, 88, 121
   conflict with Pakistan, 105–107, 113–116, 335

in Gorbachev's global strategy, 2, 5–6, 9, 78, 86, 89, 93–95, 98–102, 117, 122–123, 170, 199, 310–311
   nuclear program, 91, 113
   relations with China, 92, 97–98, 101
   relations with Pakistan, 111–115
   relations with the US, 90–92, 96–97, 110
   submarine program, 118–120
   and the war in Afghanistan, 105, 116
   see also Sino-Soviet-Indian "triangle"
Indonesia, 138–139
"Inseparability of politics and economics" see "seikei fukabun"
Institute of Oriental Studies (Russia), 207, 209, 245, 282
Interkit, 16–18, 23
IOC (International Olympic Committee), 210–213, 315
Iraq, 91, 108, 335
Iran
   and Afghanistan, 105
   Soviet rapprochement with, 108–109, 311
Ishibashi Masashi, 71
ISI (Inter-Services Intelligence, Pakistan), 93, 107–108, 116
ISKAN (Institute of USA and Canada Studies), 22, 77, 189
Islamic fundamentalism, 103, 110, 116
Israel, 91, 111
Itochu (trading firm), 80–83
Ivanov, Ivan, 209, 261
Ivanov, Vladimir, 191

Japan, 3–4, 51, 53, 93, 101, 137, 146, 160, 168, 198, 221
   and the Cambodian settlement, 139, 146
   and Brezhnev, 58–59, 74
   in Gorbachev's global strategy, 2, 5, 7, 68, 70, 77, 86
   as a perceived threat to Soviet security 38, 57, 60, 64–66, 70, 72, 78, 254, 332
   relations with China see China, relations with Japan
   relations with North Korea, 200–205, 235, 244

Ma Xusheng, 34
Mahathir, Mohammed, 149
Mahlow, Bruno, 18
Malaysia, 149
Maldives, 117
Malta, 2, 268
Mal'kevich, Vladislav, 260–262
Mal'tsev, Viktor, 34
Mansfield, Mike, 66, 82–83
Mao Zedong, 13, 16–17, 24, 26–28, 49,
    128, 166, 168, 172, 182–184
Marshall, George, 29
Martynov, Vladlen, 230, 233, 283
Massoud, Ahmad Shah, 105
Mathers, Bill, 140
Matsunaga Nobuo, 83
McDermott (oil company),
    263–264
McGiffert, David, 27
Medvedev, Vadim, 131–134, 141, 220,
    281–282, 296, 316
Mikoyan, Anastas, 13
Miller, Robert, 263
Milyukov, Anatolii, 278
Misawa Airbase (Japan), 57
MITI (Japanese Ministry of
    International Trade and Industry),
    80–81, 272, 297
Mitsubishi (company), 84, 281
Mitsui (company), 264, 281
Miura Kineji, 70
Miyamoto Yuji, 66
Miyazawa Kiichi, 69–70, 297
MMMM Consortium, 264
Mochtar Kusumaatmadja,
    137
Moiseev, Mikhail, 185
Molotov, Vyacheslav, 166
Mondale, Walter, 30
Mongolia, 2, 259, 365
    democratic revolution in, 183
    Deng Xiaoping's complaints about
        Soviet meddling in, 166, 168
    Soviet military exercise in, 128
    Soviet troops in, 13, 15, 26, 37–38,
        49, 151
Moscow Olympics of 1980, 15
Murray, Geoffrey, 137
Mussolini, Benito, 201
Myanmar see Burma

Nagorno-Karabakh, 175
Najibullah, Muhammad, 104–105,
    109–110, 116, 227
Nakao Eiichi, 297–298
Nakasone Yasuhiro, 93, 200, 256, 271, 302
    and China, 64–65
    courted by Moscow, 60
    and LDP politics, 69, 76
    prioritizes relations with the US, 53,
        55–59, 71, 82–87, 99, 309
    seeks a breakthrough in
        Soviet-Japanese relations, 54, 62,
        66–68, 70, 72–74, 78, 251–253,
        281–282
Nakayama Taro, 270, 273, 287, 293, 297,
    299–300,
Nam, Lyudmila, 215
Namibia, 239
"National reconciliation"
    in Afghanistan, 105, 110, 308
    as a model for Cambodia, 138, 141
NATO (North Atlantic Treaty
    Organization), 65, 81, 84, 280
New Zealand, 78, 266
Ngo Tat To, 148
Nguyen Co Thach, 139–140, 144,
    148–149, 152
Nguyen Van Linh, 133–135, 139,
    148, 156
Nguyen Van Phuoc, 148
Ni Yaoli, 192–193
Nikaido Susumu, 69
Nikolaev, Mikhail, 293
Nishioka Takeo, 295
Nissan (company), 73
Nixon, Richard, 28, 32–33, 41–42, 48,
    90, 106
Non-alignment (Non-aligned
    movement), 6, 94, 205, 212
"nordpolitik" (South Korea), 206–207,
    216, 218, 230, 247
"northern territories" see
    Russo-Japanese Territorial Dispute
Nuclear (non)-proliferation
    and India, 6, 96, 113, 117–120
    and Iran, 109
    and Japan, 56–57, 66, 75
    and North Korea, 8, 200, 203–204,
        206, 228, 235, 241, 244–246
    and Pakistan, 90–91